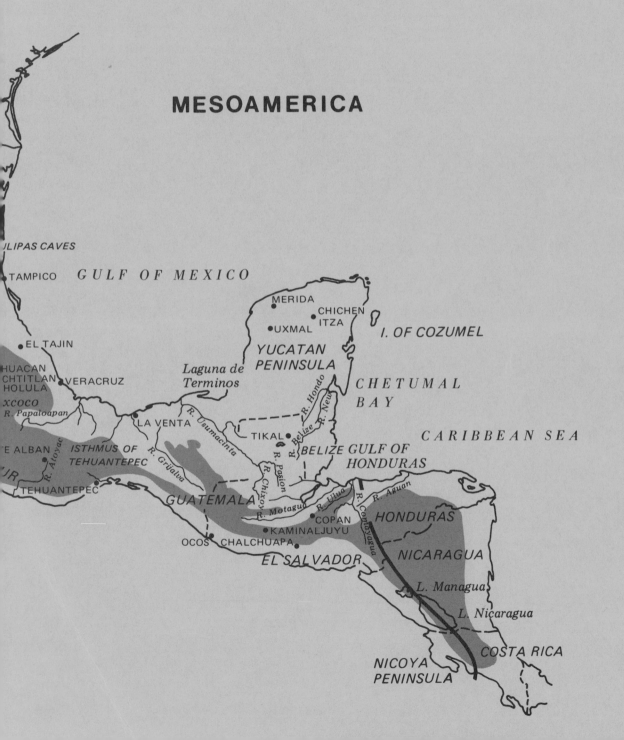

MESOAMERICA

LIPAS CAVES

TAMPICO

GULF OF MEXICO

MERIDA

CHICHEN
ITZA

UXMAL

I. OF COZUMEL

EL TAJIN

*YUCATAN
PENINSULA*

HUACAN
CHTITLAN
HOLULA

VERACRUZ

*Laguna de
Terminos*

*CHETUMAL
BAY*

xcoco

R. Papaloapan

LA VENTA

R. Usumacinta

R. Hondo

R. New

TIKAL

R. Belize

CARIBBEAN SEA

E ALBAN

R. Atoyac

*ISTHMUS OF
TEHUANTEPEC*

R. Grijalva

R. Pasion

R. Chixoy

BELIZE

*GULF OF
HONDURAS*

TEHUANTEPEC

GUATEMALA

R. Motagua

R. Ulua

R. Aguan

COPAN

R. Comayagua

HONDURAS

KAMINALJUYU

OCOS

CHALCHUAPA

EL SALVADOR

NICARAGUA

L. Managua

L. Nicaragua

*NICOYA
PENINSULA*

COSTA RICA

The Aztecs, Maya, and Their Predecessors

ARCHAEOLOGY OF MESOAMERICA

Second Edition

This is a volume in

Studies in Archaeology

A complete list of titles in this series is available from the Publisher upon request.

The Aztecs, Maya, and Their Predecessors

ARCHAEOLOGY OF MESOAMERICA

pg 271 origin of civilization

Second Edition

Muriel Porter Weaver

ACADEMIC PRESS, INC.
Harcourt Brace Jovanovich, Publishers
San Diego New York Berkeley Boston
London Sydney Tokyo Toronto

ACADEMIC PRESS, INC.
San Diego, Caliifornia 92101

United Kingdom Edition published by
ACADEMIC PRESS LIMITED
24-28 Oval Road, London NW1 7DX

Library of Congress Cataloging in Publication Data

Weaver, Muriel Porter.
  The Aztecs, Maya, and their predecessors.

  (Studies in archaeology)
  Bibliography: p.
  Includes index.
  1. Indians of Mexico--Antiquities. 2. Indians
of Central America--Antiquities. 3. Mexico--
Antiquities. 4. Central America--Antiquities.
I. Title.
F1219.W42 1981   972   80-2344
ISBN 0-12-785936-5

PRINTED IN THE UNITED STATES OF AMERICA

 89 90 91 92   10 9 8 7 6 5 4

FOR HAROLD, JEAN, AND LESLIE

Contents

CHAPTER 7

Early Postclassic Developments: Tula and Chichén Itzá   357

CHAPTER 8

Strife, Empires, and Europeans: The Late Postclassic Period   405

List of Illustrations

Preface to the First Edition

The continuing interest in the pre-Columbian cultures of Mexico and Guatemala has, over the years, led to the accumulation of a tremendous amount of literature to be found in field reports, widely scattered articles, and books by scientists, scholars, and art lovers. The student who wants to learn something of the events that took place in this region prior to the Spanish Conquest is confronted by a bewildering assortment of books and articles, some of which are hard to locate in the most richly stocked library.

This book was conceived as an answer to a frequently asked question, "Can you give me the name of a single volume that will cover the archaeology of both central Mexico and the Maya area?" The question reflects the need for synthesis, for an attempt at generalization, and to fit the scattered knowledge of pre-Columbian history into some comprehensive framework. As such this book is the first of its kind.

As the student begins to understand how the ingenious life of hunters and gatherers evolved into a complex civilization, he or she will also become aware of how great is our debt to archaeology; how with the increasing advantages of interdisciplinary studies, more can be learned from the past; and precisely how it is possible to combine archaeological facts and theories. This book is planned as a general introduction to the archaeology of Mesoamerica. For some students this may represent their only involvement with the field of archaeology, and if so, they will see how the evolution of one of the highest civilizations in the New World came about, as well as gaining an appreciation of archaeology as a science. For others this volume will serve as a point of departure for specialized research. It is my hope that many will be stimulated to expand their interests to examine specific field reports and monographs, to rethink theories and challenge ideas presented here. For those primarily interested in the primitive art of this area, the book will help them view their objects in a cultural context, thus giving them meaning and perspective.

Rather than deal with the sequence of events by geographical areas, I have chosen to treat Mesoamerica as a whole, emphasizing major cultural changes and trends beginning with the earliest inhabitants of 38,000 B.C. (?) and ending with the arrival of the Spanish in 1519. After some description of the physical setting, the scene is focused on the earliest known beginnings of farming in the highland area of the Tehuacán Valley, and then shifts to the lowland cultures of the Gulf Coast region where the Olmec civilization was centered. Following these remarkable developments, the key areas become central highland Mexico, which never again relinquishes its leadership, and the lowland jungles of Guatemala, followed by the Yucatán Peninsula. These regions taken together provide us with a mainstream or central core of complexity to which cultures of other areas can be related, compared, and contrasted.

The absorbing history of Mesoamerica's culture, however, can be ultimately understood and appreciated only when given the perspective of other New World developments. In this regard one should remember that Mesoamerica was not a static geographical area; its sixteenth-century contours do not have the same boundaries of the twelfth and ninth centuries. These fluctuations involve neighboring peoples and their interaction with those of more complex civilizations. More widespread relationships with South American cultures of Colombia, Ecuador, and Peru, that is, the role of Mesoamerica within Nuclear America and the Intermediate area, are part of this perspective. These contacts are touched on briefly, as well as current trends in Transpacific studies. Finally, I have presented my views on Mesoamerica as a civilization and mentioned some of the problems to be faced by the archaeologist in this part of the world. Many of these problems can be met and resolved by an appreciation of the past. It is here that we will begin.

ACKNOWLEDGMENTS   I have made a conscious effort to avoid complicated terms as well as all but the most vital current debates on issues and interpretations. "Try to make it understandable" was the hope expressed at the outset by Dr. Daniel F. Rubín de la Borbolla, to whom I owe my initiation into Mesoamerican archaeology. As a founder and director of the Escuela Nacional de Antropología and subsequent director of the Museo Nacional de Antropología in Mexico, no one could have offered more encouragement, stimulation, and opportunity to a student than he gave to me. I also recognize a long-standing debt to the late Alfonso Caso, Miguel Covarrubias, and Paul Kirchhoff, and to Ignacio Marquina, Wigberto Jiménez Moreno, Ignacio Bernal, Román Piña Chán, José Luis Lorenzo, and to all my Mexican teachers and colleagues who throughout years of intimate involvement with Mesoamerica have treated me as one of their own. In the direct preparation of this book, I would like to extend very special thanks to Arturo Romano, who as director of the Museo Nacional de Antropología, Mexico, generously put all his resources at my disposal.

Discussions and conversations with others in this field have been invaluable, and a number of colleagues generously made available to me unpublished material. In this respect I am very grateful to Isabel T. Kelly, Robert H. Heizer, Michael D. Coe, Paul Tolstoy, David Grove, and Ellen and Charles Brush. In addition, Paul Tolstoy and Pedro Armillas read parts of the manuscript and Michael D. Coe the whole. I greatly appreciate their helpful comments and suggestions, although the responsibility for all shortcomings is mine alone.

To Mary Beth Stokes, who prepared the art work with both talent and interest, go my heartful thanks. I am grateful, too, to Frederick J. Dockstader for innumerable favors and time spent on my behalf. The photographs from the Museum of the American Indian are the work of Carmelo Guadagno, many of which were specially prepared for this text.

The art work and photography were made possible through the interest of Dean Ruth G. Weintraub and by a Doctoral Faculty Research Grant from the City University of New York. To those many institutions and individuals who provided photographs and granted permission for their publication, I am deeply grateful. Tana Agoras and Jean Kemp typed the original manuscript.

I also wish to express my appreciation to the following publishers who have graciously permitted the reproduction of figures redrawn from their publications to appear here: Alfred Knopf, Inc., American Museum of Natural History, Carnegie Institution of Washington, Field Museum of Natural History, Fondo de Cultura Económica, Instituto Nacional de Antropología e Historia, International Congress of Americanists, McGraw-Hill Book Company, Museum of the American Indian, Peabody Museum of Harvard University, R. S. Peabody Foundation, Sociedad Mexicana de Antropología, Smithsonian Institution of Washington, Stanford University Press, Universidad Nacional Autónoma de Mexico, University Museum, Philadelphiha, University of Texas Press, and Wenner-Gren Foundation for Anthropological Research.

One of the most rewarding experiences in preparing this book was the opportunity to meet and work with staff members of Seminar Press. The production of this volume in an age characterized by computerized, stereotyped relationships has been a delightful personal experience.

The tasteful design of the book, the very difficult task of fitting in my vast disarray of illustrative material, and the precision and detail work necessary to see Mesoamerica's past properly recorded are all very much appreciated.

I realize, however, that it was only through the encouragement, understanding, and countless considerations of my husband, Harold M. Weaver, that the long-standing desire to write this book has been realized.

Preface to the Second Edition

The excellent reception accorded to the first edition of *The Aztecs, Maya, and Their Predecessors* encouraged me to embark on a second which, like the first, is directed toward students and travelers with more than casual interest in the archaeology of Mesoamerica.

Our knowledge of both central Mexico and the Maya regions has changed substantially since 1972. Although the broad outlines of the rise to civilization were already delineated by that date, the vast amount of fieldwork, research, and new ideas in more recent years has added tremendous dimensions to our understanding and perception of these early peoples and their society.

Fieldworkers have been particularly active in the Maya area, Oaxaca, and highland central Mexico. Results from team efforts from these regions are now available. Central Yucatán is better understood chronologically and archaeologically. Belize has produced and continues to yield remarkably early material, and its preceramic remains being studied by R. S. MacNeish, S. J. K. Wilkerson, and A. Nelken–Terner promise a sequence extending back to 9000 B.C. El Salvador's western history amplifies our knowledge of the southern periphery, which may help us to understand some features of lowland Maya development. The intensive and sophisticated methods of agriculture now believed to have been practiced by the Maya in the Classic period have altered older views of their settlement patterns and society. Settled life in the lowlands is now known to be far older than previously suspected. In central highland Mexico, the Projecto Puebla–Tlaxcala has contributed enormously to our knowledge of an important and long-neglected region, while the long-known sites of Teotihuacán and Tula continue to produce new remains and stimulate new ideas. In Mexico City itself, the Aztecs have once again captured the world's attention with the uncovering of their most revered temple along with vast treasures.

Not only has the physical volume of knowledge increased, but much interpretation and rethinking of ideas has been going on. We now have enough models, theories, and hypotheses to nourish generations to come. Two conferences have been devoted exclusively to the origins and collapse of Classic Maya civilization (Culbert 1973; Adams 1977c). All of these are very stimulating. Some of the most significant contributions have come from art historians: H. B. Nicholson, E. Pasztory, G. Kubler, and their students, who through their scholarly work on iconography are giving us a clearer understanding of the relationships between the major centers of Mesoamerica. Meanwhile another group of scholars (D. H. Kelley, M. Greene, P. Mathews, L. Schele, and F. G. Lounsbury) have been deciphering more Maya hieroglyphs; in doing so, they are telling us more about the rulers and dynasties of ancient Maya cities. Although it has already been a record-making decade of research in Mesoamerica the research continues at a rapid pace—even while the presses are in action. Already more rulers are being identified. The geneaological and astronomical studies of David H. Kelley currently under way will substantially clarify many of the chronological and historical problems of the Postclassic that are underscored here. Readers are advised to keep an open mind regarding the Quetzalcóatls, the Toltecs, and Tula–Chichén chronology. Meanwhile, new discoveries continue. Word comes of the great cave of Naj Tunich in Guatemala's Maya Mountains, replete with painted figures and many hieroglyphic texts.

The outlines of this second edition follow the presentation and scheme of the first, but the contents provide a more holistic view of the life and times of these ancient Americans. One inevitable result of this massive research is to burden students with an increased volume of material, names, and dates. With this in mind, I have provided additional photographs and both more plentiful and more comprehensive maps. I have attempted to include every site mentioned on at least one map.

The temporal relationships between sites and areas have been consolidated into one master chronological chart located for easy reference on the back endpapers. This includes both the traditional phase terminology—Preclassic, Classic, Postclassic—as well as an alternative scheme of periods often applied to the Basin of Mexico (see discussion in the Introduction). Finally, a special effort has been made to compile a detailed and comprehensive index.

ACKNOWLEDGMENTS   The second edition has been prepared with continued help from my many colleagues who have so generously provided me with photographs, reprints, unpublished and hard-to-get publications, and who shared with me their ideas and thoughts. Yet the responsibility for the interpretations that follow is mine alone.

Special appreciation goes to Isabel Kelly, Arturo Romano P., Evelyn Rattray, Christine Niederberger, Esther Pasztory, and John A. Graham, each of whom has taken time to show me, teach me, and keep me informed. I also wish to acknowledge a scholarly debt to Gordon R. Willey, to whose opinions and writings I continually turn.

Much of the research for this edition was made possible by Allan D. Chapman, who gave me access to the Robert Goldwater Library of Primitive Art of the Metropolitan Museum of Art in New York, at a time when it could not have been convenient to have me underfoot. To him and to his able staff I extend my thanks. The final checking was greatly facilitated by the help of Malcolm McLeod and his team at the Museum of Mankind Library of the British Museum, London.

I am again indebted to my husband, Harold, who nudged me along on this second edition.

Introduction

As in any area of the world, the ancient culture history of a people prior to their possession of a written language is gradually pieced together from that material evidence of their civilization that has managed to survive the ravages of weather, time, and man. The archaeologist first recovers what he or she can, methodically and scientifically, and then interprets this material in terms of temporal or geographic change.

One admitted shortcoming of this traditional approach lies in the difficulties and limitations it poses in explaining the processes involved. There is increased interest in attempting to explain rather than merely describe. The many new approaches and trends in archaeology represent a breakthrough in both theory and scientific method. Archaeologists are becoming more aware of the importance of thoroughly understanding the environment or paleoecology of prehistory, and this is leading to unprecedented collaborations with geologists, nuclear physicists, veterinary anatomists, zoologists, botanists, and an entire spectrum of specialists in other fields. New interpretations and inferences are also being offered in such areas as ancient social affiliations, residence patterns, population densities, and political institutions, making use of both archaeology and ethnographic and historical documents. There is a new trend toward reinterpretation and reevaluation of past work. Thus, archaeological methods are being improved, a higher precision becomes possible, and the field of archaeology is branching out into new areas of investigation, which involve both cultural and noncultural phenomena such as ecological factors. All of this has been made possible, however, by years of "dirt" archaeology, which provides the material evidence for speculation and testing of theories.

Thus, the cultural evolution of Mesoamerican civilization is understood as a result of cumulative efforts from many years of digging in
the field. In this case the task is very complex. In the geographical area
encompassing Mesoamerica, which embraces most of Mexico and part
of northern Central America, the extraordinary diversity of altitude,
climate, natural resources, fauna, and flora have contributed to an equal
diversity of ecological adaptations and cultural manifestations. About
80 years of intensive archaeological study have been required to reach
a point where one can begin to speak about characteristics, trends,
patterns, and traditions. It has taken a very long time to understand
what happened in Mesoamerica, and archaeologists are far from satisfied. Such explanations are just being initiated.

Primarily this is a history of cultural events in Mesoamerica rather
than a testing of theories, although one does not exclude the other.
The unfolding of sequences will help illuminate the processes and
mechanisms at work. In the final chapter I have presented an overview
of the archaeology of Mesoamerica, not a summary, but a review of
the long history of events stressing the interrelationship of areas, the
interplay between highland and lowland peoples, and setting forth
some general trends in the evolution of Mesoamerican civilization.

The history, however, is based primarily on fragmentary remains
which are subject to constant revision and reinterpretation. There is
also another factor of which the reader should be aware. The people
who developed these extraordinary cultures lived in a world with values
and ideals that differed greatly from those of modern times. By our
standards, some of these people might be classified as savages or barbarians, with complete disregard for human life. Through studying
their history, beliefs, and discipline, however, one hopes to view them
as human beings coping with the universal problems of mankind everywhere, but solving them in their unique way. Artists, astronomers,
gifted craftsmen and architects, merchants, warriors, royalty, peasants,
and slaves will be found—all with a singular dedication to their society
and religion. In order to understand the complex world of the Aztecs,
Maya, and their contemporaries, one must learn first about the long
chain of cultural events leading up to the culmination of these great
civilizations. And in the process, the oft-asked question comes to mind:
"Were our American cultures developed independently in the New
World, or do they owe their initial stimulation to influences from the
Old?" In addition, there is much one can learn today from the evolution
of a past civilization that, when viewed in perspective of its own life
and times, was probably as great as one feels ours is today.

I have attempted to present a cultural history of Mesoamerica—the
account of how this area of the New World reached spectacular heights
of civilization from the more modest hunting and gathering base shared
by most of the western hemisphere. Why did it happen here? What

was the role of agriculture, of irrigation? What factors contributed to the rise of urban centers such as Teotihuacán in central highland Mexico and Tikal in the Petén region of Guatemala? How, precisely, does Mesoamerica qualify as a high civilization?

In order to understand the cultural evolution that did take place, it is necessary to consider the area as a whole. Much has been written on the Aztecs and the Maya, who occupied adjacent geographical areas connected by a narrow corridor of land, the Isthmus of Tehuantepec. A kind of dichotomy has grown up over the years between the central Mexican cultures and the Maya and their predecessors. Indeed, there are few archaeologists who have done extensive work both east and west of the "Isthmus." The complexity and extreme diversity of cultures has justified such past specialization to some extent.

At the same time, it is generally agreed that these components form a cultural unit—hence the term *Mesoamerica*. Thus, despite interior diversity, the central Mexican cultures have more in common with those of Guatemala than they do, for example, with southwestern United States or the Caribbean islands—in fact, they have much in common. Such themes as certain religious concepts, a calendrical system, hieroglyphic writing, human sacrifice, a ball game with rings, a periodic market system, the use of lime mortar, and many other such elements constitute a common denominator uniting those people who share them, and in turn distinguish them from their "have-not" neighbors.

It will be helpful in the study of this complex geographical and cultural entity which is Mesoamerica to think in terms of four main areas: (1) the central highlands of Mexico, (2) the highland Valley of Guatemala, (3) the great northern Maya lowlands including the Petén region of Guatemala and the Yucatán Peninsula, and (4) the intervening coastal and piedmont regions. If it seems that there is a weighing of highland versus lowland development, we are already touching on a very crucial aspect of the whole cultural evolution: the interplay of ecological zones in which altitude and resources are a major factor.

To facilitate the mental moves between coast and highland as well as east and west of the Isthmus of Tehuantepec, we have placed a general map of Mesoamerica on the front endpapers of the book, and a chronological time scale of events on the back endpapers. In using these we are already dealing with the heart of archaeological research, the dimensions of time and space. Boundaries of both should be mentally drawn with great flexibility. For example the Olmec heartland has recently been extended to include the major site of Laguna de los Cerros. It also seems that Kaminaljuyú shared the Valley of Guatemala with a site of equal complexity and size. The well-known site of Tula, Hidalgo, is not so well known after all. The limits of this great urban center are only now being determined, and its anticipated dimensions are greater than anyone imagined. If spheres of influence and boundaries are hard to perceive in major centers, how much more difficult to delineate the so-called "empires" of Teotihuacán or the later Aztecs? Thinking of the studies in the Basin of Mexico by Sanders and his team, and Blanton's work in Oaxaca, I can say we are getting closer, but we are still relying on sherd counts to estimate size and distribution of population.

In working out the chronology of cultures in this area, our starting point is the year 1519, marking the arrival of the Spaniards, and from this date we move back in time. Although the Spanish Conquistadores destroyed much, they provided excellent accounts including letters written by Cortés himself. *The General History of the Things of New Spain,* often considered to be the first full-fledged ethnology, was written by Fray Bernardino de Sahagún. A truly remarkable scholar, he trained young Aztec nobles to write their native tongue, Náhuatl, in Spanish script. With their aid and his own questioning of informants, Sahagún produced this monumental work. Another sixteenth-century source is Bernal Díaz del Castillo's eye-witness account of the conquest of central Mexico. In Yucatán, Bishop Fray Diego de Landa, who gave the orders that resulted in the burning of many Maya *códices,* the Indians' native books, partly offset this great loss by recording much of Maya life himself. We also rely on local native chronicles for Yucatán called the Books of Chilam Balam. Fortunately for us too, the Spanish monarchs requested detailed information about New Spain, much of which has been preserved. These sixteenth-century sources by Spanish chroniclers and members of native orders of Franciscans, Augustinians, and Jesuits, as well as native documents, provide a firm cultural base from which to start. Logically it follows that cultural remains lying beneath Aztec and Maya materials are earlier, but how much? "Dirt" archaeology is indispensible for providing the relative sequence of remains, followed by the painstaking task of correlating nearby sites and regions. Even the best relative chronology, however, can indicate only that B, for example, is older than A and perhaps C older than B.

The thread of Mesoamerican chronology was first worked out by the correlation of the Maya with the Christian calendar, thus providing our earliest absolute dates. If, for example, one can be sure that July 26, 1553 corresponds to a certain Maya date, then once the Maya system of calendrics is understood, one should be able to translate into the Christian calendar the dates of Maya monuments as they are found. Unfortunately, it is not at all that simple. The Maya Long Count, yielding absolute dates from an ancient year 1 in the past, was discontinued before the Spanish Conquest and a more abbreviated form was substituted. The correlation with our calendar then becomes a problem of interpretation. For example, the just-mentioned date, July 26, 1553, is given by Landa for the founding of the Yucatecan capital of Mérida. To which date in the Maya calendar does it correspond? There are two proposed solutions: the Goodman–Martinez–Thompson (GMT) or 11.16 correlation, and the Spinden or 12.9 correlation. The difference of opinion is one of 260 years. Although the GMT correlation is more commonly used, both can be justified and the problem has not been definitely resolved. The new data from the northern and central Maya lowlands can now be interpreted as supporting either correlation. The problem is still there, but the time gap is narrowing.

Chronological charts are the despair of every archaeologist. Vertical columns represent various centers arbitrarily selected for representation, but the horizontal lines are the nemesis of all. These may be dotted, sprinkled with question marks, diagonals, interlocking bands, broken blocks and bands, every possible device to denote that "this is how I see it at the moment, but it is tentative and subject to change." In looking at charts it is the sequence rather than the absolute date that is likely to endure. Viewed with these reservations, charts are helpful and I have accordingly contributed mine (back endpapers).

The continuing problem of how to deal with regional sequences is still under review. The dilemma is not merely between choosing among periods and using a block of time arbitrarily, or selecting stages that deal with levels of achievement regardless of absolute time. Indeed, both schemes are possible and have been used with success in New World archaeology. In Mesoamerica the terms *Preclassic, Classic,* and *Postclassic* have been used with relatively little variation. I am aware that a given period may be stretched to fit all of Mesoamerica where it may not seem applicable. As a result one finds the florescence of the Mixteca–Puebla culture occurring in the *Post*-Classic and that of the Olmec civilization in the *Pre*-Classic. Several authors have voiced such discomfort with this system that at a New Mexico conference in 1972 they decided to adopt a different chronological scheme using periods defined in absolute time. This system was worked out for the Peruvian material by John Rowe in 1960 as a welcome method for organizing the archaeological data for that region. A similar scheme has been attempted for Mesoamerica and is used by Wolf (1976), Sanders, Parsons, and Santley (1979), Millon (1976), and Tolstoy (1978).

In this volume, however, I retain the conventional nomenclatures of Preclassic, Classic, and Postclassic. This terminology is so thoroughly ingrained that it has long since lost any evolutionary implication it may have originally had; it has in effect become simply a means of designating convenient time frames. The conventional nomenclature has the great advantage of providing a useful guide to the vast literature. Any designations could arbitrarily be applied, but I find this system less confusing and easier to deal with. In order to facilitate handling certain articles, I have incorporated both systems into the master chronological chart. To date, the New Mexico conference chronology has been applied almost exclusively to the Basin of Mexico.

There is, however, a more significant modification in our chronology. I have placed the Preclassic period from 2500 B.C. to A.D. 1; the Classic thus begins at A.D. 1 and continues until A.D. 900; the Postclassic follows thereafter. This in effect starts the Classic with the beginning of Teotihuacán instead of with the first Petén Initial Series, which dates about three centuries later. The Teotihuacán civilization had the most widespread impact of any in Mesoamerica, and the first nine centuries of our era can be more readily understood if this period is set apart. Within this Classic time frame, we will single out the great Middle period and the years A.D. 400–700 as the time of Teotihuacán's maximum influence and achievement. This refinement of the Classic chronology permits, I believe, a more comprehensible interpretation of the great Maya civilization that was influenced by central Mexican developments. We do not have all the answers to the often asked questions about the origins and collapse of Maya civilization, but rearranging our focus to correlate with events in highland Mexico makes explanations more logical and understandable.

The Postclassic period is likewise subject to considerable adjusting. Many features long considered to be evidence of Toltec Postclassic presence in Yucatán may have been Classic Maya assimilations of Mexican influence, which in turn were transmitted back to central Mexico to be manifested at Xochicalco and Tula. Chronologies for the northern and central Maya lowlands have been greatly clarified bringing the whole development of Postclassic Maya culture in line with what we know of events elsewhere in Mesoamerica. Here again we can use our convenient Classic and Postclassic time frames, with the provision that we are willing to adjust our thinking to the changes being brought about by archaeological research.

For absolute dating, carbon-14, fluorine tests, and obsidian dating have been used with considerable success. Methods in carbon-14 dating are the most widely used isotopic method and have recently been improved and refined. Whereas the upper effective limits were approximately 25,000 years, with newer methods, dating is possible up to 40,000–50,000 years. Dendrochronology studies on the bristlecone pine have shown that as one moves back in time, the deviation in carbon-14 values increases. Thus to a date of 4500 B.C. radiocarbon time, 800 years should be added to approximate the actual date. A helpful gauge is given by M. D. Coe (1980) as follows: A date of 1000 B.C. can probably be corrected to read 1200 B.C. Likewise, 2000 B.C., when corrected, would become 2500 B.C. and 3000 B.C. becomes 3700 B.C. Thus in some literature one may find reference to radiocarbon time (RT) and sidereal (ST) or calendar years. As yet there is not complete agreement among scholars as to the calibration curve which only extends back to 5000 B.C. Dates here, unless noted specifically, will deal in radiocarbon or uncorrected time (see Taylor and Meighan 1978).

We know more about obsidian dating now even though results have been very uneven. Originally this dating was worked out on the belief that a new but exposed surface of obsidian absorbs moisture from the surrounding atmosphere at a constant rate. When the thickness of the hydration layer is measured, this might provide a means of calculating the length of lapsed time since the fresh surface was made. The chemical variability in the physical and chemical mechanism of obsidian hydration has now been recognized but as yet it has not been possible to establish a correction for obsidian hydration values. In addition, each geographic source presents unique chemical characteristics, so hydration rates will have to be worked out accordingly. A trace element analysis is also needed for each obsidian source. Meanwhile, it has been possible to identify the sources of many obsidian artifacts, which has helped to identify exchange networks and flow of goods.

Also very promising is the possibility of being able to date lime mortar by using the carbon-14 method (Folk and Valastro 1976). Still in experimental stages, the technique would have a far-reaching influence in Mesoamerica where rebuilding was done at frequent intervals. The reader is referred to Taylor (1978) for more thorough coverage of current dating methods.

Of these absolute dating systems, the carbon-14 method has been tremendously successful in recent years. As helpful as modern scientific methods are, however, reliance on a single sample can be risky, for laboratory errors have been made. Obviously a whole series of dates provides a check and is more reliable, but multiple samples are not always available. The archaeologist must also be cautious in gathering the sample, not only to avoid contamination but to be sure he or she knows exactly what is being sampled (i.e., a geologic ash layer or a burned building). Because all of the problems have as yet to be worked out of radiocarbon dating, it is safe to say that ceramic studies will not be supplanted in the near future.

I should also say a word about references to mounds, tombs, and monuments such as stelae and altars. In the process of identifying such objects, it is a long-standing custom of archaeologists to assign arbitrarily numbers or letters to each find in the order of its appearance at each site. Hence the reader will come upon mention of Mound J and E–VII–sub, Tomb 7, Stela 29, and Altar Q. Such is the nature of archaeological labeling and recording.

The words *Aztec* or *Mexica* are used to designate those late inhabitants of central highland Mexico. Because they are better known today as Aztecs, this term is used more frequently, but the two words can be used interchangeably.

In this second edition, I have continued the general plan of the first, that is, to begin with the earliest finds and progress upward in time to the Spanish Conquest in A.D. 1521. To do this, I have concentrated on the major focus of development in each period. The older periods receive the most complete coverage, which means that as the Conquest is approached, the selection of material has been greater, necessitated by its sheer abundance. I have not attempted to present a complete account of sixteenth-century Maya and Aztec cultures. It is the sequence of events, the rise to civilization, rather than a description of civilization's fulfillment that is emphasized here.

Mesoamerica: The Area and the People

In the course of the cultural development of pre-Columbian civilizations in the western hemisphere, two areas pulled ahead of their neighbors and attained high peaks of civilization unparalleled elsewhere in the New World. These regions, roughly the Andean area and the Mexican–Guatemalan complex, together form what is called Nuclear America, implying centers of high cultural development. The complexity of these civilizations may be readily appreciated by reading first-hand appraisals of these cultures written in the sixteenth century by eye witnesses—the Spanish Conquistadores and chroniclers.

The northern center of development is called Mesoamerica. Geographically it forms part of tropical America, including, at the time of the Spanish Conquest in A.D. 1521, central and southern Mexico with the peninsula of Yucatán, Guatemala, El Salvador, and parts of Honduras, Nicaragua, and northern Costa Rica. (See Map 1; because this map will be referred to constantly, it may also be found on the front endpapers.) The northern boundary at that time, drawn from west to east, begins at the mouth of the Sinaloa River in northwest Mexico, dips south in the central plateau of the middle Lerma River valley, and then climbs north and east to meet the Gulf of Mexico at the mouth of the Soto la Marina River above Tampico. The southern limits, from north to south, begin at the mouth of the Ulua River on the Gulf of Honduras, extend west to the Choluteca River and then south across the Nicaraguan lakes, and end at Punta Arenas on the Pacific coast of Costa Rica. On what basis were these geographical limits defined, and what makes this a distinctive culture area? In 1942 Paul Kirchhoff made a distributional study of culture traits or elements and found that many of them were restricted to the area within these limits; others were found only rarely among the neighboring groups to the north and south (Kirchhoff 1943).

The northern boundary roughly separates hunters and gatherers without a knowledge of agriculture from their more sophisticated farming neighbors to the south. There was a direct confrontation of the Aztec and Tarascan states with these nomadic northern bands, a rather rare situation. Armillas (1969) calls this boundary a hard frontier. The southern limits of Mesoamerica are less sharply defined culturally. In the sixteenth century the higher cultures of Mesoamerica blended into those of Nicaragua and Costa Rica, which form part of an intermediate area between the centers of Nuclear America.

These boundaries of Mesoamerica were drawn up largely on the basis of ethnographic and linguistic data as known at the time of the Conquest. What were some of these diagnostic traits of Mesoamerica? A few of the most important were:

ball courts with rings
cacao, chocolate
chia cultivation, a plant raised for food, drink, and oil
chinampa agriculture, a system of cultivation in drained swamplands, in which soil is renewed by resurfacing with muck from the lake bottom
clay pellets for blow tube
coa, digging stick
códices, books made of amate paper or deer skin
grinding of corn mixed with ash or lime
hieroglyphic writing
human sacrifice
labrets, lip ornaments
one-piece warrior outfits

periodic market system
polished obsidian
position numerals,
pyrite mirrors
rabbit-hair weaving
ritual use of paper and rubber
sandals with heels
stepped pyramids
stucco floors
turbans
use of 13 as ritual number
volador, ritual ceremony in which several men "fly" down to earth from a high pole
wooden clubs with flint or obsidian chips for blades
year of 18 months of 20 days plus 5 extra days

Most of these are in some way related to a rich complex of religious ceremonialism and interactions between groups and regions involving exchange of goods and ideas. These features and their influence on the lives of the people played a large part in the cultural development of Mesoamerica. Combined with many other factors, they gave rise to a civilization unique in content and imaginative in concept, which conforms only in part to the expected patterns and theories that have emerged from studies of other civilizations.

Mesoamerica is therefore a term that refers to this geographic region where a particular pattern of civilization is identified as prevailing in the sixteenth century. What can be said about the preceding years? How far back in time can Mesoamerica be recognized as having a pattern of its own? Does archaeology verify the study by Kirchhoff? It is not possible to reconstruct as precisely as he has done the former extensions of Mesoamerica throughout its long pre-Columbian history.

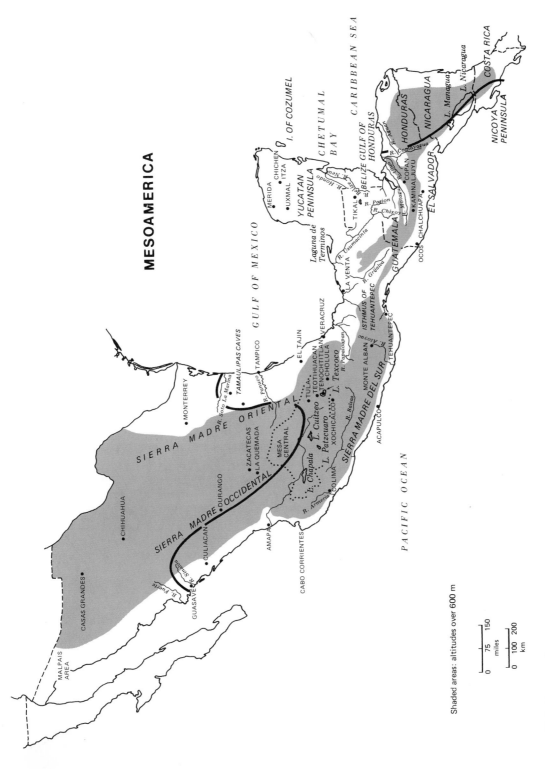

MESOAMERICA

Shaded areas: altitudes over 600 m

0 — 75 — 150 miles

0 — 100 — 200 km

MAP 1. Mesoamerica.

11

Nevertheless, archaeology shows that some considerable changes took place before the appearance of Mesoamerica as it was just defined.

The northern boundary, for example, was far from stable. Pedro Armillas (1969), Beatriz Braniff (1974), and Eric Wolf (1959) all have concerned themselves with the fluctuations of the northern extension of agriculture. Prior to A.D. 500 the boundary of Mesoamerica was pushed northward between the twenty-second and twenty-third parallels, extending from San Luis Potosí in the east to southern Chihuahua in the west (Map 1). Armillas believes that during these years a buffer belt, or soft frontier, lay between Mesoamerica and the areas to the north. In this buffer zone farming groups constructed hilltop fortresses such as La Quemada, while the outer groups on the far frontier manifested a more equal balance between hunting and gathering and farming (Armillas 1969). This situation could reflect adjustment to a new cultural scheme as well as adaptation to a different environment. The northward push of farming peoples was, we believe, contingent on an adequate water supply; a slight fluctuation in rainfall would make the vast territory to the north alternately suitable either for agriculture or for hunting and gathering in a desert-like environment. We shall see, when dealing with the Toltecs, the importance of this fluctuating northern frontier.

For earlier times, it is questionable whether the region of west Mexico properly belongs within the boundary of Mesoamerica. The peoples living in the area of Michoacán, Jalisco, Nayarit, Colima, and Sinaloa manifested a cultural development quite unique in flavor and apparently did not share in the major events taking place in the heart of Mesoamerica.

During the long Preclassic period, west Mexico had a very distinct regional culture of its own with shaft-and-chamber tombs and some pottery styles that more closely resemble South American cultures in Colombia and Ecuador than Mesoamerica. However, based on excavations at Amapa, Nayarit, which reveal groupings of structures around plazas oriented to the cardinal directions, west Mexico had become part of Mesoamerica by A.D. 600.

The southern boundary is less well defined as it fluctuated with the ebb and flow of events in the Maya area and lower Central America. Work in El Salvador and Honduras has helped bring this southern periphery into sharper focus and places the boundary near the modern border between Honduras and Nicaragua.

We do not know who these Mesoamerican people were. We only know what they called themselves at the time of the Conquest in the sixteenth century. In pre-Columbian times a great variety of languages were spoken. Fortunately for us, linguists have grouped them into families and have been able to study relationships and changes between them. Because changes are believed to have taken place at a constant rate, linguists, through comparing basic vocabularies, are able to estimate how long it has been since two related tongues branched off from a common ancestral form. Thus, they can reconstruct the linguistic past.

An excellent summary of Mexican languages and their history is found in the volume by Wolf (1959), which is briefly summarized here. Prior to 4000 B.C. all languages in Mesoamerica may have been related, but soon after that the great Uto-Aztecan strain can be distinguished, which probably had its roots somewhere in western Mexico. This group in turn split into many subdivisions, Nahua being the most important, and its close relative Náhuatl became the language of the Aztecs. It is still spoken today by many rural groups in central highland Mexico. Náhuatl is beautiful and melodious and became, as did Maya and Quéchua, one of the literary tongues of ancient America used for recording epic poems, proverbs, flowery rhetoric, and hymns to the gods. Nahua-speakers may have been around well before the Aztecs came to power but probably the earliest ones are no older than those of the Coyotlatelco culture in the Basin of Mexico (Kaufman 1976). The Toltecs probably spoke Náhuatl but not the Teotihuacanos. Later, Náhuatl-speaking Aztecs carried this language throughout Mesoamerica in the course of their late expansion. Náhuatl had great influence on speech and spelling as far south as lower Central America, though its center remained in the Basin of Mexico.

Another large group was made up of Macro-Mayan speakers who spread through the southern lowlands of the Gulf Coast and the eastern highlands. Huastec and Mayan languages are closely related; available evidence indicates that these people once lived side by side along the Gulf Coast and spoke a Mayan language. A linguistic map shows a very complex assortment of tongues, which indicates much shifting and mixing of peoples (see Map 2). The Olmec heartland on the southern Gulf Coast may have been the early home of the Maya. Glottochronological evidence of certain Maya tongues correlates well with the early Preclassic archaeological complexes of the Huasteca, Olmec, Gulf Coast, Yucatán, the Petén region of Guatemala, the Guatemalan highlands, and the Pacific coastal area of Soconusco. In a stimulating article, Joesink-Mandeville (1977) makes a strong case for the dispersal of people from the southern Gulf Coast region northeast to Yucatán along the coast, southeast into the Petén via the great Usumacinta drainage network, and along the west coast of Chiapas and Guatemala. The Olmecs were almost certainly Mixe-Zoque speakers. The Huastecans probably left the southern Gulf Coast and went north around 2200 B.C. prior to the Olmecs' great civilization at San Lorenzo. This same heartland spun off the Yucatecans to Yucatán and the Cholans to the Petén around 900–800 B.C. The other great migrations took place at a much later time from central Mexico to El Salvador.

A great number of other languages are found in central and southern Mexico. The Otomian group is composed of Otomí, Matlatzinca, and Mazahua. Mixtecan languages, such as Mixtec, Chocho, Popoloca,

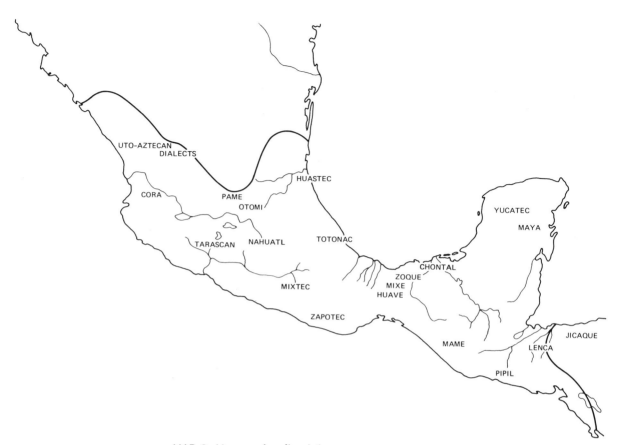

MAP 2. Mesoamerica: linguistic groups.

Mazatec, and Ixcatec, together with Zapotec, are all related in the distant past to an ancient Oto-Zapotecan stock. An interesting language unrelated to other Mesoamerican tongues is Tarascan, which is still spoken around the region of Lake Pátzcuaro; it formerly was the language of most of the state of Michoacán.

Today the vast majority of Mesoamerica's inhabitants speak only Spanish, but a minority is still bilingual, speaking an additional autochthonous Indian language. Though the native languages are diminishing with each new generation, a process accelerated by modern communication and mass media, the mark of the past is left indelibly on modern Mexican Spanish.

NATURAL AREAS   The map of Mesoamerica is shaped like a tilted bow tie, with the left side slightly higher than the right. The knot in the center is the Isthmus of Tehuantepec, a narrow corridor of land uniting western Mesoamerica with the Maya area to the east (Map 1).

In the western section, two great mountain systems run like backbones down each coastline until they are interrupted by an east–west chain of volcanoes. These mountain systems enclose the central high-land plateau or the Mesa Central, one of three highland centers in Mesoamerica, the cultural and political domination of which was felt for centuries. The Mesa Central is still the focus of the leading social, political, and economic forces in Mesoamerica today. The most important area in the Mesa Central is the Valley of Mexico, more accurately described as an inland basin. At one time its waters drained off to the south into the great Papaloapan and Balsas rivers, but a chain of volcanoes rose up to cut off this flow, thus forming a large Mexican inland basin with no outlet. Five shallow lakes were created in the basin floor which were swampy at the shoreline and offered many attractions to aquatic life. East and west of the Basin of Mexico lie two other river basins that figure prominently in the history of Mexico. Puebla, lying to the east over the mountains, is even more suitable for habitation than is the Basin of Mexico because rainfall is more plentiful. This region drains to the east, the principal river system being that of the Pánuco, which empties its waters into the Gulf of Mexico near Tampico. In the opposite direction, the Basin of Toluca is the gateway to all western Mexico and gives rise to the mighty waterway of the Lerma-Santiago, which eventually pours into the Pacific Ocean.

The volcanic chain, called the transverse volcanic axis (West 1964), lends excitement to the landscape. Majestic and terrifying, commanding respect and awe, the great volcanoes soar upward 4000 to over 5000 m and, with occasional tremors and shakes, remind those in the valleys below that they are still the older, dominating force. To them the people owe the fresh springs on the southern escarpments, the swarms of cinder cones, wide lava flows, ash falls, mud flows, and the enriched soils that permit man to grow food more advantageously. They have also provided the volcanic glassy rock, obsidian, for man's tools and andesites and basalts for construction work. The largest volcanoes from east to west are Orizaba and the Cofre de Perote in Veracruz; the Malinche in Puebla; Popocatépetl and Iztaccíhuatl, which guard the eastern rim of the Basin of Mexico; Nevado de Toluca at the entrance to west Mexico; and Tancítaro and the Volcán de Colima in the far west. One may often be in sight of two or three of these peaks at the same time.

South of this volcanic chain, the land falls off sharply into the Balsas depression (Photo 1), an area dominated by two enormous drainage systems, the Balsas River, which empties into the Pacific, and the slower, more tranquil Papaloapan, which winds eastward to the Gulf of Mexico. The southern highland plateau of Oaxaca is the only relatively flat land in the entire depression. The western mountains, Sierra Madre del Sur, border the Pacific Ocean in southern Michoacán, Guerrero, and Oaxaca, leaving a strip of coastal plain offering a natural corridor for movements of peoples. The narrow coastal plain, backed by a wet, hilly piedmont area, continues eastward along the Isthmus of Tehuantepec and southward through Guatemala, forming a region

PHOTO 1. View from Mil Cumbres toward the Balsas depression. (Photographed by the author.)

known as Soconusco (Maps 1, p. 11, and 12, p. 458). Behind Soconusco and past the Isthmus of Tehuantepec, the Sierra Madre de Chiapas rises boldly to prominence and continues down the Pacific coast of Guatemala, bends eastward, and crosses into northeastern Honduras.

East of this range, and also sprouting at the Isthmus, are the mountains of northern Chiapas. Presenting a high and difficult terrain, this system stretches into central Guatemala and forms the highlands of Alta Verapaz and the Sierra de Santa Cruz. There are many minor ranges and intervening depressions, but these two dominant mountain systems enclose the third highland area of Mesoamerica, the plateau where Guatemala City is located today, and border the great tectonic depression from the valley of Chiapas that extends through the Motagua Valley of central Guatemala to the Caribbean. This plateau has greatly benefited from volcanic activity, which spread ash and pumice to the Pacific Coast, preserving the richness of the soils and contributing substantially to the advantages of the environment.

Like central Mexico, the highland country of southern Mesoamerica has both suffered and prospered from its volcanic setting. Human footprints in consolidated mud near Managua, human remains buried under ash fall and pumice, and the earthquakes that shatter men's plans and dwellings attest to the risks of inhabiting this area. Yet the region provides excellent materials for building and for making tools, rich soil derived from weathering of basic volcanic ejecta, and an aesthetic setting with dramatic peaks, clear blue lakes occupying collapse pits or depressions, clear fresh air to breathe, and an invigorating climate in which to live and work. These advantages perhaps outweigh the hazards.

One block of land not yet mentioned is the low-lying limestone peninsula of Yucatán. Having risen from the sea in recent geologic times, this area is an almost level shelf except for the little hills of Campeche. Indeed, Yucatán is the only flat surface of any size in the whole of Mesoamerica.

Although, for the most part, Mesoamerica lies below the Tropic of Cancer, hot, humid climates do not predominate, for altitude is equally as important as latitude. Because of the physical exaggerations of the landscape, early man was offered a wide variety of environmental choices when he ceased to follow wild game and eventually settled down to raise food crops.

In the Mesa Central, an area typical of cool, tropical highland environments, man found many intermontane basins with evergreens and deciduous oaks and pines, and open woodlands abounding in white-tailed deer and rabbits. Higher on the mountain slopes were forests of firs and white pines. Since the region was volcanic, lakes and springs were plentiful and large lakes in the Basin of Mexico contained a variety of fish, reptiles, amphibians, aquatic birds, and insects that provided an easy daily food supply. The climate was cool; rainfall, though mostly restricted to June through November, was adequate to produce one crop per year. This was essentially the same environment as that offered by the highland plateau of Guatemala. The southern highland plateau of Oaxaca was slightly lower in altitude and therefore warmer.

For those preferring a tropical climate, the lowlands of the east or west coasts provided distinctive choices. The Pacific Coast was favored by early peoples. The vegetation consisted largely of tropical deciduous or semideciduous forests. The northern area from southern Nayarit to Sinaloa has a coastal plain as wide as 50 km in places. Many indications of human occupancy are found along the wide natural levees and flood plains. To the east lies the escarpment of the Sierra Madre Occidental. Just north of San Blas the great Río Grande de Santiago crosses the narrow coastal plain to empty into the Pacific Ocean. This is the termination of the Lerma–Santiago river system that rises in the Toluca Valley of central Mexico and is known simply as the Lerma River as it passes through the western states to Lake Chapala. Thereafter it is called the Río Grande de Santiago, but the hydrographic system is one and the same. Of enormous importance to the inhabitants of this area, it influenced settlement patterns and facilitated travel to and from central Mexico and the west coast. South of Cabo Corrientes, the alluvial

**CLIMATE AND
FAUNAL RESOURCES**

plains become narrow and the coast is rugged and mountainous. The Sierra Madre del Sur gives rise to a great many rivers that carry alluvial soil across the level coastal plain, making a shoreline of marshes, lagoons, and mangrove swamps. The Balsas River, bordering the states of Michoacán and Guerrero, is Mexico's second largest river system. Its waters served as main thoroughfares for early travelers, and in later times this same route was used by those carrying tribute to the Aztecs in their central highland capital.

Throughout its history, coastal Guerrero has provided man with food from both land and sea and excellent shelter for sea-going vessels once they reached the great delta of the Balsas River. Mangrove swamps and lagoons, common from the Isthmus of Tehuantepec to the southern borders of Mesoamerica, support abundant fish, mollusks, and varied aquatic bird life and, accordingly, were appreciated as early habitation sites.

The Pacific coastal area provided a moderate annual precipitation and a long dry season. This region was heavily populated at the time of the Spanish Conquest, and Acapulco became the center of Spanish trade with the Orient and Peru. Even today this shore boasts a greater density of population than the east coast.

The eastern seaboard of Mesoamerica is more varied in land forms since it includes the Veracruz and Tabasco coasts on the Gulf of Mexico, areas with low coastal plains; the rather unique Yucatán Peninsula, which forms a special subarea within the tropical lowland environment; and the coastal strip of the Gulf of Honduras, an area of dense, evergreen rain forest, characteristically hot and humid (West 1964). This true rain forest of the east coast contrasts sharply with the Pacific seaboard, although scattered areas of savannas and tropical deciduous woodlands can also be found here. Cultural remains are most abundant along the natural levees where the land was fertile and out of the reach of floods. The east-coast rivers from south to north notable as zones of habitation are the Aguan, Ulua, and Chamelecón in Honduras; the Motagua River in Guatemala; and the Tonalá, Mezcalapa, Grijalva, Usumacinta, and Papaloapan rivers in Mexico. In these zones are found the giant ceiba tree, the mahogany tree, the rubber tree, and a great variety of palms.

An area known as the Petén forms part of this lowland rain-forest environment (Photo 2). The Petén is a modern department of Guatemala but geographically and culturally includes the southern two-thirds of Yucatán and adjacent regions. It presents a series of hilly limestone formations, numerous lakes and swamps, and a lush tropical forest that, paradoxically, has both aided the preservation and speeded the destruction of archaeological remains.

Two lowland tropical east-coast areas present notable variations. The extreme northern part of Veracruz has been so altered by mankind that it is difficult to speculate on its original state. At the present time, it

PHOTO 2. *(Right)* Tropical forest, Petén, Guatemala. (Courtesy of The Tikal Project, University Museum, University of Pennsylvania.)

PHOTO 3. *(Below)* Xlopah *cenote*, Dzibilchaltún, Yucatán. (Courtesy of the Instituto Nacional de Antropología e Historia, Mexico.)

offers environments ranging from savanna grasslands to tropical deciduous forests. As on the Pacific Coast, the natural levees and river terraces of the Pánuco were favorite habitation sites.

The other special situation is that provided by the Yucatán Peninsula. Although lying within a tropical lowland area, it is at present characterized by a tropical scrub vegetation. The natural environment has been greatly modified by slash-and-burn agricultural methods, but it is a naturally dry area with a special hydrographic pattern based on underground water channels. The peninsula is basically a limestone plain devoid of surface streams and is made habitable by natural steep sided pockets called *cenotes,* where rain water accumulates (Photo 3), and by natural wells called *aguadas,* which are funnel-shaped sink holes. Removed from the coast is an area of small limestone hills that lacks even these natural reservoirs.

Aside from these markedly contrasting environments of cool tropical highlands and varying tropical lowlands, there are also areas of near-desert conditions such as those near the northern frontiers of Meso-america. Even in some parts of the Mesa Central, like north and south-eastern Puebla, semiarid conditions exist, the vegetation consisting largely of a thorn scrub and cactus growth.

Thus, when human beings settled in Mesoamerica, they could live at an elevation of 2400 m, at sea level, or at intermediate points. They had a wide choice of dwelling sites: alluvial plains, terraces, caves, valleys, inland basins. They could choose to live near a lake, spring, or river in areas with abundant rainfall, or choose a dry, semidesert climate. Lush tropical forests, savannas, deciduous forests, and barren desert-like terrain offered very different opportunities for exploitation. In some regions they could live where several ecological niches were within easy reach. These are known as microenvironments (Coe and Flannery 1964). As we shall see, groups did not fully exploit the pos-sibilities of all or even one niche, but perhaps utilized a small selection of plants and animals, ranges of which cut across several environments.

In the cool highlands of Mexico and Guatemala, white-tailed deer and rabbit were probably the most common game animals. Bears were to be found in the northern area only. Peccaries, coyotes, bats, raccoons, and a great variety of rodents and other small mammals were typical of the entire area. Especially common in the tropical lowlands were howler, marmoset, and spider monkeys and tapirs, ocelots, jaguars, and opossums. Turtles, lizards, iguanas, crocodiles, and many varieties of snakes were common reptiles. Common birds included ducks, geese, swans, teals, and coots, which were often a valuable addition to the food supply. Owls lived at all elevations; vultures and birds of prey were important as scavengers. Lakes and streams as well as the two lengthy coastlines afforded abundant fish, mollusks, and crustaceans; deep shell middens attest to their importance as a basic food supply (West 1964).

Of special significance to the Indian were the rattlesnake, which was often associated with a rain cult, and the quetzal bird, a native of the humid mountain cloud forests highly prized for its brilliant plumage. Eagles and fish are found as recurrent themes in art. Perhaps most important of the symbolic animals are the jaguar and crocodile, used as principal motifs in the first great art style, which as we shall see, influenced others that followed.

Man Arrives and Occupies Mesoamerica

Geologists tell us that this very irregular land mass, which is responsible for the great diversity of the Mesoamerican landscape, can boast of rock formations dating back at least as far as the Paleozoic era and possibly pre-Cambrian times. But only the approximate contours are known for these ancient geologic periods; the really basic outlines were laid down in the Mesozoic period, many millions of years before humankind was to appear. The great volcanoes forming the transverse volcanic axis rose during Pliocene times, causing existing animals to migrate hurriedly to the nearest zone of safety, probably to the eastern shores. The major climatic zones were already differentiated, but even more violent activity was to modify the landscape and environment further in the Pleistocene or Quaternary period (Maldonado-Koerdell 1964).

The very earliest remains of human beings, bones, and tools date from the Pleistocene period, and thus the geological events at this time are vitally important to us. About 500,000 years ago, more volcanoes erupted explosively and violently. They dammed up the river outlets south of highland Mexico, thus creating the great enclosed basin, the Valley of Mexico. Two great volcanic chains were then defined: one running from east to west in Mexico, the other running diagonally from north to south from Chiapas to Panama. Only the peninsulas of Yucatán and northeastern Honduras have no extrusive rocks, as this area was formed by a gradual emergence of the land from the sea.

The Pleistocene period is best known as the Ice Age; in the New World it was marked by four major ice advances, the Nebraskan, Kansan, Illinois, and Wisconsin, separated from each other by warmer interglacial intervals. The longest interglacial interval was the second, but the best known is the third, known as Sangamon, which lasted approximately 100,000 years and was succeeded by the final advance of the ice caps, the Wisconsin glaciation.

In the region of Mesoamerica at the end of the Pleistocene period, the circulation of warm southern winds led to a greater humidity, resulting in more rain and thus ultimately causing a recession of the mountain glaciers. As the ice melted, rivers flowed swiftly to lower levels, carrying along all sorts of loose material swept up on the way. Winds also helped to erode the face of the land. Today, on the volcanoes of Popocatépetl and Iztaccíhuatl, one can see striated rocks and terminal and lateral moraines, visible evidence of the presence of these ancient ice caps.

When water from the melting ice flowed down the western slopes of these volcanoes, it found no outlet, and the inland Basin of Mexico became a veritable reservoir for water and eroded materials. This central highland area has been more thoroughly studied than other regions, but what happened here is probably similar to the climatic and geological events that occurred at the time of man's appearance in other highland areas of Mesoamerica.

MAN ENTERS THE SCENE

Physical anthropologists tell us that man first entered the New World via the Bering Straits of Alaska. There are many points on which anthropologists differ, but agreement is general that man originated in the Old World and was a fully developed species, *Homo sapiens*, when he came to the Americas. No remains of any other species of man have ever been found. It is also important to note that the highest type of primate found in the western hemisphere is the American monkey, and no one places these creatures in man's direct line of evolution. Thus, fossil evidence leads one to believe that *Homo sapiens* was the original settler of North and South America.

Man had spread over all suitable areas of habitation in the Old World by mid-Pleistocene times. Having developed a taste for the meat of big-game animals, he had learned how to kill them. Where the bison, the woolly mammoth, and the tundra-loving musk-ox wandered, man followed. During the height of the Wisconsin glaciation, which was marked by two major advances of the ice separated by a relatively ice-free interval ending approximately 25,000 years ago, the water was locked up into great ice sheets, and the sea level was lowered at least 90 m and possibly as much as 300 m. This created the massive Berengia land bridge connecting what is now Siberia and Alaska, a 1600-km-wide strip of land that would have permitted easy access to America from Asia (Jennings 1968). It is interesting to note that areas of central and northwestern Alaska were never covered by the ice. When Asia and America were thus united by land, the horse and camel passed from the New World to the Old, while Old World elephants, deer, elk, and moose entered the Americas. Man too, pursuing big game, could easily have passed into the western hemisphere unawares, since climate and resources presented no change requiring adaptation.

When did man first cross over into the Americas? The event is not easily estimated chronologically, for the land bridge must have opened and closed at different times. The broadest interpretation places man's entrance into the New World no earlier than 50,000 years ago, during the latter part of the Wisconsin glaciation. However, optimum conditions would have prevailed about 20,000 years ago, when the forests had retreated due to glaciation and the resulting tundra vegetation and animal life in open country would have been more appealing to the hunter than a forest setting. We shall see that most of the absolute dates for early man in the New World fall between 12,000 and 6000 B.C., but a few are considerably older.

The Berengia land bridge in the Bering Strait region would seem to have been the only available land route for entry into the New World, but speculations have been made regarding other possible means of entry. No scientific data support any hypothesis involving a lost continent now submerged that might have furnished such a bridge.

The postulated route is that of an ice-free corridor east of the Rocky Mountains where high plains would make movement easy. Where many dry lakes exist today, water was more plentiful then. An alternative route has been proposed by Fladmark (1979) who believes it more likely that man moved down along the coast using watercraft to cross difficult places in the summer and traversing the ice in the winter, eventually moving inland via river systems like the great Columbia River. Much of the coastal area was submerged after the Pleistocene and no archaeological remains have been found to lend support. However, Fladmark points out that marine and terrestrial resources would have made food plentiful along coastal tundras and grasslands, and people may have brought along the tool kit of the Diuktai Culture of northeast Asia: pebble tools, pebble flake cores, leaf-shaped and stemmed bifaces, blades and burins. In support of a shore migration is the fact that the early archaeological finds that have been made are all south of Canada where man could have been traveling in any direction. The California record goes back at present to about 38,000 B.C., and no one believes that the first inhabitants have been found. It is interesting that man seems to have entered California from the south (Meighan 1978).

There is evidence that man reached southern Chile by 7000 B.C., and new finds from highland Peru indicate that man was present around 13,000 B.C. (MacNeish 1970). Numerous radiocarbon dates indicate human presence around 10,000 B.C., and recent excavations at Tlapacoya in the Basin of Mexico suggest that man may have lived in that region 22,000-20,000 years ago (Lorenzo 1970). How much earlier he entered the New World is a matter of speculation. If man spread out very quickly, his very wide distribution need not necessarily imply a much greater antiquity. It is usually felt that man has inhabited the western hemisphere for at least 20,000 years, and some specialists feel justified in extending this to 40,000 years.

What we know of this early Paleo-Indian is based on fragments of skeletal remains and a great many tools made to kill and dismember big-game animals and to scrape their skins. Most of these stone knives, blades, scrapers, and projectile points show a technique shared by the Levallois–Mousterian tradition of the Old World. The art of shaping a tool by chipping and flaking from both sides (termed *knapping*) may have originated independently in America. If so, it is remarkably similar to that of the Old World.

Many finds of early man have been made in both North and South America. The big-game animals—camels, bison, woolly mammoths, and mastodons—became extinct at the end of the Pleistocene period as the climate changed and became too warm for them. But the presence of man-made artifacts accompanying the bones of these early grazing animals testifies to man's presence here at the same time. Many "kill" sites have been found where groups of men drove the animals over cliffs, or perhaps into swampy lake shores where their movements were restricted by the deep mire and they could be killed by projectile points, darts, and, no doubt, hurled stones.

Similar scenes were enacted over and over again throughout the Americas. Everywhere man's problem was the same—to subsist. It is beyond the scope of this book to discuss even the most important skeletal remains and artifacts dating from this period. We mention only the pertinent traces of the Paleo-Indian from the particular geographical region that was to become Mesoamerica. Nevertheless, what happened in this area is probably typical of man's development throughout the western hemisphere during the late Pleistocene period.

Undisputed evidence of the presence of the first inhabitants of Mesoamerica is of two kinds: (1) human skeletal remains, and (2) tools unquestionably fashioned by man which are often associated with the remains of extinct Pleistocene mammals. Numerous finds have probably been lost to science because of the manner in which they were recovered. Since the skeleton of a Paleo-Indian is virtually indistinguishable from that of a present-day Indian from the same region, geological and paleontological data must usually be relied upon as the best means of authenticating the antiquity. Thus, only if a skeleton is carefully excavated and studied *in situ* in relation to the stratum in which it is found and the strata proved to be undisturbed subsequent to burial can the skeleton be accorded an antiquity coeval to that of its strata.

The techniques of carbon-14 dating and fluorine analysis are the modern arbitrators of disputes, and in several cases these tests have substantiated or altered existing hypotheses. The same approach also applies to associated artifacts. Surface remains and fortuitous finds can be studied on typological grounds, but their antiquity remains strictly a matter of guesswork and opinion.

Some traces of these early hunters have been found in the present area of the United States and Canada where intensive work has been done. It is believed that the culture of the earliest Paleo-Indians was very simple. The only tools and implements used by these nomads consisted of the very crude scrapers, knives, and chopping tools that they and their ancestors had made in eastern Asia. This level of culture is sometimes called a preprojectile horizon, and it is postulated as characteristic of the very earliest migration from Asia. All authorities do not recognize this early period, but whenever man entered the New World, it is believed that he brought his current knowledge of tool making with him.

At least 20,000–10,000 years ago, these big-game hunters made a great technological change in their tool production. More specialized implements have been found, among them the innovative lanceolate and fluted points. Outstanding is the fine Clovis projectile point (Figure 1), made by careful percussion and pressure flaking to form a channel or broad groove extending part way up the shaft from the base, on one or both sides. Undoubtedly derived from this is the well-known Folsom point (Figure 1), which is more refined and delicate in technique

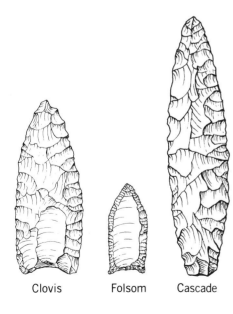

Clovis   Folsom   Cascade

FIGURE 1. Early American projectile points. Shown at one-half actual size. (From *Prehistory of North America* by J. D. Jennings, copyright © 1968 by McGraw-Hill, Inc.; used with permission of McGraw-Hill Book Company.)

and found in a relatively restricted geographical area including eastern
New Mexico, Colorado, Wyoming, and parts of adjacent states. The
Clovis and related points have been found over a very large area from
Alaska to Panama.

The Clovis and Folsom points, together with other long lanceolate
points and projectiles, make up what is called the Big-Game Hunting
tradition. Many of these tools have been found at kill sites near the
edges of lakes and marshes where animals were butchered.

Another great North American tool complex, the Old Cordilleran
tradition, probably originated in the Pacific Northwest area. A different
projectile type, known as the Cascade (Figure 1), was the dominant
tool. It was shaped like a willow leaf and was pointed at both ends.
This point is associated with a series of unspecialized artifacts. Although
there is some evidence of the Big-Game Hunting tradition in Mesoamerica, the Old Cordilleran had the widest distribution in both Meso-
and South America. In age, it would appear to be at least partly contemporaneous with the Big-Game Hunting tradition, and probably gave
rise to the Desert tradition that prevailed in Mesoamerica after 7000
B.C.

With these brief remarks on the major tool traditions that concern
us here, let us examine evidence of the Paleo-Indian's occupation of
Mesoamerica.

**EARLY MAN IN
MESOAMERICA**
By looking at a map of the western hemisphere, one sees immediately
that to reach South America by land man must have passed through
northern Mexico and squeezed through the Isthmus of Tehuantepec
in order to continue his journey south. Whether this trip was made by
large groups or small, it is nonetheless surprising that man left, or that
we have found, so few traces of his passage.

There are indications of his presence in the desert region of northwestern Sonora around 17,000 B.C. Malpais represents a very early
complex of chopper–scraper unifaced tools. No projectile points have
been found. Shells were used for small knives, scrapers, and gouges
(Hayden 1976). Clovis and Clovis-like fluted points are reported as
surface finds from the states of Coahuila, Sonora, Durango, and
Jalisco.

Most of the earliest remains of man come from central highland
Mexico. This area is rich in cultural remains of people from Preclassic
to Aztec times, which are found in a geologic layer known as Totolzingo.
It is necessary to dig down to deposits underlying this formation to
find remains of more ancient occupation. To search for Paleo-Indian
remains in the Basin of Mexico, one may look for the Becerra formation,

which is divided into upper and lower layers (De Terra, Romero, and Stewart 1949). The Upper Becerra formation yields abundant fossils of extinct fauna dating from the upper and terminal Pleistocene. This formation is conveniently separated from the more recent Totolzingo layer by the Caliche III, or Barrilaco Caliche, a formation that effectively seals off the Pleistocene beds. Caliche III represents a severe dry period that may have contributed to the extinction or migration of many Pleistocene animals.

There is some question about how widespread this arid altithermal period was. In Oaxaca, for example, conditions may have been considerably wetter. In the Tehuacán Valley of Puebla, not much change can be seen from post-Pleistocene times to the present. It is possible that the water table was higher and, thus, that mesquite forests and some grasslands covered part of the valley, but no drastic climatic changes have been detected. The recent excavations at Tlapacoya, an ancient site in the Valley of Mexico, do not support the Becerra–Caliche–Totolzingo sequence, and its value is limited to certain localities (Lorenzo 1970).

Even with modern techniques of dating and excavating, the traces of earliest occupation are difficult to assess. Dating is very insecure and estimates may vary by several thousand years or more. If, however, man was making stone tools in Peru by 22,000 B.C. (Paccaicasa phase, Ayacucho), we must be very flexible in our thinking (MacNeish, Nelken-Terner, and García Cook 1970).

PREPROJECTILE REMAINS

Far more tools have been found than skeletal traces of man himself. Speculation about the existence of a preprojectile horizon is narrowed at present to central highland Mexico and northern Belize.

Tequixquiac (see Map 4, p. 86), just north of the old Lake Texcoco in the Basin of Mexico, has long been known for its rich fossil beds of upper Pleistocene date (Aveleyra 1950). Of the many remains found, 20 implements, some of bone, are considered to be of human manufacture. Artifacts recovered *in situ* include a variety of end- and side-scrapers, unifacial blades with lanceolate contours retouched by pressure flaking, and bone awls. These were found in gravels and sands rich in fossil remains of mammoth, horse, bison, camel, ground sloth, and mastodon. The well-known sacrum bone of a camelid carved slightly to resemble a dog or coyote is also from Tequizquiac (Photo 4).

Twenty-five kilometers east of Mexico City, Tlapacoya, which was an island or peninsula depending on the fluctuations of the lake, was apparently an early living site. It has yielded some hearths and heaps

PHOTO 4. Sacrum of extinct llama, carved to resemble the head of an animal. Tequixquiac, Mexico. Width: 18 cm. (Courtesy of the Instituto Nacional de Antropología e Historia, Mexico.)

of animal bones discarded by the residents. The stone artifacts from this site were made mostly of local andesite, but the obsidian, basalt, and quartz used to fashion other tools must have been imported, because these materials are not available in the area. These remains are presently dated around 19,000 B.C. (Tolstoy 1978).

The Valsequillo reservoir (see Map 3, p. 63), located south of the city of Puebla, is another very ancient site. It, together with Hueyatlaco, has rich Pleistocene fossil gravels. Although large collections have come from these deposits, precise dating is lacking. Some charcoal buried by volcanic ash has yielded an astonishing carbon date of 36,000 B.C. Tolstoy (1978) is somewhat more conservative in his estimate but believes the Valsequillo deposits could reach back to 28,000 B.C. Geologists believe that this deposit is as old as that overlying the man-made artifacts. But since the charcoal is not from the same outcrop as the tools and the date is considerably older than any others in the area, future excavations are necessary to confirm or deny the antiquity of the artifacts. A fragment of the pelvic bone of a large Pleistocene elephant bears some crude incisions or scratches that have been interpreted by some, in particular its discoverer Juan Armenta Camacho, as truly early art, representing a bison, a tapir, and mammoths. Whether or not this is pictorial art, there seems little doubt that the bone is of Pleistocene date, as are the incisions, made while the bone was in a fresh state.

On the southeastern edge of Mesoamerica, a very unusual situation has been called to our attention by Dennis Puleston (1975). In looking for ridged fields in northern Belize in 1972, a preceramic site at Richmond Hill (see Map 3, p. 63), rich in crude flint tools, may prove to be of great antiquity. The incredible abundance and patination of the tools and general similarity to MacNeish's Ayacucho material was a lure not to be neglected. In 1980 MacNeish located a number of promising sites along coastal Belize with preliminary estimates ranging as old as 9000 B.C.[1]

After 10,000 years, information becomes less speculative and it is easier to reconstruct the kind of life that prevailed. There was some hunting of large game animals but this never assumed the importance in this area that it did further north in the U.S. Great Plains region.

HUMAN REMAINS, KILL SITES, AND TOOL ASSEMBLAGES

The remains of two imperial mammoths (*Mammuthus imperator*) discovered at Santa Isabel Iztapan provide undisputed evidence that these beasts were pursued by men and driven into the swampy edge of old Lake Texcoco, where they were killed and dismembered (Aveleyra 1956; Aveleyra and Maldonado-Koerdell 1953). A surprisingly large variety of tools was found: obsidian side-scrapers, flint blades, a fragment of a bifacial knife, three projectile points, and prismatic knives of obsidian, all of which are common in later archaeological horizons (Figure 2). The projectile points are of considerable interest, because one is a generalized knife that vaguely resembles a shouldered point called the Scottsbluff type, which is found in the Great Plains area of the United States; one is a Lerma type, a leaf-shaped projectile in the Old Cordilleran tradition; and one is a lanceolate point without a well-defined relative. The kill-site setting and certain tools are in line with the Big-Game Hunting tradition, but the Lerma-type point represents the Old Cordilleran tradition. This latter tradition prevailed during later times in this area. The mammoth finds are currently dated around 7700–7300 B.C. (Johnson and MacNeish 1972).

FIGURE 2. Tools found with Iztapan mammoths. Shown at one-half actual size. (From Aveleyra 1964, copyright © 1964 by the University of Texas Press.)

[1] Although the Richmond Hill tools may not be of such antiquity, Belize has yielded evidence of early hunting and gathering peoples believed to have exploited marine resources along the coast in the dry season and thereafter moved inland to collect seeds. Five long periods are postulated as follows: *Lowe Ha* (9000–7500 B.C.) includes Plainview and fishtail points; *Sand Hill* (7500–5500 B.C.), woodworking chert blades and projectile points, grinding of seeds is probable; *Belize* (5500–4200 B.C.), stone bowls for food preparation; *Melinda* (4200–3300 B.C.), known largely from a coastal fishing village site; *Progreso* (3300–1000 B.C.?), overlapping with the sedentary farmers of the Swasey phase at Cuello (manuscript in press, R. S. MacNeish, S. J. K. Wilkerson, and A. Nelken-Terner. R. S. Peabody Foundation, Andover, Mass.).

PHOTO 5. Reconstruction of "Tepexpan Man." (Courtesy of the Instituto Nacional de Antropología e Historia, Mexico.)

Of approximately the same date is "Tepexpan Man," actually a woman, interred on the former northeastern shore of Lake Texcoco. No more than 5 feet 2 inches (1.6 m) tall, the unfortunate creature was found face down with her legs flexed. There were no associated artifacts (Photo 5). Because of the circumstances surrounding the excavation, authorities were hesitant to accept the skeleton's Pleistocene antiquity. More recently, however, fluorine analysis bears out a date coeval with that of the Santa Isabel Iztapan finds and other fossils of the Upper Becerra formation, roughly 8000 B.C. As a result, "Tepexpan Man" now occupies its rightful place in the record as an early resident of Mesoamerica (Heizer and Cook 1959). The Xico child is probably of an age comparable with "Tepexpan Man" as substantiated by fluorine tests. This find consists of the jaw of a human infant from Xico, a site on the southern shores of Lake Chalco (Map 4, p. 86).

These are the most important human remains of the Paleo-Indian found to date (Aveleyra 1964). Undoubtedly, more will be forthcoming as interest grows in the search for early man, as dating methods are perfected, and as improved excavation techniques lessen the chances of human error.

Although not associated with human remains, ice age fauna have been found on the coast of Veracruz at La Conchita near the mouth of the Tecolutla River (Map 3, p. 63). The giant ground sloth, horse, glyptodont, and mastodon from this area are estimated to be roughly 10,000 years old (Wilkerson 1980).

The other remains of this period consist of assemblages of a great variety of tools which were used to prepare wild plant foods and small game. The Diablo focus in southeastern Tamaulipas (Map 1, and front endpapers), once thought by MacNeish to be older than "Tepexpan Man," is now dated to about the same age (Tolstoy 1978). No projectile points were found and the tool inventory consists of primitive pebble end-scrapers, unifacial flake scrapers with both percussion and pressure retouching, and crude bifacial tools, choppers, and ovoid blades.

The Lerma phase, a stratigraphic layer overlying the more controversial Diablo focus in northeastern Tamaulipas, is important for its laurel-leaf projectile points, which are similar to that just mentioned from Iztapan. It is interesting that these points, together with other bifacial flaked tools, were found with remains of modern animals including deer but with no remains of extinct varieties. The same type of hunting culture has its counterpart in the Ajuereado complex in the Tehuacán Valley in the state of Puebla (MacNeish 1958, 1961, 1962; MacNeish and Nelken-Terner 1967).

Farther north in Tamaulipas, near the Falcon International Dam, surface finds include a Plainview and an Angostura point. These are well-known types more commonly found in the Great Plains of the United States. Specifically the Plainview point is an unfluted projectile or knife, carefully pressure flaked, with a slightly convex base, and no stem or shoulder. The Angostura is a distinctive, long, graceful lanceolate point characterized by a diagonal rippled flaking. It has no shoulders or stem but has a flat or slightly indented base. These two points together with the Scottsbluff type form part of a tool complex that followed the Folsom and Clovis. The fluting characteristic of the latter is no longer found. The Scottsbluff, Plainview, and Angostura points are thought to date from about 7000 B.C. Such isolated finds as these are relatively common, particularly on the northern frontier of Mesoamerica. Clovis-type fluted points, which should be slightly earlier than the complex just mentioned, have been reported from Baja California, Sonora, Coahuila, Chihuahua, Nuevo León, and Durango. Lake deposits in Jalisco present a geological situation similar to that of the Basin of Mexico, and Pleistocene fossils abound near the lakes of Chapala, Zacoalco, and Sayula (Aveleyra 1950). One Clovis point of yellow flint was found on the surface near Apizaco, Tlaxcala (García Cook 1973).

South of central Mexico, evidence is scanty but increasing. Shook (1951) reported the finding of early fossils of glyptodon, elephant, and mastodon from various parts of Guatemala. A preceramic level at Copán, Honduras yielding lithic artifacts and separated from the Preclassic Maya material by a sterile layer was reported by Longyear in 1952. There has been no additional information on this ancient strata. An obsidian Clovis point was picked up near Guatemala City (M.D. Coe 1960b) and another Clovis fragment recovered at Los Tapiales in the Guatemalan highlands. The latter site may represent a small camp-site located on a pass in the Continental Divide, which yielded a variety of tools such as scrapers, blades, and burins, but as yet no skeletal remains. Near Huehuetenango, mastodons and horses were butchered, their bones together with crude stone tools providing further evidence of man's presence on a Pleistocene lakeshore in the Guatemalan high-lands by approximately 9000 B.C.

Further south, a Clovis-like point of flint has been reported from the Guanacaste Province in northwestern Costa Rica (Stone 1972). From El Cauce, on the shores of Lake Managua, human and bison footprints in hardened volcanic mud have been known for a long time but the geologists tell us that these probably do not antedate 3000 B.C.

Thus far, most of the evidence of man's occupation of Mesoamerica comes from the north and central regions. Skeletal material is admittedly very scarce, but the tool inventory is essentially similar to that of man's contemporary north of the Río Grande. Both the Big-Game Hunting and Old Cordilleran traditions are represented in projectile points, and after 7000 B.C. these give way to another era in man's existence, which can best be understood as an extension of the Desert tradition in western North America and which probably developed from the Old Cordilleran and persisted in some areas into historic times.

DESERT TRADITION   Several essential changes marked the shift to a new way of life. It did not take place uniformly nor everywhere and may date in some areas as early as 10,000 B.C., but because some regions share a generalized pattern, it is feasible to speak of a Desert tradition. These shared traits include:

1. Hunting techniques and tools were adapted to exploit the smaller fauna that replaced the big-game animals; thus, projectile points were made smaller and broader. Tools include a variety of choppers, scrapers, gouges, pebble mullers, mortars and *manos*.
2. People lived in extended family groups, probably numbering no more than 25–30 individuals, who were engaged in cyclical wandering in search of food; they were not truly nomadic.
3. Few material possessions were needed; remains of basketry and milling stones predominate in the archaeological record.

In the Tehuacán sequence this Desert tradition corresponds to Ajuereado and El Riego and in Tamaulipas, El Infiernillo (Chronological Chart, back endpapers; Maps 1 and 3). In Oaxaca similar material comes from caves at Cueva Blanca and Guilá Naquitz near Mitla (Schoenwetter, 1974) (Map 6, p. 121). Another cave site further east in Chiapas, Santa Marta (Map 3, p. 63), fits into this complex and the carbon dates are roughly in agreement, falling into a time span of 9000 B.C. to 6700 B.C. (Johnson and MacNeish 1972; MacNeish and Peterson 1962). When found together, these traits represent the almost blind first steps toward the cultivation of plants.

We call this a period of incipient agriculture, and it lasted approximately from 7000 to 2000 B.C. The beginning of this period conforms very closely to the appearance of the pattern of traits listed before; this pattern was shared by many groups in North America (Jennings 1968). During these 5000 years, Mesoamerica gradually pulled ahead of her neighbors until by 2000 B.C. a year-round sedentary village life was possible. From this time we can begin to see the emergence of the distinctive Mesoamerican culture.

The shift from a hunting and gathering existence to a sedentary life sustained mainly by agriculture is one of the most exciting accomplishments in the history of mankind. Cultivation of plants did not, however, "produce" a sedentary way of life, for such a mode of existence could be sustained in certain regions by harvesting and collecting wild food, trapping and hunting game, or exploiting marine and freshwater environments. Indeed, it apparently took man a very long time to rely predominantly on domesticated plants. But the eventual dependence on agriculture seems to have cleared the way for a chain of events that could, and in this case did, lead to the development of a high, complex civilization. In the following chapter we shall examine the critical events that took place in the period called Incipient Agriculture and look for explanations of the processes involved in these changes.

Incipient Agriculture: Man Settles Down

CHAPTER 3

The origins of New World agriculture have long been a subject of interest, debate, and speculation. Agreement is now general that agriculture was developed independently in the New World. The reasoning is convincing. Domestication of plants in Mesoamerica seems to have taken place as long ago as similar processes at work in the Near East, the accepted cradle of Old World civilizations. The principal New World crops—maize, squash, beans, and manioc—form an inventory differing greatly from the Old World staples of wheat, barley, and rye. Moreover, the wild ancestor of each plant was restricted to either the New or Old World, respectively. Distinctive patterns of cultivation and its accompanying technology further reinforce a belief in independent origins. This much seems clear, but in trying to answer questions of when, where, and how agriculture arose in the Americas, opinions vary.

For a very long time, little progress was made in this field. Data on primitive agriculture in Mesoamerica lagged far behind information on pottery types and ceremonial centers because visible ruins usually attract attention first. Although the importance of agricultural origins has long been acknowledged, early researchers did not know where to look or exactly what to look for. Thus, remains that could shed light on the beginnings of agriculture were generally unsought and perhaps even overlooked.

Initially there was little agreement on what crops were raised first. Some felt that root crops might have led the way to domestication because they are easy to plant and require little or nothing in the way of tools. Others felt that the answer would be found in the history of corn, *Zea mays*, because it eventually became the basic crop of much

35

of the New World. It was felt that the beginnings of maize cultivation would coincide with the threshold of civilization, so closely is civilization linked to agriculture. Despite this close association, we know now that maize was not responsible for agricultural beginnings, but the history of the plant is of fundamental interest. Moreover, botanical investigations of the ancestors of maize have helped to unravel the history of other domesticated plants, including squash and beans, the cultivation of which apparently preceded maize.

THE SEARCH FOR CORN Many years ago Spinden (1917) suggested that the origins of agriculture most logically would be found where life was not too easy, such as in a semiarid environment. He assumed, as did many at that time, that corn was the first cultigen, and visualized this environmental hearth as a healthy setting free of dense vegetation, pests, and many diseases and as a result one that would stimulate man to experiment with plants. It now seems that Spinden was partially correct. The chosen environment does seem to have been in the highlands, but the earliest corn we know comes from both semiarid and well-watered regions. In the search for corn, much has been revealed about other New World plant domestication. Over the years, much literature and many controversies have been directed to the study of the origin of maize. Now we think its evolution has been clarified and may be considerably simpler than once thought. The following is a synthesis of ideas drawn from Mangelsdorf (1974), Flannery (1973), and Galinat (1975).

The story centers around three main protagonists: *teosinte*, tripsacum, and a hypothetical wild maize. *Teosinte* is maize's *(Zea mays)* closest relative, a widespread true wild grass native to semiarid subtropical regions of Mesoamerica from southern Chihuahua to the southern limits of Guatemala. Tripsacum is a wild grass with a larger range, from Texas to South America.

Mangelsdorf's modified tripartite theory of the origin of maize postulates the existence of a primitive kind of wild pod–popcorn. The kernels were enclosed by a chaff rather than a cupulate fruit case as in *teosinte*. He sees *teosinte* as being an offspring of this wild primitive corn and tripsacum.

Galinat believes that maize (*Zea mays*) was domesticated from an ancient form of *teosinte*. Tripsacum has no real part in the story of maize. The maize found at Tehuacán was not wild, but merely a primitive domesticate brought in from somewhere else.

It seems that Galinat, along with Beadle and Harlan (Flannery 1973), is correct and the earliest stages of agriculture were already under way before the first phases at Tehuacán. In fact, man has been gathering and influencing the selection of food plants since approximately 8000

B.C. As we will see, *teosinte* was not a major food plant and did not offer much nourishment in the beginning, but it could be popped or ground. The wild ancestors of maize first established themselves quite by accident near early campsites, where their seeds were dropped. Some unintentional selection was made even then, as the early gatherers would have brought back the best husk-enclosed spikes that were less likely to be blown away by the wind before they could get them home. Naturally some seeds would be dropped near threshing and grinding areas. *Teosinte* thrives in such disturbed areas. Over thousands of years, a type was produced that was more suitable to harvest. Man would have recognized the advantage of a harvestable plant and deliberately saved seeds to sow. Then a dramatic transformation took place as *teosinte* became dependent on man for dispersal. Other types of maize were introduced by communication and movement of people, and changes in the ear of corn adapted the ear to man's use. The chaff became softer, easier to shell and hull. Kernels grew larger, yields were more productive, and maize became Mesoamerica's staple food.

Another question often raised is whether maize was native to the New World, since no wild corn is found here today. The recovery of very ancient wild maize pollen, probably 80,000 years old, from deep borings beneath Mexico City proved that there once was a truly wild maize in the Americas.

The corn we know cannot disperse its own seeds or kernels because they are tightly enclosed within a husk. Early corn seeds, however, would have been self-dispersing. Botanists' speculation about what form this early corn might have had were ended in 1948 when tiny cobs of corn were discovered at Bat Cave in New Mexico. These cobs, only 2 to 3 cm in length, were actually the prototype of an early race of corn known as *chapalote*; carbon-14 analysis of the cobs yielded a date of 3600 B.C. Similar cobs were found by R. H. Lister in Swallow Cave in Sonora, Mexico. These are probably of the same *chapalote* prototype, but so few were recovered that they could not be sacrificed for analysis and hence are undated.

Soon after the Bat Cave discovery, two excavations of dry caves by MacNeish in the state of Tamaulipas, Mexico, produced other remains of corn. Some of these cobs were slightly larger, later in time (2500 B.C.), and belonged to the *nal-tel* race, a variety of corn that still exists. Other cobs from southwestern Tamaulipas, dated at 2200 B.C., had some resemblance to the Bat Caves types. The search for primitive corn had started (MacNeish 1958, 1961, 1962, 1967; Mangelsdorf *et al.* 1967). Now one had some idea of what to look for and where. These finds directed attention to a semiarid environment and indicated that under certain conditions it was possible to recover perishable materials. Since Tamaulipas lies on the very northeastern frontier of Mesoamerica, MacNeish felt that evidence of earlier domestication might lie farther south. Accordingly, he made a survey of possible sites in Honduras and Guatemala, with disappointing results. He next excavated the Santa Marta rock shelter in Chiapas and found preceramic remains but no traces of corn prior to 1500 B.C. (MacNeish and Peterson 1962). His efforts were finally rewarded in central highland Mexico, for in a series of dry caves in the Tehuacán Valley he found the earliest corn known.

The corn samples from Tehuacán are so well preserved that all parts of the plant were recovered including cobs. The tiny cobs date from 6000 to 5000 B.C. and were first thought to be wild. However, if *teosinte* is the ancestor of corn, then these cobs show that domestication was already under way and the evolution of maize is still unknown. Beadle (quoted in Lathrap 1975) suggests the area around the Río Balsas in Guerrero as a logical area of origin since dense stands of *teosinte* still thrive there today. What does this mean in terms of chronological development? Beadle tells us that 1000–2000 years must be allowed for corn to have reached the level of genetic modification seen at Tehuacán.

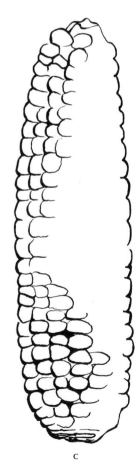

FIGURE 3. Comparison of early and modern dent corn: (a) reconstruction of early ancestral corn (?); (b) Coxcatlán phase corn cob, Tehuacán Valley; (c) modern dent corn. Shown at actual size. (From Mangelsdorf, MacNeish, and Galinat 1967, copyright © 1967 by the University of Texas Press.)

a   b   c

Thus, experimentation must have begun around 7000–8000 B.C. The early Tehuacán corn, the cobs of which ranged from 1.9 to 2.5 cm in length (Figure 3), was too small to offer much nourishment as food. However by 2300 B.C. its response to cultivation was notable and by 100 B.C. the size of the cob had increased to 10 cm in length with tougher and harder glumes and rachises. Curiously enough, in other respects, this is substantially the same corn we know today; it has maintained the same botanical characteristics for 7000 years.

It is hard to trace the actual origins of incipient domestication, as dry caves with early material are not abundant. *Teosinte* does not grow wild in the Tehuacán Valley today. There is a native race of *teosinte* (Chalco) of the Basin of Mexico, whose seeds have been recovered at Tlapacoya dating to 5000 B.C., but neither is this thought to be the earliest. Some small pollen grains of a wild variety were found at Guilá Naquitz Cave in Oaxaca which may be earlier still (Schoenwetter 1974). Deep in the Petén region of Guatemala borings were made in sediments of lakes to the south of Lake Petén-Itzá. These contained traces of *Zea mays* associated with burned grass fragments, dated at 2000 B.C. As yet there are no cultural remains that early in this region, but it is proof of early Maya agriculture in the southern lowlands. This is in accord with the information from Belize where the sophisticated Swasey complex dates to 2000 B.C. At least by 1500 B.C. and probably by 2000 B.C., domesticated maize was important enough to warrant clearing fields and cultivating it.

We believe that a primitive race of cultured maize spread south through Central America and was passed along among agricultural groups to the eastern foot of the northern Andes. The findings of *Zea mays* in Rosamachay Cave near Ayacucho in highland Peru (3000–2500 B.C.) precedes its appearance on the coast (MacNeish 1969). Lathrap believes it spread to the highlands from the eastern foot of the Andes along with other cultigens (Lathrap 1975). Although we now know more about the history of maize, there are still surprises.

The Valdivia culture (3400 B.C.) of Ecuador has pottery decorated with corn kernels, and even a charred kernel itself was preserved, embedded in the soft clay of the pot prior to firing. If this corn is *Zea mays*, it might mean that large kernel, eight-row flint corn was being cultivated earlier in Ecuador than in Mesoamerica, where the evolution had not progressed that rapidly (Zevallos *et al.* 1977). It would also mean that we still have much to learn about the beginnings of corn domestication.

OTHER PLANTS AND THEIR ORIGINS

Although corn became Mesoamerica's most important domesticated plant, one surprising fact is that its cultivation was preceded by that of avocados, chili peppers, squash, and beans, which were undoubtedly more useful for food until maize was produced with enlarged cobs. *Teosinte* had grown for thousands of years alongside beans and squash. This highly successful planting arrangement whereby the beans and squash climb up the corn stalks was not invented by men, merely copied by him from nature's early *barrancas* and still practiced today (Photo 6). As Flannery (1973) points out, with the addition of avocados, Mesoamerica had its common staples by 1300 B.C. Maize supplied car-

PHOTO 6. Cornfield with beans growing up the stalks near San Miguel de Milagro, Tlaxcala. (Photographed by the author, October, 1979.)

TABLE 1
Origins of Selected New World Plants

Plant	Origin	Appearance and comments
Maize (*Zea mays*)	New World	5000 B.C. Basin of Mexico and Tehuacán Valley. Valdivia, Ecuador (?)
Peanuts (*Arachis hypogea*)	New World, probably tropical South America.	
Grain amaranths (*Amaranthus cruenthus L*)	New World	4500 B.C. (?) Tehuacán Valley 5000 B.C. Playa 1, Tlapacoya
Bottle gourd (*Lagenaria siceraria*)	New World	7000 B.C. Guilá Naquitz, Oaxaca. Ocampo phase, Tamaulipas.
Cotton (*gossypium* sp.)	?	Possibly 3183 B.C., Tehuacán. Still complicated and unresolved.
Coconuts (*coco nucifera*)	Polynesian origin likely. Could have floated across to America without the aid of man.	
Sweet potato (*Ipomoea batatas*)	Could have been hybridized in both the Americas and Polynesia.	

bohydrates, squash and beans were sources of plant protein, and avocados provided the fats and oils.

Summarized in Table 1 is the current status of a few New World plants whose origins have been the subject of controversy over the years (Baker 1971; Flannery 1973). Our best-documented sequence of the earliest cultivated plants came to light as a result of excavations in southeastern Puebla in the Tehuacán Valley. This work was coordinated by the Tehuacán Archaeological Botanical Project under R. S. MacNeish who directed work in the field from 1960–1965. A landmark in Mesoamerican archaeology, this project utilized the services of botanists, geologists, geographers, ethnographers, and specialists in irrigation and human and animal remains, all of whom worked with MacNeish and his team of archaeologists in a highly successful interdisciplinary study. A long stratified sequence revealed traces of cultural evolution from an early hunting-and-gathering economy to a fully agricultural village community, which in turn led to the complex ceremonial pattern achieved by Classic and Postclassic cultures.

EXCAVATIONS IN THE TEHUACÁN VALLEY

The Tehuacán Valley is located in southeastern Puebla at an elevation of 1400 m (4500 ft.) (Map 3, p. 63). Long and narrow, it is almost completely surrounded by high mountains that help create the extremely hot and dry environment with rainfall limited to 2 months of the year. Although this is a desert environment, a close scrutiny of the

immediate vicinity reveals that man actually had several microenvironments available for exploitation. The alluvial valley floor, with a spotted
covering of mesquite, cactus, and spiny scrub, was adequate for primitive maize agriculture with natural rainfall. The slopes on the western
side of the valley were also suitable for growing maize and tomatoes
or trapping cottontails. Farther up the mountain slopes thorn and pine
forests provided seasonal wild fruits as well as deer and abundant small
game. Deer might also have been hunted in washed-out canyons or
barrancas, which otherwise had little to offer. However, large caves in
the dry vegetation zone furnished convenient shelter, and from them
man could carry on his varied activities. This concentration on several
ecological niches enabled man to survive seasonal variations in food
supplies and therefore furnished ideal conditions for the establishment
of farming communities. Botanists tell us that the beginnings of agriculture would logically have taken place in just such a setting, where
dry and wet seasons were pronounced and the soil was thin and poor,
giving plants a chance to grow without competition from perennials
or lush tropical ground cover. Man's fertile rubbish-heaps must have
been attractive places for these weedy plants to spring up; thus man
might have found food being offered to him at the very entrance to
his cave.

Of the many archaeological sites located in the valley, 12 were chosen
for intensive excavation. Seven were caves or rock shelters that, because
of the extreme dryness, had preserved all remains of human occupation
and refuse in stratified floor deposits. The other sites were located out
in the open. In addition to plant and animal remains, foodstuffs, feces,
and other perishables such as nets, baskets, and woven cloth were
found. Utensils and tools made of stone, wood, and ceramics were also
recovered. Never before had such a complete cultural record been found
in the western hemisphere.

One of the most valuable results of the Tehuacán excavations was
the evidence they uncovered concerning the settlement patterns and
life of these early people. How much can archaeology tell us of such
remote times? If harvests were seasonally restricted, plant remains may
indicate a spring or fall occupation of the cave. Likewise, projectile
points and scrapers indicate hunting, but if these decline in number
while evidences of basketry, net making, and milling increase, we can
then say that hunting was being replaced by collecting and planting.
In the same way, the depth of a level and the corresponding horizontal
area of occupation, together with the number of hearths, provide the
basis for a population estimate. Surveys were made of floor levels both
in caves and in open sites in the valleys. Three phases, El Riego,
Coxcatlán, and Abejas, represent this period of incipient agriculture.
They are preceded by Ajuereado, a phase during which man was still
a nomadic hunter and collector.

Nomadic microbands engaged in hunting, collecting, and trapping moved their camps several times a year. Now-extinct species of horses and antelope were hunted, but small game—rabbits, gophers, rats, turtles, and birds—provided most of their meat. The enormous quantity of rabbit bones suggests communal drives. Tools include chipped flint knives and projectile points, choppers, scrapers, and crude prismatic blades. There are no ground stones or evidences of weaving, burials, or agriculture.

Ajuereado
(?–6500 B.C.)

Microbands (four to eight people each) occupied seasonal camps, but joined others in the spring to form temporary macrobands, and thus the population increased over the former Ajuereado hunters and collectors. MacNeish (1967) suggests that these people may have been organized into patrilineal bands and believes there may have been shamans who, as part-time religious practitioners, were heeded in matters of ritual and ceremony. These people subsisted primarily on plant gathering and game hunting. Deer had replaced the earlier horses and antelopes, and cottontail rabbits had become more numerous than jackrabbits. The earliest evidence of agriculture is found in this phase. Chili peppers and avocados were probably the first domesticated plants, followed by squash (*Cucurbita mixta*) toward the end of this period. Remains of amaranth (*Amaranthaceae*), a fast-growing bushy weed, well known for its brilliant red foliage, have been found, but this plant may have been collected in its wild form rather than cultivated. Although greatly in demand at later times for ceremonial and ritual uses, amaranth was utilized by the El Riego peoples for the food value of its black shiny seeds (Photo 7). Tiny maize cobs may have been sucked or

El Riego
(6500–4800 B.C.)

PHOTO 7. Amaranth (ancient *huauhtli*) in florescence in Tlaxcala. (Photographed by the author, October, 1979.)

chewed but they could not have been very important as food. Botanists tell us the plant was already on its way to domestication. Cotton, too, may have been domesticated but the evidence is not conclusive.

Flint knapping continued, but the most important innovation in tools was the manufacture of ground-stone and pecked-stone implements—mortars, pestles, and milling stones. The first evidence of weaving and woodworking occurred during this phase.

One of the amazing discoveries at El Riego was evidence of ritual burials, offerings, and cremation or human sacrifice. The burials of two children were found in pits dug into a refuse layer. The head of one had been severed from the body, placed in a basket with a string of beads, covered by another basket, and buried near the body, which was carefully wrapped in a blanket and net. After the pit had been partially filled, another headless body, flexed and wrapped, was also buried in the pit, accompanied by various baskets. Its skull, which also had been separated from the body, was found in a basket, but this skull had been roasted, the occiput smashed, and the surface scraped clean. Another instance, the multiple burial of a man, woman, and child, suggests that perhaps they did not all die a natural death at precisely the same moment.

Coxcatlán
(4800–3500 B.C.)

The macrobands had become semisedentary, perhaps splitting into microband camps only in the dry season, the most difficult time for survival. The occupation sites are fewer but larger, which leads to speculation about changes in the subsistence economy. Although still largely collectors and hunters, agriculture advanced significantly; the bottle gourd, squash (*Cucurbita moschata*), and the common bean (*Phaseolus vulgaris*) were added to the group of cultigens. Domesticated maize is common, followed toward the end of the period by white and black *sapotes* (*Casimiro edulis* and *Diospyros digyna*) that produced an edible fruit. These plants are not native to the valley; their presence indicates that they had been brought in from a wetter region and must have been carefully watered. Tool changes were slight, but a new tanged projectile point, more delicate blades, and new scrapers and choppers were developed during this period. True *metates* and *manos* are found in remains of this phase.

Abejas
(3500–2300 B.C.)

Some outstanding changes in settlement patterns occurred in this period. Some macroband settlements were located along river terraces, where groups of pit houses have been found. These may have been occupied year round. Caves were still used by hunting macrobands in the dry season. Corn was improving by this time and two new domesticated beans appeared, the jack and tepary beans (*Canavalia* sp.

and *Phaseolus acutifolius*). The presence of the latter at Tehuacán at this time is of particular interest since it antedates its previous earliest-known distribution in the western Mexican Sonoran desert region by 4000 years. Another possible domesticate was the pumpkin (*Cucurbita pepo*). Cotton also was widely used. Remains of dogs have been found, and although it is generally believed that dogs followed man to the New World across the Bering Strait from Siberia, these remains are the earliest found in Mesoamerica. Dogs soon became a favorite food.

The older techniques of tool manufacture were continued; new additions included a long prismatic obsidian blade, which became a favorite knife, stone bowls, and oval *metates*.

The hunting of large animals such as deer, pumas, and peccaries gradually gave way to trapping or collecting smaller game animals like rodents, foxes, skunks, turtles, lizards, and birds. This trend can be observed in the decline in arrow points, projectile points, and *atlatl* in favor of the slip noose, snares, and nets.

Through interpretation of the remains at El Riego, Coxcatlán, and Abejas, a gradual transition toward sedentary life can be seen in this area. The subsequent phases in the Tehuacán Valley series fall easily into the Preclassic way of life, for which there is abundant material from many sites.

EXCAVATIONS IN THE BASIN OF MEXICO

The southern part of the Basin of Mexico offers an entirely different paleoecological environment than that of the semiarid Valley of Tehuacán, Sierra of Tamaulipas, and Oaxaca highlands. Until the excavations at Tlapacoya in 1969, early settlements had been found only in xerophytic settings where life was difficult and particularly exacting. Pollen spectrum analyses have helped reconstruct the rich biotic scene in the Basin of Mexico which since has been so drastically altered by man. Between the seventh and fourth millennium B.C., Lake Chalco, a sweet-water lake, offered good riparian soils rich in peaty components (Map 4, p. 86). Forests of pines, oaks, and alders covered large areas whereas at higher levels there were fir, willow, and poplar. The lake was never very deep but was ideal for fresh-water mollusks, turtles, and fish, while the swampy shoreline was covered with cattail, reeds, water lentils, and a variety of aquatic plants. Plant remains are found to include *teosinte*, amaranth seeds, and fragments of wood. *Teosinte* seeds (*Zea mexicana*) indicate a long practice of selection and protection of the plant, but at this time it was still a minor food item. Remains of white-tailed deer, rabbit, dog or coyote, small rodents, and fish and turtles have all been preserved. Between November and May, migratory birds flocked into the Chalco region to spend a more pleasant winter. The inventory includes Canadian geese, ducks, pintails, mallards, teals, and the American coot. When we visualize the magnificent nonpolluted setting combining adequate rainfall, fine alluvium soils, a wealth of faunal and flora resources, we can see that this was an optimal ecological area in which to live.

The ancient volcano of Tlapacoya at times formed an island in the sweet-water lake of Chalco (now drained); when the lake waters receded, the island became a peninsula. Upon leaving Mexico City today, one whizzes past the much eroded hill of Tlapacoya via the super highway to Puebla. Zohapilco is a site located just south of the present town of that name on the eastern slope of the hill. It extends about 100 m on a slight incline of the ancient shore of Lake Chalco. Christine Niederberger (1979) opened a stratigraphic trench 50 m long by 1 m wide, designed to cut across the greatest number of lake and shoreline occupation levels possible. Later extensions were opened at various points. Her excavated material has provided our best information to date on preceramic settlements in the Basin of Mexico.

The two earliest levels of occupation at Zohapilco have been called Playa 1 and 2 (5500–3500 B. C.) in which permanent villages were located along the lake shore. The most abundant foods were turtles and fish but three major environmental zones were exploited: (1) the forests yielding wild fruits and fauna, (2) the rich alluvium soils which favored wild grasses such as *teosinte,* and (3) the plant and animal food from the lake itself. It was the great variety of food resources available year round such as waterfowl and fresh-water fish that made permanent settlement possible. Niederberger (1979) suggests that rice too could have constituted part of the diet. Although not recovered from Zohapilco itself, grains of wild rice (*Zyzaniopsis*) were found in the remains of food storage pits to the north at Loma Torremote, Cuautitlán, where it was grown in Lake Xaltocan (2950–2250 B.C.) (Reyna Robles and Gonzalez Quintero 1978). Although rice made up a very small percentage of each sample, it was consistently represented in the levels suggesting that it was greatly appreciated.

Other evidence consists of hearths, charcoal, and fire-cracked andesite rocks. Nearby were traces of tool production: flakes, chips of andesite, basalt, obsidian, and chalcedony debitages. Andesite, the most abundant, was available locally and made into heavy biface tools. Grey obsidian was brought in from the deposits at Otumba in the northeastern part of the Basin of Mexico, a source widely exploited throughout Mesoamerican history. Playa 2 yielded both prismatic blades and projectile points of obsidian. Scrapers, knives, and notched artifacts were made of basalt.

This exceptional combination of factors made permanent settlement possible at a very early time. The long transition to sedentary life through seasonal occupation by seminomadic bands outlined by MacNeish for the Tehuacán Valley was not necessary in the Basin of Mexico. Fully sedentary human communities were living well at Tlapacoya by the sixth millennium B.C. However prior to 3000 B.C. great volcanic eruptions devastated the Basin of Mexico and covered the southern area with a thick white pumice. Not until after the plant life was once more restored and a new biotic balance was achieved was the lacustrine region settled again. This new phase of development (Zohapilco phase) is one of the earliest of the Preclassic period (Niederberger 1976).

Although central highland Mexico has provided the most complete information about the beginnings of farming life, there is promise of more from other areas, for this was not the only scene of plant experimentation.

THE TAMAULIPAS REMAINS

The Infiernillo complex of southwestern Tamaulipas, an earlier excavation by MacNeish, is known from similarly well-preserved remains from dry caves in arid mesquite desert scarred by deep canyons. This site is contemporary with El Riego at Tehuacán; in both regions the people were primarily meat eaters during the early phases. Projectile points, flake choppers, and scrapers were recovered along with baskets, net bags, and twilled and plaited mats (MacNeish 1958).

Wood seems to have been a more important medium than skin. It was used for making fire tongs and fire drills. Sticks were peeled and whittled to desired shapes and served various purposes in traps, snares, rods, and *atlatls*. Darts were the most prominent weapon.

Fibers from the yucca and *agave* plants provided the material from which the bags and mats were made. The fibers were softened and twisted into strings and woven into a great variety of these articles. Mats are so common and present such diverse patterns that "mat maker" suggests itself as a suitable designation for this horizon. The abundant bag and net containers provided means of carrying and storing wild foodstuffs such as nuts, seeds, and fruits. The gourd, of course, was an excellent receptacle. By comparison, bone and antler tools are relatively scarce, but a few were fashioned into needles, punches, and awls.

The foods are particularly interesting as compared with those of Tehuacán. Among the wild plants utilized were *agave*, *Opuntia* (Photo 8), and the runner bean (*Phaseolus coccineus*), while domesticates included the bottle gourd (*Lagenaria siceraria*), chili pepper (*Capsicum annuum* or *Capsicum frutescens*), and possibly the pumpkin (*Curcurbita pepo*).

In succeeding phases of these dry-cave deposits in the mountains of northeastern and southwestern Tamaulipas, a greater variety of tools has been found; stone mortars and *manos* appear in the remains. Domesticated plants definitely include the pumpkin and red and yellow beans (*Phaseolus vulgaris*). Maize does not appear until after 3000 B.C. and, thereafter, the percentage of domesticated plants greatly increases.

PHOTO 8. Prickly pear bearing fruit. Planted in a tight row, it provides an excellent defense. (Photographed by the author, October, 1979.)

EVIDENCE FROM SOUTHERN MEXICO AND COASTAL SITES

Also belonging to this incipient agricultural period are the remains from caves and rock shelters near Mitla in the state of Oaxaca. The oldest remains show that deer and cottontail rabbits were hunted. The tools include flint projectile points and the usual assortment of choppers, scrapers, and knives. These remains correspond to the El Riego and Coxcatlán phases of Tehuacán. The Guilá Naquitz Cave (7840–6910 B.C.; Schoenwetter 1974) has preserved dried remains of acorns, maguey (*agave*), prickly pear (Photo 8), and organ-cactus fruits, whereas toward the end of the period squash seeds and small black beans mark the initiation of agriculture. The food remains found at another dry cave,

Cueva Blanca (3295 B.C.), roughly parallel those from the Coxcatlán phase (MacNeish and Peterson 1962).

In the state of Chiapas, the Santa Marta rock shelter near Ocozocautla has yielded preceramic remains with estimated dates of 7000–5360 B.C. These remains underlie Preclassic deposits from the cave floors (MacNeish and Peterson 1962). The tool inventory of points, knives, and scrapers is similar to the Tamaulipas complex, but no maize or maize pollen occurs prior to the Preclassic horizon. We have found no evidence of the beginnings of agriculture here; these people seem to have eaten mostly wild foods. A nearby rock shelter at Comitán likewise has yielded preceramic tools but no plant remains, while on the Pacific Coast in the Chantuto zone, the lower levels indicate that many shellfish were collected (Map 3, p. 63). Three large middens were inhabited over 1000 years from 3000 to 2000 B.C. The accumulation of debris is enormous, mostly of small clam shells. There are a few stone artifacts, some animal bones, and lots of charcoal. This could represent seasonal exploitation by inland peoples, but the vast accumulations suggest intensive occupation. The finding of a house floor tends to favor permanence, but periodic influxes of people may have come in to collect clams, fish, and maybe shrimp (Voorhies 1976). Obsidian is known from the earliest levels (3000 B.C.) indicating early contact with highland peoples.

On the Gulf Coast side, there are sites in southern and central Veracruz—Cerro de las Conchas, Palama Sola, and El Viejón—that are preceramic and probably belong to this same period. The earliest remains near Acapulco, Guerrero, and Matanchén, Nayarit are evidence of this same coastal life-style in the west (Map 5, p. 113).

The best coastal sequence we have for the Gulf area is that at Santa Luisa on the Tecolutla River, Veracruz (Wilkerson 1973, 1975, 1979, 1980) (Map 3, p. 63). The surface architecture has been largely destroyed but it is the large underlying middens that are of interest to us here. The preceramic phase (Palo Hueco: 4000–2400 B.C.) is contemporaneous with Abejas at Tehuacán, but represents a simpler version. People lived by hunting, fishing, and collecting, but a riverine orientation predominated. There is no trace of agriculture. The few tools include cracked sandstone cobbles, shells, and one projectile point. Local limestone was procured from hills to the north and obsidian from the El Paraiso mountains near Querétaro. Life was similar to that of the Tehuacán Valley with a different subsistence base.

We can begin to distinguish certain definite trends in this transitional period. Even before the large Pleistocene animals were extinct, man was hunting small game, trapping, and collecting. It is in the highland regions of semiarid environments where evidence has been found of

LIFE DURING SEMISEDENTARY DAYS

the beginnings of plant domestication. Although the dryness of the caves has made excellent preservation possible, something not to be expected in lowland regions, it is nevertheless true that the latter have not produced stone artifacts associated with agriculture. The adaptive process in the lowlands was characterized by collecting wild foods, hunting, and where possible, exploiting the sea.

The early Tehuacán material and that from the Tamaulipas caves furnish the most detailed evidence of plant domestication. It may well be that these areas were actual centers of origin for some cultigens, but they were not the only ones. As we learn more of early agriculture, it becomes apparent that there were multiple origins of New World plant domestication, and initial steps must have been in progress in many regions that interacted and stimulated each other. The dependence of lowland coastal peoples on food gathered from the sea as well as on hunting and collecting food on land reminds us that the steps toward a sedentary agriculture-based economy were not the same in every region; rather, each group developed a subsistence pattern reflecting the food available in each particular ecological niche.

Attention has been called to the similarity of this seminomadic life to that of the Desert tradition, characteristic of the Great Basin Indians who inhabited the western United States in the area of Nevada, parts of Utah, and southern California. The semiarid environment, the tool complex including *atlatl*, a seasonal occupation of camps, and milling stones and basketry are features common to both. Except for the very privileged setting of the Basin of Mexico, the Desert tradition adequately describes life in highland Mesoamerica until about 5000 B.C. After that, distinctive artifacts, along with the domestication of plants, begin to draw Mesoamerica into a unique cultural pattern.

By 2300 B.C. the major domesticated plants had probably spread throughout the highland regions of Mesoamerica. It is interesting to note that squash, avocado, chili peppers, and amaranth, followed by corn, were the first domesticates in the Tehuacán sequence, while pumpkins, bottle gourds, beans, and chili peppers preceded corn in the north. Some of these plants were probably imports to both areas. The domestication of plants was a slow unconscious process, at first merely supplementing the diet of the hunter and collector but gradually dominating the subsistence economy. There was no sudden or rapid progress, no "revolution." This transition seems to have required about 5000 years.

The adaptive processes involved in the transition from hunting and gathering to full dependence on agriculture have been the subject of much thought. Earlier searches for origins of events and "things" such as maize agriculture and pottery will always motivate archaeologists, but at present there is equal interest in attempting to explain cultural process. As a leader in this school of thought, Flannery (1968b) emphasizes the greater importance of studying the mechanisms of change and resulting counteractions. Seen in this light, the early Mesoamericans were not fumbling about to get through each day, but were astute, clever people who had learned how to extract a living from a very difficult environment. They lived on such foods as cactus fruits, maguey, a variety of wild plants, and deer and small animals, some of which were exploited seasonally. Other resources were continually available and, in order not to threaten any wild species, a definite pattern of utilization was employed to avoid upsetting the ecological equilibrium (Flannery 1968b).

For example, the sap of the maguey plant may have been utilized to make a fermented drink like today's *pulque,* but there is also evidence that the plant was exploited for food. Ample remains of masticated cud or "quid" of the maguey have been found in the caves. The maguey must be roasted from 24 to 72 hours to make it edible. Not only did these Indians know how to prepare it as food, but they also harvested the plant precisely at the time it began to die, when it was sweetest. This system of exploitation did not threaten the existing plant supply, but served to weed out the dying plants. Thus, collecting and hunting were carried out according to a planned schedule based on the availability of food resources.

As long as a group adhered to a pattern proven to be efficient, there was little inducement or pressure for change. Eventually, however, some genetic changes, perhaps very minor, took place in one or two species of plants useful to man. These deviations, insignificant and accidental as they may have been, nevertheless set in motion a whole series of events that eventually altered the entire ecosystem. Indeed, in the case of maize and bean cultivation (an excellent combination of starch and protein) as agriculture was intensified through weeding, back-crossing, and further genetic changes, this new way of obtaining food increased in importance at the expense of others. Planting and harvesting patterns would logically have led to grouping of macrobands and reinforcement of the sedentary village way of life.

In one of the most stimulating reconstructions of this period, Bray (1977a) denies the belief of any conscious attempt by man to switch from hunting and gathering to a reliance on agriculture, and furthermore believes that the change-over was not due to any necessity to increase the food supply. He does not believe any pressure or stress was involved. Rather, man drifted into agriculture by accident. The simple small house-garden of "volunteers" gradually became a hodgepodge of very useful plants, requiring little care, but proving very productive. A modern example given by Bray is a garden plot in highland Guatemala that looked haphazard but was actually very sophisticated—it included staple foods (maize, squash, beans, and *chayote*), herbs, ornamental flowers, fruit trees, maguey, cacti, coffee, all effectively enclosed by maize and *chichicaste* shrubs. Some plants protected others, helping to retain moisture and provide shade, and even fertilizing other plants. This is the type of "garden" that could easily have grown up in the ancient household rubbish heap and come to be greatly appreciated.

The archaeological record shows that as population increased, so did the percentages of cultigens in the diets of these incipient farmers. Corresponding decreases are noted in the utilization of wild foodstuffs. As each region, including the lowlands, incorporated agriculture into its local economy new techniques of exploitation were developed, and we see irrigation, terracing, flood controls, and drainage devices as conscious efforts to increase food production. These in turn permitted man to farm new lands, produce a surplus, and become involved in all the complexities of a civilization.

Although our knowledge of life during this period is based on very few sites as yet, there is evidence that as early as 2000 B.C. maize had spread to some areas of the Maya lowlands where it was cultivated along with root crops. Certainly by 1500 B.C. farming villages were common. One of the most fascinating phases in the development of Mesoamerica, the Preclassic period, in which the basic cultural pattern was formed, was about to begin.

Mesoamerica Identifies Itself: The Preclassic Period

CHAPTER 4

The span of time from approximately 2500 B.C. to A.D. 1 is known as the Preclassic or Formative period. During this time the basic patterns of Mesoamerican civilization were formulated, patterns that were to lead directly to the great Classic civilizations after A.D. 1. At the beginning of this long span of time, people were leading a very simple village life, and by A.D. 1 they had already seen the rise and fall of one great civilization, the Olmec. They were, however, approaching even greater complexities of urban life and brilliant intellectual achievements that were to culminate in the Classic period. The Preclassic reveals this transformation.

A number of cultural characteristics of Mesoamerica already have been pointed out. Nearly all made their appearance prior to A.D. 1. That is to say, the characteristic technology, architecture, ceremonialism, specialization of arts and crafts, social differentiation, and hieroglyphic writing and calendrics were initiated during this period. Agriculture was based on a variety of cultigens. Knowledge of irrigation and water control increased. Exchange networks and communications between regions were established. Population increased dramatically.

What happened, then, in these remarkable 2500 years to transform the Mesoamerican incipient farmer into a highly specialized, sophisticated agriculturist approaching the complications of urban life? Several factors were of fundamental importance: continual improvements in agricultural techniques, the addition of new cultigens, an increased knowledge of crop control, and an increase in productivity of plants by back-crossing. Hunting, gathering, and fishing still formed an important part of the economy, but gradually they came to occupy a position second to farming. Life in Mesoamerica was characterized by scattered village communities differing in climate, altitude, and type of ecological niche but sharing new techniques of plant control.

The most widely employed method of farming was slash-and-burn, or *milpa*, agriculture, in which trees were laboriously felled, the stumps burned, and the land painstakingly cleared. Planting was accomplished by pushing the fire-hardened end of a simple digging stick, or *coa*, into the soil. *Milpa* farming could be done in the same plot of earth for 1 or 2 years, but afterward the clearings had to be allowed to revert back to forest for several years to revitalize the soil. Thus, each family had to open up new *milpa* land at frequent intervals. If they were entirely dependent on maize agriculture, it follows that they would have to move about in search of more land to keep up production. The conditions imposed by slash-and-burn agriculture formed an ever present problem that had to be taken into account for any community planning, and every archaeologist must allow for the effects of this system when attempting to reconstruct life at this time. Variations of slash-and-burn agriculture included fallowing systems in which only certain sections were planted, alternating with others left idle. This is known in Mesoamerica as *tlacolol* (Sanders and Price 1968) and was practiced over large areas of the highlands. There is great divergence of opinion as to the size of population these systems of agriculture could support on a permanent basis. To make any meaningful population estimates based on this kind of information, we would need to know what races of maize were available, how many crops were produced per year, and what other potential food sources were available. Now we know the Preclassic community was not wholly dependent on slash-and-burn agriculture, that is, it did have sufficient alternative food resources, so the necessity of periodic village transfers could be avoided in many cases. As we shall see, villagers were not restricted to maize, and in some areas they became very ingenious in exploiting their local environments for a great variety of other foodstuffs.

In some areas such as the Basin of Mexico, sedentary life was possible even before agriculture was known. This was true also for many lowland settlements in Mesoamerica. People in these areas could exploit tropical forests, tidewater rivers, and lagoons and estuaries, all of which provided plant and animal resources that made sedentary life possible at a very early date (Photos 9 and 10). Along the Pacific and Gulf coasts of Veracruz and Tabasco, great natural food resources of many varying microenvironments made a seminomadic life or seasonal occupation unnecessary. Thus, knowledge of maize cultivation, which came to the coasts from highland regions effected no immediate great change in coastal settlements. Maize was easily cultivated on the alluvial flats without causing any dislocation in an already thriving economy based on collecting, fishing, and perhaps manioc cultivation (Coe and Flannery 1967; Green and Lowe 1967).

PHOTO 9. Dugout canoe of type used for travel in the swamps and estuaries of the Chiapas Pacific Coast near Pampa El Pajón. (Courtesy of Maricruz Paillés and the BYU–New World Archaeological Foundation.)

PHOTO 10. Riverine–estuary environment on the southern Isthmus of Tehuantepec near Juchitán. (Courtesy of Robert and Judith Zeitlin.)

The appearance of pottery, weaving, and stone grinding at this time parallels developments in Neolithic settlements in the Near East during the fifth and sixth millennia B.C. Many general similarities between Mesoamerica at this time and Old World Neolithic cultures can be found. Notable differences lie in the particular food plants brought under cultivation and the presence in southwest Asia of wild sheep, goats, cattle, and pigs, as well as possession of the wheel.

The construction of planned religious centers in Mesoamerica, which was initiated during this period, is evidence of further important changes. A sizable labor force was needed, suggesting a considerable increase in population. It also means that by this time not every man was needed as a full-time agriculturist. Farmers must have constituted the bulk of the population, but there must have been a sufficient agricultural surplus to support those engaged in religious functions, civic duties, and craft specialization. Although we know of no great concentrations of population at this time, village residents might have made pilgrimages to religious centers that represented a unifying factor in their lives. In addition to its religious function, the center could also have served as a meeting place for exchange of goods and gossip, gradually formalizing the activity into the typical market system known today, which fulfills both economic and social needs. A jungle rendezvous or marketplace leaves no such obvious traces as a temple-pyramid, but inferences can be made and tested archaeologically. We are impressed today by the size and planning of ceremonial centers, which reflect the power wielded by religious and political leaders and the unwavering devotion of the people. Perhaps the farmers' participation was greater than is often implied. The ceremonial center further signifies a shift in attitude. The scattered villages no longer looked only to themselves; although the clusters of villages may still have been widely separated, they came to share a common religious and political center occupying a separate, specific, awe-inspiring place. In many areas these ritual centers did not appear until the very end of the Preclassic or the beginning of the Classic period. On the other hand, they emerged in some lowland regions around 1000 B.C.

It is helpful to think of Preclassic remains in terms of three, and in some cases four, phases of development. In the early phase man lived in settled villages and demonstrated his ability to maintain a sedentary life based on agriculture. The appearance of pottery and the very first religious centers also belong to this phase. The middle phase was rich in fine pottery, ceremonial objects, and well stocked burials and saw the spread of mound building. The late phase was marked by an increasing amount of ceremonial architecture and greater complexity of material goods. In some areas an additional, transitional phase is justified, the Protoclassic, in which a blending with Classic-period features is apparent. This term is applied to certain regions that developed more rapidly than others.

Traditionally, these phases are rather arbitrarily divided into Early, Middle, Late, and sometimes a Terminal Preclassic or Protoclassic phase, divisions that may be more meaningful in some areas than others. The most outstanding development of Preclassic years was the rise and apogee of the Olmec civilization. Thus it is easy to think of the Preclassic in terms of Early (Pre-Olmec), Middle (Olmec Horizon), and Late (Epi-Olmec) phases. The beginning of the Early or Pre-Olmec phase at 2500 B.C. is marked roughly by the appearance of pottery and lasts until the first Olmec phase (Chicharras) at San Lorenzo Tenochtitlán (1250 B.C.). The Middle Preclassic or Olmec Horizon itself had a wide Mesoamerican impact and can logically be set apart (1250–400 B.C.), combining its two best known manifestations at San Lorenzo and La Venta. A final Late Preclassic phase, Epi-Olmec, deals with the immediate legacy of the Olmec civilization and subsequent development until A.D. 1. This scheme allows some flexibility for the appearance of pottery and correlates roughly with Tolstoy's chronology as compared in Table 2.

The discussion will proceed along chronological lines, but the reader will want to consult the Chronological Chart (found on the back endpapers) and Maps 1, 3, 4, 5, and 6 to place the material in the proper perspective.

The very earliest material (2500–1500 B.C.) comes from such diverse regions as west Mexico, the Basin of Mexico, Tehuacán Valley, Guerrero, and Belize, a very spotty cross-section of Mesoamerica.

THE EARLY PRECLASSIC (PRE-OLMEC)

Matanchén, Nayarit

The Matanchén complex is represented by the remains from one midden on Matanchén Bay, Nayarit, near the base of a hill (see Map 5, p. 113). The site is located in the northwest corner of the bay and covers 3600 m² with debris 7 m deep. Nonceramic and possibly seasonal, Matanchén was a coastal adaptation that may have been typical of cultures from Panama to the United States border. The small sample of artifacts includes obsidian flakes for opening shells, cobble hammerstones, chop-

TABLE 2
Chronology of the Preclassic Period

	Simplified scheme	Tolstoy (1978)	
A.D. 1			
	Late Preclassic or Epi-Olmec	First Intermediate phases 5–9	500 B.C.–A.D. 1
400 B.C.			
	Middle Preclassic or Olmec Horizon	First Intermediate phases 1–4 Early Horizon	900–500 B.C. 1400–950 B.C.
1250 B.C.			
2500 B.C.	Early Preclassic or Pre-Olmec	Initial period	2400–1400 B.C.

pers, and a few remains of fish, turtle, and bird bone. Mountjoy believes this to have been a food-extraction station with the preparation of food done elsewhere. It is dated about 2000 B.C. (Meighan 1974; Mountjoy 1970, 1978).

The Basin of Mexico

Although people lived around the lake of the Basin of Mexico as early as 5000 B.C. and exploited its rich resources and other environmental niches, life was brutally interrupted around 3000 B.C. by a violent volcanic eruption that destroyed life in the southern zone and deposited a thick layer of white pumice over the valley.

It was not until 2500 B.C. that life began to renew itself and the plant equilibrium was restored. This period is known as the Zohapilco phase at Tlapacoya (Niederberger 1976, 1979). There is evidence that during this period of renewal farmers were busy cultivating and controlling plant life. Grains of *Zea* pollen have been recovered that are much larger and three times as numerous as in Playa levels. Squash, peppers, amaranth, and *chayotes* have been found. Fish and snakes were eaten as well as migratory birds such as American coots, pintails, and mallards. Basalt and obsidian, mostly grey but some green, are found at the site which means that they had been brought in from neighboring regions. There is a notable increase and better quality of grinding tools: bifacial *manos, metate* fragments, and circular and oblong mortars. Although no pottery vessels were found, one clay figurine was found in a hearth area (Photo 11). Made from local clay and fired, it represents a pregnant female with four depressions for the eyes and is devoid of mouth or arms. The charcoal in association produced a date of 2300 ± 100 B.C.

The lacustrine environment of the Basin of Mexico had permitted fully sedentary communities since the sixth millenium B.C. By 2500 B.C. farming communities were still exploiting the lake and forests with no clear division between food-gathering and food-producing stages. The shift in dependency was very gradual and it was a shift in emphasis only, for gathering of food continued. This was a different pattern of adaptation than that of the Tehuacán Valley.

The only other material from the Basin of Mexico that may be this early (1870 ± 100 B.C.) is that from Cuicuilco postulated as the Tlalpan phase (Heizer and Bennyhoff 1958a, 1958b). The thin, burnished pottery bears some resemblance to later Ixtapaluca phase ware from Tlapacoya, but Tolstoy (1978) thinks a separate earlier phase may be justified. The main problem to date is that this complex is known largely from mixed fill and has been separated out on a typological basis. Since its excavation in 1957, no additional material has been forthcoming to support it (Figure 4).

PHOTO 11. Clay female figurine, recovered from hearth at Zohapilco, Tlapacoya. Height: 5.7 cm. Dated 2300 B.C. Shown twice actual size. (Courtesy of Christine Niederberger.)

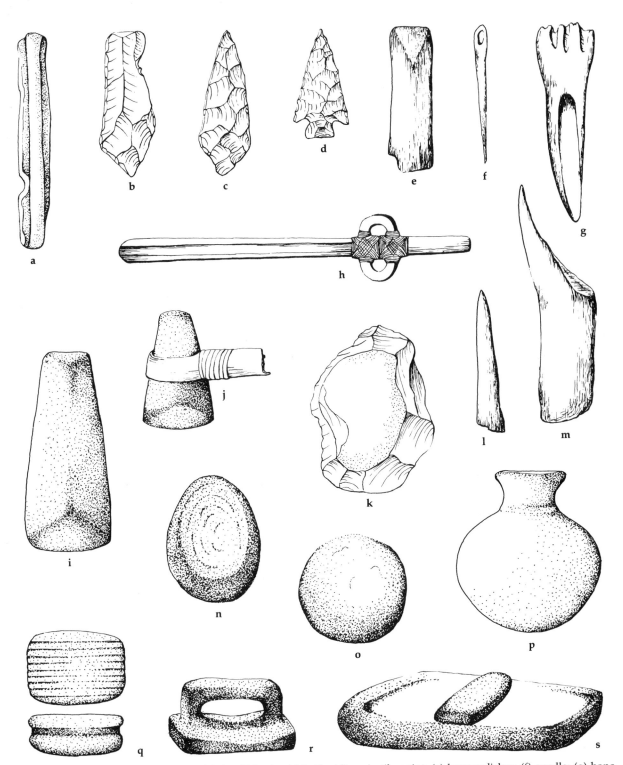

FIGURE 4. Man's tools: (a) obsidian blade; (b) burin; (c) knife; (d) projectile point; (e) bone polisher; (f) needle; (g) bone auger; (h) *atlatl*; (i) chisel; (j) hafted axe; (k) scraper; (l) bone stone-flaker; (m) bone perforator; (n) hammer stone; (o) stone ball; (p) pottery *olla*, (q) stone barkbeater; (r) stone polisher; (s) *metate* and *mano*. (Adapted from Piña Chán 1955.)

Tehuacán Valley   Settled villages were well established by this time at Tehuacán, and a new hybrid maize had been added to the growing list of cultigens. The outstanding innovation in this Purrón phase was pottery, which appears at approximately 2300 B.C. (Johnson and MacNeish 1972). The presence of pottery indicates that man had already learned to select a clay, dampen it, add "something" to it, and fire it. This "something" is called a temper, which may consist of sand, powdered shell, pieces of grass (fiber-tempering) or even ground-up bits of pottery. The addition of temper to the clay strengthens it and also prevents shrinkage in the drying process. The Purrón pottery, known from two cave occupations, has a coarse, gravel-like temper and is crude and crumbly, but its production nevertheless represents a major achievement. The two dominant Purrón vessel forms are the *tecomate* (see Figure 6-m, p. 76) and the flat-bottomed bowl with low, flaring sides. MacNeish (1961, 1962) draws attention to the fact that these two shapes are similar to stone vessel forms of the previous Abejas phase. Could one origin of pottery lie in a desire to duplicate in a lighter material a shape already known in stone? This phase is one of the least well defined in the long Tehuacán sequence, and has been dated partly by a comparison of pottery with that called Pox from Acapulco.

Guerrero   Fiber-tempered pottery very similar to Purrón and of equal antiquity has been found at Puerto Marqués, a site near Acapulco on the Pacific Coast (Brush 1969). Here too *tecomates* are believed to be the dominant form, but the distinguishing ceramic feature common to both Tehuacán and Puerto Marqués is the pitted secondary surface on the sherds, giving rise to the term *Pox pottery*. Figurine fragments, both hollow and solid, make their appearance shortly after. Some of these can already be described as Olmecoid in style. As yet this early period is very imperfectly known, so coastal areas of Guerrero and Oaxaca may yet have much more to yield.

Ceramic remains in the lowlands of Veracruz, Tabasco, Chiapas, and the Yucatán Peninsula during the Early Preclassic fall into two well-defined rather exclusive traditions. The first is found in the Yucatán Peninsula, the second in the coastal lowlands area astride the Isthmus of Tehuantepec region associated with Mixe-Zoque peoples. The fact that these two traditions exist at the same time with no blending of traits not only suggests a singular lack of communication but also different origins or roots, or perhaps different ethnic components. The Yucatecan tradition, ancestral to the Maya Mamom, is characterized by necked *ollas*, spouts, and handles, as well as the absence or rarity of hand-modeled clay figurines. In the coastal lowlands, early material is much more abundant and includes the Ocós complex which underlies and contributed to the Olmec tradition. This region includes and extends out from the Olmec heartland. At this early Pre-Olmec period, there was much activity in small settlements that were widespread on both sides of the Isthmus. We will first look at the Yucatecan tradition that is known from Belize and northern Yucatán.

In the early 1970s not much consideration was given to finding early sites in the eastern Maya lowlands of Belize, the assumption being that it, along with Yucatán and northern Guatemala, was largely uninhabited. This view has radically changed with a great amount of work done in northern Belize and with reports of possible preceramic remains from Richmond Hill (Puleston, 1975).[1] Northern Belize is an ecological frontier lying between the northeast edge of the central rain forest of the Yucatán Peninsula and the dry karstic plain of the north. In depressions between parallel ridges of limestone run the major rivers. Swamps and lagoons are found along the shallow edges of Chetumal Bay. An ancient tropical forest vegetation once covered the limestone ridges, and aerial photographs show extensive ridged fields in the lower swampy areas. It should have come as no surprise for Norman Hammond and his team to discover on one of these ridges at Cuello stratified deposits underlying material known as Chicanel and Mamom. These deposits yielded pottery, remains of architecture, and burials that are at least as old, if not older, than all others in Mesoamerica (Hammond 1977b; Hammond *et al.* 1979). Uncovering remains of such an early sedentary settlement generated tremendous excitement.

Belize

This early material is now known as the Swasey complex, dated by 12 carbon-14 samples at 2000–1000 B.C. The pottery, about as old as anything on record, is far from primitive but is technically well made and sophisticated. This pottery has now been recognized at Nohmul, San Estevan, Santa Rita, and El Pozito in northern Belize and represented by a few sherds at Becán, Campeche (Map 3). In these sites, Swasey sherds are mixed with Mamom remains. Only at Cuello have they been found in a pure, unmixed, stratified layer underlying Mamom material. Outstanding forms include pattern-burnished water bottles, spouts, and necked *ollas* with handles. Most are red-slipped. Decoration is by simple pre-slip incision and more rarely by modeling and appliqué. The complex shows great continuity with little change apparent during the entire phase.

Seven burials, earth or bedrock graves, were accompanied by offerings of pottery, shell-bead bracelets, two jadeite beads, and powdered hematite. Material for flint and chert tools at the site would have been available from nearby Colhá, a distance of only 27 km, but the single fragments of a *mano* and a *metate* of reddish quartzite must have been brought down from the Maya Mountains, and the jadeite possibly from the Motagua River valley.

[1] See footnote 1, p. 29.

Architecture consists of plastered platforms to support pole and thatch superstructures. Possibly pine was used in construction since it provides straight trunks and its resin content keeps out the termites, but above all, it was available only 20 km away. The earliest structure is a low round platform 6 m in diameter; a larger one is apsidal in form.

These people cultivated maize and root crops, and possibly cacao and the breadnut tree as soil conditions were favorable. The raised fields were being used at least by the end of the Swasey phase at 1000 B.C. The Swasey people certainly fished, kept dogs, perhaps for food, also hunted deer, armadillo, and turtles.

When compared to other early complexes, Swasey is the most developed and is believed to be the forerunner of the Maya Mamom pottery. Its ceramics are much more sophisticated and technically superior to either Purrón or Pox pottery and share neither form, color of slip, or techniques of decoration. Nor are they at all similar to the earliest Chiapas and Guatemala material which is related to the Olmec culture.

Further north in Yucatán, the Maní Cenote narrow-mouthed and pointed-bottomed jars found by George Brainerd (1951, 1958) have finally found companionship. For years, these curious pattern-burnished jars from the deep *cenote* cave deposit stood out as curiosities. Now they fit comfortably into a Swasey-type pattern, dated at 1500 B.C., and belong to the early Yucatán tradition (Lowe 1978). As we will see, more bottles and spouted vessels come from eastern Honduras, and although dated somewhat later (Middle Preclassic), they may reflect a continuation of this early tradition. The early Yucatán tradition is seen as being an early, widespread lowland Maya sedentary manifestation contemporary with, but distinct from, pre-Olmec culture in the Gulf–Isthmian lowlands.

Soconusco and Veracruz

Pre-Olmec remains are found to be more abundant in the regions of the Olmec heartland, in the lowland regions of the Isthmus of Tehuantepec, and the Pacific coastal area of Guatemala known as Soconusco (Map 3).

Excavations at Altamira on the Pacific Coast of Chiapas near the Guatemalan border have led to an examination of the possibility of root-crop agriculture. Altamira is located on the flat, hot, relatively dry coast and has a backdrop of a tall rain forest. It is an area where small-scale flood-plain farming could have been practiced with ease.

One particular mound yielded pottery and a great abundance of obsidian chips. Known as the Barra phase, this oldest material has been dated at 2000–1500 B.C. (Lowe 1975). Barra pottery is characterized by abundant *tecomates*, squash and gourd forms, flat-based jars, open bowls, incising, zoned-punctuating, red-slipped rims, some with spec-

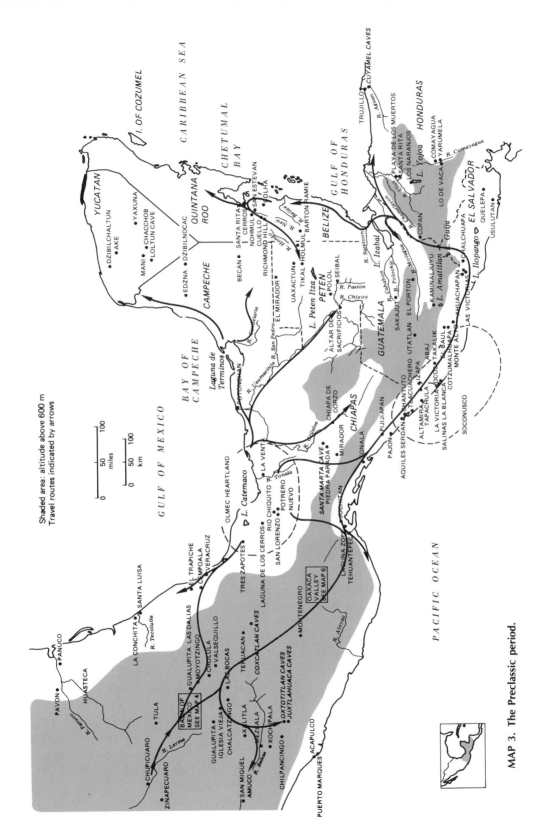

MAP 3. The Preclassic period.

Shaded area: altitude above 600 m
Travel routes indicated by arrows

63

cular hematite and a small amount of red- and white-slipped wares. External similarities are found with contemporary material at Valdivia and Machalilla in Ecuador, the Barlovento phase, north coast of Colombia, Monagrillo and Sarigua, Panama, and the earliest pottery from Ometepe Island in Nicaragua (Lowe 1975) (see Map 13, p. 487). The Barra people show no indications of having exploited their fish or shellfish, nor were they maize farmers, for none of their stone tools could be used for grinding corn. The abundant small obsidian flakes might have served as blades in manioc graters, logically ending up in the household dump where they were found. Identical obsidian chips are also found in the oldest phase at Aquilés Serdán, along with stone vessels, pottery, mortars, and a great variety of small animal remains. Obsidian chips are also reported in the Lagunita phase at Laguna Zope (1500–1100 B.C.) coastal Oaxaca (Zeitlin 1978). Still more Barra-like material comes from Tlacuachero, south of Escuintla in the mangrove swamps, indicating that Barra was not unique, but suggesting that this type of economy was representative of Soconusco.

Not only did it extend south, but also across the Isthmus and north to central Veracruz where the Palo Hueco people had lived earlier without the benefits of pottery or agriculture. After a hiatus of 700 years, four Early Preclassic occupations share much of the Barra–Ocós ceramic tradition including obsidian chips. With the introduction of maize, the latter soon faded away (Wilkerson 1979).

The possibility of manioc cultivation is a stimulating one and would explain how settled communities such as these could have sustained themselves without relying on maize, fishing, or shellfish gathering. Manioc is commonly prepared by baking or frying on *comals,* or stone slabs, but nothing like this has been found. Perhaps it was made into a kind of pudding or bread that was steamed, in which case the *tecomates* would have been ideal receptacles. Corn is easier to deal with as it can be stored and is more easily transported. The archaeological sequence shows that once maize was introduced, obsidian chips disappear from the record. Although Flannery (1973) has reservations about manioc cultivation because no remains have been preserved, Lathrap says that preservation would be very unlikely in such a climate. He believes that manioc cultivation along with pottery-making and religious beliefs moved northward out of the tropical lowlands of northwestern South America, but manioc lost out in competition with maize (see discussions in Lathrap 1973, 1975; Lowe 1975). Elsewhere in Mesoamerica there are indications that manioc cultivation reached Tamaulipas by 1000 B.C. probably via the coastal lowlands, but not until 400 B.C. is there any trace of the plant at highland Tehuacán (MacNeish 1967). In both these areas maize had been farmed for many years. No obsidian chips are found at these highland sites, implying another type food preparation.

Not far east of Altamira, just over the border in Guatemala on the hot Pacific Coast, is the related site of La Victoria. It lies on a narrow strip of coastal plain of savannas crossed by sluggish rivers, creating an alluvial zone. Inland lies an elevated sloping region or piedmont with a luxuriant rain forest. This coastal site furnishes a good example of an Early Preclassic village that, in contrast to Altamira, did exploit its rich coastal environment but does not have the previously mentioned obsidian chips (M. D. Coe 1961). Such foods as clams, oysters, turtles, crabs, iguanas, and a variety of fish were supplied by the brackish-water estuary system while maize was cultivated in the alluvial flats. Maize was probably first traded down from the central Mexican highlands prior to 2000 B.C.

The earliest phase at La Victoria is called Ocós; at this time houses were being built on low platforms of earth as a flood precaution. Construction was simple: Poles were covered by mud and whitewashed. It is believed that the population density was low, and there is nothing to indicate deliberate village planning. Because this coastal region was ideally suited for permanent villages due to the food resources of its lagoon–estuary system and alluvial farming, the sheer number of villages per square kilometer in this area may well have exceeded that of the Tehuacán Valley in the contemporary Ajalpan phase.

In general Ocós pottery is hard, well polished, and technically sophisticated. Like Barra, it too has possible South American origins. Ocós shared early vessel forms with Barra, especially the grooved, gourdlike *tecomate*, but it has some surprising differences. The quality of the pottery is very fine, negating any suggestion of an experimental beginning. These were skilled ceramicists who produced cord-marked pottery, a decoration rare in Mesoamerica but more common in the Old World and northern North America. This ware was decorated by wrapping a fine cord around a paddle and pressing it against the unfired clay vessel, leaving a characteristic imprint. Another most unusual find at Ocós is pottery decorated with thin stripes of iridescent paint, which give an almost metallic luster to the finish. Identical sherds of comparable age have been found in Ecuador, again leading to speculation of intercontinental travel at this time (M. D. Coe 1960a; Lathrap 1975; Meggers, Evans, and Estrada 1965). There is increasing evidence of early contacts between the two continents. For example, Ocós rocker-stamped pottery, both plain and dentate, has been found at many other contemporary sites in Mesoamerica, as well as in the Andean region.

Rocker-stamping is a particular type of incising made by "walking" a sharp edge (a shell?) back and forth over the soft clay before firing, which produces a curved zigzag design (see Figure 6-o, p. 76; Plate 4-m, p. 94). If the edge is notched, it then becomes a dotted zigzag or dentate rocker-stamping. The combining of zones roughened by various kinds of stamping, cord-marking, or fabric impression with smooth areas was a common decorative style. *Tecomates* with tall tripod supports or poorly made solid-slab supports are Ocós features found elsewhere. Small obsidian chips related to manioc preparation, although not found at La Victoria, do form part of the Ocós horizon.

This has now been found to extend over a wide contiguous area from the Olmec heartland south across the Isthmus of Tehuantepec including the Grijalva River basin and coastal Chiapas. The Ocós-related phase (Ojochí) at San Lorenzo is the earliest one at that site and is pre-Olmec.

It is difficult to know how self-sufficient these littoral cultures were and the extent to which the reliable marine resources influenced the growth of villages. Shellfish and fish were exploited, but it is not always easy to know if these were just areas of seasonal habitats, that is, extensions of the inland village. The material from Pajón (Paillés 1978) suggests that these pre-Olmec villages were self-sustaining units in their own right.

By 2000 B.C. pottery making was firmly established in Mesoamerica but, except for MacNeish's suggestion that earlier stone vessels may have inspired a ceramic craft, there is no evidence of its beginnings. Mesoamerica is not unusual in this regard, for nowhere in the world have the initial steps in pottery making been preserved. It is possible that the invention was made at numerous times and places. In the case of Mesoamerica, the idea of making pottery could have come from cultures to the south, where between 3400 B.C. and 2100 B.C. potters at Valdivia in Ecuador and Puerto Hormiga in Colombia were already turning out ceramics (Chapter 9). It may be significant that both Puerto Hormiga pottery and Pox pottery are fiber-tempered as is the earliest pottery in the southeast of the United States. Pottery-making itself and root-crop cultivation are currently regarded as having been transmitted to Mesoamerica from South America, either via Central America or by sea, or both.

THE MIDDLE AND LATE PRECLASSIC (OLMEC AND EPI-OLMEC)

What is known as the Olmec heartland is the area around the Tuxtlas, Veracruz, and western Tabasco (Map 3), so-named because this seems to be where the extraordinary Olmec civilization was developed. There are several major sites: San Lorenzo and La Venta being the most important along with Potrero Nuevo, Río Chiquito, and Tres Zapotes. More recently Laguna de los Cerros is thought to be a cultural and political center that may prove to be of importance equal to San Lorenzo with which it was contemporary. The main cultural developments as we know them come from the excavations at San Lorenzo and La Venta and these names are given to the two Olmec phases: San Lorenzo (1200–900 B.C.) and La Venta (from 900–400 B.C.). Although La Venta rose to prominence as San Lorenzo waned, both were wilfully destroyed, and by 400 B.C. the Olmecs were becoming legendary figures.

The Olmec heartland is too hot, too humid, and too tropical and rainy to be singled out by anyone today as a choice place to live. Yet this is a very rich agricultural area that offered an almost inexhaustible food supply: Fish, aquatic birds, dogs, toads, crocodiles(?), and people were all eaten. Curiously enough, not much hunting was done so the natural resources were never exploited to their fullest capacity. When first discovered, the abundant remains of toads caused no little interest, for what known group has a predilection for toads? It was later found that eating the flesh of this particular kind of toad (*Bufo marinus*) produces hallucinations.

The Olmecs are probably most famous for their monumental stone carving. Colossal heads, "altars," figures, and stelae were all carved in a distinctive style. The basalt heads are amazingly uniform (Plate 1-g,h). They represent a huge head with infantile or Negroid-type features, wide thick lips, and a curious close-fitting cap often compared to the American football helmet. The heads are complete monuments in themselves and had no bodies, whose dimensions would have staggered the imagination. The tallest heads measure 3 m in height and weigh up to 20 tons. They are believed to be actual portraits of Olmec leaders distinguished by the headgear (M. D. Coe 1972). The colossal heads are restricted to this climax area with the exception of Abaj Takalik (see p. 133), a site promising some antecedents for the Olmec sculpture, which until now has had no known precedent (M. D. Coe 1965b).

Stelae, tall shafts of stone, were also carved in basalt. Some show figures in relief, as do the misnamed "altars," large blocks with flat tops used as thrones (Grove 1973). A beautiful example of Olmec style is Monument 34 at San Lorenzo, representing a half-kneeling figure, now headless, which originally may have had articulated arms (Plate 1-f). Sculptures were painted in bright colors and must have represented power and authority.

Clay figurines, both hollow and solid, are amusing when compared with the huge carved-stone figures, for the same stance and heaviness of feeling have been faithfully reproduced in small ceramic sculptures.

Before going into any further detail of Olmec civilization, it would be helpful to know something of the developments at the sites of San Lorenzo and La Venta.

San Lorenzo

Located in southern Veracruz in the Coatzacoalcos River basin, this site has the longest history of all those studied (M. D. Coe 1968a, 1970). The very earliest occupation at San Lorenzo is called the Ojochí phase (1500–1350 B.C.). It ties in with the Barra and Ocós phases of Soconusco, but the pottery lacks cord-marking and iridescent paint. The forms are comparable, however, and figurines are present.

a

b

c

d

PLATE 1. Preclassic-period stone sculpture.
a. Stela 2, La Venta, Tabasco. Height: 2.46 m. (Courtesy of the Instituto Nacional de Antropología e Historia, Mexico.)
b. Stela 21, Izapa, Chiapas. Height: 1.78 m. (Courtesy of the Instituto Nacional de Antropología e Historia, Mexico.)
c. Carved stone ''altar'' (throne), Altar 5, La Venta, Tabasco. Height: 1.53 m. (Courtesy of the Instituto Nacional de Antropología, Mexico.)
d. ''Danzante'' relief stone slab depicting a sacrificed prisoner. From Building L, Monte Albán. Height: 1.22 m. (Photographed by the author.)

68

e

f

g

h

PLATE 1 (Continued)

e. Olmec god. Tlaloc, Monument 52, San Lorenzo. Height: 99 cm. (Courtesy of M. D. Coe.)

f. Monument 34. San Lorenzo. Height: 79 cm. (Courtesy of M. D. Coe.)

g. Re-carved Olmec colossal head (note ear). Monument 23, Abaj Takalik, Guatemala. Height: 1.85 m. (Courtesy of John A. Graham.)

h. Colossal stone head, Monument 1, San Lorenzo. Height: 2.74 m. (Courtesy of M. D. Coe.)

Even in the following Bajío phase (1350–1250 B.C.), there is still little that looks Olmec, but the San Lorenzo people were already busily hauling and dumping fill according to their planned ridge construction. Pottery featured the *tecomate,* bottles of the early Yucatecan tradition, rocker-stamping, and added the differentially fired white-rimmed black ware (Plate 4-l, p. 94).

It is in the Chicharras phase (1250–1150 B.C.) at San Lorenzo that Olmec culture can first be recognized. The differential firing became common, and kaolin ware made of very fine-textured clay appeared, accompanied by various kinds of rocker-stamping and some cross-hatching and hematite-slipped *tecomates*. Olmec figurines of fine-texture white clay are found in this phase as are *metates* with two supports. Monumental stone carving was initiated, although the truly great phase of San Lorenzo is currently dated from 1200–900 B.C.

The site of San Lorenzo is, in a way, a gigantic artifact itself. Situated on a platform rising some 50 m above the surrounding savannas, it is regularly inundated each year. The escarpment on the eastern side of the plateau is rather even, but the other three sides are sharply cut by deep ravines. These are manmade, for the ingenious Olmecs hauled up basket after basket of fill to create the artificial ridges that reach out like fingers, not haphazardly but in a definite pattern. M. D. Coe (1977) now thinks this might have represented a gigantic effigy mound, like a bird flying east, much on the order of those at Poverty Point, Adena, or Hopewell in North America.

There are many mounds atop the plateau, the main cluster being aligned along a north–south axis with rectangular courts surrounded by pyramids. Structures are made of earth and colored clays. There was no stone available locally, and although the Olmecs did not hesitate to move huge chunks of basalt for their monuments, these were not used in construction.

As numerous huge stone carvings were uncovered, it became clear that they had been purposely mutilated before burial. Some represented human or animal figures, others were sculptured thrones or columns. The great colossal heads, perhaps the best known of all Olmec monuments, were also defaced and buried. Although sometimes found deep in ravines, they had originally been ceremonially buried in a line along the tops of the artificial ridges. The time and effort expended by the Olmecs in moving these great stone carvings is staggering. M. D. Coe estimates that to drag Monument 20 to where it was found, presumably with ropes, would have required at least 1000 men. The stone itself was quarried 70 km away and was probably floated on rafts down the meandering rivers.

Another special feature of San Lorenzo is the location of buried drains on the slopes of the ravines, one of which is 200 m long. They are composed of neatly shaped sections of basalt with lids. There are two of these aqueduct systems on either side of the plateau. One seems to have carried water from a ceremonial pool to Monument 9, a kind of fountain. These systems, also known from La Venta and Laguna de los Cerros, are unique features of the Olmec heartland.

The resident population of San Lorenzo, Rió Chiquito, and Potrero Nuevo (Map 3, p. 63) combined was estimated at 2500 persons, which clearly was not enough to get the work done. San Lorenzo as well as its partial contemporary and successor, La Venta, relied on a large outlying hinterland population.

A great variety of artifacts and new materials was imported, particularly toward the end of the San Lorenzo phase. Colored obsidians, serpentines, mica, and schist, together with small sandstone slabs for lapidary working are all signs of increased contact with the outside world. From analysis of trace elements in a large number of San Lorenzo obsidian specimens it now seems evident that the Olmecs procured this material from many sources, ranging from highland Guatemala to highland Mexico (Coe and Cobean 1970). Jade, so intimately associated with Olmec civilization, was apparently not worked at San Lorenzo, nor does it appear there archaeologically.

Many ceramic features are shared with other contemporary sites but two outstanding traits are characteristic. The first is the hollow baby-face figure made of fine-paste clay. The emphasis, almost obsession, with babies is a distinctive feature of Olmec civilization. These hollow "dolls" are also found in the central highlands of Mexico (Plate 2-e) and are considered to be of San Lorenzo date. They were not made at La Venta. The second noteworthy ceramic trait is the deeply carved or excised technique of decoration (Plate 4-g, k, p. 94), often executed on one side of a vessel only. Frequently, red paint was rubbed in the design areas.

In the Nacaste phase (900–700 B.C.) Olmec civilization at San Lorenzo came to an end. New pottery types, typical of Middle Preclassic settlements elsewhere, replace the old; figurines stare out of strange, large punched eyes, a style unknown to the Olmecs. The mutilation of monuments was general, and the defacement by smashing faces, knocking off heads, and marking with axes gives some indication of the effort expended in terminating the Olmec occupation. What brought about the sudden disorder is not known. New wares and figurines are indications of outside interference. The systematic destruction of monuments and their methodical concealment suggest that the Olmecs themselves chose this fate for their great stone carvings. The Nacaste invaders, whoever they were, did not share in or perpetuate the Olmec tradition. The succeeding phase, Palangana, introduces new pottery suggestive of contacts with La Venta, Tres Zapotes, and Mamom peoples.

It was also at this time that the ball court was constructed—Mesoamerica's first. Located in the very heart of San Lorenzo, the Olmecs built a court of earth and clay, basin-shaped and enclosed by ridges on all four sides. This is the land of rubber and it is natural that the game would have developed in such a setting. Abundant clay figurines depict the players in their sporting attire, wearing a heavy belt or yoke. The well-known elegant stone yokes are of Classic date (see p. 248) and form part of the paraphernalia of a ball-game cult. These early yokes may not have been preserved and may have been made of some perishable material such as wood or leather. The game was spread by the Olmecs to highland Mexico where figurines of ball-players are known from Tlapacoya and Tlatilco, contemporary settlements in the Basin of Mexico.

All activity seems to have ceased around 400 B.C., and San Lorenzo, although reoccupied in Postclassic years, never regained the prominence attained by the early Olmecs. San Lorenzo is only one of many sites to be investigated. Río Chiquito and Potrero Nuevo, minor satellites of San Lorenzo, are less well known, but they too have mounds around plazas, colossal heads, and carved-stone monuments. Sherds with differential firing, rocker-stamping, and cord-markings hint of other Preclassic settlements probably contemporary with San Lorenzo.

Laguna de los Cerros is located in today's sugar-cane country 35 km south of Lake Catemaco (Map 3, p. 63). This is another huge archaeological zone with clay and earthen structures with plazas aligned as at San Lorenzo and La Venta. The major mound is oriented 8° west of north as is one at La Venta and at San José Mogote in Oaxaca. Colossal stone heads, Olmec torsos, Olmec reliefs on a huge rectangular block, and small figurine heads in pure Olmec style, as well as carved-stone drains, leave little doubt of the importance of this site in the

---

PLATE 2. Olmec artifacts.

a. Stone seated figure with child, Tabasco? Height: 11.4 cm. (Courtesy of the Metropolitan Museum of Art, The Michael C. Rockefeller Memorial Collection of Primitive Art, Bequest of Nelson A. Rockefeller, 1979.)

b. Hollow figure wearing caiman pelt, Atlihuayán, Morelos. Height: 23 cm. (Courtesy of the Museo Nacional de Antropología, Mexico.)

c. White-slipped seated figurine, Las Bocas, Puebla. Height: 7.6 cm. (Courtesy of the Museum of the American Indian, Heye Foundation, N.Y. [23/5495].)

d. Black stone carving representing a kneeling Olmec figure with hollow in the top of the head. Incense burner? Height: 24.8 cm. (Courtesy of the Museum of the American Indian, Heye Foundation, N.Y. [15/3560].)

e. Hollow seated baby figure, Las Bocas, Puebla. Typical of San Lorenzo phase. Height: 33 cm. (Courtesy of the Metropolitan Museum of Art, The Michael C. Rockefeller Memorial Collection of Primitive Art, Bequest of Nelson A. Rockefeller, 1979.)

f. Large stone votive axe, carved on one side. Height: 29 cm. (Courtesy of the Museum of the American Indian, Heye Foundation, N.Y. [16/3400].)

Olmec world. Bove (1978) believes that Laguna de los Cerros was a major center contemporary with San Lorenzo and that it controlled a hierarchy of nearby sites and could have served as a central place for the control and redistribution of long-distance trading operations.

La Venta   After the destruction of San Lorenzo, Olmec civilization lived on at La Venta from 900–400 B.C., no doubt the most important site in all Mesoamerica at this time (Drucker 1952; Drucker, Heizer, and Squier 1959). La Venta, only 30 km from the Gulf of Mexico, is located on a small, swampy, stoneless island near the Tonalá River. At the time the Olmecs settled there, food was abundant. Tapirs, armadillos, peccaries, howler monkeys, and jaguars were common, and all sorts of reptiles and aquatic life flourished in the swamps and sluggish rivers. But the varied animal life also included dangerous snakes and insects, and, for a farming people, the dense vegetation was a constant opponent to be cut back again and again.

Here on this low island, on about 5 km^2 of dry land, the Olmecs selected a north–south axis on which to erect a well-planned ceremonial center (Figure 5). The largest of the clay and earth constructions is a massive structure 110 m in height and shaped like a fluted cone, with the exterior surface presenting an alternating series of 10 ridges and 10 valleys (Heizer 1968). Although the point is still debated it seems that it is not the result of natural erosion but was consciously constructed. It resembles a giant volcano and was perhaps inspired by a local example. No access to the top is provided by a ramp or stairway; there is only a steep incline of about 30°. We do not yet know if it was meant to be scaled, if it supported some kind of structure, or if it might instead be a burial mound or repository of caches and offerings.

North of this mound lies a great court containing two smaller mounds, bordered by two long low mounds. Beyond this area is a rectangular compound ending in another low central mound (Figure 5). The compound was once fenced in by 2-m basalt columns set in an adobe brick wall. It has been suggested that the whole ceremonial center might have depicted a gigantic jaguar mask. Three massive mosaic pavements, each consisting of about 485 blocks of green serpentine, were laid out to form jaguar masks. Two were found on platforms to either side of the great court, and the third just north of the main pyramid. These gigantic mosaics occupy an area about 4.5 by 6 m each, some portions being filled in with colored clays. The entire pavements were carefully buried soon after they were completed. For this reason it is supposed that these identical mosaic pavements represent massive offerings. One lay under 20 jade and serpentine celts arranged in a cross-shaped design with a concave hematite mirror found at the intersection.

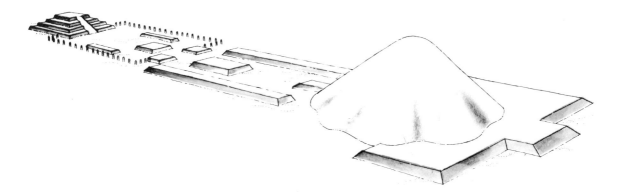

FIGURE 5. Ceremonial center of La Venta. (Adapted from M. D. Coe 1968b, © 1968 American Heritage Publishing Company.)

The entire complex, rising out of a clearing in the jungle, must have been an impressive sight with its painted constructions, colossal stone heads, and numerous stelae and altars. Like those at San Lorenzo, all these great stone monuments were hewn from enormous blocks of basalt quarried some 80 air miles to the west and floated on rafts down the rivers. La Venta is best known for its ceremonial center and stone carving (M. D. Coe 1965a; Stirling 1943). In view of the poor preservation, burials, as might be expected, are few. However, one famous basalt column tomb was found in Mound A–2 (see Figure 7, p. 114). Two youths had been wrapped separately and heavily covered with vermillion paint. The offering laid around them on the limestone floor indicates the special status of these dead, for it includes beautiful jade figurines, beads, a sting-ray spine of jade, and other jade objects. Although burials are scarce at La Venta, a number of spectacular caches or offerings have been found, usually rich in jade and serpentine objects. The jade was polished to a glossy finish with sand and water, a technique requiring tireless persistence. Of all materials available to Mesoamerican artists and craftsmen, jade was the most highly prized.

Jade is often associated with the Olmecs, but was only introduced after 900 B.C. at La Venta, where it has been found in abundance. This was a predilection shared with the Maya. One cache reported by M. D. Coe (1977) at Arroyo Pesquero contained 25 life-sized jade masks and 1000 jade and serpentine celts. Material for these were all laboriously imported and carved, only to be taken out of circulation by burying them in caches. Of course, this would have brought prestige to the elite donor and helped maintain their high value. Although caches and offerings are commonplace in all periods in Mesoamerica, in no other area at any time will we see the great quantity of luxury items in caches that are found at Olmec sites.

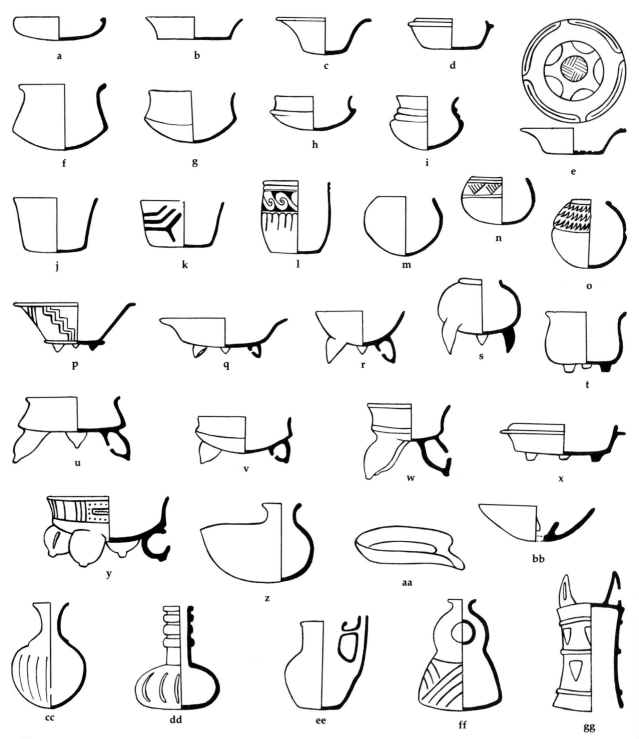

Perhaps the most extraordinary objects discovered in the offerings are concave mirrors made of magnetite and ilmenite, so highly polished that they can reflect images or be made to produce fire. Perforations indicate that they were suspended, and some figurines are shown with just such an object being worn around the neck. Such an exotic pectoral was probably restricted to the Olmec rulers (M. D. Coe 1972).

The usual household remains and refuse deposits are not found at La Venta, and even pottery, so abundant at other places, is not very plentiful. The large hollow dolls or baby-faced figures were no longer made. The outstanding change in pottery is the replacement of the heavy excised pots by a hard white ware incised with the double-line-break. This is a distinctive rim decoration consisting of two incised lines, one of which is interrupted and the ends turned upward (Figure 6-e).

It was during these 500 years at La Venta that the Olmecs were reaching out in all directions, searching for exotic minerals, dealing with the elite in other prominent centers, and leaving their mark from Guerrero and Morelos south to El Salvador. How curious that such a ceremonial center in the swampy lowlands could make such an impact. La Venta seems to have functioned as the traditionally envisioned ceremonial center with a great hinterland population traveling in by water and foot for special events. Heizer (1960) suggested a population of 18,000 might have supported this center. The island itself could not

FIGURE 6. Preclassic-period pottery forms (exceptions: t and x are marble): (a) simple bowl, La Venta; (b) flat-bottomed bowl with flaring walls, La Venta; (c) black-brown bowl with flat rim, Miraflores, Kaminaljuyú; (d) rim-flanged bowl, Chicanel; (e) "grater bowl" with double-line break, Tlapacoya; (f) black-ware composite silhouette, Zacatenco; (g) black ware, composite silhouette, Zacatenco; (h) basal-flange grey ware, Monte Albán I; (i) thin black ware, Zacatenco; (j) deep bowl, Tlatilco; (k) deep bowl, excised decoration, Tlatilco; (l) black-brown, fine-line incised ware, Miraflores, Kaminaljuyú; (m) *tecomate*, Tehuacán Valley; (n) incised *tecomate*, Tlatilco; (o) rocker-stamped *tecomate*, Tlatilco; (p) fine red incised tripod, Miraflores, Kaminaljuyú; (q) composite silhouette tripod, Zacatenco; (r) tripod bowl, Ticomán; (s) *tecomate* tripod, Ocós, La Victoria; (t) marble tripod bowl, Miraflores, Kaminaljuyú; (u) grey-ware tripod bowl, Monte Albán I; (v) composite silhouette tripod, Ticomán; (w) grey-ware tripod bowl, Monte Albán I; (x) marble vessel, flanged tripod, Miraflores, Kaminaljuyú; (y) tetrapod, mammiform-shaped supports, incised, Holmul I; (z) shoe-shaped vessel, Monte Albán; (aa) spouted tray, Tlatilco; (bb) burner bowl with three inner horns, central vent, Chiapa de Corzo; (cc) gadrooned bottle, Tlatilco; (dd) reconstructed bottle, La Venta; (ee) grey-ware vessel with spout, Monte Albán II; (ff) black-brown grooved stirrup-spout bottle, Tlatilco; (gg) incense burner, Las Charcas type. (From the following sources: a, b, dd reproduced by permission of the Smithsonian Institution from *Smithsonian Institution Bureau of American Ethnology Bulletin 153 (La Venta, Tabasco: A Study of Olmec Ceramics and Art)*, by Philip Drucker: Figures 9, 38a, 38c, 40b, Washington, D.C.: Government Printing Office, 1952; c, t, x, Shook and Kidder 1952; d, Smith and Gifford 1965, copyright © 1965 by the University of Texas Press; e, Porter Weaver 1967, courtesy of Museum of the American Indian, Heye Foundation, N.Y.; f, g, i, q, Vaillant 1930, r, v, Vaillant 1931, courtesy of the American Museum of Natural History; h, u, w, z, ee, Caso and Bernal 1965, l, p, gg, Rands and Smith 1965, bb, Lowe and Mason 1965, all copyright © 1967 by the University of Texas Press; ff, reprinted from *Tlatilco and the Pre-Classic Cultures of the New World*, by Muriel Noé Porter, Viking Fund Publications in Anthropology, No. 19, copyright 1953 by the Wenner-Gren Foundation for Anthropological Research, Incorporated. New York; m, MacNeish 1962; o, aa, Piña Chan 1955; s, M. D. Coe 1966; y, Marquina 1951.)

have housed more than a very few elite families. But by 400 B.C. this was no longer a problem. La Venta's monuments had also been smashed and destroyed insofar as possible, but the Olmec culture had already left a lasting imprint on Mesoamerica.

Olmec Art and Iconography

The massive constructions of the Olmecs and their dexterity in moving and carving huge basalt blocks and small jade and serpentine objects are indeed notable, but the impact of their culture on a large portion of Mesoamerica was accomplished by the spread of their beliefs, portrayed in a distinctive art style (M. D. Coe 1965b, 1965c, 1968b).

The idea that the jaguar was the central theme of Olmec religion is now discarded (M. D. Coe 1977). There is however a pervasive jaguar symbolism combined with human baby features. Infantile expressions, linked with snarling mouths turned down at the corners, fangs, a prominent thick upper lip, toothless gums, a deeply notched or V-shaped cleft in the head, and perhaps a full chin, are all distinctive features of Olmec art (see Plates 1 and 2). One interpretation of this strange combination of human and jaguar elements is based on Monument 3, discovered at Potrero Nuevo. According to Stirling (1943), the remarkable carvings depict a woman copulating with a jaguar, a union that might have given rise to a mythical offspring combining jaguar and human characteristics. This theme is also repeated at Laguna de los Cerros and at Río Chiquito. There are many instances of peoples who believe in complete interchangeability of form between man and animals, as well as traditions in tropical South America in which the jaguar appears as the original mother or father.

The were-jaguars, commonly portrayed by the Olmecs, were believed to be the children of this early jaguar–female pair. They were known by the cleft at the top of the head representing the sagittal furrow on the jaguar's head. There may be a close correlation between the jaguar-babies and the sky or rain. The Mexican artist Covarrubias (1946) has suggested that all the various rain gods of Monte Albán, Teotihuacán, Tajín, and the Maya may have been derived from this Olmec were-jaguar.

M. D. Coe (1972) believes this jaguar element can be equated with the later Aztec deity of Tezcatlipoca. Herein lies a fundamental concept that is basic to an understanding of Olmec civilization as portrayed in their art and is related to the origin myth common to all Mesoamerica. Part of the myth reveals that kings are descended from the fire-god and Tezcatlipoca. It was believed that these deities not only created the sun that lights our world today, but also created man in a different form from the deities.

Of particular interest here is the clear separation of royalty (of divine origin) and commoners. Rulers are divine, being descended from the fire-serpent and his offspring, Tezcatlipoca. Versions of this myth are found in Mesoamerica wherever we have legendary history. Because Maya and Aztec accounts are so similar, they are believed to have a common root: the Olmec. Linguistic evidence would lend support. Tezcatlipoca's most prominent attribute is a foot transformed into a mirror, a symbolism that could stem from the wonderful iron-ore mirrors of the Olmec used by royalty. M. D. Coe (1972) points to a close association between the jaguar and royalty in the Olmec cave paintings of Oxtotitlán, Guerrero (see p. 111), in which an Olmec ruler, known by his quetzal-feather headdress, is shown symbolically demonstrating his power to procreate jaguars.

Stocker *et al.* (1980) suggest that the emphasis on jaguars in Olmec art has been exaggerated. Jaguars are indeed present, but many animal representations assumed to be jaguars actually depict the crocodile or caiman. One such example is the well-known clay figurine from Atlihuayán, Morelos (Plate 2-b, p. 72), wearing a skin now considered to be that of a caiman. These authors interpret the cleft head, hand–paw, flame eyebrows, up-turned lip, and crossed teeth as crocodilian symbols.

As we will see, the crocodile will be found to occupy a prominent place in Izapa iconography as well as among the Maya. It is readily identified at a later time on reliefs of stone columns at Tula, Hidalgo; by Conquest times, the *cipactli* (or crocodile) had become one of the Aztec day signs (Figure 11-a, p. 169). As we become more conscious of the crocodile iconographically, we find it to occupy an increasingly prominent role pervading Mesoamerican art from the Middle Preclassic to the arrival of the Spaniards.

There are, however, divergent opinions as to the interpretation of figures and their identification with animals and deities in Olmec art. Joralemon (1971) has refined and tested some of Coe's ideas and believes the Olmec worshipped a number of deities that are the prototypes of many found in later Postclassic contexts. According to him most Olmec art is filled with abbreviated symbolic statements. By breaking these images into their component parts, he compiled a series of symbols and through their combinations or clusters of traits, identified 10 major deities. God I, for example, is shown to be the fire-god, Tezcatlipoca, or the Olmec dragon, associated with the previously mentioned jaguar or crocodile(?). The flame-eyebrows, crossed bands, excised hand–claw, hand–paw–wing combinations all refer to this god. Some of the other well-defined deities would include God II, the maize god, symbolized by a corn plant sprouting from the cleft of the head and God VI, known by a band passing through the eye and across the cheek. This god became known in later times as Xipe Totec, god of springtime. God VII is the feathered serpent to become famous as Quetzalcóatl.

This suggests a great continuity in Mesoamerican religion based on using a direct historical approach as a working hypothesis (Nicholson 1976a). However, not everyone feels comfortable with the identification of Olmec jaguars or crocodiles with Tezcatlipoca, an Aztec deity who followed so much later in Mesoamerican history. Kubler warns us that this assumption can be very misleading, because the stability of form does not necessarily apply to meaning as well, and he advises caution in attributing Aztec meanings to Olmec art (Kubler 1972). Still other interpretations have been offered.

Pohorilenko (1977) thinks that Olmec art is made up of elements that must have been "read," a kind of visual communication using specific signs. He does not believe these composite representations depict deities at all, but a curious anthropomorphic fetish to which belonged certain spirits. The Olmecs lived in a world of spirits and invisible masters. When hunting, fishing, and planting, the Olmec destroyed something of nature and this disruption had to be compensated through ritual and offerings. Pohorilenko interprets Olmec art as containing the seeds of later hieroglyphic iconography which lay the groundwork for the writing system developed later at Monte Albán. Marcus echoes similar ideas regarding deities and the development of writing (Marcus 1976b, 1978).

Of equal importance to the central motifs and themes of Olmec art is its mood or feeling. Olmec art is never cluttered; space is an important ingredient. A pottery vessel, for example, may have a single design engraved or incised on one side only, leaving the remaining portions plain. These people did not have the desire, so common in later Mayan art, to neatly fill the whole field. To the Olmecs, space, slowness of rhythm, and design were essential. Corners are gently curved or rounded. Whether small or monumental, sculptures are usually three dimensional, made to be seen from all sides. Indeed, even small objects seem large and grand, and, when measured, are smaller than anticipated.

Extent of Olmec Influence

The portable Olmec artifacts—mainly small jade and serpentine figurines, plaques, beads, and pendants—moved over great distances in Mesoamerica in Early and Middle Preclassic times (M. D. Coe 1965b; Flannery, 1968a; Grove 1968b). Sculptured objects turn up sporadically across the central highland area, but are particularly abundant in southern lowland Mexico, and extend in an arc from Veracruz south and west to include the state of Guerrero. Although more portable Olmec artifacts can be attributed to Guerrero than anywhere else, the center of the culture is still believed to lie in the region of the great stone monuments.

Distribution of Olmec remains seems to correspond to that of Ocós sites spreading up river basins and in estuary zones. To the northeast Olmec figurines and pottery have been found at Tierra Blanca and Trinidad, Tabasco (Rands 1977), while about 105 km from Palenque in the Usumacinta region an Olmec stela was found during the construction of a road. The whole figure is enclosed in a cartouche. The arms and legs are badly eroded, but the head is portrayed in Olmec style with the characteristic V-cleft (Hernández Ayala 1976). Mirador, Miramar and San Isidro, Chiapas might be considered as way stations along an Olmec route between the Gulf Coast and the Pacific. At Tonalá, Chiapas at the site of Tzutzuculi carvings of the were-jaguar and stylized serpent–dragon flank the stairway of a pyramid dated at 410 B.C. (McDonald 1977). Continuing south, sculptures and rock carvings are known from Mazatán, Chiapas, and San Isidro Piedra Parada in Guatemala. Olmec stone carvings are known from coastal Chiapas around Pijijiapan where Olmec-style life-size reliefs are carved on three huge granite boulders (Navarrete 1974) (see Map 3, p. 63). The area from Salinas la Blanca to Pijijiapan is rich in Olmec remains and carved jadeite pieces. Many can be seen in the regional museum at Tapachula and in private collections. Further south still, the round stone heads at Monte Alto, Guatemala are surely Olmec inspired as well as some of the sculpture at Abaj Takalik. The Olmec impact was felt as far away as El Salvador in the Tok phase ceramics of Chalchuapa and from the stone reliefs pecked on boulders at nearby Las Victorias. These figures are far simpler and cruder than we will find at Chalcatzingo in the Mexican highlands, but they are unmistakably Olmec. Curiously, Olmec objects beyond the borders of the heartland often depict warriors and military themes unknown at home. Olmec influence reached the very southern periphery of Mesoamerica a little later in the Preclassic. At Quelepa in eastern El Salvador a huge jaguar altar with feline face and lateral heads suggests Olmec-derived influence as well as that of Izapa. There is a jadeite axe covered with cinnabar paint at Los Naranjos, Honduras (Jaral phase) and an incised stylized animal on a black cylindrical vase from the Cuyamel Caves—both are clearly Olmec related.

In the opposite direction, west and north of the Isthmus of Tehuantepec, Olmec influence is found in Oaxaca and many highland sites in small portable works of art and in pottery where the were-jaguar, crocodile, and the fire-serpent motifs were copied. Chalcatzingo, Morelos is outstanding as the only highland site with Olmec rock reliefs. These narrate some very violent episodes along with more peaceful views of a royal figure. Cave paintings and a stela in Guerrero are evidence of more distant Olmec penetration. These will all be referred to again in the regional discussions that follow.

Although the Olmecs extended their influence over a very wide portion of Mesoamerica, it should be pointed out that two areas seem little affected: the lowland Maya region which was to see the great flowering of the Maya civilization and the Basin of Mexico.

It could be that these Maya lowlands were very sparsely settled at this time and perhaps received their greatest population boost only upon the demise of the Olmec heartland centers; then peoples may have migrated up the great river systems. Linguistically they are believed to be related groups.

We know that people in the Basin of Mexico were exposed to Olmec culture, and contact is evident as we will see in the ceramics of Coapexco, Tlapacoya, and Tlatilco. But the Olmec ingredient remained very minor in the overall Basin of Mexico culture, whereas in neighboring Morelos to the south, it was a strong influence during the years of La Venta's apogee. The answer may lie in the interests of the Olmecs themselves. The Basin of Mexico offered little to them, whereas Morelos, specifically Chalcatzingo, was the highland gateway to the exotic minerals of Guerrero. For commercial purposes it was not necessary to pass through the Basin of Mexico. Logical routes lay from Las Bocas (Puebla) and Oaxaca, directly to Morelos (see Map 3, p. 63). The Basin of Mexico remained marginal to the Olmec world.

Tres Zapotes   About 160 km northwest of La Venta, near the foot of the Tuxtla Mountains, is the site known as Tres Zapotes. Most of the remains there postdate La Venta, but the earliest may be partially contemporaneous with La Venta. Two colossal heads not easily moved about may well be of Middle Preclassic data and six more heads have recently been reported. What does seem certain is that Tres Zapotes became the most important center after La Venta was destroyed. At this site the Middle Preclassic blends into the Late Preclassic phase (Weiant 1943).

About 50 mounds stretch approximately 3 km along the Arroyo Hueyapan at Tres Zapotes. They are arranged in groups of four around plazas. In front of one of the highest mounds was the lower part of Stela C associated with a flat stone altar. This stela is the most significant find at the site, for it is inscribed with one of the earliest Long Count dates known (see Plate 6-a, p. 166). When the lower portion was found by Matthew Stirling in 1939, he speculated that the missing bar and dot baktun would be a seven. It was not until 33 years later that the missing portion of the stela was found by a farmer near Tres Zapotes, and Stirling was proven correct. Translated into our calendar, Stela C bears a date of 31 B.C. Nothing at La Venta hints of bar-and-dot dates, but we can reasonably assume that some steps were being taken there toward the development of the calendar and hieroglyphs.

The reverse side of Stela C depicts a rather abstract were-jaguar mask executed in an Olmec-derived style. Small Olmec jades sometimes bear hieroglyphs, and although these have no meaning for us as yet, they imply that calendrics and hieroglyphic writing were already being developed in the Middle Preclassic or even earlier.

In addition to Stela C there are other interesting aspects of the Late Preclassic period at Tres Zapotes, including a rectangular pyramid faced with cut stone, but no use of lime mortar (a later development), and the continuation of oxidized white-rim pottery and flat-bottomed dishes. In other respects the ceramics differ from La Venta and Middle Preclassic lowland sites. Bowls with wide everted rims and grooved and modeled decorations became common, a feature shared with Izapa and some Petén sites, and the composite-silhouette bowls are distinctly late in flavor. Five figurine types have been distinguished, all solid and made by hand. Some of these too are credited with Olmecoid features (Drucker 1943a).

A few kilometers west of the ruins of Cempoala on the banks of the Chachalacas River is a site called El Trapiche, known through excavations of José García Payón. Zoned rocker-stamped and excised pottery, as well as white-rimmed black ware, are known to come from the lowest deposits, along with clay figurines similar to highland D types (Ford 1969).[2]

Olmec Society and Its Decline

Today few would disagree that Olmec society was authoritarian with absolute power in the hands of royal kings. This was not an egalitarian social system, but one in which semidivine kings descended from a mythical union of a jaguar–female couple and had their portraits immortalized on huge colossal stone heads. This birthright was constantly reaffirmed in art as a means to reinforce royal power.

As a practical matter, this resulted in the huge public-works projects that are found at San Lorenzo, the first "capital." Built in a very rich productive area, it could nevertheless support only a small percentage of the thousands needed as a labor force, which was drawn from the great tropical forest hinterland. Special commodities were deemed necessary for ritual and prestige such as iron-ore mirrors and jade, while obsidian was in demand for cutting tools. Cacao was another valuable commodity, whether for use both as a drink and as currency is not known. The procurement of all these items and many more would involve various exchange networks, accounting for Olmec "presence" in the many different areas cited. The mechanisms of operation are not known, but probably elite items were exchanged only with the elite of

---

[2] This type of classification, often encountered in the following pages, refers to the system of figurine identification devised by George Vaillant (see Table 3, p. 99).

other groups. Possibly crocodile meat and pelts were an Olmec export (Stocker *et al.* 1980). Obsidian would have circulated in another network with a wider distribution and was procured from various sources. At San Lorenzo most came from Guadalupe Victoria and El Chayal (see Map 8, p. 206). What did the Olmecs offer in return? They probably offered to other elite the promise of power, prestige, an association with kings and a religious cult, a chance also to become semi-divine, control the populace, and exact tribute and labor.

What caused the violent end of San Lorenzo and the vicious destruction of the monuments is not known. A comeback attempt was made in another setting at La Venta, with similar catastrophic results. Drennan (1976) has attempted to explain these phenomena by applying a theory of R. A. Rappaport, that illustrates the cost of ritual sanctification and demonstrates how in a limited situation a fatal cycle can result. Increased production can only lead to increased expenses; this in turn demands greater production that ultimately cannot be met and results in a total collapse of the economic system and society. Two solutions are possible. Either production is increased through technology or some change is made that puts a ceiling on the ritual expenditures. Such a change could be a dictatorial state system of tight controls. The first alternative was probably beyond the Olmecs' capabilities and the second, if tried, was unsuccessful.

We will find similar problems later among the Classic Maya. The Olmec collapse is seen as a faulty hierarchy that lost control. M. D. Coe would agree, as he visualizes a social revolution that destroyed the monuments. Grove (personal communication) proposes that a ruler's monuments were destroyed at his death and buried in clusters as we will find happened among the Maya. This could account for the defacement of the monuments, but the total devastation suggests a massive dissatisfaction with the whole social fabric.

The Huasteca

Farther north, early material is found on the very periphery of Mesoamerica in the Gulf Coast region known as the Huasteca (see Map 3, p. 63). This area is believed to have been settled around 2200 B.C. by people from the Olmec region (Joesink-Mandeville 1977; Kaufman 1976). Just west of the Pánuco River and only about 160 km southeast of the Sierra de Tamaulipas, two large stratigraphic excavations have proved most rewarding. The phases named Pavón and Ponce probably antedate 1000 B.C. and fall within the range of the Early Preclassic period (MacNeish 1954).

Stone tools were not frequent in either phase, but fragments of *metates* and *manos*, scrapers, and flints, followed by obsidian flakes, all point to corn agriculture supplemented by hunting. The earliest pottery, that of Pavón, is some of the poorest quality found to date in Mesoamerica.

It is crumbly and granular—some pots were not even fired. Forms are few and simple: *ollas* and flat-bottomed bowls. When present, decoration consists of simple cylindrical punchings. Figurines are notably lacking. After a slight gap in time, the Ponce phase continues with some Pavón traits, adding obsidian, some simple new bowl forms, and five figurine types. The quality of the pottery is not as fine as at contemporary sites in the south. The Huasteca (Ekholm 1944) conforms generally to the emerging lowland Preclassic pattern, sharing monochrome wares and the lack of vessel supports, but there is nothing specifically suggestive of the Olmecs. The greatest Olmec influence lay to the south and west, from where it spread to the highlands.

The Basin of Mexico

We now come to the Basin of Mexico, where archaeology of the Preclassic horizon has been extremely difficult to interpret for several reasons. First, in addition to nourishing its own local cultures, the Basin of Mexico received influences from many other directions. Thus, there are many different features from many different peoples who met, mingled, and competed. Some cultural traits lost out, others survived, and some were altered almost beyond recognition. Into this veritable stew of cultural remains the unsuspecting archaeologists dug their first trenches, which, as it turned out, produced selected slices of Middle and Late Preclassic material. Only now, after 25 years of probing, erring, and revising, do we have a chronological sequence for this complex region that promises reasonable cross correlations with the lowlands and Maya area. The presentation that follows is a much simplified version of events based on Niederberger's (1976) work at Zohapilco–Tlapacoya and Tolstoy's work at various Basin sites including Coapexco (Tolstoy 1975; Tolstoy *et al.* 1977; Tolstoy and Paradis 1970, 1971; Tolstoy and Fish 1975). (See Map 4.)

   Preclassic events after 1500 B.C. in the Basin of Mexico have been grouped into three large chronological divisions of Ixtapaluca, Zacatenco, and Ticomán. Each of these in turn have been fractured into a number of subphases that are almost indistinguishable one from another to all but the experts who have the material at hand. Here, only the broadest outlines will be attempted; further details are available in Tolstoy (1978).

The earliest full ceramic phase from the Basin of Mexico is Nevada, estimated to have lasted from 1400 B.C. to 1250 B.C. The Nevada material correlates with Tierras Largas in Oaxaca and Ocós on coastal Guatemala. (Niederberger hesitates to include the Nevada phase within Ixtapaluca,

THE IXTAPALUCA PHASE (1400–800 B.C.) (EH 1–4; FI 1–2)[3]

---

[3] Abbreviations for chronology used by Tolstoy (1978) and Sanders, Parsons, and Santley (1979): IP, Initial Period; EH, Early Horizon; FI, First Intermediate; MH, Middle Horizon; SI, Second Intermediate; LH, Late Horizon. See Chronological Chart, found on back endpapers.

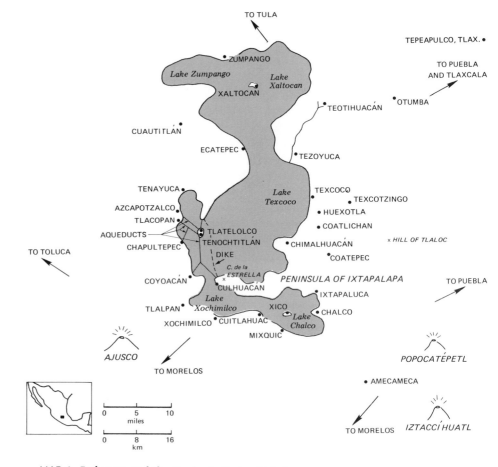

MAP 4. Early man and the Preclassic Basin of Mexico.

which accounts for the question mark on the chart on the back endpapers.) This material in the Basin of Mexico is known from a strata at Zohapilco–Tlapacoya lying directly on sterile soil and containing some elements of the Ayotla subphase which lay above (Niederberger 1976). Although the sample is admittedly small, the Nevada farming community made stone andesite tools and sophisticated pottery. The latter is thin and well-polished with forms including semispherical bowls, *ollas* with out-curved rims or short necks, plates, and low-walled vessels with flat bottoms. Characteristic decoration is by fine channeling, zoned-thumbnail, rocker-stamping, and red slip, with or without specular hematite. A clay figurine without a mouth, but with rudimentary arms is somewhat similar to the earlier Zohapilco figurine (Photo 11, p. 58).

Directly above Nevada, Niederberger found remains of the Ayotla complex, dated at 1250–1000 B.C. Ceramic forms include *ollas*, flat-bottomed bowls, small *tecomates,* and jars with short, wide necks. Decorations consist of opposed spirals, St. Andrews's cross, excised or carved motifs, such as wing–paw and flame brows, incised geometric lines in zones and rocker-stamping, and negative painting that is rather hazy in whitish or grey tones, sometimes combined with incised decorations. Differentially fired wares also occur. So-called Olmec figurines and types D-1, D-2, and K are typical of both Ayotla and the following Manantial subphase as are representations of ball players and acrobats. These two phases also share work in obsidian, basalt, andesite, and chalcedony.

Within the Ayotla time-frame is Coapexco, an early sedentary community unusual in several features and dated by Tolstoy (1978) from 1150–1100 B.C. Coapexco is not a bottom valley site but is located at an elevation of 2600 m on the flanks of Iztaccíhuatl, an altitude higher than any settlement either before or after its brief occupation. The precise size of Coapexco is hard to assess but remains cover an area of about 50 ha. The surface material was found concentrated in numerous patches of high density, which contained not only pottery vessels but figurine fragments and *manos* and *metates*. The concentration of surface debris suggests that it accumulated in and around domestic structures that are estimated to number 53 in an area of 8000 m². When compared with the results of test pits and trenches, the authors are inclined to double this estimate of structures (Tolstoy and Fish 1975). Coapexco can probably be classified as a large dispersed village, perhaps numbering 2650 persons. Although all structures may not have been dwellings, there is nothing to suggest specialization other than a possible production of *manos* and *metates*. Coapexco pottery is strongly related to that of San Lorenzo on the Gulf Coast. Although the pottery shares many features with the Ayotla subphase material in the valley below, Tolstoy feels that the general assemblage is sufficiently distinct to warrant a separate subphase.

With this exception, most of the small villages that characterize these early phases were located in deep alluvium soil in the southern part of the valley which offered the finest soil and most reliable rainfall. Tlapacoya, which as we have seen has perhaps the longest history of settlement in the Basin, was thriving during these Ixtapaluca years.

Manantial, the next subphase in the Basin of Mexico chronology, in many ways marks the peak of the Preclassic development in this region (1000–800 B.C.) Many Ayotla ceramic features continue as Manantial does not represent an abrupt break but rather an elaboration of earlier styles with an added new ingredient or emphasis. During this time differentially fired ware is imitated by painting white rims on bowls. Pottery forms are of infinite variety. In addition to bowls and *ollas,* there are kidney-shapes, long-necked bottles, basket handles, flower pots, stirrup-spouted vessels, and effigies of human, animal, and imaginary figures. The entire range does not appear at every site with Manantial material which may signal a distinction between grave goods and rubbish. For example, no stirrup-spouted vessels have been found to date at Zohapilco–Tlapacoya, although such vessels are known from the Tlatilco graves across the lake. Large hollow figures often called dolls, typically with spread, chubby legs and baby-faces, are found in both Ayotla and Manantial subphases. One was found by Tolstoy in his Ayotla subphase. Of the same complex is the seated figure sucking its finger from Las Bocas, Puebla, a truly remarkable ceramic sculpture (see Plate 2-e, p. 72). Of the tools, small pointed-stem projectile points and *metates* without supports are typical of all related sites. The Manantial phase at Zohapilco–Tlapacoya has several distinctive features. Interregional contact is much in evidence with crystals of specular hematite, twice the early number of obsidian specimens (in particular the prismatic knives), while clays too were imported from various regions. A Oaxaca grey ware and pottery from the Gulf Coast and Pánuco regions have been identified.

Although this Preclassic occupation is still very imperfectly known there are as yet no indications of ceremonial structures. There was, however, some construction at Zohapilco because Niederberger reports finding cut pieces of *tepetate* and some flooring of red earth. She believes that conditions were somewhat drier and that the lake level receded, but the production of maize was the greatest of any time in the long occupation of the area.

That these early residents were farmers is indicated by the presence of *metates, manos,* and even tiny maize cobs at Ayotla. Pollen grains of *Zea mays* constituted 35% of the botanical fossil remains at Zohapilco. This diet was supplemented by deer, rabbits, gophers, and domesticated dogs. Mud turtles, waterfowl, fish, and reptiles were also eaten.

Across the lake to the northwest of Tlapacoya (see Map 4, p. 86), the lake-shore settlement of Tlatilco began to increase in population reaching its apogee in the Manantial subphase. This became one of the most densely settled areas in the Basin. Although excavations were begun by the Instituto Nacional de Antropología e Historia in 1947, the site is still poorly known and has now disappeared under modern Mexico City. The site is famous for the beauty of its figurines and the exotic pottery shapes and decorations (Piña Chan 1958; Porter 1953; Tolstoy and Paradis 1970, 1971).

Although simple clay-surfaced platforms are believed to have been raised at Tlatilco, the only documented architecture here are fragments of wattle-and-daub house walls. It was another simple farming community. The residents dug deep triangular bottle-shaped pits (Photo 12) into the earth to store their food, but when found by archaeologists

PHOTO 12. Bottle-shaped food storage–rubbish pit at Tlatilco. (Courtesy of Arturo Romano P.)

they were filled with general household debris, pottery and figurine fragments, burned pieces of walls from huts, animal bone, ash, and charcoal.

Tlatilco in the 1940s was a brickyard where clay was removed from vast areas and molded into sun-dried brick for building. In the process, untold remains of the Tlatilco inhabitants were destroyed or redistributed. Several hundred burials (Photo 13) and some refuse debris have been excavated, revealing a very long occupation of the site. Some burials had few or no offerings, but others were lavishly supplied with pottery vessels, figurines, masks, tools, and jewelry. A great range of vessel forms include flat-bottomed vessels, composite silhouettes, *tecomates*, goblets, tripods, long-necked bottles, and stirrup-spouts (Figure 6, p. 76; Plate 3-a,b,d; Plate 4-b,d,e) together with a great variety of effigy and whistling vessels portraying both human and animal forms. Consider the range of fauna represented: peccaries (Plate 4-m), ducks, fish (Plate 4-k), birds, opossums, frogs, bears, armadillos, rabbits, and turtles, along with some purely imaginary grotesque forms. Decorations include banded geometric incised designs, rocker-stamping, differential firing (Plate 4-1), cinnabar rubbed into incised designs (Plate 4-g), the double-line-break, and white-on-red painted wares.

PHOTO 13. Graves at Tlatilco cemetery, Valley of Mexico. (Courtesy of Arturo Romano P.)

PLATE 3. Preclassic-period figures and figurines.
a. D-1 figurine, Tlatilco. Height: 11 cm. (Courtesy of the Museum of the American Indian, Heye Foundation, N.Y. [22/4692].)
b. D-2 figurine, Tlatilco. Height: 14 cm. (Courtesy of the Museum of the American Indian, Heye Foundation, N.Y. [22/710].)
c. Chupícuaro figurine of local style. Height: 8 cm. (Courtesy of the UCLA Museum of Cultural History collections, gift of Miss Natalie Wood [X69W-422].)
d. Shaman (?) wearing animal skin, wig, and mask, Tlatilco. Height: 10 cm. (Courtesy of the Museo Nacional de Antropología, Mexico.)
e. H-4 figurine, Chupícuaro. Height: 8 cm. (Courtesy of the UCLA Museum of Cultural History collections, gift of Miss Natalie Wood [X69W-319].)
f. Figurine with slab base, Cuitzeo, Michoacán. Height: 4 cm. (Courtesy of the Museum of the American Indian, Heye Foundation, N.Y. [23/9352].)

a

b

c

d

e

f

g

h

i

j

PLATE 3 (Continued)

g. Gesturing figure from Colima, Mexico. Height: 35 cm. (Courtesy of the Metropolitan Museum of Art, The Michael C. Rockefeller Memorial Collection of Primitive Art, Bequest of Nelson A. Rockefeller, 1979.)

h. Effigy figure from Buena Vista, Colima. Height: 22 cm. (Courtesy of the Museum of the American Indian, Heye Foundation, N.Y. [22/5100].)

i. Polychrome figure of a woman holding jar, Nayarit, Mexico. Height: 27 cm. (Courtesy of the Museum of the American Indian, Heye Foundation, N.Y. [23/2275].)

j. Hollow figure, Gualupita, Morelos. Height: 33 cm. (Courtesy of the Museum of the American Indian, Heye Foundation, N.Y. [22/1351].)

PLATE 4. Preclassic-period pottery.
a. Jar decorated in Usulután resist technique, Cobán, Guatemala. Height: 9 cm. (Courtesy of the Museum of the American Indian, Heye Foundation, N.Y. [9/9473].)
b. Stirrup-spout, brown ware. Height: 18 cm. Tlatilco. (Courtesy of Arturo Romano P.)
c. Black trifid vessel, Gualupita, Morelos (?). Form and decoration are distinctive features of the Capacha complex, Colima, but this is an unusually elegant example. Height: 29 cm. (Courtesy of the Museum of the American Indian, Heye Foundation, N.Y. [23/3034].)
d. Black-brown bottle. Tlatilco. Height: 20 cm. (Courtesy of Arturo Romano P.)
e. Brown bottle with neck and grooves painted red, Burial 90, Tlatilco. Height: 19 cm. (Courtesy of Arturo Romano P.)
f. Large red-ware hollow dog, Colima. Height: 13 cm. (Courtesy of the Museum of the American Indian, Heye Foundation, N.Y. [23/8366].)

PLATE 4 (Continued)

g. Black excised *tecomate,* cinnabar paint in roughened areas, Las Boca, Puebla. Height: 10 cm. (Courtesy of the Museum of the American Indian, Heye Foundation, N.Y. [23/7832].)

h. Red-on-buff spider-leg tripod, Chupícuaro, Guanajuato. Height: 16 cm. (Courtesy of the Museum of the American Indian, Heye Foundation, N.Y. [22/5691].)

i. White-on-red cylindrical tripod, Valley of Mexico. Height: 18 cm. (Courtesy of the Museo Nacional de Antropología, Mexico.)

j. Goblet or vessel with pedestal base, decorated in *al fresco* technique, polychrome, Tomb 2, Tlapacoya, Valley of Mexico. Height: 19 cm. (Courtesy of the Museo Nacional de Antropología, Mexico.)

k. Black, excised fish effigy from Tlatilco, Burial 53. Height: 14 cm. (Courtesy of the Museo Nacional de Antropología, Mexico.)

l. Differentially fired black and white bottle, Burial 162, Tlatilco. Height: 20 cm. (Courtesy of Arturo Romano P.)

m. Hollow effigy vessel in form of peccary, with rocker-stamped decoration, Tlatilco. Height: 18 cm. (Figure is enlarged to show decoration.) (Courtesy of the Museum of the American Indian, Heye Foundation, N.Y. [23/6193].)

To date nearly 400 graves have been found. Ordinarily this would constitute a fine sample but at Tlatilco where the same terrain was inhabited over a long period of time and new burials disturbed older ones, the chronology is particularly vexing, which accounts for changing and differing interpretations. (See Niederberger 1976.) The discrepancies throughout the Preclassic remains of the Basin of Mexico may reflect social distinctions, differences between funerary or domestic pottery, geographic location, actual time differences, or any combination of these factors. It was by cross-correlations with the stratigraphic sequence of Niederberger's Tlapacoya excavations, and Grove's material at Chalcatzingo (Grove 1974), together with his own explorations at Coapexco and other Basin sites that finally allowed Tolstoy to make some sense out of the Tlatilco grave material that spans Ixtapaluca and Zacatenco periods. Now we think the Olmec-like traits there are earliest and belong to the Ayotla subphase. These include flat-bottomed dishes, spouted trays, Olmec designs, and thin-walled *tecomates*.

Other ceramic traits known as the Tlatilco tradition (also called Río Cuautla or Amacuzac style) belong to the succeeding Manantial subphase (1000–800 B.C.) and comprise carinated tubular-necked bottles, stirrup-spouted vessels (Plate 4-b), masks (Plate 5-d), and certain effigies. The occurrence of the stirrup-spout in Preclassic Mesoamerica is sometimes, but not always, accompanied by the long-necked bottle (Plate 4-d,e). For example, they are found together in central Mexico during the Manantial subphase of the Basin of Mexico and in the contemporary Barranca phase at Chalcatzingo, Morelos. But although the stirrup-spout is found in the Capacha complex of Colima, long-necked bottles are not part of west Mexican assemblages. They do occur far to the southeast in Honduras. The Cuyamel Caves (Map 3, p. 63) have very similar bottles, as does the pre-Olmec Bajío phase at San Lorenzo. Only two stirrup-spouted vessels have been reported from these regions: one of Playa de los Muertos style in the Poponoe Collection from Honduras (Porter 1953) and another in the Ceramoteca of the National Museum of Anthropology, Mexico, attributed to La Venta (Lowe 1978). Neither bottles nor stirrup-spouts are considered to be Olmec traits but form part of the Tlatilco tradition in central Mexico after 1000 B.C.

Decorations of this tradition include gadrooning, ribbing, lobing, modeling, and painting; the most diagnostic figurines are D and K types. These features are all well represented in the Manantial subphase at both Tlatilco and Tlapacoya.

The small, hand-modeled figurines, a popular product of Preclassic peoples, are particularly abundant in central highland Mexico and merit a brief digression. Those of Tlatilco are the most spectacular examples. We see mothers holding babies or dogs, while men are depicted as ball-players, shamans, musicians, or acrobats. The dwarfs, hunchbacks, and monstrosities with two heads or one head with three eyes are

a

b

c

d

curiosities the meaning of which eludes us. Styles of clothing, coiffures, and body adornment of the figurines suggest uses of some of the minor artifacts. For example, pyrite mirrors are shown hanging from the neck, and elaborate clay stamps produce designs similar to those painted on the bodies of the figurines. Since clothing was minimal, often limited to a saucy skirt or fancy bloomers, an animal skin, or even just a turban or necklace, exposed portions of the body were decorated by stamped colored designs. For humor, imagination, and mimicry (?), and certainly for sheer perfection of execution, the Tlatilco figurines are superb (Plate 3-a,b,d).

Preclassic figurines are always hand modeled. Thereafter though produced by molds, some kind of small solid figurine was in vogue until the Conquest, and even after, into Colonial times. Although some represent males, the great majority are females. Some exhibit exaggerated sexual characteristics or are obviously pregnant. Others depict women in childbirth and mother and child groups. Ball-players are known from Tlatilco, Cuicuilco, Dainzú, Xochipala, and San Lorenzo. Usually figurines are recovered from household refuse and therefore are broken. Burial of figurines, as practiced at Tlatilco where as many as 60 were found in a single grave (Photo 14), preserves specimens complete, but after the earliest Zacatenco phase, they were no longer placed in graves. This practice was more common in central Mexico than in the Maya area. Why, one wonders, were the figurines made?

A number of functional interpretations have been suggested, for the making of clay figurines is shared with other parts of the world, notably the Near East, where a parallel is seen in the mother goddess figures. Among some contemporary Indians of Mexico and Colombia a figurine may have special curing powers bestowed on it by a shaman. After it has performed its function it is kept around the house or thrown out. The Aztecs strung them over cornfields as a talisman or for protection and also used them in ritual (Lee 1969). Among other groups figurines are used as protective fetishes during pregnancy. In primitive magic

---

PLATE 5. Various Preclassic-period artifacts.
a. Stone sculpture with mask of the Long-Nosed God. Height: 147 cm, weight: 117 pounds. (Courtesy of the Museum of the American Indian, Heye Foundation, N.Y. [9/6718].)
b. Cylindrical clay stamp or seal, Las Bocas, Puebla. Height: 9 cm. (Courtesy of the Metropolitan Museum of Art, The Michael C. Rockefeller Memorial Collection of Primitive Art, Gift of Nelson A. Rockefeller, 1965.)
c. Jade mosaic mask representing Bat God, Monte Albán II grave. Height: 17 cm. (Courtesy of the Museo Nacional de Antropología, Mexico.)
d. Small clay mask with two perforations for suspension, Tlatilco. Diameter: 12 cm. (Courtesy of the Museum of The American Indian, Heye Foundation, N.Y. [23/5589].)

PHOTO 14. Tlatilco Burial 95. Note the figurines heaped on the feet. (Courtesy of Arturo Romano P.)

and religion, miniatures often play a vital role. Figurines in Mesoamerica are too plentiful to have been luxury objects. This fact, together with their appearance in household refuse, suggests that they formed part of a popular household cult and perhaps served as talismans or charms.

So abundant were figurines at El Arbolillo, Zacatenco, and Ticomán (see Map 4, p. 86) that George Vaillant based his Preclassic chronology, the first ever devised, on an intricate figurine typology (Vaillant 1930, 1931, 1935). Indeed, his basic classification by letters and numbers is still used, though it has since been amplified. Difficulties and confusion have arisen from attempts to apply this classification to Mesoamerica as a whole. Then it loses its usefulness, for the figurines of each region are sensitive to local tastes and styles, and only in a general way can some correlations be made. The finest Preclassic figurines are the D–1, D–3, and D–4 types, well represented in Tlatilco graves. A simplified summary is found in Table 3.

Returning now to the Basin of Mexico sequence, Manantial is the final subphase of Ixtapaluca. This period of perhaps 500 years (Nevada [?] through Manantial) saw great prosperity and activity in the central highlands. Coapexco was in touch with Gulf Coast peoples, and the serpentine beads, iron ore, and mica fragments at that site are certainly imported. Wares from Oaxaca and the Huasteca along with

TABLE 3

Chronology of Preclassic Figurines in the Basin of Mexico[a]

Preclassic phase Basin of Mexico	Figurine types[b]
Ticomán	Figurines E–1, E–2, H–2, H–4, H–5, B, F, and A Somewhat later, H, G, I, and L
Zacatenco	Figurines C–3, C–5, B, F, and A C–1 and C–2 especially characteristic Generally cruder type figurines
Ixtapaluca	Figurines D and K types Plow-eyed (Pilli and related forms) Baby-face types

[a] Based on Niederberger 1976 and Tolstoy 1978.
[b] From Vaillant 1930, 1931, 1935.

crystals of specular hematite and abundant obsidian were brought in to Tlapacoya. Kaolin pottery could have come into the Basin of Mexico from a number of areas, but Morelos was a reliable source. Jadeite is never common, but does appear in some Tlatilco graves.

Belief in the supernatural is deduced from representations of deities in the ceramic art of these sites. Basing our identifications on Joralemon's (1971) Olmec iconography, we can recognize four gods of Olmec derivation: God I, with features of the fire-serpent or Xiuhcoatl; God III, a kind of avian monster with maize fertility associations; God VI, with attributes of the fertility deity the Aztecs later called Xipe; and God X, who is less well understood (Tolstoy *et al.* 1977). The fire-serpent was dominant at Tlatilco, and Xipe heads the list at Tlapacoya as its tribal ancestor (?).

To summarize, the Ixtapaluca phase of the Basin of Mexico corresponds to the Olmec horizon. The Ayotla subphase, including the Coapexco material, shares features with San Lorenzo, whereas Manantial corresponds to the early years of La Venta. Olmec influence in the Basin of Mexico is found in particular ceramic styles and decorations, baby-faced figurines, and "dolls." We find no monumental stone carving or reliefs. The Olmec influence never constituted a major ingredient or exercised a strong impact on these peoples.

The Tlatilco tradition represents a different strain stemming from unknown roots, which appears after 1000 B.C., thus found simultaneously with the later Olmec traits at Tlatilco and Zohapilco–Tlapacoya. As we will see, both the Olmecs and the Tlatilco tradition are strongly represented just over the mountains to the south in Morelos, to which the Basin of Mexico probably occupied a marginal position in the Ixtapaluca phase.

We somehow have a better picture of Ixtapaluca than we do of the following Zacatenco period, perhaps because after Manantial life seems less affluent, a little harder, and much less exciting.

ZACATENCO
(800–400 B.C.) (FI 3–5)

The beginning of the Zacatenco phase is marked by a real population explosion in the Basin of Mexico. Larger settlements continued on in the southern part of the valley, but now people moved around to settle in small hamlets even in arid regions such as the Teotihuacán Valley, Cuautitlán, and Texcoco regions. The population was more dispersed, and people took up residence in the piedmont areas. Some distinction can be seen between large and small villages, but no one center dominated (Sanders, Parsons, and Santley 1979).

The population at Zohapilco–Tlapacoya was very dense in the early years of Zacatenco. Inhabitants erected buildings with well-cut blocks of *tepetate* sometimes combined with undressed stones held together with clay. Remains of walls indicate that rooms were rectangular in shape (Niederberger 1976). But Zohapilco–Tlapacoya did not retain its former momentum, and by 500 B.C. much of the population moved away.

Cuicuilco, however, is believed to have begun the first ceremonial mounds at this time, although the extent of construction is not clear. The best evidence of social stratification in the Zacatenco period continues to be the difference in grave goods in which many of the Tlatilco tradition traits now disappear along with any lingering trace of the Olmec.

The most important ceramic change is the great increase in white-paste wares accompanied by incised sunburst decorations on the interior of bowls and the incised double-line-break on the rim. This cluster of traits is a reliable Middle Preclassic marker with a broad-based distribution from the Basin of Mexico to coastal Guatemala and including Guerrero and the Huasteca. It was very common earlier at Zohapilco–Tlapacoya in the Manantial subphase but seems to become even more widespread in the Zacatenco period. Tolstoy *et al.* (1977) call it the Double Line Break tradition. The double-line-break is found on an orange-brown ware as early as 1500 B.C. at San Miguel Amuco, Guerrero (see Map 3, p. 63), and this, together with its long history in the Basin of Mexico, hints of a highland origin (Tolstoy and Fish 1975).

Other Zacatenco ceramic features are dark bay wares in *olla* and composite-silhouette forms, annular bases, *comals*, and oval shapes. White-on-red painted wares come in late, and at the very end of the period a red-on-black appears.

Despite the population boom, there is a general drabness of Zacatenco remains not found earlier. Burials contain fewer and simpler offerings; imports are negligible. More arid land was farmed and small-scale irrigation experiments were being conducted on the floor of the valley by 700 B.C.

The Ticomán phase is distinguished by even greater population growth and the first civic–ceremonial architecture at Cuicuilco. This settlement had grown from a tiny hamlet founded about the same time as Coapexco. Around 400 B.C. these people, in deciding to construct an oval truncated cone of adobe, initiated religious architecture in the Basin of Mexico. The main pyramid was built in four stages, and a smaller one of six stages was erected at nearby Peña Pobre. After 300 B.C. the cone structure at Cuicuilco was altered and enlarged, resulting in a round temple platform (80 m in diameter) faced with stone and having two ramps leading up to the double altars at the summit, 27 m above the ground (Photo 15). Almost a kilometer to the east, 11 additional mound structures have been cleared. Cuicuilco emerges as a bustling hub of activity dominating the southern Basin of Mexico in the Late Preclassic times. Population is believed to have reached 20,000 concentrated in an area of 400 ha, which is as far as Cuicuilco was ever to expand.

Cuicuilco was not the only center to experience a tremendous population explosion. This was typical of the entire Basin of Mexico, which doubled its numbers in the area of Chalco and Ixtapalapa (see Map 4, p. 86). Smaller regional centers grew up in the same area with respectable nucleations of 1500–4500 people. One of these was Tlapacoya, where a permanent platform for rituals was raised (Photo 16). Pottery at the village not only resembled that of its valley neighbors, Ticomán, Zacatenco, and Cuicuilco, but also that of Chupícuaro from the northwest.

On the eastern saline lakeshore of Texcoco, groups settled for the first time in the marshes no doubt to exploit the lake, for this was well away from agricultural land. Perhaps these were only seasonal dwellers, yet they might have engaged in a dependable lacustrine specialization.

TICOMÁN
(400–100 B.C.) (FI 6–8)

PHOTO 15. Pyramid at Cuicuilco, Valley of Mexico. (Courtesy of the Instituto Nacional de Antropología e Historia, Mexico.)

PHOTO 16. Pyramid at Tlapacoya, Valley of Mexico. (Courtesy of the Instituto Nacional de Antropología e Historia, Mexico.)

Loma Torremote (Atlamica) on the northern periphery of the Basin is an example of a large nucleated village of 500 B.C. It occupied about 30 ha on a long low ridge near the headwaters of the Río Cuautitlán at a time when oak forests may still have been thriving. The town consisted of perhaps 400–475 individual house compounds which were grouped into clusters. The fundamental unit was composed of wattle and daub, a floor of *tepetate*, patio of packed earth, and a small garden with storage pits, all enclosed by an adobe wall. Certain households within the compound stood out as being of higher rank; these would have housed the lineage head.

The ranked household had duties of redistribution of goods, for within the compound were obsidian workshops; agricultural surplus was stored in bottle-shaped pits and there was some part-time pottery specialization and perhaps cutting of *tepetate* blocks for construction. Assuming the village brought in its own obsidian to be worked, this required a group of laborers. It would have been a local-operated economy, not a market system. The lineage head was also in charge of ritual activities. Individual households had figurines and censers whereas the lineage as a group observed religious practices in the patio. Associated with the ancestral shrine were more than 200 figurines and censer fragments along with pottery, masks, and shells.

Large nucleated villages, such as Loma Torremote with an estimated population of about 2500 people, represented a radical change in social structure and a more varied economy than seen earlier. Sanders, Parsons, and Santley (1979) suggest that such communities with powerful lineage heads could have collaborated in the procurement and redistribution of raw materials such as obsidian. One result of an effort to increase their control and be nearer the sources could have been the settlement and growth of population in the Teotihuacán Valley.

The initial settling of Teotihuacán had taken place around 900 B.C. in the form of several small hamlets located in the drainage of the Barranca de San Lorenzo. This dry northern area was almost uninhabited for many years while the main Basin of Mexico was culturally far more active. It is not until the late Preclassic period that Teotihuacán began to grow and make her presence felt. Gathering momentum almost overnight, Teotihuacán caught up with developments at Cuicuilco to equal it in size and complexity. This huge regional center is estimated to have occupied about 8 km² with a population of 20,000–40,000 inhabitants. The first settlements were located at the head of a large alluvial plain, near a group of permanent springs. In this dry northern section with less reliable rainfall and more subject to frost, the water resources were of primary consideration. One cannot help but ask why the area was heavily settled now, if it was a location not very favorable for agriculture and at least 10 km away from the waters of Lake Texcoco? Sanders, Parsons, and Santley (1979) feel that this nucleation is closely associated with canal irrigation and a more central political system, for some control over land and water would have been mandatory to sustain such a large population. The *why*, however, is still unexplained although the case of Loma Torremote may furnish a clue. Knowing what we do of the later mercantilism and expansion of Teotihuacán, we are tempted to suggest that the location was selected for its strategic position from which to control the great obsidian deposits to the northeast. The nearby sources of lime for building would also have been attractive.

PATLACHIQUE
(100 B.C.–A.D. 1) (FI–9)

By the final Preclassic phase (Terminal Preclassic or Patlachique) (FI–9), two huge centers equal in rank had emerged: Cuicuilco to the south and Teotihuacán to the northeast. Not only did each of these dominate its immediate area and attract population but they must have competed with each other for land, resources, and services. The other regional centers were infinitely smaller and possibly already under domination of one of the big two.

Some hints of conflict or competition between Teotihuacán and Cuicuilco can be detected in massive stone retaining walls on the southeastern corner of Lake Texcoco and by an increasing number of hilltop sites. The chronology of the latter, Tezoyuca centers, is still unclear but they belong to this somewhat unsettled terminal Preclassic period. Thirteen such hilltop centers of approximately 300–600 people have been identified and all have some modest public architecture in an isolated, steep-sided setting which looks good for defense. Chronologically they may represent a short phase between Ticomán and Patlachique, or they may be contemporaneous with the latter. At this time valley peoples were subjected to various pressures or influences from the east and northwest that resulted in cultural diversification. Population continued to increase, and if the Texcocan region reflects the prevailing settlement pattern, the great majority of people lived in large concentrated centers characterized by ceremonial or public works. Tlapacoya had by this time ceased to be of any importance. Temesco on the eastern lake shore and the remains at Cerro del Tepalcate (literally "potsherd hill") high above Tlatilco probably related to this period, which basically continues the Cuicuilco tradition.

One source of new influence was Chupícuaro, a Late Preclassic site on the Lerma River, some 128 km northwest of the valley (Map 3, p. 63). From this center, elaborate polychrome vessels and H–4 figurines, a kind of mouse-faced flat type with slanted eyes, were traded into the basins of Mexico, Tlaxcala, and also Morelos (Plate 3-e, p. 91). Bennyhoff (1967) feels that additional ceramic features were introduced into the valley from the area of Puebla. These include flat-based bowls, more resist-painted decorations, *comals*, and perhaps the idea of modeling figurines to represent deities.

The local pottery at this time had replaced the early dark bay ware with a tan or buff pottery, and a polychromed red-on-buff appeared. Tripod supports, especially large bulbous ones, are common. Of the competing styles and forms at this time, Chupícuaro was the loser, and it is the eastern influence that blends with the older Cuicuilco–Ticomán tradition to emerge as Classic Teotihuacán ceramics.

Despite all influence and machinations, Cuicuilco was doomed. But her end was not quite as sudden as once thought. Instead of one, there were two calamities. The first volcanic eruption of nearby Xitli occurred in the Patlachique subphase around 50 B.C. and reduced the great center to a small community leaving Teotihuacán as the only major center. The ash and lava of a second eruption in the Early Classic put an end to all activity in the southwestern region. The events that follow—the rise of Teotihuacán—belong to the Tzacualli phase (A.D. 1–150) which I have considered Early Classic, and will be taken up in Chapter 6. Before, however, we should look at those Preclassic developments elsewhere in Mesoamerica that have a bearing on the Classic period civilizations.

Intensive field work over the years in the Puebla–Tlaxcala region under **Puebla–Tlaxcala** the direction of Angel García Cook has borne very fruitful results. In cultural achievements and development, this region was about 300 years ahead of the Basin of Mexico, which because of its later civilizations is always assumed to have led the way. Now it seems that, throughout the entire Preclassic period, Puebla–Tlaxcala was a cultural jump ahead.

This may be explained in terms of its more favorable environment and geographic location. There is much more agricultural land available, much less risk of frost, at least for a shorter time, and it receives about 25% more rainfall than the Basin of Mexico. (Sanders, Parsons, and Santley 1979). It is not a closed interior basin but gives rise to the headwaters of the Atoyac River and many minor streams leading eastward to the Gulf lowlands. Strategically Puebla–Tlaxcala is much better situated for dealing with Oaxaca, the southern and eastern lowlands, and the Maya region; in fact, across it lay the major routes of communication in Classic and Postclassic periods and probably Preclassic as well.

By the year 1500 B.C. villagers were already cultivating plants and continued to supplement their diet by hunting and gathering. Nineteen different sites have been located belonging to the Tzompantepec phase. Although sites are scattered, people made similar pottery, placed their houses on terraces near agricultural fields, and practiced some kind of ritual activities. The Puebla Valley consistently follows a regional variant of the larger Puebla–Tlaxcala culture. At this time it had contact with people in the Basin of Mexico but more importantly with areas to the south. The rest of Puebla and Tlaxcala were more closely related to the Tehuacán Valley and the north–central Gulf Coast region.

The 400 years between 1200–800 B.C. (Tlatempa) (García Cook 1978) are marked by a sharp rise in population with 150 sites recorded, almost five times the number of earlier settlements. Characteristic are ceremonial platforms, pottery-making, canals for irrigating cultivated terraces, and increased ritual activities seen in the production of figurines and incense-burner lids. The same earlier dichotomy is observed: The Tlatempa culture dealt with Tehuacán, Oaxaca, Puebla Valley, and Morelos, while in addition the Puebla Valley is related to the Basin of Mexico.

The Texoloc phase (800–300 B.C.) is marked by the founding of towns in addition to the earlier small villages and hamlets. Moyotzingo near San Martin Texmelucan, Puebla, is just such a town with small platform house remains, pyramids, bottle-shaped pits, and abundant Middle Preclassic pottery (Aufdermauer 1973). Although it did yield one carbon-14 date of 1330±85 B.C., most of the material dates to the Texoloc phase. A streaky finish on the pottery links it to early pottery in Morelos and the Tehuacán Valley. Craft specialization may have been a full-time occupation for potters and weavers for much paraphernalia of these trades have been recovered including spindle whorls (*malacates*). Both Huehuéteotl and Tlaloc are represented. Social organization at this time was more complex, for priests, craftsmen, farmers, and merchants must have existed. Already trade was brisk. More than 275 Texoloc sites have been located covering most of Tlaxcala. In addition to earlier contracts, a relationship with west Mexico developed.

The next 400 years (Tezoquipan phase, 300 B.C.–A.D. 100) saw the cultural peak of Tlaxcalan development and a consolidation of the technological and ideological processes. Villages were now transformed into a dozen regional centers or cities and into more than 40 towns. The technological advances and urban aspects are illustrated by the large planned ceremonial centers with streets, plazas, drains, ball courts, common use of stucco, *talud–tablero* architecture, and complete hydraulic systems of terrace cultivation, irrigation canals, dikes, and ridged fields. Institutionalized religion was a major concern and the government is believed to have been a theocracy.

Three colonies from west Mexico moved into the northwestern part of the State of Puebla at this time, one of which is represented by Gualupita las Dalias (see Map 3, p. 63), located on a hill surrounded on three sides by deep *barrancas*. The very position suggests a defensive location, borne out by look-out posts and an entrance point that could have been guarded easily. About 17 structures have been located, of which 3 are pyramids and the rest are low residential platforms. A series of bottle-shaped pits were found containing rubbish as at Tlatilco. Among the inventory of remains are solid earspools, *malacates*, and quantities of clay figurines types H–3 and H–4 along with pottery decorated by negative painting or polychromed, at times with mammiform supports or made in kidney shapes. García Cook and Rodríguez (1975) believe these remains to be those of colonists from the area around Chupícuaro, Guanajuato or neighboring Michoacán, dating to the years 500 B.C. to A.D. 1. We have already noted the presence of similar material at Cuicuilco and Tezoyuca sites in the Basin of Mexico.

Contacts in general between Tlaxcala–Puebla and the Basin of Mexico were strong during these years. Just as ceremonial architecture was started in the Basin of Mexico, so a Preclassic population at Cholula constructed a small pyramid only 17 m in height and decorated it with creatures resembling mythical insects painted in red, black, and yellow. Meanwhile, the Tlaxcalans were working closely with the Basin of Mexico masons, demonstrating their technique of stuccoing and building in the *talud–tablero* style which was to become the hallmark of Teotihuacán. Figurine types E and C–10 along with some pottery styles were also shared. Some groups with early Teotihuacan culture (Patlachique–Tzacualli) were living in the western and extreme northern parts of Tlaxcala. We will return to this area when dealing with the Classic period, because it was closely involved with the fortunes of Teotihuacán (García Cook 1978).

Morelos

Bearing westward across southern Puebla, the traveler finds a natural opening in the hills leading to Las Bocas, an Olmec site located at the base of a large hill or cliff at the eastern edge of the Izúcar de Matamoros Valley. Las Bocas is known largely from the spoils of looting parties, which have brought out large hollow baby-faced figures, white-rimmed black ware, spouted trays, and black-excised pottery with the jaguar–paw–hand motif (Plate 2-c, e; Plate 4-g). Across the valley, one of the few passes in the mountains affords access to the central Morelos plains. At the Morelos end of the pass is Chalcatzingo, perhaps the most important Olmec highland site and unique for having the only Olmec-carved bas-reliefs in the highlands (Grove 1968a). It could have served both as a religious center and as a traffic or trade control point. There are several groups of carvings, which seem to deal with agriculture, fertility, and rain. Some convey a suggestion of militarism. The human figures, scrolls and volutes, clouds, rain, and flame eyebrows are in purest Olmec style.

The location of Chalcatzingo parallels that of Las Bocas. Both are situated at the base of a tall cliff and both would have been well situated to check on travelers arriving from or leaving for Gulf Coast regions. Chalcatzingo could have controlled three-way traffic: south to Guerrero, north to the Basin of Mexico, and southeast to the Olmec heartland on the Gulf Coast.

At an altitude of 1370 m, Morelos enjoys a temperate year-round climate that today attracts thousands of visitors to the city of Cuernavaca to bask in the continual sunshine and escape the more rigorous highlands. Open forests of pine and oak, numerous streams, and abundant summer rainfall would have made the Morelos valleys favorable habitation sites in ancient times as well.

There are other Preclassic sites in Morelos, and most of them show some Olmec influence. Gualupita was one, but this has now been absorbed by the city of Cuernavaca and we know it largely from George Vaillant's published accounts (Vaillant and Vaillant 1934). While making a road cut at Atlihuayán on the Yautepec River, workers came across a magnificent hollow Olmec ceramic figure, seated, and wearing a caiman skin (see Plate 2-b, p. 72). Excavations were subsequently made in this area by Grennes-Ravitz at a site known as Iglesia Vieja. His material has many similarities to the Tlatilco grave goods and to that found at Chalcatzingo (Grennes-Ravitz 1974). It is the latter site, however, that provides the most complete record of the Preclassic in Morelos (Grove *et al.* 1976).

Chalcatzingo is located in the Amatzinac River valley about 100 km southeast of Mexico City where farmers could have practiced simple canal irrigation. More ideal farm lands and climate would be hard to find.

Earliest remains date to 1500 B.C. (Amate phase) when only a small settlement of farmers lived in the valley but who, even at that early time, began erecting some permanent structures. Analysis reveals that these people got most of their early obsidian from Otumba (see Map 8, p. 206) with small quantities coming in from Veracruz and Oaxaca. After 1000 B.C. these were substituted by Hidalgo and west Mexican sources, presumably Zinapécuaro. The pottery resembles that of the Nevada subphase of Ixtapaluca in the Basin of Mexico as well as Tierras Largas in Oaxaca. By 1150 B.C. the pottery begins to look much like that from the Tlatilco graves. This material, formerly called La Juana, is contemporary with the San Lorenzo phase, yet shows no specific relationship to that Olmec site. The flat-bottomed cylindrical bowls, zoned rocker-stamping, roller stamps, spouted trays, white-rimmed black wares, and a few red-on-brown bottles are not specifically Olmec, but rather reflect the southern lowland tradition of Ocós.

In such a favorable environment it is no surprise to find that after 1100 B.C. (Barranca phase) Chalcatzingo expanded to cover 20 ha. To this phase belong the famous Olmec bas-reliefs. A whole hillside was terraced and water was so plentiful that dams were built to divert the excess. Aside from the massive terracing, a central plaza was laid out adjacent to the area of bas-reliefs and a large mound was raised (70 m × 40 m × 4 m). Ceramics of this phase (formerly called San Pablo) correlate very nicely with the Manantial subphase of the Basin of Mexico, sharing form, decoration, and general inventory of ceramic remains. Bottles reach their peak of popularity and variety as well as cylindrical bowls, kaolin ware, excised Olmec designs, stirrup-spouts, and white wares with double-line-break. Here again we find the familiar Tlatilco or Río Cuautla style. It is at this time that contact has been postulated with west Mexico (Green and Lowe 1967; Kelly 1970; Grove 1971).

The last phase of Chalcatzingo (Cantera phase 700–550 B.C.) is the culmination of the Preclassic in Morelos. Three terraces support stone-faced platform structures, an elite residence yielded elaborate offerings from beneath the floor; there are workshops in obsidian, hematite, and serpentine, all indicative of a very sophisticated society with a busy commercial life. Of special interest is a large stone altar made of 18 stone blocks that is very similar to Olmec ones. This may have been made earlier and reassembled. The relief of a "flying Olmec" shows a La Venta-style figure with a torch in the right hand. A broken stone stela was associated with a platform. These objects have no known highland antecedents. Grove believes Olmec rulers were actually in the area (Grove *et al.* 1976). Their presence is manifest in some ceramic motifs but more specifically in the stone bas-reliefs, stela, and altar belonging to the Cantera phase.

The Preclassic cultural boom in the Amatzinac Valley was fomented by its commercial activities. Chalcatzingo is what Hirth (1978b) has called a gateway community, located at the convergence of natural corridors of communication where the flow of trade to Guerrero, the Basin of Mexico, Puebla, or Oaxaca could be conveniently controlled (see Map 3, p. 63). The Amatzinac Valley was a source of kaolin, cotton, lime, and hematite. Obsidian and salt could be obtained from the Basin of Mexico; jadeite magnetite, hematite, and other minerals came from Guerrero (see Map 8, p. 206). Goods could have been procured, produced, or refined, and redistributed from this center. Although population estimates are not yet completed, the sophistication of farming techniques, the civic–ceremonial architecture, and residences indicate a sociopolitical integration of a sizeable population unequalled anywhere in the central highlands at this time.

We have already seen the positioning of other communities with Olmec monumental art all along a trade route extending down the Guatemala coast to Chalchuapa, El Salvador. Chalcatzingo was the central highland link in this network. Middle Preclassic commerce had gone beyond the simple exchange of goods. Now several exchange networks functioned at different levels handling different products. Chalcatzingo undoubtedly moved agricultural produce, but its greatest wealth would have derived from handling scarce exotic products destined for the elite heads of lineages, the most prestigious individuals. For example, the raw materials procured from Guerrero could be finished by specialists in the Amatzinac Valley where they would be held for redistribution by the privileged leader of the ranked sociopolitical system. This scheme involved the pooling and redistribution of commodities in a system of interregional commerce. There may have been other such gateway communities in the central highlands, but Chalcatzingo offers the best example on record.

By 500 B.C. the whole system collapsed; Chalcatzingo was abandoned, and its population relocated. For reasons still unclear, trade with Oaxaca and the Gulf Coast and Puebla abruptly ended. However, just beyond the mountain passes to the north, the people at Cuicuilco were enlarging their circular pyramid and this center was soon to dominate the whole southern part of the Basin of Mexico, a development which must have affected the Amatzinac Valley or, perhaps with other emerging centers, contributed to the disruption of the commercial network.

Guerrero

As mentioned already, Morelos was at the hub of three choice routes of communication. One of these, of course, connected via Puebla with Oaxaca and Gulf Coast points. The Basin of Mexico was easily accessible if one ascended another 900 m through the mountains north of Chalcatzingo to enter the valley from its southeastern corner. The third route, perhaps the most exciting and challenging of all, followed the Cuautla–Amacuzac River south and west to the great Balsas River, which traverses Guerrero and offers a natural thoroughfare to the Pacific Ocean. Why, one may ask, would anyone leave the temperate climate and pleasant life in Morelos or Oaxaca to penetrate the difficult, rough, and often forbidding terrain of the Balsas depression? Guerrero was the land of tin, copper, silver, gold, and semiprecious stones. But more important than the rich deposits of metals and minerals, some of which were not appreciated this early, Guerrero was a probable source of jade, the most prized of exotic materials. The common green stone referred to as jade was known to the Aztecs as *chalchihuitl* (translated as herb-green jewel-stone). A translucent emerald-green jade was the finest of all; this the Aztecs called *quetzalilztli* from the iridescent green feathers of the quetzal bird. A dark green variety may refer to chloronolanite or to omphacite (Hammond *et al.* 1977). Langenscheidt (personal communication) has suggested that the word *chalchihuitl* be used more extensively in Mesoamerica to refer to the many green stones treasured by the Indians, as many of these are not jade. Pure jade, nephrite, is rarely found in Mesoamerica, but was made into simple celts in South America. Although most Mesoamerican "jade" came from the Motagua River valley in Guatemala, Guerrero has small but numerous deposits which were undoubtedly exploited. One boulder of 15–20 kilos was found along the Atoyac River (Langenscheidt, personal communication).

We also suspect that even in early times the immense delta of the Balsas River was an exciting port, offering shelter to ocean-going crafts as well as being the terminal of the vast interior communication line to the highlands. Another logical corridor for movement of peoples lay along the coastal strip that stretches south from the delta to Oaxaca. There is ample archaeological evidence that Preclassic peoples looked beyond the grubby cactus- and mezquite-covered hills and found their way to the rich river valleys and to the coast itself.

At Puerto Marqués near Acapulco, pottery and figurines are clearly related to the Preclassic Mesoamerican tradition (C. Brush 1969; E. Brush 1968). A very early pitted pottery like that of Purrón Tehuacán has already been mentioned, and this is followed by a long sequence of remains. Olmec-type baby-faced figurines had a wide distribution on this coast during Middle Preclassic times, only to fade out completely in the late phase.

Preclassic material is also known from the Balsas delta itself, but even richer remains have come from inland areas around Iguala and Chilpancingo; some of these areas relate to the Basin of Mexico through red-on-brown wares, the double-line-break, and D-1 figurines.

No other region can rival Guerrero's production of portable Olmec art treasures such as green stone plaques, masks, figures, and celts. Olmec merchants not only exploited the natural resources but also lived and worshipped around Chilpancingo, where two caves are decorated with remarkable paintings executed in pure Olmec style. Just east of Chilpancingo and only 6 km apart are the caves of Juxtlahuaca and Oxtotitlán, each high above the river valley. The Juxtlahuaca paintings, some of the oldest known in the New World, date from perhaps 3000 years ago. Lying little more than a kilometer inside the mountain, they are painted in black, green, red, and yellow. A great bearded (?) figure with a quetzal-plumed headdress, tunic, and cape wears gauntlets and leggings of jaguar skin. He holds out a rope-like object toward a smaller, crouching figure. In the next chamber a bright red serpent on a slab of rock faces a smaller feline creature (Gay 1967).

Oxtotitlán, about 6 km to the north, is located high up a hillside, and some paintings decorate the very mouth of the entrance. Although not all the details are well preserved, one painting depicts a human figure seated on a jaguar–monster head. Themes include water or fertility and possibly mythical origins. A similar association of the jaguar–monster–mouth cave is seen in the relief carvings at Chalcatzingo and probably can be symbolically associated with the jaguar stone "altars" of the Olmec Gulf Coast sites. The interior cave paintings, in polychrome black or red, portray jaguars, baby faces, and the earliest known occurrence of the speech scroll, so common in later Mesoamerican art. M. D. Coe (1977) believes the paintings of the Juxtlahuaca caves to date from the San Lorenzo phase. The Oxtotitlán murals are slightly later, contemporaneous with La Venta (see Map 3, p. 63).

One must be impressed by the distances these Olmecs traveled from their Gulf Coast heartland to record their favorite themes of human figures, jaguars, and serpents on the walls of Guerrero caves. Surely these represent some kind of shrine, and the large bearded Olmec is certainly a figure to be respected.

The area from Chilpancingo north to Xalitla is sometimes known as the Mezcala area from which numerous small stone carvings have come. It is also the area of Xochipala, important for Preclassic pottery and figurines that have "surfaced" in private collections and are often cited for their Olmec traits.

Paul Schmidt of the Universidad Nacional Autónoma de México has excavated in the area and to him I am indebted for the following information. About 90 sites have been recorded near the modern town of Xochipala, which is part of an extensive central Guerrero tradition. Characteristic are red-on-white and black-on-white granular wares dating from the Middle Preclassic through Early Classic. *Tecomates*, bowls, and a later flat-bottomed jug are frequent. In general the pottery shares Middle Preclassic trends of white-slipped bowls with the double-line-break followed by the polished composite-silhouette incised bowls. It is of interest that nothing specifically Olmec was found.

The dating of the Xochipala figurines remains an enigma since these figurines only occur in graves, and no graves have been found by Schmidt. These figurines are described and illustrated by Gay (1972) and Griffin (1972). Perhaps representing dancers, some are very naturalistic, showing gestures such as a raised hand and great freedom of movement. Some are ball-players outfitted with knee pads and yokes. Hollow yellow or red painted types as large as 66 cm are also found in a characteristic stance with flexed legs. There are reports of round shaft-tombs 2 to 3 m deep, sealed with a stone slab, but as yet no undisturbed tombs or graves have been located. As a speculation, Schmidt suggests a Late Preclassic–Early Classic date for the Xochipala figurines.

In 1967 an Olmec stela at San Miguel Amuco (see Map 3, p. 63) near Coyuca in the Middle Balsas area was discovered—a full standing figure wearing a cape and holding in his arm a bundle of reeds (?) much resembling the later Aztec year symbol, the *xiuhmolpilli* (Grove and Paradis 1971). This is a rare example of an Olmec monument of this nature in a setting outside the Gulf Coast heartland. There is no longer any doubt that the Olmecs themselves lived in Guerrero. They even may have irrigated the river valleys in order to stay on. The Preclassic remains already reported, together with abundant sites awaiting excavation, indicate that this region formed part of the mainstream of Mesoamerican culture at this early period.

West Mexico   Preclassic remains west of the Basin of Mexico are still sporadically known, but considerable work over the years is rapidly increasing our knowledge of this vast region. West Mexico is composed of the modern states of Michoacán, Jalisco, Colima, Nayarit, and Sinaloa. Zacatecas and Durango are sometimes considered separately as the northwest frontier, and the state of Guanajuato lies directly between these two groups. With the exception of Guanajuato, the remaining areas can probably be considered as lying outside Mesoamerica at this time.

The most distinctive feature of Preclassic west Mexican cultures is the hundreds of shaft-and-chamber tombs that occur in a great arc from north of Ixtlán del Río, Nayarit, through Jalisco to Colima (Map 5). Typically they contain (apart from skeletal remains) conch-shell trumpets and pottery, including large hollow ceramic sculptures. Chronologically they range from approximately 1500 B.C. to A.D. 400. Although abundant, they have usually been thoroughly ransacked before the arrival of an archaeologist. The tombs, often beehive-shaped, consist of a vertical shaft usually 4–6 m deep that leads to one or more horizontal chambers. The deepest tombs are frequently located in high

MAP 5. West Mexico.

places overlooking the surrounding country, preferably in a row along a ridge with the tombs facing west into the setting sun.

Several such tombs were excavated many years ago near Jacona at El Opeño, Michoacán (Noguera 1942; see Figure 7). These tombs, surprisingly well made, were cut into the *tepetate* to a depth of 1.1 m. Entrance was gained by steps leading down to an underground antechamber connected to the stone-lined tomb. In one of these tombs, the dead, stretched out on the floor, had been buried with notched and

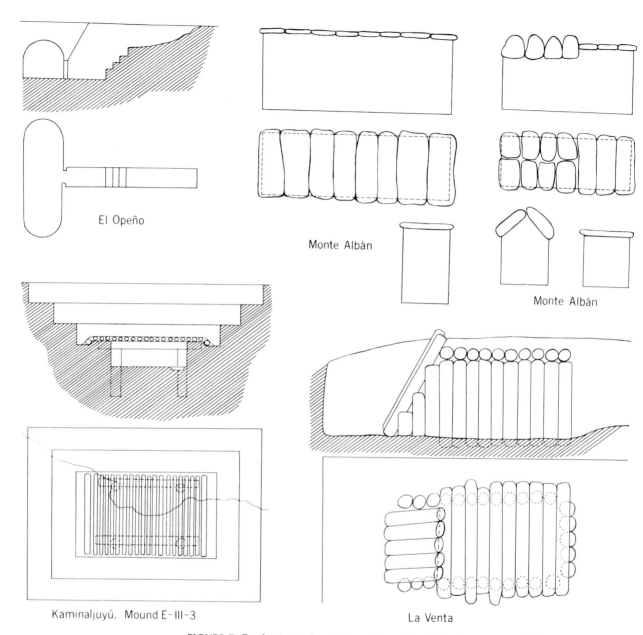

El Opeño

Monte Albán

Monte Albán

Kaminaljuyú, Mound E-III-3

La Venta

FIGURE 7. Preclassic tombs. (Adapted from the following sources: El Opeño, Noguera 1942; Monte Albán, Marquina 1951; Kaminaljuyú, Shook and Kidder 1952; La Venta, reproduced by permission from the Smithsonian Institution from *Smithsonian Institution Bureau of American Ethnology Bulletin 153 (La Venta, Tabasco: A Study of Olmec Ceramics and Art)*, by Philip Drucker: Figures 9, 38a, 38c, 40b, Washington, D.C.: Government Printing Office, 1952.)

stemmed arrowpoints, a green stone reclining figure, jade earplugs, and pottery figurines and vessels. The assemblage resembles that of the Ticomán–Cuicuilco horizon of the Basin of Mexico.

The Mexican archaeologist Arturo Oliveros (1974) had the long-awaited opportunity to open two unlooted tombs in highland Michoacán. The first tomb excavated by Oliveros contained skeletal remains with offerings that postdated the tomb construction. The tomb itself was 4.45 m deep and was entered through a shaft with four steps. The chamber, sealed by three stone slabs, contained skeletal remains of 10 individuals, pottery, and figurines. A second tomb contained two adult male skeletons. The pottery reflected the local style of negative painting, geometric designs, and red-and-buff on cream, rather like Chupícuaro. The rest was similar to the Río Cuautla or Tlatilco style of the Basin of Mexico and Morelos. A few sherds closely resemble Capacha pottery from Colima specifically in form and decoration (Kelly 1970, 1980). Sixteen figurines of C and D types were piled in the interior passageway of one tomb. Some are ball-players with knee pads and a bat (?) in hand. Others from the second tomb, beautifully made of kaolin clay, seem to have been intentionally broken before being placed in the tomb. A basalt *yuguito* like examples from Tlatilco, Tlapacoya, and Guerrero, a greenstone pectoral carved with a St. Andrews cross, obsidian projectile points, and tools probably used in chopping the tomb out of the *tepetate* were left inside the burial chamber. The ^{14}C date for this tomb is 1500 B.C., roughly coeval with the Capacha date of 1450 B.C.

What we believe to be the total contents of one tomb near Etzatlán, Jalisco came to rest in the Los Angeles County Museum. They consist of nine articulated skeletons and jumbled bones of three others without skulls. The nine deceased were accompanied by 17 hollow polychrome figurines ranging in height from 27.5 to 51.5 cm, 40 polychrome dishes and bowls, several rectangular ceramic boxes with lids, shell and obsidian ornaments, and conch-shell trumpets. Of the conch-shell trumpets, one proved to be of Caribbean and one of Pacific Coast origin. It is not uncommon to find Caribbean trumpets in the shaft tombs. This one yielded a ^{14}C date of 266 B.C.; the west-coast shell from this tomb is dated at A.D. 254. These dates refer, of course, to the death of the mollusks, not to their placement in the tomb. This particular tomb was studied by Long (1966), who concluded that it had been reopened and used at three different times over a period of 200 years.

Another shaft tomb, from Tequilita in the southern temperate highlands of Nayarit, yielded a date around A.D. 100. Thus, in west Mexico during the Late Preclassic times people were greatly preoccupied with burial of the dead and dug these curious tombs, which in themselves are far more characteristic of north-western South America than Mesoamerica and may be the result of direct contact by sea (see Chapter 9). Chronologically Mesoamerica has the priority (Kelly 1980).

The region of Colima, Jalisco, and Nayarit has produced a great variety of hollow and solid figurines as well as effigy vessels. These are often found in the shaft tombs, which keeps the tomb looters' enthusiasm alive.

The large hollow Colima figures (Plate 3-g, h, p. 92), often of highly polished red or brown clay, portray adults and children in a variety of activities such as carrying jars; some are abstract figures that may well have a symbolic meaning as yet unidentified. Nayarit figures like-wise portray a variety of human activities in a somewhat different style (Plate 3-i). Particularly charming are small figures forming scenes of people grouped around a house or temple. Musicians beat drums, shake rattles, and play flutes while others dance and do acrobatics. This gaiety and frivolity is in marked contrast to the later macabre sobriety of altiplano art. The Colima modeled pottery flutes are among Mesoamerica's finest. The red dogs of Colima (Comala phase, Plate 4-f, p. 93), found in shaft tombs, are avidly collected by art dealers. They are usually believed to have been made for interment in order to carry the soul of the deceased across a river, one of the obstacles to be overcome before reaching paradise. Much could be learned from the dress, ornamentation, and polychrome designs of these ceramic sculp-tures, but no definitive study has been attempted.

Not all the ceramic sculptures come from tombs. At Cerro Encantado in northeast Jalisco the same complex is found in graves. Bell (1972) relates these remains to those of Chupícuaro and to Chalchihuites sites in the north around A.D. 100–250.

Aside from the widespread preoccupation with funerary rites which produced such a proliferation of magnificent ceramic sculptures, several regional excavations have provided some cultural sequences.

COLIMA   In 1970 while pursuing her long involvement with the archaeology of Colima, Isabel Kelly identified a distinctive ceramic assemblage which she named the Capacha phase (Kelly 1970, 1974, 1980). This is the earliest Colima material known, and consists largely of ceramics once placed in graves but subsequently disturbed and smashed by looters. It is probable that shaft tombs were also a Capacha trait.

Capacha ceramics occur inland at elevations ranging from 186 to 800 m and stretch from Colima into Jalisco (see distribution on Map 5, p. 113). As yet there is no information on living sites, possible mounds, or the economy of these people. But the ceramic assemblage provides not only the earliest material from Colima, but suggests exterior rela-tionships that make it of more than routine interest. Most typical is a huge open-mouthed *olla* with cinctured body, which the local farmers call a *bule*. Kelly's largest specimen for example, measures 38 cm in height by a rim diameter of 36 cm. Many are undecorated but others may have several navel-like depressions with radiating incised lines. Forms include: *tecomates*, small open-mouthed *ollas*, two animal effigies, and miniature vessels. One stirrup-spout was found. More common is the curious trifid form (Plate 4-c). There are no shallow flat bowls, no grinding bowls, supports, or negative painting. Bottles are not part of the complex. This material is only known from graves and the one corrected ^{14}C date is 1870–1720 B.C. (radiocarbon date is 1450 B.C.) (Kelly 1970, 1980).

Although material from this early time is scarce, comparable ceramics believed to be from the area around Apulco, Jalisco have been reported by Greengo and Meighan (1976). A lot of 21 vessels including several stirrup-spout pots, probably all from looted graves, comprise the early material from this area.

Specific resemblances to the Capacha complex can be found with ceramics from some of the El Opeño tombs with which Capacha is contemporary (see chart on back endpapers.) Several trifids from central coastal Sinaloa and a stirrup-pot from Baja California are other west Mexican ties. Looking inland, Capacha may have some relationship with the Tlatilco or Rio Cuautla style, sharing the stirrup vessel and curious cinctured or constricted body forms as well as general decorative features of zoning and punctuating. Even stronger similarities, including the stirrup-spout vessel, are to be found with northwest South America, an area renowned for its shaft tombs. The possible implications of these occurrences will be dealt with in Chapter 9.

Following the early Capacha material, there is a gap in our knowledge until the Ortices phase from approximately 500 B.C.–A.D. 100. The Ortices phase is known from tombs excavated by I. Kelly in the Los Ortices district and one at Chanchopa near Tecomán. The Ortices phase is characterized by small solid figurines and fine quality cream to gray wares with shadow-striping, a technique that appears to be the forerunner of the *blanco levantado* in the region of Guanajuato, Querétaro, and Hidalgo. True *blanco levantado* appears later on in the Colima phase of the Classic period (Kelly 1978). Tombs were cut out during the Ortices phase, but reopened, cleared out, and reused in the following Comala phase, which includes the best-known Colima pottery: beautiful red vessels, black-on-red decorated pots, engraved monochrome vessels, and an almost infinite number of large hollow human and animal effigy figures.

Another site with Preclassic remains in Colima is Morett, on the Jalisco border, where the early phase is dated from 300 B.C.–A.D. 300 (Meighan 1972). There are no mounds or structures; remains are from a midden some 3 m in depth. Tripods, tetrapods, negative painting, zoned-hatchure decoration, and white-on-red pottery conform to the general feeling of Preclassic Mesoamerica. Nothing specific relates it to the Ocós horizon and Meighan sees more affiliation with Conchas of Guatemala, Playa de los Muertos in Honduras, and even to Ecuador where Chorrera and Tejar phases share many of these features. He believes some kind of relationship existed between Colima, Guatemala, and Central and South America prior to the Christian Era.

NAYARIT   While the highland areas were engaged in the shaft-and-chamber cult, the coastal pattern of Nayarit was somewhat simpler. Early material from coastal Nayarit comes from San Blas where the earlier nonceramic Matanchén complex was followed by the San Blas phase (700–450 B.C.). The latter is known from two sites located at the southernmost point of the Sinaloa–Nayarit coastal plain, just north of where the Sierra Madre Occidental mountains descend to the ocean. Its economy was oriented toward the sea and estuaries. The monochrome wares and a life based on marine exploitation form a complex reminiscent of the earlier Ocós, on the Guatemalan coast. Some of the ceramic traits (forms of jars, clay figurines, and some stone ornaments) are vaguely suggestive of Pioneer Hohokam features in the southwestern United States (Mountjoy 1970).

At the site of Amapa located on the delta flood-plain 5 km north of the Río Grande de Santiago, the main occupation belongs to the Classic period following A.D. 600. The Preclassic phases at the site (Gavilán and Amapa) consist of refuse mounds only. Houses were of wattle-and-daub construction. Nothing is known of the burial customs. Ceramics are decorated with white-on-red and an elaborate polychrome. Hand-modeled figurines, including Chinesca types, both hollow and hand-modeled, are part of the widespread tradition and bear similarities to those of the Early Ixtlán complex (Meighan 1976b).

JALISCO   One of the few Preclassic sites with architecture is Etzatlán, Jalisco excavated by Weigand. Extensive surveying yielded 348 sites which have been grouped into (a) hunting stations and kill sites; (b) small simple villages with a central mound or altar, with three to six outlying mounds and temples; (c) larger sites with more complex mounds and tombs with very elaborate offerings; and (d) Ahualulco, a large and most impressive site with eight separate mound circles, each with a huge central mound. These belong to the Arenal phase (? B.C.–A.D. 200) where perhaps each mound circle represents a lineage. The smaller centers suggest an occupation by several lineages of more or less equal rank. Ahualulco is a curious site located on high ground surrounded by valleys and old lake beds. Tombs were found in the central mounds containing typical shaft-tomb pottery as just described. Since reusing tombs was a common practice, the study of the remains is always difficult as contents were moved about and mixed up. I. Kelly (1978) relates that, to clear out one Colima tomb for reuse, its contents were dumped into the shaft of another. In other cases, shafts remained open for deposition of any rubbish, adding to the tribulations of the archaeologist. As noted earlier, the famous Etzatlán tomb from this region of Jalisco was probably used three times.

Despite evidence of obsidian workshops and much household debris at Ahualulco, the population remained small until A.D. 150. About that time, colonizers from Teotihuacán came in, probably to exploit the local obsidian, turquoise, agate, and opal deposits (Ahualulco phase). With their arrival, the shaft-tomb practices were discontinued. Thin Orange pottery and Teotihuacán ceramics replaced the older ones, and the whole area was integrated into one major center at Ahualulco. Thus, the Etzatlán region was exposed to Teotihuacán culture early in the Classic period (Weigand 1974).

On the banks of the Lerma River in the southern part of the state of Guanajuato lay the village of Chupícuaro, a long-known site that exerted considerable influence on pottery styles of west, northern, and central Mexico. Thousands of complete pottery vessels from this site stock museums and private collections around the world, but the site itself is now covered by an artificial lake created by the Solís Dam, completed in 1949. Prior to the inundation, extensive excavations undertaken by the Instituto Nacional de Antropología e Historia of Mexico uncovered nearly 400 richly stocked graves, a veritable cemetery located along the top of a hill at the confluence of the Lerma and a small tributary. The only remains of construction were stone alignments somewhat similar to those on the Cerro del Tepalcate and burned clay fragments presumably from floors (Porter 1956). People lavished pottery figurines and small artifacts on the dead, so great was their preoccupation with events after death. Scattered throughout the cemetery were rectangular mud-packed basins filled with fine ash, around which were strewn burials. We imagine that interment took place while fires burned in the sunken basins.

Pottery can be divided into two distinct lots: (1) the black-brown unpainted wares, typical of Ticomán types as seen in composite silhouette, mammiform or plain tripod shapes and (2) elaborate polychrome wares decorated in combinations of red and black, brown-on-buff, and red-on-buff bichrome. Designs are geometric without exception. Variety lies in form: elongated and kidney shapes, shallow bowls with great long "spider leg" supports (Plate 4-h, p. 94), effigy vessels, and the stirrup spout again. The H-4 figurine was produced with great enthusiasm and traded into the Basin of Mexico and Morelos, while several other related styles were limited to the locality (Plate 3-c, e, p. 91).

CHUPÍCUARO

Musical instruments—clay *ocarinas*, flutes, whistles, and rattles—were interred with children at death. Dogs were carefully buried, and sometimes they too were given offerings. Horizontally cut skulls, painted red and perforated for suspension, were stacked on the knees of some bodies. Decapitated skeletons and skull burials further emphasize a well-developed death cult.

The practice of decapitation was very widespread in Mesoamerica and there are many Preclassic examples from La Venta, Tres Zapotes, Izapa, Monte Albán, the Pacific Coast of Guatemala, Uaxactún, and Tikal. The custom increased in the Classic period, especially in Late Classic when decapitation was intimately associated with the ball-game cult. The practice is very well documented for the Postclassic period. The precise meaning it held for Preclassic peoples is not known, but it is assumed to have formed an integral part of ceremonial life, related to warfare, personal achievement and/or ancestor worship (Moser 1973).

There are probably two successive phases represented in the Chupícuaro graves, an early one including the brown polychrome and H–2 figurines; and a later one with the majority of the remains in which black paint replaced the brown. Both fall within the late Preclassic horizon (Porter 1956; Porter Weaver 1969).

All activity ceased by Classic times; these people must have either moved off or been absorbed by others, as this period is not represented in the region. Although the end of the Preclassic spells the end of Chupícuaro, its geometric patterns and the red-on-buff pottery tradition were kept alive by the Bajío and northern cultures and we will see it reassert itself many years later in the Postclassic Matlatzinca culture of the Toluca Valley and in the Coyotlatelco tradition (Porter Weaver 1969).

Another west Mexican trait that became very widespread and enjoyed great popularity is the decoration called *blanco levantado* or Tula Watercolored. Hard to describe, but easy to spot even on a sherd, this curious decorative style may have developed from the early shadow-striping of Colima, but became very common among later Classic settlements across the upper Lerma Basin in the states of Guanajuato, Querétaro, and San Luis Potosí (Braniff 1974; Kelly 1978). It has been reported from Tula, Hidalgo, and the Valley of Mexico along with Mazapan and Coyotlatelco pottery. Long considered a Postclassic pottery style, it can now be traced back to the late Preclassic in the Bajío and ultimately to Colima.

The Preclassic period in west Mexico seems to have early ties to central Mexico around 1500 B.C., but thereafter remained culturally very independent developing a special regional cult centering around the shaft-and-chamber tomb complex. Pottery and tombs hint of stronger ties with northwestern South America than with Mesoamerica, where stone-faced mounds around plazas, temples, and pyramids were already being erected. It was not until A.D. 600 that these features spread to the west coast.

An area we will often refer to in chapters ahead is the Valley of Oaxaca, **Oaxaca** situated in the southern highlands of Mexico at an average elevation of 1500 m. Blessed by a warm, temperate, semiarid climate and drained by the Atoyac River and its tributary, the Salado or Tlacolula River, the area has one of the longest and most informative cultural sequences in Mesoamerica. Three valleys converge at the modern city of Oaxaca: Etla Valley to the north, Tlacolula to the east, and Zaachila or the Valle Grande to the south (Map 6). Etla and Zaachila valleys are drained by the Atoyac River and the Río Salado joins the Atoyac just south of Oaxaca City.

Near this modern city, the famous site of Monte Albán stretches over five hills which rise sharply from the valley floor. The remains of Monte Albán have been the object of intense study by Caso and Bernal (1952, 1965), Acosta (1965), and Blanton (1978). The Preclassic history has been reconstructed from settlements in Oaxaca Valley and from the first two periods of occupation at Monte Albán. The early history has been the subject of a large project headed by Flannery and a team of investi-

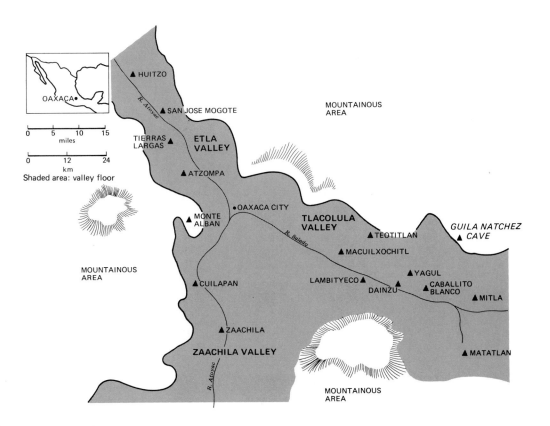

MAP 6. The three valleys of Oaxaca.

gators. The results of this work have implications far beyond the Oaxaca region. Archaeologically, they have provided not only a wealth of new data, but also fresh ideas and techniques, many of which can be applied to other geographical areas. For this reason, more detail will be included.

The earliest Preclassic material known comes from the Valley of Etla, northwest of the city of Oaxaca, where a concentration of early sites is located in a region drained by the Atoyac River (Flannery, Kirkby, Kirkby, and Williams 1967). Here, soon after 1500 B.C. people lived in settled communities on the high alluvium flood-plain. Since the water level is only 3 m below the surface, this land was not farmed by the slash-and-burn method, but by "pot irrigation," a technique in which water was hauled up from wells sunk in the corn fields and then distributed around plants. This system is still in use today among modern Zapotec Indians of Oaxaca, and remains of ancient archaeological wells confirm a long tradition of the practice.

EARLY HISTORY   Atop a long promontory jutting out into the Etla Valley overlooking the Atoyac River, the village of Tierras Largas furnishes an example of an early Preclassic settlement and its name has been given to the first phase (Tierras Largas phase: 1500–1200 B.C.). The village was composed of approximately 10 households or clusters, each consisting of a wattle-and-daub house, with associated features of storage pits, burials, drainage ditches, ovens, and refuse deposits. The storage pits are similar to those at Tlatilco, Ajalpan, Moyotzingo, Chiapa de Corzo, and Las Charcas, probably used first to store food and later for rubbish. At Tierras Largas they were dug into soft, decomposed rock and, when sealed with a flat stone, could store grain very efficiently for years. There are no public buildings at Tierras Largas itself or at most of the other contemporary hamlets in the Oaxaca Valley. However, at nearby San José Mogote one building is believed to be ceremonial in nature for it was swept clean, contained no household rubbish, and was oriented at 8° west of true north like Olmec sites.

The following phase, San José (1200–900 B.C.), is contemporaneous with the Olmec site of San Lorenzo. Contact between the two regions is seen in Olmec pottery designs among the dozen or more sites of this period. San José Mogote is unique in being 10 times the size of any other settlement and having four distinct residential wards, corresponding roughly to the four cardinal directions. Ceramics can be cross-dated in form and decoration with other contemporary lowland sites and those in central highland Mexico. The differentially fired white-rimmed black ware, excised designs, Olmec motifs, rocker-stamping, and figurines of C and D types are familiar markers.

It has been suggested that Olmec motifs were limited to elite groups associated with two major descent groups: the were-jaguar and the fire-serpent (Pyne 1976). In studying the distribution of their respective motifs, they were found to be mutually exclusive, that is, those San José Mogote residents claiming the fire-serpent as their mythical ancestor lived in the eastern and western wards, whereas were-jaguar descendants resided in the south. Had these ceramics been purely ritual, one would expect to find them associated exclusively with ceremonial structures and in graves, but they occur in residential contexts as well, and even with children, suggesting that the affiliation is inherited rather than acquired. Special features of San José Mogote suggesting ritual are painted circles and a circular area in a court that had been plastered and painted red.

Drennan (1976) has pointed out that this was a period of intense ritual activity and that perhaps the clay masks and the curious figurines in costume or special paraphernalia, often with exaggerated facial expressions, may represent dancers or people undergoing some religious experience. Sting-ray spines used for bloodletting, sharks teeth, turtle-shell drums, and conch-shell trumpets were all part of the ritual inventory. Since these items are products of lowland cultures, they had to be procured through a network of exchange with outsiders.

This brings us to a discussion of Preclassic exchange networks for which San José serves as a good example. Deposits of magnetite and ilmenite in the Oaxaca Valley were exploited to make small iron-ore mirrors. Clay figurines show that these were worn on the chest, surely a distinction of the elite. Most were produced in San José Mogote where fragments, chips, unfinished as well as finished and broken products, and lumps of raw material were found in several clusters in one household. Debris indicates that this craft had been carried on through generations as a part-time specialization. Just how the finished mirrors were distributed is not known. Since the mirrors were restricted to high-status individuals, an elite network exchange of some sort is indicated, of which Morelos, Nochixtlán, and Veracruz were a part.

Iron-ore mirrors and ritual paraphernalia are examples of rather exotic items. Jade, turquoise, and mica are others. However, food products and many other kinds of goods moved around also. Some were available to everyone, whereas others were highly restricted and involved another type of commercial mechanism.

The movement of obsidian is an interesting example of still another kind of exchange taking place. There were nine main sources of obsidian of which four were of primary importance: Guadalupe Victoria in eastern Puebla, El Chayal, Guatemala, Barranca de los Estetes near Otumba in the Basin of Mexico, and Zinapécuaro, Michoacán (see Map 8, p. 206). In the earliest periods in Oaxaca, households probably procured their own material, for a variety of sources were utilized; chips, flakes, and general debris are common in the houses. After 900 B.C. some basic changes occurred that coincide with the appearance of elite residences. The prismatic blade became much in demand, which eliminated Guadalupe Victoria from the obsidian market as its obsidian was of rather mediocre quality and unsuitable for blade production. Barranca de los Estetes and Zinapécuaro stepped up their activity accordingly (see Map 8, p. 206). Now we begin to see a new factor called *pooling,* a central agency that handled the distribution. This practice had been gradually building up and now became firmly established. The increasing value of prismatic blades may have triggered the idea. The result was that some individuals became very wealthy and gained enough power to control and manipulate the exchange process. How the pooling was actually carried out is not known, but it could have been handled by the most prestigious individual who began by supplying his immediate family and followers.

The Gulf Coast cultures had been a good market for San José Mogote's iron-ore mirrors. But around 900 B.C. San Lorenzo was being defaced and La Venta growing prosperous. For some reason, there was no more demand for small flat magnetite mirrors. Now they wanted large, concave mirrors of ilmenite or hematite, and these were probably made locally. At the same time there was a decline in the demand for shell products. These shifts in commercial activities probably reflect social changes that are less easily observed archaeologically.

In the long run, the earlier chiefdoms were gradually replaced by a more formal state political system, resulting in a restructuring of the exchange networks. Instead of many varied networks operating in terms of the type of commodity involved, the use to which it was put, the market for which it was intended (general populace or elite), commerce now approached a statelike enterprise in which products were made regionally on demand. This resulted in the expansion of local industries and a reduction in long-distance trade, which altered the whole character of commodity exchange, paving the way for the mercantilism that developed in the Classic period (Pires-Ferreira 1976; Pires-Ferreira and Flannery 1976).

Continuing the Oaxaca Valley sequence, in the Guadalupe phase (900–700 B.C.) the Olmec influence fell off rapidly, although white-slipped baby-face figurines continued. The incised double-line-break reached a popularity peak which was to taper off in the next phase (Rosario). Small solid figurines resemble "A" types, which have a characteristic eye with a well-defined punched pupil. The "A" figurine is known from the Basin of Mexico and the Santa María phase at Tehuacán and is generally distributed throughout lowland sites as far east as the Petén.

Architecturally, some fundamental Mesoamerican planning was taking shape in Oaxaca, for at Huitzo a public building preserves the 8° west of true north orientation seen at San José Mogote and La Venta. This forms one of a group of structures placed around a court. Public buildings became more plentiful from this time on.

By the Rosario phase (700–500 B.C.) there were numerous small chiefdoms in the Oaxaca Valley. Each contained one village with some public buildings which served as the local civic–ceremonial center for a series of nearby hamlets. At the same time an elite residence became a prominent feature in the center of town. Differentiation of size and complexity of settlements is seen as good evidence of a class system. San José Mogote was one of the more prestigious centers and had been among the first to erect a civic–ceremonial building. It was here that one household had specialized in the production of ilmenite mirrors. And it was in this rather precocious town that the earliest example of the 260-day cycle was found.

This was a ritual cycle that was extremely influential in the lives of Mesoamericans and effectively determined day-to-day activities. It will be taken up in Chapter 5, but it should be noted that it was already in operation in Oaxaca at this early date. Its archaeological documentation is rather dramatic. A carved slab of stone depicting a sprawled figure was set on the threshold of a public building where one would naturally tread. A date of "1 Earthquake" is carved on the glyphs between the figure's legs. He represents a captive and is only the first of hundreds of such slabs which postdate 500 B.C. to be found at Monte Albán. Perhaps "1 Earthquake" was the name of the unfortunate creature, for it was common practice to be named for the day on which one was born.

It was probably about this time (500–400 B.C.) that the decision was made to build a capital at Monte Albán. The site chosen was a unique hilltop location 300–400 m above the valley floor, without water or arable land, in a rather inaccessible area for commercial activities. The valleys were inhabited by numerous chiefdoms probably competing and quarreling with one another. Population had increased to the point where less desirable land on the upper piedmont slopes had been taken up for farming. Given these circumstances, Blanton (1978) suggests that Monte Albán was founded as a special-function community, or capital of the Oaxaca settlements. Speculating that a kind of confederacy or league had developed in the valley with conflict and rivalries leading to worrisome threats of military action, Blanton proposes that there was need of a central authority in a neutral setting. Monte Albán provided an ideal place.

Although this is admittedly speculative, Blanton feels there is some evidence that the three early residential areas around the Main Plaza represent distinct ethnic groups, and this would support his basic premise of league representation. One group may have come from San José Mogote which was abandoned precisely at this time.

In Monte Albán I, the Main Plaza (300 m × 150 m) was laid out, occupying the summit of the hill (see Figure 23, p. 238). People moved

MONTE ALBÁN

up, creating a resident population of 10,000–20,000. Toward the south-western corner of the Main Plaza, a structure (Building L) with a great gallery along its eastern side to display low-relief carvings of captives and sacrificed victims was erected. An estimated 300 such slabs were carved, a truly tremendous display of military power, matching the enthusiasm of the young expansionist state.

The slab-relief figures were arranged in four superimposed rows; on the bottom, which was most visible, were placed the best carvings with finest details. These so-called "Danzantes" represent nude male figures (nudity itself being a humiliation for Mesoamerican peoples), with rubbery lifeless limbs, half-closed eyes, and mouths that droop at the corners, sagging open in death (see Plate 1-d, p. 68). Sex organs are depicted in elaborate flower designs, possibly representing blood flowing from castration or from ritual penis blood-letting with sting-ray spine. Name glyphs often accompany a figure as on the threshold stone at San José Mogote. Unfortunately stones were subsequently moved around and Building L was partially destroyed in antiquity so the sequences and exact location of each slab cannot accurately be re-created. This collection of so many captives or slain prisoners would have given any potential insurgent cause for reflection.

The inhabitants of Monte Albán were given normal burial, but the more prestigious were placed in tombs. Tombs were built in simple rectangular shapes roofed over with slabs of stone (see Figure 7, p. 114). Much of the early pottery is found in these tombs as well as from valley sites. The fine-paste gray ware was to dominate the many periods that follow. For daily use, cream and brown wares were preferred. A variety of very small vessels with a fine polish and slip are characteristic, and bridged spouts are a prominent special form (see Figure 6-ee, p. 76). Hand-modeled figurines are known, but were not produced in quantity.

This was a period of population growth both in the valleys and on Monte Albán. Monuments were carved in regional styles and local traditions continued uninterrupted.

The growth and consolidation of Oaxaca as a state took place during Monte Albán II (200 B.C.–A.D. 100). The exposed north, northwestern, and western sectors of the mountain were sheltered by 3 km of wall, rising 4 m high in places. Although this would offer a good defense, there is no evidence that conflict ever took place. As time went on, we see that the residents seemed obsessed with privacy so perhaps the walls served other purposes such as to control access or levy taxes. An irrigation system was added on the east side below the Main Plaza. It consisted of a dam laid across a *barranca* to catch water and combined with a canal system that conducted the water for 2 km around the mountain.

In the Main Plaza, Monte Albán continued to publicize her military victories but with far fewer monuments. Mound J, an arrow-shaped building, was erected in the plaza itself toward the southern end (see Figure 23, p. 238). This odd structure is larger, but very similar to one at Caballito Blanco, some 50 km to the east. There seems to be a tendency in Mesoamerica to identify towers and odd-shaped structures as astronomical observatories, and Mound J is no exception. Aveni and Linsley (1972) studied this possibility and in effect found a possible zenith sighting tube and concluded that the building could have been oriented to the heliacal rising of the bright star, Capella, during the solar zenith passage. They discovered no other lunar or solar coincidences. Although not everyone is convinced (Marcus 1976b), planets and heavenly bodies were observed from somewhere, for calendrical knowledge as well as writing was well advanced.

Monte Albán at this time already had its emblem or place sign, was using bars and dots for recording dates, manipulating the 260-day ritual calendar, and observing the very Mesoamerican practice of using one's birth date as a name. Oaxaca was the hearth of one of Mesoamerica's writing systems as well as the scene of some of the earliest steps in developing the calendar system which was later carried to its fullest expression by the Maya. These intellectual achievements are discussed separately in Chapter 5.

In addition to any scientific purpose it may have served, Mound J provides a record of conquests. More than 40 additional carved slabs decorated with reliefs of sacrificed corpses are set into the lower walls of the building. These differ from those of Building L in having many more hieroglyphs. Not all the glyphs can be "read" but Marcus thinks that four may refer to towns conquered by Monte Albán within 140 km. Thus the conquest slabs could delineate Monte Albán territory. For example, Cuicatlán, whose toponym has been identified, was a fortified mountain between Oaxaca and the Tehuacán Valley. Monte Albán II pottery has been found there but not beyond. Although Period II has only 50 carved slabs as compared to 300 in Period I, the glyphic writing is much more informative and many Zapotec glyphs appear (Marcus 1980).

There are also ball courts that date from Period II but have not been excavated because they lie inside later structures. Two-room temples with columns were another innovation. One of these lies inside Mound X northeast of the Main Plaza (see Figure 23, p. 238). This was a period of militarism, expansion, and glory. The city had reached its maximum growth and attention focused on consolidating its position.

Monte Albán is the best-known and the largest site of this period but by no means is it the only prominent one. Mitla, well known for its Postclassic occupation, was actually founded in the San José phase.

Dainzú, near the village of Tlacolula, has proved to be an extensive site that has traces of Olmec flavor. Although there is a large pyramidal platform, the stones at the base of the structure have attracted the most interest. Mound A was constructed directly over a rock base. The lower wall is completely covered by two superimposed rows of bas-relief drawings. Two figures are humanized jaguars; others may portray priests(?), perhaps dressed as deities; but 32 represent ball-players wearing wide pants, knee guards, visored helmets, gauntlets, and holding the ball in their hands. Some are shown with yokes around the waist (Bernal 1973). If these figures accurately depict the game, the rules at this site (500–100 B.C.) must have differed from those of the Postclassic, for we know that in the latter the sport was played without hands. (See Chapter 6.)

Still another site, Montenegro, located west of Monte Albán in the Mixteca, was occupied only during Middle Preclassic times. It is considered to be a pure Monte Albán I site, yet the material is not identical. No slab-reliefs of captives, numerals, hieroglyphs, or evidence of the 260-day cycle have come to light. A very typical pottery form is a tall, simple urn decorated with an Olmec-like face on one side. With streets and public architecture, Montenegro has many features of a major center (Paddock 1966a). The site was apparently abandoned by 300 B.C. and we hear nothing more of it. At Monte Albán, however, there is a gradual transition from the Preclassic into the Classic period.

LAGUNA ZOPE

The Zeitlins' work at Laguna Zope (Zeitlin 1978) near Juchitán on the Isthmus of Tehuantepec has provided a much needed Preclassic sequence in a cultural intersection of Mesoamerica. Throughout the Preclassic period, no settlement on the Oaxaca coast could rival Laguna Zope in size or importance for these people had their choice of contacts and products. The initial settlement was most likely due to nothing more than the area's fine alluvium soil, availability of marine and estuary resources, and good water (Photo 17). In its early phases it shared the basic lowland ceramic tradition of Barra and Ocós. Here too the very small obsidian flakes are plentiful, but as elsewhere, there is nothing to either prove or disprove their use in processing manioc.

By 800–400 B.C. Laguna Zope had grown to a site of 90 ha due to its participation in an interregional exchange network. Obsidian sources and pottery styles fluctuated and were modified as relationships shifted from the Gulf lowlands to the Maya region to central Mexico. Although more obsidian was brought in to meet the demands of a greater population, the per capita distribution remained about the same. It is the tremendous increase in quartz and shell that suggests commercial production of ornamental shell. This was an item found in many Preclassic centers, in ceremonial contexts, and in graves of high-status individuals; and by being in scarce supply the shell was valued as a symbol of wealth and prestige. Thus shell ornaments were widely distributed,

PHOTO 17. Riverine–estuary environment on the southern Isthmus of Tehuantepec near Juchitán. (Courtesy of Robert and Judith Zeitlin.)

triggering an economic prosperity that transformed a rather undistinguished coastal settlement into a major Preclassic center.

Between 400–200 B.C. intimate relationships were developed with the Maya area; the lustrous brown and waxy orange wares of the Maya were brought in from the east, along with Usulután ware which came from as far away as El Salvador. Laguna Zope marks its northern limit.

Thereafter the momentum was lost. By 200 B.C. some sort of breakdown severed ties to the Maya region including the El Chayal contact which had been supplying Laguna Zope with obsidian for as many as 1200 years. The slack was taken up by Altotonga and Zaragoza, Puebla, but the ornamental-shell exchange was badly damaged. As might be expected, with the decrease in importance of the shell industry, the quartz tools diminished accordingly.

The fortunes of Laguna Zope, its growth and decline, can only be understood in terms of other regional developments. The social changes that affected Monte Albán were felt here also and the cessation of ornamental-shell production is a reflection of the new political alignments taking place elsewhere.

Pacific Lowlands and Piedmont Areas of Chiapas and Guatemala

We return now to coastal Guatemala and continue the Preclassic sequence following the Ocós horizon (see p. 65) at the site of Salinas la Blanca (see Map 3, p. 63). Here, two mounds were built up of accumulated household debris, one of which was excavated by stratigraphic levels by Coe and Flannery (1967). Two successive Preclassic phases, Cuadros and Jocotal, were found to follow Ocós chronologically. All Cuadros and Jocotal sites are located toward the backwaters of estuaries where villagers could travel by canoe but at the same time could be within walking distance of the mixed tropical forest lands. Vessel forms are essentially the same as Ocós, predominantly *tecomates* and the flat-bottomed bowl with sides slanting outward accompanied by rocker-stamped decoration, but there are important differences. Cuadros has no figurines, no iridescent painting, and no cord-marked pottery. Jocotal evolved from Cuadros and shows the same pottery types, with the addition of a white-rimmed black ware achieved by differential firing.

Flannery has reexamined the material in an effort to reconstruct household clusters as had been done so successfully in the Oaxaca Valley. Few sites are excavated with this in mind, and when digging arbitrary levels, a house and associated activities are not apparent. Until more excavations are done with the purpose of looking for settlement data, there is almost nothing known about Preclassic households outside of the Oaxaca Valley. Taking Salinas la Blanca as an example, Flannery reconstructed a Cuadros phase household as follows (Flannery 1976a).

The village was located on the edge of a mangrove swamp where the banks had been artificially raised by alternating layers of clay with domestic refuse. The house foundation was dug into this base and a hard-packed clay floor placed on top. Small posts were set close together for the wall, whose interstices were chinked with clay. General house dimensions could not be estimated. Remains of a *petate* (woven straw mat) on a floor suggested a sleeping arrangement, although today this is hammock country. Outside was a large red hearth and several smaller ones, all dug into the courtyard. These contained small roasting stones and remains of crabs and mollusks that had been opened by the heat. Pits had been dug to extract clay for daubing the house walls, and over to one edge of the built-up base was a sherd-and-shell midden where all trash was thrown.

The most widespread and important local development took place during the Middle Preclassic period (Conchas I and II phases). Population on the coast reached a peak of density not to be attained again until the Late Classic period. Villages were not necessarily larger, but simply more numerous. Clay platforms and pyramidal mounds announce the appearance of ceremonial architecture. The two Conchas phases share Middle Preclassic pottery traits with both lowland Gulf Coast areas and highland developments in central Mexico and Guatemala. Examples of these are the composite silhouette forms, the double-line-break, "grater bowls" with interior scoring (Figure 6-e, f, g, p. 76), and naturalistic figurines.

Late Preclassic times saw a great reduction in coastal population, paralleled by a shift of interest or influence away from lowland neighbors, and toward inland and highland centers such as Izapa in Chiapas and the Miraflores settlements at Kaminaljuyú. A veritable network of Late Preclassic sites covered the slopes of the Pacific, including the Crucero phase at Salinas la Blanca, Ilusiones at Bilbao (Parsons 1969) and Abaj Takalik (Graham 1976, 1977; Graham, Heizer, and Shook 1978). Coastal pottery reflects strong highland influence. Crucero wares are slipped and polished, consisting of orange monochromes, red-on-orange, and streaky brown-black vessels accompanied by Usulután, an early resist-painted pottery (see Plate 4-a, p. 93). By the year A.D. 1, coastal Guatemala had become marginal to major developments in the highlands.

We must also call attention to the long continuous occupation of sites in the region of Chiapas, where careful and detailed excavations have been carried out for a number of years by the New World Archaeological Foundation (Lowe 1959; Lowe and Mason 1965). The important site of Chiapa de Corzo is located in the great central depression of Chiapas near the modern town of Tuxtla Gutierrez, an area that has a dry tropical climate. Chiapa I (Cotorra), the lowest level of one of the longest sequences in Mesoamerica, yielded pieces of adobe plaster from some kind of early construction. In its pottery forms we again find the *tecomate* and flat-bottomed bowls with straight or flaring walls and jars with necks. There is a variety of decorative techniques: punctating, rocker-stamping, filleting, and pattern incising on a white-slipped ware, and red-and-white bichrome. Solid, hand-made figurines also form part of the first complex. The earliest Chiapa phase correlates with the Cuadros material from the Pacific Coast, and six more phases (Chiapa II-VII) follow, bringing us to the threshold of the Classic. The Chiapas sequence is an important scale for comparison of remains both west and east of the Isthmus. Stone architecture had begun by Chiapas III, as seen in stone-faced terrace platforms and foundations of small boulders. Toward the very end of the Preclassic a poor-quality lime mortar was being used. Although we believe that contacts were made with the Petén residents and that travelers may have seen corbelled arches being constructed, none are found in Chiapas.

Another Chiapas site with early architectural remains is Izapa, located on the Pacific coastal plain of Chiapas near Altamira. This site has yielded pottery affiliated with Chiapa de Corzo, as well as the Soconusco coastal sites with the exception of the very early Barra phase. The earliest material is represented by sherds from Mound 30A, a stepped pyramid faced with uncut stone, which in its final stages is estimated to have been approximately 9 m high. Post holes indicate that it originally had supported a small temple on its summit (S. M. Ekholm 1969). Corrected carbon dates of the Duende phase structure average 627 ± 177 B.C., which is the earliest date for a pyramid in eastern Mesoamerica. The platforms and plazas are oriented on a north–south axis, the same basic plan as that of Teotihuacán. The way was now prepared for the extraordinary development that Izapa displayed in the late Preclassic and Protoclassic years.

Izapa became an enormous center of activity with 80 temple–pyramids arranged around courts and plazas. Its special iconography was related to a very complex religious cult that is portrayed on many of the 250 stone altars, stelae, and boulders. There are familiar Olmec motifs such as the St. Andrews cross, the U-shaped design, a long-lipped deity believed to be derived from the were-jaguar. The art depicted here is full of motion. Combined animal-and-human figures fly, paddle canoes, descend from the sky, and wrestle. Some are busily decapitating a victim while others burn incense. Izapan figures are free to move between earth, sky, and heaven. Above all, these combined human, bird, jaguar, crocodile–serpent figures are narrations. The result is exciting, wild, confusing, and cluttered. Turning to the art historians for help, we are told that although Izapan art may be Olmec-derived, it contains some Maya elements (Quirarte 1976, 1977). For example, it is possible to trace the ancestry of the Mayan long-lipped rain deity back through Izapan figures of crocodiles, serpents, and jaguars to the Olmec were-jaguar (Quirarte 1973, 1976; see also opinion of M. D. Coe 1980). Izapa art was pictorial, narrative, and maybe mythic, but is not accompanied by hieroglyphic texts (see Plate 1-b, p. 68). Once thought to have been a cult which spread over a wide area of the coastal lowlands with influence reaching beyond, this idea is now less convincing. What has frequently been attributed to Izapan may be Olmec or early Maya, for the styles of these people were also present (Graham 1976). The sculptures of Abaj Takalik are helping to distinguish the differences.

At Abaj Takalik, Department of Retalhuleu, Guatemala both Maya and Olmec sculptures occur together. This is a large site at 600 m elevation where the heavy tropical forest vegetation has been replaced by sugar-cane and coffee plantations. The eastern edge is delineated by a deep, steep *barranca* with a small stream at the bottom. The site consists of many earthen mounds on wide terraces cut back into the hillside. There is no cut stone masonry but some use may have been made of stone cobble for facings. Excavations to date have concentrated on mapping and on the abundant stone monuments. These show a remarkable sequence of sculptural development beginning with the use of natural boulders to which eyes or certain other elements have been added by incising or grinding. The famous "pot-belly" sculptures (see Monte Alto later in this chapter) developed out of these early sculptures to finally produce a naturalistic sculpture in the round and the emergence of the Olmec style. An Olmec colossal head of Gulf Coast type was reused (see Plate 1-g, p. 69) and the carving of the nose and lips altered to represent a figure seated on a cushion. The entire range of Olmec sculptural art can be found at Abaj Takalik with the exception of the large rectangular "altars" (John A. Graham, personal communication).

In the Late Preclassic period, during the few centuries prior to A.D. 1, Maya portrait stelae with hieroglyphic texts appear. Figures are represented wearing traditional elements of Maya attire. This whole complex marks a clear break with the earlier sculptural tradition. It is the result of a long development somewhere else, but its antecedents are not found at Abaj Takalik. Graham calls attention to a related style on Altar 1 at Polol (see Map 3, p. 63). The limestone piece is small enough to have been brought in from elsewhere in the Petén, and he believes it to contain a Cycle 7 Initial Series date, the earliest known in the Petén (John A. Graham, personal communication).

From the excavations at Abaj Takalik over the last few years, stelae have been recovered not only with traditional Maya-style dress and emblems but with Initial Series dates, predating the southern Classic Maya stelae known at present (Graham 1977). Stela 5 (Plate 6-f, p. 167) with an Initial Series date of A.D. 126 is an outstanding example.

The front figures are both dressed in Maya-style like that of the Leyden Plate and one holds a long serpent, the forerunner of the later ceremonial bar in Maya art. The side figures may represent visitors from Izapa rendered in Maya fashion (Graham, Heizer, and Shook 1978). This stela predates the earliest known dated lowland one (Tikal's Stela 29) by 166 years and is surely preceded by a long period of antecedent development.

Stela 2 is too damaged to read unequivocally but is probably no later than the first century B.C. This stela shows two figures facing each other over a vertical column of hieroglyphs (Proskouriakoff 1950). The identifying period and cycle glyphs are missing, but those present clearly depict position numerals. This remarkable stela shows a large bearded head surrounded by dragon masks and scrolls. If the postulated date is proved correct, Stela 2 from Abaj Takalik would provide one of the earliest recorded dates in the New World. It was accompanied by Altar 5, a large unsculptured stone found at its base. Another interesting monument is Altar 13, originally erected as a stela and later laid horizontally before a plain stela to serve as its altar. The main human figure wears a long beaded-trellis skirt, a feature usually associated with the late Classic period. Yet here, so similar is its style to that of Stelae 1 and 2 that it probably belongs with sculpture of the first century A.D.

The finding of Olmec and Maya monuments together at Abaj Takalik raises the question of the relationships of these to Izapa. It would seem that we are dealing with three styles that overlapped: Olmec, Izapa, and Maya. Although Izapa has often been considered as transitional to Maya, this is not necessarily the case. Maya art is historical in content and concentrates on the human figure with information as to name, date, and deed described in a hieroglyphic text, none of which suggests Izapa iconography. In some cases Olmec can be seen to overlap with Maya; thus, the end result is three different art styles.

At El Baúl, halfway between the Valley of Guatemala and the Pacific, another stela with glyphs, some of which are numerals, was associated with Arenal (Late Preclassic) pottery. In this case also, the hieroglyphs are badly eroded, but there is further confirmation of early recording of Long Count dates. M. D. Coe (1957, 1980) reconstructs Stela 1 at El Baúl as having a baktun 7 coefficient (see Plate 6-d, p. 167) thus reading 7.19.15.7.12 or A.D. 36 in our calendar (see Chapter 5). This interpretation credits El Baúl with another of the very early dated monuments in the Maya area.

Monte Alto, a site in contact with Kaminaljuyú, is only 40 km from the Pacific Coast on the fertile alluvial plain, ecologically transitional between the rain forest and savana zone. There are a number of badly weathered earthen mounds spaced in two rows enclosing a plaza, but the most outstanding feature is the stone sculpture. It falls into the Late Preclassic sequence after 500 B.C. (?) The curious boulder sculptures for which the site is famous have an Olmec look about them—Olmec-derived or pre-Olmec? Two are colossal human heads, and three are round human figures with wrap-around limbs and closed eyes; they are nude, sexless, and bald. Another boulder has a carving of a jaguar-monster mask.

Similar carved boulders have a wide distribution including Bilbao and sites as dispersed as Piedra Parada, Abaj Takalik, and Utatlán to Kaminaljuyú in the highlands and south to Copán, Honduras. Associated pottery includes white-rimmed black ware, thick-rimmed *tecomates,* and glossy white-paste wares (Parsons and Jenson 1965).

The site of El Bálsamo, only 9 km west of Monte Alto, promises a good ceramic sequence for this area which would help place the sculpture chronologically. Sharing many traits with Monte Alto, its history extends back in time to the Cuadros phase, thus spanning the years from approximately 1150 B.C. to about 200 B.C. This should be helpful because pottery from surrounding areas, such as the Valley of Guatemala, was brought in permitting cross correlations. Left unexplained in an otherwise lengthy ceramic history is the scarcity of Conchas phase material (Shook and Hatch 1978).

Not so many years ago it was thought that the story of the Maya began in the central region, the lowlands of the Petén, but we now know that although there were Preclassic settlements in the lowlands, even north to the tip of the peninsula of Yucatán, the most extraordinary advances were being made in the highlands of Guatemala at Kaminaljuyú, the outskirts of the modern capital.

Bordered by lofty volcanoes jutting above the surrounding hills, the broad green plateau at 1493 m above sea level, where Guatemala City sprawls today, has always been favored as a living site for man. Offering a temperate climate that varies little throughout the year, with rainfall often adequate for two planting seasons, the area possesses rich volcanic soil, small game in the pine and oak forests in the surrounding higher country, and abundant resources of minerals and plants. Few areas could offer more advantages to the farmer, the builder, and the artisan. Of more than 35 prominent archaeological sites in the valley, we know most about the large settlement on the western edge. Known to us as Kaminaljuyú, it was the scene of great activity throughout Preclassic and Classic times (Borhegyi 1965; Kidder *et al.* 1946; Sanders and Michels 1969; Shook and Kidder 1952).

No habitation mounds have actually been excavated of the earliest phase (Arévalo), but again many burned adobe fragments show impressions of poles and vegetal material. Living sites were scattered, open, and undefended. The quality of the pottery is outstanding, even superior to some of later periods. The variety in form and decoration shows that some potters were in complete command of their craft. Monochrome wares are red, black, buff, white, or gray-brown; bichromes are largely combinations of red and white or buff. Small hand-modeled figurines, clay stamps, and hollow effigy whistles all conform to similar developments elsewhere.

The earliest phase, Arévalo, was followed by Las Charcas and Providencia (Middle Preclassic) and Late Preclassic phases known as Miraflores and Arenal. Las Charcas is best remembered for its bottle-shaped pits like those of Tlatilco and beautiful white kaolin pottery handsomely painted with abstract designs, dragon masks, or realistic portrayals of monkeys. Clay temple–pyramids were probably already being constructed by these people.

During the Late Preclassic years (400 B.C.–A.D. 100), religious architecture got off to a good start. Temple–pyramids, which in some cases served also as burial mounds, were arranged along both sides of a long rectangular plaza or avenue. Religion was the driving motivation, and all nearby peoples must have contributed heavily, in time and muscle, to the necessary labor force. Apparently there was no fear of outsiders since the sacred or civic centers were located on open valley floors

The Highland Maya

VALLEY OF GUATEMALA

without visible means of protection. Sanders and Michels (1969) suggest that these centers may have been utilized largely for ritual burials of chiefs.

A brief look at the Miraflores phase may serve to exemplify the peak of Preclassic development in the highland area (Shook and Kidder 1952). Huge earthen mounds were brightly painted, and two to eight staircases led to a hut-like temple on top. But these mounds were not built to their final height of 18 m all at once. One such mound may contain as many as seven interior structures. The custom of enlarging a pyramid periodically is a common feature of Mesoamerican builders. Thus, the oldest structure will be the smallest and form the initial interior core of a mound, with successive pyramids superimposed upon it. All this was done at Miraflores, but just prior to one of these periodic enlargements the builders dug through the top of an existing pyramid and excavated a rectangular-stepped opening to be used as a tomb (see Figure 7, p. 114). The corners were carefully braced by wooden uprights, and then the privileged deceased, covered with red paint, was carefully extended on a litter in the center. In the case of Tomb 2 in Mound E-III-3, both adults and children were offered in sacrifice, along with more than 300 objects, to accompany the distinguished corpse in afterlife. These objects were items of great luxury, such as jade beads, mosaics, and masks; beautifully carved vessels of soapstone, fuchsite, and chlorite schist (see Figure 6-t, x, p. 76); sting-ray spines, symbols of self-sacrifice; stuccoed gourds; sheets of mica; fine implements of obsidian and basalt; bone; quartz crystals; fish teeth; and quantities of fine pottery vessels. The contents complete, the tomb was then roofed over with crossbeams and rush mats, the flooring restored, and construction of a new, grander pyramid accomplished by covering the entire mound according to plan. Two such tombs were found, both occupying prominent positions in pyramidal structures. Mound E-III-3 is the largest and best-known structure of the Miraflores people. Actually it forms part of a small compact group of nine mounds which were arranged around a plaza. Two other such groups of public buildings have also been identified which contain similar though smaller constructions. Each of these has a high terraced temple platform and a low sprawling platform presumed to be the substructure of an elite residence. These buildings constituted what must have been the administrative center adjacent to which the local population lived in a tightly knit group. In turn, these groupings of administrative centers, each with some local residents, were well spaced. Sanders estimates the total population around 5000 (Sanders 1977a).

A very distinctive pottery, called Usulután ware, was much in style in Late Preclassic times (Plate 4-a, p. 93 ; also see later in this chapter). Although clay figurines, stamps, and whistles were made in abundance by the Miraflores people, none was found among the numerous articles in the tombs. One suspects, therefore, that these were not prestigious goods and were destined only for daily usage among the general populace.

The possible significance of toads as a hallucinogenic medium was mentioned earlier in relation to the San Lorenzo inhabitants. We again encounter the toad or frog represented on stone mortars and pottery bowls among the contents of Tomb 1 at Miraflores. A "mushroom" stone was also found in the same tomb. These stones are curious objects not yet explained to anyone's complete satisfaction. They are cylindrical shafts of stone set on annular or tripod bases with mushroom-shaped caps (Plate 10-i, p. 290). Some are plain, while others are decorated by human figures or animals (jaguars, toads or frogs, rabbits, deer, or birds), which may replace the shaft. They may represent some kind of mushroom cult with hallucinogenic connotations, or they may symbolize a totem of some kind. Mushroom stones are distributed throughout the Guatemalan highlands and Pacific slopes, and more rarely in the lowlands, Chiapas, and El Salvador. They were made during Preclassic and Classic times, but apparently their manufacture ceased thereafter (Borhegyi 1965). Effigy mushrooms of clay are known from the Zoned-Bichrome period (Chapter 9) of the Nicoya Peninsula of Costa Rica, where they are associated with Usulután decorated pottery. They form part of an early complex of Mesoamerican features that penetrated lower Central America (Stone 1972).

The larger stone sculpture at Kaminaljuyú reflects the result of a long history of Preclassic monumental carving shared by the Pacific slopes and the region of the Isthmus of Tehuantepec. As elsewhere, this sculpture seems to be primarily religious in nature, and at Kaminaljuyú uncarved plain stelae are often associated with mounds. Boulder sculptures related to those of the Pacific slope are also found here. The sexless figure commonly represented is fat, heavy shouldered, and usually clasps his flexed knees. With a flat nose, thick lips, fat cheeks, and long ears adorned with spools, he is a distinctive personality. A vague resemblance is noted by some to the colossal heads found in the southern Veracruz and Tabasco areas. Those at Kaminaljuyú were deliberately smashed and suffered heavy damage, which recalls the treatment given to the San Lorenzo and La Venta monuments. We have seen sculptures of similar style at Monte Alto and Abaj Takalik. To a slightly later time belong the pedestal sculptures that depict jaguars, *pisotes*, monkeys, and some human figures capping a long square shaft. Although most numerous at Kaminaljuyú, they have also been found throughout the highlands, on the Pacific slopes, and in Honduras.

The peak of Preclassic sculpture is exemplified by two great sculptured stelae from the Miraflores phase of Kaminaljuyú, both of which exhibit a style related to that of Izapa (M. D. Coe 1980; Stirling 1943). Stela 11 shows a single standing human figure, attired in a cape and bearing four different varieties of the dragon mask. Standing on an Izapa-type platform and observed from above by the sky god, he carries in his left hand a kind of ceremonial hatchet and an "eccentric" flint like one found in the Miraflores tombs. The most important sculpture is Stela 10, made of black basalt, which unfortunately was deliberately smashed and mutilated before being buried with Stela 11. It depicts an anthropomorphous jaguar, a human figure, and probably a god. Below a pair of outstretched arms is a long hieroglyphic text, which cannot be read and looks non-Maya, unrelated to any known script (M. D. Coe 1976).

There are also some sculptures in the round, such as a handsome frog altar presently in the Guatemala Museum, toad mortars, three large monuments closely related to the much-discussed masks flanking the staircases of the E-VII-sub pyramid at Uaxactún. These exhibit elements of the serpent, Chac the rain god, and perhaps a tinge of Olmec flavor. The Kaminaljuyú monuments are executed in Miraflores style although they were found in association with an Arenal structure. Other sculptures attributed to the Late phase are tenoned or "silhouette" figures. These stones have a projection at the back which permits them to be embedded in walls or floors.

The glory and luxury evident at Kaminaljuyú can only signify a high degree of social stratification with wealth, power, and prestige in the hands of an elite few. The trend toward standardization of ritual material and the exclusion of certain artifacts such as figurines from the rich tombs suggests that religion was becoming formalized and rigidly patterned. The Protoclassic phase, Santa Clara, shows clearly that decline had set in, for the building boom ended, population declined, and people fell upon hard times.

As we have seen, Preclassic remains are strongly represented all through the regions of Chiapas, the coastal and Pacific slopes of Guatemala, and the southern highlands around Kaminaljuyú. Remains of Preclassic people in the northern highlands are few in comparison and until 1972 it was thought that the northern Guatemalan highlands were largely unpopulated until the Classic period. However, since the University of Minnesota survey was made, two Preclassic settlements have been found, Sakajut and El Portón (Sedat and Sharer 1972; see also Map 3, p. 63).

Sakajut in the pine forests of Alta Verapaz is precisely the point from which native peddlers leave today following the old foot paths north to the Petén and east to the Polochic Valley. It is 4 days' travel on foot to Guatemala City and a week or less to the Petén. It probably took no longer in Preclassic days. Close to sources of jade, quetzal feathers, and obsidian, Sakajut functions as a gateway to the lowlands. Preclassic remains include five mounds grouped around a plaza across a small river from another similar grouping of eight mounds and an open-ended ball court. Ceramics are largely Middle Preclassic in date with white-rimmed black ware, zoning, appliqué on *tecomates*, and flat-bottomed bowls.

El Portón is located nearby at the head of the Salama Valley near San Jerónimo, Baja Verapaz. More to the point is that it is located at a pass between the Sierra de Chuacus and Sierra de las Minas, both sources of jadeite, and only 30 km northwest of Manzanal, the most important jade area in all Mesoamerica. Here in a shallow pit in a low mound of rubble and earth, a Preclassic sculpture was found. Only one side of the 2.3-m-high schist slab was carved and it has been badly eroded or defaced (?). Scroll motifs and a possible dragon mask are suggestive of Izapa and Olmec iconography. A horizontal row of irregular hieroglyphs may be an ancient text. The estimated date is 600 B.C.–A.D. 100 (Sharer and Sedat 1973).

Chalchuapa in eastern highland El Salvador is the more comprehensive term for a large area that includes the site known as Tazumal, which now is but one of a series of four mound groups. Located at an altitude of about 640 m between the Pacific coastal plain and the Maya highlands, the ruins dominate the valley of Río Paz with a cultural record reaching back to 1200 B.C. (Sharer 1978b). At this earliest period of settlement, ceramics affiliate the region with the general lowland tradition of the Cuadros phase further north.

CHALCHUAPA, EL SALVADOR

We know much more about the Middle Preclassic period (900–650 B.C.) because during these years the Olmecs came south. In this case it was probably a commercial venture to gain control of the cacao production, hematite, and Ixtepeque obsidian. Once again the differentially fired white and black bowls, incised double-line-break, everted tabs, excised designs, and Olmec-style figurines are found.

The valley narrows sharply about 25 km west of Chalchuapa, and there at Ahuachapan a number of Olmec serpentine and jade figurines have surfaced. We know that the Olmecs liked such strategic control points. The huge El Trapiche (E-III 1 and 2) pyramid at Chalchuapa is of this date and ranks as one of the largest in Mesoamerica in its day.

Late Preclassic remains look remarkably like contemporary ones at Kaminaljuyú. Usulután pottery was produced by the ton. The name refers to a very distinctive resist decoration in which a series of wavelike lines were applied after the vessel had been fired to a light buff color. A second firing removed the resist substance, exposing the original cream slip, while the rest of the vessel turned orange or brown. It seems a rather complicated process; at times the lines were made with a multiple brush, but at others less care is evident and cloudy blotches were the result. No matter, the style enjoyed a tremendous success and was manufactured in El Salvador and western Honduras for almost

1000 years. Usulután vessels have a continuous range in western Honduras, El Salvador, Guatemala, and even neighboring Nicaragua. There are few examples from Mexico, the northern limit being Laguna Zope on the Oaxaca coast (Zeitlin 1978). Chronologically Usulután ware is of Late Preclassic date, but it persisted into Classic times in the extreme southern regions of Mesoamerica (Andrews V 1977) and is found as far south as the Nicoya Peninsula.

Southern Lowlands

Turning east from El Salvador to the southern lowlands of the Yucatecan peninsula, we enter the dense tropical jungle, a rather unlikely place for a civilization to develop, where the rain forest growth of Spanish cedars, mahogany, and sapodilla trees join overhead, only occasionally letting through the dazzling sunlight, while underneath, young trees, vines, and palms thrive in the hot, humid shade. Today this area holds little interest for the outside world, except perhaps as the home of chewing gum, made from chicle, the thick, milky sap of the sapodilla tree. However, its importance in Mesoamerican history is great, for it was also the chosen home of Maya Indians, who found here the inspiration to achieve one of the greatest civilizations of the western hemisphere. Despite the difficulties of scientific investigation, Preclassic remains of this region have been well known for a long time, for the long sequence at Uaxactún served as the basic yardstick for Maya chronology and archaeology prior to modern dating techniques.

The earliest Preclassic remains in this area belong to the Xe complex, a ceramic sphere of influence centering in southern and southwestern Guatemala. This material (early Middle Preclassic) comes from the sites of Seibal and Altar de Sacrificios on the Pasión River. At Seibal, a site located on a 100-m-high bluff overlooking a great bend of the Pasión River, rubbish left by Preclassic peoples underlies later constructions—floors, buildings, and patios. Their remains are also known from a few pits. The pottery is known as the Real Xe complex, which is closely affiliated with the Xe pottery at Altar de Sacrificios. The *tecomate* form, monochrome wares, and double-line-break are all familiar, but the Real Xe also has a white ware with thick slip and a large bolstered *tecomate* form. As far as we know, this Xe complex is limited to this region. Of outside areas, it is most closely related to the Late Dili–Early Escalera phases at Chiapa de Corzo, but ties can also be found with the Guatemalan Pacific coast (Conchas) and the Gulf Coast cultures as far north as the Huasteca (Willey 1970).

Other pre-Mamom pottery has been found at Dzibilchaltún, that extraordinary site in Yucatán with abundant remains spanning Middle Preclassic and Conquest times (Andrews 1960, 1965). The earliest Preclassic remains there (the Zacnicte complex) show little similarity to other lowland sites and represent rather a local development of black-on-tan and black-and-red-on-tan polychrome decoration of simple forms.

About 600 B.C. remains of the Mamom horizon are reported from central and eastern Maya lowland sites. It was first identified as a complex at Uaxactún and Tikal—sites located in the dense tropical jungle of northeastern Petén (Kidder 1947). Mamom remains consist largely of pottery and figurines. The monochrome pottery—red, orange, black, grey, brown, or cream—may be decorated by daubs of red in bands. The ware has a characteristic waxy feel owing to a glossy slip that makes up the bulk of any Mamom pottery sample. Common shapes are flat-bottomed bowls and cuspidors. The figurines are not unlike some from Chiapas and the highlands, being fashioned by punching and filleting. However, they are all monotonously alike, presenting none of the vigor, imagination, and sophistication displayed by their contemporaries in the Basin of Mexico. The horizon includes a few artifacts of stone and obsidian but no evidence of construction. Despite these generalities, there is considerable diversity between sites, and relationships between complexes are not always clear.

A pure Mamom cache was found in a *chultun* at Tikal, only a few miles south of Uaxactún. A *chultun* is a pit hollowed out of limestone bedrock; it is composed of one or more inner chambers and is closed with a stone lid. These are found both at Tikal and Uaxactún in association with living quarters and are located on high ground. Various suggestions have been made as to their possible use but Dennis Puleston (1971) has proved rather convincingly that they were used for storing the fruit of the breadnut or ramon tree (see p. 275). Mamom must have been a simple village culture and as we shall see it reached northern Yucatán and Belize.

Late Preclassic remains, called Chicanel, are both more extensive and more uniform than Mamom. The complex includes virtually all the southern Maya lowlands and extends throughout the peninsula of Yucatán. All indications lead us to suppose that it represents a long period of intense occupation of the Maya lowland. The contrast with Mamom is enormous. Complexes now show a great degree of similarity. Chicanel people left behind them a variety of pottery forms, mostly legless, but they did add wide-everted rims and flange protuberances. Usulután and some waxy wares are diagnostic. Figurines, which in Mamom faithfully conformed to the prevailing trend, now virtually disappeared. The most exciting innovations were architectural. A variety of structures were suddenly erected, including rich tombs, temple-pyramids, great plazas, terraces, and primitive corbelled vaults decorated with painted murals. Many of these changes did not occur until Late Chicanel, around A.D. 1, and about this time rapid strides were made toward full Classic status. At this time there were distinct signs of the emergent Maya civilization (Thompson 1965a).

The beautiful white-stuccoed pyramid known as E-VII-sub of Uax-actún is a Chicanel structure (Photo 18). Preserved intact by later su-perimposed buildings, this squat little pyramid, measuring only 8 m in height, is famous for its 18 grotesque monster masks that flank the staircases, which lead up all four sides. Some masks have elements of the jaguar, such as curled tusks and flat snouts, but others suggest the rain god or the serpent. This carefully stuccoed and adorned structure, set off by its own plaza, may have formed part of a solar observatory (Coggins 1980).

A somewhat similar pyramid with painted stucco masks, also of Chicanel date, has been uncovered at Tikal (W. R. Coe 1967). Some Chicanel temples were built with masonry walls, and excavations have shown that the great plaza and much of the planning of Tikal was done at this time. Temples and tombs were adorned with mural paintings, the earliest of the Maya area. As might be guessed, the theme is re-ligious. The style is Izapan. The presence of obsidian is good evidence of contact with the highlands. Tombs equal in splendor to those of their highland contemporaries at Miraflores have the unique distinction of being roofed over by a primitive corbelled arch.

PHOTO 18. Pyramid E-VII-sub at Uaxactún, Petén region of Guatemala. (Courtesy of the Peabody Museum, Harvard University, copyright © by the President and Fellows of Harvard College.)

Much is made of this corbelled or "false" arch for several reasons. It was the most sophisticated arch known in New World architecture, and we believe it was developed by the Maya for roofing their tombs and was later used to support roofs of temples, palaces, stairways, and passageways (see Figure 25, p. 284). It is called a "false" arch because it lacks the central keystone that can support an enormous weight and permits wide doorways and graceful curves. The corbelled arch results in narrow, dark rooms and necessitates thick, massive walls. It is built up from the top of a column or wall, each successive stone jutting slightly out over the one below, eventually closing the gap with a capstone. The corbelled arch is always associated with fine Classic Maya architecture, and its primitive beginnings in Late Chicanel tombs at Tikal and Altar de Sacrificios are of considerable interest (W. R. Coe 1967; Thompson 1954).

A good challenge to the archaeologist is offered by El Mirador, a site in the Petén excavated by Ray Matheny (New World Archaeological Foundation) and Bruce Dahlin (Catholic University) to whom I am indebted for the following information. This is a huge site 128 km north of Tikal and twice its size. Although El Mirador has an enormous amount of truly monumental architecture, there are no vaulted roofs and it was practically abandoned by A.D. 300. It may in fact be the oldest city of the Maya lowlands.

The pottery indicates that its cultural climax was during the Late Preclassic to very early Classic. Ceramics do not tie in with neighboring sequences of Tikal, Uaxactún, or Becán, but more closely resemble those from Cerros in northern Belize. Slab feet and "cream pitchers" suggest early Teotihuacán contact; the Protoclassic horizon (Floral Park) is represented by a few Usulután-type sherds and mammiform vessel supports. Several stelae carvings are in the late Preclassic style of Kaminaljuyú.

There are two main groups of buildings rather poorly preserved. The monumentality is staggering. For example, Structure 704 in the East Group has a pyramidal base measuring six times larger than Temple IV at Tikal, thought to be the lowlands' largest. Ancient causeways lead out from the site and are the earliest occurrence of causeways on record. Could they have served some other purpose as well as walkways?

The codirectors have tentatively advanced the hypothesis that the people of El Mirador were forced to abandon the site due to extreme desiccation of the area. Pollen profiles from the lake region to the south support this possibility. It is an area with very poor agricultural potential. It has been ascertained that these particular *bajos* were never lakes, that is, had never contained much water, certainly not enough to have sustained ridged-field agriculture (see p. 276). The ancient Maya added lime to the poor soil, which, together with salt accumulations from the shallow gypsiferous bedrock deposits, effectively exhausted agricultural endeavors. Maize could never have been raised under such conditions, so it is root and fruit-tree cultivation that may have been staples here. Water would have been an almost daily preoccupation since there was no supply other than surface water captured in swamps and man-made reservoirs. This is a curious site, somewhat of a maverick in the Petén. It is hoped that the results of current work will provide more information about incipient urban growth and failure.

The lowland Maya were rapidly catching up with their highland counterparts and now had the corbelled arch to their credit; but what about monumental stone carving, writing, and dates? A rock carving near the entrance to Loltún Cave, Yucatán boasts a hieroglyphic inscription, but few others have come to light. It may be that monuments were battered and defaced and have been more effectively hidden by the jungle than in other areas. If so, they still await discovery.

Discussion of the Protoclassic (Floral Park) phase which logically follows this sequence has been included as an introduction to the lowland Maya Classic period in Chapter 6. It is a special manifestation limited to the southern periphery of Mesoamerica affecting many sites in Belize and the Petén.

Central and Northern Yucatán Peninsula

The forest and brush areas of central Yucatán and the northern plains were uninhabited prior to 700 B.C. After that time these areas were settled by people from the southern lowlands having Mamom pottery who spread throughout the northern regions via the great river systems. Preclassic remains have appeared at so many sites that a general framework has emerged for an area formerly felt to be unattractive to early settlers.

The fact that they brought with them the Mamom ceramic tradition, except for late markers such as Mars Orange and resist-decorated pottery, shows that they left the southern heartland before the appearance of these wares there around 500 B.C. With this base they established themselves and gradually developed a regional culture of their own. The Chicanel pottery horizon is well established at Bećan by 300 B.C. (Paklum phase). This very homogeneous ceramic tradition stretched across the Yucatán Peninsula from Cerros in Belize in the east, to Laguna de Términos in the west. Ball (1977b) visualizes a social organization based on a segmented tribe dependent on slash-and-burn agriculture, living in small scattered hamlets. The presence of some obsidian blades from Jilotepeque, Guatemala signals the tremendously important role trade was soon to play, but during the Middle and Late Preclassic, tools were usually made of chert, which, though not as good as obsidian, was plentiful locally.

The Late Paklum phase (50 B.C.–A.D. 250) is marked by a tremendous socioeconomic change, with the sudden appearance of formal architecture, more extensive agriculture, and a gradual increase of population. Expansion was confined by their precocious Maya neighbors to the south and the arid northern sector of Yucatán. These factors may have led to conflicts, alliances, and stronger central authority. Population pressure together with competition for arable land were the two main factors Ball believes responsible for the development of larger and more complex communities (ranked chiefdoms) in the central region. It was just after this (A.D. 100–250) that Becán constructed its famous moat or dry ditch with proportions of 16 m in width by 5.3 m deep and 1.9 km in circumference. The inner parapet formed a vertical wall of 5 m, so from the bottom of the moat any intruder was confronted with an obstacle of nearly 11 m in height. Seven causeways or natural limestone bridges led across the great ditch to Becán itself. This is the most outstanding defensive system of the Maya on record, and the labor required for its construction must have been enormous (Webster 1976). Apparently this was built for protection against pressure from the southern groups pushing into this region perhaps in an effort to establish direct communication with northern Yucatán, the great salt resource. It is even possible that Tikal, as the most powerful leader at this time, might have conquered Becán (Webster 1977). In turn there may have been some attempt from the north to encroach or expand southward, as these people were eager to take up more arable land. The early Classic remains bear out a long unsettled history of disturbances in this central region.

In other areas of Yucatán a somewhat parallel development occurred. By the seventh century B.C. small settlements have been identified at Chichén Itzá, Yaxuná, Maní, Chacchob, Ake, and Dzibilchaltún, as well as at other less well-known sites. Simple houses were put together of mud and loose stone walls, and were roofed over with thatch. They resembled the modern Yucatecan house but were apsidal in shape and had only one door instead of two. Typically a low platform faced with stone and stuccoed might be raised close by. This arrangement might eventually be enlarged to include a sweat house.

Mamom-like traits unite the area ceramically although regional variation is considerable. Spouted and gadrooned jars and *tecomates* are common. Decoration may be by preslip groove incision or a resist technique of orange-on-buff.

Dzibilnocác ("painted vault") erected a pyramid and stone walls. The associated Chicanel-type pottery with a "waxy" slip is so similar to that of the Petén that it may have been made on the spot with local calcite temper by a Petén craftsman. At the same time, northern plain opaque wares were circulating (Nelson 1973).

In Campeche at Edzná there is a large pyramid and entire Preclassic settlement just west of the better known Late Classic palace structure. A large canal extends out from the palace possibly to the Champotón

River. Ceramically all these sites have been coordinated with the sequence from Becán, which is well documented.

The major development took place in the Late Preclassic on the northern plains where Dzibilchaltún outstripped every other site. Buildings were erected in great number and size. A single acropolis with courts and terraces reached the incredible height of 8 m. The quantity of jade and exotic luxury goods conjures up visions of a sudden wealthy elite who encouraged local salt production to attract long-distance merchants.

Ball (1977a, 1977b) attributes this sudden prosperity to population pressure and conflicts arising from the limited agricultural land. At the same time, high-status commodities furnish evidence of communication with other Maya regions via coastal exchange networks. This economic boom was short-lived and Dzibilchaltún was hopelessly collapsed by A.D. 250. Its bankruptcy was a local affair for other centers continued on unaffected. Perhaps its redistributive monopoly of exotic products built on coastal traffic was undercut by an overland route through the central region (Freidel 1978).

Belize   All along the east coast of Yucatán, Preclassic remains have been reported, not only from mainland sites such as Cuello, Nohmul, and Xcaret, but also from Cozumel, Quintana Roo, and the Bay Islands, Honduras. The latter provide proof of early Maya canoe travel, for it is a precocious and skilled paddler who ventures out into the treacherous waters of the Caribbean and Gulf of Honduras.

One of the most interesting sites along this eastern littoral is Cerros, Belize for it became a thriving commercial center in the Late Preclassic period only to be abruptly abandoned thereafter. Freidel's interpretation of its rise to prosperity, in relation to emergent Maya civilization in the Petén and Dzibilchaltún in northern Yucatán, bring the interrelationship of these areas into sharper focus (Freidel 1978, 1979).

Cerros is located at the tip of a peninsula on Chetumal Bay (see Map 3, p. 63) where, in addition to marine exploitation and contacts with coastal canoe traffic, it controlled the mouth of the New River, a canoe route leading to the southern Maya heartland. Exploiting the marine resources was probably of greater importance than agriculture. Deer and peccary provided additional protein.

It is believed that the earliest settlement grew up near a lagoon where a stone platform may be what is left of an ancient docking facility. This simple village of perhaps 30 dwellings was so successful in procuring marine–estuary resources and fostering trade with canoe-traveling merchants that a wealthy status-minded center emerged. The buildings at the site itself are not grouped around plazas or courts, but the large pyramid complexes are clumped together with plazas leading out from them—a very different arrangement, but one affording maximum accessibility. Fine residential quarters adjoined the public buildings and dispersed settlements were slightly removed. Four pyramids were built; the staircase of one (Structure 6B) was flanked by massive modeled stucco masks comparable to those at Uaxactún and Tikal. Polychrome fresco is another trait shared with Tikal as are other decorative details. Corbelled vaulting may be present. Cerros has architectural features of other sites as well. For example the outset stairways are shared by sites as distant as Dzibilchaltún and Chalchuapa. Cult paraphernalia presage the approaching Classic period. There may be some stylistic resemblances to Izapa art, but ceramically there are few ties to other contemporary developments with the possible exception of El Mirador. For the energetic people of the interior at El Mirador, Cerros could have functioned as their link to highland Guatemala.

Freidel believes that Cerros' success is due not simply to a strategic location in a favorable environment, but to cultural factors involving the greater Yucatecan peninsula.

As the ceremonial centers of the Petén region sought exotic goods such as jade, crystalline hematite, serpentine, and exotic marine products to satisfy status and ritual demands, Cerros could provide these, located as she was in the very center of coastal and riverine exchange networks operating north and south. At this time in northern Yucatán, Dzibilchaltún rose to prominence through exploiting salt resources. As long as these two interaction spheres (Dzibilchaltún in the north and the Petén with littoral Belize in the south) operated via the coast, the symbiotic relationship worked to mutual advantage. Cerros prospered as the nexus of a large exchange network acting as a kind of eastern Petén port. However, toward the end of the Preclassic period, the southern interior centers pushed northward through the center of the peninsula competing with a northern penetration south. Archaeologically this tension and conflict is documented at Becán. The southern centers eventually prevailed and established direct exchange relationships with northern Yucatán. Once this occurred, Cerros had no further role and was subsequently abandoned.

This explanation illustrates several important points. As in the case of Laguna Zope, the sudden prosperity and collapse of Cerros cannot be understood in terms of a local framework, but only by studying the whole Preclassic development of Yucatán. The early symbiotic relationships between interior and littoral peoples contributed to the rise of Maya civilization; not that the goods involved were necessary for subsistence, but they were the means of reinforcing stratification in the complex emergent social system. But for the cultural activity of the Late Preclassic, Cerros could have remained one more simple coastal settlement.

The Southern Periphery   Unfortunately archaeological work on the southern limits of Mesoamerica has been both spotty and sporadic, but we do have sequences
now for eastern El Salvador at Quelepa and the Ulua–Comayagua drainage area as well as some information from northeastern Honduras.

Quelepa is a long-known major site on the banks of Río San Esteban
in eastern El Salvador. Residential mounds and pyramids are grouped
along the north bank of the river separated by a small spring-fed stream,
while south of the river is the cemetery. A large platform terrace and
several ceramic caches are the earliest Preclassic material from the site
(Uapala phase; 500 B.C.–A.D. 150). Usulután ware comprises 60% of the
pottery assemblage which represents a spread of the technique out of
western El Salvador in the Middle Preclassic. The famous jaguar altar
of Quelepa discovered in 1926 has a carved feline face flanked by feline
heads. It is a huge sculptured stone 3 m² by 85 cm in height, presently
in the National Museum in El Salvador. Andrews V (1976) suggests
Olmec-derived influence, rather than actual Olmec presence in the
region.

The stratigraphic work at Los Naranjos by Baudez and Becquelin
(1973) has brought all the material from the general area of the
Ulua–Comayagua drainage into focus (Canby, 1951). Los Naranjos is
located on the northern shores of Lake Yojoa. The Jaral phase (800–400
B.C.) fits comfortably into the Middle Preclassic Mesoamerican pattern
with Olmec-like figurines, pottery, and fine jade including a jadeite axe
covered with red cinnabar. Jade was placed with high-ranking individuals in graves. Mounds also exist, but the most outstanding feature of
the Jaral phase is a formidable defensive ditch which, with measure-
ments of 1300 m length by 15–20 m width and 7 m depth, would have
been very efficient. It extends from the main group of ruins to the lake.

The Lake Yojoa monochrome pottery excavated in this region many
years ago (Strong, Kidder, and Paul 1938) has now been equated with
the Jaral phase. It was found in the lowest levels of two pits beneath
Maya polychrome horizons, sealed by a 1-m sterile layer. The complex
includes plain wares, very little paint, some tetrapod supports, and
simple, hand-modeled figurines.

Probably of similar date are the Ulua River sites of Playa de los
Muertos and Santa Rita. At Playa de los Muertos, richly stocked graves
yielded some fine jade artifacts. The presence of zoned and excised
decorations, rocker-stamping, bottle forms, a stirrup-spouted effigy
vessel, and hand-modeled figurines relate this material to Middle Preclassic remains at Tlatilco and Morelos in central highland Mexico.

Returning to the sequence at Los Naranjos, following the Jaral phase
in 400–100 B.C. (Eden I phase) seven large mounds were erected. Structure IV was a stepped platform supporting four structures on top; it
was aligned to the cardinal directions. The core was entirely of earth
faced with undressed limestone blocks. No use was made of stucco or

cement. The earlier ditch had been such a success that they now built a larger one, this time enclosing not only the main buildings but a sizeable area of agricultural land.

In eastern Honduras, just south of Trujillo, more Preclassic material was found in caves. The Cuyamel Caves, located in the vertical face of a steep hill, are accessible only by dropping a rope 15–30 m from the top through a natural opening in the limestone. For their efforts Healy and team (1974) were rewarded by finding three undisturbed caves extending over hundreds of meters. Great quantities of human bones, mostly in lateral alcoves, which were the driest areas, led Healy to believe the caves had been a depository for secondary burials over many years. More than 50 ceramic vessels were intact or restorable. The predominant form is the long-necked bottle well known from Tlatilco and Morelos in central Mexico (Plate 4-e, p. 93). The same bottle form was found in the caves near Copán, excavated by Gordon in 1898. Four of his eight vessels were long-necked bottles now in the collections of the Peabody Museum at Harvard University. At Cuyamel, gadrooning, cinctured forms, double bottles, composite bottles, and flat-bottomed bowls with flaring walls made up the inventory. A hand-modeled effigy vessel is similar to one from Playa de los Muertos. An excised bowl in Olmec-style forms one more link in the long chain of related Middle Preclassic sites. Healy dates the Cuyamel Caves from 1200–600 B.C.

Two well-defined cultural phases have emerged for this southern area. The earlier one has long-necked bottles, excising, burnishing, zoning, fine hand-modeled figurines, Olmec-like designs, and jade. Sites and phases include Cuyamel and Copán caves, Yojoa monochrome, Yarumela I and Jaral phases, probably Lo de Vaca I and Playa de los Muertos material. Estimated dates are 1000–500 B.C.

This is followed by a uniform ceramic complex that spread rapidly throughout eastern El Salvador and western Honduras in Late Preclassic times. Usulután resist technique was the outstanding new feature. It represents a strong wave of Mesoamerican influences from the west prior to 300 B.C., possibly a migration. Andrews V (1977) calls it the Uapala ceramic sphere made up of such elements as Usulután ware, a red-slipped group, *tecomates, comals,* single- and composite-silhouette bowls with four nubbin feet, and some fine whitish-paste figurines. The Uapala ceramic sphere would include the Eden I phase at Los Naranjos, Copán's Archaic, Lo de Vaca II, and Yarumela II in the Comayagua Valley, and the Ulua Bichrome at Santa Rita, Honduras.

The years between 2500 B.C. and A.D. 1 saw the transformation of Mesoamerican life from one of small farming villages through the rise and fall of its first civilization to the very brink of urbanism at Teoti-

SETTING THE MESOAMERICAN PATTERN

huacán and up to the rise of Maya civilization. The changes and innovations of these 2500 years read like an inventory of Mesoamerican culture. These were the most creative years in its long culture history.

Most lowland settlements lived by exploiting a marine–estuary environment combined with hunting and gathering. Root-crop cultivation may well have been transmitted from South America and formed the basis of the economy of small settlements on the Pacific Coast as well as in Belize. Maize was a highland development which, upon reaching the lowlands around the second millennium B.C., immediately became the staple food. It thereafter underwent genetic changes that resulted in a larger, more productive ear, the consequence of which was an increase of population and eventually a more complex society. Agricultural techniques and cultigens were improved. Irrigation canals, dams, and pot irrigation were all innovative hydraulic works initiated during these years.

Between 1200 and 400 B.C. we see the rise and fall of the Olmec civilization, centered in the eastern Gulf Coast lowlands. Unusual for their tremendous constructions of earth and colored clays, monumental stone carving (with a trend from three-dimensional to narrative themes), carved stone drains, and huge caches of jade and serpentine (La Venta), the Olmecs left a legacy of other features that became characteristic of later Mesoamerican peoples. These include orientation of buildings, high value of jade, a distinctive art style and iconography, the ball court, several deities, elaborate exchange networks involving interregional communication, development of ranked society, semidivine rulers, and centralization of power and authority.

The first of Mesoamerica's writing systems, the Zapotec, evolved in Oaxaca. Hieroglyphs denote place names, birth dates, conquests, year, month, and day signs. The earliest evidence for the 260-day cycle appeared in a public building at San José Mogote, Oaxaca in 600 B.C. From Oaxaca the knowledge spread to other areas. Long Count dates appeared around the beginning of the Christian Era at Tres Zapotes, Chiapa de Corzo, El Baúl, and Abaj Takalik.

Architecture advanced in planning, construction, and decoration. The basic Mesoamerican plan of grouping buildings around courts or plazas (the patio-group arrangement) became standard. These are believed to have housed extended families or lineages. The larger settlements were clusters of these patio-groups. Stone was cut and used to face public buildings and in temple construction. Lime stucco was used for flooring, plastering, and decorations. Astronomical orientation of buildings became standard; platforms, tombs, and temples were constructed. Houses were varied; special features occur such as ovens, drains, storage pits, areas of craft specialization, larger households, residential wards, and even elite housing. Disposal of the dead varied from simple graves to elaborate masonry tombs at Monte Albán, basalt columnar tombs at La Venta, tombs of wooden beams at Kaminaljuyú, and shaft-and-chamber tombs in west Mexico.

Housing and burial practices indicate the gradual emergence of a highly stratified society. Richly stocked tombs of the elite can be compared to simple interments beneath a house floor without offerings of any kind. Class lines began to be drawn and were more sharply defined in the Classic period. Already status distinctions could be made between slaves, farmers, builders, laborers, craftsmen, priests, merchants, and kings. Specialization is seen in production of domestic and fine ceremonial pottery, lapidary arts (jade and serpentine), iron-ore mirrors, ornamental shell, and prismatic obsidian blades.

The development of exchange networks is believed to be one of the most important factors in the rise of the Olmec civilization as the elite sought to reinforce their status by possession of hard-to-get goods like sting-ray spines, iron-ore mirrors, jade, and serpentine. Pires-Ferreira and Flannery (1976) list six different kinds of networks that could have operated at this time, each operating under different conditions, to serve a different purpose, destined for a different, even highly restricted, market. The exchange system stimulated craft specialization, encouraged merchants, and bolstered stratification. At the same time, other developing cultures were exposed to the Olmec model of society, one of power, prestige, kings, and commoners. As the networks functioned, the Olmecs spread their great art style and iconography, symbolism, and ritual emphasizing jaguars, crocodiles, and fire-serpents.

Early roots of the ball game, which became an important cult in the succeeding Classic period, can be found in the first known ball court at San Lorenzo, Dainzú bas-reliefs, and numerous ball-playing figurines.

Pottery is characterized by fine quality, great variety of form and decorations, and a proliferation of hand-modeled figurines.

- *Early Preclassic:* oldest known pottery from central highland Mexico, coastal Guerrero, and Cuello, Belize. Two traditions identified: Yucatecan (Swasey complex) and Ocós.
- *Middle Preclassic:* three traditions: Olmec, Tlatilco, and double-line-break.
- *Late Preclassic:* Usulután ware in the southern regions; central highland Mexico: tripods, composite silhouettes, and development of polychrome pottery.

Warfare and conflicts are in evidence. Examples are: Chalcatzingo reliefs, Las Victorias battle scenes, walls and possible fortifications at Monte Albán, protective ditches at Becán and at Los Naranjos, Honduras.

In general it is a period marked by the emergence of many regional styles, great experimentation, imagination, and innovation. The single artistic horizon style is that of the Olmec. Social changes include: increase in population, growth of more and varied settlements (ceremonial centers, large nucleated villages, hamlets), increasingly complex sociopolitical organization, expansion of intercommunication and exchange networks, accumulation of wealth and power. The foundations were laid for the basic pattern of Mesoamerican culture.

SUMMARY

Early Preclassic (Pre-Olmec: 2500–1250 B.C.)

This was a crucial period in which settled villages were established in both highland and lowland areas to exploit a variety of environmental resources. The highland maize, when transmitted to the lowlands around 2000 B.C., became the staple crop, permitting population growth. Pottery made its appearance, possibly being transmitted from South America along with root-crop agriculture. Ocós and Swasey complex are the first recognizable pottery traditions, both found in the lowlands. *Metate* and *mano* and obsidian prismatic blades became standard tools.

Middle Preclassic (Olmec Horizon: 1250 B.C.–400 B.C.)

The Olmec civilization rose in a tropical lowland setting. Its influence was most strongly felt in Morelos, Guerrero, Oaxaca, lowland areas of the Gulf Coast, Soconusco, and piedmont areas of Guatemala. Various exchange networks operated to circulate exotic, ritual items, foodstuffs, and utilitarian goods. The period was marked by great interregional communication between highland and lowland peoples. Sociopolitical complexity increased. The development of wealth, power, and well-defined class structure was not limited to Olmec, but could be found in other developing regions. Craft specialization developed. The first great Mesoamerican art style (Olmec) evolved. Olmec heartland sites collapsed.

Late Preclassic (Epi-Olmec: 400 B.C.–A.D. 1)

Monte Albán was founded as the political capital between 500–400 B.C. The Zapotec writing system developed and the first evidence of the 260-day cycle appeared in Oaxaca. As Olmec centers collapsed, Monte Albán prospered. The Basin of Mexico was dominated by two major regional centers: Cuicuilco and Teotihuacán; the latter soon controlled the entire valley. The exploitation of nearby obsidian sources supported by intensive hydraulic irrigation was seen as a contributing factor to the rise of Teotihuacán.

Hieroglyphs from the southern lowlands and Pacific slopes of Guatemala initiated the Long Count dating system. Miraflores people in the Guatemala Valley constructed huge mounds containing elaborate tombs with fine grave goods, denoting the emergence of a complex stratified society. The southern Maya lowlands were populated by immigrations of settlers along all the major river systems. These practiced slash-and-burn agriculture. Small villages displayed their prosperity in ceremonial centers, the most spectacular development taking place in the Petén at El Mirador, Uaxactún, and Tikal. The widespread distribution of Chicanel ceramics illustrates the degree of communication and sharing of ideas throughout the eastern lowlands regions. By the end of the Preclassic they were set on a course already recognizable as Maya, having the corbelled arch, elaborate tombs, and ceremonial architecture.

Somewhat removed from these developments, west Mexican peoples went a different route, displaying a unique regional culture preoccupied with shaft-and-chamber tombs that date back to 1500 B.C. Both tomb construction and early ceramic styles suggest early maritime contact with South America. In this regard, the Capacha complex of Colima is of fundamental significance.

The Written
Record

CHAPTER 5

The recording of dates and hieroglyphic inscriptions are among the most important contributions of Mesoamerican civilization. Before examining the events of the Classic period, let us first look in some detail at the unusual scientific achievements of the Mesoamerican peoples: their counting systems, calendrical recordings, methods of writing, and the kind of information they give us. I have relied on the following sources for the material in this chapter: Caso (1967), M. D. Coe (1976), D. H. Kelley (1962a, 1962b, 1962c, 1972), Knorozov (1958, 1967), Marcus (1976b, 1980), Morley (1915, 1956), Nicholson (1978), Satterthwaite (1965), Thompson (1962, 1965b, 1975), and Troike (1978).

Mesoamerican peoples in general were fascinated by the passage of time. The entire written record—their calendar, commemorative dates, and books—shows an obsession with permutating cycles, the recording of elapsed time, and predictions for the future. At first glance, one might imagine that these Indians were dedicated to the advancement of astronomy. Upon careful scrutiny, however, other reasons for this preoccupation seem more likely. Whether one is considering the Maya Indians of the Petén region of Guatemala, the Zapotecs of Oaxaca, the Mixtecs of Puebla, the Nahua of the Basin of Mexico, or the Tarascans of Michoacán, the predominating reason for such an exact record of passing time and the attendant writing systems seems to have been intimately related to astrology and prognostication of the future. Only by being able to predict accurately or receive forewarning of future events—eclipses, seasonal changes, movements of the sun, moon, and other planets, forthcoming period endings, and cyclical concurrences—could these men prepare themselves to deal with the gods, the forces of good and evil, by making the necessary offerings and sacrifices to ensure their continued support. The chronological events of a ruler's personal life, his major victories, and proud achievements—his past—were recorded in stone to stand in public places of honor. Such a recording of the past may have served as a kind of religious insurance against an uncertain future, but of more immediate concern was to reinforce his claim to power in the present.

We know from the Spanish accounts of the sixteenth century that only a small fraction of Maya society could read and interpret the inscriptions. Indeed, only an even smaller group, probably made up of nobles and religious leaders, had a working knowledge of all the scientific details. Undoubtedly traders and merchants had a rudimentary knowledge of the inscriptions, enough to handle their own accounts and identify place-name glyphs of towns on maps. The general populace, however, relied on its leaders, first religious and later secular, to tell them when it was time for a new-year festival, or whether a certain day would be auspicious for a wedding ceremony or the baptism of a child. It is easy to understand the respect and awe granted a priest if, after his prediction of an eclipse of the sun on a certain day, the event took place as scheduled. There would be no reason, then, to doubt his advice on far simpler matters. The scholarly priests undoubtedly controlled the people for many years, at least during the early centuries of the Christian Era. Even under the more militaristic governments of the Postclassic, religion remained a powerful force linked to every aspect of daily life.

SOURCES OF MESOAMERICAN HIEROGLYPHS, INSCRIPTIONS, AND WRITING

Maya hieroglyphs were carved on vertically set shafts of stone called stelae (see Plate 6, pp. 166–167 and Figure 16, p. 174), on stone altars, and on stairways and lintels. Others were worked in stucco or painted on pottery, on the walls of temples and tombs, and in the books (Photo 19). Occasionally some inscriptions are found carved in shell, bone, or semiprecious stones. We already have seen that hieroglyphics were in use by Late Preclassic peoples in Oaxaca, the piedmont and highland areas of Guatemala, the Isthmus of Tehuantepec, and Veracruz. The Zapotecs, Teotihuacanos, and later central Mexican peoples all recorded dates.

According to M. D. Coe, of all the writing systems in Mesoamerica, Maya script was the most complex. Four others are somehow connected: Teotihuacán, Xochicalco, Ñuiñe, and Zapotec of Monte Albán. Other writing systems include: the Borgia group and Mixtec; Aztec from the Basin of Mexico; Cotzumalhuapa; Toltec, which is somehow related to Xochicalco; Tajín, possibly related to the Borgia–Mixteca group; and

Kaminaljuyú, whose Stela 10 has a script unrelated to any other. All these people shared the Calendar Round of 52 years.

Joyce Marcus approached the study of the Zapotec writing system by starting with historic Zapotec sources of the sixteenth century and projecting back in time through the archaeological record. In a region such as Oaxaca, with a very long continuous history characterized by a relative isolation and conservatism, her efforts were well rewarded. After A.D. 900 or 1000 it may be possible to work with *códices*, but for earlier years there is no other source of writing but hieroglyphic inscriptions from stone monuments and wall paintings in tombs.

Mesoamerican books, called *códices*, were a kind of picture album made by gluing together pieces of paper to form a long strip 10 m or more in length; the strip was then folded like an accordion. The Maya made the paper for these *códices* from the inner bark of a variety of trees. The bark was pounded, the fibers were separated by soaking in lime water, and they were beaten to form a smooth surface. Once dry, the paper was covered with a thin coat of calcium carbonate, at which point the page was ready to be painted. Some central Mexican groups wrote on deer skin, but demand often exceeded supply, and the bark of the amate tree was often substituted. Paper also was in constant demand for decoration and making offerings, and for this reason was frequently listed in tribute payments.

Only three pre-Conquest Maya *códices* and fragments of another have survived (Villacorta and Villacorta 1930). Their subject matter involves astronomy, chronology, disease, hunting and agricultural ceremonies, and deities. By far the most useful, the Codex Dresden, which is preserved in its entirety in Dresden, Germany, resembles an almanac in that it is filled with tabulations for consultation (Photo 19). It also includes material copied from an earlier manuscript. The Codex Tro-Cortesiano, now in Madrid, is not complete, nor is it as finely executed as the Codex Dresden. It contains much that is not understood, probably some errors and confusion of glyphs. The Codex Peresiano in Paris dates from the period of Mayapán's supremacy and deals with predictions and prophecies as well as the 52-year cycles. However, two pages are missing and it is in a poor state of preservation; hence its value, archaeologically speaking, is minimal. In 1971 a fragmentary codex of bark cloth, known as the Grolier Codex, was on temporary exhibit in New York City. The history of this document has never been fully disclosed and its authenticity is still in doubt. If genuine it would date from A.D. 1230 and deal with the Venus cycle depicting deities beautifully drawn in the Toltec–Maya style (M. D. Coe 1973).

Despite the scarcity of pre-Conquest Maya documents, other valuable sources of information on ancient Maya life are preserved in the Books of the Chilam Balam, which were compiled in the Colonial period after the Indians had learned to write with the Spanish alphabet. The word

PHOTO 19. Page from the Codex Dresden. (Courtesy of Arturo Romano P.)

Chilam is derived from the name of a famous prophet, *chilan*, known as jaguar (*balam*). The so-called Books of Chilam Balam are in fact documents which bear the name of the towns in which they were kept: Chumayel, Tizimin, Maní, and Kaua. Information found in these ancient records other than the usual calendrical material includes songs, recitations, magical formulas, medicinal knowledge, and notations on prominent families. The Popul Vuh, literally "Book of the Community," of the highland Maya is an invaluable collection of documents on mythology, astronomy, history, religion, and the legends of the Quiché and Cakchiquel people. The original Quiché manuscripts have never been found, but are believed to have consisted of pictorial writings or paintings. An anonymous transcription was made into the Quiché language about 1554, and modern versions are based on this document (Recinos 1950).

Many more *códices* are known from northwestern Mesoamerica than from the Maya area, and the subject matter differs according to region. Pre-Columbian *códices* from the Valley of Mexico deal largely with the Tonalpohualli, or 260-day cycle. Since the gods regulated the lives of men, events were not left to chance, and it was deemed important to know which deity would be presiding over particular days and scheduled ceremonies. Accordingly, the Tonalpohualli could be consulted if one needed to know whether a day would be lucky or unlucky, if one wanted to select an auspicious date for a marriage or trading expedition, or which days were propitious to plant and harvest. The Mixtec *códices* are particularly valuable, for they provide historical and genealogical information about Oaxaca and probably the region of Puebla as well. The Borgia group includes those Mixtec *códices* known as the Borgia, Vaticanus B, Laud, Fejéváry-Mayer, and Culto del Sol, all of which deal predominantly with the luck of the days, directions, sacred numbers, and ritual (Photo 20). These books may have been written in the Puebla–Tlaxcala region as the style resembles that of the mural paintings of Tizatlán, Tlaxcala. The Vidobonensis, Nuttall, Bodley, Selden, and Becker *códices* give unique historical information about the ruling dynasties in the region of Oaxaca; all are beautifully drawn in great detail.

A whole revaluation of the Mixtec *códices* is under way at the moment. They were originally interpreted by Caso, who, by applying central Mexican concepts to the Mixtec area, advanced some ideas that were accepted as fact for many years. What follows are a few comments by way of anticipating the trends or kinds of new material we may expect from the newer studies done since Caso.

The *códices* probably date from the years A.D. 900–1000 and therefore Mixtec history may be considerably shorter than formerly thought. Much information deals with origins and activities of Mixtec rulers, at the same time providing interesting facts about social and political organization. The Codex Colombino–Becker, for example, relates the

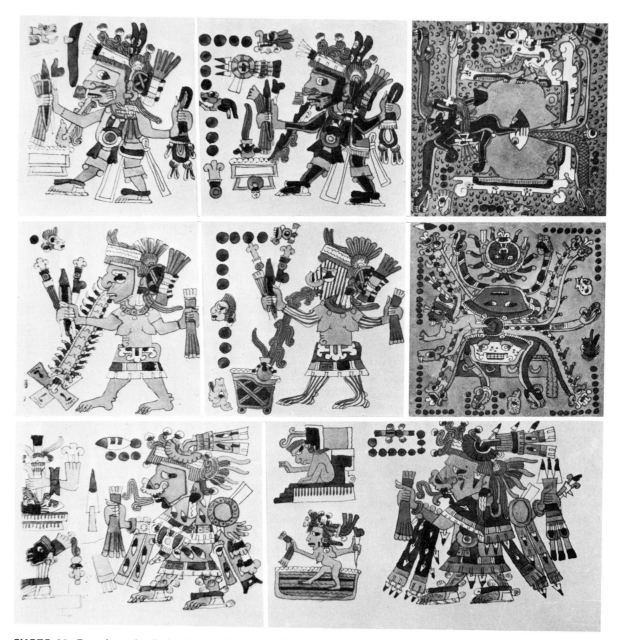

PHOTO 20. Page from the Codex Borgia. (Courtesy of the Instituto Nacional de Antropología e Historia, México.)

rise to power of a ruler "Eight Deer" who, for his efforts to create an empire, is finally sacrificed. He is the first ruler of Tututepec; he then co-rules Tilantongo with an older half-brother who is murdered (Caso 1960). Politics with threats and challenges are the consuming theme of Eight Deer's life; his five marriages and numerous children are not mentioned. We learn that having one's nose pierced is an honor, a mark of nobility.

It is not always easy to separate myth from actual fact, a problem central to Toltec history. Another problem is dealing with "gods," a term we are comfortable with, but probably misleading as applied to the Mixtecs. Supernatural beings, spirits, dead ancestors, "forces" may all be more apt. The pictorial system of each codex is related to the language represented, and only by studying the language will the signs and symbols be understood. Of particular interest is the study of gestures and postures, clearly meant to convey specific information to the reader. It is an exciting suggestion that when these are understood, the meanings may perhaps also apply to paintings, pottery, and sculpture.

The studies in progress on the Mixtec códices will no doubt spark enthusiasm for reviewing those from other areas. Aztec códices, most of which are post-Conquest, also provide a vast amount of material not preserved in any other medium. Many of their hieroglyphs were pictographic, that is, the message is portrayed by pictures, while in others ideographs were used to register both concrete and abstract ideas.

There are various ways in which Aztec códices might be read; from bottom to top, top to bottom, or even right to left, or left to right. Once the manner of reading was established, consistency was maintained. Of post-Conquest códices, some of the most important are the Tira de la Peregrinación, which relates the migrations of the Aztecs (Mexica) until they settled in the Basin of Mexico; the Tonalamatl of Aubin, with calendrical cycles; and the Codex Mendoza or Mendocino. The latter was drawn up upon orders from the Viceroy Antonio de Mendoza and deals with Aztec conquests, the tribute they exacted from various towns, and an account of Aztec daily life.

The Maya had several ways of representing numbers (Figure 8). The most common was a dot for 1 and a bar for 5. Thus, three bars placed side by side represent 15; two bars with three dots equals 13. As this system was quite cumbersome if one wanted to write a larger number, such as 843 or even 45, the Maya devised a vigesimal system of position numerals based on the unit of 20, comparable to our decimal system using the unit 10. Instead of progressing from right to left as we do,

MESOAMERICAN NUMERAL SYSTEMS

The Maya "Zero," Numbers, and Counting

they proceeded from bottom to top. The value of each unit was determined by its position, which progressed by twenties. That is, the first position included numbers from 0 through 19; in the second position, each unit had the value of 20; in the third position each unit was worth 400; and so on. However, in order to represent 20 by a single dot in the second position, the first position had to be occupied by a "zero" or, more accurately, a symbol for completion.

The invention of the zero, or symbol for completion, is a basic necessity to higher mathematics and calculation. Kroeber (1948) attributed the failure of the Romans to develop higher mathematics to their lack of the concept of zero. For example, even the simplest of mathematical problems became unwieldy because they could only express 1888 as MDCCCLXXXVIII. Anderson (1971) has shown that arithmetic can be carried out using Maya numerals, but these procedures were probably not utilized by the Maya. How they actually performed their calculations is not known. Very simple additions and subtractions may have been scratched in the soil, with the possible aid of some kind of counter.

To our knowledge, the zero was invented only twice in the Old World. The best known is its formulation by the ancient Hindus, who eventually passed it on to the Arabs from whom the zero made its way to the Western world. The other Old World inventors of zero were the ancient Babylonians, who in all likelihood developed it to assist them with their weights and measures but used it only a short time. The Mesoamerican zero may have been in use as long as the Hindu one, whose estimated origin is around 500 B.C., for although we have no recorded dates of that age, the fully developed calendrical system was probably known by 36 B.C., and the zero was a necessary prerequisite for its evolution.

Once the Mayan concept of zero was understood, the result of the scholarly studies of Ernst Förstemann, the door was open for him to work out the position numeral systems and subsequent calendrical calculations. Whether the Maya themselves or some of their neighbors invented the concept of the zero is not yet clear, but certainly it was the Maya who took the early invention of the 260-day cycle and the vague year of 365 days and elaborated upon them, eventually evolving the very complex calendrical system known as the Long Count (see pp. 172–175).

The number glyphs used for carving in stone were different from those used for painting on the *códices*, due undoubtedly to differences in medium and technique. Although the bar-and-dot numbers are most common, numerals sometimes had head variants when carved in stone. For example, 4 could be represented by the head of the sun god with a very square eye, 6 by a head with a cross in the eye, and 8 by a representation of the young corn god. The number 10 was a death's head, and the glyphs for larger numbers were composed of a death's head (10) plus the attributes of the lower number. For example, 14 equals 10 plus 4, or a death's head (10) plus the attributes of the sun god (4); 18 is formed by a death's head (10) plus the attributes of the young corn god (8) (see Figure 8). Not all the numerals from 0 to 19 are as easily deciphered as this may sound, for variations are great and the glyphs are often badly weathered.

Among the Aztec, who also used a vigesimal system, numbers from 1 to 19 were made up of the corresponding numbers of dots or circles (Figure 9). Symbols were arbitrarily selected to represent greater quantities. A flag equaled 20, strands of hair or a feather 400, and a bag of copal incense 8000. Only rarely was a bar used to signify 5 as was done among the Maya and in some Mixtec and Zapotec regions. The bar

Aztec Numerals

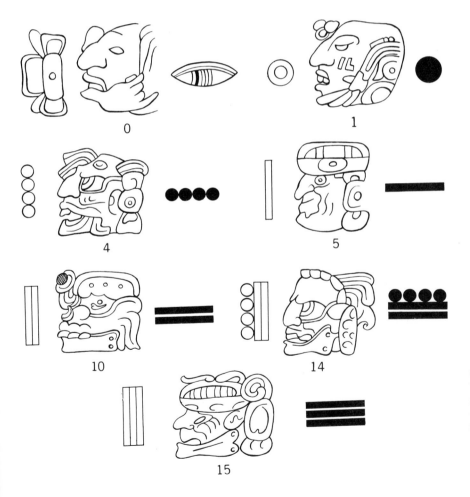

FIGURE 8. Maya numerals. Left: bar or dot numerals in stone; center: head variant in stone; right: painted numerals in *códices*. (From Thompson 1942, by permission of Field Museum of Natural History, Chicago, Illinois.)

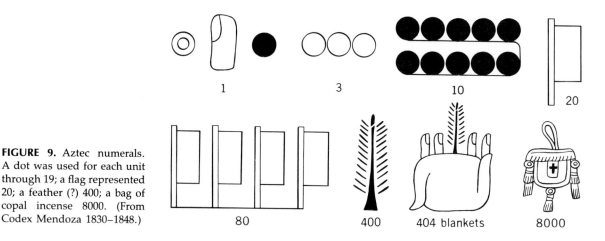

1

3

10

20

FIGURE 9. Aztec numerals. A dot was used for each unit through 19; a flag represented 20; a feather (?) 400; a bag of copal incense 8000. (From Codex Mendoza 1830–1848.)

80

400

404 blankets

8000

seems to have been in early use at Teotihuacán, Xochicalco, and Tenango, but it was later replaced by dots (Caso 1967). There is no sign for zero among the Aztec, for they did not make use of position numerals. These numerals were essential for recording Long Count dates, but such dates are not found among the central Mexicans.

MESOAMERICAN CALENDARS

Origins

We have already seen that glyphs were being carved in relief as far back as the seventh century B.C. in Oaxaca. The calendar of the Classic Maya was the most sophisticated of any used in Mesoamerica; hieroglyphs representing days and months were elaborately carved in stone sometimes in the form of a human figure or animal. Totally apart from the information conveyed, the relief carvings were frequently artistic masterpieces. As we will see, not all glyphic inscriptions include calendric material, but many record one or more dates. No other group can equal the Maya for beauty or quantity of inscriptions, but the calendar itself may have originated among their neighbors: the Zapotecs and groups in the lowlands of the Isthmus and western regions of Guatemala.

The Olmecs are often credited with having invented the Mesoamerican calendar, but this remains an unsolved problem. There are no Olmec calendrical inscriptions. Four astronomical Olmec symbols (sun, moon, Venus, and celestial bands) were transmitted to the Maya and incorporated by them as elements of their calendar, but we do not know if they had this function among the Olmecs. The Olmecs may have laid the groundwork in the sense of using representational symbols that had a widespread meaning, and they were masters at stone carving which became the preferred medium for writing.

Our earliest calendrical data comes from a stone carving at San José Mogote, Oaxaca dated at 600 B.C. (see p. 125). In Marcus' opinion there may be such carved monuments as far back as 1000 B.C. At the Zapotec capital of Monte Albán, many glyphic notations are found in the years following 600 B.C. Most deal with noncalendrical material but some calendrical hieroglyphs occur. Among them day signs with numerical coefficients have been identified (see Figure 14, p. 172), which is evidence of the 260-day cycle. A roster of the earliest Mesoamerican dates is found in Table 4.

TABLE 4
Early Mesoamerican Dated Monuments

Monument	Date	Comments
Stela 2, Chiapa de Corzo	December 9, 36 B.C., assuming a baktun 7. Badly damaged and date is reconstructed.	One of eight broken stela fragments in a mound. Bars and dots are arranged horizontally, which indicates position value notation.
Stela C, Tres Zapotes (Plate 6-a)	31 B.C.	One column of glyphs reads from top to bottom. Above dates is a noncalendrical text.
Stela 12–13, Monte Albán (Figure 14-f)	Estimated date 500–400 B.C. (?)	The combined glyphs may form a single text. Evidence for 260-day cycle, year-bearer, year sign, maybe 20-day months (?)
Stela 10, Kaminaljuyú	300 B.C.–A.D. 1 Miraflores phase	Black basalt, cannot be read. Four-column text; could be precursor of Maya system.
El Trapiche, El Salvador	200 B.C.–A.D. 200 (?)	Eight columns or four paired columns, definitely Maya. Badly battered.
Stela 1, El Baúl (Plate 6-d)	A.D. 36	Glyphs are paired in columns, Maya-style.
Stela 5, Abaj Takalik (Plate 6-f)	A.D. 126	Figures in Maya dress with traditional Maya emblems. Well preserved Long Count date.
Tuxtla statuette	A.D. 162	Jadeite carving. Nine columns of incised glyphs, nonpaired columns. Maya-type text.
Stela 29, Tikal (Plate 6-b)	July 6, A.D. 292	First appearance of vertical bars and dots, acting as coefficients for specified period glyphs. Introductory glyph, first emblem glyph.
Leyden Plate	A.D. 320	Jade plaque. First appearance of Supplementary Series.

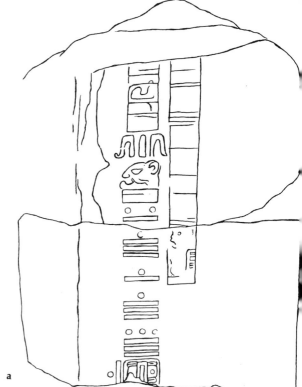

b

PLATE 6. Stone stelae with hieroglyphic texts.

a. Stela C (rear view) from Tres Zapotes, Veracruz, one of the earliest dated monuments in the New World, 31 B.C. Left: lower part of stela with partial inscription. (Courtesy of Museo Nacional de Antropología, Mexico.) Right: drawing of completed Initial Series date, following recovery of upper part of stela in 1972. (Courtesy of M. D. Coe.)

b. Stela 29, Tikal, Guatemala, with a drawing of the inscription. This is the earliest known lowland Maya inscribed monument, dated at A.D. 292. Height: 1.33 m. (Courtesy of the University Museum, University of Pennsylvania.)

c. Part of finely carved hieroglyphic text of Stela 26, Tikal. (Courtesy of the University Museum, University of Pennsylvania.)

d. Stela 1, El Baúl, Guatemala, which bears a partially eroded hieroglyphic text. Assuming a 7 baktun, the date corresponds to A.D. 36 in our calendar. Height: 1.80 m. (Courtesy of the Peabody Museum, Harvard University, copyright by the President and Fellows of Harvard College.)

e. Stela C, Copán, with double figures and lateral hieroglyphic texts. The figures are bearded and entire monument was painted red. The Long Count date (9.17.12.0.0) corresponds to A.D. 782. Height: 3.52 m. (Photographed by the author.)

f. Stela 5, Abaj Takalik, bearing Initial Series date, A.D. 126. Height: 2.11 m, height of sculptured panel: 1.66 m. (Courtesy of John A. Graham.)

There is a growing list of monuments of possible Preclassic date from the area of southern Veracruz, the Isthmus region, Oaxaca, and the Pacific slopes of Guatemala. Not all may be correctly interpreted at the present time, but evidence is mounting in favor of an origin of the calendar outside the Maya region in the lowlands. The fauna represented in the day glyphs support a lowland origin, because crocodiles, monkeys, and jaguars—jungle animals—would not be likely selections of a highland people. The calendar probably evolved prior to writing.

The Calendar Round

The basic unit of time was the day. Neither the Maya nor any other Mesoamerican groups broke time down further into hours, minutes, and seconds. The 260-day cycle, already in use during Preclassic times, formed a basic part of all Mesoamerican calculations. Among the Aztecs, this cycle was known as the Tonalpohualli, as mentioned earlier; the Maya called it the Tzolkin. This cycle was composed of 20 day signs, which ran consecutively, combined with a number from 1 to 13 as a prefix. A day would be designated, for example, as 5 Atl (water) or 8 Tochtli (rabbit) in the Tonalpohualli. In order for the exact day 5 Atl to come around again, 260 days would have to elapse (or 20×13, since there is no common denominator). This 260-day cycle is not based on any natural phenomenon and we do not know how to account for its invention (Figures 10 and 11).

In addition to the Tonalpohualli or Tzolkin, another cycle ran concurrently, resembling our solar year of 365 days. This was made up of 18 months of 20 days each ($18 \times 20 = 360$), plus 5 additional days of apprehension and bad luck at the end of the year. Days were numbered from 0 to 19. The Aztecs called the 360-day year the Xíhuitl, and the 5-day period of bad luck the Nemontemi. The equivalent Maya periods were named the Haab (360 days) and Uayeb (5 days) (Figures 12 and 13).

In the rotation of days, only 4 could occupy the first position in any month. In 365 days the 20 day names would revolve constantly, but at the end of the year there would always be a remainder of 5 days ($365 \div 20 = 18$ cycles + 5 days). Dividing these 5 days into the 20 day names shows that only 4 of them will constantly turn up to begin the new year, or any month. The Maya called these 4 days the Year Bearers because one of the 4 days, Ik, Manik, Eb, or Caban, always started the new year. At a later date, a shift took place and Ben, Eznab, Akbal, and Lamat became the Year Bearers. At the time of the Conquest, the Year Bearers were Muluc, Ix, Cauac, and Kan, indicating still another slip forward. In the same manner the central Mexicans recognized 4 days as rotating Year Bearers. The system was exactly the same; only the names varied. The Aztec Year Bearers were Acatl (reed), Técpatl (flint), Calli (house), and Tochtli (rabbit).

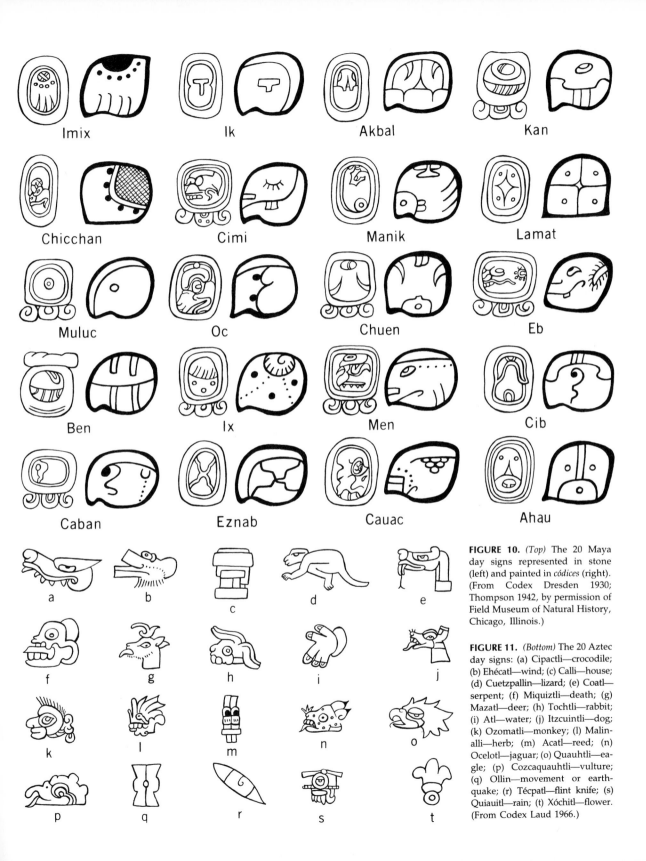

Imix   Ik   Akbal   Kan

Chicchan   Cimi   Manik   Lamat

Muluc   Oc   Chuen   Eb

Ben   Ix   Men   Cib

Caban   Eznab   Cauac   Ahau

a   b   c   d   e

f   g   h   i   j

k   l   m   n   o

p   q   r   s   t

FIGURE 10. *(Top)* The 20 Maya day signs represented in stone (left) and painted in *códices* (right). (From Codex Dresden 1930; Thompson 1942, by permission of Field Museum of Natural History, Chicago, Illinois.)

FIGURE 11. *(Bottom)* The 20 Aztec day signs: (a) Cipactli—crocodile; (b) Ehécatl—wind; (c) Calli—house; (d) Cuetzpallin—lizard; (e) Coatl—serpent; (f) Miquiztli—death; (g) Mazatl—deer; (h) Tochtli—rabbit; (i) Atl—water; (j) Itzcuintli—dog; (k) Ozomatli—monkey; (l) Malinalli—herb; (m) Acatl—reed; (n) Ocelotl—jaguar; (o) Quauhtli—eagle; (p) Cozcaquauhtli—vulture; (q) Ollin—movement or earthquake; (r) Técpatl—flint knife; (s) Quiauitl—rain; (t) Xóchitl—flower. (From Codex Laud 1966.)

FIGURE 12. The 18 Maya months with 5 remaining days (Uayeb). (Reproduced by permission of the Smithsonian Institution from *Smithsonian Institution Bureau of American Ethnology Bulletin 57 (Introduction to the Study of the Maya Hierglyphs)*, by Sylvanus Griswold Morley: Figure 19. Washington, D.C.: Government Printing Office, 1915.)

The Tzolkin and the Haab ran concurrently, like intermeshed cogwheels, and to return to any given date, 52 years, or 18,980 days, would have to elapse (because both 365×52 and $260 \times 73 = 18,980$). In other words, the Tzolkin would make 73 revolutions and the Haab 52, so that every 52 calendar years of 365 days one would return to the same date. A complete date in this 52-year cycle might be, for example,

FIGURE 13. The 18 Aztec months with 5 remaining days (Nemontemi): (a) Izcalli; (b) Atecahuallo; (c) Tlacaxipe-hualiztli; (d) Tozoztontli; (e) Hueytozoztli; (f) Tozcatl; (g) Etzalcualiztli; (h) Tecuilhui-tontli; (i) Huey tecuilhueitl; (j) Miccailhuitontli; (k) Huey micaeilhuitl; (l) Ochpaniztli; (m) Pachtli; (n) Huey pachtli; (o) Quecholli; (p) Panquet-zaliztli; (q) Atemoxtli; (r) Tititl; (s) Nemontemi. (From Caso 1967.)

2 Ik 0 Pop (2 Ik being the position of the day in the Tzolkin, 0 Pop the position in the Haab). Fifty-two years would pass before another 2 Ik 0 Pop date returned.

One cannot overemphasize the significance of this 52-year cycle for Mesoamerican peoples. It is called the Calendar Round or Sacred Round. Aside from the Maya and Aztecs we know it was in use by the Mixtecs, Otomís, Huastecs, Totonacs, Matlatzinca, Tarascans, and many other groups (Figure 14). The cycles of time are believed to have been primarily divinatory in purpose. When these coincided, it was an event of great importance, marked by special ceremonies and perhaps by the enlargement of architectural structures.

It was expected that the world would end at the completion of a 52-year cycle. At this time, among the Aztecs in the Valley of Mexico, all fires were extinguished, pregnant women were locked up lest they be turned into wild animals, children were pinched to keep them awake so that they would not turn into mice, and all pottery was broken in preparation for the end of the world. In the event the gods decided to grant man another 52 years of life on earth, however, a night time ceremony was held in which the populace followed the priests through the darkness over a causeway to the top of an old extinct volcano that rises abruptly from the floor of the Basin of Mexico, known today as the Hill of the Star, the hill above Ixtapalapa. There, with all eyes on

FIGURE 14. Various glyphs from Zapotec, Mixtec, Toltec, and Aztec calendars; (a) day sign, Zapotec; (b) month sign, Zapotec; (c) year glyph, Monte Albán II; (d) fire-drilling glyph over Ome Acatl or 2 Cane (1351), completion of the 52-year cycle; (e) year glyph, Mixtec *códices*; (f) Stela 12, Monte Alban I—from top: year sign, day, and numeral 4; two unknown glyphs; bottom: a day sign with numeral 8 below cartouche; together with Stela 13 (not shown) provides early evidence for 260-day cycle, probable date 500–400 B.C.; (g) Aztec day sign, 8 Técpatl; (h) Toltec year sign, 4 Acatl. (From the following sources: a, b, c, f, Caso 1965b, e, Caso 1965c, copyright © 1965 by the University of Texas Press; d, Codex Mendoza 1830–1848; g, h, Acosta 1956–1957.)

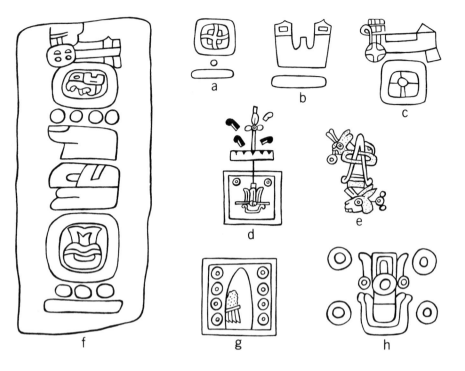

the stars, they awaited the passage of the Pleiades across the center of the heavens, which would announce the continuation of the world for another 52 years. When the precise moment came, a victim was quickly sacrificed by making a single gash in his chest and extracting the still palpitating heart. In the gory cavity the priests, with a fire drill, kindled a new flame that was quickly carried by torches across the lake to the temple in Tenochtitlán, and from there to all temples and villages around the lake. This was known as the New Fire Ceremony among the Aztecs, and in some way this same completion and renewal of each 52-year cycle was recognized by all Mesoamericans (Figure 14-d). It was probably rare for a person to witness more than one of these celebrations in his or her lifetime, so undoubtedly it was an event approached with great anticipation and relived many times after its passing.

CALENDRICAL AND ASTRONOMICAL CALCULATIONS: THE MAYA LONG COUNT

Most Mesoamerican peoples were satisfied with calculating this 52-year cycle and being able to place a date accurately within that span of time. The Maya, however, were more demanding of their calculations. In addition to situating a date within the 52-year cycle, they wanted each cycle itself to be related to the beginning of time. Thus, the elaborate Long Count or Initial Series dating was developed so that they could tell how many days had passed since the beginning of their calendar, their starting point in time. This is exactly what we do when writing any complete date such as March 10, 1955. What we are saying is that 1955 years, 2 months, and 10 days have passed since the beginning of our record of time, which is the birth of Christ in A.D. 1. In like manner the Maya recorded Long Count dates, for example, 9.14.8.0.0, which means that 9 baktuns, 14 katuns, 8 tuns, 0 uinals, and 0 kins had passed since the beginning of their record of time (Figure 15). Each position represents a period of lapsed time as follows:

$$
\begin{array}{lll}
1\ baktun & = & 144,000\ days \\
1\ katun & = & 7,200\ days \\
1\ tun & = & 360\ days \\
1\ uinal & = & 20\ days \\
1\ kin & = & 1\ day \\
\end{array}
$$

It will be seen that a uinal is 20 kins, a tun is 18 uinals, a katun is 20 tuns, and a baktun is 20 katuns. There are even larger units, such as the pictun, which equals 20 baktuns. To be consistently vigesimal, the tun should logically be 20 uinals or 400 days, but when recording calendrical time, the Maya made the tun equal to 18 uinals or 360 days, more closely approximating the solar year.

(Introductory)

Baktun

Katun

Tun

Uinal

Kin

FIGURE 15. Maya calendrical hieroglyphs. (From Thompson 1942, by permission of Field Museum of Natural History, Chicago, Illinois.)

We find Long Count dates carved on altars, stairways, stelae, and lintels (Plate 6-b, e). The usual stela inscription shows a large introductory glyph heading two vertical rows of hieroglyphs (Figure 16). Beginning at the top and proceeding from left to right are the baktun, katun, tun, uinal, and kin glyphs, each prefixed by the proper numeral in either the bar-and-dot or head variant. Immediately following is a glyph that represents the day in the 260-day cycle reached by the recorded Long Count date, and after approximately eight more glyphs, the corresponding month glyph is found. The intervening glyphs tell which of the Nine Lords of the Night presides over the specified day involved and give information on the day-by-day moon age count of the current lunar month on this particular Long Count date (D. H. Kelley 1972). These last glyphs make up the Supplementary Series.

The Maya starting date of 13.0.0.0.0, 4 Ahau 8 Cumkú, is 3113 B.C. according to Goodman–Martínez–Thompson correlation, which is followed here. This is the Maya "zero" date because after 13.0.0.0.0 baktuns had passed, the Maya began to count again with 0 baktun. The date 4 Ahau 8 Cumkú is the beginning day and month of the new baktun cycle. This was probably just a mythological event in the past, since no recorded contemporary Long Count dates are known to be that old. Remember that the oldest contemporary Long Count date from the lowland Maya is from Stela 29 at Tikal, which reads 8.12.14.8.15 or A.D. 292, and the most recent is A.D. 909 from Quintana Roo.

The so-called lunar series might include up to eight glyphs. The lunar calendar consisted of 29 and a fraction days between two successive new moons. In addition to keeping track of a vague year of 360 days, a solar year of 365 days, the 260-day cycle, and the phases of the moon, the Maya also displayed great interest in the movements of the planet Venus. All Mesoamericans considered this planet to be sinister and a threat to man's affairs on earth. The Maya divided the Venus cycle of 584 days into four periods of 236, 90, 250, and 8 days, corresponding to the appearances and disappearances of Venus as the morning and evening star. The Dresden Codex has lengthy tabulations of the Venus cycles, and it is with this planet that this codex deals.

INITIAL SERIES

Stela E, Quiriguá

FIGURE 16. The Long Count or Initial Series. The date is read from top to bottom and left to right. Under the introductory glyph it begins with the baktun glyph with the bar-and-dot coefficient for 9. To the right of the baktun glyph is the katun glyph with its coefficient for 17. Continuing below in order, the reading is 0 tuns, 0 uinals, 0 kins. The following glyph is 13 Ahau, the day in the 260-day cycle reached by this Long Count date. The corresponding month glyph is not found until the very end, 18 Cumkú. Between the 13 Ahau and 18 Cumkú glyphs are the glyphs of the ninth deity, Lord of the Night, who presides over this particular day, and those dealing with the position of the moon and its age. (Redrawn from *The Ancient Maya*, Third Edition, by Sylvanus Griswold Morley, revised by George W. Brainerd, with the permission of the publishers, Stanford University Press. Copyright © 1946, 1947, 1956 by the Board of Trustees of the Leland Stanford Junior University.)

In addition to the Maya region, observation points for the planet Venus were located in Tehuacán, Puebla, and Teotitlán del Camino, Oaxaca. The central Mexicans also took into account the Venus cycle of 584 days, which was apparently of considerable significance, and they, as the Maya, were aware that 8 solar years exactly equaled 5 Venus periods. More spectacular still was the completion of 104 years, at which time several cycles coincided: the 584-day Venus period, the 365-day solar year, the 52-year cycle, and the Tonalpohualli. This event was the cause of great rejoicing and special ceremonies.

Aside from these calculations, there are Maya glyphs recording the dates of katun period endings or fractions thereof. There also are dedicatory or commemorative dates, which serve as base dates for further calculations. These may reach back several katuns or more. Recording of future dates was rare.

By the sixteenth century, the Maya of Yucatán had replaced the Long Count by a shorter system known as the "U kahlay katunob" or Short Count. Rather than a time-distance count such as the Long Count, this abbreviated system started from the end of katun 13 Ahau, and used tuns and katuns. Tuns were numbered; katuns were named. The katun was the time span of greatest concern. In this system, the cycle always ended on a day Ahau; thus, katun 13 Ahau was followed by katun 11 Ahau, and katuns 9, 7, 5, 3, 1, 12, 10, 8, 6, 2, and 13; after 260 years, katun 13 Ahau was repeated. Prophecies, most of which were unlucky, were associated with each katun. Therefore, certain events were expected to repeat themselves accordingly, thus compounding the problems of the historians.

Can any hieroglyphs be "read" then, aside from dates and numbers? Yes, indeed they can, and it is now felt that the inscriptions are largely historical.

The códices contain approximately 287 different signs, which were published in 1956 by G. Zimmermann. Since then Thompson (1962) has published the first comprehensive catalog of glyphs in which the preceding and following glyphs in each context are included. There is a need for analyzing whole Maya texts and for publishing complete photographs and drawings of monuments to facilitate hieroglyphic studies (Kelley 1962c).

Perhaps the greatest contributions to understanding the structure of ancient Maya writing have been made by Thompson, who has supplemented archaeological evidence with that from early colonial documents and studied traces of the ancient calendars among present-day Indian groups. In his studies of Maya hieroglyphic writing (Thompson 1959, 1975), he identified dozens of glyphs and outlined many basic

NONCALENDRICAL INSCRIPTIONS AND WRITING

concepts that have been accepted by Maya scholars. There are many isolated glyphs such as those for sun, moon, colors, directions, death, and eclipse for which the meaning is clear. But it is possible to go beyond simple identification of certain glyphs. Thompson does not see good evidence for syllabic writing, and in his approach to decipherment lies an attempt to connect affixes with sounds. He believes that grammatical particles were expressed as affixes, for example, *al, il,* and *ti,* while some affixes made use of the rebus principle (in which a picture stands for an abstract idea that is a homophone).

Rebus Writing   An examination of glyph writing during the historic period of contact with the Spanish in central Mexico gives us some idea of the processes involved in reading earlier hieroglyphs. Using the mid-sixteenth-century Codex Xólotl as an example, we can see clearly that these glyphs are ideographic, representing a kind of play on homonyms or rebus writing. The central Mexicans had no real alphabet, but combined pictures of objects to give a meaning (Figure 17). For example, to represent Tenochtitlán they would combine a picture of a stone (*tena*) with a picture of nopal cactus (*nochtli*); similarly Chapultepec was represented by a grasshopper (*chapullin*) sitting atop the glyph for hill (*tepec*) (Figure 17-d). A path was indicated by a row of footprints, while footprints plus water signified a bridge. The figures are characteristically shown in profile; no perspective was attempted, and depth of field was indicated by placing an object higher on the page. Speech was simply represented by volutes in front of the mouth, and song, therefore, consisted of speech scrolls decorated with flowers (Figure 17-c). Charles Dibble (1940), who has made thorough studies of Náhuatl documents, points out that there is no evidence of any use of an alphabet, but as Spanish influence increased, so did the rebus-type writing. Eventually the glyphs were read from left to right in a line instead of from bottom to top as in pre-Conquest examples. This principle of rebus writing was easily applied to the Maya language, which was largely monosyllabic.

FIGURE 17. Aztec picture writing. (a) Warrior receiving insignia for having taken three prisoners of war; (b) priest playing *teponaztli* drum; (c) symbol for song (speech scroll adorned with a flower); (d) glyph for Chapultepec, from Náhuatl *chapulin* (grasshopper) and *tepec* (hill); (e) glyph for Coatepec, from *coatl* (serpent) and *tepec* (hill); (f) glyph for Cuernavaca (near a tree); (g) goldsmith at work; (h) priest observing the stars; (i) boy fishing; (j) temples of Huitzilopochtli and Tlaloc in Tenochtitlán; (k) King Huitzilíhuitl—glyph is a hummingbird's head and five white down feathers; (l) the conquest of Azcapotzalco—*azcatl* means ant, and *putzalli,* sand heap; thus, Azcaputzalli signifies ant heap. *Co* means in. Thus the translation of Azcapotzalco is "in the ant heap" or the place of dense population. The temple toppled by flames is a sign of conquests. (From the following sources: a, b, d, e, f, g, h, i, j, k, l, Codex Mendoza 1830–1848; c, Codex Borbónico 1899.)

a

b

c

g

d

e

f

h

i

j

k

l

Thompson (1965b) gives several examples that use representations of animals. A dog glyph might be used to symbolize drought in the Books of Chilam Balam, or be associated with disease in other texts. *Pek* means dog and "worthless rains"; it is also the name of a skin infection in Yucatec. The reader would be expected to choose which meaning best suited the text.

Phoneticism, Ideographs, and Old Yucatec

Attempts at deciphering Maya hieroglyphs have gone through various stages of study and each step has had a profound effect on contemporary and succeeding work. Thus, in 1904 when Cyrus Thomas became discouraged and repudiated his own attempts at discovering phoneticism in Maya hieroglyphs, studies in this field were abandoned for many years. When Landa's Yucatec day and month names were published, it was hard to see that these corresponded in any way with the hieroglyphs of the monuments. As a result, scholars were discouraged from looking for any phonetic approach and decided that the Maya hieroglyphs were largely ideographs and required no knowledge of the ancient Maya language. Ideograms or any recognizable representation could be dealt with on a very mechanical basis in much the same way that one can work with mathematics using Arabic numerals, without needing to know the English language.

Therefore, throughout the 1930s and 1940s studies centered around the deciphering of dates and calendrical information, while the remaining inscriptions were largely ignored. Now, due in part to some controversial articles of a Russian epigrapher, Yuri Knorozov, the existence of phonetic glyphs is being examined once more, and this entire field of research is being revitalized by serious studies.

Knorozov began publishing articles in 1952. As his early work was filled with errors of interpretation, and as he also had antagonized Western scholars by suggesting a general lack of competence, his New World counterparts were very unfavorably disposed toward him and his work. However, despite exaggerated claims of success and poor presentation and style, his scientific work is now regarded by some to be a major contribution to the decipherment of Maya script. D. H. Kelley and M. D. Coe are among those who feel he has demonstrated the existence of some phonetic glyphs.

One fundamental difficulty hampering this research is our ignorance of the language in which the hieroglyphs were written. We are faced with hieroglyphic texts of an ancient Maya language nearly 2000 years old. The closest related language Knorozov calls Old Yucatec, used in the Colonial sources of Yucatán in the sixteenth century such as the Books of Chilam Balam. Old Yucatec has been subjected to many changes as a result of the influx of Toltec, Putún Itzá, and Xiu groups. Nevertheless, Landa's information was recorded in this language and it forms a basis for study. His writings probably date to about 1566, and although the original manuscript was lost, parts of preserved copies were first published in 1864 (see Tozzer, 1941). Landa compiled 27 signs which he called a Maya alphabet. Landa's glyphs are genuine Maya glyphs, but he was mistaken in believing they were simple consonant and vowel signs. They seem to be Maya sound symbols for Spanish names of the alphabet and probably were recorded incorrectly by the native informant. Knorozov thinks that these signs can be better understood when viewed as a syllabary rather than an alphabet.

If Maya texts were simply composed of pictographs, then one would expect to find that these glyphs occurred with the same frequency throughout. In the Maya texts, however, the number of newly appearing signs diminishes as one progresses, which is a hint that one is dealing with recurring speech sounds. Knorozov believes that the Maya alphabet is a mixed morphosyllabic system. Some of the signs represent phonemes, forming parts of morphemes, whereas others represent morphemes. His best work is a monograph published in 1963, of which three chapters have been translated into English by Sophie Coe (Knorozov 1967). This very scholarly work includes many illustrations of hieroglyphs and provides a base for the testing of this theory. Probably Knorozov's most important point is that single morphemes with a consonant–vowel–consonant pattern may be written by two phonetic glyphs of the consonant–vowel pattern, thus creating syllabic signs, which have no semantic connection with the word. All phonetic glyphs consist of an initial consonant and vowel, and when paired, the final vowel is not pronounced. Conflicting views at present deal with the nature and extent of phoneticism and the frequency of true ideographs. The hieroglyphic texts include historical, astronomical, and ritualistic information. There are probably many logographic glyphs, that is, glyphs with one or more morphemic referents, and a knowledge of the language is a necessary prerequisite for deciphering both logographic and phonetic glyphs.

In comparing Maya hieroglyphic writing with Old Yucatec, the word order was basically the same, and there were several structural similarities. Ancient Maya was considered sacred and carefully preserved by the priests for generations. There is some evidence that the *códices* sometimes were buried with the priests. The spoken language changed greatly, owing to outside influences. Thompson has been able to demonstrate that the affix *te* in the Dresden Codex shifted to the sound *che* in Yucatec; in other cases *ch* changed to *c*. These problems must be considered in any study of phonetics.

To prove any theory, of course, one must put it to the test. In this case, the correctness of a phonetic reading of a syllabic sign is found when the sign is read the same way in different words. Once the sound is established, the semantics must be worked out. This is where our ignorance of the ancient Maya language is keenly felt. Though a great deal of work lies ahead before anyone can "read" Maya script, the nature of the system has probably been identified and scholars are once more hopeful of deciphering a real writing system.

Historical Studies

Tatiana Proskouriakoff, well known for her beautiful drawings and reconstructions of Maya sculptures and architecture, has also been analyzing and studying the hieroglyphs. In observing the carved stone stelae at Piedras Negras, her attention was caught by the repetition of certain glyphs on groups of monuments related to a particular temple. Investigation of the dates revealed that these stelae were erected at 5-year intervals, and that all the dates of a single group fell easily into the life span of a single individual. Her curiosity thoroughly aroused, she embarked on a complete study of 35 monuments at Piedras Negras and others at Yaxchilán and Naranjo, with astounding results (Proskouriakoff 1960, 1961). She now believes that each group of monuments represents the reign of a single individual or lord. The figures carved in relief are not gods and priests, as formerly assumed, but the current ruler. For example, the first monument erected typically depicts a young man seated in a niche accompanied by two glyphs. One of these, the "up-ended frog" glyph (Figure 18), probably records the birth date of the ruler and may be repeated on later monuments. The other glyph, dubbed the "toothache," or "accession," glyph, is believed to mark the ascension of the young man to power (Figure 18). In one case, a later monument shows a woman and child. Personal names and some titles are believed to have been identified, so that a set of monuments is interpreted as dealing with the life of one ruler and recording his birthday, the events of his reign, his marriage, birth of offspring, and perhaps military victories. Since it is known that the Maya were astrologers rather than astronomers, one can assume that these dates were not simply historical records, but provided a basis for predictions of good and evil events in the reign. Confirmation of these interpretations lay in the examination of the next set of monuments associated with the erection of another temple. Once again, a young man seated in a niche accompanied by "up-ended frog" and "accession" glyphs unfolded the subsequent story of a new reign.

Another landmark in glyphic studies was Berlin's identification of "emblem glyphs," that is, glyphs that appear at a single center and more rarely at others. He felt these glyphs could stand for the name of the center, or region, or possibly the dynasty (Berlin 1958). A number of emblem glyphs have now been identified for Copán, Quiriguá, Tikal, Naranjo, Piedras Negras, Palenque, Seibal, and Calakmul (?) (Figure 19). As a result of these studies, we have some information on the history, genealogies, data on marriages, and possible alliances for a number of the Petén cities that are mentioned here.

toothache

bird jaguar

kin jaguar

birth date

name

hand & fish

FIGURE 18. Maya historical glyphs. (Hand and fish from Proskouriakoff 1960 and reproduced by permission of the Society for American Archaeology from *American Antiquity*, 25(4):470, Fig. 8b, 1960; toothache, bird jaguar, kin jaguar, birth date ["upended frog" glyph], and name from Proskouriakoff 1961 and reproduced by permission of The University Museum, University of Pennsylvania.)

Copán

Seibal

Naranjo

Piedras Negras

Quiriguá

Palenque

Tikal

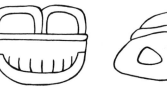

Yaxchilán

FIGURE 19. Emblem glyphs of Maya cities. (From Berlin 1958.)

Basing herself on the studies of Berlin and Proskouriakoff, Marcus (1976a) has set forth a political history for the Classic Maya in which she divides the southern lowland area into four regional centers, each under jurisdiction of a city. This scheme has not been accepted by all scholars and is not without problems, yet it serves as a working model and hypothesis and should be viewed as such. Coggins (1979), Jones (1977), and Haviland (1977) have put together a remarkable history of Tikal. Quiriguá and Copán can be better understood by the writings of Kelley (1962a) and Sharer (1978a), and Palenque's personalities and family problems are perhaps best known of all (Mathews and Schele 1974; Schele 1976). These histories are brought out in Chapter 6.

At Yaxchilán there is evidence of some kind of a jaguar dynasty but the record is far from clear at present. There seems to be a relationship between the ruler and the jaguar as his protector. It is hoped that the Yaxchilán hieroglyphs will someday tell us something about prevailing politics and local conflicts, as no other Maya site portrays so many militant battle scenes.

The most complete history of writing for one area is that described for the Zapotec in Oaxaca (Marcus 1980). As long suspected, the earliest hieroglyphs are calendrical in nature, a simple date is our earliest evidence of the 260-day ritual cycle in 600 B.C. The following years see a great proliferation of pictorial bas-reliefs at Monte Albán. Between 500–200 B.C. over 300 stone carvings are known which represent sacrificed victims and captives (see Plate 1-d, p. 68). Thereafter the carved reliefs continue, but, while they are numerically fewer (only 15), they convey much more information as the glyphic content becomes more complex. These are the stones celebrating Zapotec conquests, displayed as reminders and badges of Zapotec power (200 B.C.–A.D. 100). Year, month, and day signs can be "read." Place names are represented by several glyphs which combine to identify the "Hill of the Bird" and the "Place of the Song." Other sequences show the toponym combined with an upside-down human head wearing a distinctive headdress which conveys the idea of conquest. Writing was used as a means of propaganda, aimed at discouraging resistance and promoting enthusiasm for the emerging state.

By the Classic period (Monte Albán III), four stone monuments describe the visit of an important person at Monte Albán. By combining pictographs and hieroglyphs and by faithfully representing the regional dress and styles, the arrival of an important person from Teotihuacán at Monte Albán is very well portrayed. This was Monte Albán at the peak of its power, prestige, and diplomacy. After the Zapotec capital was abandoned around A.D. 700, the tradition of writing was carried on in the important towns of the Oaxaca Valley. From A.D. 700–900 texts reflect the political changes that took place. The single capital was replaced by small competitive centers. Power belonged to those who could manipulate kinsmen, establish alliances through marriage, and reinforce their nobility. Thus old militaristic themes were replaced by genealogical records of ancestry, birth, marriage, death, succession, which were all important. Stones were still carved, but were smaller in size, to be read close up. Texts began at the bottom and zig-zagged up to the most recent information at the top. These are known as genealogical registers and were placed in elite residences or in tombs. In no other area has the history of writing been so thoroughly documented.

The study of hieroglyphs was for many years confined almost entirely to the decipherment of dates in the belief that these were recorded solely for their astronomical and calendrical significance. Now not only are other explanations feasible but we are beginning to see a variety and originality in approaches to the decipherment of all scripts. A true phonetic writing system would be very good news indeed, but no one, including Knorozov, expects to be able to read all texts in the near future. Even if his system proves to be essentially correct, a determination of values for all Maya signs will have to be worked out, a Herculean task.

If Thompson is correct about the nonsyllabic character of the hieroglyphs, then we can expect progress to be even slower, for the solution to the meaning of one glyph would not necessarily reflect on others. Advancement in any case will be greatly accelerated by a more comprehensive recording and publishing of complete texts. To this end, Ian Graham is currently working under the auspices of the Guttman Foundation to compile a record of ancient Maya glyphic material, which at present is widely scattered, inaccessible, and incomplete.

Nearly 100 years have passed since Alfred Maudslay struggled into Copán, his team of mules hauling 4 tons of plaster of Paris, with the determination to make molds from the stelae. Eventually the molds reached England, casts were made, and from them the drawings that set Ernst Förstmann on his way to calculate the first Long Count dates. Equally dedicated to the study of the ancient Maya was Sylvanus G. Morley, who combed the jungles in his search for new inscriptions. His enthusiasm kindled the interest of the Carnegie Institution of Washington and led to the extensive program of excavation and restoration at Chichén Itzá and Copán. All studies of Maya glyphs are based on the early works of pioneer scholars in this field such as Paul Schelhas, Teobert Maler, Herbert J. Spinden, John E. Teeple, Herman Beyer, Thomas Barthel, and more recently J. Eric Thompson. We are only now beginning to reap rewards of many years of dedicated study.

The Era of Teotihuacán and the Maya: The Classic Period

CHAPTER 6

The cultural achievements in Mesoamerica immediately prior to A.D. 900 were so remarkable that these years of development have long been called the Classic period. It used to be defined as beginning with the earliest recorded Long Count dates from the Petén and ending with their cessation. Now, however, in reappraising and refining our concept of the Classic period, we need to extend its limits further back in time and to revise its subphases.

In its very broadest interpretation it embraces the first 9 centuries of the Christian Era. By starting the Classic period at the year A.D. 1 as in the chart (back endpapers), the Protoclassic is included, while at the other end of the chart we find a Terminal Classic phase. What each phase is called, how the years are divided up, or where one draws the line are only organizational aids for ourselves. Although a Protoclassic phase is a useful segmentation in an area like Belize, for example, it has less meaning in the central Yucatán development. Phases are but guidelines; the cultural events in each region, while linked to those in other areas and affected by what happens there, at the same time retain a character of their own. At first the local characteristics of each area, or regionalism, seemed to predominate, but due to intensive work in a number of areas since the 1960s, a more holistic view is easier to achieve as the interrelationships of various areas come into focus. The best example of this is to be found in the Classic period history of Teotihuacán and its relationship with the great civilization of the lowland Maya and their respective neighbors.

The story of the Classic period is one in which regional cultures shared ideas, art styles, and intellectual knowledge to produce a magnificent display of brilliant achievements, only to collapse a century or two later. New centers rose to take their places but rather than producing much that was innovative, the result was rather another type of regionalism in which existing norms, institutions, and patterns were reorganized and consolidated.

For many years the Classic period was divided into an Early (A.D. 300–600) and a Late phase (A.D. 600–900). Somehow this break at A.D. 600 was awkward and did not correspond to cultural events. Now the concept of a Middle Classic period has come into use, a refinement that has helped bring the events between A.D. 400–700 into sharper focus and has proved to be a logical and useful division (Lowe 1978; Pasztory 1978b). The term was originally proposed by Parsons (1969) as a result of his work at Bilbao on the Pacific slopes of Guatemala. The greater Classic period is conveniently broken down as follows and is the framework to be used here:

- *Early Classic (A.D. 1–400)* in which the earlier Preclassic peoples made rapid socioeconomic and intellectual advancements. The years are marked by experimentation and innovation, a period characterized by regionalism. A Protoclassic phase is a further convenient subdivision for the first years in some areas.
- *Middle Classic (A.D. 400–700)* further divided into an Early Middle (A.D. 400–550) and Late Middle (A.D. 550–700). The former is marked by the greatest expansion and influence of Teotihuacán. After the collapse of this great central Mexican center, others rose to prominence: Tajín, Xochicalco, Ñuiñe, and Cotzumalhuapa. This Late Middle Classic development is devoid of direct Teotihuacán influence.
- *Late Classic (A.D. 700–900)* in which the southern lowland Maya attained their peak of intellectual, artistic, and socioeconomic development. The last 100 years saw the collapse of their brilliant civilization and the subsequent rise of regional centers in northern Yucatán and at Tula, Hidalgo, in central Mexico.
- *Terminal Classic period (A.D. 800–1000),* a convenient segment of time used in some areas as a transitional phase from Classic to Postclassic development, particularly applicable to the Yucatán sequence.

During these 9 centuries we see an increase of population, true urban development or the rise of cities, more elaborate ceremonial centers, increased socioeconomic differentiation of the population, and intensified extensive trade networks. I have considered any concentration of population in the tens of thousands as a city or urban development. With urbanism or city life we may also expect to find nonfarming residents, occupational specialization, a class-structured society, and the concentration of capital wealth. This broad, flexible definition of a city permits the inclusion of great contrasts in Mesoamerica, as urbanism in highland Mexico is very different from a special kind of urbanism among the lowland Maya.

In this Classic period skilled architects throughout Mesoamerica directed the erection of pyramids, temples, buildings with many rooms, and stone masonry ball courts. Each region developed its own basic architectural style, but the vaulted or corbelled arch was a distinctive feature of the lowland Maya, where sculptors were in particular demand for executing stone carvings, decorating facades, and carving altars, stelae, tablets, and inscriptions. Mural painting was an important medium of liturgical expression at Teotihuacán and was used more realistically at Tikal, Uaxactún, Bonampak, and Mul-Chic. Ceramicists specialized in elaborate decorative techniques, and distinctive regional wares were traded between important centers, which indicates extensive trade and travel. Advanced knowledge of calendrics and astronomical calculations permitted the priests to predict cosmic events with accuracy. Among the lowland Maya, Long Count dates and genealogies were carefully and methodically recorded as rulers became obsessed with establishing their legitimacy to the throne via their ancestors. No physical effort was spared in erecting huge ceremonial centers; no task was too great or required too much patience if a stucco sculpture, a carved mirror, or a champ-levé vessel was needed for an approaching ritual or for exchange with a foreign dignitary. Activity was constant. Whether one walks down the Avenue of the Dead at Teotihuacán or looks out at Palenque's temples banked against the jungle-covered hills, one is awed by the magnitude of the undertaking, the depth of inspiration that made it possible, and the painstaking physical labor that was expended upon its materialization. In short, the Classic period signifies what we traditionally think of as the cultural peak of Mesoamerican culture.

We know when events took place. However, the questions of how and why they came to pass are not so easily answered. One wonders what motivated these people to achieve such creative heights and how, with their neolithic culture without metal tools, they were able to build majestic cities that, even lying in ruins as we see them today, are stunningly impressive.

It is helpful to focus attention on three key areas of development at this time: (1) central highland Mexico (Map 7), (2) the Maya lowlands (Map 9, p. 257), and (3) the coastal lowlands (Map 8, p. 206). The latter have been called the Peripheral Coastal Lowlands comprising the Gulf Coast of Veracruz and western Tabasco, and the Pacific Coast of Chiapas, Guatemala, and El Salvador, actually forming a single cultural and geographic unit with similar environment (see Map 8, Parsons 1978). These coastal areas united by the Isthmus of Tehuantepec were, as we have seen, the scene of major Preclassic advances, the home of the Olmecs. Once again this region plays a very important role, but this time it is peripheral to the great civilizations that rose to the east and west. Although a little to one side geographically and culturally, Monte

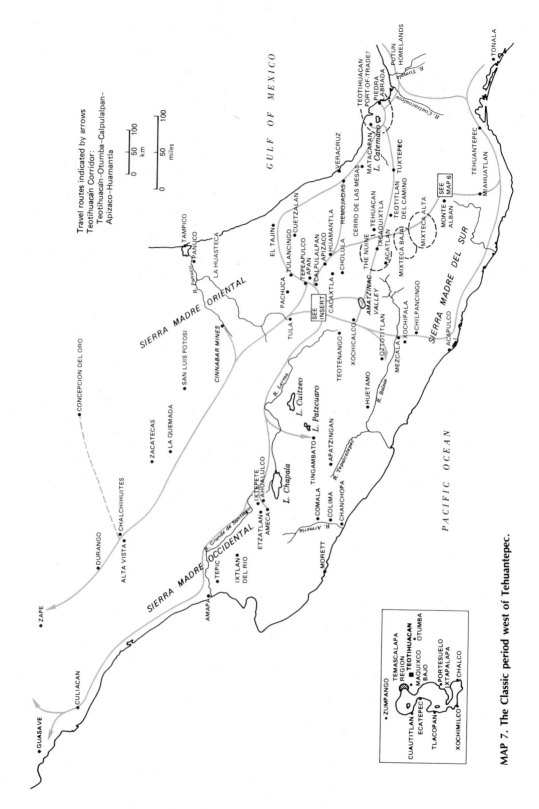

188

MAP 7. The Classic period west of Tehuantepec.

Albán in Oaxaca, important in Preclassic days, enjoys a regional flor-escence which in turn reflects the fortunes of her neighbors. In our treatment of this period, let us take up once again the events in the Basin of Mexico, first examining Teotihuacán and her neighbors. We will then turn to the Classic Maya.

Although some small villages were settled in the Valley of Teotihuacán as early as 900 B.C., this northern region had no major Preclassic centers and was culturally marginal to the more active peoples around the lakes in the Basin of Mexico. In the Late Preclassic period, settlements began to diversify and there were a few signs of occupational specialization such as lacustrine exploitation, salt-producing centers, and obsidian workshops. Of the two main regional centers, Teotihuacán in the north and Cuicuilco in the south, Teotihuacán soon outdistanced its southern rival. Realistically, Cuicuilco had nothing to develop—no resources at hand, no growth potential. In any event, Cuicuilco was completely obliterated by a volcanic eruption of Xitli. With Cuicuilco eliminated, there would be nothing to stand in the way of Teotihuacán for nearly 300 years.

TEOTIHUACÁN: THE GROWTH OF A CITY

During the Tzacualli phase (FI–10), people began to pour into the city, swelling the population to 70,000 or even 100,000. Teotihuacán is estimated to have held 80–90% of the total population of the Basin of Mexico, the remaining percentage consisting of small scattered hamlets (Sanders, Parsons, and Santley 1979).

It was about this time that a great drop in population is noticeable in the Tenanyecac phase east of the Basin of Mexico in Tlaxcala. In the preceding Tezoquipan phase (300 B.C.–A.D. 100) civic–ceremonial architecture had been erected there in a *talud–tablero* style with wide balustrades. Great advances had been made in agricultural technology for terracing, canals, irrigation, and dams have all been documented. García Cook suggests that many of these skilled technicians and laborers moved over the mountains and helped build Teotihuacán. Demographically and chronologically the hypothesis fits (García Cook 1974, 1978).

What triggered the ambitious rise we do not know exactly, but there must have been a few brilliant minds with leadership qualities. R. Millon (1973) has suggested that economic exploitation and specialization of obsidian together with religion played the most important roles. Sanders and Price (1968) feel that the need to control water for agricultural purposes led to the formation of centralized authority and eventual statehood. The answer surely lies in a combination of factors that are not fully understood, but it seems clear that the control of the Tepeapulco obsidian industry would have been paramount to the location and prosperity of Teotihuacán.

By Tezoyuca–Patlachique phases this complex commercial operation was initiated. The network exploited four different obsidian sources and provided for production and redistribution of finished products, coinciding with the dramatic increase of population and urban development at Teotihuacán (Charlton 1978). Local workshops in the city indicate that at least some tools were produced or finished there, and it is believed that by Late Preclassic times 2% of the population was already working full time at the trade.

By the Early Classic phase of Tzacualli (A.D. 1–150) the city exhibits extraordinary complexity. Intensive farming was the occupation of nearly all the inhabitants. Irrigation systems are believed to have been elaborate and complex, essential for food production, if the city was to prosper.

By the end of Tzacualli, the city center extended over 20 km². Under pressure of gods and priests, workers toiled as never before, and by the end of this period most of the Pyramid of the Sun and perhaps the first structures of the Pyramid of the Moon were completed. Although we know Teotihuacán was a planned city (Figure 20), it is seldom that we know exactly why specific sites were selected for building. Among the thousands of visitors that climb to the summit of the Pyramid of the Sun, few know that almost directly beneath them are a series of natural caves, roofed over with basalt slabs, whose walls are still plastered with mud. The natural formations have been somewhat enlarged, for this must have been a very sacred place, at one time containing a spring.

Doris Heyden has compared this cave to the legendary Chicomoztoc or Seven Caves which, according to Aztec mythology, spawned those people of the sun (Heyden 1975). No one knows where Chicomoztoc was, if indeed it had an earthly location, nor can we be sure that the Teotihuacanos had the same beliefs. But if so, Chicomoztoc could refer to any number of symbolic locations, of which this could be one. In any event, it would have been a natural attraction for pilgrimages. The way leads in via a deep pit, a partially destroyed stairway cut into bedrock, then through a natural tunnel terminating in several chambers. The caves held no skeletal remains when found in 1971 but Heyden suggests they may have been used as the scene of rituals, sacrifice, investiture of chiefs, special meetings, or even as tombs for ancient rulers. It can be no coincidence that directly above these caves rises the great Pyramid of the Sun.

Even legends current at the time of the Conquest refer to the Pyramids of the Sun and Moon, and unlike most labels given to ancient structures, these probably correctly relate to the gods honored at each temple. The Pyramid of the Moon guards the northern end of the central axis, the Avenue of the Dead. The Sun, located just east of the great avenue, faces west (Photo 21). A hasty and faulty reconstruction done many years ago completely destroyed the exterior facing, and although it is mammoth in size at present (61 m high by 213 m base length), the

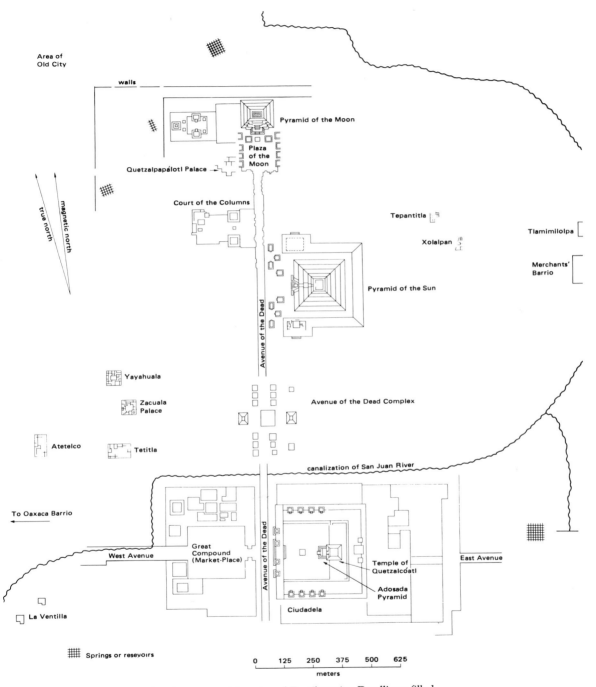

Area of
Old City

walls

Pyramid of the Moon

Plaza
of the
Moon

Quetzalpapálotl Palace

true north

magnetic north

Court of the Columns

Tepantitla

Xolalpan

Tlamimilolpa

Merchants'
Barrio

Pyramid of the Sun

Avenue of the Dead

Yayahuala

Zacuala
Palace

Avenue of the Dead Complex

Atetelco

Tetitla

canalization of San Juan River

To Oaxaca Barrio

West Avenue

Great
Compound
(Market-Place)

Avenue of the Dead

Temple of
Quetzalcóatl

East Avenue

Adosada
Pyramid

La Ventilla

Ciudadela

Springs or resevoirs

0   125   250   375   500   625

meters

FIGURE 20. Simplified map of civic–ceremonial center of Teotihuacán. Dwellings filled the spaces between constructions shown. From Pyramid of Moon to Great Compound: 2000 m. (Information from R. Millon 1973; Millon, Drewitt, and Cowgill 1972.)

191

PHOTO 21. Pyramid of the Sun with associated structures along the Avenue of the Dead, Teotihuacán. (Courtesy of Compañia Mexicana Aerofoto, S. A.)

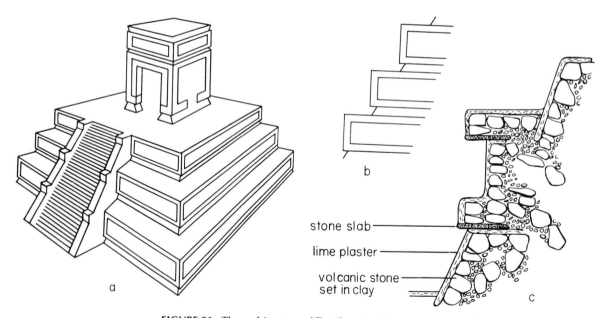

stone slab

lime plaster

volcanic stone set in clay

FIGURE 21. The architecture of Teotihuacán: (a) reconstruction of a Teotihuacán pyramid and temple, based on an excavated stone model; (b) profile of *talud–tablero* architecture; (c) *talud–tablero* construction. (From the following sources: a, Salazar 1966; b, c, Acosta 1964.)

Pyramid of the Sun was once even larger. We believe the original was built up with the typical *talud* and *tablero* facing, in four tiers (Figure 21). The *talud–tablero* is an architectural feature that typifies Teotihuacán, and many other groups who saw it carried the idea home with them, and copied or modified it to suit their special tastes. It consists of a rectangular body (*tablero*) with recessed inset, which rests on an outward sloping basal element (*talud*). Elsewhere, the relative proportions varied, but at Teotihuacán the *tablero* always was larger than the *talud*. In the case of the Pyramid of the Sun, the interior was built up of adobe bricks. These were faced with volcanic stones set in clay and plastered over with a smooth coating of lime. The staircase located on the west side was divided at the base, then merged in the final ascent to the thatched huts on top, the two sacred temples (Millon 1976). Construction was basically of this type throughout the city, interiors consisting of adobe or rubble faced with stone set in clay and finally covered with a lime plaster.

The center of the religious complex lay about 3 km farther south where the Avenue of the Dead met another great group of structures, the Ciudadela. The Temple of Quetzalcóatl, begun at this time, was part of this group. Probably the East Avenue was also laid out as part of an east–west axis that, together with the Avenue of the Dead, divided the ceremonial center into quarters. The intricate drainage system whose weblike pattern eventually covered the whole city was also initiated. Nothing approaching the magnitude of such planning had ever been attempted before, and by A.D. 150 Teotihuacán had achieved total domination of the Valley of Mexico and perhaps even the entire highland area (Figure 20).

The next 100 years (A.D. 150–250), known as the Miccaotli phase (FI 11), marks the maximum expansion of the city, which came to occupy 22.5 km^2 The population swelled accordingly. About this time groups of people from Oaxaca moved into the area; about 3 km west of the center of the city, typical Monte Albán II pottery, including two effigy urns, has been found. This district retained its ties to Oaxaca throughout the life of the city and is known as the Oaxaca Barrio.

Upon the laying out the East Avenue, which roughly bisects the Avenue of the Dead at the center of the Ciudadela, the fundamental planning was completed (Millon, Drewitt, and Cowgill 1973) (Figure 20). The city was laid out in quarters, containing public religious structures, palaces, and multifamily dwellings. Climbing to the heights of the Pyramid of the Moon marking the northern end of the great Avenue of the Dead, one can look straight down the great axis of the city and marvel at this urban planning (Photo 22). Directly in front of the pyramid is a great plaza flanked by three pyramids on either side. On the right, behind Structure 5, is the sumptuous Palace of Quetzalpapálotl, (the Butterfly–Quetzal Palace) with its inner patio lined with sculptured

PHOTO 22. Aerial view, northern sector of Teotihuacán. Pyramid of the Moon at upper left, Pyramid of Sun at right center. (Courtesy of Compañia Mexicana de Aerofoto, S. A.)

columns of polychromed bas-reliefs (see Photo 26, p. 202) and murals in surrounding rooms painted with motifs associated with water and Tlaloc.

Looking once more down the Avenue of the Dead past the Pyramid of the Sun, the eye will finally reach the Calle de los Muertos Complex, located about half way between the Ciudadela and the Pyramid of the Sun. The Calle de los Muertos Complex consisted of a cluster of tiered temple-mounds, platforms, stairways, patios, and possibly some residential quarters, arranged around a central court. Its prominent location in the very center of the main axis suggests that it played an important but as yet undefined role in the ceremonial life of the city. Beyond this lies the huge Ciudadela, facing the Great Compound which is believed to have served as a marketplace. So great is the distance that these structures are barely discernable from the Pyramid of the Moon. Both sides of the main avenue are lined with civic and religious buildings. Narrow, alley-like streets lead off into residential areas, which are crowded in between the more important religious edifices.

By the time one has trudged down the Avenue of the Dead, ascended and descended countless staircases, and crossed seemingly endless sunken courts, one may be tempted to agree with the opinion of the visitor who said that Teotihuacán presents the dullest architectural form since the sand castle. The *talud–tablero* combination is repeated throughout on every platform, shrine, and altar (Figure 21). The repetition of this terraced profile emphasizes its privileged form, which is restricted to religious structures. The *tablero* often served as a frame for painted or sculptured motifs, much of which has deteriorated so completely that one can see only the stone base. Architects did not continually erect *talud–tablero* forms for lack of imagination, but in order to communicate a religious symbolism (Kubler 1970) (see Photo 24 and Figures 21 and 27, p. 316).

The Ciudadela is not only an excellent example of the size, precision, and long-range planning that marked the culmination of Teotihuacán architecture but also provides a hint of how the structures really looked in their days of glory. The Ciudadela is actually a gigantic square, approximately 400 m long, which is limited by a wide platform on the north, east, and south sides. Each supports four smaller pyramids on top with the exception of the eastern side, which has three. A wide staircase on the west affords access to the entire compound (Photo 23). The Ciudadela can be considered a palace where perhaps rulers lived. It has been suggested that Teotihuacán had dual rulers, one heading the Quetzalcóatl faction, the other, less well identified, more militant. The gigantic square may have been the scene of large celebrations in honor of the passing of calendrical cycles (Drucker 1974). The platforms built in the Miccaotli phase enclose a huge patio toward the back of which is the famous Temple of Quetzalcóatl, a six-tiered structure of typical *talud–tablero* construction that was partially covered over by a plain structure, probably soon after A.D. 300 in the Tlamimilolpa phase. The facade of this spectacular temple is elaborately carved with undulating feathered serpents, which are bordered by shells and marine motifs (Photo 24). Serpent heads protrude from a kind of flower with 11 petals. These alternate with Tlaloc or rain-god heads with large circular eyes and straight bar moustaches, from which hang two fangs. These tenoned heads, which have an extension that is imbedded in the wall, represent some of the finest stone carving in the city, for unlike the Maya and Gulf Coast cultures, the Teotihuacanos rarely carved stone on a monumental scale. Remains of red and white paint are still preserved. Imagine the dramatic sight this must have been in the fourth century, when the six-tiered pyramid was complete, its carved and tenoned heads protruding from a stuccoed and brightly painted facade

PHOTO 23. The Ciudadela, Teotihuacán, enclosing a central court (precinct arrangement). The old Temple of Quetzalcóatl appears as an earthen mound with the later Adosada Pyramid in front. (Courtesy of Compañia Mexicana de Aerofoto, S. A.)

and capped by a proud temple lit by sacrificial fires and torches. The monotony of the repetitious architectural scheme is relieved if one imagines the entire city ablaze with color, for as we shall see, Teotihuacán was indeed a painted city.

During the Tlamimilolpa phase (MH 1–2) most of the structures we see today were completed in an enormous building boom. The Ciudadela was finished and in the name of progress the old Temple of Quetzalcóatl was partially buried by a larger, plain-tiered platform-pyramid of *talud–tablero* style known as the Adosada. The latter was erected after A.D. 300, perhaps representing a shift of power from the Quetz-

PHOTO 24. Carved facade of the Temple of Quetzalcóatl, Teotihuacán. (Courtesy of the Instituto Nacional de Antropología e Historia, Mexico.)

alcóatl faction to the more secular. This trend toward secular, expansionist, commercial interests is archaeologically supported by the mural paintings and ceramic objects. As a result, the Adosada displays less craftsmanship than the structure it has helped to preserve.

Perhaps the most dramatic change, certainly as it affected one's daily life, was the construction of permanent housing. Until this time, energy had been spent on public architecture. Now stone walled residential compounds were built, housing as few as 12 or as many as 60 or even 100. Built as a unit, conceived with the whole plan in mind, each compound possibly housed members who all worked at the same trade.

These high-walled compounds converted streets into alleyways and must have changed the whole complexion of the city. Nor were these the only walls. Massive, long, free-standing walls were concentrated in the northwestern area, behind the Pyramid of the Moon (see Figure 20). Sections have been preserved up to 5 m in height with a base width of 3.5 m. The extent of the walls is not known, nor is their purpose clear. They never encircled the city. As a defense mechanism, they would have been easy to circumvent, but combined with a healthy cactus fence, they could have been very effective. The walled compounds could have also impeded the advance of any enemy, although there is no evidence that walls or compounds were ever put to this test.

By the end of the Early Classic period (A.D. 400) the city of Teotihuacán extended so far south that it effectively blocked passage from the valley eastward to Puebla and Veracruz. The city was thus placed in the only exit to the east, at the same time positioning itself at a kind of trade-route intersection.

The Middle Classic period at Teotihuacán is represented by the Xolalpan and Metepec phases (MH 3–5), when the city's peak of power and influence was reached. Teotihuacán's fortunes were rising rapidly, and as fast as luxury items could be produced, they were packed off by merchants in every direction or taken to sell in the great marketplace along with the foreign goods brought in by outsiders. We will soon see how a great commercial enterprise was developed and how through mercantilism the influence of Teotihuacán reached the outward limits of Mesoamerica. This foreign involvement depended on a firm supportive foundation at home. The basic economy, goods and services, had to be provided locally. The entire Basin of Mexico became a kind of rural extension of the civic–administrative–ceremonial center of Teotihuacán.

With no advance warning that we can see, fortunes changed abruptly and the great decline seems to date from the time of a fire that devastated part of the city. This must have taken place around A.D. 650(?). A recovery was never made. Metepec is the phase that depicts these sad events, yet some people prospered. Teotihuacán remained the largest settlement in the Basin; some of the finest murals were painted, and wonderful trade goods were still brought in. It is a fascinating period and one with many problems still to solve. The population of the great city fell off rapidly to a mere fifth of its earlier peak, as people moved away into the areas of Texcoco and even toward Chalco and Ixtapalapa. All across the north, population dropped. With no compelling reason to remain in the Basin and no authoritarian voice to follow, one-third of the population went over the mountains in some direction.

There was no single replacement for Teotihuacán. By the Late Classic period (A.D. 700–900) three northern centers can be identified. An estimated 50,000 people lingered on at Teotihuacan itself, 20,000 more at Tenayuca–Cuautitlán, and perhaps 5500 at Zumpango, while three notable concentrations in the south were located at Portesuelo, Cerro de la Estrella, and Xico (see Map 4, p. 86). Politically the scene was in shambles and we have to look outside the Basin proper for leadership. This is the configuration in brief. Let us now go back and take a closer look at life in the city itself and try to understand how it functioned and what weaknesses lay behind the sudden decline of such a brilliant civilization.

It is not hard for us to visualize Teotihuacán, as it was a city in our sense of the word: busy, crowded, bustling with commercial and religious activities, and laid out in a grid pattern with multifamily dwellings crammed in to utilize every bit of space. The only open areas were those in the Avenue of the Dead and the marketplace. The main axis, the Avenue of the Dead, was the civic–ceremonial center with the most elegant residential section located toward the northern end. Middle-class housing was slightly removed from the main thoroughfares and the outskirts of the city were the least desirable as living quarters. The city had to house not only craftsmen and skilled workmen, but also a considerable number of religious leaders, some of whom, if not all, must have been full-time practitioners to judge from the size and number of temples under their supervision. The increasing secularization that became apparent by the Middle Classic period meant that civic officials and administrators were important and had to have appropriate housing.

The Housing Problem

Remember that two-thirds of the population were farmers, living in the city and traveling every day to their outlying fields. Their homes were the least well constructed and used more adobe than stone. Much wood was used in general construction which made the city easy prey to the final conflagration. Finer housing was of stone, roofed over with wooden beams.

Tlamimilolpa (Photo 25) was probably a lower-class dwelling and is the largest compound of its type. It was located east of the Pyramid of the Sun and offered rather cramped quarters with poor light and little air. It was partially excavated many years ago by Linné (1942). Its 3500 m² area contained an estimated 176 rooms, 21 patios, and 5 larger courts, plus numerous alleys. Although the sunlight of Teotihuacán is dazzling today, one must bear in mind that the city was so solidly filled in with structures during Classic times that the small interior rooms must have been gloomy and conditions crowded. Inhabitants lived under the constant threat of a violent storm that might damage the drainage system or a sudden fire that could leave a resident hopelessly trapped in the narrow alleys or cramped quarters. Perhaps the incon-

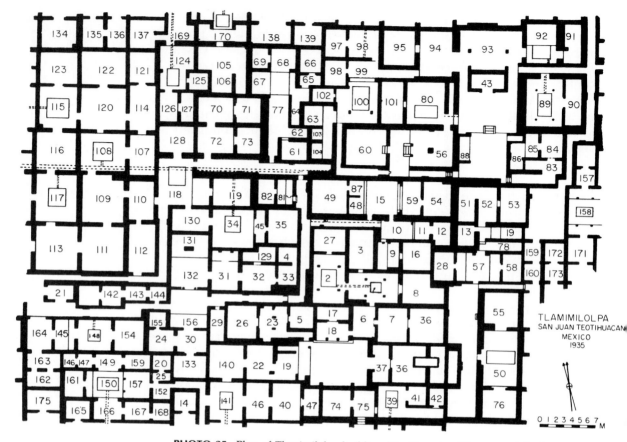

PHOTO 25. Plan of Tlamimilolpa building, Teotihuacán. (Courtesy of the Instituto Nacional de Antropología e Historia, Mexico.)

veniences of dark, damp, crowded living were offset by the advantages of living close to work and the market, amid the excitement of seeing the frequent arrivals of foreign traders and pilgrims. Indeed, where else was one to live? We think that the urban leaders controlled agricultural land as well as rural settlements. If one were to move to a planned rural community such as Maquixco Bajo, the living would have been almost identical. (See pp. 201–203.)

A step up in the social scale, and closer to the Avenue of the Dead, were other residential compounds of which Tetitla, Tepantitla, Zacuala, and Xolalpan, famous for their mural paintings, have been partially excavated. These are composed of clusters of rooms arranged around small open patios with central altars. Rain-water drained into a kind of cistern in the patio and was conducted from there to the outside by an interior drainage system. There were no windows, but small patios and courts admitted additional light and air. Miller (1973a) believes that paintings and murals were designed at the same time as the buildings. Thus patios and wall space were planned in advance and accordingly alloted, so the murals were not simply added as a decorative after-thought. Only a few of the many murals that existed have left a trace, but it is believed that most buildings were painted. The architectural pattern of 50–100 rooms was quite standardized in the 2000 structures of this type that have been identified. Size varied, smaller units housing perhaps 20 individuals while larger compounds could accommodate 100. Kitchens, remains of storage wares, cooking utensils, and debris leave little doubt as to the purpose of rooms. According to excavated compounds, each had its own temple or shrine, drainage, and some sort of sanitary facilities, all enclosed within a wall, providing privacy but also permitting a close administrative control.

The most sumptuous living was close to the main street, and a good example is furnished by the Quetzalpapálotl Palace (Acosta 1964) (Photo 26), located at the southwest corner of the Plaza of the Moon. It is a curious combination of public rooms and residential quarters. One en-ters this elegant palace by way of a wide stairway and porches leading to a magnificent court. This is bordered by a veranda with sculptured piers carved to represent owls in frontal view, originally painted in red and green with inlaid obsidian eyes. Others piers are carved with the profile of a quetzal bird. The owl is a common war emblem and its association with the quetzal here could have a meaning related to a lineage and warrior cult (Kubler 1967). We know this structure postdates A.D. 500, by which time Teotihuacán was becoming more and more materialistic and there was an increasing interest in personalities, lin-eages, and a warfare cult. Behind the court and public rooms are living quarters, a jumble of rooms resembling those in other apartment-like dwellings.

As already mentioned, life in the rural villages would have been similar, for we think they were controlled directly by the city authorities. The small community of Maquixco Bajo, excavated by the Teotihuacán Valley Project in 1961–1972, furnishes an example of a planned rural settlement of Middle Classic date (Sanders, Parsons, and Santley 1979). Located on the edge of an alluvial plain only 2 km west of Teotihuacán and occupying 8 ha, it probably accommodated 140–150 families, roughly 500–600 people.

Housing consisted of either individual households or apartment-like compounds of 10–12 nuclear families. Farming was the principal occu-pation and possibly sap was extracted from the maguey plant and made into *agua miel* or *pulque* to bring in extra money. The unusual number of obsidian scrapers can best be accounted for by this kind of activity. The stucco work was so far superior that it might represent a special-ization. Otherwise there was little variety and life looks monotonous

PHOTO 26. Interior patio with columns carved in relief, painted cornice. Quetzal-Butterfly Palace, Teotihuacán. (Courtesy of the Instituto Nacional de Antropología e Historia, Mexico.)

indeed. Basic staples were provided locally but there was no craft specialization, no innovations, nor were any seemingly encouraged, for access to raw materials was controlled. The picture presented is one of little flexibility or variety, for each family bought the same pots and products at the Teotihuacán market.

Heading up this community was a politician rather than a religious leader to judge from the local temple–pyramid and unimpressive paraphernalia associated with it. For important ceremonies, one went into the city to participate in its pageantry. Meanwhile, household artifacts suggest it was important to observe daily household ritual where the individual could most effectively communicate with the gods on a personal basis. Typical are broken clay figurines, incense burners, *candeleros*, and some fine tripod vessels, all found among debris. Larger houses had special rooms presumably for storing such objects, but no household could leave to chance the outcome of everyday fortunes. From our point of view, it would seem that the greater decisions of its sociopolitical economy were made in the big city.

In Mesoamerica one can usually look to the graves or tombs accompanied by lavish offerings for evidence of status and rank of a society. Teotihuacán is the exception, for no remains of any ruler or very important personage have been found to date. Contrary to what one might expect, no elaborate tombs and few cemeteries have been found. Simple, slab-lined graves were sometimes placed under floors of the residences, but the deceased were usually carefully wrapped and then cremated. Offerings such as finely painted vessels, utilitarian artifacts, textiles, and food were then placed with the remains. Infants were often interred in altars. At Teotihuacán class differences and the layers of hierarchical authority are inferred from the amount of space given over to courts and patios, the size of rooms, floor plans, some special furnishings, and perhaps mural paintings.

Earning a Living

The subsistence economy was based on the cultivation of maize, squash, and amaranth, supplemented by a variety of other cultigens; essentially it was the same diet established in Preclassic times. Dogs were probably eaten as well as turkeys, but hunting even of white-tailed deer does not seem to have been very important, and the daily food supply depended heavily on local crop production. For a flourishing urban center, with commercial interests and a complex sociopolitical structure, an agricultural surplus was a paramount necessity. Members of the religious hierarchy were surely not expected to till the soil in addition to attending to the temples and daily demands of the populace. Likewise, specialized artisans devoted the greater portion of their time to their trades.

Fortunately Teotihuacán was blessed with a dozen or more large permanent springs, which initially encouraged settlement. Eventually the tributaries of the San Juan River were harnessed further north, and this river was canalized and led along the eastern confines of the city past Tlamimilolpa and the Merchants' Barrio, then westward, traversing the city center just north of the Ciudadela and Great Compound to flow out the southwestern regions (see Figure 20, p. 191). Four reservoirs, wells, and small canals helped distribute water to the city. All these hydraulic systems enabled Teotihuacán farmers to produce their staples within about 15 km of the city limits. Sanders, Parsons, and Santley (1979) calculate that during the Classic period 9700 ha of land were under permanent irrigation which could easily maintain the enormous population of the city dwellers. Additional foods would have come in from other areas in the Basin. We must think in terms of supporting a city of 150,000 to 200,000.

It is now felt that not only did Teotihuacán control the entire Basin, but that certain areas were carefully colonized to exploit specific resources. Thus the southern regions of Chalco–Xochimilco, Ixtapalapa, and southern Texcoco were settled by people who hunted deer and provided the oak and pine timber for building. Others exploited the lake by fishing and taking waterfowl. The most substantial rural settlements were concentrated in the west–central region of Tacuba, Tenayuca, Cuautitlán, and Temascalapa to the east, where multifamily dwellings like those of Teotihuacán were erected. Ecatepec seems to have been a salt-producing station. Special stone, earth, and various clays were in demand for building and pottery making. Maguey fibers were always needed for clothing and cordage. The lakeshore provided reeds from which baskets and mats were woven. And farmers everywhere raised staples. The settlement at Zumpango in the extreme northwestern corner of the Basin may have been located to extract lime in the Río Salado drainage. Extensive lime quarries have been located that could have met the demands of the builders and masons of the great metropolis. Thus the Basin itself could have supplied most of the necessary basics and can be viewed as a giant resource area for the maintenance of the city.

A city of this magnitude would have required any number of skills, since clothing, household furnishings, and luxury objects for ceremony and trade, such as fine stone masks and exquisitely decorated tripod vessels with lids, were manufactured here and either sold in the market place or exported in all directions. Other specialized workshops include domestic pottery (i.e., not ritual), clay figurines, lapidary work, ground stone and basalt tools, and slate ornaments. Leather and wood workers, feather workers, weavers, and basketmakers must have also had their own shops, but being perishable, their materials are not preserved. This constant movement of raw materials and finished products entailed much going and coming of people who earned their living backpacking tump-lines. The network of lakes in the Basin of Mexico provided easy access around the central valley, but there was no waterway that could be used to reach Teotihuacán, and no beasts of burden.

All routes led to the marketplace—the heart of the city. The group of structures directly west of the Ciudadela, across the Avenue of the

Dead, has been named the Great Compound and is believed to have served as the daily marketplace, replacing an earlier one in front of the Pyramid of the Sun (R. Millon 1973). This huge secular complex is surrounded by wide streets and plazas, providing more air space than anywhere else in this busy city. A market complex such as this was vital to the proper functioning of the city. Since all members of the society—farmers, craftsmen, builders, and even religious leaders—had interdependent functions, a well-organized market served as a necessary and perfect vehicle for the distribution and exchange of goods as well as an instrument of social control (see Figure 20, p. 191). It was here that everyone could circulate on a daily basis: city and country dweller, venders and buyers, traders, pilgrims from all parts of Mesoamerica, especially from over the mountains to the east and south—people from the Gulf Coastal lowlands, Oaxaca, and the Maya area.

We have seen how Teotihuacán housed and fed its urban population, but this does not account for its great prosperity. What was the basis of its great commercial empire? One answer is probably obsidian. We will take time here to discuss some of the larger implications of this prime resource.

The study of obsidian permits us not only to appraise the tools into which it was made, but to see the functioning of exchange networks. Along with pottery, obsidian is one of the most informative objects a Mesoamerican archaeologist can find. This black volcanic glass, found only in highland areas of volcanism, is formed by rapid cooling of igneous ejecta and has the advantages of being durable, datable by modern techniques, and easily transported. With practice it can produce a very sharp cutting edge and was the favorite knife of Mesoamericans since the earliest tool found with the Iztapan mammoth (see p. 29). Although obsidian looks black, when a thin flake or transparent edge of obsidian is held to the light, it proves to be green or gray, and it may be streaked, cloudy, or have spots. Still another variety is reddish-brown in color from an as yet unidentified source and was exploited on a small scale in Classic times (Moholy-Nagy 1975). By trace analysis studies, a number of sources in highland Guatemala and Mexico have been identified and it is now possible to locate the place of origin of many obsidian artifacts. For example, the great hill of obsidian near Pachuca, Hidalgo (which fairly glistens when seen just after a rain) is the only known source of green obsidian. Gray is far more common, and therefore less precious, with at least 15 sources (Nelson *et al.* 1977) (Map 8). Some sources provided a better quality raw material than others. Guadalupe Victoria's obsidian, for example, was of rather poor quality, being unusually brittle and hard to work, and so was less in demand.

Obsidian has already been mentioned with some frequency as being one of the earliest traded goods, but it is during the Classic period that

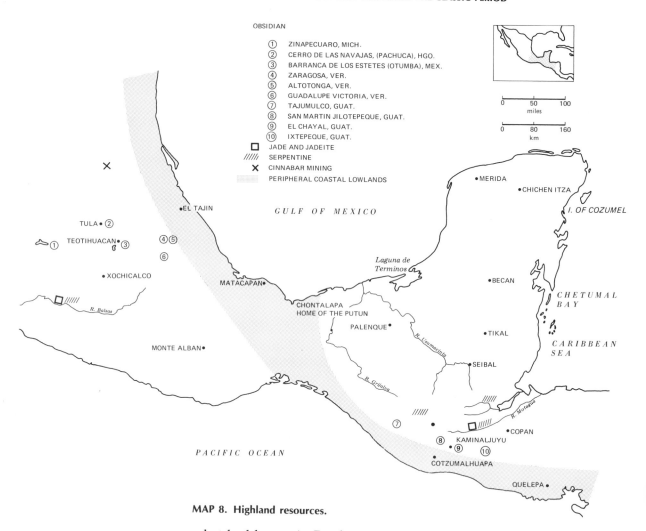

OBSIDIAN

① ZINAPECUARO, MICH.
② CERRO DE LAS NAVAJAS, (PACHUCA), HGO.
③ BARRANCA DE LOS ESTETES (OTUMBA), MEX.
④ ZARAGOSA, VER.
⑤ ALTOTONGA, VER.
⑥ GUADALUPE VICTORIA, VER.
⑦ TAJUMULCO, GUAT.
⑧ SAN MARTIN JILOTEPEQUE, GUAT.
⑨ EL CHAYAL, GUAT.
⑩ IXTEPEQUE, GUAT.
☐ JADE AND JADEITE
///// SERPENTINE
✕ CINNABAR MINING
▨ PERIPHERAL COASTAL LOWLANDS

MAP 8. Highland resources.

what had begun in Preclassic times as an exchange system was transformed into a major industry.

In the case of Teotihuacán, bear in mind that sources of green and gray obsidian were only 50 and 22 km away. In the Late Preclassic period (Patlachique) the Old City of Teotihuacán used large quantities of points and knives of gray obsidian. By the Tlamimilolpa phase, numerous workshops near the Great Compound produced exclusively green blades, a very successful commercial enterprise suggesting the takeover and incorporation of the Pachuca obsidian mines into the network. After the decline of the city, it is significant that gray obsidian was once more used, implying the breakdown of the Tepeapulco network, which did not operate again on a large scale until later Toltec times.

The Tepeapulco obsidian industry just mentioned is believed to date from Late Preclassic times and, with the exception of the hiatus after the fall of Teotihuacán, remained a major commercial enterprise until the Conquest and even into the Colonial period (Charlton 1978). Obsidian was taken in the form of cores and blanks from the source areas of Cerro de las Navajas (Pachuca), Barranca de los Estetes (Otumba), Paredón, and Tulancingo to Tepeapulco where factory workshops have been identified by heavy concentrations of obsidian in the form of unused and unretouched flakes, broken tools, and the near absence of cores.

The beginning of the line was extraction of the raw material from Otumba, Pachuca, Tulancingo, and Paredón (Map 7). At the quarries shallow pits are found with obsidian debris where cores and tool blanks were formed. These partially prepared tools were then carried, or in the case of Paredón taken by boat across Lake Tecocomulco, along natural routes for foot travel to Tepeapulco for final production and redistribution. Both this site and Huapalcalco in the Meztitlán Valley are well located at natural exits to the coast and undoubtedly their situation helped regulate the trade. Redistribution probably centered around Calpulalpan, a gateway center located at the beginning of routes to the southern lowlands via Tlaxcala (what García Cook, 1974, calls the Teotihuacán Corridor). Calpulalpan is directly reached from Teotihuacán by starting out at the East Avenue and following the natural drainage system and ridge tops, marked by a line of ancient remains, through a pass to the east. Charlton has walked all these routes and reports finding Thin Orange pottery and small sites along the way.

The efficient operation of this commercial enterprise and its strict control by Teotihuacán reveals a degree of sophistication previously undetected. It is interesting to note that although the city had workshops within its confines, the main industrial center was located away from the urban development itself.

It now seems likely that the trade networks and market system in Teotihuacán proper and the Basin of Mexico functioned separately from the Tepeapulco industry. The latter's production may have been destined exclusively for export to regional and long-distance markets (Carlton n.d.). Calpulalpan probably functioned as a major control point for both raw materials moving in and finished products moving out of the city. Obsidian was one important export. As we will see Thin Orange pottery vessels were another. The complex organization of the Tepeapulco obsidian enterprise is an example of how Teotihuacán managed and controlled its great commercial empire.

Religion and Art

Religion was seemingly the key factor in the integration of Teotihuacán society. One has only to see the clusters of temple-pyramids, shrines, altars, and quantities of smaller temple mounds to realize how religion dominated the lives of these people. Religious leaders at the same time may have been the supreme rulers, combining the powers of church and state. As an intellectual elite, the priest–scholars were able to interpret the Tonalpohualli, calculate the ever-recurring cycles, recite the procession of days and months, and issue instructions for forthcoming events (Caso 1967).

Teotihuacán artisans turned out beautiful pottery in great variety but preferred polished monochromes to the multicolored vessels of their ancestors and Maya contemporaries. Having developed from the local Preclassic tradition, many ceramic features continued to be used, but it is the changes and innovations that help identify a particular period of development. The four phases of Classic Teotihuacán are more easily distinguished in the ceramics than in the architecture or in settlement patterns.

Figurines continued in popularity but were made in distinctive Teotihuacán styles, and after the Late Tlamimilolpa phase, about A.D. 400, they were turned out by molds (see Plate 9-a, p. 252). The "portrait" figurine is a very standardized, easily recognized type. In addition to a triangular-shaped face, there is usually a depression in the top of the head. Articulated figurines with movable limbs were another innovation (see Plate 9-b). Although many fragments have been recovered, complete figures are rare. Through the studies of figurines and vessel decorations, in addition to Huehuéteotl, the old fire god, two more deities have been identified: the fat god, a deity represented with his eyes closed, who may have been associated with a second god, Xipe Totec, god of springtime. The latter is also called the masked god, and was honored by a priest wearing a flayed human skin, symbolizing the new vegetation covering the old. The cult of Xipe is believed to have had its origin in the Guerrero or Oaxaca region (Plate 7-e) (Caso and Bernal 1952).

During the Tlamimilolpa phase, contact was close with Gulf Coast cultures, and toward A.D. 450 Maya influence can be recognized. These contacts are evident in both form and style of ceramics as well as in the mural paintings. The Tajín-style scroll, appliqué ornamentation, and the first plano-relief decoration appear on vases, and these elements are continued and more fully elaborated in the great phase that followed. The lidded cylindrical tripod, Teotihuacán's single most distinguished pot, became popular at this time. It was decorated by painting, plano relief, fresco, incising, or was simply burnished. This pottery form has been called the hallmark of Teotihuacán, and was produced in quantity and traded widely. In the great Xolalpan phase, potters took this form and carved intricate designs in plano relief that were set off by combinations of colors and textures (Figure 22-g). Symbolism and life-figure styles replaced the Tajín scroll, and resist painting became more popular.

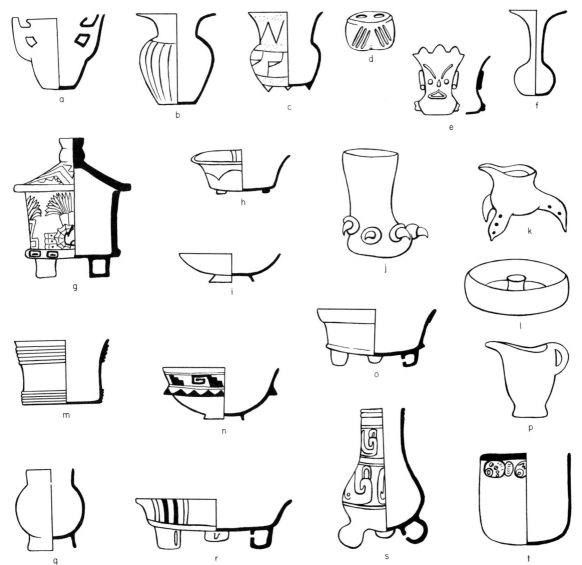

FIGURE 22. Classic-period pottery: (a) black-ware jar with two spouts, Teotihuacán (Xolalpan); (b) black incised jar, Teotihuacán (Xolalpan); (c) polychrome vessel with three tiny solid supports, Teotihuacán (Xolalpan); (d) *candelero* (incense burner); (e) so-called "Tlaloc" vase, Teotihuacán (Tlamimilolpa); (f) *florero* form, Teotihuacán (Xolalpan); (g) painted cylindrical tripod with lid, Teotihuacán (Xolalpan); (h) incised brown tripod bowl, Teotihuacán (Xolalpan); (i) Thin Orange bowl, annular ring base, Teotihuacán (Tlamimilolpa); (j) gray-ware vessel in the form of a jaguar foot, Monte Albán IIIa; (k) gray-ware spouted tripod cup, Monte Albán IIIa; (l) bowl with interior cup, incense burner (?), Monte Albán IIIa; (m) cylindrical vessel with moldings, Cerro de las Mesas II; (n) polychrome basal-flanged bowl, Early Classic, Copán; (o) negative-painted black tripod bowl, basal molding, hollow cylindrical feet with a square vent on the inner side, Early Classic, Nebaj, Guatemala; (p) brown-ware Tzakol pitcher, Kaminaljuyú; (q) vessel with ring stand, Uxmal; (r) polychrome Tepeu tripod, Uaxactún; (s) Fine Orange Tepeu tripod, Chichén Itzá; (t) Polychrome Tepeu vessel banded by glyphs, Zaculeu. (From the following sources: a, b, c, g, Piña Chan 1960; d, e, f, h, i, Sejourné 1966; j, l, Caso and Bernal 1952; k, Caso and Bernal 1965, r, s, Smith and Gifford 1965, t, Rands and Smith 1965, all copyright © 1965 by the University of Texas Press; m, reproduced by permission of the Smithsonian Institution from *Smithsonian Institution Bureau of American Ethnology Bulletin 141 (Ceramic Stratigraphy at Cerro de las Mesos, Veracruz, Mexico)*, by Philip Drucker: Fig. 12r, Washington, D.C.: Government Printing Office, 1943; n, Longyear 1952; o, Smith and Kidder 1951; p, Kidder, Jennings, and Shook 1946; q, Ruz Lhuillier 1963.)

PLATE 7. Classic-period pottery.

a. Large orange jar with stamped decoration. Teotihuacán, Metepec. Height: 20 cm. (Courtesy of the Museo Nacional de Antropología, Mexico.)

b. Black-brown vessel with excised and incised decoration, Teotihuacán, Late Tlamimilolpa. Height: 20 cm. (Courtesy of the Museo de Antropología, Mexico.)

c. Thin Orange effigy vessel: Early Classic Teotihuacán type. Toluca, State of Mexico. Height: 31 cm. (Courtesy of the Museum of the American Indian, Heye Foundation, N.Y. [16/6067].)

d. Cylindrical tripod vessel with incised panel decoration. Lid has modeled parrot at apex, Kaminaljuyú, Guatemala: Esperanza phase. Height: 35 cm. (Courtesy of the Museum of the American Indian, Heye Foundation, N.Y. [16/6235].)

e. Life-size cerámic sculpture representing Xipe Totec, who holds a jaguar-paw vessel of Monte Albán type in his right hand: Teotihuacán culture. Height: 122 cm. (Courtesy of the Museo Nacional de Antropología, Mexico.)

f. Funerary urn representing goddess "13 Serpent," Monte Albán III. Height: 50 cm. (Courtesy of the Museo Nacional de Antropología, Mexico.)

g. Grey-ware funerary urn representing the god Cocijo, who wears a mouth mask with forked serpent tongue, Monte Albán IIIA. Height: 48 cm. (Courtesy of the Museum of the American Indian, Heye Foundation, N.Y. [23/5554].)

h. Maya cylindrical vessel of Tepeu phase. Polychrome figure and band of hieroglyphs. Height: 17 cm. (Courtesy of the Metropolitan Museum of Art, The Michael C. Rockefeller Memorial Collection of Primitive Art, Gift of Nelson A. Rockefeller 1967.)

i. Black incised bowl with basal flange, jaguar lid, Holmul, Guatemala: Early Classic Maya. Height: 24 cm. (Courtesy of the Peabody Museum, Harvard University, copyright by the President and Fellows of Harvard College.)

j. *Incensario* typical of Middle Classic Teotihuacán with hour-glass-shaped base and ornate lid. Height: 60 cm. (Courtesy of the Instituto Nacional de Antropología e Historia, Mexico.)

211

Thin Orange pottery is a very distinctive fine-paste ware whose production and distribution were controlled by Teotihuacán. Its enigmatic history has been the subject of investigation ever since it caught Seler's eye in 1915. Evelyn Rattray, as a ceramic specialist of R. Millon's Teotihuacán team, has reviewed the whole development of Thin Orange (Rattray 1980). It is one of the best markers for Teotihuacán, as it came and went along with the city's fortunes (Plate 7-c).

Teotihuacán was undoubtedly the center of distribution but the source of clay has yet to be determined. Because it is such a distinctive orange ware, one would suppose its place of manufacture would not be difficult to identify. In fact, this location is growing more elusive. Recent neutron activation analysis has shown that the examples from Teotihuacán, Kaminaljuyú, Copán, and El Salvador have a single origin. The often-cited area of Ixcaquixtla in southern Puebla is not the source, nor is Acatlán or Huehuetlán, Puebla, nor the Gulf Coast, the clays of which have now all been analyzed.

Production probably took place in Teotihuacán itself. Rattray suggests clay could have been brought in during late times as raw material, and vessels produced in the city; or pottery such as the very characteristic bowl with annular base (Figure 22-i) could have been made outside, stacked in a basket, and brought in by tump-line for final decoration and distribution. It is estimated that a man could easily carry 300 pots for a long distance this way. We know too that only the finest examples were exported, probably passing to the east through Calpulalpan for redistribution over great distances. When Teotihuacán collapsed as an urban center, Thin Orange was no longer produced.

Numerous masks of green stone, serpentine, onyx, and obsidian, sometimes encrusted with turquoise mosaic or having inlaid eyes of cut shell and obsidian, are attributed to Classic Teotihuacán (see Plate 8-e, p. 246). Oddly enough, not one of these masks has been found *in situ*, and it is therefore impossible to date them with any accuracy, or in some cases to be certain of their authenticity. Thin clay masks found in the household rubbish of Yayahuala and Tetitla are believed by Séjourné (1966) to have been tied to the wrapped and bundled deceased before cremation.

The art of Teotihuacán, which is profoundly religious, is manifested in new forms and media. When compared with the much earlier Olmec civilization, one is surprised that Teotihuacán has produced so little stone carving. It has been suggested by way of explanation that decoration of buildings and temples may have been in such demand that the more rapid technique of painting was substituted for the slower and more painstaking one of stone sculpting and carving. The Teotihuacán paintings have been the subject of considerable study (Kubler 1975; Miller 1973a; C. Millon 1966; Pasztory 1974, 1976a; Quirarte 1973). Murals are found in temples, palaces, public buildings, shrines, and even private dwellings (Photos 27 and 28).

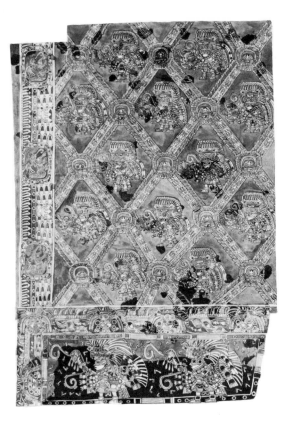

PHOTO 27. Mural from Atetelco patio, Teotihuacán. Repetitious designs show both profile and frontal views of a priest (?). Patterns were possibly used here. Figures are sometimes cut off in a corner like unmatched wallpaper. (Courtesy of the Instituto Nacional de Antropología e Historia, Mexico.)

PHOTO 28. Tlalocan mural paintings from Tepantitla, Teotihuacán. The rectangles at the lower edge of the picture across the river are thought to represent irrigated fields. (Courtesy of the Instituto Nacional de Antropología e Historia, Mexico.)

The quality of the workmanship as well as the subject matter vary even in the same house. Pasztory thinks the mural painters may have constituted a kind of guild. Walls were first prepared by applying a thin layer of clay over which another layer of lime mixed with fine quartz sand was spread. A red wash was then applied and figures were outlined in black or red. Blues and greens were added last of all and, being already too dry, were the first to flake off. A final burnish was achieved by rubbing the whole surface with a hard stone (Pasztory 1976a).

The art style is very austere and almost monotonous in its overwhelming liturgic character, with the notable exception of the Tlalocan murals at Tepantitla, which depict little figures dancing, singing, and frolicking about (Photo 28). Of particular interest in this scene is the border beneath the river, interpreted as representing irrigated fields. With few exceptions, whether the painted object is a mural or a pottery vessel, the theme is religious ritual or prayer, usually related to agricultural fertility. The common motifs of flowers, butterflies, fish, and quetzal birds are related in some way to a god or religious cult.

The lively Tepantitla mural just mentioned shows a ball game in progress, which is of some interest since no ball courts as such have been found. In the painting the limits of the court are marked by some kind of end-marker or post, and the game is being played using a bat, a different form of the usual Mesoamerican game. A composite stela from La Ventilla interpreted by Aveleyra (1963) as being such a ball-game marker furnishes supporting evidence of this sport among the Teotihuacanos (see Plate 8-i, p. 247). The hip-ball game is depicted on another wall at Tepantitla (Pasztory 1972). The ball game and courts are discussed elsewhere (see pp. 249–250) but the ball-game complex is believed to be an innovation of the Veracruz people and its presence at Teotihuacán reflects this contact.

There are different interpretations of Teotihuacán mural art. Kubler cautions against identifying Teotihuacán figures with Postclassic deities and Pasztory warns us not to consider every goggle-eyed representation a Tlaloc rain deity.

There are so many Tlalocs all over Mesoamerica that we are indebted to the art historians for sorting them out for us (C. Millon 1973; Pasztory 1974, 1979). To digress for a moment let us look at some of these different representations; there seem to be at least four. One is *the* exclusive rain deity represented with crocodilian features, perhaps related to Izapa art, intimately associated with fertility, water, water lilies, and often shown with his rainmaking equipment, a vessel and staff. A second Tlaloc, a god of water and of the underworld, has jaguar features and net symbols. He can be related to Cocijo at Monte Albán and perhaps ultimately back to Olmec art. A third Tlaloc combines the features of both the jaguar and rain with a warrior cult and special headdress; the headdress was first identified by C. Millon (1973) as representing a symbol of a high-status group. This Tlaloc (Pasztory's Tlaloc "B," 1974) has a long bifurcated tongue, fangs, and the tasseled headdress. In addition to fertility and water, he is associated with weapons and war. It is his face that appears on the shields of warriors on Tikal's Stela 31 (see Plate 10-d, p. 289). He is found more often on foreign soil than at Teotihuacán which suggests his connection with a ruling dynasty or he may even be a patron deity of Teotihuacán. These Tlalocs are found in art of the fifth to seventh centuries, but, with the fall of Teotihuacán, they too disappear.

Still another Tlaloc follows in the seventh and eighth centuries, also of Teotihuacán derivation and found in political and dynastic contexts. Easiest of all to identify, this Tlaloc has the year-sign, usually on his headdress. This one has retained the attributes of the rain deity with crocodilian features and often occurs in Late Classic and Postclassic Maya contexts. His distribution includes Xochicalco, Horcones, Tikal, Bonampak, Piedras Negras, Aguateca, Dos Pilas, Yaxchilán, Copán, and Uxmal. At Tula, Hidalgo, the Toltec capital, two stelae with bas-relief warrior figures wear headdresses with this Tlaloc and year-sign, and there is even one example on a later Aztec *chacmool*. It is little wonder that Davies (1977) calls Teotihuacán the city of Tlaloc, for he and his symbols are everywhere.

Although the glyphs at Teotihuacán have led to many opinions, an in-depth study has never been made. Glyphs appear on pottery as well as in the murals, apparently at random, but we cannot be sure. Place names at Teotihuacán have not been identified, nor anything corresponding to the Maya emblem glyphs. The Teotihuacanos were in touch with both the Zapotecs and the Maya and surely saw their writing and understood the principle behind it. The only glyphs we can understand seem to relate to the calendar (Pasztory 1976a).

The truly great mural paintings are those from Tepantitla, Tetitla, the Zacuala Palace, and Teopancaxco. They not only help us identify the prominent gods of the Teotihuacán pantheon but also provide information about distant contacts.

In the murals we see evidence of relationships with Oaxaca, the Gulf Coast, and both highland and lowland Maya areas. The "Pinturas Realistas" show a "long-nosed deity," certainly a stranger to Teotihuacán. These paintings portray foreigners such as Mayoid peoples with distinctive slanted eyes, body paint, masks, and dress. The bands of glyphs placed in a row are clearly Maya inspired. Gradually a trend toward painting in tones of red became widespread all over the city, along with a great predilection for detail. Finally, in the Late Classic period, armed deities and priests appear for the first time along with warriors, shields, spears, and *atlatls*. Style changes occurred, and motifs varied according to period, but one figure is recurrent, Quetzalcóatl, the feathered-serpent deity who adjusted to each new phase and survived the catastrophe that finally engulfed Teotihuacán.

The evolution of mural painting shows a gradual trend away from religious ritual to militarism and glorification of the warrior. This is more subtle than it sounds for one has to learn how darts and *atlatls* are represented. To the uninitiated a priest and a warrior may look alike. Sex is indicated only by clothing, so the sex of the Tepantitla figures remains an enigma.

Warfare and Expansion

For many years the Classic period in Mesoamerica was envisioned as a time of complete peace and harmony. Now this concept of Classic life is obsolete. After A.D. 500 a trend away from purely religious symbolism toward individual glorification and warfare can be seen at Teotihuacán in the carved reliefs and Metepec figurines as well as in pottery, murals, and sculpture (Kubler 1967; C. Millon 1966). Weapons that might have been used against either man or beast include clubs, knives edged with obsidian, axes, large knives, *atlatls*, slings, harpoons, and, after A.D. 500, bows and arrows. A warrior priest in the Tepantitla fresco holds a bunch of arrows in one hand and a tiger claw in the other. The drops of liquid often associated with drawings of weapons or knives could represent water, but blood is a more likely possibility. A figure on one pottery lid represents a warrior with a shield and *atlatl*. Among the clay figurines we find helmets to protect the head and both round and rectangular shields. Some figurines wear a garment that suggests the padded cotton shirts worn by later Aztec warriors.

Although no battle scenes, sacrificial victims, or prisoners are represented in the murals, for narrative scenes would be out of character at Teotihuacán, the finds mentioned before indicate that the Classic years were not spent exclusively in pious devotion to theocratic pursuits. Warfare is proving to be a long, deep-rooted tradition.

Thus far we have been concerned with the growth and socioeconomic organization of the city and have made mention of foreigners only in passing. So extensive is the influence of Teotihuacán in other areas that it is tempting to speak of an empire. However, only at Kaminaljuyú in the Guatemalan Valley is there convincing evidence of actual colonization by the Teotihuacanos, with perhaps way stations along the route such as Matacapan. There were also special groups sent out to colonize and exploit mineral resources. It seems likely that Teotihuacán's culture was spread by merchants and it would be more accurate to speak of a commercial empire. Its products were in great demand, especially finished obsidian tools, fine quality pottery, which was gorgeously and expertly crafted and decorated, figurines, and minor crafts. The architectural *talud–tablero* style was widely copied and adapted regionally. Probably the greatest and most lasting impact was made in the fields of art and iconography.

The early Middle Classic years saw a tremendous expansion of Teotihuacán influence. We have seen evidence of centralized authority in the city but we do not know the exact nature of the power structure. Religion was a key integrating force and the city authorities could well have combined religious and civic duties, or had a dual system of government. The priests of the main temples must have belonged to the top-ranking social group. With time, certainly by the Metepec phase, the secular forces appear to be equally strong. Whatever the combination, the system was efficient and worked remarkably well for several hundred years.

Essential to the continuing prosperity was long-distance trade operated by professional traders whom we imagine to be organized like the later Aztec *pochteca* (see p. 453). These were armed representatives of the state and one may wonder how peacefully trade relationships were initiated and maintained. Was there a choice? It is usually felt that the great expansion of Teotihuacán in the early Middle Classic was accomplished at least in part by military persuasion (R. Millon 1976).

Archaeological evidence of militarism is largely confined to those representations just mentioned for the Metepec phase. As time began running out, the Teotihuacanos were put on the defensive. Toward the very end of Metepec walls were added to the upper part of the Ciudadela. By then it was already too late.

Outsiders in the City

The Oaxaqueños had established a district or barrio of their own in very early times west of the city. They and their descendants continued living in this same area, retaining ties to Oaxaca while adopting much of Teotihuacán's way of life. Several hundred years later (A.D. 400) in the Tlamimilolpa phase, both fine ceremonial pottery and every-day wares from Oaxaca were still being used in this barrio. A typical Zapotec stone-lined tomb with antechamber dates to the seventh century A.D. An old building stone from Teotihuacán had been reused, put in the wall, and the number 9 carved on it in Zapotec style. No one questions that it was carved in Teotihuacán, for the stone weighs 600 pounds. A close relationship with Oaxaca lasting 300–400 years is thus documented. People from the Gulf Coast and the Maya area preferred to live in the Merchants' Barrio to the east which would have been closest to their point of entry into the city. There was, however, no other colony as permanent or distinctive as that from Oaxaca.

Xolalpan and Metepec remains provide ample evidence of nonlocal traits at Teotihuacán. From Veracruz came the cult of the ball game, recorded in the Tepantitla murals, the Ventilla ball-court marker, stone yokes, and figurines. A particular double-scroll motif, the hallmark of Tajín, is prominently displayed on pottery and on the Ventilla ball-court marker (see Plate 8-i, p. 247). We now have proof by neutron activation analysis that the Lustrous Ware at Teotihuacán was made at Tajín (Rattray 1978). Thin Orange pottery, another Classic-period indicator, is closely associated with Teotihuacán, which handled its distribution. As has been noted, the source of the clay is still undetermined. Other fine-paste wares have been traced to Los Tuxtlas, Veracruz, and the Huasteca. A Thin Slate ware in late Xolalpan and Metepec phases came from Yucatán.

Influences from Izapa and early Classic Maya are seen in the murals: a profile of a priest-figure seated cross-legged, Maya personages with glyphs at Tetitla, other priest-figures carrying bags of incense before them, the presence of the quetzal bird, water drops, isolated human eyes are all typically Maya elements. The glyphs may be Maya inspired but could also represent influence from Veracruz, Xochicalco, or Monte Albán. They are not a local tradition.

It seems clear that Teotihuacán grew out of the earlier Preclassic cultural traditions of central highland Mexico. Pottery styles were largely a continuation of Basin of Mexico types and, while there is no precedent for the *talud–tablero* style in the Basin, it has earlier antecedents in northern Tlaxcala. It will be remembered that extensive trade networks had been highly developed at an early time, obsidian being one of the products in constant demand. The symbiotic relationships between highland and lowland areas that were significant throughout Mesoamerica's cultural development were clearly operating in the Classic period. The spectacular rise of Middle Classic Teotihuacán was accompanied by a renewal or revitalization of the ancient Preclassic trade mechanism. Once communications were established and trade began to flow, the system would tend to perpetuate itself, demanding greater political expansion to assure a continual market for exports as well as a source of foreign products. Although Teotihuacán dealt mainly with the Peripheral Coastal Lowlands and the Maya, it also opened up extensive relationships to the north and west in its quest for turquoise and mineral resources.

External Affairs During the Classic period, the frontier of Mesoamerica was pushed northward, for during these years rainfall was more plentiful and farmers extended their cultivation accordingly. Thus along the eastern foothills of the Sierra Madre Occidental lay a corridor-like area inhabited by sedentary farmers that extended north through the states of Zacatecas and Durango to the southern boundary of Chihuahua. This narrow region of cultivation, limited on the west by the juniper, pine, and oak forests of the foothills and by the great interior desert plateau on the east, has been found to have a great number of archaeological remains consisting of fortresses combined with ceremonial centers. The fortified settlements are usually situated on hilltops with village–farming communities occupying terraces and the alluvial plains in the valleys below. These remains are evidence of the Chalchihuites culture (J.C. Kelley 1971).

This culture is known from a number of sites that stretch from La Quemada and Alta Vista as far north as Zape in northern Durango, all of which share similar Mesoamerican traits. These first appear in the Canutillo phase (A.D. 1–250) when the ball game and court were introduced. Teotihuacán was probably searching for turquoise at this time.

Thereafter another invasion, believed to be of Teotihuacanos, introduced around A.D. 250 (Alta Vista phase) formal ceremonial centers with buildings grouped around plazas, cut-stone and adobe-brick architecture, colonnaded halls, and pyramids, accompanied by the cults of the plumed serpent and Tlaloc, with characteristic Mesoamerican features such as priesthoods, heart sacrifice, and speech scrolls. Mesoamerican culture had arrived in an area previously devoid of elite centers.

The Teotihuacanos are believed to have been lured north by deposits of jadeite, turquoise, hematite, and flint. Deep pits and tunnels several kilometers long have debris taluses identified as mining operations. The defensible hilltop or mountain sites protected the commercial enterprise as well as the frontier, for there is evidence of perpetual conflict with the nomadic Chichimecs. Even so, mining operations were extensive. Not only was the Chalchihuites region exploited, but expeditionary trips were made as far north as Cerrillos, north central New Mexico, for chemical turquoise from that area is found at Alta Vista sites. This means that Mesoamericans were in the Southwest during the Basketmaker culture. A second source of turquoise, one within Mexico, was the Concepción del Oro region on the Coahuila–Zacatecas border (see Map 7, p. 188). Here there were small natural outcrops of turquoise, and exploitation was always solely by expeditionary groups, not colonizers (Weigand, Harbottle, and Sayre 1977).

The Alta Vista mines were exploited until A.D. 500 and then, upon the withdrawal of Teotihuacán, prosperity ended; the mines closed. Population dropped rapidly as people left for northwestern Durango to take up residence at the Schroeder site. Here too a ball court was built, but it looks very unlike that at Alta Vista. It is from Schroeder that the ball-game complex is thought to have been transmitted to the Hohokam culture of the southwestern United States between A.D. 500–700. The withdrawal of Teotihuacán around A.D. 500 did not create major repercussions, and the Chalchihuites culture was carried on by other centers that continued to thrive. The area maintained its contacts with the Southwest, and the Cerrillos turquoise continued to flow south.

Teotihuacán's main interest was mining, because, in addition to the operation at Alta Vista, exploitation of cinnabar deposits in northern

Querétaro were also undertaken. These mines had been known and exploited long before by the Olmecs, but the most intensive mining operations were carried out toward the end of the Middle Classic period. Judging from pottery and stone yokes recovered at the site, both Teotihuacanos and central Veracruz groups were there. We do not know how the mines were controlled, but the objective was cinnabar, one of the special commodities prized for decorating fine pottery and deemed necessary for ritual. It was also the source of red paint for pyramids and elite residences.

From Langenscheidt's reconstruction of the mining operation, this would have been a hard way to earn a living. The rock face of the mountain was attacked with hammers of diorite or andesite. Attrition eventually created great cavities, actual pits, rooms, and galleries. Where possible, hard wooden wedges were driven into cracks to break off fractured pieces of rock. The debris was allowed to accumulate, which raised the level of the floor and permitted the miners to get at the roof. Remains of baskets and cordage indicate how the stone was removed to be subsequently pulverized and subjected to a flotation process. The Querétaro mines have been exploited periodically since 300 B.C. (?) and, although deposits are not yet exhausted, the destruction of a round temple, terraces, and walls near the face of the mountain are rather thorough. It is possible, although undocumented, that native mercury was also exploited (Langenscheidt 1970).

To the west, an area still very inadequately known, Teotihuacán-style stone carvings, vessel shapes, and Thin Orange pottery are found sporadically in the states of Michoacán, Jalisco, Nayarit, and Colima. Ancient commercial transactions are usually credited with the spread of these portable objects throughout the west. However an increasing number of structures with talud–tablero-style architecture are being reported, which suggests a more substantial contact. At Ixtepete on the outskirts of Guadalajara, Jalisco (Map 7, p. 188), a structure of this form is made of large adobes and painted white. Others are reported from this same Atemajoc Valley. Usually considered to be of Classic date, Schöndube and Galván (1978) feel the Ixtepete structure to be later.

The most convincing evidence of direct Teotihuacán influence is found in the Etzatlán region of Jalisco where there was actual colonization from central Mexico. This is the area mentioned in Chapter 4 with Preclassic mound circles and tombs in large mounds at Ahualulco. About A.D. 150–200 tomb construction ended, coinciding with the arrival of Teotihuacán groups. Weigand (1974) compares the situation to the colonization in the north of Alta Vista, Zacatecas. Closeby are extensive beds of turquoise, red obsidian, opaque gray obsidian, agates, and good basalt material for metates. It is not at all unlikely that the Teotihuacanos were searching out such resources at this time. Teotihuacán pottery including Thin Orange suddenly appears, and the entire region is integrated and centralized at Ahualulco, which became the ceremonial–civic capital of the area.

Excavations by Piña Chan in Michoacán have exposed Teotihuacán *talud–tablero* architecture on huge platforms and on an I-shaped ball court at Tingambato near Uruapan (Photos 29 and 30). No central Mexican ceramics have been recovered to date. Tingambato is chronologically placed between A.D. 500–1000.

It was during the late Middle Classic period that extraordinary changes took place in Nayarit at the site of Amapa near the mouth of the Río Grande de Santiago. It will be recalled that there were considerable Preclassic remains here (Gavilán and Amapa phases). Following a hiatus (A.D. 400–600), Amapa suddenly looks very Mesoamerican with mounds grouped around plazas oriented to the cardinal directions

PHOTO 29. Large platform supporting a series of rooms. Construction in *talud–tablero* style of Teotihuacán. Tingambato, Michoacán. (Courtesy of Román Piña Chan.)

PHOTO 30. Narrow end-zone of ball court, constructed in *talud–tablero* style. Tingambato, Michoacán. (Courtesy of Román Piña Chan.)

and some cut stone used in stairways and on trim of buildings. Pottery became very elaborate with polychrome and engraved decorations. Special cemeteries were initiated in which the dead were placed in a seated position surrounded by many grave goods and metal artifacts (Meighan 1976a).

The appearance of metal here is one of the earliest on record, and not just a single find but in abundance: copper awls, needles, tweezers and knives, rings, beads, bracelets, but most common of all were copper bells which were placed in graves. Documented finds of metallurgy in Mesoamerica are all of Postclassic date with the exception of a few Late Classic pieces traded to the Maya area from Central America (Bray 1977b). Objects of gold, never as abundant in Mesoamerica as copper, are largely confined to the Late Postclassic period. The abundance of metal on the west coast suggests an introduction from northern Peru or Ecuador around A.D. 800–900 (Meighan 1976b). It appears in quantity, in a variety of forms, full-blown, with no sign of local smelting

operations, and continues on through the following Izcuintla phase
(A.D. 1000–1300).

At present it seems that Teotihuacán made some attempts to exploit
mineral resources in Jalisco and in doing so extended the sphere of
Mesoamerican influence westward. Although it is not Teotihuacán presence that is found in Nayarit, the radical architectural innovations that
took place there after A.D. 600 were typically Mesoamerican. They were
of such lasting effect that they continued until the Conquest.

Teotihuacán influence was more strongly felt on the coast of Guerrero where C. F. Brush (1969), E. S. Brush (1968), and G. Ekholm
(1948), reported Teotihuacán-type pottery and mold-made figurines.
Even the unspectacular but highly characteristic *candelero* (see Figure
22-d, p. 209), cylindrical tripods, and figurines found their way down
to the Pacific Coast. The relationship seems to have been broken off
abruptly, however, to be replaced by one with a more Maya-type flavor.
This latter was not limited to the coast, for a double-corbelled Maya
vault roofed a tomb at Oztotitlán in the northern Río Balsas. Large
Maya-like stone sculptures are also reported in the area (Moedano 1948).
Further west in the Middle Balsas Valley both Teotihuacán and Maya
influences are found in the region of Huetamo, Michoacán (see Map
5, p. 113). A variation of the *talud–tablero* architecture, resembling that
of Xochicalco with the flaring cornice, along with sculptured Maya-like
stelae are reported. Guerrero and the eastern Tierra Caliente of Michoacán are known only from very spotty data such as these, but what
there is indicates that the Río Balsas drainage, though not densely
populated, was well traveled.

Many objects showing Teotihuacán influence are known to come
from the upper Balsas River basin near Mezcala, again exposed by
looters rather than scientific explorations. Because of their style, these
Mezcala stone artifacts have been tentatively placed in an Early Classic
context, but some may prove to be earlier. Stone vessels; masks; human
and animal figures; tools such as axes, chisels, and punches; and curious
models of columned temples in a severe and rectilinear style are typical
(Plate 8-a, b, p. 246). Strangely enough, more Teotihuacán masks come
from Guerrero and Puebla than from Teotihuacán itself, and the Guerrero examples are too numerous to be explained by trade alone. Preferred stones were serpentine, jadeite, andesite, white nephrite, quartz,
turquoise, chalcedony, amethyst, garnet, alabaster, soapstone, and
diorite. Having these natural resources at hand, Guerrero became a
major production center. Pottery of Teotihuacán style is also reported,
but it did not figure as prominently as stone.

Trade routes had been well established in Preclassic days and a major
thoroughfare from Teotihuacán to the east is plotted by García Cook
and Merino (1977). Known as the Teotihuacán Corridor, it led from
Teotihuacán east to Otumba–Apan–Apizaco–Huamantla, from where

one could proceed to either the Gulf Coast or go south to Oaxaca (see Map 7, p. 188). From Tepeapulco one could also go north to Tulancingo and east to the Gulf, probably the shortest route to El Tajín. It is interesting that although Teotihuacán dominated the entire Basin of Mexico, its influence in Tlaxcala was limited to the northern part of the state. The well-known site of Cholula to the south has a paucity of Teotihuacán artifacts and cultural remains at this time, being far more heavily influenced by the Gulf cultures, particularly in the Late Middle Classic (Dumond and Muller 1972; García Cook and Trejo 1977).

The Peripheral Coastal Lowlands were the geographical link between highland central Mexico and the Maya. These regions were of primary interest for Teotihuacán, who gazed down on the rich rubber and cacao-producing regions with a greedy eye.

And down they went. Their artifacts are liberally distributed throughout central and southern Veracruz and northern Tabasco. Matacapan looks like a small Teotihuacán colony (Map 7). Cerro de las Mesas, though perhaps never a colony, kept in close contact until A.D. 550. On the southern side of the Peripheral Coastal Lowlands there are thousands of cylindrical tripods, Teotihuacán-style, found near Escuintla; this region was the gate into the Valley of Guatemala, where a Middle Classic port-of-trade operated. The Kaminaljuyú excavations there revealed such a surprisingly strong Teotihuacán presence that foreigners are thought to have settled, married into the elite, and managed a thriving commercial enterprise while maintaining ties with their central Mexican homeland. Teotihuacanos also penetrated the Petén, perhaps marrying into the ruling lineage at Tikal. At Altun Há and Becán, Teotihuacán obsidian has been found in quantity. Teotihuacanoid pottery and artifacts, representations of deities, and art styles exist throughout the Maya lowlands. But actual colonization or political control were never realized there.

Oaxaca, located between the Peripheral Coastal Lowlands and central highland Mexico, was well situated for travelers going back and forth across the Isthmus. A close and special relationship existed between Monte Albán and Teotihuacán, reflected in the Oaxaca Barrio on the city's edge. At the great site of Monte Albán itself, however, Teotihuacán influence is rather subdued and there are few actual trade pieces.

The only major region not mentioned here is Yucatán, which may have had only indirect relations with Teotihuacán. As we will see, there are central Mexican traits to be found there, but the nature of the contact is not clear. They may have been diffused through the filter of the Peripheral Coastal Lowlands.

Collapse   The exact date of the fire is not known. An estimated date is around A.D. 650 at which time the northern end of the great city was set on fire with devastating results. There are no signs of warfare within the city, no evidence of outside intruders or invasion. Selective burning and looting looks like it could have been the work of well-informed malcontents. During the Late Xolalpan and Metepec phases (MH–4 to SI–1) business had never been better. The Merchants' Barrio has yielded Thin Slate and several other Yucatecan wares, Striated Ware from the Grijalva area, and various types from the Gulf region including Los Tuxtlas. Although the fire marks the catastrophe, Teotihuacán declined over decades and was not immediately abandoned. What seemed to collapse rapidly were the political system, power, prestige, and control. By the end of Metepec, A.D. 800, the city had suffered a major calamity from which it would never recover. The population was drastically reduced, the area of habitation shrank, and a general degeneration in artistic quality was the result.

Prominent in the waning Classic days were mold-made figurines with complex headdresses (see Plate 9-b, p. 252) and very ornate incense burners. Important ceramic features include annular-based bowls and imitation of Thin Orange forms, pottery stamps, and possibly the annular-based *florero*. Stamped decorations (see Plate 7-a, p. 210) and spindle-whorls are characteristic of the period. Hundreds of clay Metepec figurines depict warriors. It is surely significant that defensive walls were added to the upper part of the Ciudadela, the city's political center.

Oxtoticpac (SI–1) is a poorly known phase, which is based on pottery that postdates the collapse. It may represent small groups who moved in to live on top of the debris of the city.

The last Classic phase is called Xometla-Coyotlatelco (SI–1), the latter also being the name given to a red-on-buff decorated pottery that was made in many places. The ware is found in the Valley of Toluca, the Basin of Mexico, and large parts of the Puebla–Tlaxcala region, but is limited to central highland Mexico. The largest center of production was at Teotihuacán where 15 workshops have been located in the Old City northwest of the Pyramid of the Moon. Through the study of this postcollapse product, Rattray (n.d.) has shown how complete the destruction was, affecting religion, craft production, procurement of raw materials, long-distance trade, the colonization program—the whole state political organization was upset. Although the monopoly of the Pachuca mines was lost, an effort was made to produce tools of gray Otumba obsidian.

People still lived in the old residences at Tetitla, Atetelco Tepantitla, and Yayahuala (Rattray n.d.). There must have been serious problems and it is tempting to look with suspicion at the powerful secular groups. Another source of trouble could be any abrupt alteration in the ecology affecting water resources and distribution or food production, which would disturb the delicate balance between the demands of man and nature's resources. The role of external factors can be judged by a study of Teotihuacán's neighbors. Teotihuacán had been successfully exploiting them for years, and in the process, rival centers at Tajín, Xochicalco, and Cholula (?) grew wealthy, learned the trade, and cut into the competition, perhaps blocking access to the Teotihuacán Corridor.

About A.D. 650 the Olmeca–Xicalanca took Cholula in the Puebla Valley and established their capital at Cacaxtla. At this time there were people of Mixtec and Tajín affiliation who, in addition to the local groups, were struggling for supremacy and regional control. It is possible that they collaborated in closing the Teotihuacán Corridor (García Cook and Merino 1979). Evidence of this conflict would not leave traces at Teotihuacán, which was simply cut off from a distance. Very likely the Toltecs too can share the blame. They had settled at Tula by the eighth century and may have encroached on Teotihuacán's arable land. Diehl thinks Tula was one of the growing regional centers that eventually turned on Teotihuacán with the blessings and possible collaboration of the others (Diehl 1976).

MORELOS

Amatzinac Valley

After the lucrative Amatzinac commercial network of the Preclassic period no major regional center emerged for many years. Following 500 B.C. the presence of Ticomán pottery in eastern Morelos indicates contact with Cuicuilco in the Basin of Mexico. But as Teotihuacán grew and reached out to consolidate her power, Morelos, with its fine cotton and rich agricultural products, loomed as a desirable objective. The first signs of Teotihuacán contact are the presence of Tzacualli pottery in the Amatzinac Valley. A curious local political scene developed about this time. Two distinct chiefdoms occupied the northern and southern sectors with a kind of no man's land between. Each chiefdom had its own ceremonial center and elite residences. Smaller villages with their civic centers were scattered about, but no one lived in the dividing zone. This appears to have been an entirely peaceful arrangement and a purely local affair (Hirth 1978a).

But as Teotihuacán increased in size and power, it incorporated this eastern area of Morelos into its tributary domain. Under new outside control, the former dichotomy disappeared and local administration was concentrated around the southern chiefdom. Agriculture was intensified and rural settlements were encouraged under a system of hierarchical order: small settlements reporting to the next larger ones in a coordinated network. Thus, this sustaining hinterland of Teotihuacán was organized around one nucleated administrative center and dispersed rural hamlets. The important crop was probably cotton for the spinning industry of the great metropolis. When Teotihuacán experienced major problems after A.D. 600, a noticeable change took place in eastern Morelos. The rural settlements broke up and people moved into fewer and larger settlements, shifting again toward the north.

There a nucleated population presumably of nonfarmers consumed their own local agricultural surplus, thus reducing outside commercial activities. Other people went west, for it was around this time that Xochicalco began to be of some importance.

Forty kilometers west of the modern town of Cuernavaca is the major fortified site of Xochicalco, "Place of the House of Flowers." Xochicalco had been settled briefly and abandoned in the Late Preclassic period, and it had not shared in the Amatzinac trade of earlier days centered at Chalcatzingo. This region, although in contact with Teotihuacán in the Early Classic, never became part of its domain. A glance at the map will help keep in mind the locations of eastern and western sites in Morelos, for they have very different histories of development. Xochicalco, in contrast to the eastern valleys, is located on a steep hillside, and water was supplied from springs, lakes, and rivers.

Xochicalco

The site was important during the years A.D. 600–900, rising to prominence just as Teotihuacán faltered and fell. The construction of walls and ditches at Xochicalco suggests a growing hostility between the two centers. Xochicalco retained its independence and developed its own commercial relationships with the Valley of Mexico, Guerrero, Oaxaca, the Peripheral Coastal Lowlands, and the Maya area. Obsidian was procured from sources outside the domination of Teotihuacán.

The main group of public buildings was constructed on a steep terraced hill where it could be defended by a series of moats and walls (Sáenz 1962; Sanders 1956). The most imposing structure is a pyramid supporting remains of long walls on top (Photo 31). The profile is

PHOTO 31. Main pyramid at Xochicalco, Morelos. Feathered serpents carved in low relief adorn the *talud*. (Courtesy of the Instituto Nacional de Antropología e Historia, Mexico.)

PHOTO 32. Detail of sculptured relief of main pyramid at Xochicalco, Morelos. The seated figure shows Maya influence. (Courtesy of the Instituto Nacional de Antropología e Historia, Mexico.)

basically *talud–tablero* construction but in proportions different from those at Teotihuacán. Here the *talud* is tall and the *tablero* short. The latter contains no niches or recessed panels but is surmounted by a flaring cornice, typical of Tajín (Marquina 1951). The *talud* is faced with slabs of andesite carved in reliefs depicting feathered serpents. Their undulating bodies enclose human figures wearing elaborate animal headdresses seated in typical Maya postures (Photo 32). Some glyphs have been identified as day and year signs and are enclosed in cartouches, also Maya-style. The upper gallery has a carved frieze of warriors armed with darts and shields.

A small building complex called Structure A is located about 30 m south of the main pyramid that houses the Temple of the Stelae, named for three finely carved stone stelae found in the debris of the sanctuary (Photo 33). These magnificent monuments had been intentionally defaced and broken and were only completely assembled after archaeologists broke through the stucco floor to uncover the remaining fragments. They are carved on all four sides and constitute a set. The reliefs depict three deities (Tlaloc, the Sun God, and his wife: a fertility and moon goddess) and deal with major events in the agricultural cycle. They were erected between A.D. 600–700 as a prayer or appeal for bountiful crops. Pasztory (1976c) has demonstrated that this deity triad also characterizes the Peripheral Coastal Lowlands in the later Middle Classic period. Its presence at Xochicalco on the three stelae confirms the close ties that existed with Tajín, Bilbao, and Palenque at this time. Associated with the stelae were Teotihuacán figurines, eccentric ob-

PHOTO 33. Stelae depicting a deity triad constituting a set. Probably erected around A.D. 600 in an appeal for a good harvest. Height: 178 cm. (Courtesy of the Instituto Nacional de Antropología e Historia, Mexico.)

sidians, and shell, jade, and turquoise beads, as well as Late Classic pottery of Teotihuacán, Toltec, Mixtec, and Fine Orange types (Sáenz 1961).

Extensive terraces were so densely occupied by dwellings that they are difficult to study in terms of household units. Other residences were scattered between major terraces on low platforms. These often hold three structures each and the platforms were clustered at distances between 10 and 20 m. Residences might be built on several levels connected by ramps or stairways. No large multifamily apartment-like structures have been found such as characterize Teotihuacán. Xochicalco housing resembles more the arrangements we will see at Tula. Food was probably stored in nearby caves.

Paved causeways linked groups of structures within the site and also connected it with outlying areas. One leads down the hill to a ball court (Photo 34), which originally had rings and is almost identical to one at Tula. The style is that of many Classic Maya courts, especially that of Cobá (Kubler 1975). Two other roads extend for 3 km out into the country, without any discernable destination.

Ceramically Xochicalco forms a link between central highland Mexico and Guerrero and the Pacific Coast, with minimal ties to the Valley of Toluca (Cyphers Guillén in press). A very distinctive granular ware is shared with Xochipala, Guerrero, which constitutes the greatest per-

PHOTO 34. Ball court with stone rings in lateral walls. Xochicalco, Morelos. (Courtesy of the Instituto Nacional de Antropología e Historia, Mexico.)

centage of imported pottery throughout the various periods. Fine Orange pottery from the lowlands and Teotihuacán and Mazapan sherds indicate outside relationships, but these constitute a small ingredient of the total ceramic assemblage which has a strong local flavor.

Xochicalco is one of the most puzzling and fascinating highland sites. Its importance lies in its geographical and chronological focus, both important for the reconstruction of the rather vague epi-Classic period. We know Xochicalco ceased to be of any importance after A.D. 900. Therefore it did not replace Teotihuacán as a major center of the Postclassic period, nor could it have offered Tula much competition, for by Toltec times it was of little significance. The pronounced Maya features of Xochicalco are of considerable importance as the thrust of this southern civilization is believed to have reached Tula from a Pacific route that extended northward via Guerrero and Morelos. In fact, Litvak-King (1978) attributes the demise of Xochicalco at the end of the Classic period to a shift in trade patterns and political power that left it isolated.

PUEBLA–TLAXCALA

The big site of Cholula in Puebla has been well known and visited by thousands since the Spaniards first publicized it in the sixteenth century, yet it is only in recent years through work by the German Foundation of Scientific Investigations and through renewed interest and field work by the Instituto Nacional de Antropología e Historia of Mexico that a general perspective of the highland areas of Puebla and Tlaxcala is emerging.

The great pyramid at Cholula was begun in the Preclassic period and the site was remodeled and expanded many times in succeeding years. Archaeological sequences in general parallel those of the Basin of Mexico. Some of the structures are built in the *talud–tablero* style of Teotihuacán. An example of this can be seen south of the pyramid where an elegant residential palace is decorated with 50 m of murals of beautiful polychromed frescoes, dubbed "the Drunkards." Life-sized figures are shown serving one another and drinking *pulque*. All the figures have different faces and are a rare example of realism. More than a dozen of the illustrated vessels can be duplicated in the archaeological collections (F. Muller personal communication).

The influence of Teotihuacán is most notable in the Early Classic phases at Cholula, but in later years the Gulf cultures are more strongly represented. The Classic period looks rather impoverished when compared to other areas of Mesoamerica at this time. Teotihuacán influence, which one might expect to be strong, is actually rather vague. Pottery of the two sites is similar, but not identical. There are no frescoed vessels or *candeleros* and few Tlaloc effigy vessels at Cholula. Thin

Orange occurs but is often smudged black or painted red. Thin Orange pottery is found largely in the spheres of Teotihuacán influence, that is, in northern Tlaxcala in the so-called Teotihuacán Corridor.

Around A.D. 650–800 Cholula was apparently depopulated without any sign of major destruction. Some flooding occurred in the area but the extent of the damage is not known (Dumond and Muller 1972). Perhaps people moved over to Cerro Zapotecas where a considerable population is noted about this time.

Cerro Zapotecas (Mountjoy and Peterson 1973), only 3.2 km west of Cholula, is an extinct volcanic crater rising 240 m from the floor of the valley. Most remains date from late Middle to Late Classic period (Metepec–Oxtoticpac–Xometla). Considerable building includes two temple–pyramids, possible residential structures on terraces, and a ball court. Stone-lined ditches and some kind of waterworks were found in association with the upper residential terracing. The presence of Plumbate and Fine Orange pottery points to a later occupation, but in general Late Classic–Early Postclassic remains are rare.

Presumably people left Cholula and went to Cerro Zapotecas for refuge after the take-over of Cholula by the Olmeca–Xicalanca around A.D. 650. Jiménez Moreno believes the latter to have been a tri-ethnic group from the Gulf Coast area who were merchants and dominated Cholula from A.D. 800–1292 (Jiménez Moreno 1966). Others believe they were already present by A.D. 650 (Davies 1977; García Cook and Merino 1979). Their arrival coincided with other groups in the valley such as the Cuauhtinchan–Mixtecos in the southeast, people in the north with Tajín affiliations, and the local Tenanyecac population. These groups were all in conflict and struggling for supremacy and regional control (García Cook and Merino 1979). About the time the Olmeca–Xicalanca arrived, the various groups got together and closed the Teotihuacán Corridor, only to continue fighting thereafter among themselves, resulting in a very unsettled period in the history of the valley. The Olmeca–Xicalanca made Xochitécatl–Cacaxtla their capital and maintained a hegemony in the Puebla Valley and central Tlaxcala area only until A.D. 850 (?) when they were driven out. This version would explain the rather weak cultural manifestations at Cholula itself. After the collapse of Teotihuacán and the eventual expulsion of the Olmeca–Xicalanca, which some place as late as the twelfth century, more stable conditions returned and the Cholultecan city was reestablished near the old pyramid.

Cholula is the best known site, but there are hundreds more, and the Puebla–Tlaxcala region constitutes a key geographical link between highland and eastern lowland cultures. Local phases include Tezoquipan (300 B.C.–A.D. 100), Tenanyecac (A.D. 100–650), and Texcalac (A.D. 650–1100). Accordingly, Tezoquipan material would be largely Preclassic, but developmentally the three phases should not be separated and will all be treated here.

Tezoquipan is in fact the florescent period of the region, represented by more than 25 planned civic–ceremonial centers. Architecture abounds: temple–pyramids, ball courts, *talud–tablero*-style platforms, terraces both for cultivation as well as habitation, the use of stucco, and drains. Technical knowledge of waterworks shows a remarkable sophistication including irrigation canals, dams, and dikes. Cultural ties are strong with the Basin of Mexico as seen in pottery, figurines, and *talud–tablero* architecture. The enormous number of Teotihuacán figurines has been a great help in working out the chronology. There is a huge ball court with a playing field 105 × 12 m with walls 2.5 m high. Religion was institutionalized and maybe even some kind of rudimentary calendar system was in existence. As noted earlier, this region seems to be a jump of several hundred years ahead of the Basin of Mexico.

In the years A.D. 100–650, no new hydraulic constructions were built nor was more land cultivated. In fact, a kind of cultural stagnation ensued and even religion seems less important. Smaller, more dispersed rural settlements and fewer sites with formal architecture are characteristic. Of particular interest is the appearance of fortified sites such as Tetepetla and settlements located in defensible positions. The sharp decline in the general quality of material culture can be seen in pottery and in the absence of, or poorly made, figurines. Outside of the Teotihuacán Corridor or extreme northwest region, there is little or no visible contact with Teotihuacán.

By the following phase (Early Texcalac A.D. 650–850) regional development was renewed and more fortresses were constructed. It is at this time that the murals at Cacaxtla were painted.

Cacaxtla is the best-known center, but it actually forms part of a large archaeological complex composed of the ruins of Xochitécatl, Atoyatenco, Atlachino, and Tepenberna. The fortified site of Xochitécatl has Preclassic remains, although the ditches or moats, like those of Cacaxtla, are believed to belong to the Postclassic period.

The hill of Cacaxtla is built up with terraces, platforms, shrines, palaces, and altars. The peak period should be around A.D. 600–850. Foncerrada de Molina (1978) suggests a date of A.D. 700–900 for the murals. The paintings were discovered in October, 1975 by looters who tunneled into Building A and suddenly found themselves looking up at some of the most remarkable paintings in Mesoamerica. Fortunately, they were so overwhelmed that they reported their finds to the local priest, who immediately notified the Instituto Nacional de Antropología e Historia. Controlled scientific excavations followed revealing the truly spectacular murals that are now open to the public.

The ruins are tucked behind the site of Xochitécatl, not far from Texmelucan, Tlaxcala. The local springs, serving the needs of the modern community, may well have been an important factor in choosing this site for ancient settlement. The ruins of Cacaxtla occupy the hilltop of a promontory less imposing than Xochitécatl, but command an impressive view nonetheless, sweeping over the Tlaxcala Valley to the great volcanoes of Iztaccíhuatl and Popocatépetl. The entire summit is covered by a ceremonial area of shrines, rooms, patios, altars, and palace structures.

The murals of Building B are seen immediately as one reaches the great patio. They decorate either side of the small stairway leading up to a long chamber with seven doorways. Colors are vivid: bright blue, brick red, white, and black. A sense of movement is especially well achieved by these life-sized figures and viewers feel they have arrived just in time to witness the end of a very bloody battle.

Two protagonists are portrayed: victorious jaguar-men and less fortunate bird-people (Photo 35). The former are shown richly attired in jaguar skins worn like a poncho with the jaguar head and feet hanging down over a kind of short skirt. They went into battle wearing sandals, leggings, belts, and elegant adornments. At this moment, *atlatls* still aloft, they are jabbing the bird-men in the noses or in the abdomens with spears, spilling blood and internal organs. The bird-people, so-called for a great bird helmet and beak, wear many personal ornaments but no clothes. Heads are visibly deformed, and they wear a Maya-like pectoral. Most of the bird-people are already down on their backs, legs doubled under, chests thrown back, with heads facing their victors above. Perspective is remarkable, as one can see the victor's leg placed between those of the victim's, the latter's foot being flexed backward with the toenail in full view. Presiding over the scene to the right of the stairway is a giant Teotihuacán-style owl. It may sometimes be associated with water, but here it is overseeing the war.

A stairway to the right leads up to Building A whose murals were discovered by the looters. These paintings consist of one large figure on either side of a doorway to a palace room, jamb paintings, and a longer mural on the far wall of the room which must have been the most important of all. Unfortunately, deterioration of the latter is complete. The entrance murals are very different from the lower war scenes. Foncerrada de Molina estimates they were executed about 75 years later. Here there is only one figure on each side and on each of the door jambs, a much simpler pattern but equally fine execution. To the right is the bird-man again, holding a huge ceremonial bar which ends in a stylized serpent head. By now his social standing has improved for he wears elegant clothing and receives equal billing with the jaguar-man across the doorway. Both the bird-man and the figure on his door jamb are painted black and the facial characteristics are strikingly Mayan. There is a curious glyph to the left of the bird-man's face with footprints as shown in the *códices* and at Teotihuacán. Below this is a feathered eye, a symbol recalling Xochicalco.

Across the doorway is a giant figure in the form of a serpentine jaguar. The familiar face is that of the victor in the battle-scene below,

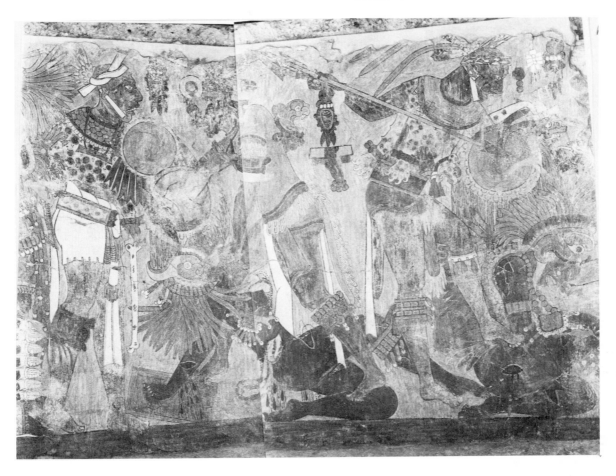

PHOTO 35. Scene of a battle between the jaguar-men and the bird-people. Mural paintings, Building B, Cacaxtla, Tlaxcala. (Photographed by the author. Reproduced by permission of the Instituto Nacional de Antropología e Historia, Mexico.)

also painted black, but it is not a Maya-like face. He is completely dressed in a jaguar skin. Instead of a ceremonial bar, he carries a quiver dripping water. The figure on his corresponding door jamb, the north one, wears a long-nosed mask, a very recurrent theme in Maya iconography. The cross-band motifs on belts of the main figures are similar to those at Palenque. Other features have parallels at Seibal. Despite the Maya flavor of certain features, the Cacaxtla murals should be seen as an eclectic art, developed out of central Mexican highland cultures of the Classic period with inputs from the coastal lowlands and Maya areas. (The murals have been reproduced and discussed in Foncerrada de Molina 1978 and Abascal *et al.* 1976.)

OAXACA

The Zapotecs at Monte Albán

The Classic period in Oaxaca is represented by hundreds of sites, but the great Zapotec capital is Monte Albán (Acosta 1965; Bernal 1965; Blanton 1978; Paddock 1966b). We have seen that the Zapotecs established residence in the Oaxaca Barrio at Teotihuacán, and at Monte Albán the visits of some Teotihuacán emissaries are graphically recorded in stone. This relationship between the two great centers was apparently peaceful, but not as intimate as that which existed between Teotihuacán and El Tajín or with Kaminaljuyú, for example. Monte Albán always remained staunchly Zapotec and is in many ways unique as a major center of Mesoamerica.

Resuming the history of this hilltop capital, the Classic remains belong to periods III (IIIa and IIIb) and IV. The cultural peak was III when the city occupied more than 6 km^2 with a population estimated at 30,000. The heart of this city is the Main Plaza designed for public ceremonies. This had been laid out when Monte Albán was founded around 500 B.C. By the Classic period, Building L was very visible at the southwestern corner of the Main Plaza with the galleries of prisoners and sacrificed victims on display, and Building J was located so that people could walk all around it to be reminded of the city's conquests. At least three distinct residential (possibly ethnic) groups lived close to the plaza and all were sheltered by a wall that enclosed 3 km of the hilltop on the north and northwestern sides.

For the next 500 years, Monte Albán would have no rival for power in the southern highlands. During the Classic years the city reached its maximum expansion. These were also prosperous days for Teotihuacán, and no doubt the two cities had each other under surveillance.

In Monte Albán IIIb, the great South Platform was built at the end of the Main Plaza; it was a gigantic pyramid 15 m high, measuring more than 100 m at the base along one side. At each of the four corners stood a stela carved in relief to show two figures and hieroglyphs. The message on all four stelae is the same. The scenes show a Teotihuacán ambassador (known by his tasseled headdress) leaving his Tepantitla-like home at Teotihuacán and traveling to Oaxaca where he is greeted by a Zapotec official upon his arrival. At the foot of the stela at each corner was a stone box containing special offerings of sea shells, jade, and Classic Monte Albán pottery. No dates are given, but perhaps the recorded scene took place upon the dedication of the South Platform. All participants are decked out in fine ceremonial attire, the Teotihuacanos bearing their incense pouches of copal as they do in their own painted murals (Marcus 1980).

On another occasion a Teotihuacán emissary named "Eight Turquoise" came to Monte Albán to confer with "Three Turquoise," a Monte Albán lord. This meeting is recorded on a *tecalli* plaque known as the Lápida de Bazán found in 1931 in the debris of Mound X. The carved monuments from the Classic period number around 15, very few compared to 300 in Monte Albán I, but those that do exist convey much more information because of the advances made in writing and pictorial manner of describing events. Outside of Monte Albán proper, regional styles had ceased to exist. Monte Albán had set a standard adopted by all.

The North Platform also built at this time was reached by much wider, highly visible stairs, leading to a colonnaded hall overlooking a huge sunken patio enclosed by high pyramidal platforms. As a public building, this was stunningly impressive. The rest of the Main Plaza was bordered by 14 buildings, perhaps each representing one of the 14 Oaxaca barrios. There is no archaeological documentation for this assumption but the existence of 14 buildings and 14 known Oaxaca barrios seems more than random coincidence (Blanton 1978). The main ball court occupied a prominent location at the northeast corner, rather effectively confining the Main Plaza by construction (Figure 23). The latter was no more accessible to the general public than other areas of the city, which were enclosed by steep walls and passageways.

To find one's way into the ruler's house (at least an especially fine residential palace) required all one's wits. From the sunken patio of the northern public building, one climbed a short staircase and passed through a gate into a narrow hallway. Up another stairway, through a room with two columns, a door to a hall, eventually reaching the central patio. This sense of seclusion was typical of elite residences. Access was restricted and probably controlled. Happily in this case the owner had a small private entryway via a discreet gate. The desire for privacy is reflected throughout construction on the hilltop and is one of Monte Albán's most distinctive features. Barrio Siete Venado, built at the end of Period IIIb, surrounded itself with double walls. Even the two main roads from the north led to points in the residential areas on east and west sides of the mountain, but not within easy access of the Main Plaza. The modern tourist road, which leads to a parking lot near the restored ball court, has been built over a vertical ancient wall.

When the hilltop of Monte Albán itself was so built up that it could accommodate no more, additional settlements were made on the slopes and tops of other nearby hills. During Period IIIb, all terraces were occupied and the maximum population is estimated at 15,000–30,000 inhabitants.

In regard to construction, facades form a series of rectangular *tableros* in two planes that alternate with recessed spaces. Also, rather than standing out as separate additions, many staircases are set into the structures (Photo 36). The large, handsome, I-shaped ball court is located at one corner of the Main Plaza. Here, as elsewhere in the Oaxaca area, the ball game was played without rings. As if to compensate, two

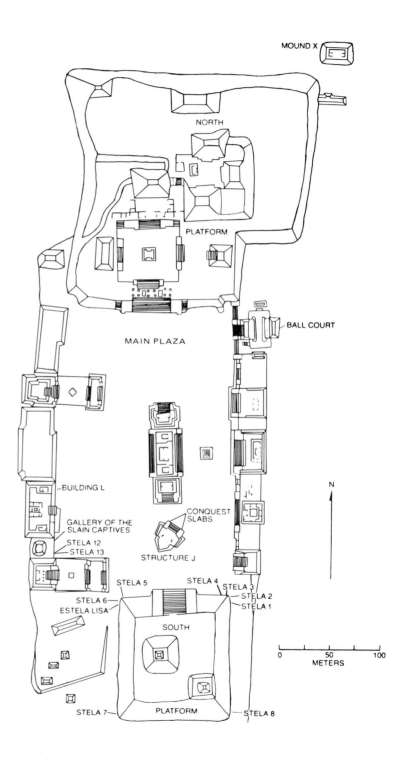

MOUND X

NORTH

PLATFORM

BALL COURT

MAIN PLAZA

BUILDING L

GALLERY OF THE
SLAIN CAPTIVES

STELA 12
STELA 13

CONQUEST
SLABS

STRUCTURE J

STELA 5

STELA 4

STELA 3

STELA 2

STELA 6

STELA 1

ESTELA LISA

SOUTH

N

0   50   100
        METERS

STELA 7

PLATFORM

STELA 8

FIGURE 23. Main civic–ceremonial center of Monte Albán. (From "Zapotec Writing" by Joyce Marcus. Copyright © 1980 by Scientific American, Inc. All rights reserved.)

PHOTO 36. Building complex (System IV) at Monte Albán, Oaxaca. (Photographed by the author.)

niches were placed in opposite diagonal corners, though we do not know if they were involved in scoring or if they were perhaps designed to hold idols of the game's patron deities.

The typical gray ceremonial ware of Monte Albán persists, so it is the form or ornamentation of the vessel rather than the color of the ware itself that signals change. Some of the earlier types survived, including spout handles, spider-foot vessels, perforated incense burners, and bird-shaped bowls, but new forms reflecting Teotihuacán tastes were added, such as *floreros* (see Figure 22-f, p. 209) and *candeleros* (Figure 22-d), stucco coating, cylindrical tripods, so-called Tlaloc jars (Figure 22-e), ring bases, and some Thin Orange ware and resist painting. These all make their appearance in the transition to the full Classic period at Monte Albán itself, as well as at many sites in the valley below. Distinctive local developments are a serpentine motif and the urn, in particular the funerary urn, a Zapotec specialty (see Plate 7-f, g, p. 210). Made of gray, unpolished clay, it is composed of a very elaborate deity usually but not always seated cross-legged against a cylindrical receptacle.

Mural paintings are largely confined to tombs where mineral colors were applied *al fresco* to a white base color. People and animals are shown in profile without shading. The best preserved of all painted tombs is Tomb 104, where on an urn a god wearing a Cocijo (the Zapotec rain deity) as a headdress gazes down from his niche over the entrance. The people in the murals are toothless old men with protruding chins. They are reminiscent of the figures in Teotihuacán's Tepantitla. A scene in Tomb 105 shows nine paired gods and goddesses in a procession.

At Monte Albán murals are found in tombs and these together with the elaborate pottery urns have been the main source of our information on deities and religion. Caso and Bernal have pointed out how closely Monte Albán adheres to the general Mesoamerican religious pattern: Cocijo as the equivalent of the rain god (Plate 7-g); Tlaloc, a bat god associated with fertility and maize (Plate 5-c, p. 96); the serpent associated with Quetzalcóatl, especially in his role as the wind deity and even a flayed deity which is later known as Xipe (Plate 7-e, p. 210). Nearly all the art and architecture now visible date from Period IIIb.

As a political capital it is not too surprising to find that workshops are scarce, for this hilltop would not have been a very likely production center. Throughout the Classic period, obsidian was never very plentiful and undoubtedly limited to the elite. The few obsidian workshops identified are therefore logically situated near elite dwellings, along with several others that crafted exotic items from marine shells and special minerals. Other utilitarian crafts were produced away from the capital itself. Some conflicting evidence is provided by the discovery of two pottery kilns located 1 km northwest of the Main Plaza. Could the plaza have been used after all as a marketplace where pottery could have been displayed (Winter and Payne 1976)?

A different kind of specialization, or even perhaps experimentation, comes from the medical profession. Monte Albán provides the best evidence of skull trepanation in Mesoamerica. Ten adult skulls, six of which were female, all dating to Period IIIb, showed drilling, scraping, and cutting of the bone. Since none were buried in tombs, they were presumably of low social rank. One individual endured five operations before he expired, and most had undergone two. Apparently only two lived long after surgery (Wilkinson and Winter 1975).

The general character of Monte Albán is very different from other centers examined up until now. Although it is easy to understand why Teotihuacán might have wanted exclusive control over the fertile valleys of Oaxaca, Monte Albán always remained independent. As Teotihuacán expanded her interests abroad, it is assumed that Monte Albán felt threatened and responded by reinforcing the hilltop capital, but there is as yet no documented evidence that Teotihuacán attempted exploitation, colonization, or coercion. The meetings recorded in stone are peaceful encounters. Nonetheless Monte Albán continued a massive construction program, implying that greater contributions were required of all Oaxaca communities. When Teotihuacán lost its great power and prestige, it no longer constituted a threat to Monte Albán and, to the relief of the Oaxaca populace, there was no longer a pressing need to maintain the great capital city. The Main Plaza was abandoned, and though a few more walls were erected, the population declined. There was no wholesale destruction and some people continued to live on the hilltop, but by A.D. 950 only 18% of the former population remained.

It is possible that contacts with Teotihuacán were not as close as this discussion implies. Paddock (1978) remarks that Teotihuacán had very little impact on the Zapotec center. Actual Teotihuacán imports are very few. From 2000 residential terraces, not one import from Teotihuacán could be identified (Blanton 1978). Aside from some mural styles, most of the influence is seen in portable goods which could have come in indirectly from the Ñuiñe or Xochicalco. Ceramics of Teotihuacán form were usually from tombs. The most convincing evidence of direct contact with Oaxaca is that in Teotihuacán itself and in the two relief carvings recording meetings. The ball courts and ball-game paraphernalia reflect lowland influence. Of course, the game was played very early at Dainzú, so it had a very long tradition in the Oaxaca area, but yokes and *hachas* are cult paraphernalia of the Classic period. Overall, Monte Albán seems very individualistic, conservative, and reflects regional isolation.

Like Teotihuacán, Monte Albán was not depopulated overnight. But a house abandoned one year and one abandoned 25 years later are both reduced to ruins before long; 1500 years later it is not easy to establish a chronology of abandonment if they have not been reoccupied. Logically, people would have gradually returned to their place of origin in the valley. The old regional centers had begun to prosper in the Late Classic period as if anticipating the end. After A.D. 700 all the valley settlements expanded rapidly. Prominent centers mentioned by Marcus (1980) include Cuilapan, Zaachila, Macuilxóchitl, Mitla, Matatlán, and Lambityeco (Map 6, p. 121).

Lambityeco

Lambityeco is an interesting example of a Monte Albán IV site. The pottery of this period is impossible to distinguish from IIIb at Monte Albán itself as ceramic assemblages there are identical. But the ceramic sequences continue at valley sites such as this, and we realize that the collapse of the hilltop capital had little impact on village daily life.

When Monte Albán was founded, Lambityeco was but a village. Its occupation overlaps in part with the Zapotec capital, but its most prosperous days are those from A.D. 700–775. Its flourishing could be based on mining salt from the earth. This produces a poor quality salt, but if, as has been suggested, salt could no longer be obtained from the Isthmus, its production would have been a good business (Peterson and MacDougall 1974). At best it would have been a short-lived venture because the Zapotecs themselves moved down to the Isthmus when alien groups began to enter the Oaxaca Valley.

Architects at Lambityeco copied the Monte Albán style of profiles and recessed panels, but decorated them with stepped frets and figures modeled in stucco. The mosaic frets and use of stucco reflect Maya influence and these will be found over and over again in the buildings of Yucatán.

Of special significance is the presence of Maya-like spiked incense burners of Balancan (Z) Fine Orange pottery; Plumbate and the later variety (Y) Fine Orange do not yet appear. This information ties in nicely with that from several sites on the east coast of Oaxaca where Fine Orange, Fine Gray, and Fine Black wares appear together. These are not local developments but have their origin in the western Maya regions (Long 1974). The Oaxaca Coast would have been a good route for the Maya to reach Guerrero, the Middle Balsas region, and central Mexico.

Another feature of Lambityeco is the appearance of paired male and female figures in tombs, on platforms, or facades sometimes modeled in stucco. These are an innovation of the seventh century, believed to represent elite marriages. Marcus (1980) describes the stone monuments of this period from several sites which she calls genealogical registers and which were carved between A.D. 700–900. A typical arrangement is to depict the man and woman seated on mats, sharing a cup of *pulque* or chocolate, or perhaps burning incense. Their names (which are, as we have seen, actually their dates of birth) are often included, while in the sky a glyph denotes their royalty or high birth. When the political capital of Monte Albán collapsed, power was left in the hands of ruling families who were anxious to record their genealogies for the same reasons as the Late Classic Maya. And, as among the Maya, a "good marriage" could establish a political alliance and be very advantageous. Thus, epigraphically, themes shift from conquests to personal histories: birth, marriage, and ancestry. These stones are read from bottom to top and alternately from left to right and right to left, as though winding up a set of mountain switch-backs.

Following the demise of Monte Albán, small rival centers competed for power and prestige. The Oaxaca Valley was not politically unified until the arrival of the Spanish in 1529. As Paddock (1978) points out, I and II were the creative periods in Oaxaca, and thereafter in the Classic period, Oaxaca passively retained its regional flavor while the rest of Mesoamerica went literally and figuratively a different route.

The Ñuiñe   The Ñuiñe as defined by Paddock (1966a) refers to an area and a style. The area is the low Mixteca between highland Cholula in Puebla and the Mixteca Alta region of Oaxaca (see Map 7, p. 188). Once thought to have been the center of Thin Orange production, this has now been disproven (Rattray 1980). It is, however, the region of *cabecitas colosales*, small colossal heads. Unlike the early stone Olmec ones, they are here made of clay. But like the Olmec heads, these had no bodies or necks, and stylistically relate to the central Veracruz sculptures. All come from Acatlán.

In addition to a handsome stone carving style, the Ñuiñe glyphic writing system has some correspondences with Xochicalco. Despite proximity, it is not Mixtec and has no connection with the pictographic writing of the *códices* (Troike 1978).

The Ñuiñe emerges as a kind of buffer zone between the major centers of Teotihuacán and Monte Albán, and was surely closely related to events at Cholula. At the same time the map shows it to be a kind of low-altitude path between the Gulf lowlands, Xochicalco, and Guerrero. For several hundred years Ñuiñe people enjoyed a close commercial relationship with Teotihuacán, and when the great city collapsed, Ñuiñe was one of the regional centers that prospered. Perhaps it remained a friendly area to which Teotihuacanos turned as refugees (Paddock 1978).

THE PERIPHERAL COASTAL LOWLANDS

El Tajín and the Ball-Game Cult

Sites in the Veracruz area are less extensively excavated than those of the highlands so it is possible that the importance of this region has been greatly underestimated. At one time, a very important development was centered at El Tajín, Veracruz, 8 km southwest of the town of Papantla in the humid, heavy tropical rain forest where the present-day Totonac Indians make their home.

In the Early Classic, El Tajín was a small settlement closely allied to Teotihuacán. The visible ruins belong to the Middle and Late Classic period at the peak of prosperity (García Payón 1957). They are deceptively small since the exposed buildings are tightly clustered, but untouched mounds extend for 5 km² into the lush tropical growth that covered the surrounding small hills. Although Krotser has estimated a maximum population at 3000–3500 for the cultural peak between A.D. 600–900, a large sustaining area could perhaps triple this figure (Krotser and Krotser 1973). The core area is composed of more than 200 mounds, consisting of temples, courts, elite residences, and no fewer than 11 ball courts, for as we will see, this was one of the regions where the elaboration of this cult took place.

The most important and commanding structure is the Pyramid of the Niches built in six tiers over a similar earlier one. It is outstanding for its variation of the *talud–tablero* form in which it incorporates 365 niches into its facing, surmounted by a flaring cornice (Photo 37). The niches may have been symbolic or purely decorative. It is tempting to imagine that each niche held a figure, but this is undocumented. Nearby are 2 of the 11 ball courts. The vertical walls of one are elaborately carved with narrative bas-reliefs in the interlaced outlined scroll-and-volute pattern for which the site is famous. The relief represents a scene in which a ball-player is about to be sacrificed (Photo 38).

PHOTO 37. Pyramid of the Niches, El Tajín, Veracruz. (Courtesy of the Instituto Nacional de Antropología e Historia, Mexico.)

Beyond El Tajín's ball courts and the Pyramid of the Niches and at a slightly higher level are a series of palace-like structures, Tajín Chico, with roof combs and corbelled-vaulted rooms with great colonnaded doorways all reminiscent of the Maya area. Particularly interesting is the massive masonry, constructed of a concrete mixture of sand, seashells, and wood, poured in sections using wooden molds. Numerous relief carvings reveal a predilection for toads, jaguars, serpents, and human beings. Bar-and-dot numerals associated with day glyphs are also found, so we know that the people of El Tajín had their own Tonalpohualli (260-day) and Xíhuitl (365-day) cycles.

Special architectural features include the use of niches, mosaic decorations found mostly on residential structures, friezes of frets, a flaring cornice, flat roofs, and corbelled arches. The most distinctive pottery is an ivory-type fine-paste ware made of kaolin, which was popular throughout Classic and Postclassic periods.

Many references are made to Tajín's art style of ornamental spirals and interlaced outlined ribbons found on yokes, *palmas* and *hachas*, pyrite mosaic mirrors (Plate 8-c), and bas-relief carvings. This style, remarkably comparable to motifs on Chou-period bronzes of ancient China (Ekholm 1964), was widely copied from central highland Mexico to Honduras. It is found in paintings at Teotihuacán, on monolithic stone stela–altars at Cholula, on the back of carved stone mirrors in

PHOTO 38. Relief carving of south ball court showing sacrificial scene. El Tajín, Veracruz. Length of this panel: 1.98 m. (Courtesy of the Instituto Nacional de Antropología e Historia, Mexico.)

Guatemala, and on marble vases along the Ulua River Valley of Honduras (Plate 10-k, p. 290). It is closely identified with Tajín but is possibly Izapa derived.

Tajín became very influential in the late Middle Classic period. No other outside art is as pronounced at Teotihuacán as that of Tajín, seen in pottery, murals, and architecture. Between A.D. 600 and 800 Gulf influence at Teotihuacán no doubt reflects the growing power of regional competitors like El Tajín. Gulf Coast people moved into the city's areas of La Ventilla and the Merchants' Barrio. A distinctive pottery called Lustrous Ware has been found in excavations near the Ciudadela, Tetitla, and La Ventilla. The results of neutron activation analysis place

PLATE 8. Various Classic-period objects.

a. Stone figure, Mezcala style, Guerrero. Height: 35 cm. (Courtesy of the Metropolitan Museum of Art, The Michael C. Rockefeller Memorial Collection of Primitive Art, Gift of Luis de Hoyos, 1959.)
b. Stone model of a temple, Mezcala style, Guerrero. Height: 18 cm. (Courtesy of the Metropolitan Museum of Art, The Michael C. Rockefeller Memorial Collection of Primitive Art, Bequest of Nelson A. Rockefeller, 1979.)

c. Hematite mirror back with perforations for suspension, El Tajín, Veracruz. Diameter: 8 cm. (Courtesy of the Museum of the American Indian, Heye Foundation, N.Y. [22/6252].)
d. Wheeled pottery cart in form of a crocodile, Veracruz, Mexico. Length: 25 cm. (Courtesy of the Museum of the American Indian, Heye Foundation, N.Y. [22/5562].)
e. Green-stone mask, Teotihuacán type, Santiago Tlaltelolco. Height: 27 cm. (Courtesy of the Museum of the American Indian, Heye Foundation, N.Y. [2/6607].)

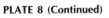

PLATE 8 (Continued)

f. Stone figure, with incisions and cavities for inlays, Teotihuacán. Height: 30 cm. (Courtesy of the Museum of the American Indian, Heye Foundation, N.Y. [10/7462].)

g. *Hacha* or thin stone head with projecting tenon. Height: 29 cm. (Courtesy of the Museum of the American Indian, Heye Foundation, N.Y. [16/3474].)

h. *Palma* or palmate stone, Veracruz. Height: 20 cm. (Courtesy of the Museum of the American Indian, Heye Foundation, N.Y. [16/3473].)

i. Composite stela used as ballcourt marker (?), volute carving in Tajín style, La Ventilla: Teotihuacán culture. Height: 211 cm. (Courtesy of the Instituto Nacional de Antropología e Historia, Mexico.)

j. Stone representation of Tlaloc with a serpent tongue, subterranean structures, Teotihuacán. Height: approximately 80 cm. (Courtesy of the Museo Nacional de Antropología, Mexico.)

k. Stone yoke carved with Tajín style volute, El Tajín, Veracruz. Length: 44 cm. (Courtesy of the Metropolitan Museum of Art, The Michael C. Rockefeller Memorial Collection of Primitive Art, Bequest of Nelson A. Rockefeller, 1979.)

the origin of this pottery near El Tajín (Rattray 1978). Other pottery with incised figures of ball-players and fine-paste wares are believed to come from Los Tuxtlas or Chachalacas as further indication of Gulf contacts. It was at La Ventilla that the famous ball-court marker was found (Plate 8-i). Yokes and Gulf Coast shells come from the same part of the city. Although Teotihuacán was receptive to the Veracruzanos and probably held them in high esteem, the ball game was never embraced with great enthusiasm at the highland city.

It has been suggested that El Tajín was a Teotihuacán colony, an ally, or a subordinate because of the sharing of pottery, art, and architectural styles. The political relationship we do not know, but the archaeological record makes it clear that, as Teotihuacán began to decline in the sixth century, El Tajín prospered and increased its power and prestige to become one of the major centers of the seventh century. Part of this glory may have come through the elevation of the ball game to a state cult.

Pasztory (1972) places the peak of the ball game cult from A.D. 450–700, a period of great mercantilism throughout Mesoamerica. At this time most of the representations of the ball game are found in the Peripheral Coastal Lowlands. There were three major centers for the game: El Tajín, Cotzumalhuapa, and Chichén Itzá. The Tajín and Cotzumalhuapa cultures are of Middle Classic date, as is possibly the Great Ball Court at Chichén Itzá (see discussion, p. 399).

Associated with the Classic ball-game cult were objects we know as yokes, *hachas*, and *palmas* (Plate 8-g,h,k). The U-shaped stones called yokes, often elaborately carved on the outer surfaces and weighing from 40 to 60 pounds, were imitations of protective belts worn by ball players. Clay figurines and sculptured reliefs, such as the ball-court scene mentioned before, show such belts being worn (Plate 9-d). The *palmas*, or palmate stones, are tall stones, 15–80 cm in height, and are usually fan shaped, notched at the top, and have a concave surface at the base as if meant to be supported by a curved edge. The back is smooth and left plain. The front may be decorated with such motifs as birds, iguanas, human figures, or inanimate objects. Pictorial representations suggest that the *palmas* rested on the yokes. Certainly they were designed to be viewed from the front. The *hachas*, or thin stone heads, were somehow associated with the yokes and the ball game. Their use is not known. *Hachas* often have a deep cut or notch at the back, or an undecorated projecting tenon. Like *palmas* and yokes, they are beautifully carved to represent human, bird, or animal forms. Neither *hachas* nor *palmas* can stand without support. On stylistic grounds, the thicker *hachas* may be Early Classic, the thinner ones later (Plate 8-g), and the *palmas* (Plate 8-h) later than both *hachas* and yokes (Plate 8-k) with a much more restricted distribution (Proskouriakoff 1954). Artistically these are some of Mesoamerica's finest stone sculptures.

Through a study of the art and iconography of the relief panels and associated paraphernalia, together with the later written chronicles, Pasztory believes the game reenacted a myth in which the sun god descends to the underworld and is reborn as the maize god, representing fertility. A plant usually figures in the sculptured narrative panels whether maize, cacao, or even maguey. Wilkerson (1980) suggests that *pulque*-drinking was an important part of ball-game ritual. The sun god is often shown with his twin brother, the planet Venus. The ritual game may have been played to hasten the rains and ensure fine crops for the forthcoming season.

Cacao was used both as currency and as a ritual drink and is therefore closely associated with traders. Travel at this time may almost be thought of as a "cacao route," for areas of major production lie in the Peripheral Coastal Lowlands, the scene of the ball-game cult. In fact, clay figurines of ball-players from both Jaina and Lubaantún may wear cacao-pod pendants. There is a close association of traders, cacao, and the ball game.

The first evidence of the game as a cult is to be found in the Dainzú relief carvings in Oaxaca (see p. 128), by which time sacrifice was an important ingredient of prescribed ritual. The stone stelae at Cotzumalhuapa show players carrying off freshly severed heads. At Chichén Itzá, the reliefs depict beheading with a flint knife, and heart sacrifice is shown in the Tajín reliefs (Photo 38).

Some version of the game had been played in Preclassic times, for there are numerous ball-players represented in the clay figurines of San Lorenzo, Tlatilco, Tlapacoya, Cuicuilco, and Xochipala who are often represented with padded knees, wrapped hands, and wearing protective belts. The earliest ball court on record is that of San Lorenzo. We do not know exactly how the earliest games were played but some elements in Izapan iconography seem to anticipate the Classic cult. Hellmuth, in a study of ball-game scenes from Maya vases, believes the Maya game differed from that of the Peripheral Coastal Lowlands and central Mexico by the use of a huge ball which could be bounced off the stone markers to force it out of bounds. Players wore a great deal of padding and a kind of deflector which fit up under the armpit and could bounce the ball off the chest (Hellmuth 1975).

Cohodas (1978b) reconstructs the game at Chichén Itzá. The playing field of the court was divided into equal halves lengthwise, the end zones serving as goals. Teams faced each other across the central line; to score a point, the ball had to pass through the ring (automatically ending the game) or reach the opponents' end zone.

The game has also been described for us by the early Spanish chroniclers who witnessed these competitions (Sahagún 1946). They tell us that the game was very rough and that it was played by two opposing teams, each numbering from 2 to 11 men, with a solid rubber ball that might measure nearly 30 cm in diameter and weigh as much as 5 pounds. According to the rules of the game, the ball had to be kept in motion by using only the hips, knees, and elbows, but no hands or feet. The players often were seriously injured or even killed, but the dangers in no way diminished the enthusiasm for this sport. Accounts from central Mexico at the time of the Conquest describe the elegant spectators who arrived in their jewels and fine clothes to watch and root for their team from the reviewing stands on the sides. If perchance the ball passed through the stone ring, a difficult and not too common feat, the game was immediately won, and to the winners belonged the right to claim any wearing apparel of the spectators. As a consequence, upon seeing the ball pass through the ring, the audience fled with the winning team in hot pursuit. These games had religious significance, and matches sometimes were scheduled as a form of divination to determine the outcome of future events or to make decisions.

The form of most Mesoamerican courts was I-shaped, but the lateral benches vary from being very low and sloping as at Copán (Photo 40, p. 301), to tall and vertical as at Chichén Itzá (Photo 67, p. 394). Within this general framework there were many variations. At Teotihuacán, for example, the game was not played in a stone masonry court, but in an open space with end markers. In the Tepantitla murals, some figures play ball using bats, but another scene shows the more typical hip-ball game in progress (Pasztory 1972). In west Mexico, the court at Amapa, Nayarit has a central marker topped with a cup (Figure 24). This is unique for center markers are more frequently in the form of tenoned heads, either animal or human. In Yucatán at Cobá rings appear for the first time and this style was followed by many other sites in Yucatán as well as in Toltec and Aztec courts (Clune 1976).

The game itself dates from the Preclassic, and by the end of the seventh century it had become a state cult in which human sacrifice was the predominant feature. It was transmitted by cacao traders from its original homeland in the Peripheral Coastal Lowlands until by the Middle and Late Classic periods a ball court had become a standard feature of all major sites. After A.D. 900 the game was still played but it underwent major changes, no longer being a cult but maintaining religious and divinatory overtones without utilizing yokes, *hachas*, and *palmas*.

Central and Southern Veracruz

The ruins of El Tajín are not unique: There are others with niches, profiles with flaring cornices, and step-fret designs. With slight variations, the complex extended into the Sierra de Puebla, a good example being Cuetzalan, Puebla on the very edge of the altiplano. This site has a pyramid with niches like that of Tajín with stepped frets up the balustrades, a ball court with vertical low walls, yokes, and *palmas*.

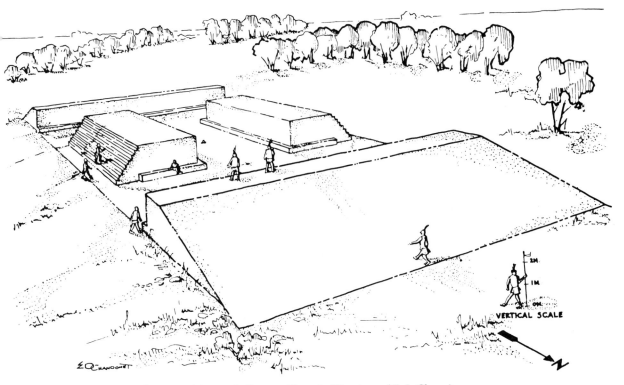

FIGURE 24. Perspective drawing of Amapa ball court, Nayarit. (Courtesy of F. J. Clune.)

Not far from the port city of Veracruz the potters of Remojadas busied themselves producing molds from which masses of hollow figurines flowed. Mostly of Late Classic date, these figurines are quite distinctive, although they may have some affinities with those of the Classic Maya. Their jolly, laughing faces often expose filed teeth through great smiles (Plate 9-g). Men and women as well as infants are represented, along with some ball-players and warriors. Black asphalt paint, from natural outcroppings in the area, was used to highlight the features and ornamentation (Medellin Zeñil 1960) (Plate 9-c,f). The jolly figures may depict a forced gaiety as the result of drinking hallucinogens in preparation for being sacrificed. To have met this fate looking gloomy would have been considered an evil omen (Heyden 1970.)

This is also the region where small wheeled animals have been found, which look at first glance like children's pull toys. One explanation sees them as imitations of ancient Chinese bronze carts in miniature (Ekholm 1964) (Plate 8-d). They are of considerable interest because their wheels are the only ones known in the New World; apparently the principle was never put to any practical use. These wheeled animals have a wide but not abundant distribution in the Gulf Coast region.

PLATE 9. Classic-period figures and figurines.

a. Pottery mold for producing figurine head (photo enlarged to show detail): Gulf Coast cultures. Height: 10 cm. (Courtesy of the Museum of the American Indian, Heye Foundation, N.Y. [22/9145].)

b. Mold-made figurine made for articulation: Teotihuacán culture. Height: 25 cm. (Courtesy of the Museum of the American Indian, Heye Foundation, N.Y. [24/6664].)

c. Solid clay figurine with asphalt paint on legs, Pánuco, Veracruz. Height: 19 cm. (Courtesy of the Museum of the American Indian, Heye Foundation, N.Y. [23/8592].)

d. Hollow figurine representing ball-player wearing yoke about the waist: knee and arm guards. Santa Cruz, Quiché, Guatemala. Length: 37 cm. (Courtesy of the Museum of the American Indian, Heye Foundation, N.Y. [12/3347].)

e. Hand-modeled figure in a pod, Jaina. Campeche: Late Classic Maya. Height: 21 cm. (Courtesy of the Metropolitan Museum of Art, The Michael C. Rockefeller Memorial Collection of Primitive Art, Bequest of Nelson A. Rockefeller, 1979.)

f. Remojadas standing figure decorated with asphalt paint. Central Veracruz. Height: 32 cm. (Courtesy of the Metropolitan Museum of Art, The Michael C. Rockefeller Memorial Collection of Primitive Art, Bequest of Nelson A. Rockefeller, 1979.)

g. Hollow "laughing face" figure, central Veracruz: Remojadas culture. Height: 36 cm. (Courtesy of the Museum of the American Indian, Heye Foundation, N.Y. [23/3925].)

h. Hand-molded pottery figurine representing a warrior–priest, Jaina, Campeche: Late Classic Maya. Height: 29 cm. (Courtesy of the Museum of the American Indian, Heye Foundation, N.Y. [22/6348].)

i. Clay red-ware effigy rattle, mold-made, Jaina, Campeche: Late Classic Maya. Height: 18 cm. (Courtesy of the Museum of the American Indian, Heye Foundation, N.Y. [21/4632].)

j. Bearded male figurine, Jaina, Campeche: Late Classic Maya. Height: 37 cm. (Courtesy of the Museum of the American Indian, Heye Foundation, N.Y. [23/2573].)

k. Female figurine body (mold-made) from Lagartero, Chiapas, Mexico: Late Classic. Height: 10.5 cm. (Photograph courtesy of Susanna M. Ekholm and the BYU–New World Archaeological Foundation.)

l. Female figurine head (mold-made) from Lagartero, Chiapas, Mexico: Late Classic. Height: 6.5 cm. (Photograph courtesy of Susanna M. Ekholm and the BYU–New World Archaeological Foundation.)

m. Male figurine (mold-made) from Lagartero, Chiapas, Mexico: Late Classic. Height: approx. 20 cm. (Photograph courtesy of Susanna M. Ekholm and the BYU–New World Archaeological Foundation.)

Some belong to the Late Classic period of the Remojadas culture. A tomb at Lambityeco, Oaxaca contained 50 such vessels, the greatest number recovered to date. They have also been reported from central Mexico, and one from Nayarit in western Mexico shows a man sitting on a wheeled platform. Five curious examples from Cihuatán, El Salvador came from a very late (probably Postclassic) horizon heavily influenced by Mexico. The El Salvador examples also functioned as whistles.

In southern Veracruz, Cerro de las Mesas, whose roots go back to 600 B.C., is also an important center of Classic times. Although its several dozen mounds have been known for a very long time, little scientific work has been done at the site. Among the stone monuments, carved stelae with bar-and-dot numerals bear Long Count dates of A.D. 468 and 533. Some glyphs look derived from Oaxaca, whereas many stone carvings resemble Cotzumalhuapa and Izapan. Very specific resemblances can be found between Stela 4 at Cerro de las Mesas and Monument 9 at Cotzumalhuapa. Other carvings and inscriptions remain to be studied.

A famous Classic-period cache reported many years ago by Drucker (1943b) is a reminder that this was formerly Olmec country. It included jade heirlooms, many carved pieces of jade, serpentine, and other stones, altogether over 800 selected pieces of elite property. But the cylindrical tripod vessels, *candeleros*, mold-made figurines, and large clay sculptures of familiar deities such as Huehuéteotl and Tlaloc are unmistakable Teotihuacán relics.

Activity at Cerro de las Mesas ended with the withdrawal of Teotihuacán influence, emphasizing its dependency on the highland city. It should be remembered as marking the northern limits of the Long Count dating system as well as being squarely in the path of the merchants moving their goods back and forth from Atlantic to Pacific and to points north and south.

A short distance to the southeast is Matacapan, which is located between Lake Catemaco and the slopes of the San Martin Tuxtla volcano. The Teotihuacano tradesmen selected this fertile plain as a pleasant stop on their long way south, and the presence of Maya elements shows that goods flowed in both directions (Rattray 1978). Matacapan laid out its mounds in typical Classic form, oriented slightly east of north. The pottery, artifacts, and *talud–tablero* architecture all label this as a small outpost of Teotihuacán.

Neighboring sites of Matacanela and Piedra Labrada with carved stone boxes, a basin, and a stela carved in Teotihuacán style have led Parsons (1978) to suggest this Lake Catemaco zone (Malacapan–Matacanela–Piedra Labrada) as a Teotihuacán port-of-trade (Map 7, pp. 188). It is certainly ideally situated in neutral ground between Teotihuacán and the Petén.

Tonalá, Chiapas is another site that testifies to the flow of Middle Classic traffic. It has wide paved ramps to connect its acropolis with other structures and groups called precincts, an arrangement paralleled at Cotzumalhuapa.

Cotzumalhuapa and the South

This latter site lies further south, constituting a major regional center perhaps equalling the power of Tajín in the north. Cotzumalhuapa is the name given to a distinctive art style on the south coast of Guatemala. The type site is Bilbao, a short distance northeast of the town of Santa Lucia Cotzumalhuapa, located on the sloping piedmont area in a natural rain forest 50 km from the Pacific Ocean. In actual practice the names Bilbao and Cotzumalhuapa are used interchangeably. Today the area is under coffee cultivation as was the archaeological zone at the time of excavation.

Remains show occupation during Middle Preclassic into the Postclassic period (Parsons 1969). The ceremonial center is made up of four main groups that include 17 pyramids, plazas, and courts faced with stone rubble or adobe plaster along with some finely dressed stone-block stairways. A number of large ball-player stelae may once have marked off a ball court, but these were moved to Berlin many years ago. There are six stone monuments still *in situ,* and many more have been illustrated in publications, through which the Cotzumalhuapa style has become well known.

Five pyramids enclose a central court with adjoining pairs which has been called the precinct arrangement. This idea of enclosing a court is paralleled at the Ciudadela at Teotihuacán, Systems M and IV at Monte Albán, and with other groups of structures at Xochicalco and Kaminaljuyú.

Until the archaeological sequence was clarified by excavations at nearby El Baúl, the art style of Cotzumalhuapa was difficult to place chronologically. It can now be dated from A.D. 400–700 corresponding to the Middle Classic period. Indeed it was the study of the Cotzumalhuapa remains that led Parsons to initially define the Middle Classic concept in 1969. During the late Middle Classic, Cotzumalhuapa became the most important regional center of the south. Prior to this the area may have been under the domination of Teotihuacán as its merchants made their way through here to the Valley of Guatemala. But when Teotihuacán hegemony was disrupted, and in this region direct influence seems to wane around A.D. 500, it is Cotzumalhuapa that assumed the leadership.

Characteristic are the stone-carved narrative scenes, centered around the ball-game cult, its ritual, and sacrifice. Decapitation, graphically illustrated, is a predominant theme and old Izapa subjects such as the diving god and the "tree of life" are still in style. Stones are carved in full round or relief and depict deities, skulls, serpent heads, and sacrifice. Carved hieroglyphs, though enclosed in cartouches, look more Mexican than Mayan. The distinctive style extends locally from Abaj

Takalik south to Cara Sucia, El Salvador, including highland Kaminaljuyú, and even further afield to Tajín and Yucatán.

Foreign contact with Teotihuacán, Tajín, and the Valley of Oaxaca is in evidence throughout this general area. Teotihuacán's influence is well brought out in Hellmuth's publications on the nearby Escuintla region (Hellmuth 1975, 1978). Hundreds of cylindrical tripods have been turned up by bulldozers preparing the land for cultivation of sugar and cotton. Mold-impressed designs as well as carved decorations record scenes of ball-players and decapitation. On one single cylindrical tripod vessel, motifs can be recognized from Teotihuacán, Chichén Itzá, Cotzumalhuapa, Monte Albán, or Xochicalco. Not only was this an eclectic art, but it provides good evidence of the contemporaneity of styles. The *incensarios* typical of the region are essentially that of Teotihuacán (Plate 7-j, p. 211). The ornate lid is used over an hour-glass shaped base, the latter usually abandoned or smashed in the field as not being worth saving. *Candeleros* are also found throughout the Escuintla region, which is curious in view of their paucity nearby in the Valley of Guatemala.

The rapid spread of the ball-game cult with its associated yokes, *hachas*, and *palmas* is well documented in the Peripheral Coastal Lowlands. Although Cotzumalhuapa was a major cult center, these carved stones are not found in southern Guatemala and western El Salvador. It therefore came as a surprise to find yokes *palmas*, and one *hacha* south of this distributional gap in eastern El Salvador in a cache at Quelepa.

This distribution may furnish a clue to a less suspected trade route leading around the Yucatecan peninsula from Veracruz, up the Motagua River and south via tributaries and valleys to El Salvador via Copán. This would explain the early Mexican influence and ball courts we will see at Chichén Itzá, as well as the presence of stone yokes and Chenes architecture at Copán, Honduras (Kubler, 1975; Parsons 1969). The ballplayer figurines wearing cacao-pod pendants at Jaina and Lubaantún would have been directly on this projected route of sea-going merchants (Map 9).

It is now time to look at these vast and varied regions occupied by the Maya, for only after that can the Classic years be appraised with some perspective.

THE HIGHLAND MAYA

The transition from Late Preclassic to the Early Classic period is more easily seen on the Chronological Chart (back endpapers) than in the Valley of Guatemala to which we now turn. Many Late Preclassic centers continued without interruption, and some architectural styles and techniques were still in use in A.D. 300. Ceremonial offerings were thrown into the waters at Lake Amatitlán, presumably to ask favors

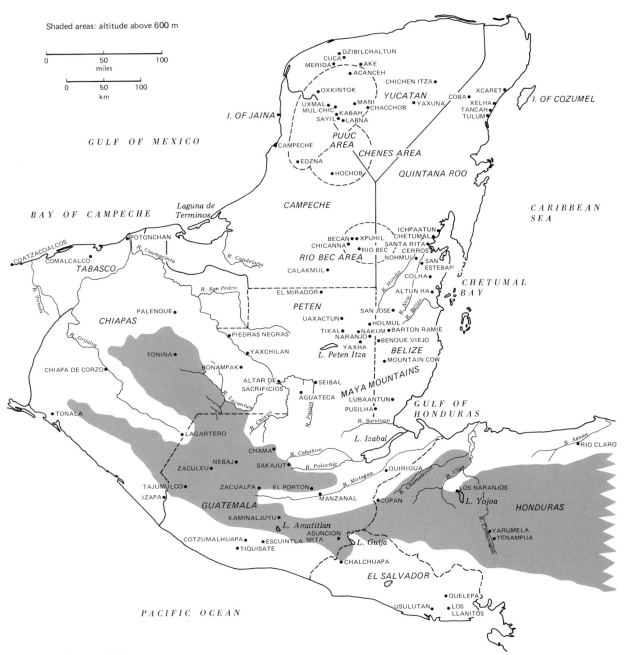

MAP 9. The Classic Maya.

of or placate the gods. Results were very beneficial indeed to judge from the tremendous increase in the practice by Late Classic times. Lake Amatitlán remained a center for all groups throughout the long history of the valley. Its location at the southern entrance to the valley lay directly on the path of many travelers. The lake region was utilized for resources such as fish, waterfowl, and salt, but it was also an area rich in vital raw materials such as columnar and vesicular basalt, and thin slabs of rocks (*lajas*) useful in lining stone drains. These *lajas* occurred as natural outcrops. Wild amate trees supported a growing industry of cloth and paper-making to judge from the presence of stone bark beaters. Though the first Classic phase, Santa Clara, seems drab compared to its predecessors, and the following phase of Aurora is undistinguished, by A.D. 400 the outlines of society and the economic patterns of the great Esperanza phase had been formulated.

This remarkable phase, corresponding to the Middle Classic period, provides us with a wealth of knowledge that reveals much about interrelationships between major centers in Mesoamerica at this time. For many years archaeology of the Valley of Guatemala meant archaeology of Kaminaljuyú, because not only was it the best excavated site, but the spectacular contents of tombs reported in 1946 (Kidder *et al.* 1946) focused attention on the presence of central Mexican influence. Ed Shook and other members of the Carnegie group were well aware, however, of many other mounds in the valley which they systematically reported when making preliminary surface collections.

The groundwork was therefore laid for the team from Pennsylvania State University who arrived in 1969 with both funds and theories to spend three field seasons of investigation. From 1968 to 1970 the massive ceremonial building complexes were reappraised and tests were conducted for remains in residential zones; extensive pits and trenches were dug at the main centers and in the surrounding sustaining areas. Results are truly astonishing. The reader is referred to articles by Brown (1977a, 1977b), Cheek (1977a, 1977b), Michels (1977, 1979), and Sanders (1977a), whose data and ideas are summarized here, in addition to the earlier work of Kidder, Jennings, and Shook (1946).

The ecological and geographical scene was the same as that in which the Miraflores people had sealed their great tombs in Mound E–III–3, but socially and culturally the valley was radically altered by A.D. 400. Now it is clear that the Valley of Guatemala had two chiefdoms, huge centers of great complexity: Kaminaljuyú to the north, and Amatitlán (Frutal) to the south. There was a smaller settlement of Sólanos in between.

Kaminaljuyú consisted at this time of two major areas of mounds known as the Palangana and the Acropolis, which together are referred to as the Park. Originally estimated to have occupied 7.5 km, the area known today as the Kaminaljuyú Park, set aside by the Guatemalan

Government, probably occupies about 3% of the ancient site, the rest having fallen prey to weather, looting, and the bulldozer as the modern capital expanded to the north.

The Kaminaljuyú chiefdom was composed of five subchiefdoms of which El Incienso and Santa Rosa were the most important. The former controlled access out of the valley to the north, mineral resources, and craft barrios. The latter controlled the rich obsidian deposits of El Chayal.

Population estimates were worked out by obsidian dating since sherds were too eroded to use. Aerial photographs were divided up into square meters and each site was carefully surveyed on foot. If the dates of two of four specimens from each site fell into a single phase, then the site was dated accordingly. Four dates were calculated for each. A standard house lot was assumed to be inhabited by seven people, and each lot was estimated at 2500 m². By this means of calculation, the population for the Kaminaljuyú chiefdom peaked in the early Late Classic period (A.D. 650) at 22,712 for the core, with a sustaining area population of 16,244. By early Postclassic (A.D. 900), the population had dropped almost 75%.

The great period of development corresponds to the Middle Classic or Esperanza phase. At this time Teotihuacanos were actually in residence, there being no signs of resistance. The study of the Kaminaljuyú chiefdom by Michels (1979) shows that the foreigners, however prestigious they may have been, do not exhibit great freedom. They lived in one particular area in the northeast where all the wealthy economic activities were concentrated. They probably married locally, which would have helped neutralize their impact. Teotihuacán-style architecture was confined to the Kaminaljuyú Park area and to Mounds A and B.

The building activity is estimated to have taken place over a period of perhaps 100 years. Architecture shows a combination of local styles and techniques using puddled mud but with strong Teotihuacán influence including the familiar *talud* and *tablero* combinations. Almost all the buildings are placed on new ground instead of being superimposed on old buildings. Some are faced with neatly cut volcanic-pumice blocks covered with clay and plastered in white.

Tombs were still constructed according to the old Preclassic practice of building rectangular burial chambers roofed with logs. On the floor of the burial chamber the honored dead were laid in an extended position, accompanied by retainers—men, women, and children—and lavish offerings of pottery, jade, obsidian, and pyrite mirrors. Eventually the dead were seated cross-legged, a custom unknown from Teotihuacán, but reported from Mirador, Chiapas (Agrinier 1975). Instead of placing the tomb in a prominent position in the mound as the Miraflores people did, the Esperanza builders now located the graves in front of the structure or in the subsoil beneath. These tombs are plain rectangular pits, very different from the elaborately constructed tombs of their predecessors. The rich contents—objects of pottery, shell, jade, obsidian—show strong Teotihuacán influence. The familiar lidded, slab-leg cylindrical pot (Plate 7-d, pp. 210), Tlaloc vases, *candeleros*, *floreros*, and Thin Orange ware are proof of central Mexican intrusions, for surely these well-stocked tombs belonged to an elite, the highest ranking and most powerful members of society. It is interesting to note that some pottery made in Kaminaljuyú has been found at Teotihuacán indicating a flow of goods in both directions.

Household debris indicates that fine objects of jade, eccentric obsidians, and fine cylindrical tripod vessels with matching lids were not available to all. None of these items were found in household debris of the general population, not even in elite residences where they might be expected.

It comes as somewhat of a surprise to find that Kaminaljuyú had very real competition from another huge chiefdom only 13.5 km to the south known as Frutal or the Amatitlán chiefdom. Spread out on the flat valley floor, San Antonio Frutal was as large as, if indeed not larger than, Kaminaljuyú and boasted its own acropolis and 30 principal mounds, with approximately 200 others scattered about. Less well known and less extensively excavated, the ceramic remains clearly show that Frutal residents dealt not with Teotihuacán, but with traders from Copán and Guaytán to the south, Nebaj, Zaculeu, and Chamá to the north, and the piedmont area of the Pacific slope. Frutal seems to have been exclusively Maya, and unaffected by the central Mexicans. Among ruins belonging to a ball court now completely destroyed lay a tenoned ball-court head-marker, depicting a parrot much in the style of Copán. Not a trace of Teotihuacanos.

Thus the Amatitlán chiefdom with its center at Frutal was in close contact with other parts of the Maya world. It controlled the southern part of the Valley of Guatemala which afforded access to the southern highlands, the Motagua River, and its tributaries. It also controlled the strategic Escuintla Pass leading to the Pacific Coastal plain. This is a curious situation which finds two political chiefdoms facing each other over a common frontier on which was located a smaller settlement, Sólanos.

Sólanos is located in a 5-km stretch between the two large chiefdoms of Kaminaljuyú and Amatitlán. It occupies a tongue of land between two deep *barrancas* and is the smallest of the sites. It is estimated to have had 15 mounds grouped around three plazas and an acropolis. Teotihuacán influence is manifested in both architecture and material goods, along with traditional Maya remains. Fine exotic goods are present from virtually every direction. Obsidian workshops have also been identified. Brown (1977a) believes the population to have been small but dense and tells us that Sólanos had a very long occupation.

How can we account for these remarkable developments in the Valley of Guatemala during these 300 years? The architectural data give some idea of the influence of the Teotihuacanos at Kaminaljuyú and Sólanos. Around A.D. 400 evidence of contact with the foreigners is seen in pottery, but building styles and techniques remained essentially Maya. By A.D. 450–500 the foreigners were influential enough to recruit labor for building, resulting in the construction of Mounds A and B which reached their maximum height in A.D. 550. They caused the most spectacular tombs to be built. Thereafter something crucial occurred. Sanders believes the aristocratic chiefdom was replaced by a state-type political system. Whatever happened, Mounds A and B were abandoned. Although the massive Acropolis complex of Teotihuacán style was built after this, tombs are few in number and their contents are shabby as compared to earlier ones. Quality visibly declined. Everyone owned a Tlaloc incense burner and, as if searching for some solution to a problem, people cast theirs into Lake Amatitlán. Simple stelae were carved as a tribute to Teotihuacán deities, but no longer were the old three-pronged incense burners produced, which had served the masses so faithfully during the difficult days of the Late Preclassic and Early Classic. Gone too are figurines, frog-effigy altars, and the old Izapa-style relief-carved stelae.

The nature of the foreign intrusion is not entirely clear. Was it merely a convenient trading relationship? Was the labor expended in building exerted purely to attain favor, benefits, and prestige through association with these outsiders? Was there a real choice? We know the Teotihuacanos were knowledgeable in the arts of warfare. We have only to recall their murals depicting shields, *atlatls*, and darts (C. Millon 1973), yet the Guatemala Valley has produced no weaponry, defense systems, or signs of physical conflict. To outward appearances, this was a peaceful relationship.

Society may have been organized along the structure of conical clan chiefdoms, at least at Kaminaljuyú. Michels visualizes a class hierarchy of four statuses: peasants, commoners, a secondary elite, and a top-ranking elite. The five subchiefdoms at Kaminaljuyú each had a ranking lineage divided into two moiety units. Although the Teotihuacanos made a great impact (A.D. 500–550), they were probably not in complete control (Michels 1979).

Brown (1977a) accounts for the extraordinary deposition of archaeological remains by postulating that the valley in Middle Classic times was an inland port-of-trade. He believes the situation fulfills all the necessary prerequisites (as listed by Chapman 1957) and his reconstruction of the events runs essentially as follows. The valley acted as a center for traders from central Mexico, the northwest Maya highlands, the northern Maya highlands, and the southern Maya lowlands. Lake Amatitlán with the towns of Contreras and Mejicanos would have constituted a main entry-point. Kaminaljuyú and Frutal were residential–administrative centers of their chiefdoms. Sólanos may have been an actual trading post in a buffer zone controlled by the two rulers of the independent political chiefdoms. Perhaps the whole system grew up originally by exchanging cacao and obsidian between the two chiefdoms (Michels 1979). As trade increased, what choices a consumer might have had!

From the lowland Maya cities came lime, so indispensable for building, and other products such as pelts, feathers, and eccentric flints. Basal-flanged Tzakol vessels (Plate 7-i, p. 211), a lowland Maya style, stood side by side with the cylindrical tripods from central Mexico (Plate 7-d). Commerce was mutually beneficial, for lowlanders were eager for highland jade, obsidian, volcanic ash (used for tempering pottery), cinnabar (often used to cover jades and graves), specular and crystalline hematite (for painting pottery), and the feathers of the quetzal bird, which could only be found at altitudes above 1500 m. Obsidian was readily available from El Chayal only 25 km to the east, and also from Ixtepeque not far to the south (Map 8, p. 206). This was an exclusive highland commodity and its procurement alone warranted the arduous trip up the rivers and footpaths from the Petén or Pacific Coast. Jade would have come from Manzanal near San Agustin Acasaguastlán, a source conveniently exploited by Guaytán. The Pacific coastal plain had always been a natural trading partner and continued to bring up agricultural products such as cacao from the lower altitudes, along with utilitarian pottery.

The distant lines of communication that had operated throughout the Preclassic period distributing Olmec artifacts were either still open or revived. Central highland Mexicans could have descended from the altiplano to Veracruz and Tabasco, crossed the Isthmus to the Pacific Coast, and made their way along Soconusco to the highlands through the Cotzumalhuapa and Escuintla region, or, if they had business in the southern lowlands and were in no hurry, they could pass from Tabasco around the Gulf Coast and travel down the Usumacinta River to the Petén and make their way to the highlands along with Petén merchants. Or, from the Basin of Mexico, they might have taken an alternate route to Tehuantepec via Morelos and Oaxaca. Whichever the route, they looked forward to an exchange of goods, gossip, observing and storing information of use to those at home, and making contacts. With such adventures and news to share, and well stocked back-packs, why would they not be eagerly greeted upon arrival everywhere? Who else moved around but traders, or warriors?

Sanders (1977a) proposes the ethnographic analogy of the Aztec *pochteca* (see Chapter 8). A Teotihuacán-type *pochteca* would have been a highly prestigious foreigner, a professional trader well armed to be able to cross hostile country. If contact were by means of merchants, this would explain the absence of Teotihuacán goods in residential areas since the Teotihuacán women would have stayed at home in central Mexico, while Kaminaljuyú households remained purely Maya. The limited imports would have had prestigious value and would accordingly be confined to ceremonial complexes.

Startling as it has been for us to find Teotihuacán influence so far from home, perhaps the majority of the valley's population went on about their usual Maya business undisturbed by what the odd ones at Kaminaljuyú and Sólanos were doing. The Kaminaljuyú home itself was never indoctrinated, so the foreign culture was only a veneer. At Teotihuacán, supervision was maintained over the whole populace, which lived crowded into planned quarters where their lives and resources were strictly controlled. This was not true of Kaminaljuyú, where the earlier pattern of small pole-and-thatch homes around courts was never replaced. Small scattered hamlets were common. Life continued in some areas relatively untouched by the outsiders who were strictly confined to one area. This would indicate that the intrusion never penetrated very deep. Participation in civic events was either partial or vicarious. The foreigners never constituted a real colony in the sense of transplanted families making a new home.

Somehow the whole system overreached itself and inequalities got out of hand. Competition must have been intense. Perhaps the Teotihuacanos began to assume more control; certainly the north became the dominant area. Once the port-of-trade system collapsed, the foreigners seem to have pulled out completely (Brown 1977a). About A.D. 550, tump-lines taut and packs filled, the outsiders left, and the local Maya reverted to their older life-styles. Did something happen to disgrace the Teotihuacanos? Did they leave in shame? Loss of face? Did problems at home force a return? We do not yet know the details as to why they left, but leave they did, not only the valley but the Pacific Coast and the southern Maya lowlands as well.

It is generally agreed that the Teotihuacán–Kaminaljuyú relationship was of commercial nature, perhaps stemming from an initial desire by Teotihuacán to control the cacao production of the Pacific coastal regions. There are in addition, however, other interesting highlights from excavations in the area. During the Middle Classic period a significant advance in agricultural technology was made. The older methods of swidden farming were altered by the introduction of short fallowing cycles. Terraces were constructed and farming was extended to marginal soils. The stone hoe blade was widely adopted making the work easier. As we will soon see, these changes come about at the same time that agricultural methods were improved in the Maya lowlands. Was this just coincidence, or another example of highland–lowland interaction?

The gradual breakdown of the Guatemala Valley cultures, culminating around A.D. 800, although not entirely understood, shows a sequence of events that probably reflects the withdrawal of the foreign power in the sixth century. Population had expanded so much that arable land could hardly cope with demand. Friction and competition between chiefdoms and then within the moieties themselves led to a marked deterioration of the former pattern of living.

The Late Classic phases are known as Amatle (A.D. 650–800) and Pamplona (A.D. 800–1000) and are well represented. The prominent Mexican influence, so strong during the earlier Classic manifestation, is no longer in evidence. At the beginning ceremonial centers continued to be constructed in tightly knit, compact groups in open country such as valley floors, where stone and *talpetate* masonry platforms were built. One architectural innovation was the huge basin-shaped or *palangana* ball court. Cotío, just a few kilometers west of Kaminaljuyú, is a typical Amatle site. Construction there made use of boulders, clay, earth fill, adobe, and lime mortar. Toward the end of the Amatle phase, the valley sites were abandoned for more favored defensive positions along hilltops.

Pottery is degenerate when compared to the finer quality and taste of Esperanza wares. Pots were rarely painted, but some ceramic ties can be traced through the presence of Tepeu-like polychrome wares. Although the pottery as a whole is drab, new types appear, such as the Fine Orange and San Juan Plumbate wares. The latter (Shepard 1948), thought to have originated in the Pacific slopes of Guatemala, is a distinctive, fine-textured ware with a high percentage of iron compounds. Upon firing, the surface acquired a hard metallic luster. In this respect it resembles the Postclassic Tohil Plumbate, but differs from the latter in paste, shape, and decoration. San Juan Plumbate was made into tall cylindrical vessels that contrast sharply with later effigy forms.

In the Late Classic another variety of Plumbate may have been produced in the region of Veracruz. Still another centers making a kind of imitation arose in El Salvador in Early Postclassic times (Bruhns 1980). The hard metallic-like finish of these wares remained in vogue for several hundred years.

In our next encounter with Guatemala Valley people, we will find them all living on hilltop sites, concerned with defense. But this takes place around the year A.D. 1000, the beginning of the Postclassic period.

In highland Chiapas to the west, Late Classic settlements were already located on hilltop sites or on ridges bordered by easily defended ravines or cliffs. The building of ceremonial–residence centers on higher land in preference to the valleys is a change that suggests a need for defensive positions (R. M. Adams 1961).

THE LOWLAND MAYA

By Late Preclassic times, the character of Maya civilization had begun to emerge. Remember that among the lowland Maya, the corbelled vault had already appeared; ceremonial centers and the beginning of dated monuments all demonstrate a gradual movement toward a distinctly Mayan civilization. Though certain roots may well stem from a Peripheral Coastal Lowland tradition, Maya culture certainly experienced a vigorous development on its own in the lowland jungle of the Petén, exemplified by such sites as Uaxactún and Tikal. Unlike central highland Mexico where Teotihuacán had no rival in power and influence, the lowland Maya had many centers of varying degrees of importance.

We will look first at the southernmost areas as a convenient approach to developments in the Petén region of Guatemala.

Near the southern periphery, about 100 km southeast of the Valley of Guatemala, the large site of Chalchuapa[1] in El Salvador (Map 9, p. 257) had maintained a close contact with the peoples of the Guatemala Valley since Late Preclassic days as well as relationships with other Mesoamericans by way of the Peripheral Coastal Lowlands. The role of Chalchuapa in the transitional period of Preclassic to Classic is of considerable importance, as the dramatic events that took place there affected the southern Maya lowlands.

Chalchuapa got off to an inspired start in the Preclassic in which we have already seen a lively trade with the Olmecs and their contemporaries. By 400 B.C. these people were operating a major center: El Trapiche Structure E-3-1 was rebuilt and enlarged to enormous proportions, along with new platforms and an artificial plaza. A comparison with structures at Kaminaljuyú shows that Chalchuapan people must have been sharing their architectural ideas. Sculptors were artistically sophisticated, the market for Usulután ware was still expanding, and the intellectuals were becoming involved with writing and calendrics as witnessed by a long hieroglyphic inscription on Monument 1 in the El Trapiche group. Population rapidly increased and just as a budding civilization was gathering momentum, rumblings were heard from the throat of Mt. Ilopango, 75 km to the east. The volcanic eruption of A.D. 250 was so disastrous that pumice covered the entire valley and much of the southeastern lowlands. Given time, life could begin again, but for most Chalchuapa families, their homes and belongings had disappeared under the ash. Apparently many decided to get out.

By A.D. 650, Tazumal was once more enlarged and relationships were restored with some central Petén sites. Merchants were getting in some elegant polychromes from Copán, Honduras and from Nicoya, in what is today Costa Rica. Along with the latter came some of Mesoamerica's earliest metal. Although spirits lifted somewhat, El Trapiche was never freed from the ash deposits and the earlier momentum was lost. People continued to live in the valley, but Chalchuapa became peripheral to major events in Mesoamerica. The Classic years passed effortlessly into the Postclassic marked in the archaeological record by the introduction

---

[1] Elevation of 640 m, see p. 139.

of Tohil Plumbate ware. At least these people were spared many of the problems that the lowland Maya had to face.

The Motagua River valley leading from highland Guatemala to the Gulf of Honduras may have witnessed the exodus of many victims of the Ilopango eruption. It is easy to imagine straggling refugees making their way across the Lake Güija Basin to the Motagua River tributaries and from there following that great system to the Caribbean coast. Deep layers of ash have been found at Copán, Honduras and also at the Ulua River sites of Playa de los Muertos and Santa Rita in Honduras. In Barton Ramie on the Belize River in northern Belize, there is archaeological evidence that fresh-water mussels suddenly disappeared as well as univalves, so possibly Ilopango blew its detrimental ash that far east. The ceramic history in a number of riverine and coastal sites shows intrusive elements that would correlate with a postulated migration.

The new complex is known as Floral Park, included here in the Early Classic period, but on a regional basis it is often set aside as a Proto-classic phase called Matzanel (A.D. 250–300) (Dahlin 1979). The Floral Park complex is most evident at Holmul and Nohmul on the Río Hondo, also at Santa Rita and San Esteban, Barton Ramie on the Belize River, and Altar de Sacrificios on the Pasión River (see Map 9, p. 257). The most outstanding features are true polychrome painted pottery, using combinations of orange paint; a ware known as Aguacate Orange, a distinctive new-shaped, Z-angled bowl with four large mammiform supports (Figure 6-y, p. 76), spouted jars; annular-based bowls; pot-stands; and Usulután-type decoration. Bark beaters and spindle whorls may also accompany the complex. The diagnostic tetrapodal vessels with mammiform supports is already familiar, occurring among Pre-classic wares of Monte Albán in Oaxaca (tripod illustrated, Figure 6-w, p. 76). In the Maya lowlands these traits are found with Chicanel pottery or even Tzakol, not disrupting the established traditions but rather enriching them. Some researchers (Adams 1971; Ball 1977b; Dahlin 1979; Sharer 1978b, vol. 3; Sheets 1979) feel that Floral Park manifestations are the result of actual migrations from El Salvador, but Willey and Hammond (1979), who have worked in Belize sites as well as in the central area, are not certain if actual movement of people is involved, or if this is a matter of diffusion at work. Dahlin reasons that cacao cultivation could also be part of the intrusive complex and its introduction might have been an important factor in sparking the great Classic development. The issue is still being debated but whatever the vehicle, direct or indirect, it does seem certain that the area of western El Salvador was a source of many of the new features (see discussion in Pring 1977).

Other noteworthy changes in northern Belize during the Early Classic are a general increase in population, expanded agricultural techniques, the appearance of raised fields where beans, maize, squash, and possibly root crops, cacao, and cotton were grown. Nohmul, a large site on the Río Hondo, is a good example of such a mixed economy. Norman Hammond (1975a) suggests that the raised fields, which could be renewed annually by silt from the canals, were constructed in response to the demands of an increasing population. As a result, the growing community was placed under firmer control. The massive building projects must have required a large labor force and at the same time commercial activities expanded. Most settlements were easily reached by water and Belize was strategically situated both to receive and distribute goods along the major river system leading into the heart of the Petén area as well as to have access to highland Guatemala and points beyond the Motagua River.

The site of Colhá is neither riverine nor coastal but commercially dependent on others that were (see Map 9, p. 257). Its large settlement around a ceremonial center was sustained by production of eccentric flints. All sorts of tools, chips, and nodules identify this as a specialized craft town, thriving prior to A.D. 900 at which time it was abandoned in the company of San Estevan and many other neighboring Maya settlements.

Altun Há is another important Belize site remembered for its rich tombs, jade, and famous cache of eccentric obsidians. Buried in the upper level of a pyramid near the main ceremonial center, a great cache contained shells, pottery, jadeite beads, and 245 eccentric green obsidians along with 13 green stemmed obsidian blades. Not only is the workmanship fine, the quantity staggering, but the green obsidians could only have come from the Cerro de las Navajas mines in central highland Mexico.

Barton Ramie, 45 km east of Holmul, is one of the best known sites in the area with a long history of occupation, mostly of ordinary house mounds. So great was activity in this eastern region that by Late Classic times Belize had the greatest number of tightly packed ceremonial centers of all the Maya lowlands. This eastern development of Maya culture is atypical in that sites are strung out along river banks in linear fashion. The distinctive life-style that developed around the use of waterways and raised fields was shaped by the build-up of an economic network of exchange, depending completely on outside trade. We will return later to the role of commerce among these settlements.

Rise to Civilization

At this point (A.D. 1–100) the Maya are poised at the brink of their greatest development, and it seems fitting to examine here some of the prevailing ideas concerning the evolution of their civilization. Although I have only highlighted certain sites in the surrounding regions, parallel cultural developments were widespread.

It seems clear that the Maya drew on cultural roots from the Peripheral Coastal Lowlands and perhaps also from the Guatemalan highlands. But these areas provided only some ingredients of the final product. The Maya had many companions thus far, but from this base they took off on their own and developed a civilization that is unique in many ways among pristine societies. This final quantum jump took place in the tropical rain forests of Guatemala, in that remote region where Tikal is located, farthest from outside influence. The how and why have fascinated many, and some of their ideas are examined here.

We have already seen that the adaptations to diverse ecosystems that resulted in economic symbiosis and hydraulic agriculture are thought to have been important catalysts toward the evolution of urban civilization in highland central Mexico. In the case of the Maya some of these processes were at work along with other factors more difficult to grasp, perhaps because the setting and circumstances are more alien to our modern way of life. Most archaeologists feel that Carneiro's hypothesis of circumscription as an explanation of the rise of the state has some application to the case of the Maya. As we examine the most outstanding sites, it will be useful to bear his main points in mind (Carneiro 1970). His reasoning is outlined in the following.

In some areas, as population grows, demands are placed on the limited resources available, such as water or agricultural land. Efforts are made to intensify exploitation methods or to expand existing supplies somehow. Competition inevitably leads to friction, perhaps even intertribal war, with the result that wealth and authority accumulate in the hands of a few. This concentration of authority may result in the establishment of the state. In a situation such as this, defeated groups have no choice but to submit, because there is no more room in which to expand, no other resources to tap. This situation may arise where there is local competition between chiefdoms, and a need or compelling desire to remain in place. Population pressure and military conflicts are therefore important ingredients of the theory. Competition could arise over any number of local issues or, for example, control of foreign trade, limited resources, or status benefits. Under these conditions, it can be seen how a state with centralized authority could arise from a simple village base. Predictable results follow, such as increased economic specialization and a number of changes in social and political structure. Adams (1977a) suggests that in the case of the Petén Maya, the constricting catalyst could have been the need to control water, always a serious problem with an expanding population. We shall see how the Maya devised ingenious means for storing this vital resource and how proximity to a water supply inevitably influenced settlement patterns.

For many years the Maya were thought to be extremely devout and religious to the point of fanaticism. Every sculptured figure was a god; religion explained all. In the writings of J. Eric S. Thompson, the Maya are beautifully and convincingly portrayed as moderate, peace-loving, kind, and pious. The role of religion was undoubtedly important to

Maya society and may have been a factor in the emergence of a dominant lineage among the earlier Preclassic settlements. However, Classic Maya are now believed to have been highly competitive, engaging in constant local warfare. We have begun to take note of the battle-scenes, trophy heads, portrayal of warriors, bound captives, and torture, which, together with retainer burial practices, have obliterated the peace-loving image. The pious peasant-and-priest concept has been somewhat modified as we have learned that priests either became, or were replaced by, semidivine earthly rulers, who commissioned sculptors to record their dynastic history, alliances, ascent to power, and eventual death. Before the pendulum swings too far to earth, we must not forget the abundant temples, deified ancestors, and proliferation of ritual paraphernalia.

Haviland (1975) suggests that this old Preclassic theocratic base played a determining role in the origins of Maya civilization. The ceremonial centers, which were the earliest architectural form in Mesoamerica, were where people gathered to propitiate the gods. Consequently they took up residence closer to the temple-pyramid centers. To avoid long trips to the field, agricultural techniques were intensified. Priests became full-time religious practitioners; therefore a surplus of food was required to provide for nonfarmers, who in addition to priests included sculptors, masons, ceramicists, and other full-time specialists needed to maintain the center. At Tikal a stratified society was visibly on the way to urbanization by 200 B.C.

Although agricultural pursuits would have engaged the bulk of Tikal's population, these other specialists formed an important part of the community. For example, the abundant supply of native flint not only provided local material for tools but could have been exported either raw or as a finished product. Exchange of goods and commodities is found over and over again along with the emergence of both New and Old World civilizations. Rathje (1971, 1973) sees long-distance trade as a major integrating force in the young civilization. He points out that the Petén region lacks three essential household commodities: salt, obsidian for sharp knives, and *metates*, the standard grinding quern in every household. Although the Petén has ample limestone deposits, this is too soft a stone for a *metate*, as it leaves particles of grit in the corn during the grinding process. Of the 2000 *metates* found at Tikal, 85% are of imported hard stone (Culbert 1970). In addition, hematite, jade, slate, pyrite, and marine materials were brought in (Haviland 1970). The presence of Petén polychrome pottery in both the Guatemalan highlands and northern Yucatán is evidence that long-distance trade was reciprocal.

Here again the civic–ceremonial center is seen as the central axis around which all activity was concentrated. To stimulate the flow of foreign goods, a center should be grand and prosperous to greet a traveler after a long trip through the jungle, for what merchant felt rewarded to arrive and find a common hamlet? Then as now, he was looking for a good investment and an expanding economy. Thus, according to Rathje (1977), a frenzy of building required full-time specialists to cut the huge blocks of stone, plaster and stucco floors and exteriors, carve wood, sculpt stone, paint, and provide all the amenities of civilized life. This required administrative skill and organization which in turn created an elite group, who would have controlled the trade networks and distribution of products, ultimately resulting in increased specialization, stratification, and population growth.

Although both Rathje (1973, 1977) and Webb (1973, 1974) see trade, especially long-distance trade, as fundamental to the rise of Maya civilization, there is little agreement on the control and distribution of the scarce commodities in the Petén. In fact the actual functioning of the Maya economic system is not yet understood. The importation of many exotic goods from highland and coastal areas is, however, well documented, showing that long-distance trading networks were in operation at this time.

Sanders, who once saw the tropical lowlands as a very ecologically homogeneous region that would have stifled any motivation for interaction among communities, has now altered his view. Upon a closer look, he sees in fact that there are many different kinds of agricultural opportunities available in the Petén. Following an ecological approach, he believes Tikal was settled because it has the most fertile soil of the Petén and this encouraged a concentration and saturation of population. Competition for control of land would have resulted in the emergence of an elite group of property owners. This model accounts for Maya florescence strictly in terms of local events, an *in situ* explanation (Sanders 1973; Sanders and Price 1968).

If excellent environmental potential was such an important factor, Culbert (1977) asks, why did the agriculturally rich southeastern Maya region around Copán not develop faster and earlier? There is no single cause for Maya civilization arising where it did, but Willey (1977b) implies that being well situated for receiving outside stimuli may also have been important. Thus, a marginal area, regardless of its environmental blessings, may remain peripheral to main events that would predictably be found where cultural contacts are greatest.

Webster (1975, 1977) postulates conflict and warfare as a contributing cause of stratified society. Having studied the fortifications at Becán in central Yucatán, he feels that a strong centralized authority would have been the response to the needs of a people with limited resources such as land. Aggressive expansion would be one way to solve a land shortage and at the same time alleviate any internal conflicts over land. This would tend to increase the role of leadership and permit concentration of wealth, power, and authority. The warrior's opinion would have carried some weight in managing the affairs of the community. Concentration of wealth in turn stimulates trade and reinforces the high-status positions. The elite would promote militarism as a process that had permitted their rise to power. In a sense this explanation of a class system arises from a local application of Carneiro's circumspection theory. Most hypotheses see warfare as an ingredient of a rising state, though not necessarily the principle force.

Another suggestion, drawn from northern Yucatán, is provided by Ball (1977b), whose model is related to the one just described. His area is limited, or circumscribed, by the Gulf of Mexico, the Caribbean Sea, and the Petén area to the south. Having little room for expansion, the soils being rather thin, and the population increasing, an inevitable conflict between settlements is seen as the cause of the Late Preclassic development at Dzibilchaltún. Because of this center's ultimate concentration of power and authority, civilization there was imminent.

Cerros, a site already mentioned on the east coast of Yucatán on Chetumal Bay, provides still another situation. Here a building boom in Late Preclassic times set the stage for a surge of activity in the Classic. Analyzing these events, Friedel (1979) points out that Cerros is strategically located for riverine contact with the core of the Petén as well as being in touch with the Pacific Coastal Lowlands via highland Guatemala. Florescence in this case was the result of the interaction of cultural spheres on the Yucatán Peninsula in which long-distance exchange supplied marine estuary resources in return for jade, obsidian, and other nonlocal products. The main point emphasized is that this is not a question of adaptive responses to natural and environmental conditions, rather Maya civilization was born of cultural phenonema that specifically reinforced social stratification by important status goods (see p. 146).

Most explanations have to do with outside contact. Thus Lamberg-Karlovsky and Sabloff (1979) as well as Graham, Heizer and Shook (1978) suggest that cultural diffusion plays a vital part in the evolutionary process and point to the contact between highland and eastern lowland Maya regions just prior to the latter's great fluorescence. Both a Mexican art style and hieroglyphic writing may thus have been transmitted to the lowland peoples (M. D. Coe 1976; Marcus 1976b).

There is no simple explanation of the origin of Maya civilization, but we are drawing closer to an understanding of the processes at work. We see the gradual replacement of an early base of a theocratic agricultural society by a stratified, nonegalitarian, more materialistic one. Important factors in this transformation seem to be population increase, warfare, cultural diffusion, and well-developed exchange networks at work in some kind of socially circumscribed environment in which arable land is limited.

In order to understand Classic Maya civilization, it is necessary to have some background regarding settlement patterns, the economic base, and social organization as a prelude to the archaeological record at specific sites. We will focus next on these important factors.

Population and Settlements

The Petén region is believed to have had few inhabitants in the early Preclassic years. Settlement was eventually made by people following the rivers to the interior (see Maps 3, p. 63, and 9, p. 257). As Tikal is located in a remote area of the tropical rain forest, its setting serves as a good example. Rivers are rare in this area, and the most reliable sources of water were water-holes called *aguadas*. These were favorite habitation sites, as were the level ridges of natural or artificial elevations, the edges of lakes, and *bajos,* low areas that become swampy in the rainy season. The rains fall mostly between June and December, contributing an average of 135 cm annually. Tikal was settled in this hilly, tropical terrain, which was obviously unsuited for a grid plan of settlement. The choice of location was apparently dictated by the local topography, and such requirements as water resources and drainage. The large natural supply of flint, valuable for tools, is another advantage which may have played a part in the selection of the site.

Central Tikal alone can boast of five great pyramid-temples as well as "palaces," shrines, terraces, ball courts, ceremonial platforms, sweat baths, and thousands of structures considered to be housing units. Individual houses were constructed of wood, mud, and thatch, of which nothing remains. A large number of walls, temples, and "palaces" still stand because they were built of limestone and mortar and faced with stucco. The walls of these structures typically were very thick and solid, and the windowless rooms, which today are usually damp and clammy, were very small in proportion to the walls. We would not consider such quarters to be habitable, but the ancient Maya might have used some "palaces" as prestigious residences for the elite. Imagine the city at its prime, with the vegetation cut back and the plaster pavements kept in repair—measures that alone would go far toward preventing humid, moldy conditions. Adams (1970) visualizes these rooms as dry and cool, furnished with benches, skins, mats, and textiles. Benches seem to be a particular feature of residential "palaces." Other such multiroomed structures were probably used for storage or administrative functions. A "palace" may often be identified as residential by its general arrangement and appearance, which is but a larger all-masonry version of the smaller perishable house. Other evidence of habitation would be the presence of household rubbish, ordinary burials, and the absence of traces of ceremonial activity (Haviland 1970).

House mounds and residential units have been studied in the same way to determine their function. The presence of utilitarian artifacts denotes living quarters as opposed to workshops or rooms designated for ceremony or ritual. With this in mind, the structures on strips of land 500 m wide by 12 km long that radiate in the four cardinal directions from the Great Plaza have been carefully mapped and studied (W. R. Coe, 1962). Tikal reveals a concentration of ruin mounds close to the core that falls off in density farther from the center. There the structures are distributed around plazas, but these groupings in turn are scattered at random. Nevertheless, the general pattern is a dense central core which is surrounded by a less densely populated periphery.

The basic pattern that had been laid down in Preclassic times is that in which low platforms supporting houses were grouped around patios. The simplest house was made of pole and thatch while improved housing made use of stone. Living quarters, kitchens, storage facilities, and sometimes work rooms can be identified. As we will see, one building facing the main plaza of several such groups tended to be outstanding for having no domestic function. This is believed to have been used as a shrine. The patio-groups are thought to have housed extended families or lineages. A cluster of these groups might include several extended families, and larger and more complex settlements were simply aggregates of the same features. The civic–ceremonial center itself can be seen as the final elaboration of the simplest patio-group in which the size of the area, the height of the buildings, the amount of dressed stone used, and the replacement of the shrine by a temple–pyramid completed the transformation.

We will see this pattern in the Copán Valley. It is similar to the clusters of settlements, small and major centers, in central Belize at Barton Ramie (Willey and Bullard 1965; Willey *et al.* 1965). A riverine environment such as northern Belize presents a somewhat different situation as groups and structures there tend to be strung out along the rivers at a greater distance from one another.

An additional feature of city planning is the causeway or Maya road called *sacbé*. These are found at Copán as well as at Tikal and El Mirador in the Petén where they link residential areas or intersite features. Their greatest elaboration took place in the flat plains of northern Yucatán where they connected cities at great distances and might be spanned by monumental arches. The most outstanding example is one that extended for 100 km linking Cobá with Yaxuná by way of six lesser centers (see Map 9, p. 257).

Although some sites may have been selected because of their riverine location, proximity to *bajos*, (swampy depressions) or resources such as flint, the patterning of Maya settlements is looking less and less random as we come to know more about it.

Estimating population of Maya settlements is a very complex task. Some of the difficulties involved in using the "house-mound count" methodology can be appreciated when one realizes that the Maya often had the disconcerting habit of moving out of their huts after burying a dead person therein. Thompson (1971) cites various examples of this practice from Postclassic sources but believes the custom very probably was followed in Classic times as well. Other than a death in the family, house mounds could have been abandoned for a number of reasons, such as the exhaustion of the soil, epidemics, fear of an enemy, or even to avoid oppression or some other undesirable social situation. The physical move would involve only a small expenditure of time and labor, for the Maya did not accumulate household goods on the scale that we do today. To make matters more confusing, houses might be rebuilt at a later time and mounds reoccupied. How then can the archaeologist cope with such deranging factors? Any meaningful population estimate would have to be based on the number of houses inhabited simultaneously. If excavations showed that pottery styles remained unchanged while remodeling of the house took place, this would be one clue favoring continual occupation. If abandonment and reoccupation at a later time had taken place, some observable accumulation of debris would result. The fact that the great majority of burials in the structure platforms of Tikal remained undisturbed is viewed by Haviland (1970) as additional proof of continuous occupation. Archaeologists at Tikal have been aware of these problems and have attempted to control the necessary variables in making their calculations.

At the same time, in addition to house counts which presumably deal with the nuclear family, the larger residential arrangement of patio-type groupings would have included extended families. It is very difficult to estimate population for these residential units. Summarizing data in Ashmore (1980), Willey cites figures of 72,000 in 120 km² at Tikal, calculated at 800 persons per km²; 500 persons per km² around Becán, Río Bec, and Xpuhil; as well as 2000 persons per km² at Dzibilchaltún in northern Yucatán in its Late Classic zenith. The overall population of the Maya lowlands must have been in the millions (Willey 1980).

Food Production

The economy of Tikal was probably based on slash-and-burn agriculture of maize, squash, and beans but not exclusively as once thought, nor as primitively accomplished. We now know that agricultural knowledge was sophisticated and one is left feeling that the ingenious Maya wrung every possible vitamin out of their forest environment through resourcefulness and hard work. Swidden agriculture is not an easy life. First the land must be laboriously cleared, and the subsequent burning off may take several days. Planting is done at the beginning of the rainy season by dropping one seed at a time in a hole made by a sharp stick and covered over. After working a field for about 3 years, the land must be fallowed for at least 4, possibly 8 years, to replenish the minerals, after which the cycle is repeated. This usually results in a shifting population, although the evidence from Tikal shows that some house platforms were in continuous use from Preclassic to Classic times. This indicates that a slash-and-burn economic base need not always require nomadic farming. Numerous studies comparing yields of slash-and-burn agriculture have shown that a crop surplus is possible (Carneiro 1960; W. R. Coe 1957; Cowgill 1962; Drucker and Heizer 1960; Dumond 1961).

In addition, the combination of maize, squash, and beans makes optimum use of the natural resources: the vines of the squash protect the soil from erosion; the corn grows tall, breaking the force of the rain; and beans grow up the corn stalks, increasing the foliage. For a vivid description of the farming cycle in detail, the reader is referred to Adams (1977a).

Another source of dependable food was the breadnut or ramon tree (*Brosimum alicastrum*) that yields a fruit of high nutritional value. By a series of experiments, Puleston discovered that these nuts could be stored in underground chambers called *chultuns* up to 18 months, whereas maize rotted within 2 weeks. Once planted, the breadnut tree will last for nearly 100 years, requires no tending, and is not so dependent on rainfall. It may not have been delicious, but it certainly would have provided a substantial vegetable protein in the Maya diet. The abundance of *chultuns* at Tikal, one per household group, indicates that this was more than just a famine food (Puleston 1971). The tree is not so plentiful along the Pasión River (Willey 1973), so perhaps the Tikal example of exploitation may be restricted, which might account for its economic longevity. It is of interest that in 1958 at Altar de Sacrificios such foods as avocados, cacao, vanilla, and tomatoes were growing wild and there is no reason to believe this had changed over the years. The workmen on the archaeological project planted their own beans, squash, maize, manioc, chili peppers, and sweet potatoes with great success, possibly following a very old tradition (Willey 1973).

Although archaeological evidence of root-crop agriculture is difficult to find, it is now commonly believed that the Maya cultivated manioc. Mention is made of root crops in the early Spanish histories and a variety is farmed by the modern Maya. For a people inhabiting a dense rain forest, root crops offer greater subsistence potential than maize (Bronson 1966). At present it seems that manioc cultivation may have spread north from the South American lowlands in the second millennium B.C. (Lathrap 1973).

Marine resources undoubtedly provided additional food and the sea was heavily exploited all around the Yucatecan coast. Fish may have been trapped and bred in canals between raised fields along the levees, an idea advanced by Thompson (1974) when studying the Río Candelaria Basin. Fish could also have been dried and traded inland. Apparently fresh-water snails, *Pomacea* and *Pachychilus*, provided a supplementary source of protein (Moholy-Nagy 1978; Nations 1979). *Pachychilus,* once thought to have been consumed in great quantities, was not eaten, but its shell was burned and added as powder to boiling water in the preparation of maize, thus providing a wonderful source of alkali. The *Pachychilus* is abundant in rivers and streams of eastern Chiapas and the modern Lacandón Maya still utilize it in this form. Although the Petén is rich in limestone, this source is not pure enough to use in cooking. Our present knowledge of the archaeological distribution of *Pachychilus* shells includes Piedras Negras, Tikal, Uaxactún, and some Belize sites.

Evidence of rather sophisticated food-producing techniques have been forthcoming from various regions in late years. Hundreds of thousands of stone-walled terraces line the hillsides around Río Bec in central Yucatán. These may not all be agricultural, as terraces also make good living sites, but the vast majority were designed to intensify food production (Turner II 1979). Not only did they serve to impede erosion with carefully planned drainage techniques, but short-crop fallowing could have been facilitated. Pot irrigation could have improved the yield in dry seasons. It is not known exactly how old these earthworks are, but some were in use by Middle Classic times and widely used in the Late Classic.

Distribution of sites suggests the use of ridged fields and *bajos,* ancient lakes (?) for a *chinampa*-type agriculture. In this system, soil or muck is piled up in an area of swampy or seasonally wet lands, creating ditches or canals between ridges or plots of higher ground. The result is an extremely fertile plot for agriculture. These were first identified as ridged fields along the Río Candelaria in Campeche (Siemens and Puleston 1972) and have also been found along the Río Hondo in northern Belize where they have been dated to 1100 B.C. (Puleston 1977). The raised-field patterns of Quintana Roo indicated that *bajos* there had been cultivated. It seems likely that the Petén region may have been settled according to the availability of *bajos* where this type of agriculture would have contributed substantially to the food supply (Harrison 1977; Harrison and Turner II 1978). The *bajos* at El Mirador seem to be an exception and apparently were not suitable for agriculture (see p. 143).

Additionally, in the Río Bec area of central Yucatán, Eaton (1975) has been able to identify what he calls farmsteads. A farmstead accommodating 8–10 people would consist of a house or group of houses with walled enclosures or courtyards set aside for storage or work rooms containing tools, utilitarian pots, and debris. These houses would be adjacent to agricultural land. The farmsteads, in contrast to ridged fields and agricultural terraces, have been dated to the Late Classic period in the Río Bec area. They seem to have been rather privileged landholdings, some houses having benches (perhaps sleeping platforms), and floors were plastered as skillfully as in the temples.

Another special situation is that of northern Belize where, as we have already seen, settlements were strung out along the rivers. Here both cacao and cotton could have grown on the ridged fields whose soil was renewed from the canals or swampy depressions between the ridges. Cacao needs high rainfall and humidity and these conditions were excellently met in both northern and southern Belize. The area around Lubaantún was a large cacao-producing center in Late Classic times as it is today (Hammond 1977a). Cacao is pollinated by midges, which Dahlin says would breed in the swamps; their larvae also provide good food for fish, which could have been exploited by traps as well (Dahlin 1979).

Although hunting does not seem to have been a major food-producing activity, a number of different animals were presumably eaten at Cuello, Belize: white-tailed deer, musk-turtle, armadillo, pond turtle, and brocket deer were the most abundant, but dogs, rabbits, and peccaries were also found.

All told, a variety of food was available to a people willing to work hard to exploit this tropical environment that was subject to dry periods and yearly fluctuations in rainfall patterns. By developing special farming techniques of ridge-field agriculture, *chinampa*-type cultivation in the *bajos*, terracing, trapping fish, storing breadnuts, and controlling and storing water, the Maya were energetic, resourceful, and imaginative farmers.

Commercial Enterprises

Early settlements were primarily concerned with providing food, but even in the Preclassic period there is ample evidence that the Maya maintained contact with the rest of its world and did not live in isolation. Trade played an important part in the complex development of the eastern lowlands, but, throughout the rest of the lowlands too, we can see that commercial activities resulted in sharing many new styles of art, architecture, pottery, weapons, tools, and fashion, as well as other innovations inferred in social and political organization. Early routes of settlements and trade between the Pacific Coastal Lowlands and the Petén region have already been mentioned. These avenues continued in use into the Classic period at which time Teotihuacán revived and expanded the ancient networks of central highland Mexico via both Veracruz and Oaxaca.

We have already seen how the source of many obsidian artifacts can be traced (p. 205; Map 8). Among the lowland Maya it seems that the earlier Preclassic source of San Martin Jilotepeque was replaced in the Classic period by El Chayal. Proximity to a source did not necessarily dictate usage. For example, Cerro de las Navajas obsidian from central Mexico has been found at Tikal and Uaxactún in the Petén, in northern Belize at Altun Há, at Becán in central Yucatán, and at Dzibilchaltún in northern Yucatán in the early Classic period (Hammond 1972, 1977a). Closer sources such as El Chayal, Ixtepeque, and San Martin Jilotepeque were also exploited, so the importation of Pachuca obsidians from such a distance must mean it was particularly prestigious.

From the finding of many cores in sites like Tikal, we infer that obsidian was imported in that form for local tool production and re-distribution. Certainly it would have been less risky and more practical to carry a bag of cores than the delicate finished product. However, at an early time, at least in central highland Mexico, this was not always the case. Pires-Ferreira reports that prismatic blades (see Figure 4-a, p. 59) were probably exported from Otumba (Barranca de los Estetes) to the Oaxaca Valley as finished products. Some blades were found care-fully wrapped in bark cloth in a Tehuacán cave, presumably to protect them from breakage (Pires-Ferreira 1975). Possibly the exportation of cores is an indication of a more established market system.

Although El Chayal exported to Tikal, Uaxactún, the Usumacinta River sites, Becán, Lubaantún, Belize Valley, and the Toledo District of southern Belize, merchants with Ixtepeque obsidian were after some of the same markets: the Caribbean coast of Belize, northern Yucatán, and northeastern Petén. It was not at all unusual for a center to import from several sources (Jack *et al.* 1972). Seibal, for example, imported from both El Chayal and San Martin Jilotepeque and even has one specimen from Zaragoza, Puebla, 800 km to the northwest (Graham *et al.* 1972).

Another very marketable commodity was volcanic ash for tempering pottery. The vicinity of Chalchuapa, El Salvador, was the source of ash for the Early Classic pottery at San José, Barton Ramie, Benque Viejo, and Uaxactún. From the east coast merchants bearing ash could have traveled the earlier Preclassic river routes inland to the Petén. Ash-tempered pottery also became abundant in the southwestern and south-eastern Petén as well as in northern Yucatán during the Late Classic, but different sources were used, suggesting that several networks were in operation. Only Dzibilchaltún, which probably controlled the salt monopoly, received the earlier high-quality ash. The enormous quantity of ash that was transported indicates a sea-borne route. Chichén Itzá may have eventually controlled the volcanic-ash trade, for it ceased with the decline of the city (Simmons and Brem 1979).

Ash and obsidian were not the only highland commodities in de-mand. Jade from Manzanal on the Motagua River was the most highly prized article of all times. The mark of the truly elite was to be buried with a jade bead in the mouth, jade ear ornaments, rings, and a figurine or two or as many as the family could afford. The term *jade* is used rather loosely to apply to a number of green stones. The Olmecs pre-ferred a dark blue-green jade (Frontispiece); there was also a fine trans-lucent emerald-green color especially prized by the Maya, but many varieties exist and all were considered gems, enhanced no doubt by its scarcity. Most jade was made into jewelry, plaques, beads, pendants, earspools, mosaics, even dental inlays, but one famous 9-pound lump was turned into the head of the sun god at Altun Há (Pendergast 1969).

Products mentioned so far have been highland exports to the lowlands. What lowland products would have made the return trip? Salt, being a universal necessity, was a major item, obtainable only from salt lakes, streams, wells, or the sea. Cacao was another product in great demand in the highlands, used both for ritual and as currency. Cacao cannot be grown everywhere as it requires shade, moisture, and good drainage. The Petén region would not have been suitable nor would Yucatán where soil and climate were not amenable. Irrigation is necessary.

Hammond (1975a) believes cacao would have been a good cash crop for the eastern lowlands, and Dahlin (1979) thinks that the immigrants from El Salvador could have introduced both cotton and cacao cultivation to Belize. The finding of spindle whorls is usually taken as a good indication of cotton cultivation. Both cotton and cacao were crops that the Salvadoreños were accustomed to growing, and northern Belize would have appealed to them as a region in which to settle, for here they could continue the farming occupations that they knew best. With this in mind, the inhabitants of both the Petén and Yucatán would have been good, regular customers for Belize merchants.

Although many products were exchanged, few are preserved to indicate how the movement of goods took place. Again we turn to obsidian for a clue as to how trading networks functioned (Hammond 1972). From highland Guatemala there were several routes to the northern lowlands (which could well be the ancient routes of original settlement): from Alta Verapaz via Sakajut and El Portón down the Chixoy and Pasión Rivers to the Petén (Map 9, p. 257). From there down the Usumacinta River system to the Gulf of Mexico, north to some point along the coast, and overland to the final destination in Yucatán. Another route would be down the Motagua River valley to the Gulf of Honduras for redistribution from the east coast riverine sites. Adams (1978) calculates a canoe trip could be made from northern Belize to El Cayo, 250 km into the Petén, in about 8.5 days, traveling 10 hours per day at 3 km per hour. From there it is another half day to Naranjo and 3 more to Tikal. Simultaneously, porters (*tamemes*) probably made the trip overland even as they do today along the flanks of the Maya Mountains. Foot travel is not hampered by the obstacles we encounter with wheels, and coping with changes in altitude, ravines, and rivers would have been easier on foot. An overland route could have been used all the way to Yucatán via northeastern Petén, at which stop the merchants might have added polychrome pottery to their loads. The return trip from northern Yucatán surely included salt, honey, and textiles. These commercial activities undoubtedly contributed to the importance of Dzibilchaltún in Yucatán as a major gathering and redistribution point.

Highland Guatemala probably got most of its cacao and cotton from Soconusco and the Escuintla region, which are very convenient, but the eastern lowlands were a viable alternative source. From the tropical forest itself came such marvelous items as jaguar skins, feathers from the toucan, parrot, macaw, and hummingbird. Quetzal feathers, a gorgeous emerald-green iridescent color, went the other way, from highland to lowland, for these birds live only in the cloud forests of the southern highlands, between 1200 and 2700 m elevation (Dillon 1975). Also from the lowlands came flint and polychrome pottery, both heavy items which would have traveled easier by canoe than by tump-line (see chapter ornament, Chapter 2, p. 21).

None of these routes is easily traveled today and it is more and more amazing to realize how well the Classic Maya maintained contact with their contemporaries. In the Classic period many of these commodities moved via the inland rivers, precisely to facilitate the transfer of heavy and bulky items such as volcanic ash. As we shall see, ocean or coastal trade became more profitable in the Late Classic and Postclassic periods, thus eliminating some of the older cities from active participation.

Sociopolitical Organization

The transition from Preclassic society to Classic was gradual, and it is impossible to say exactly when the older theocratic priest–ruler was replaced by a more secular one and when a strongly stratified community appeared. The basic system was probably worked out by 100 B.C., preceded by a building up of class distinctions. Certainly by A.D. 300, at least in Tikal, a strong hereditary ruler (Jaguar Paw) was in command. Again, not all centers proceeded at the same pace, and as always there were groups reluctant to change their ways.

Archaeologically the emergence of power from an early political and religious authority of a family lineage can be demonstrated by the Preclassic data from Altar de Sacrificios. The earliest information on residential patterns there shows a patio-group arrangement believed to house an extended family. When rebuilding took place, one particular group was considerably enlarged. By the end of the Preclassic period, this same patio-group had been transformed into a temple–palace complex of the typical Maya center (Willey 1980) graphically illustrating the growth of power of one lineage.

Haviland (1975), working with data from Tikal, has suggested a hypothesis for the development of centralized authority along similar lines, which seems very plausible in view of what we know of the complexity of construction and the extent of accumulated material wealth. Society is believed to have been patrilineal (see Chapter 5). Therefore, as craft specialization developed, it would be logical for this to take place along family lines or lineages, with the sons apprenticed to their father and growing up in the trade. These lineages might easily have become endogamous castes and a ranking of craft specialties would lead to ranking of lineages. Four main social classes, each with its ascribed status, would line up as follows:

1. The top ranking hierarchical class was probably semidivine, at least originally. Occupations associated with this group would logically have included administrative posts, religious activities, warfare, and trading. In representations painted on pottery or in murals, figures engaged in these pursuits are always decked out in elegant attire, indicating that these would surely have been prestigious positions. In fact, what we know of early warfare would seem to indicate that this was a small-scale enterprise, certainly no large organized affair, and could have been engaged in rather constantly among the elite without affecting the rest of the populace at all.
2. Another social rank might include scribes, accountants, skilled sculptors.
3. Artisans such as potters, tool makers, weavers, and featherworkers would follow.
4. The lowest strata would belong to the peasants who offered nothing more than their manual labor in the fields, which, of course, made the whole system possible.

How flexible was the class structure? Not very. Any social mobility was probably confined to permanent urban residents of the top-ranking or ruling elite. Rathje (1970) has hypothesized that the accumulation and redistribution of wealth became a circular movement limited to a few families. Perhaps warfare eventually became an activity in which one could gain prestige and improve one's social status. A talented sculptor who could portray in bas-relief a ruler with his elegant trappings for all to gaze upon surely merited royal blessings. The archaeological record supports the existence of a strong centralized authority with an aristocratic ruling elite. The recent historical and dynastic studies indicate its presence by the Early Classic period.

Tikal was the first center known to have an emblem glyph, which appears on Stela 29 in A.D. 292, thus emerging as the earliest center of political power. By A.D. 495 we can speak of a Maya state, which had spread to its maximum extent as shown by adherence to the stela cult. This extension to the margins of the lowlands was realized in the reigns of Curl Snout and Stormy Sky (see pp. 285–287). Upon the latter's death, there was some disruption at the government level, and for about 60 years (A.D. 534–593) no dates were inscribed. Coggins feels there may have been a trial reign with corulers, military and civilian, which if true did not prosper, for by A.D. 731 the Jaguar Paw dynasty was once more reinstated to power and Maya civilization embarked on its greatest florescence.

At this time Stela A at Copán records four important Maya centers with their emblem glyphs. Berlin (1958) suggested that these might be regarded as regional capitals. He identified Tikal, Copán, and Palenque, and Marcus has suggested Calakmul (?) as the fourth (Marcus 1976a). These four regional centers were in control of the Maya world by A.D. 731. Each one had its dependencies, and lesser centers in turn controlled smaller ones. Communication and coordination were well organized, and on at least one occasion, at Altar de Sacrificios, it seems that several rulers (Yaxchilán, Tikal, and one from Alta Verapaz) gathered to pay their respects to a deceased female ruler. This event was recorded on a pottery vessel dated at A.D. 754 (Adams 1977b).

The years between A.D. 687–756 were a period of great uniformity in which 60% of all Maya monuments were erected. Throughout the Maya lowlands, a standardization of the lunar calendar was adopted within a period of 10 years. There was also a marked homogeneity in certain styles and motifs, so at this time the evidence shows close contact and coordination of political structure of the Maya state.

The studies of Haviland (1977), Marcus (1976a), and Coggins (1979) allow us to flesh out some areas of Maya society that were conjectural earlier. It is now possible to think in terms of family trees, alliances, conquests, marriages, and foreigners. For example, it seems that Seibal, Aguateca, and Dos Pilas may have tried to raid Tikal in A.D. 735. Seibal could not have been very enthusiastic as Tikal was the source of its polychrome pottery, but being closely allied to Aguateca, how could it refuse support?

There is also some evidence linking Naranjo and Tikal by marriage. A prominent woman at Tikal is portrayed as the mother of Scroll Squirrel, heir to the throne of Naranjo. She was greatly honored at Naranjo after the birth of her son, and when he became ruler, the event was highly publicized. Indeed, Naranjo mentions Tikal 47 times. The political advantages of royal marriages and alliances were clearly appreciated. Another member of Tikal royalty went up to Pusilhá to be married. For a time Dos Pilas seems to have been linked to Tikal by family alliance. Women became very prominent in Late Classic years, even ruling Palenque and Altar de Sacrificios, but never at Tikal. As we will see, Tikal's ruling house may have helped start lineages at Copán and Quiriguá (Sharer 1978a) and exercised considerable influence at Becán, whether through conquest or alliance is not known (Webster 1977).

For some reason, perhaps presaging the collapse, there was a shift in capitals at a late date. By A.D. 889 Tikal and Calakmul retained their capital status, but Motul de San José (?) and Seibal replaced Palenque and Copán. It could have been a time of retrenchment, a shrinking of the state back to a more solid core, because the two discarded capitals lay on the southwestern and southeastern frontiers respectively.

By the year A.D. 900 the Maya ceased to record Long Count dates. Copán seems to have been suddenly abandoned after the carving of its final date A.D. 800. Stelae were smashed and some construction was halted in the very building process, as at Uaxactún. No more palaces or temples were built. At Quiriguá and Piedras Negras, A.D. 810 is the last recorded date. Seibal recorded one of the last dates of all, A.D. 889. One by one throughout the ninth century, city after city ceased all construction and sculpting. Some of the last stelae carved are but sad imitations of an earlier grandeur.

How very much different the Maya political structure was from that of Teotihuacán! That they were in close contact in early years is well confirmed as is the fact that this relationship had a profound influence on the fledgling Maya civilization. There is much yet to tell, but let us continue the Classic period as viewed from the sites themselves, starting with Tikal, continuing with Copán and Quiriguá, and finishing with the western site of Palenque and its riverine contemporaries. One of the last recorded dates is from Seibal whose history will take us to central and northern Yucatán.

Although northern Belize and the Pasión River sites of Seibal and Altar **Tikal** de Sacrificios were apparently settled first, it was northeastern Petén that became the first political power. Both Uaxactún and Tikal began erecting stelae at an early date, but Tikal rapidly assumed the leadership and maintained it until the ninth century. We can properly refer to this region as a central core area or heartland of Maya civilization.

Most of the structures one sees today at Tikal are of Late Classic date because the earlier ones were not only lower in height but have been razed and covered over by succeeding public works until what is left of the first structures is best seen via tunnels. We do know that by 100 B.C. the first platform of the North Acropolis was built and it was mounted by four stairways. By A.D. 250 this building complex was approaching its final layout. These builders already had grandiose plans for Tikal, as the Great Plaza (1 ha) and North Terrace were laid down in such proportions that no subsequent enlargement was necessary. Early platforms were gaily painted and stuccoed, faced with huge masks of the long-nosed god, exemplified by Structure 33–3 (Coe and McGinn 1963). When this was rebuilt, the next platform was even more elaborate, having stairways flanked by fantastic heads with serpents emerging from ear ornaments and carved masks on the temple facade. The corbelled vault was first used in Preclassic tomb construction, but by A.D. 250 it had become the standard way to support a roof whether in a passageway, palace, or temple (Figure 25).

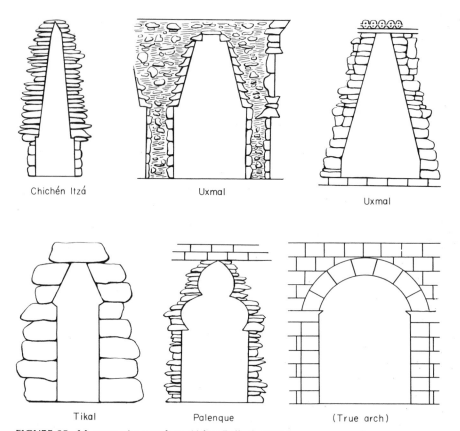

Chichén Itzá   Uxmal

Uxmal

Tikal   Palenque   (True arch)

FIGURE 25. Mesoamerican arches. (After Pollock 1965.)

Four kilometers north of the Great Plaza of Tikal, archaeologists came upon the remains of an Early Classic-period wall and ditch or moat that continued 9.5 km in an east–west direction before disappearing into the swamp. This great moat, bridged by narrow causeways, was a defensive mechanism to guard Tikal from raids or warring groups whomever they may have been (Puleston and Callender 1967). Another earthwork of similar nature was located to the south, about 8 km from the main center. Both are dated about A.D. 350. These fortifications at Tikal and the great moat at Becán are the most impressive of their time.

Tikal is not only the best-known site archaeologically, but was the very earliest center on record to have its own emblem glyph which appeared on Stela 29 as a "tied pouch" (see Figure 19, p. 181). The presence of an emblem glyph reflects Tikal's status as some kind of a leader in the area, perhaps dynastically or politically.

Numerous stelae have been found at Tikal, many uncarved, others bearing Initial Series dates (W. R. Coe, 1962, 1965) (see Plate 6-b, c, p. 166). Uaxactún has even more. Between them, they account for half of all dated monuments erected between A.D. 514 and 534. Stelae are found most frequently in prominent positions in courts or plazas, before stairways and buildings, and are usually paired with altars. It was once believed that stelae were erected to stand throughout eternity to commemorate important calendrical events, but now we know that they were dedicated to, or erected by, a particular ruler or important dignitary and might commemorate his birth, accession to power, or some important historical event, as well as recording calendrical and genealogical information. At Tikal they are often deliberately broken and smashed; some were placed in tombs, while others were reused and even reassembled upside down at a later date as in the case of Stela 4. After the death of a ruler, they were sometimes fragmented to accompany him to his grave. Thus, rather than being public monuments designed to last forever, stelae were personal records, sometimes honored only during one individual's lifetime.

The oldest dated lowland Maya stela known is Stela 29 (Plate 6-b, p. 166). This stela was found neither in a tomb, in temple debris, nor in a court or plaza, but it had been cast aside about 20 m west of the Great Plaza, where it lay for centuries, buried in the forest under soil and leaf mold (Shook 1960). It too had been broken and one part was recovered on the slopes of a nearby mound. This remarkable stela, carved in bas-relief, bears a Long Count date of 8.12.14.8.15 (July 6, A.D. 292), antedating Uaxactún's famed Stela 9 by 36 years. Stela 29 is fairly representative of Early Classic stelae. This one was not recovered *in situ*, but other stelae of this period often are accompanied by a small round altar. The large limestone slabs usually have a single male figure, typically represented with the shoulders in full front view and the head and lower limbs in profile on one side, and hieroglyphs on the other.

These early Maya were, as we have seen in Chapter 5, obsessed with cycles of time. Time was closely tied up with their concept of cosmology which they conceived of vertically—the earth beneath and their deified ancestor in the sky. Horizontally, east and west were of primary importance. On early stelae, the ancestor was usually depicted as a face gazing down from above, providing a kind of pedigree for the ruler. There may have been three early ruling lineages, but our first clue is a ruler (Burial 22) belonging to the Jaguar Paw family whose descendants make a later claim to power. He might be the figure standing over a bound captive shown on the famous Leyden Plate. In any event, he was buried about A.D. 376.

We know more about Curl Snout who ascended the throne at Tikal in A.D. 378 (8.17.2.16.7). He is remarkable for being an outsider, from Kaminaljuyú perhaps or from Teotihuacán, for he surely brought many central highland Mexican elements along with him. He is supposed to have come in from the north, perhaps no further north than Uaxactún

20 km away, where a stela portrays a foreigner bearing weapons. His ascent to power is depicted on Stela 4 where he is seated frontally Mexican-fashion with his legs hanging down and dressed as a Teotihuacano. He has no ancestor in his sky, so no one can vouch for his birth-right; furthermore, the stela records not a Long Count date but a Calendar Round date, more in keeping with Mexican traditions. He introduced this recording of 20-year period endings, 20 of which covered a 260-year period, resembling the 260-day period celebrated in western Mesoamerica. Along with this shorter cycle of a ritual calendar, probably rather popular among the people as being more easily understood, Curl Snout introduced the manikin scepter, a national emblem. This is a kind of ceremonial bar, and later rulers are shown regally holding one. The *atlatl*, or spear thrower, also appears in sculpture for the first time. Curl Snout opened wide the doors of trade and the following years see strong influences from Teotihuacán. This was a great period of mercantilism, and, just as we saw the *talud–tablero* architecture at Kaminaljuyú along with other hallmarks such as the cylindrical tripod, we find similar traits now penetrating the Petén. The 100 years from A.D. 380 to 480 were a period of intense foreign influence. When Curl Snout was laid to rest in A.D. 425 (in Burial 10), among his lavish grave goods were imitations of Thin Orange pottery, a token reminder of where his roots lay.

He was succeeded by Stormy Sky, over whose fortunes Curl Snout could watch as the ancestor in the sky recorded on Stela 4. Now in his ancestor role, Curl Snout is shown as the long-nosed deity which is later to become Chac, the emblem of this Mexicanized Maya dynasty. Stormy Sky is immortalized on Stela 31, one of Tikal's most famous (W. R. Coe, 1962) (Plate 10-d). The front figure is the ruler himself, barely recognizable in his elaborate paraphernalia as a Maya ruler. He flaunts his Mexican connections by wearing a skull on his helmet and a quail on his wrist. The Teotihuacán owl can be seen in the headdress of the mask above his upraised hand. In contrast to his gorgeous trappings, the accompanying warriors of lower status are much more simply attired. They carry *atlatls* and shields. Their tasseled headdresses may be special insignias of power, perhaps for foreign-relations officers; the Tlaloc-like representation on the shield may represent a war deity (C. Millon 1973).

Stormy Sky did much to further trade relations, and judging from his final rites, he retained his high status to the end. He was given a very sumptuous burial in a painted tomb tunneled into bedrock under a succession of temples in the North Acropolis. Prior to interment, both head and hands were removed. He was buried in a seated position but his bones eventually collapsed into a heap. Befitting his high rank, not only was he accompanied by the bodies of two teenagers, but the walls of the tomb itself were stuccoed and painted with an Initial Series date of 9.1.1.10.10 (A.D. 457). Among the rich offerings were elegantly decorated pots, a particularly fine Teotihuacán type cylindrical tripod covered with painted stucco, and a fine alabaster bowl also stuccoed in pale green and decorated with a band of incised glyphs. Made of beautiful Motagua River valley jade were hundreds of beads and two pairs of earplug flares. Marine products, food offerings, and greenish obsidian from Cerro de las Navajas gave the deceased ample supplies for any eventuality in afterlife. Such treatment was only given to rulers and members of his dynasty. Commoners were usually interred under the floors of their houses, so nothing resembling a cemetery has been found.

It is interesting that both burials of Curl Snout and Stormy Sky (Teotihuacán-dynasty rulers at Tikal) are contemporaneous with Early Tomb A–III and A–V and B–1 at Kaminaljuyú. It has been speculated that these rulers may have come to the Petén from the Guatemalan highlands (Haviland 1977), but the possibility also exists that the Teotihuacán influence went the other way, with Tikal being donor rather than receiver (Coggins 1979). It is a point not to be settled here, but certainly the central Mexicans made a strong impact on the southern Maya lowlands at this time. The great cache of green obsidians at Altun Há, Belize has already been mentioned. At Becán, in Structure XIV a curious cache was recovered in the rubble of a building when preparing to rebuild. A large hollow Teotihuacán-style figurine contained 10 small solid ones representing Teotihuacán-style deities and warriors along with jade ornaments. The large figure was placed in a typical cylindrical Maya tripod, elegantly carved with a Chac-like seated personage (Ball 1974a).

The foreign intrusion is very evident in materialistic aspects of Maya culture. The Pachuca obsidians, Becán hollow and small figurines just mentioned, the diagnostic cylindrical tripod vessel, and *talud–tablero* architecture are all striking Teotihuacán features, but of more lasting effect is the foreign impact on the iconography, the introduction of the Tlaloc cult, the *atlatl*, and recording of katun endings. This intrusion was seemingly easily absorbed because the traditional Maya life-style continued thoroughly Maya in conception and orientation, erecting dated monuments, temples, and vaulted ceiling. Intrusive elements were fitted into the established traditional scheme. Throughout this period of maximum foreign input, Maya centers were in close contact. By A.D. 400 the stela cult had almost reached its maximum geographical spread. A standardized art style had crystallized and Tikal was a recognized prestigious political power.

The Middle Classic period at Tikal falls into a 200-year span following the death of Stormy Sky, that is, A.D. 480–680. It is a puzzling period archaeologically and historically, and when we learn more of these particular years we will better understand the upheavals, restructuring,

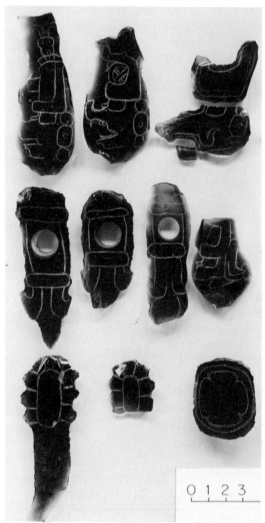

b

c

PLATE 10. Various objects from the Maya area.
a. Late Classic incised obsidian flakes and blades, often found in caches, Tikal, Guatemala. See scale for dimensions in centimeters. (Courtesy of the Tikal Project, the University Museum, University of Pennsylvania.)
b. Shell carving of seated Mayan man with a pearl inlaid in ear spool (greatly enlarged), Palenque, Chiapas. Height: 7.3 cm. (Courtesy of the Museum of the American Indian, Heye Foundation, N.Y. [22/4955].)
c. "Eccentric" flint of ceremonial use, considered of great value and widely traded, Río Hondo, Orange Walk, British Honduras. Length: 36 cm. (Courtesy of the Museum of the American Indian, Heye Foundation, N.Y. [13/5547].)
d. Drawing of front and lateral faces of Stela 31, Tikal, Guatemala. The main figure is Stormy Sky, elaborately dressed, accompanied by two warriors, carved on lateral sides of stela. They carry *atlatls* and shields. Tlaloc's face is visible on right-hand shield. The tasseled headdress of the two minor figures is insignia denoting authority. Height of Stela 31: 2.30 m. (Courtesy of The Tikal Project, the University Museum, University of Pennsylvania.)
e. Lintel 15 from central chamber of Structure 21, Yaxchilán, Petén, Guatemala. Fine, yellowish limestone. Probably eighth century. Elite figure on viewer's right is being addressed by an ancestral figure who emerges from a serpent's mouth. Classic Petén-style carving. Height: 86 cm. (Reproduced by courtesy of the Trustees of the British Museum.)
f. Beautifully modeled life-size stucco head believed to represent Pacal. Found on the floor of the funerary crypt, Temple of the Inscriptions, Palenque, Chiapas. Height: 31 cm. (Courtesy of the Museo Nacional de Antropología, Mexico.)

288

(Continued on p. 290)

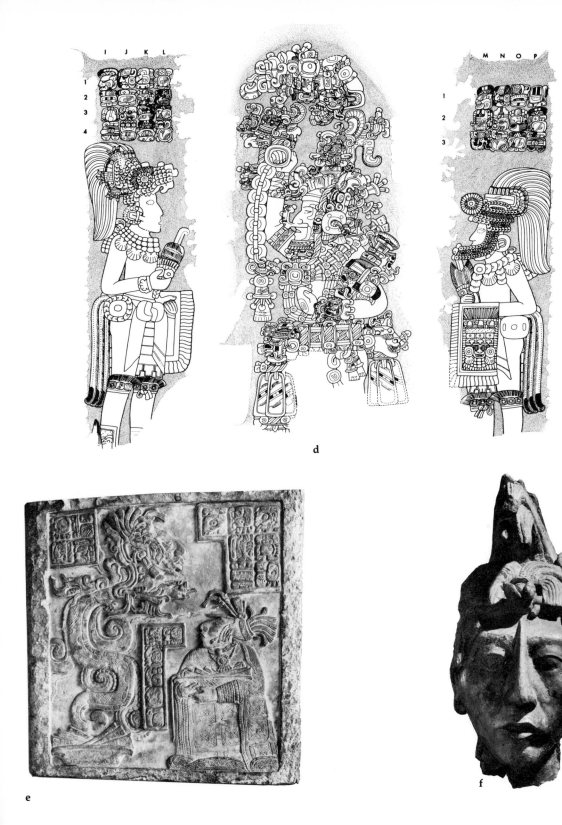

d

e

f

g

h

i

j

k

PLATE 10 (Continued)

g. Jade mosaic mask with eyes of inlaid shell and obsidian. Found as death mask of Pacal in sarcophagus of funerary crypt. Temple of the Inscriptions, Palenque, Chiapas. Height: 24 cm. (Courtesy of the Museo Nacional de Antropología, Mexico.)

h. Carved wooden figure, Tabasco. Height: 36 cm. (Courtesy of the Metropolitan Museum of Art, The Michael C. Rockefeller Memorial Collection of Primitive Art, Bequest of Nelson A. Rockefeller, 1979.)

i. Human-effigy mushroom stone, Momostenango, Guatemala. Height: 33 cm. (Courtesy of the Museum of the American Indian, Heye Foundation, N.Y. [9/8304].)

j. Carved jadeite figure, Copán, Honduras. Height: 20 cm. (Courtesy of the Museum of the American Indian, Heye Foundation, N.Y. [10/9827].)

k. Marble vase carved in Tajín style, Ulua River valley, Honduras. Height: 13 cm. (Courtesy of the Museum of the American Indian, Heye Foundation, N.Y. [4/3956].)

or realigning of power that took place in central Mexico as well as in the Maya area. Between the Long Count dates of 9.5.0.0.0 and 9.8.0.0.0, roughly 40–60 years (A.D. 534–593), construction work seems to have paused and few stelae were erected. This lack of activity is noted throughout the southern lowlands. At Tikal this hiatus, as it is often called, appears to be marked by instability, there are very few rich graves, few carved stelae, and construction was limited to very minor enterprises. Any direct connection with Teotihuacán was not just interrupted; it had ended. The rupture was complete. A break with highland Guatemala about the same time is undoubtedly related, as the Teotihuacanos pulled out of Kaminaljuyú as well.

In trying to reconstruct events at Tikal after the break with Teotihuacán and death of Stormy Sky, we enter more speculative ground. Politically some unrest and instability is manifested. Although it seems that the Teotihuacán dynasty was well received, it is very possible that tensions built up between the older Maya traditions and the foreigners, which culminated in a dispute over succession to the throne. Coggins (1979) thinks there is reason to believe that Tikal tried a corulership with Kan Boar, representing the new militarism with only a Calendar Round date, and Claw Skull, advocating a return to basic Maya principles. The latter was a decendant of the original Jaguar Paw dynasty and his stela bears a Long Count date. Not many stelae were erected during these uncertain years. The issue is further confused by Stela 26 being commemorated to Claw Skull posthumously.

The history of Stela 26, known as the Red Stela (see Plate 6-c, p. 167), serves as one example of the treatment given to monuments erected at this time (Shook 1958). When clearing away accumulated debris in the back room of one of the temples (Structure 34) of the Northern Acropolis, investigators found this spectacular stela ruthlessly smashed and broken. Apparently it originally had stood at the back of the room facing the doorway in a position of prominence. The front of the stela was carved with an elaborate figure of Claw Skull. Double rows of beautifully made glyphs adorn the lateral sides, and the entire stone was painted bright red. One fatal day, however, the monument was tumbled, the face was smashed, and chunks were broken off, chips flying. All these fragments were gathered and heaped into pits dug into the floor, other rich offerings were added, and the floor was sealed over. To conceal the base of the stela, a stone altar was raised above it, upon which ceremonial fires were kindled. Eventually the altar too was defaced and partially destroyed. What curious furor possessed these Tikal Maya to vent such destruction upon the Jaguar Paw dynasty? Certainly it was not a rage of disrespect, for the cache offerings accompanying the stela fragments are some of the finest and most exotic known. A great variety of marine material was included, including fish vertebrae, sponges, coral, shells, and sting-ray spines, as were fragments of jade and obsidian and a mosaic plaque of jade and crystalline hematite mounted on mother-of-pearl that could only have been traded down from the highlands of Guatemala. The eccentric obsidians and small incised obsidians in this cache represent some of the finest and rarest objects uncovered to date (Plate 10-a).

The hiatus reflects some severe breakdown which is still imperfectly understood, but we do know that somehow the Maya straightened themselves out, and after A.D. 600 such a great surge of activity and vitality ensued that it is often called the Maya renaissance. Once again burials were stocked with luxurious goods, plazas and courts bristled with freshly dated stelae and altars. Indeed, 60% of all Maya monuments were now erected. Greater and loftier temples were raised, more stucco applied, floors were newly plastered, no effort was spared to glorify the Maya realm. These were the 100 years of the period of uniformity, roughly A.D. 680–780.

Although cultural stimulation from Teotihuacán had ceased, its earlier influence is still much in evidence. Structure 5D–57 in the central Acropolis at Tikal is one of the first manifestations of the Maya renaissance. One of the walls has a large figure with headdress and features carved in relief very much in Teotihuacán style. Another facade sculpture on the same building portrays two figures: a seated, captive Maya bound by a cord or rope held by a stiff Teotihuacán-like figure covered with elaborate detail. Maya glyphs flank the scene. Foreign influence is still common. Some Thin Orange pottery has been found at Uaxactún, a full-face Tlaloc figure outfitted in Teotihuacán style is carved on Stela 11, Yaxhá. In fact, Tlaloc had become a cult that was publicly displayed on monuments and represented in ceramics. At Copán, Tlaloc's head became the manikin-sceptor deity. All of these examples, and many more could be cited, illustrate the lasting impact of the earlier contact. By this time Teotihuacán was facing serious problems. Its days of great mercantilism were over, and whatever the forces were that brought about its destruction, they were hastening the end of that city at this time.

In the Maya lowlands the earlier political unrest and instability had somehow resolved itself. If the old traditions had been challenged, objections had been overcome by about A.D. 680, the next 100 years were prosperous beyond recall. Perhaps, and this is only speculation, the efforts of a strong leader who emerged at this time contributed greatly to revitalizing the society. Ruler A, also known as Double Comb and a descendant of Stormy Sky, emerges as a man of action, dedicated to the state's well being, and interested in commerce. His was a long reign of perhaps 53 years, filled with great prosperity. Possibly he built up trade again, not with Teotihuacán, which was no longer a vital center, but within the Maya world and with Gulf Coast cultures. Pop-

ulation increased and Structure 5D–33–1 at Tikal may have been raised
under his auspices. It is interesting that Ruler A came from the "west"
and ruled at Tikal by virtue of his marriage to a ruler's daughter.
Succession was patrilineal, and if, as is apparent in this case, no heir
was available, then a royal daughter's husband was granted the throne.

By contrast, his son, Ruler B, was more concerned with his personal
image, in asserting his ancestral birth-right and legitimacy, albeit with
great sculptural originality. As at Palenque, each ruler planned his own
tomb and temple, so it seems fitting that Ruler B lies beneath Temple
IV, a huge structure on a hill, looming over Tikal.

The final ruler, Ruler C, showed less originality as he merely copied
other stelae. He was, however, greatly impressed by monumentality.
His twin-pyramid groups are gigantic, apparently his greatest contribution (Jones 1977).

Returning now to our example of Tikal as a city-center, what would
it have looked like in the Late Classic days of renaissance? The very
core of Tikal now consisted of an East, West, and Great Plaza and the
huge complexes of the North and Central Acropolis. Two temples, I
and II (also known as the Temple of the Giant Jaguar and the Temple
of the Masks, respectively), are located on the Great Plaza. These giant
temple-pyramids with their high roof combs soar to a height of 161 m;
together with lower buildings, courts, and plazas, they make up the
central ceremonial cluster (Carr and Hazard 1961). From this nucleus,
three causeways flanked by parapets and separated by two ravines lead
to other structures and groups of buildings, all of which have vaulted
ceilings. The exteriors, which once had flying facades, are very simple,
with relatively little stone carving, whereas the combs were elaborately
decorated with stucco masks. The Temple of the Inscriptions marks the
end of the southeastern or Mendez Causeway, while the Maler Causeway originates behind Temple I and runs north to three twin pyramid
complexes known as Q,R, and O. The pyramids are accompanied by
stelae and altars, some of which are magnificently carved and bear
Initial Series dates. Continuing north, this causeway terminates at a
large plaza bordered by two temples, another twin-pyramid complex,
and acres of other structures, many of which are still untouched by
the archaeologists. This entire area is now called the North Zone. The
third or Tozzer Causeway leads northwest from the central area to
Temple IV, the tallest (65 m) of all standing New World structures,
which is connected by the Maudslay Causeway to the North Zone and
the Maler Causeway, thus completing a huge triangular thoroughfare.
These causeways were a Late Classic innovation here as well as in
Yucatán where they appear spanned by monumental arches. From the
height of Temple IV, or from the base of the enormous roof comb, if
one is bold enough for the climb, the view of all Tikal is superb. Imagine

this magnificent jungle city at this time, a bustling wealthy center where priests, merchants, artisans, and administrators circulated through the paved courts and causeways, temples, palaces, and accessory buildings, all stuccoed and painted, roof combs and stelae erect—and the luxuriant jungle cropped back to the city limits.

The Great Plaza, which had by now been replastered four times since it was laid out in the Late Preclassic period, was the heart of ancient Tikal. Temples I and II, built about A.D. 700, face each other across the plaza, while between them on the north side is Tikal's single most complex structure, the Northern Acropolis. Occupying 1 ha, it alone supports 16 temples and conceals nearly 100 buildings underneath.

The new additions and changes altered the profile of the city. The Temple of the Giant Jaguar underwent many stages of construction to bring it to its present form. Prior to the initial construction, however, a large vaulted tomb was dug deep into the Great Plaza. Its main occupant, Ruler A (Double Comb), was lavishly buried with the finest offerings available: 180 pieces of worked jade, pearls, alabaster, and shells. Quite remarkable is a pile of 90 bone slivers, located in one corner of the dais on which the deceased had been extended. Thirty-seven of these bones were delicately carved depicting deities in naturalistic scenes such as traveling by canoe, and some of these have hieroglyphic texts. Ruler A's tomb (Burial 116) is admittedly one of the finest, but apparently other important interments were frequently made prior to starting construction of a temple–pyramid. Archaeologists conducting a dig can usually tell when they are approaching an underground tomb because quantities of chips of obsidian and flint appear in the fill (W. R. Coe 1967).

Above Ruler A's tomb, the Temple of the Giant Jaguar rises to imposing heights, its nine sloping terraces supporting a temple of three rooms at the summit. These rooms, recessed one above the other, are small and dark and typical of the period, for not until later times were doorways wider and more plentiful and walls thinner. Each vault was supported by *sapote* wood, the exceedingly hard wood of the sapodilla tree, which fortunately has resisted the decomposition characteristic of the tropical forest, preserving some magnificent carving. The exquisitely carved lintels of Tikal are well known, as some have found their way to foreign museums. Fortunately, others still perform their intended function. Not all the beams and lintels were carved, and as a rule, outer doorways have plain lintels. Over the wall of the last of the three temple rooms, rises a tall, two-leveled roof comb, the face of which was decorated with stone blocks representing an individual seated between scrolls and serpents that are now badly weathered. The entire limestone temple once was painted red, with a roof comb of red, cream, and perhaps blue or green (Photo 39; Figure 26).

PHOTO 39. Temple of the Giant Jaguar (Temple I) at Tikal, Guatemala. Height: 4.4 m.
(Courtesy of The Tikal Project, The University Museum, University of Pennsylvania.)

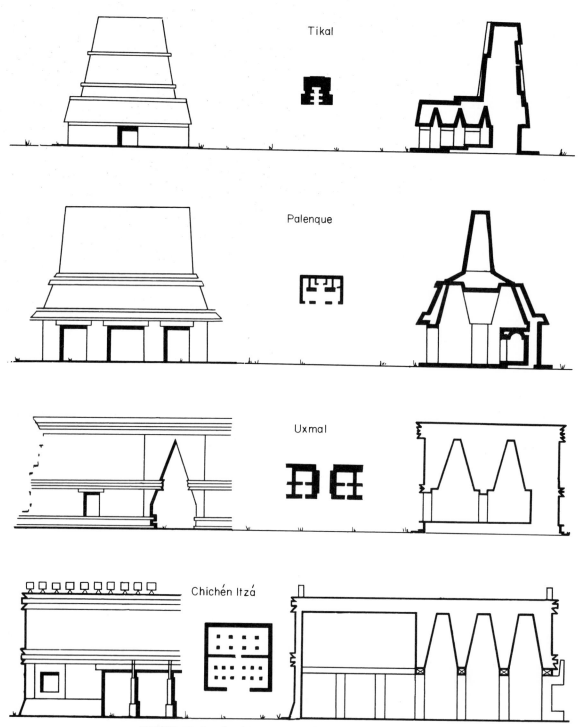

FIGURE 26. Lowland Maya temples, floor plans, and profiles. (Adapted from Marquina 1951.)

There are also sweat houses consisting of a single room with a low doorway from which a channel leads to a firepit at the rear. Sweat baths, or *temescals*, which probably were of ritual significance and may have been associated with the ball game, are known from both lowland and highland regions.

Tikal also subscribed to the ball-game cult. A small ball court with low sloping benches, much like one at Copán, was located in the Great Plaza. A second was found in the East Plaza, and another in the Plaza of the Seven Temples contained a triple court. None had markers and all are open-ended, as is typical of lowland Maya ball courts. The game is believed to have originated in the Gulf Coast lowlands from which region it spread as a cult throughout Mesoamerica in the Late Middle Classic period. The ball court, as has been noted elsewhere, is not typical of Teotihuacán, and its presence signals Peripheral Coastal Lowlands influence. Likewise, it is not the Teotihuacán *talud* and *tablero* seen in some Tikal construction, but the modified form with flaring cornice as found in Tajín (see Figure 27, p. 316). Although Teotihuacán influence is present at Tikal, there is no evidence that these foreigners were ever in control.

A distinctive Late Classic feature is the twin-pyramid and stela-room complex. These pyramids are relatively low and have stairways on all four sides, a radial plan. They usually face each other across a courtyard and are associated with a long, narrow room across a court to the north, which presumably was roofed over with thatch and contained an altar and a stela. These commemorate a katun ending and show the ruler in the act of scattering seeds (?), a scene found on Stela 27 (A.D. 514) at Yaxchilán. Similar themes are found at Teotihuacán. Opposite this stela–altar building was a long single-storied multiroom structure. The whole complex may have been evolved from the earlier distribution of buildings in the Great Plaza. Coggins suggests that these buildings were designed for public participation in the katun-ending rituals which popularized Tlaloc, who became the long-nosed Maya Chac. These celebrations might have paralleled those held in the Ciudadela in Teotihuacán. The new religious cult and the idea of erecting stelae to commemorate 20-year periods were innovations introduced by Curl Snout, the Mexicanized foreigner (Coggins 1980).

Another idea is put forth by Guillemin (1968) who believes this architectural design could relate to the path of the sun as it crosses the sky and descends to cross the underworld, and might be symbolically compared to the life and death of the ruler before he joined his ancestor in the sky. This double connotation would have had popular appeal. Its ritual was introduced by the Late Middle Classic. By Late Classic times, Tikal stelae were fashioned wider and taller than previously, with figures carved in high relief, and women are shown for the first time. A general change notable in these later stelae is that of presenting the body in full front view with feet pointing outward. The altars of this phase, like the stelae, also were heavier and larger than earlier ones. Wall painting and elaborate burials of important personages emphasized class distinctions and social rank.

After A.D. 830 Tikal began to lose inhabitants, and a number of changes presage the Maya collapse. Before proceeding, however, I want to discuss briefly certain other centers, beginning with Copán, the beautiful southern capital with many special features, located near the southern fringes of Mesoamerica.

Copán   Slightly removed from the mainstream of the Petén nuclear region and representing the most important and spectacular of the southern Maya sites is the main group of ruins at Copán in southwestern Honduras (Longyear 1952; Morley 1920, 1956; Stromsvik 1947; Thompson 1965a) (Map 9, p. 257). Located not in the tropical forest but on the banks of a small river in a valley surrounded by forested hills, Copán occupied an enviable natural setting. Flowing westward, the Copán River soon crosses into Guatemala to join the Motagua River on its course to the Caribbean. Thus, geographically Copán was accessible to traders or travelers passing from the western highlands to the whole of Belize, the Petén, and Yucatán towns to the east. Ceramics also show contact with the Ulua–Yojoa cultures of Honduras, and it is possible that travelers to Quelepa coming from Yucatán passed through Copán.

The valley had very rich agricultural lands, but also offered many other advantages. At 610 m above sea level, its climate was temperate, and forest game, fish, and bird life were abundant. Excellent building stone was available close by in the form of a greenish volcanic trachyite that was easy to cut and work when freshly quarried, but hardened upon constant exposure to air. The light green cast of Copán buildings and sculptures is both distinctive and pleasing.

We do not know when Copán was originally settled. There are Preclassic remains in nearby caves and from a pre-Mound 26 midden near the hieroglyphic stairway of the Acropolis. The extent and importance of Preclassic settlement is yet to be determined. It is possible that Copán and nearby Quiriguá received new settlers in the Classic period about the same time, who came from the Petén, perhaps from the royal house of Tikal (Sharer 1978a).

The Copán Valley is naturally subdivided by the hilly terrain and one of the widest sections along the river is where the ancient ruins were constructed. People lived on either side of the great ceremonial center on both sides of the river.

In 1976 the Peabody Museum of Harvard University initiated a settlement study of the Copán Valley which is to form part of a larger

Copán project to be undertaken by the Honduran government. This new research is badly needed to provide some information on the surrounding area which has been neglected, as attention until now has been directed to the main Acropolis. To date, various living zones have been located but only the Copán pocket itself has been excavated (Willey and Levanthal 1979; Willey *et al.* 1978). This is the section where the valley widens out to 2–4 km along the river for a distance of 12.5 km. The flood-plain or first terrace of the river shows no signs of habitation, but the second terrace of the valley bottomland, where the main ceremonial center is located, was favored for living.

Settlements are also found all along the northern foothills with mounds occupying natural terraces or small hillocks. Finally there are small clusters of housing units apparently scattered at random in outlying areas. A cautious population estimate for the Copán Valley or pocket is 10,000 persons.

The preliminary results of the Copán Valley project now provide some of the most specific information on Maya living arrangements. The residential settlements were ranked in four types from simple to complex (Types 1 to 4). Type 1 sites had only three to five mounds no more than 1.25 m in height around smallish courts and were built of undressed stone rubble. CV–20, an example of a Type 2 site, consisted of five mounds around a main plaza and three smaller mounds grouped above a minor court. One mound, Building B, located on the east overlooking the main plaza, was a special-function structure, believed to have served as a temple or shrine as it contained a single room with the only well-polished and plastered floor in CV–20. It was the only main mound that did not contain an earlier structure. Dating from A.D. 450–650, CV–20 was rebuilt and enlarged at various times and used until possibly A.D. 800. Burials with polychrome pottery and some elite goods were found under the plazas and buildings, but the finest grave goods were placed in the mound of Building B. CV–20 did not house royalty but was inhabited by moderately wealthy extended families.

The unit CV–43 is an example of a Type 3 settlement. It was connected to the main road or *sacbé*, which led to the main ruins of Copán by a narrow road 1 m wide. Consisting of five patio-groups, mounds reached as high as 4.75 m and more dressed stone was used; in other respects the general plan was much like that of CV–20. The most outstanding feature was a large pyramid, Mound A, mounted by a staircase leading to three vaulted and painted chambers, containing masonry benches along the back walls. The overhang of the bench in the central room was inscribed with a hieroglyphic text containing a dedicatory date of A.D. 780 and 13 full-figure glyphs. The long bench was upheld by four false columns of Atlantean figures, the Bacabs, deities who held up the Maya sky at its four corners. Whereas the other structures were all domestic in function, Mound A served as the temple or shrine.

The most elite residential areas were located close to the main center of Copán to the north and east and were connected to it by a fine *sacbé*. Structures were larger, more complex, and contained the finest offerings with graves. It was a Type 4 grouping that yielded the only imports from central Mexico. The settlement study at Copán gives us a range of living schemes from simple to complex. It is possible to see how the Maya temple eventually evolved from the special-function building of the Type 2 site, while the basic Mesoamerican design of mounds facing a court was a very ancient idea.

The Copán flood-plain was not large, but extremely rich, so by refining their agricultural techniques, the relatively small settlement at Copán must have lived privileged lives. A dam built between A.D. 650–800 indicates that there were sophisticated members of the populace who, not content to rely on the whims of nature, decided to exercise some control over the flow of water. Built of neatly cut stone blocks and mortar, the dam extends 4 m across the channel of a small tributary in the foothills just below a spring (Turner II and Johnson 1979).

Although Long Count dates at Copán range from A.D. 465 to 800, the cultural peak was in the seventh century. Most of the ruins visible today date from this part of the Classic period.

The main group of ruins consists of a massive cluster of constructions known as the Acropolis, which is composed of repeated constructions overlying earlier buildings. The principal multiroomed structures and temples are ornately decorated with roof combs and flying facades. The top of the Acropolis may be reached by the famous monumental hieroglyphic staircase, which is 27 m high and 9 m wide. The riser of each of the 63 steps is intricately carved with hieroglyphs, 2000 in all, constituting the longest Maya text in existence. Spaced at intervals up the steep flight of steps are five seated figures of stone, each almost 2 m high.

From the top of the Acropolis one commands an impressive view of the Copán River far below, in addition to the main courts and their surrounding buildings and stepped terraces. One is also struck by the imposing view of the great plaza, which is over 210 m long and studded with handsome stelae and altars elaborately carved with personages and hieroglyphs in high relief. It was built between 9.12.5.0.0 and 9.13.0.0.0 as a center for the monuments, some of which were brought in from other areas nearby and re-erected here. It is at Copán where figures most closely approximate true sculpture in the round. Altars are intricately carved in heavy relief, and hieroglyphs are particularly ornate and imaginative (see Plate 6-e, p. 167). The individuals depicted on stelae are characteristically stiff and sedate in posture, but richly attired and gigantic in size. Mention is often made of the oriental cast of the Copán style of stone carving with its curious bearded individuals.

There is no doubt but that Copán represents something special in regional development.

Copán is outstanding not only for the beauty but also for the abundance of its stone carving. Facades are lavishly decorated with human, bird, and animal figures; altars, stelae, stairways, and temples provide a wealth of hieroglyphic inscriptions, many of which still await scholarly interpretation.

The buildings are of massive proportions and combine simplicity with intricate relief sculpture in stone and stucco. The Temple of Meditation (Temple 22) is an example of such cyclopean masonry. One mounts the enormous stairway and enters the temple through a doorway carved in the form of a gigantic serpent's mouth, a feature usually associated with Río Bec architecture. The facade was originally decorated with rain gods, huge grotesque masks, gargoyles, and seated human figures. The inner doorway to the temple is carved with naturalistic human figures seated on skulls and accompanied by elaborately intertwined motifs of grotesque monsters. The temple has been accurately restored by the Carnegie Institution, following a careful description by Maudslay, even to such details as holes near the doorways for inserting poles, probably to support a curtain or mat.

On the northern side of the court of the hieroglyphic stairway lies one of the most beautiful ball courts known (Photo 40). Following the

PHOTO 40. Ball court at Copán, Honduras. (Photographed by the author.)

typical plan of an elongated H, the long playing alley had crosswise rectangular end zones and floor markers. Wide sloping benches on either side border the playing area and are studded with three pairs of large parrot heads set into the upper edges. This court overlies two earlier ones.

The stone carving at Copán is particularly fine and the wealth of inscriptions is notable. This was, of course, the southeastern capital of the Maya realm from A.D. 731–790. We do not know as much about reigns and rulers of Copán as we do for some of the other centers but a few have been identified (Marcus 1976a). The history of Copán is closely linked to that of neighboring Quiriguá, which for some years was subject to the larger center. Ruler XVIII-Jog at Copán ruled contemporaneously with Cauac Sky (Two-Legged Sky) at Quiriguá. Some sort of conflict between the two centers took place in A.D. 737 from which Quiriguá emerged victorious and apparently gained its independence. Before long it displayed its own emblem glyph and its fortunes rose. The date of A.D. 737 is prominently and frequently recorded at Quiriguá, but preferably ignored at Copán which came off badly. Perhaps Ruler XVIII-Jog was captured, killed, or Copán was humiliated in some other fashion. However it was, Copán takes a break of 20 years before it resumes recording inscriptions.

The next ruler, son of XVIII-Jog, New Sun-at-Horizon or Yax Macaw, is more visible. We see him sitting on a throne on a sculptured altar bearing a Long Count date of 9.16.12.5.17. His accession to the throne may be the scene depicted on Altar Q (Photo 41) in which 16 local lords of Copán are seated on one or more glyphs and the name of XVIII-Jog is recorded as Yax Macaw's father. We assume the personages to be local leaders since no emblem glyphs are represented. The next ruler was Yax Bat (Hand–Leaf–Sky), whose birth and accession dates we do not know. The inscriptions of Copán differ somewhat from those of other centers in that they deal more with ceremony and ritual than with dynastic successions. The last recorded date at Copán is 9.18.10.0.0 (A.D. 800) and by then Copán had declined in power and prestige, having lost its position as regional capital.

Quiriguá   A 2-day walk north of Copán in today's banana land of the Motagua River valley of Guatemala, some of the tallest sandstone stelae known were carved by the inhabitants of Quiriguá. This site was never a large densely nucleated center and perhaps its proximity to Copán eclipsed its importance for many years. The structures here in no way compare to those of Copán or Petén, but hieroglyphic inscriptions representing fantastic mythical monsters were masterfully carved on stelae and gigantic flat boulders. Quiriguá is unique in many ways, and its singular history is providing us with many details about the functioning of a

PHOTO 41. Altar Q, Copán, Honduras. The stone may commemorate accession to the throne of ruler Yax Macaw. (Courtesy of the Trustees of the British Museum.)

secondary center, in contrast to a capital center. The story of Quiriguá that follows is based on Sharer's (1978a) reconstruction.

The Acropolis was built in four stages of construction spanning the years A.D. 550–850. Construction materials progress from the oldest period, using river silt and cobbles, to cut rhyolite blocks, followed by the use of sandstone, and finally marble. A ball court was built between A.D. 720–740 and a second one in the years between A.D. 740 and 810. At this time a very ambitious building program was undertaken, remodeling, enlarging, and substituting older structures with new ones. Much of the Acropolis was rebuilt between A.D. 810–850 adding a new platform with sandstone staircase. The Acropolis contained the finest residential complexes, providing the occupants with such amenities as benches, curtain holders, and windows. There were also areas for services, storage, and less elegant living quarters nearby. The Great Plaza, as at Copán, was the focal point for displaying stelae and other great monuments such as zoomorphic sculptures and some of the largest monuments. Although some of the peripheral residences were located downstream on higher terracing, most settlements were spread along the river on the first terraces.

Clues to Quiriguá's beginnings probably lie well buried below ruins and silt, but the site could well have Late Preclassic remains. Sharer thinks Quiriguá was settled as early as Copán, and the two sites may share common origins. A good guess would be that some Early Classic elite settled here from the northern lowlands. This is not idle speculation for the Caan glyph identifying the Sky dynasty of Quiriguá's rulers is associated with Tikal's Early Classic dynasty as well as that of Copán. Kinship ties may have existed between these three sites.

Of the five rulers at Quiriguá, it is the first, Cauac Sky, who is the most colorful and to whom Quiriguá owes its greatest debt. He ascended the throne prior to A.D. 730. We know nothing of his origins but he could have inherited his power from a line of leaders from the Petén or Belize area. In any event, Quiriguá seems to have spent its early days as a dependency of Copán. Cauac Sky (or Two-Legged Sky) who lived regally in elaborate quarters in the southwest corner of the Acropolis, led his people during the A.D. 737 conflict with Copán. Emerging victorious, Quiriguá gained its independence, its own emblem glyph, and henceforth had complete control of the Motagua River valley trade route. Probably the movement of jade and obsidian from the Motagua River valley to the Caribbean accounts for its great prosperity. Control of this route became even more important in the Late Classic period, when trade routes began to shift away from the Petén resulting in the circumnavigation of Yucatán.

This cleverness seems to have isolated Quiriguá, for it is not even mentioned by other sites. There are no records of intermarriages or alliances. Indeed Sharer wonders if it was ostracized by its contemporaries. Ceramically Quiriguá does not share wares with its neighbors. Almost entirely lacking is the ubiquitous polychrome found at Copán and most Classic Maya centers.

Not greatly concerned, Cauac Sky undertook a massive building program and constructed a huge monumental plaza enclosed on three sides by the Acropolis. Here he housed his five portrait stelae (Photo 42).

His successors could hardly equal these feats. Sky Xul (A.D. 784–795) was probably Cauac Sky's son and ruled 11 years. Imix Dog reigned only a few years to be followed by Scroll Sky who occupied the throne for a short time in A.D. 800. His record is very vague but Jade Sky ascended to power in A.D. 805 and renewed the building program. The hieroglyphic frieze on Structure 1B–1 has the last recorded date at Quiriguá of A.D. 810. And 20 years later, the largest structure ever erected at Quiriguá was completed (Structure 1B–5). This may have been Jade Sky's living quarters.

PHOTO 42. Detail of Stela C, portraying ruler Cauac Sky, A.D. 775. Quiriguá, Guatemala. (Photographed by the author.)

Quiriguá was probably not abandoned until about A.D. 850, and even then the abandonment was not total. Some inhabitants in the Postclassic left behind Plumbate pottery, copper objects, and even a *chacmool* (Richardson 1940).

A few sites among many will suffice to portray the flavor of the Classic period in Belize. These were largely riverine-oriented.

Belize

In southern Belize, the site of Lubaantún (Hammond 1975b) furnishes a good example of life in this part of the Maya realm. Not a huge ceremonial center, its location was well chosen, having the economic potential of exploiting the foothills of the Maya Mountains to the north where most of the population lived and grew corn and beans and hunted deer, peccary, and birds. Cacao would have done well here since abundant rainfall and humidity provide ideal conditions. The coastal plain was accessible by a short trip down the Río Grande to the Caribbean shores, where a secondary population hunted waterfowl and gathered copal incense from the trees, while those living right on the shore had access to a wealth of fish, shell fish, and even deep-water marine life (mackerel and sharks). Of the animal bones recovered at Lubaantún, 40% were of marine origin.

Life centered around trade, for Lubaantún could reach Alta Verapaz in highland Guatemala and have access by river and coastal waters to the southern and central Maya sites as well as to northern Yucatán. A healthy trade is documented by highland volcanic stone and much obsidian. Jade is rare at Lubaantún. The 1970 excavations turned up an eighth-century clay figurine of a musician wearing a cacao-pod pendant. In another instance, two figurines were found made from the very same mold, but one of these was discovered many years ago in Cobán in the Guatemalan highlands, and the other in Lubaantún. Seldom does the archaeologist recover such clear proof of trade.

The site itself is located on a ridge between two streams and consists of about 25 clusters of large rubble-filled platforms grouped about plazas. Dated inscriptions, stelae, and vaulted buildings are not found here, and the perishable superstructures are gone. Rich graves are lacking but a multiple tomb containing 18 individuals (a family?) has been reported. The associated pottery was all Late Classic (Hammond 1975b).

Lubaantún is strictly a Late Classic site, having no early history of settlement and having been abandoned not long after A.D. 830. Further north in central Belize, Barton Ramie and Benque Viejo did not end so abruptly but neither did they contribute much at a late date.

Stretching along the Belize River, Barton Ramie and Benque Viejo had both been occupied since Preclassic days (Willey *et al.* 1965). The early development of Barton Ramie parallels that of the northeastern Petén, sharing ceramic traditions and architectural developments. The Middle Classic period is essentially represented by the Tiger Run Phase at Barton Ramie, and Benque Viejo IIIa at Benque Viejo. These mark the transition from Early to Late Classic ceramically, a long gradual change on the Belize River (A.D. 600–700).

The following phase at Barton Ramie, Early Spanish Lookout (A.D. 700–830) is marked by a tremendous amount of massive construction. Polychrome styles continue but the pottery looks less and less like that of the Petén. This is coeveal with Tepeu 2 in the Petén and represents the peak of cultural activity in both domestic and ceremonial construction, as well as in population.

Thereafter, in Late Spanish Lookout (A.D. 830–889) abrupt changes are noticeable. There was still contact with the Petén heartland, but Barton Ramie began its decline, whereas by A.D. 830 Benque Viejo was abandoned. No new or at least no significant structures were erected, and ceramic decoration fell off. However, people continued to occupy all the house sites, so the mass exodus seen elsewhere did not occur this early at Barton Ramie. Nonetheless, the great civilization had peaked, and the Late Phase (New Town: A.D. 950–1300) has no fine exotic goods and does not reflect its earlier prosperity. Curiously, everything was intentionally covered over with soil, so the great pyramidal structures looked like simple earthen mounds. Barton Ramie in the New Town phase has little in common with the older Classic Maya civilization, even the pottery has been replaced by that of the Central Petén Postclassic tradition.

Further north still we find Nohmul, one of the largest Classic sites and one which may well help reconstruct the transition from Classic to Postclassic in the area. It is located on a ridge between the Río Hondo and New River not far from Cuello. A large Acropolis, platforms around plazas, temple–pyramids, and a ball court suggest the traditional lowland Maya Classic site. The core area is less than 1 km² with a sustaining area of villages occupying 20–25 km². Some kind of a platform structure on the river has raised the possibility of Nohmul's role as a river port. It seems to have been actively involved with long-distance canoe trade, which in the Late Classic period was oriented toward Yucatán (Hammond 1975a, 1977a).

Trade was also important to the north and west of the Petén, for this is the region which opened up to merchants from other parts of Mexico. The impact of this foreign contact should be kept in mind, for it has some bearing on the eventual collapse of the Maya civilization.

Lagartero

Before examining the great river sites of the western Maya region, I would like to call attention to a site currently being excavated by the New World Archaeological Foundation in Chiapas, close to the Guatemalan border. This is the Late Classic site of Lagartero (see Map 9, p. 257), an island and peninsular settlement in the swamps formed by rivers and *cenote*-like lakes. Temple–pyramids, palaces, and other buildings were grouped around plazas and patios, but it is the mold-made human figurines that are of particular interest.

Lagartero figurine bodies are mold-made in two or three parts plus the head, which was formed from front and back pieces. These were not placed in graves, as we will see at Jaina (see p. 324), but were found broken in refuse deposits. In her study of these remarkable figurines (see Plate 9-k, l, m, p. 253), S. M. Ekholm points out that 60% represent women, elegantly attired and assuredly of elite status. Men are well represented too but are less numerous. The previously unrecognized art style of the figurines is closely associated with Tepeu polychrome pottery with figure painting. It is interesting that only men are represented on the painted pots. The beautifully dressed women portrayed by figurines may have had a very important role in this society (S. M. Ekholm 1979).

Altar de Sacrificios Starting with the Pasión River sites and proceeding westward we will mention only the most outstanding Maya centers in this region, well drained by the great Usumacinta river system (Map 9, p. 257). The first of these is Altar de Sacrificios (Willey 1973, 1977a, 1977b; Willey and Smith 1969), strategically located in the relatively flat plain of the Pasión River where it is joined by the Chixoy River, thus providing a trade route to Alta Verapaz. Below this juncture the river is known as the Usumacinta, a main thoroughfare of communication from the western regions of Tabasco to the Petén during the Classic period. By making a short portage to the Sarstoon River from Altar de Sacrificios, canoes could reach the Bay of Honduras on the east coast of Yucatán. Thus, Altar de Sacrificios occupied a prime location for commercial transactions, an advantage not overlooked by the aggressive Putún (Thompson 1970). A leading ceremonial center in its own right, Altar de Sacrificios flourished throughout Classic times. The first Long Count date of A.D. 455 is carved on a red sandstone stela. This stone was available about 9 km upstream, but the closest source of limestone, the preferred building material, was 21 km upstream. Obsidian, quartzites, jadeites, and other igneous rocks all had to be imported from the Guatemalan highlands. Although deep in the tropical forest environment, Altar de Sacrificios was so well communicated via river and trail systems that all these products could be obtained and are found in richly stocked graves. There is a pronounced differentiation between ordinary and ceremonial or ritual wares, or perhaps simply luxury wares for the elite. The Floral Park manifestation discussed earlier in relation to the Belize sites and El Salvador is evident here on the Pasión River. Only the strategic location of Altar de Sacrificios can explain its growth out of the Early Preclassic Xe complex, the Early Classic beginnings, and the wonderful 200 years of prosperity following the hiatus of A.D. 534–593.

Here in the southwestern Petén, the Maya erected a pyramid of 9 or 10 terraces with almost vertical walls. An elaborate staircase led up to the summit, once crowned by a perishable temple. A curious feature is the placement of stelae and altars on the stairways of platforms and buildings rather than in the courts and plazas. But consistent with prevailing trends, the buildings were arranged around courts and plazas. A ball court at the site resembles that of Copán but lacks the masonry superstructures. Toward the end of the great Classic period, one sees in Altar de Sacrificios' art faces and motifs that reflect a new strain. This outside influence is markedly apparent in the pottery and figurines from what has been called at this site the Ximba phase. Fine Orange, particularly the variety known as Y or Altar type, and Fine Gray wares predominate. Fine Orange paste was also used for the figurines that present non-Maya features.

The last dated monument at Altar de Sacrificios was erected around A.D. 780. This does not mean the center was immediately abandoned thereafter but it marks both the influx of outside ceramic styles and signs of general impoverishment.

If its location controlled the growth and prosperity of Altar de Sacrificios, so too does it explain its ultimate collapse, for eventually it was outside pressures and intrusions of foreigners who pushed up the rivers that hastened the end of this site.

J. Eric Thompson (1970), basing his observations on the study of linguistics and historical source material along with archaeological data, believed that the Chontal Maya people, whom he identifies as Putún, were responsible for the outside influences noticed first at Altar de Sacrificios (about A.D. 771–790) and later (A.D. 830) at Seibal. The Putún Maya lived in the large delta lands of the Grijalva and Usumacinta Rivers in southern Campeche and Tabasco, an area culturally marginal to the great Classic Maya centers.

These people are known to have been aggressive traders and merchant seamen who eventually controlled the sea routes around the peninsula of Yucatán to the Bay of Honduras on the east, probably seeking salt, slaves, or honey. Groups undoubtedly traveled by both land and sea to penetrate the Maya region at various times. Remember that trade routes were well established and we noted the widespread influence of Teotihuacán in the Early Middle Classic period. It is also seen at Uxmal, Becán, and Altun Há. Mexican Tlaloc representations are sprinkled throughout Classic Maya sites as far south as Copán. The Putún should not be made responsible for all evidence of foreign contact but are an example of the mercantilism practiced in the Late Middle Classic. Their center of operations was Chakanputún, a province of Putún in Tabasco (?) or possibly the name given to their capital which Ball (1974b) suggests could have been Seibal. Possessing Mexican neighbors, they naturally intermarried and absorbed some Mexican tastes and habits. In Late Classic years, these Putún made incursions by canoe up the Usumacinta River, thus accounting for the blend of Maya and Mexican elements that appears at this time along interior river sites. The Putún may also be the producers of Y (Altar) Fine Orange, a fine-paste ware prominent in the Petén and the area drained by the Usumacinta River. These Putún seafaring merchants will be referred to often in the pages ahead.

Seibal

As Altar de Sacrificios declined in power and influence around A.D. 751, its neighbor, Seibal, located 100 km upstream, gradually rose to take its place. Like Altar de Sacrificios, Seibal's roots date back to Preclassic times, particularly Late Preclassic, but Seibal has few remains from the Early Classic period. It might even be considered semiabandoned for a short time, as no stelae were carved from about A.D. 500–650 (Willey et al. 1975).

Three groups of ruins are located on a range of limestone bluffs precisely at a bend of the Pasion River. They are connected by causeways, the entire building area occupying about 1 km². The high location would have been advantageous for defense, which was a factor to consider in Late Classic times. The highest elevations available were selected for building, undoubtedly for better drainage but possibly also for purposes of communication. The structures themselves were of the ceremonial type typical of the organized religious hierarchy believed to have been in existence. At Seibal most of the populace lived outside the main nucleus in small peripheral clusters grouped around central courts. More than 43 structures have been excavated revealing corbelled vaults and open-ended ball courts, as well as a round three-terraced structure (Structure 79) with a large jaguar altar located at the end of a causeway. This is the only round structure known from the Petén. Dated at A.D. 830–928, it belongs to the last cultural phase at Seibal, subject to outside ideas and influences.

Artifacts are much like those of Altar de Sacrificios with the exception of eccentric flints, which are scarce. Most of the altars are uncarved as are the majority of stelae. Those bearing dates use the Calendar Round more often than the Long Count system.

After A.D. 650 there was a steady growth in population and public construction with maximum activity in the 60 years prior to A.D. 890 when the finest architecture and sculptures were produced. Even true Puuc veneer masonry can be seen in walls and vaults of Structure A3. A close relationship with Altar de Sacrificios was maintained and ceramic traits such as Fine Orange and Fine Gray wares were shared (Sabloff 1975). The foreign elements may have been provided first hand.

There seem to have been two intrusions of outsiders (Ball 1974b; Sabloff 1975). The first took place around A.D. 771–790 (?) and a second in the early or mid ninth century. These intruders may have pushed up the rivers from the coast, or come south from Yucatán. Seibal art shows a mixture of Mexican (Toltec) and non-Classic Maya styles as seen in the ceramics and stone sculpture. The foreigners may have even replaced the elite at Seibal for a short time. These people seem not to have maintained control over Seibal for long and were not the cause of its collapse. Indeed, these intruders joined in the erection of dated stelae. Around A.D. 930, however, Seibal too was overcome by the same forces that caused the decline of the great Classic Petén centers.

Bonampak   Further along the Usumacinta drainage, western centers of Maya civilization were also constructing temple–pyramids, erecting stelae, and recording dates and events in hieroglyphic carvings. Bonampak in Chiapas, a contemporary of Altar de Sacrificios, is a site renowned for its unique mural paintings of the ancient Maya, which provide us with infinite detail of dress, processional scenes, musicians, sacrifices, sacred rites, and warfare (Ruppert, Thompson, and Proskouriakoff 1955). Bonampak lies deep in the jungle home of the modern Lacandón Indians, who bear such great resemblance to their Maya ancestors that they appear to have just stepped down from a stela. The ruins of Bonampak lie on the banks of the Lacanjá River and are so completely covered by the dense vegetation that one is close upon them before they are seen. Around a great rectangular plaza, groups of platforms support temples at varying levels. The temples are small, but all are built with vaulted roofs. Bonampak shares many architectural features with neighboring Yaxchilán such as carved stone lintels and block masonry construction. It also has Calendar Round dates.

The Temple of the Paintings contains three rooms, each with a stone lintel carved in relief, and fresco paintings that cover the entire wall from floor to ceiling. The walls were first prepared with a lime coating 3–5 cm thick, and while they were still damp the paintings were executed in orange, yellow, green, dark red, and turquoise blue. The processional figures are shown in fancy headdresses and elaborate attire, carrying children, using umbrellas for shade, wearing animal disguises and fantastic masks, dancing, and conversing. Musicians rattle turtle shells, beat drums, and shake clay (or gourd?) rattles (Photo 43) (Thompson 1954; Villagra Caleti 1949). On the walls of another room a battle scene and its consequences are depicted—the trial and punishment of prisoners (Photo 44) and a group of warriors and their leader, who wears a jaguar skin thrown over his back and holds a staff of authority in his right hand. Other scenes include bound victims whose fingers drip blood, some of whom are seminude and have disheveled hair. This sequence is completed by a painting of a decapitated skull resting on a step; in the murals of the next room victory is being celebrated (Villagra Caleti 1949). Bonampak is Late Classic in date.

We now know that these are historical scenes, relating at least in part to the investiture of authority upon a new ruler. Certainly the murals provide us with invaluable, seldom-preserved ethnographic data.

Yaxchilán

Yaxchilán, a huge site that sprawls across the Usumacinta River in the modern Mexican state of Chiapas, shares the mansard type roof and centrally located perforated roof combs with the more westerly Palenque. Architecturally, buildings of the palace type with three entrances rather than the temple–pyramid prevail, but many other features recall Petén construction with very thick walls. Two ball courts have been identified.

PHOTO 43. Wall painting showing a procession of musicians, Bonampak, Chiapas. (Courtesy of the Instituto Nacional de Antropología e Historia, Mexico.)

Despite the fact that the site has yielded more than 125 inscriptions on carved lintels and stelae, no major work has ever been done at this site. Many inscriptions bear Calendar Round dates of the seventh and eighth centuries (Graham 1973) (see Plate 10-e, p. 289).

Only fragments are known of Yaxchilán's political history. We know that a ruler called Shield Jaguar was born in A.D. 647 but not at Yaxchilán. He was an outsider who could have come from Piedras Negras or the Puuc area of northern Yucatán. He is seen on Lintel 25, which may commemorate his death. He is shown as a warrior wearing a mask with Tlaloc and the year-sign headdress. This particular combination of Tlaloc and the year-sign is found in the seventh and eighth centuries, possibly derived from Teotihuacán. It is scattered in Maya dynastic art, but its meaning is not yet well understood. It may be symbolic of a title or possibly represent a family connection, in this case between Uxmal, Piedras Negras, Bonampak, or even with Xochicalco and Teotihuacán, where it is also found (Pasztory 1979).

PHOTO 44. Wall painting showing torture of prisoners, Bonampak, Chiapas. (Courtesy of the Peabody Museum, Harvard University, photograph by Hillel Burger, copyright © 1972 by the President and Fellows of Harvard College.)

A later ruler at Yaxchilán, Bird-Jaguar, who claimed mythological ancestry, also wears the emblem. He ascended the throne in A.D. 752 and is not a descendant of Shield-Jaguar, but was also an outsider. He was one of the important dignitaries that attended an elaborate funeral of a prominent woman in her forties at Altar de Sacrificios in A.D. 754.

The scene is beautifully painted on a Tepeu polychrome vessel found at Altar de Sacrificios (Adams 1977b). The implication is that the rulers of Yaxchilán, Tikal, and perhaps Alta Verapaz who gathered at Altar de Sacrificios may have been related through marriage, thus giving an idea of the political significance of elite kinship ties.

It could be that Yaxchilán was controlled by some Putún groups for a short time prior to A.D. 750. At least some Yucatecan-style inscriptions are evident, and influence from the Campeche region is seen in a particular method of recording dates, examples being the Calendar Round dates recorded on Stelaes 18 and 20 (Graham 1973). Yaxchilán provides a hint of the unrest and change soon to come, for prominent themes in art are group compositions of strife and conflict (Proskouriakoff 1960, 1961; Thompson 1970). In late days, warfare was a favorite subject.

Piedras Negras   Nearby Piedras Negras, a settlement with no Preclassic background, is located in very steep terrain and rises from a high hill. It is typical of Usumacinta sites where height was achieved by leveling and terracing natural elevations. The ruins consist of tightly grouped courts, structures with wide stairways, two ball courts, and eight sweat houses with dressing rooms and lounging quarters (W. R. Coe 1959). Architects at Piedras Negras were slow to take up the corbelled arch, but eventually ceilings were vaulted in pure Maya style. Other Petén influence can be seen in stucco masks which flank the staircases, although the colonnaded doorways are more like Palenque. Buildings let in much more light and air than earlier Petén construction permitted (Kubler 1975).

Piedras Negras became a thriving Classic center where stelae were superbly carved, exhibiting great detail in styles of clothing and unusual care in the execution of hieroglyphs. Both wall panels and stelae distinguish Piedras Negras from other sites, and it was the groups of stelae at this site that led Proskouriakoff (1960) to her remarkable study of the personal histories of important leaders (see Chapter 5).

About 40 stelae have been found at Piedras Negras, which commonly depict a sacred person, ruler in a niche, priests preparing or making sacrifices, or a victorious warrior. The martial motifs of the seventh century often include a bound captive or prisoner at the foot of a warrior (Brown 1972). One ruler of Piedras Negras, Turtleshell, claimed to be descended from a mythological ancestor as did those at Yaxchilán and Palenque (Mathews and Schele 1974). Piedras Negras art is rich in iconographic detail exhibiting many traits not only from the Petén and Palenque, but also from the more distant regions of Cotzumalhuapa, Xochicalco, and Teotihuacán (Parsons 1969).

Widespread trade is much in evidence and was clearly important. Shells from both coasts, obsidian, and jade are common in caches.

However, the lack of deep middens and a Preclassic horizon at this site argues against a long occupation. As at Yaxchilán, themes in art eventually depict military scenes. Although few weapons are included in caches and burials, a warrior group may have been important here as well.

We come now to Palenque, a great Classic Maya center of the west, **Palenque** yet very different from anything we have yet seen. Carved inscriptions and Long Count dates abound, but only two stelae are known. There is no Acropolis, no great plazas with paired stelae and altars, no *sacbés*, no great caches of eccentric flints or obsidian. The polychrome wares typical of the Petén were short-lived, and, although misleading at first glance, there appears to be no city planning. Yet despite these differences, Palenque belonged to the Maya world and became one of its four leading centers or capitals of the eighth century.

Palenque has long been famous for the beauty of its sculpture in stucco and marvelous carved panel reliefs as well as for the harmony and charm of its crested temples with mansard roofs. Archaeologists are intrigued by the vaulted aqueduct to channel waters of the Otolum River beneath the ruins, a vaulted bridge over the river, trefoiled niches to reduce the massiveness of walls, a four-story tower structure, T-shaped windows, and a completely new concept in temple building. Temple walls are thinner at Palenque, the doors wider and more numerous, roof combs are centered over the middle of the temple roof instead of at the back. The rear room of the temple has a typical sanctuary or interior shrine with its own roof (Figure 26). The combined result is a lighter, airier temple than the dark, massive walled structures of Tikal. Palenque does share with Tikal the custom of placing tombs within pyramids, thus the Temple of the Inscriptions was the scene of one of the most spectacular funerary rites in Mesoamerica. In addition, it is here that true portraiture was developed, not just the idealized Maya figure, but naturalistic models of distinct personalities, even to portraying their physical defects.

It is little wonder that Palenque has been a favorite of visitors (Maudslay 1889–1902). Nestled in the foothills of the great Chiapas mountains which are covered with forests of mahogany, cedar, and *sapote*, the temples of Palenque command a magnificent view far out over the low coastal plain that extends to the Gulf of Mexico some 128 km away. Although a few Chicanel sherds have been recovered, and a small ball court and tomb with rather undistinguished pottery date from the Early Classic period, Palenque was in most respects just one more modest or rustic settlement until the seventh century. The extraordinary florescence of the site is confined to a mere 150-year span of time and can be attributed to the energy and inspiration of some remarkable

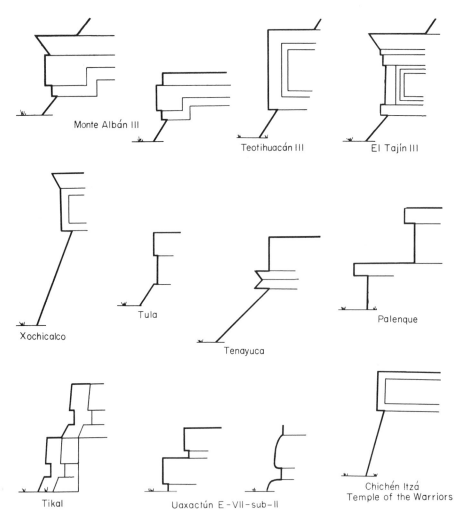

FIGURE 27. Comparative architectural profiles of Mesoamerican pyramids. (Adapted from Marquina 1951.)

personalities. The ruins we see today can be better understood by attempting a historical reconstruction beginning with Lord Shield Pacal (Mathews and Schele 1974; Robertson *et al.* 1976; Schele 1976).

This remarkable ruler was born in A.D. 603, ascended to power in A.D. 615 at the age of 12½ years, enjoyed 68 years on the throne, and merited all the pomp and ceremony accorded him upon his death in A.D. 683. He boasted of a mythological ancestry, thus establishing himself as semidivine, but the archaeological record indicates that he inherited his power from his mother, a consort whose husband was an outsider. There was some major power struggle in the preceding generation resulting in Pacal's uncle being beheaded, an event graphically recorded on a stucco relief. The uncle had a badly deformed clubfoot which, despite his unfortunate end, was viewed as a divine attribute. His sister, Lady Zac-Kuk, is depicted with a very massive head and jaw, the victim of acromegaly. She was Lord Shield Pacal's mother, and because of his youth, she ruled as regent for 15 years after her son came to power. Lord Pacal was also born with a clubfoot which he seems to have flaunted as proof of his divinity as well as his relationship to his divine but decapitated uncle. This clubfoot is significant as it was eventually conceptualized and transformed into a serpent. God K, the serpent-footed deity, rapidly became prominent as the symbol of divine rulership. After A.D. 912 we find God K, the manikin-scepter deity, with a serpent foot and a flare in his forehead as a common concept throughout the Maya realm.

As is frequent among divine royalty, intermarriages prevail, for the divine must choose for marriage one of their own rank. Thus it is possible that Lord Pacal married Lady Zac-Kuk, his mother, in name only or perhaps in actual fact. She died when he was 27 years old. He also married his sister, Lady Ahpo-Hel. The genes for physical deformities were thus closely retained and best explain the abnormalities in the Palenque ruling family. Lord Pacal fathered two sons who succeeded him: Lord Chan-Bahlum and Lord Hok, the first of whom had six toes on each foot and six fingers on his left hand, an example of polydactyly.

No other ruler reigned as long as Lord Pacal, and he and his mother are responsible for the extraordinary transformation of Palenque into a western power. He built several temples and constructed part of the Palace complex. T-shaped windows, trefoiled niches in vaulted roofs, courtyards, galleries beneath corbelled passages, and sculptured panels combine to make the Palace unique among Maya structures. The entire complex is situated on an artificial platform some 90 m long by 73 m wide. Its pillars were lavishly decorated and covered with stucco reliefs; walls were decorated with stucco masks and figures. Traces of the hieroglyphs and scenes that once adorned the walls may still be seen.

He also laid out the plaza before the Temple of the Inscriptions and had this huge temple–pyramid built to house his tomb (Photo 45). When he died in A.D. 683, his final resting place had been prepared and his funeral must have been the most sumptuous Palenque ever witnessed.

He was carefully laid out in a great stone sarcophagus with a piece of jade in his mouth and one in each hand; he wore a jade ring on every finger, bracelets, a diadem of jade disks and earplugs, and his favorite necklace; finally, his face was covered with a mosaic mask with eyes of shell and obsidian (see Plate 10-g, p. 290). Having left with his body the finest gifts they had to offer, his subjects carefully fitted a lid

PHOTO 45. Temple of the Inscriptions, Palenque, Chiapas. (Courtesy of the Instituto Nacional de Antropología e Historia, Mexico.)

over the U-shaped box, and removable stoppers were dropped into place for the last time. Over this lid, another gigantic one, 4 m long and exquisitely carved, was slowly lowered into place. This beautiful lid shows Pacal as a clubfooted young man, wearing the headdress of God K, and falling into the jaws of the underworld along with the dying sun (Photo 46). No fewer than 14 dates are inscribed on the lid, including his own birth and death dates, as well as names, dates, and pictorial representations of his ancestors. The crypt containing these sacred remains was located 1.5 m below the plaza floor. Its walls were entirely covered with stucco reliefs. Two stucco heads and pottery vessels containing food were left on the floor. The final sealing of the crypt was accomplished by fitting a triangular slab into one of the vaults, whereupon five or six youths were promptly sacrificed and left to accompany (or guard?) the privileged deceased among offerings of jade beads, earplugs, shells with red pigment, and a pearl. A solid masonry wall in turn sealed in this macabre scene, after which attention turned to concealing the crypt.

PHOTO 46. Funerary crypt underlying the Temple of the Inscriptions, Palenque. The beautifully carved stone is the lid of the sarcophagus of ruler Pacal. (Courtesy of the Instituto Nacional de Antropología e Historia, Mexico.)

In anticipation of these funeral rites, the Temple of the Inscriptions (Photo 45) had been constructed above the prepared secret chamber long before, and as the pyramid was built, so was the interior staircase with its neatly vaulted roof. The stairs turned at a landing and, keeping pace with the exterior construction, finally reached the summit. A temple was then raised in keeping with the times. Thus the Temple of the Inscriptions resembles others at Palenque with its mansard roof and central roof comb. The five entrances are framed by stuccoed figures some of whom represent Lord Chan-Bahlum as a baby with six toes. One clearly shows his left leg as a serpent (God K ?). The temple was surely finished by Lord Chan-Bahlum who ordered these portraits of himself as well as other representations of his famous father resting below. The great stone panels at the back immortalize the Initial Series date of A.D. 693. Easily overlooked among the neatly cut and fitted stones that form the paving of the floor is one with a double row of stone stoppers, the only clue to the interior staircase leading to the sealed crypt some 23 m below. When the Mexican archaeologist Alberto Ruz lifted this stone in 1949, the vaulted stairway was found entirely filled with rubble. Four field seasons later on June 15, 1952, the crypt and its secrets were revealed (Ruz Lhuillier 1960) (Photo 46).

One of its secrets was the so-called psychoduct, a small tube that passes from the foot of the sarcophagus and follows the staircase to the temple above, as though to maintain contact with the deceased. Puzzling is why the elaborate vaulted staircase was built with removable lid and stoppers if Pacal was to be sealed in for all eternity. Debris from the staircase dates from the building's construction (Griffin 1976), so access was blocked as of that time. Curious too is the evidence that the psychoduct was a slightly later addition. This is not the only temple–pyramid tomb with a psychoduct at Palenque, but it is certainly the most elaborate.

Pacal would have been gratified indeed to have witnessed his continued impact on Palenque. Lord Chan-Bahlum of the six toes and fingers succeeded his famous father in A.D. 684 and ruled for 18 very fruitful years. He must have directed the same skilled architects and sculptors to the culmination of the Palenque style. Inspired by his father and anxious to immortalize the legitimacy of his birth-right, he erected the Group of the Cross temples (Temples of the Cross, the Foliated Cross, and the Sun) which served to heap glory upon and reinforce the divinity of this abnormal family.

This group of three temples was inaugurated in A.D. 692 introducing the concept of the sanctuary within the temple. The occurrence of this feature at Dzibilchaltún in the Temple of the Seven Dolls, dated at A.D. 700, is seen by Andrews V (1974) as proof of intimate contact between Yucatán and Palenque. The beautifully sculptured stucco panels from the three temples of the Cross group depict the transfer of authority from Lord Pacal to his son, Lord Chan-Bahlum, as well as a comparison of the rule of Chan-Bahlum to the life and death cycle of the sun god associated with agriculture. The Temple of the Cross emphasizes the divinity of the lineage. The Temple of the Foliated Cross stresses its mythological beginnings in association with the gods, depicting the rebirth of the sun as the maize deity. The Temple of the Sun shows Lord Chan-Bahlum receiving his divine power of authority accompanied by all the prescribed rites of sacrifice of war victims. This type of inaugural scene depicts the accepted pattern of establishing authority as found in the sculptured altars and stelae of Copán and Quiriguá and on the murals at Bonampak. The three temples together form a set, emphasizing directional symbolism in their location on the north, east, and west sides of a court, and through their sculptured reliefs, show the preoccupation with time and cyclical events.

Lord Chan-Bahlum was not only an ingenious master planner but a realist as well. Although Pacal initiated and planned his tomb, and the Temple of the Inscriptions, without doubt it was Lord Chan-Bahlum who saw the work through to completion. He is surely the six-toed child depicted on some of the temple piers. The standing figures on some of the others which show abnormalities must be Lord Pacal and Lord Chan-Bahlum, proudly displaying their authority. A marvelous

PHOTO 47. Palace complex at Palenque, Chiapas, showing the square tower. (Photographed by the author.)

stucco head of Chan-Bahlum from Temple XIV realistically shows a very large nose, thick pendulous lower lip, and even anxiety in his facial expression (Griffin 1976). Realistic portraiture was, we believe, ordered by Chan-Bahlum, because prior to his reign we find the standard archetype Maya sculptures as for example the stucco head of Pacal found in the crypt (Plate 10-f, p. 289). Not only was sculpture standardized but also mural painting. At Palenque, as well as Seibal and at Teotihuacán, patterns or stencils were sometimes used (Miller 1973a; Robertson 1975, 1977; Sanders 1977a).

Lord Hok succeeded his brother Chan-Bahlum. By this time he was 38 years of age and reigned for the following 23 years. Each ruler looked for some way to leave a lasting mark and thus it fell to Hok to remodel the Palace (Photo 47) and extend it to its massive proportions, adding more rooms, galleries, and courtyards. Somewhat out of character are the captive figures carved on slabs in the northeast Palace courtyard. The workmanship is generally poor and inconsistent, striking a discordant note in an otherwise harmonious setting.

The curious Palace tower was probably contributed by one of Hoks successors: Lords Chaac, Chac Zutz, or Kuk. This square four-story masonry structure was supported not by corbelled arches but by horizontal beams of wood. A tower in itself suggests use as an astronomical observatory, but such seems not to have been the case at Palenque, nor are structures aligned with any clear cardinality. The tower does offer a superb view over the immense plain but seems to have been primarily a cosmic–magical symbol unifying the entire site. Schele (1976) believes the tower was placed so as to observe the winter solstice sun entering the underworld via the tomb of Lord Pacal. Experiments carried out by astronomer Carlson (1976) do not refute this suggestion. He also points out how well the sound of a conch shell trumpet carries when sounded from the tower. Could it have functioned as a kind of ancient minaret? If one looks from the doorway of the Temple of the Foliated Cross toward the Temple of the Inscriptions, one looks directly into the center of the Temple of the Sun. The distribution of space and positioning of temples may well be related to the importance of Pacal's tomb and may display a significant directional symbolism.

Palenque seems to have been extremely preoccupied with establishing the divinity of the ruler, documenting bloodlines, and the transference of royal power. It has been suggested also that this site was consciously selected as a necropolis, associating the dead with the west, the dying sun, and the underworld. The island of Jaina seems to have been such a place, but the lack of large numbers of interments at Palenque has not yet lent great support to this theory.

Lord Kuk, the last ruler of whom we have record, reigned for about 20 years until A.D. 784 (?), which is almost the last we hear from Palenque.

Thus from very humble beginnings, Palenque became the most important center in the west, a sacred city, leader, and capital, only to be eclipsed by A.D. 790. It was one of the first Maya cities to succumb to the new pressures and changing times of the ninth century. Through the years Palenque has managed to retain more of its ancient character than many other sites, for even today one feels an ageless unity between the underworld, the heavens, and the temples, which serve to join the different realms.

Only casual mention has been made of Palenque's relations to other sites, in contrast to Tikal whose rulers were involved with intersite marriage and alliances as well as long-distance trade. Palenque retained a regional character of its own. Even in the Early Classic, Palenque had few ceramic ties to the Petén heartland and none of the polychromes or orange slipped wares (Rands 1974). There is little that looks like Tzakol until the Motiepa phase (Early Middle Classic) when Petén wares were both imported and imitated and contacts with nearby Piedras Negras were strong. By Tepeu I (Otolum complex: A.D. 600–700), styles were very localized and thereafter Fine Paste wares increased and polychromes sharply declined. In Palenque's final days, Fine Gray wares and a Fine Orange of Balancan type (Z) heralded the presence of a non-Classic tradition. Most of the products were made in specialized local communities for the local market (Rands 1974, 1977).

Architecturally Palenque's influence affected northeastern Yucatán and extended to the alluvial plains of Tabasco, where the large site of Comalcalco (Blom and La Farge 1926–1927) shows similarities in art and architecture. Here are systems of courts and plazas and a huge artificial platform that supported a number of buildings constructed of kiln-fired bricks. Situated in the homeland of the Putún, or Chontal Maya, these people mingled with their Mexican neighbors. In effect, some of the stucco reliefs reflect both Maya and non-Maya features.

Jaina

Following the Gulf Coast north and east, one comes first to the extraordinary island of Jaina, 32 km north of Campeche. This site boasts two ceremonial centers, Zayosal and El Zacpool, accompanied by a small ball court. The buildings were all constructed of an earth nucleus faced with irregular stones, which were stuccoed and painted. However, had these Maya not produced beautiful figurines, probably the most spectacular of such objects in the New World, the name Jaina would scarcely be known. The life-like figurines are truly portraits in clay recording the gestures, dress, and ornamentation of the day (Plate 9-e, h, j, pp. 252–253). Animals and abstract objects are also known. The finest figures are solid and were hand modeled, while more standardized, hollow examples were produced by molds. Both techniques might even be combined in one figurine—a mold-made body and a hand-modeled head. Some examples are whistles and others rattles (Plate 9-i), but we believe that all were manufactured primarily as grave offerings (Piña Chán 1968).

Jaina was unquestionably one of the few great cemeteries of the Late Classic period, and it may have served other nearby localities as well, because ground burial is not possible in parts of Yucatán where bedrock lies close to the surface. The most common type of burial at Jaina was that in which the body of the deceased was flexed, a figurine placed in the flexed arm, and wrapped in a cloak or *petate,* and the head was covered with a tripod vessel after a jade bead was placed in the mouth. The entire grave then was sprinkled with cinnabar paint. Other offerings might include any kind of adornment, musical instrument, or utensil of bone, pottery, shell, or other form of marine life. The skulls are usually found to be artificially deformed frontooccipitally, and the teeth may be mutilated and have incrustations of jade or pyrite. Children were interred in large urns and covered by a tripod vessel or fragment of a large pot.

We know that the Maya usually buried their dead under house floors or in the ground as at Jaina. Sometimes, however, they cremated the remains or buried them in caves, *chultunes,* or urns; in the case of the privileged classes, elaborate tombs were even constructed. The practice of retainer burial, in which an important person was accompanied by others, often wives or servants, the presence of red pigment or cinnabar paint, and the placement of a jade bead in the mouth as currency for the next world are all widespread burial customs in Mesoamerica.

THE COLLAPSE OF MAYA CIVILIZATION IN THE SOUTH

Logically from these western Maya regions our history should move to central and northern Yucatán where there is much yet to be said about the Classic period. These areas, which were the scene of special regional developments, were nonetheless in contact with their southern neighbors. But before moving on, this is a good point at which to pause and view the Maya collapse close up, to bring together certain thoughts concerning internal problems and regional differences. The Maya collapse will be seen with greater perspective when related to the larger context of Mesoamerican development (Chapter 10).

Archaeological data documenting the collapse can be summarized as follows:

1. There was a widespread cessation of building activities after A.D. 900, and hieroglyphic inscriptions were no longer carved.
2. A rapid decline in population and actual abandonment of many sites took place. At other sites a greatly reduced settlement continued to live nearby but the ceremonial centers ceased to function.

3. There are signs of foreign intruders from the north and/or west, manifested in new pottery types and Mexicanized non-Maya traits in stone sculpture.
4. The western intruders may have hastened the collapse but did not cause it, as heartland Maya sites were already deteriorating.
5. Long-distance trade networks with central highland Mexico had broken down and Teotihuacán influence had been withdrawn as of the sixth century.
6. A shift in trade routes, going around the Yucatecan peninsula instead of across it, effectively by-passed the old Maya trading centers ending earlier relationships.
7. There were signs of political problems by A.D. 889, resulting in a shrinking of the Maya state within smaller boundaries.
8. The quality of ceramics was deteriorating.
9. Full lunar information ceased to be recorded toward the end, and there was widespread use of Calendar Round dates rather than the full Initial Series method.
10. There is one example of a large Maya ceremonial center (El Mirador, Petén) that collapsed in A.D. 300, due to over-exploitation or changing environmental conditions. Conceivably there could be more examples not apparent as yet.
11. That the collapse was very real, very complete, is borne out by Postclassic occupation of the southern Maya lowlands by a much smaller population having a very different cultural tradition (Chapter 8).

The collapse was not brought about by a single cause, but the many articles written on the subject still leave one reflecting on exactly why this great civilization was not able to be perpetuated. It had seemingly learned how to cope with its special environment, how to communicate, feed itself, defend itself, manipulate the supernatural, and support its dynasties as well as an extravagant elite. The pomp and ceremony of seeing a ruler ascend the throne could only be equalled by seeing him to his tomb. Some early day-to-day pressures were alleviated since breadnuts could be stored, dried fish kept well, and the steady stream of merchants kept salt in stock. Local crops were doing very nicely with new terracing and the control of water supplies. Obsidian was plentiful thanks to the shipments down from Alta Verapaz, and as soon as the thin blades could be flaked off the cores, they could be easily redistributed at a profit. Many households now had a few quality imports such as a fine *metate* of highland limestone, and if blessed by very good fortune, perhaps a few jade beads so as not to leave this world as paupers, though jade beads were becoming scarcer and harder to acquire than they had been a few generations back.

The years A.D. 680–780 were the cultural peak of Maya civilization. The population at that time is hard to estimate. In 1973 Sanders suggested a population in the Petén of 20,000–25,000 in core areas, but Willey thinks this is too conservative. Haviland suggests 45,000 for greater Tikal. Now a larger estimate of 70,000–75,000 is proposed by Dickson (1980), basing himself on the variety of food available combined with the numerous techniques of exploitation the Maya possessed. Much depends on how many people we estimate as comprising the standard household and the number of residences per platform; and then we wonder if all were occupied at the same time. Clearly the function of a city is of greater importance than sheer volume of inhabitants, and no one now questions that Tikal functioned as an urban center.

More temples and palaces were constructed now than at any other time, the palace-type being on the increase. More dated monuments were erected than at any other period in Maya history. Calakmul has the astounding number of 104 stelae. At no other time were such efforts made to perfect art, ceremonialism, and fine polychrome ceramics, as well as all types of luxury goods. Not only were artistic and intellectual achievements at their peak, but everything seemed to be growing. Population increased, centers grew larger and many new ones appeared. Dramatic too were innovations in agriculture: terracing, dams, ridged fields, short-cycle slash and burn. The Maya state had never before presented and was never again to present such an organized, well-functioning integrated pattern of civilization. In fact at Tikal there seems to have been a great acceleration of building just prior to the end, a point we will take up again.

Although the collapse seems to have happened rapidly, there were warnings. Problems began after A.D. 534 when, for the 60-year hiatus, most activity ceased. When we understand those critical years of inactivity, the process of collapse ought to become clearer.

After A.D. 700, a return to traditional values and a frenzy of building took place. This is a curious phenomenon because if the Maya could recover once, why not again, having the benefit of experience? It can only be that circumstances had changed, and even if we cannot fully understand the causes and stresses behind the hiatus, at least we can pin-point some of the changes that came out of it, for there are significant differences between the Maya civilization before and after the hiatus. This is not to say that continuity was in any way lacking. It was still thoroughly Maya, in fact the trend was one of regeneration, of renewing the older conservative patterns. It is always the lesser ingredients, the aberrant traits, that signal new trends and change; hence these lesser ingredients are often overemphasized out of proportional importance.

Looking at the 200 years prior to the collapse, the direct long-distance trade network with Teotihuacán had broken down, and Teotihuacán withdrew from the Maya world creating a serious void. The role this contact had played is hard to overemphasize. Contact with Teotihuacán had opened up entirely new horizons in religious, political, and economic fields. It is after contact with Teotihuacán that we see a new political structure develop among the Maya with every effort made to build up trade. It does not take long for what begins as a luxury product to become a necessity. The physical loss of these products was undoubtedly lamented, but think of the lack of news, the stimulation generated by the personal contacts as well as the problem of new export markets. Where would the Maya now dispose of the polychrome pottery, textiles, tropical feathers, and skins? A serious economic dislocation was the result.

In the Middle Classic years of A.D. 550–700 three platform buildings were erected at Tikal that show foreign influence. These so-called Teotihuacán-style structures are more truly a reflection of Gulf Coast influence as they have the slope, panel, and flaring cornice profile, popularized by Tajín. This was the period of Tajín's greatest influence during which the ball-game cult was widely spread. Although the Gulf Coast cultures tried to step in and fill the gap left by the central Mexicans, they were not as successful as Teotihuacán, and most of the foreign influence seen in the Petén after the hiatus can be accounted for as persisting from earlier times. Direct contact and imports from Teotihuacán had been cut off.

Tikal was no longer able to retain her former power. It was in the peripheral areas that new centers were springing up such as Copán, Palenque, Piedras Negras, and Cobá, and a multitude of smaller ones. Power likewise was redistributed and reinforced by an increase of trade throughout the riverine networks of the Usumacinta, Pasión, Sarstoon, and Motagua rivers. Webb (1973) suggests that exotic goods may have been somewhat replaced by more secular ones and no longer were long-distance traders willing to expend such an effort to penetrate the interior.

At the same time the more aggressive merchants were taking to the sea, and more and more frequently they went around Yucatán instead of crossing it by river and portage. As we will see, Campeche and Yucatán offered good products and profitable trade at their new centers, and traders continued around to their east coast counterparts on Chetumal, Cozumel Bay, and Belize. Heavy objects could be more easily transported by sea than by a river–portage combination through the jungle. For cities of the Petén, it was tantamount to being by-passed by a freeway; an all-sea route removed them from competition and participation. All the wealth they had once seen now accumulated in the peripheral areas.

The Maya political system became more rigidly structured after A.D. 700. Molloy and Rathje (1974) think that the old dynasties of Tikal, the early power, were so respected that descendants of former dynasties

a

b

328

were able to reinstate themselves and their dynastic rule. This is the time of the new centers, and authority is divided between Tikal, Copán, Palenque, and Calakmul (?). The Maya appreciated the political advantages that marriages and alliances could offer (Marcus 1976a). Tikal's dynastic history is one of conniving and scheming in order to wring the greatest benefits from political marriages (?) with Yaxchilán, Piedras Negras, Dos Pilas, Naranjo, and Pusilhá. By the end of the seventh century the Maya state stood politically strong with layers of authority radiating out from several main centers down through satellite communities. Tikal reinstated its old dynasty with a descendant of Stormy Sky after wresting power from rival political contenders. Copán dominated the southern periphery. Prosperity reached up to include Cobá in the northeast, which attained its peak at this time as evidenced by the erecting of 30 stelae in the seventh century. Palenque ruled the northwestern flank, ably accompanied by Yaxchilán and Piedras Negras. However, an ensuing political shake-up signaled uneasiness and stress of some sort. The late replacement of two of the capitals suggests a shrinking or retrenchment of the state, not a healthy sign. Exactly when this occurred is not clear, but by A.D. 889 Seibal and Motul de José seem to have replaced the authority formerly held by Palenque and Copán. This was almost the end, so this move might be interpreted as a desperate effort to save the state.

Involved is undoubtedly the role of the elite, logically a key factor in the collapse. How large a group was it? What kind of relations did they maintain with the rest of the populace, on whom they were so dependent for labor and craftsmanship as well as their food supply? A serious gulf between classes due to exploitation and inequalities has often been cited as a contributing factor to the collapse. This is hard to document but not hard to imagine when the differences in the class structure are so apparent. The widening gap between elite and commoners remains an important ingredient of the collapse. This same theme is echoed in the inflexibility of the Petén centers, which, clinging to their older conservative ways, were unwilling to invite participation by newer Maya cities (Willey and Shimkin 1973). Apparently Ruler A at Tikal was making an effort, for at least some of the art associated with him reflects contact with Piedras Negras and Dos Pilas (Pasztory 1978a).

Another hint is provided by the ceramic history. The basal-flange bowl (Tzakol phase) diagnostic of the Early Classic (Plate 7-i, p. 211), is replaced by handsome cylindrical jars with figure painting in late Tepeu phases. After A.D. 700 the polychrome jar is often rimmed with hieroglyphs and mythical scenes (Plate 7-h; Photo 48). "Waxy" and orange-slipped monochromes are also very typical of the central Petén heartland sites and diagnostic of Late Classic Maya settlements. However, in the western regions, new fine-paste wares (temper-free paste) began to appear. These were probably manufactured in the

Chiapas–Tabasco area of the Gulf Coast lowlands and widely traded. These wares made their appearance just before or after Piedras Negras and Palenque failed. By the year A.D. 830, Fine Orange Balancan and Altar types were found at Palenque, Altar de Sacrificios, and Seibal. The Fine Orange wares also made their way to Tikal and Uaxactún, but by that time, Tikal had been declining for about 60 years.

The rise of the western centers, exemplified by Palenque, was swift, marvelously productive, but short lived. It is in these western sites that the first cracks appear to presage the collapse. Looking at final inscriptions in this area we find that Piedras Negras went first (A.D. 795), followed by Palenque (A.D. 799), Bonampak (A.D. 800), Yaxchilán (A.D. 810), and Seibal (A.D. 889). It seems significant that the first indications of conflict are found along the western frontier. Scenes of raids, sacrifice, and conflict manifest themselves in wall paintings at Bonampak and in stone sculptures at Piedras Negras and Yaxchilán. On the Pasión River both Seibal and Altar de Sacrificios show evidence not so much of warfare as of non-Maya intruders. We have seen that Seibal's elite was replaced by foreigners. Other groups followed, possibly from northern Yucatán as well as directly from Tabasco. It seems that these foreigners did not cause the collapse but probably hastened it, preying on an already weak victim.

Willey and Shimkin (1973) do not attribute the collapse to the intruders since Tikal was already going under. Shimkin believes that competition between centers, even fighting among cities, bad crops, and resulting malnutrition and disease would be sufficient reason for the Maya collapse. Sanders (1973) visualizes a more complete evacuation, perhaps a migration to the Guatemalan highlands, an area already known to them through trade. Cowgill (1964) likewise suggests such a depopulation of the southern lowlands, but to the north, as the result of invasion, warfare and subsequent famine.

Speculating on agricultural problems, we note that when much of the forest was stripped away possibly the animals went also, thus curtailing fresh meat. With continued expansion, land would become more valuable as well as scarce, so farm land a little farther out would be taken up. Plant disease, insects, and weeds were potential problems in areas of high population. Malnutrition was a constant enemy, for a deficiency in protein would affect a population very severely. It will be recalled (p. 268) that an increase in population may lead to the taking up of more land, thus expanding the habitation zones and at the same time putting additional strain on limited resources such as water. A conflict in any of these areas could lead to warfare, with increased competition between centers or within a single center.

Culbert (1977) suggests that the growth rate of the civilization exceeded the limits of its environmental potential resulting in a kind of overshoot which was the basic cause of the collapse. In this case it was an economic overshoot. As the civilization grew, several regional centers developed in order to handle the distribution and exchange of subsistence goods and utilitarian products. These centers would logically enter into competition with each other especially in overlapping areas of jurisdiction. A primary problem is the production of food. In order to maintain a large population in the center itself, the center would have to rely on importing food, as the center would have no longer been self-sufficient. Specialization was not only subject to natural resources, such as flint deposits at Tikal, but also in skills and concentration of manpower and facilities. Once the system was set in motion, the economic machinery refueled itself. More labor produced more crafts; this required greater investments of time, which in turn generated more specialization and greater variety of goods. The entire system would have become committed to itself with each activity dependent on the next, thus producing a population increase in the centers, which in turn depended more and more on imported food. People who gave up producing their own food in order to specialize in other fields found themselves more dependent on the regional center to arrange importation of necessary products. Increased political control, competition between regional centers, and eventual hostility could have been the result.

The collapse is seen in this case because the build up was too great, an overshoot of the limits set by the subsistence and resource base. It happened so swiftly that there was little time to adapt. The elite had expanded to the point where its maintenance demanded an increasing share of resources. Control over the people became more difficult as food production could not be further increased, so coercion through taxes and tribute led to tighter political controls. With few incentives left, labor declined and the entire system wound down. At the roots of the system were too many people for too few resources. When these were over-exploited, there was nowhere to turn.

A contrasting view to that presented by Culbert is one in which Cowgill points out the predisposition for endemic warfare among the Classic Maya. Rejecting the idea that population increase was an overshoot, he feels it was a conscious cultural choice. Only by having a large population could one of the Maya centers achieve complete political control of the southern lowlands, and thus a large population was seen as a great political and military advantage. Drawing a parallel with the ancient city of Athens, Cowgill observes that warfare resulted in constant conflicts over a long period of time, which caused pronounced debilitation; thus a strong political unity was never achieved. Herein lay the seeds of its destruction (Cowgill 1979).

A rather alarming suggestion has been made by Puleston to the effect that the Maya, whom we know were obsessed with the concept of time and recurring cycles, may have anticipated their own demise. In a fascinating article, Puleston (1979) traced the 13-katun cycle in Yucatán and showed how the Itzá were driven from their home every 256 years, fulfilling the famed katun prophecies. He speculated that this cycle of time was also of great significance in the Classic period, at which time the scholars and priests would have been well aware of the approach of doomsday. It is not suggested that this could be the sole cause of the Classic Maya collapse, but a rather fatalistic attitude, which combined with some economic or social setbacks, would certainly have been a contributing factor.

With increased data at hand, Harrison (1977) has revived an idea suggested in 1931 by Cooke: The *bajos* found in Petén, Belize, southern Campeche, and Quintana Roo may actually have been lakes in Preclassic times in which a kind of *chinampa*-type cultivation could have taken place. As the result of soil erosion, these lakes gradually silted up to become the seasonal swamps we see today. In studying the location of Maya centers in this region, these swamps are located either on rivers or at the edge of *bajos*. We now know that several methods of intensifying agricultural yields were introduced by the Classic period: terrace agriculture, ridged fields on river levees, and short-cycle slash and burn. In addition, after study of the site surveys in Quintana Roo, it seems that the *bajos* were indeed former lakes and were exploited for agricultural purposes. Already it had been suggested that a *chinampa*-type agriculture could have predated swidden agriculture in the swamplands. The soil now filling the *bajos* is of the highest quality, logically having eroded down from well-drained slopes (Palerm and Wolf 1957; Sanders 1973). The silting in of *bajos* in the Late Classic would have put an end to any *chinampa*-like cultivation very effectively, thus resulting in the loss of a major food source.

Apparently the *bajos* at El Mirador, Petén were not of this type and could never have grown maize (p. 143). Consequently El Mirador barely made it into the Classic period. Its crisis came early yet apparently it was a purely local or limited collapse.

These thoughts about the collapse of the southern Maya will take on greater perspective when we have examined the rest of Mesoamerica. It was not a local event but was enmeshed with phenomena taking place elsewhere. There is, however, still more to say about the Classic period, which involves some of the most beautiful and fascinating sites in the Maya area.

MIDDLE AND LATE CLASSIC DEVELOPMENTS IN CENTRAL AND NORTHERN YUCATÁN

One of the most confusing periods in Mesoamerican studies is that related to Yucatán between the years A.D. 600–1200, which embraces that crucial time spanning the Late Classic and Post-Classic Maya development. Involved is the problem of dating and correlation of the archaeological remains with carbon-14 dates and the Maya calendar, the relationship between northern and central Yucatán to the collapse of the great Classic civilization in the south, and the relationship between Chichén Itzá in northern Yucatán and Tula, Hidalgo in central highland Mexico.

For many years dating of the Maya area, and by extension the rest of Mesoamerica, was keyed to the Long Count dating of Classic Maya ceramics. The preferred correlation was that known as the Goodman–Martinez–Thompson system (GMT) (11.16..0.0.0) in which the Classic period dates from A.D. 300–900. When radiocarbon dates began coming in after 1950, and ages for the early periods proved to be older than previously estimated, some Mayanists enthusiastically embraced the 12.9.0.0.0 correlation of Spinden, since it seemed to apply particularly well, pushing dates back approximately 260 years beyond those of the GMT correlation. After some dating reruns, refining of techniques, and sampling, discrepancies between the two correlations have been narrowed. In addition, intensive excavations in a number of areas both within and without the Maya area have added to the volume of study material. It is interesting and rather reassuring that in case of doubt or conflicting results, it is the basic ceramic study that is deemed most reliable (Lowe 1978).

As regards the correlation of northern Yucatán with the southern Maya lowlands, controversy has centered around the chronological placement of the Pure Florescent period characterized by the Puuc style architecture. (For a summary of ideas of Brainerd, Andrews IV, Smith, and Ball, see Lowe, 1978.) Was this development contemporaneous with the Late Classic of the south, or did it postdate it? Now, it seems it may have begun very early.

Andrews V (end note of Lowe 1978) suggests that Puuc architecture began around A.D. 790 or 800 and lasted about 200 years. He believes most Puuc architecture of Campeche and Yucatán is later than A.D. 800 and that archaeological data can now be accommodated in either the GMT or Spinden correlations. Willey welcomes this solution as it fits in with the GMT correlation used in the southern lowlands. He believes the Puuc style lasted from A.D. 800 to A.D. 1000 (Willey 1978)—years that are becoming known in Yucatán as the Terminal Classic phase.

However, it may have begun somewhat earlier than A.D. 800. Parsons (1969), Pasztory (1978a), and Cohodas (1978a, 1978b) begin Puuc and related styles in the seventh century, with the peak of development taking place in the eighth. Their reasoning will be pointed out as we go along. Allowing for the broadest interpretation, Puuc architectural style would fall between A.D. 650 and 1000.

The relationship between Chichén Itzá and Tula, Hidalgo is also a difficult one and subject to various interpretations. Usually considered strictly a matter of Postclassic concern, this is no longer the case. In striving for clarity, the problems involved may be oversimplified, but current theories relating to these important issues will be presented.

Central Yucatán

The Río Bec area (see Map 9, p. 257) is located in southeastern Campeche and southwestern Quintana Roo, a region ecologically transitional between the Petén rain forests on the south and the dry scrub plains of Yucatán to the north. Except for hunters, the area has been virtually uninhabited since ancient times. Ridges or hills are covered with dry forests of breadnut and *sapote* trees; water runs down the gullies to be caught in low-lying areas, perhaps forming lakes in early days; today these areas have been silted over due to deforestation-caused erosion creating swamps. Maya settlements were located here where rainwater could be caught in reservoirs. In this rather forbidding environment lived the Classic Maya of Río Bec, Chicanna, Becán, La Hormiguera, and Xpuhil, to name only the most important centers in a 100-km diameter.

It will be recalled that Becán dates back to the sixth century B.C. and around A.D. 100–250 fortified itself with a remarkable ditch or dry moat. The inhabitants also constructed two huge stone-lined reservoirs to alleviate their water problem. The detailed ceramic history as reconstructed by Ball (1977a) shows that Becán was in close contact with the Petén sites and shared forms and decorations. In the Chacsik phase (A.D. 250–450) there were full-time potters, and trade involved a complex redistributive system. Fine wares were brought in directly from the Petén. A curious local ware with a controlled-trickle decoration was distributed north of Becán at Acanceh, Oxkintok, Dzibilchaltún, as well as in Quintana Roo. Becán, on the frontier between northern and southern Maya areas, maintained contacts with both, and even received central Mexican green obsidian via the long distance trade network.

Some kind of violent disruption occurred in the Sabucan phase (A.D. 450–630), perhaps actual conquest by Maya (Tikal?) from north central Petén. These could have acted independently or been directed by Teotihuacán interests, but they managed to overwhelm the staunch defenders of Becán despite their fortifications. In a pure Sabucan deposit, great amounts of human skeletal remains were scattered about. Buildings were destroyed and rebuilt. This was the time of the Middle Classic hiatus in the south, when the famous Teotihuacán figurine cache was deposited at Becán (p. 287). There were several important changes resulting from this unsettled period. Petén influence became stronger, the trickle-decorated wares declined, but more important, agriculture took on new dimensions. Hillsides were suddenly terraced; 35 km away *chinampa*-type farming was undertaken, and from Campeche to Quintana Roo family farmsteads appeared (Turner II 1974). This looks as if they were accelerating toward the great cultural climax and population boom of the Late Classic.

The seventh century was marked by the great Río Bec architectural styles when Chicanna, Xpuhil, and Becán's Acropolis were built (Potter 1976). This architecture combines features of chambered palaces with pyramidal platforms. Heavy use of stucco and fine uncut masonry, vertical facades, and elaborate ostentatious decorations are very characteristic. Roof combs are sometimes replaced by towers, and masks of a long-nosed god often decorate corners and facades. Two-story structures are known in which the second story rests on solid fill. Río Bec architecture is closely related to other styles called Chenes and Puuc, which are found farther north. These three styles are now believed to be roughly contemporary (Kubler 1975).

Chicanna, 3 km southwest of Becán, an elite center of five groups of mounds and buildings, is small, but a jewel of the Río Bec region. Structure I has end towers stimulating pyramids after the style of Tikal. The facade is completely adorned with mosaic monster masks, and in passing through the doorway, one is entering the open mouth of a serpent. Appropriately named, Chicanna means "serpent–mouth–house" (Eaton 1974).

PHOTO 49. Example of Río Bec architectural style: Reconstruction of structure at Xpuhil, Campeche. (From drawing by Tatiana Proskouriakoff 1946, courtesy of the Peabody Museum, Harvard University, copyright by the President and Fellows of Harvard College.)

At Xpuhil (Photo 49) ornamental tower pyramids have front and back stairways with treads too narrow to use. Ostentatious facades of veneer masonry are heavily decorated with bas-reliefs, the final details being carved into thick stucco and brightly painted.

Just as the ceramics became very conservative, so the simulated towers may have tried to copy Tikal's pyramids. The ditch was filled in at Becán, a sign either of bravado or confidence that no enemy was near. Following the ceramic record, by Chintok phase (A.D. 730–830) pottery began to deteriorate. Puuc Slate Ware was imitated and a clear break occurred with the southern sites. Some foreign groups came in from the north, possibly Mexican-related Putún people. Certainly during the early ninth century elite warriors poured in from the northwest bringing with them Thin Slate wares, Fine Orange, and new ceramic forms. Decorative themes on pottery glorified the warrior and his battles. The enfeebled cultures of central Yucatán apparently permitted the northerners to walk right in unopposed.

From then until the twelfth century, central Yucatán was the scene of continual movement of peoples, involving the Putún or Chontal Maya. First they went northward up the coast and overland to the Puuc area and perhaps Chichén Itzá. Later they moved south through the Chenes and Río Bec regions of central Yucatán on their way to the Usumacinta–Pasión cities. These intruders left their influence on buildings as well as pottery; the Fine Orange wares.

Northern Yucatán

The shift of power away from the older southern Classic Maya centers to the peripheral areas after the hiatus and the greater utilization of sea-going trade routes are reflected in the rising fortunes of northern Yucatán in the Middle and Late Classic period. Salt and shells for ceremonial use had been major export items even in Early Classic days, but in the seventh and eighth centuries Yucatán became a major commercial center. The importance of salt is easily underestimated when it is readily available and cheap. But it should not be taken for granted, because without a minimum of 2 g of salt per day man cannot live very long. Physical labor has been known to boost the salt intake to 30 g a day. It has been estimated that to maintain the population of Teotihuacán at its peak, tens of thousands of pounds of salt per year were needed (Ball 1977b). Presented in these terms, salt-producing northern Yucatán takes on another dimension.

Classic development in northern Yucatán shows conformity to the southern sites in the sharing of some ceramic styles, presence of the corbelled-vault, Maya-styled monumental sculpture, and some similarities in hieroglyphs and calendrical inscriptions, although these were never as well developed as those in the Petén region. A few simple stelae with illegible inscriptions have been found. The stelae cult which recorded dynastic and historical data in the Petén and southern low-lands is not characteristic of the north. Neither politically nor economically was Yucatán subject to its southern neighbors. We will find Teotihuacán influence, but it was never as strongly felt here as elsewhere in Mesoamerica.

Many new sites rose to prominence at this time, among them Dzibilchaltún, and older Preclassic ones such as Acanceh and Yaxuná were rebuilt. Relationships continued with the southern Maya lowlands, with Yucatán now contributing more than it received. Particularly important to Yucatán's development were the cultural and commercial ties to the Gulf Coast cultures from where the ball-game cult was introduced.

We have seen that architecturally the styles of Chenes, Río Bec, and Puuc are closely related and can be considered as one with local variations. We are dealing here with architecture, for associated burials are not plentiful and hieroglyphic inscriptions, although present, are scarce. Again we find veneer mosaic facades, much stucco, monster-mouth doorways, and long-nosed deities on corners of buildings. Hochob is the largest of these sites and is a good example of the Chenes-type variant (Photo 50). Here, a long platform once supported three buildings. The doorway to the palace-type structure forms the mouth of a monster, and the entire vertical facade is elaborately decorated in deep relief. Other examples of Chenes architecture are known from Dzibilnocác, El Tabasqueño, and Chichén Itzá. Kubler (1975) points out early antecedents for this remarkable architecture in the elaborate facade of Temple 22 at Copán and Building A at Holmul.

The Puuc region is the most fertile and most densely populated of Yucatán. The word *Puuc* refers to a series of hills in the northern area where a number of rather well-preserved remains have been found, all located close to *chultuns,* water-storing devices. In northern Yucatán these large tanks were either cut into the limestone or built into plazas, lined with stone, and plastered. (The *chultun* of northern Yucatán therefore had a different function from the nut storage pits of Tikal by the same name.) In the western area, Puuc sites are small and rather plain when compared with the large ceremonial centers to the east. The western sites, for example Edzná, are considered to be older than sites like Uxmal and Kabah and show more originality or experimentation (Kubler 1975).

Puuc buildings do not have the ornamental towers of the Río Bec and Chenes regions, but they all share many features of veneer masonry. In this type of construction, small mosaic stones are tenoned into a rubble concrete core. In forming veneer masonry quantities of presculptured stone elements were assembled and then combined as needed into masks and geometric designs producing repetitive motifs characterized by excellent craftsmanship. This is in contrast to the older block masonry construction where big slabs of stone faced with mortar

PHOTO 50. Example of Chenes style architecture; model of temple at Hochob, Yucatán. (Museo Nacional de Antropología, Mexico, courtesy of Victoria Bach.)

carry the load. In addition, a storied effect is created in Puuc buildings by setting back rows of chambers in a staggered formation.

A very beautiful center with Puuc architecture, although hardly typical, is Uxmal, a well-known center about 78 km south of Mérida (Andrews IV 1965; Foncerrada de Molina 1965; Morley 1956; Thompson 1954). The Monjas, or Nunnery, is a huge quadrangle surrounding a great patio entered through a corbelled arch on the south side (Photo 51). The long buildings contain numerous chambers, each with its own doorway. The facades are all intricately decorated by small cut stones set in masonry. Motifs in the friezes are huts among latticed panels, rain-god masks, small columns, and serpent heads. The decoration of the north building includes Tlaloc with the year-sign headdress (Foncerrada de Molina 1965).

The Pyramid of the Magician, also called El Adivino, rises sharply just east of the Nunnery. It has a roughly elliptical base and was rebuilt

PHOTO 51. The Nunnery, Uxmal, Yucatán. The facade is composed of cut stone to form mosaics. (Courtesy of the Instituto Nacional de Antropología e Historia, Mexico.)

PHOTO 52. Detail of Governor's Palace, Uxmal, Yucatán. (Courtesy of the Instituto Nacional de Antropología e Historia, Mexico.)

at five different times. Although considered to be purely Maya in flavor, it actually contains styles ranging over four centuries; in the earliest structure ([14]C A.D. 569) one can see Teotihuacán influence in Tlaloc with the year-sign headdress (Pasztory 1978a, 1979) as well as influence from the Petén and Usumacinta regions. The lowest structure is of Puuc style covered over by a later Chenes style (Foncerrada de Molina 1965).

Impressive for its tremendous size, the so-called Governor's Palace consists of a central building and two lateral structures containing a series of chambers. The facade is decorated in the same Puuc style with rain-god masks, stepped frets, and lattice panels (Photo 52). The entire structure rests on a stepped terrace some 122 m long by 27 m wide, which in turn is supported by a natural elevation. This may well be the last structure erected at Uxmal. It overlies a well-preserved earlier one of Chenes style with plaster and stone facade, block masonry construction with a monster-mouth doorway. The reader can now begin to appreciate the overlap in architectural styles. In the construction of El Adivino, an early Puuc building underlies a Chenes one. In the Governor's Palace an early Chenes structure was found beneath Puuc construction. The answer would seem to lie in the contemporaneity of these related styles (Cohodas 1978a; Kubler 1975).

The Uxmal ball court has the high vertical playing walls and tenoned stone rings of the court typical of seventh-century Yucatán. The ball-court ring is inscribed with a date corresponding to A.D. 649. Several other badly eroded structures complete the ruins. The distribution of buildings at Uxmal does not conform to any particular plan. The site is impressive for its massive structures and geometric mosaic facades in soft shades of pink and yellow stone.

On the road from Mérida to Campeche near Santa Elena, a path leads off to the Mul-Chic ruins. This site lies between Uxmal and Kabah in the Puuc region. Although long known as a modest ceremonial center, the murals of Structure A were not discovered until 1961. The building has a roof comb with stucco figures painted in red, blue, and yellow, and on the stuccoed facade one can still see a human figure with a deer. The large mural paintings depict scenes of a gruesome battle between two groups. Some figures are taking captives; trophy skulls are shown three per person. Hanging, stoning to death, and sacrifice comprise the main theme. Names of the most important people appear above their heads as glyphs contained in cartouches. Dress and ornaments are similar to those seen on carvings at Edzná, Uxmal, Chichén Itzá, and Dzibilchaltún.

The paintings resemble those of Bonampak in some respects, but have Puuc traits. Although there is no veneer masonry, the roof comb, stucco facade, and ceramics associated with Structure A are Puuc. Piña Chan feels the paintings are closely linked to the reliefs of the Great Ball Court at Chichén Itzá, the pictorial style being Classic. He wonders if either the Puuc style lasted much longer than previously thought, or if the dating of the ball court should be reviewed. He places the Mul-Chic paintings at A.D. 600–750, which would agree with some new chronological interpretations of Chichén Itzá (see p. 399, Piña Chan 1964).

Only a short distance further on are Kabah (Photos 53 and 54) and Labná, both Puuc sites, the former renowned for a building completely faced with stone mosaic masks with long hooked noses. At Labná one can walk through an amazing arch decorated by stone mosaics that spans a short *sacbé*, a Maya causeway, built with considerable energy and imagination. Huge blocks of stone were laid, subsequently leveled

PHOTO 53. Puuc-style architecture, Kabah, Yucatán. (Courtesy of the Instituto Nacional de Antropología e Historia, Mexico.)

PHOTO 54. Monumental arch spanning a *sacbé* at Kabah, Yucatán. (Courtesy of the Instituto Nacional de Antropología e Historia, Mexico.)

with gravel, and finally paved smooth with plaster. The *sacbé* at Labná links only the temple–pyramid with the palace, but at Cobá in northern Quintana Roo, 16 such causeways connect many scattered ruins, one of which extends some 100 km to Yaxuná near Chichén Itzá. The main axis of Dzibilchaltún is just such a *sacbé*. These are often called roads and it is thought that they were constructed for religious processions. Only in Yucatán do we find monumental arches over causeways linking cities. They were an innovation of the seventh century, precisely at the time of greatly expanded commercial activities and intersite communication. This timing has led Pasztory to question their purely ceremonial use (Pasztory 1978a). Although the flat peninsula of Yucatán and the well-constructed *sacbés* seem to us well suited for wheeled vehicles, there is no indication that the wheel was ever utilized in a practical sense. The only wheel in Mesoamerica, or in the New World for that matter, is that found on miniature pottery animals in the Gulf Coast (see Plate 8-d, p. 246) and other scattered sites.

If not the most beautiful, certainly one of the most impressive and well-known sites is Chichén Itzá, 124 km east of Mérida (Morley 1956; Thompson 1954). The history of Chichén Itzá begins in the Middle to Late Classic period when some of its Puuc and early Maya structures were built. However, it also has a series of buildings that are usually considered to date from the so-called Toltec period. This will be discussed in Chapter 7, which contains the photographs of this site, but it is important to mention certain aspects of Chichén Itzá here. As we have seen elsewhere, many early remains are out of sight, some best seen via tunnels buried beneath later visible structures.

One example of this is the inner Temple of Kukulcán (the Castillo), a much smaller interior building belonging to the Classic period. Built with nine stages and a single staircase, it has a profile resembling that of Puuc structures and a temple with twin chambers on top. The temple is decorated in relief with a procession of jaguars prowling beneath a row of round Mexican-style shields. This temple houses the famous Red Jaguar Throne, a carved stone jaguar with flat back to serve as a seat or place of offerings, painted bright red with incrustations of 73 green jade disks, jade eyes, and shell fangs.

Of the same date was the west colonnade which faced the east side of the Castillo across the large court. This consisted of four rows of cylindrical columns, the southern extension being corbel-vaulted with overhangs.

South of the centrally located Xtoloc *cenote* is the Puuc Group of structures, including the Caracol or Observatory, the Nunnery or Monjas complex, the Red House, Iglesia, the Akab Dzib, and others. These are Puuc flavored buildings with vertical facades covered by elaborate stone mosaic masks (Photo 55). Both the Red House and the Monjas have associated ball courts with bench reliefs depicting ball-players,

PHOTO 55. Puuc-style architecture, examples of mosaic veneer masonry at Chichén Itzá, Yucatán: The Iglesia (the Church) and the Monjas (Nunnery). (Courtesy of the Instituto Nacional de Antropología e Historia, Mexico.)

similar to those of the Great Ball Court. If the two courts underlie the Puuc-style Red House and Monjas structures, they would support the idea of a very early Toltec or central Mexican presence (Cohodas, 1978a).

The Caracol or Observatory is a curious structure, considered by some to be a monstrosity. It consists of a round tower perched on two rectangular terraces. The interior spiral stairway (*caracol* in Spanish) leads to a small observation chamber in the tower. Square openings in the walls seem to correspond to lines of sight at the vernal and autumnal equinoxes, but the structure may have been destined for other purposes as well. Mesoamerican round structures in general are thought to be associated with Quetzalcóatl (Kukulcán), and possibly were built to represent a conch shell. Round structures, though existing since Preclassic times, are relatively rare in Mesoamerica. There seems to have been renewed interest in them in the seventh century, for in Yucatán they are found at Ake and two examples are at Edzná, in addition to the Caracol at Chichén Itzá. The latter also contains Puuc architectural and ornamental elements in its mosaic serpent-mask panels and moldings. Although later additions were made, the early construction shows Puuc style with Toltec remodeling, and dates partially to the Late Classic period. A curious mixture of Mexican ornamentation is here combined with Maya construction including the corbelled vault (Kubler 1975).

Other buildings and additions showing Toltec influence from central highland Mexico are usually considered to be Postclassic in date. Of particular interest is the fact that there is much at Chichén Itzá dating to the Classic period which shows a contemporaneity of Toltec with several styles of Maya architecture.

The 100 years following A.D. 850 (Terminal Classic) saw Putún penetration not only of the Petén but also the east coast of Yucatán including Cozumel, Bakhalal, and Chetumal. The traditional account of Chilam Balam of Chumayel (Roys 1933), written after the Conquest, tells of the Itzá invasion from Polé (Xcaret) on the northeast coast, the mainland port for Cozumel. This island, originally reached by sea from the Putún homeland in Tabasco, is presumed to be the point of departure for their journey into northern Yucatán. After considerable wandering these people who were the early Itzá settled down at Chichén Itzá in A.D. 918 (Thompson 1970) or perhaps as early as A.D. 800 (Adams 1977a).

These early Itzá brought with them some Mexican influences as seen in Tlaloc representations at Uxmal and warriors with *atlatls* on the door jambs of Kabah. Some of the Mexican influence at Chichén Itzá such as the inner structure of the Castillo with reliefs of jaguars and shields is often thought to stem from this intrusion. It would have had to have taken place earlier however to account for all the Mexican and Toltec features that are believed to be of seventh-century date. Whenever Chichén Itzá did become a local capital of an outlying Putún province, it would explain the introduction of Balancan Fine Orange ware which has been found in association with Puuc architecture at Uxmal and Kabah.

After an undetermined number of years, some Itzá left Yucatán and went to live at Chakanputún in the tenth century. Ball (1974b) speculates that Chakanputún might be Seibal and reconstructs the following scene.

Those that left Chichén Itzá moved slowly south through central Yucatán, constituting a rather large-scale migration out of northern Yucatán, taking Balancan and Altar Fine Orange pottery as well as Thin Slate wares to Becán. We have seen that Altar de Sacrificios declined in power and influence around A.D. 751 while neighboring Seibal, 100 km upstream, gradually rose to take its place. The invaders of Seibal in A.D. 830 could have been these Itzá–Putún, who, having pushed on down from Becán, arrived as elite intruders taking over an already impoverished community. One of their legacies is believed to be Seibal's Altar 17, which rests on a platform carved with prowling jaguars in Toltec style.

It was during the 60 years prior to A.D. 890 that Seibal reached its peak of prosperity. Its art is a mixture of Mexican and Mayan motifs with serpents, Tlaloc faces, speech scrolls, and martial themes. The Putún seem not to have maintained control for very long, for a decline was probably already in progress by the time they arrived. The last stela erected is dated A.D. 889.

Meanwhile in northern Yucatán, the Puuc cities prospered and the

Putún merchants built up a lucrative network of exchange centers from Tabasco to Honduras. Chichén Itzá was to dominate northern Yucatán and become the capital of the Putún in Postclassic years.

Although the question of Toltec chronology in Yucatán is not yet settled, other aspects have been clarified. Teotihuacán may not have dealt directly with Yucatán, but its influence reached the Puuc centers in the seventh or eighth centuries in the form of Tlaloc with the year-sign headdress and owls. In addition, at Acanceh near Mérida there is *talud–tablero* construction and relief figures including a feathered serpent, all in Teotihuacán style. At this time the great centers of Cotzumalhuapa, El Tajín, Xochicalco, and probably Tula itself were actively engaging in interregional trade and struggling for supremacy. This was when the ball-game cult spread over the entire Maya region. In Yucatán not only do we see the ball game, but other intrusive elements such as a phallic cult at Uxmal which may be of Huastec origin, the *greca* or stepped fret motif (Sharp 1978), (developed locally or perhaps at El Tajín?), and the use of columns (a Zapotec trait popular since Monte Albán II). In other words, we are dealing not only with Teotihuacán and Toltec traits, but Mexican traits from other sources in the Peripheral Coastal Lowlands and central highland Mexico.

Toltec influence at Uxmal is weakly manifested on platforms and altars with skulls and crossed bones, feathered-serpents in the ball court, and human figures. Likewise there is a little Toltec art at Kabah, Sayil, and Labná. Chichén Itzá manifests much stronger central Mexican ties in the Toltec reliefs of the ball courts and the inner Temple of Kukulcán, possibly through early Putún connections. The Putún were neighbors of the Nonoalca who settled around Coatzacoalcos (Maps 8, p. 206, and 9, p. 257) while other Nonoalca moved to Tula and, together with some northern Chichimecs, become the people we eventually know as the Toltecs (p. 360). Thus the Putún were closely associated with early Toltec peoples. The Putún traveled not only to Yucatán but also to the west. They could be responsible for transmitting Maya influences across the Isthmus of Tehuantepec to the Pacific coast of Oaxaca, continuing west to Acapulco and then north to Xochicalco and Tula (p. 231; Schmidt 1977). The impact of Maya culture was also felt at El Tajín, Veracruz and at Cacaxtla, Puebla (p. 234, 244). These westward travels of the Maya took place after the fire of Teotihuacán during the rise of the regional centers. Thus the Late Classic Maya of Yucatán participated in the same wave of interregional communication and readjustments to a new order that were sweeping across the whole of Mesoamerica.

THE TERMINAL CLASSIC PERIOD IN YUCATÁN A.D. 800–1000

Central Yucatán felt the intrusions of foreigners who by early in the ninth century were bringing Fine Paste wares into Becán. The influx of both domestic and funerary pottery in the Xcocom ceramic phase shows that the weakened older traditions had lost hold. During the tenth century, however, a new trading relationship opened up with the Guatemalan highlands that brought in Tohil Plumbate. Both Becán and Chicanna have yielded great amounts of this curious new foreign ware from highland Guatemala. Ball (1977b) is not certain how the contact was made, but suspects it could have taken place through the eastern area of Chetumal Bay reached from Guatemala via the Motagua River. In fact, a cross-peninsular trade route of 300 km might have functioned from east to west: Chetumal Bay to Laguna de Términos, benefiting Becán in the center. This, if true, did not prosper long, for in the eleventh and twelveth centuries, Río Bec centers were eclipsed, probably caused by coastal routes replacing the overland one.

The main development in northern Yucatán is highlighted in the florescence of the Puuc sites just described. An attempt to settle several large Puuc communities was made during the Terminal Classic in north-west Yucatán. Chacchob and Cuca were Puuc towns which are notable for their fortifications but otherwise rather undistinguished. At Cuca two enormous concentric masonry walls were constructed encircling a dense inner settlement. Causeways connected the walls to a civic center of pyramids and platforms without much formal planning. This is certainly atypical and presumably unsuccessful, for both towns have very brief histories (Webster 1978).

Puuc architecture is also late at Dzibilchaltún, which is slightly marginal to the main centers of Puuc development. Most of the datable construction at this site belongs to Tepeu 2 and the Terminal Classic phase, although the site has a very long period of occupation extending back into the Preclassic Period. Andrews V (1974) has roughly correlated the Group of the Seven Dolls construction with that of the Cross and Palace structures at Palenque (Photo 56). The ceramic evidence of the two sites that share Fine Orange types seems to support this. It was outside contact that is believed to have brought about the transformation of Dzibilchaltún from a very minor site to one of great florescence. Palenque was one point of contact, but other stimulation is attributed to the western lowlands and southern Gulf Coast as a whole.

In effect, it would seem that there was no collapse of Maya civilization in the north, but a long period of florescence lasting until A.D. 1000.

THE SOUTHERN PERIPHERY

It will be recalled that after the catastrophic volcanic eruption of Mt. Ilopango in El Salvador, many people left the valley. We do not know what happened to all of them, but some may have fled to Quelepa in eastern El Salvador (see Maps 3 and 9). In Preclassic days, this area had been part of the Uayala ceramic sphere, a cultural horizon embracing much of El Salvador and Honduras. By A.D. 150, however, it was developing a regional tradition of its own, and the fine hard Usu-

PHOTO 56. The Temple of the Seven Dolls, Dzibilchaltún, Yucatán. (Courtesy of the Instituto Nacional de Antropología e Historia, Mexico.)

lután pottery was gradually replaced by a coarser ware. Its Early Classic remains look very un-Mesoamerican with curious huge artificial terraces which support house-mounds and are reached via paved ramps. There is nothing Mesoamerican about the architecture or general layout. Almost identical construction is found at Los Naranjos, Honduras.

Toward the end of the Classic period (A.D. 625–1000), however, Quelepa became overwhelmingly Mesoamerican. Terracing went out and buildings were grouped around plazas. Three yokes, one *hacha*, and two effigy *palmas* were found in a cache associated with an I-shaped ball court, which, together with wheeled figurines and Fine Paste wares of the Gulf Coast cultures, leaves little question as to the source of this foreign influence. Puzzling though is how it reached eastern El Salvador with so few traces in Chiapas and Guatemala. Andrews suggests a migration by sea, motivated by the desire to control cacao production for which the Quelepa region had great potential (Andrews V 1976, 1977). Other ball courts are known from Los Llanitos, and at Tazumal, Chalchuapa two courts were erected. The courts at Los Llanitos and Quelepa are the most southerly ball courts in Mesoamerica. It has already been suggested (p. 256) that the Gulf Coast influences reached eastern El Salvador by a sea route around Yucatán combined with use of the Motagua River and its tributaries. This route has left a trail of ball courts and paraphernalia from Jaina to Copán (Parsons 1969).

The general sequence at Quelepa is paralleled at Los Naranjos, the site with great Preclassic ditches (p. 148). The Early Classic phase (Eden II: 100 B.C.–A.D. 550) shows so few Mesoamerican traits that Baudez and Becquelin (1973) consider it to lie outside the southern frontier. It has little Usulután ware, no Mexican influence, and the pottery bears no resemblance to Tzakol pottery of the Petén which was fashionable at this time. Meanwhile, Usulután ware, which was probably produced in various centers in El Salvador, Guatemala, or western Honduras, enjoyed a tremendous boom throughout the southern regions, eventually reaching lower Central America (see discussions in Andrews V 1976, 1977; Baudez and Becquelin 1973; and Lowe 1978).

Another major settlement was Yarumela on the Comayagua River, which by A.D. 550 had one of the largest mounds in the region, as well as a rectangular platform oriented to the cardinal directions. It is not known if it had ramps or staircases. The site of Lo de Vaca was typical of less important centers having but several dozen house sites and a single mound, whereas Yarumela and Los Naranjos can be considered ceremonial centers. Baudez (1970) thinks that the site of Tenampua may have taken over the political leadership from Yarumela as it is the most impressive site of all and is fortified. It is perched on a steep hill to which walls have been added. Within were the three largest mounds and a ball court. By this time there was a notable increase of population all over northern Honduras.

The years between A.D. 550 and 900 are known in this area of Honduras as the Yojoa phase and it is at this time that Copador polychrome became famous. It is very distinctive (red, purple, and black on buff) and well represented at Copán and western El Salvador, as well as in the Comayagua drainage. Tenampua has some of the finest painted pottery in the whole area with very imaginative designs of birds, monkeys, and people, often accompanied with bands of imitation glyphs. Even a representation of Tlaloc has appeared on one jar.

This is also the period of Ulua marble vases, so handsomely carved in the interlocking-scroll patterns of Veracruz. At this time the impact of Maya civilization reached its peak on the southern periphery but it was just limited to influence. There was no corbelled vaulting and no inscriptions. This southern area was never part of the Maya realm, but when the Maya civilization of the southern lowlands collapsed, not even these centers on the southern periphery survived. After A.D. 950 a great decrease in population took place and, thereafter, only small settlements are found such as Río Blanco at the foot of the Santa Barbara Mountains.

Northeastern Honduras has been tested by Healy (1978) at a site called Río Claro in the Aguan River valley. He did not find material as old as that of the nearby Cuyamel Caves (p. 149) but has a good Classic and Postclassic sequence. Classic constructions consist of randomly spaced irregular mounds composed of shell and earth. On the basis of present sampling, northeastern Honduras would seem to be affiliated with lower Central America.

CULTURAL CHANGE AND INNOVATION IN THE CLASSIC PERIOD

The Classic period is far more complex and more elaborate than the Preclassic, and the sheer accumulation of remains is many times greater. Aside from quantity and complexity, what kind of advancements were made and what were the basic differences? The period can be generally characterized by the appearance of urbanism, great art styles, and many intellectual innovations.

Mesoamerica expanded its geographical limits to the north and west, which did not greatly affect its overall development. With a climatic fluctuation which increased rainfall, the northern frontier was extended almost to the boundary of Chihuahua along the eastern flanks of the Sierra Madre Occidental, but dipped sharply in the central region where desert conditions prevailed and the nomadic Chichimecs lived. It was not until A.D. 600 that Mesoamerica extended its boundaries to the west coast. At that time Amapa, Nayarit looked very Mesoamerican with formal planned ceremonial centers, buildings grouped around courts oriented to the cardinal directions. By this date no more shaft tombs were being constructed and a number of sites show an increasing number of Mesoamerican characteristics.

The tools changed but little. Man still worked with his stone implements, with the addition of a new type of hoe around A.D. 500. The weaponry inventory of spears, slings, and darts was enlarged to include the bow and arrow. Diet remained essentially the same, but new varieties of maize and improved agricultural techniques permitted the production of more food and a substantial increase in population.

Some of the most important innovations took place in the field of agriculture. Techniques were improved both to increase yield and to bring more land under cultivation. Dams, irrigation canals, and terracing, were all introduced into central highland Mexico, and in addition, the southern lowland Maya cultivated ridged terraces and *bajos,* introduced short-cycle slash-and-burn agriculture, built huge reservoirs, dug wells, and learned how to cultivate, harvest, and store the fruit of the ramon tree.

Population increased dramatically. Teotihuacán at its peak may have housed approximately 100,000–200,000; Monte Albán, 30,000; Tikal at least 70,000. Thus, large urban centers growing out of the earlier Preclassic ceremonial centers are a characteristic feature of the Classic period. At least three settlement patterns are found: (1) the nucleated compact grid such as that of Teotihuacán; (2) a nucleated center with a large sustaining area of dispersed villages or hamlets, exemplified by the southern lowland Maya cities and such sites as El Tajín; and (3) although probably nonurban, the pattern in Belize, where settlements were strung out along the rivers. Monte Albán presents an aberrant special situation of a non-self-sustaining city, supported as a joint venture by the Oaxaca Valley communities. In addition there were, of course, various types of villages and coastal settlements.

Classic ceremonial centers were larger, more complex, and more properly called administrative civic–religious centers as religious practitioners gradually shared more and more of their authority with the administrative secular officials. Centers were planned, structured, and oriented to the cardinal directions, that is, slightly east of magnetic north.

In the field of religion, Teotihuacán is sometimes credited with conceptualizing high gods instead of emphasizing ancestor worship. Certainly Tlaloc was a popular god to whom everyone could appeal. Ancestors were a more elitist concept and were important for establishing one's birth-right and social position.

Intellectual achievements include a knowledge of the zero and a vigesimal system of mathematics, probably derived from the Peripheral Coastal Lowlands. But the Maya carried scientific pursuits further, learning how to predict eclipses of the moon and sun, plotting movements of the planets and other heavenly bodies. Astronomy was closely related to agriculture for predictions determined when to plant.

Increasing secularization after A.D. 600 was a new trend undoubtedly linked to mercantilism, an outstanding characteristic of the Classic-period development. Intensive communication between diverse areas exposed people to other political and socioeconomic conditions, new ideologies, new art styles. This cross-cultural fertilization of ideas had a profound and lasting effect on regional cultures.

Institutionalized long-distance trade networks have been both credited with the rise of Maya civilization and blamed for its collapse. Alone this is a simplistic explanation, but most archaeologists would agree that the stimulation of outside contacts and desire for exotic, prestigious foreign goods was an important factor in the creation and maintenance of an elite class, massive building programs, increased social differentiation, and years of economic prosperity. In turn, although not *the* cause of collapse but certainly a related event, was the closing of the Teotihuacán Corridor and the shift in trade routes around Yucatán that cut off internal Maya commercial centers. Loss of obsidian monopolies and of control over trade routes, emergence of competitors, and militarism are all related factors affecting both Teotihuacán and the Maya.

Secularization, already touched upon, is further emphasized in genealogical studies of dynasties, rulers, and their mundane desires to legitimize their status by publicizing their ancestors, recording victories, marriages, births, and using religion to document their divinity. The secular trend is present in Monte Albán's early relief carvings, but the Late Classic Maya saw that the information was clearly recorded and immortalized in sculptured panels, stelae, altars, and lintels. In doing so, they left evidence of their knowledge of equinoxes and soltices, eclipses, and astronomical data in stone that would otherwise have been undocumented. Names, portraits, intercity alliances, marriages, and conferences are subjects now within our grasp, for certain Maya cities such as Tikal, Naranjo, Calakmul, Yaxchilán, Copán, Quiriguá, Palenque and Piedras Negras inscribed this information on their stone monuments.

Whereas the Maya expressed themselves in a variety of media (stone, painting, and stucco), Teotihuacán communicated primarily by mural paintings and ceramics. Most scenes are formal and liturgical, nonetheless, iconographic studies reveal the presence of warriors, weapons, and ball games, in addition to the more common themes of ritual and priestly affairs. Cholula and Cacaxtla have rare examples of narrative eclectic art in central highland Mexico. Chichén Itzá, Mul-Chic, and Bonampak have representative surviving Maya paintings. All these murals represent a much greater elaboration and sophistication than the few Preclassic paintings known and provide much historical and ethnographic information.

Warfare is a common theme in mural paintings but is also well documented in relief carvings at Usumacinta Basin sites and in Metepec pottery figurines at Teotihuacán. There is no longer any question of militarism in the Classic period. Although small scale, conflict is portrayed often; even hand-to-hand combat is depicted in murals. There were no large organized armies at any time in Mesoamerica. Fortifications were built at Becán and Tikal. The purpose of the walls at Teotihuacán and Monte Albán is not known but they could have served as a defensive mechanism. Fortified sites in Tlaxcala date as early as A.D. 100–650. Teotihuacán may have intervened militarily to exploit mineral resources or to patrol the "cacao route" traveled by its merchants. A Teotihuacán military role at Kaminaljuyú is still debated. That the Teotihuacanos were capable of coercion, everyone agrees.

The concentration of power and authority evident at Teotihuacán has no parallel. Settlement patterns and apartment-house compounds suggest little mobility, with tight control over personal lives. Among the Maya, there were multiple administrative centers instead of one, but the power of the ruler may have been equally strong.

There is ample evidence of a well-defined class-structured society in every urban situation: an elite, merchants, craftsmen and specialists, farmers, and slaves.

In artistic manifestations Classic remains have great aesthetic appeal. The art of stucco sculpture developed at Palenque has no equal before or after in Mesoamerican archaeology. Stone carving too reached a cultural climax in the Classic period: narrative art of Cotzumalhuapa and quality of the stone carving of Copán, Piedras Negras, Tikal, and Yaxchilán. A different kind of beauty is seen in the Tajín interlaced-scroll style epitomized in the craftsmanship of yokes, *hachas*, and *palmas*. These art styles are carried over into ceramics where vessels were exquisitely carved, incised, or painted. Narrative scenes, glyphic texts, and religious symbolism are all portrayed in ceramic art, a field of study awaiting more detailed research.

Accompanying the new urbanism, extensive communication, and trade is the trend toward mass production and standardization. The use of molds for figurine production is paralleled by the repetitious pottery form such as the cylindrical tripod. Special wares were manufactured on a large scale for wide distribution such as Usulután, Thin Orange, and Fine Orange wares. The trend toward mass production is also seen in the stone mosaic decoration of Puuc sites, where small cut stones were prepared in advance and could be assembled in any number of designs. The use of patterns or stencils has been demonstrated in the murals at Teotihuacán and in stucco sculpture at Palenque. Such time-saving standardization devices are Classic-period innovations.

Mosaic facade decoration and veneer masonry were new developments in the field of architecture which were accompanied by other features that produced a whole new flavor. Walls became thinner and less massive and, together with more doorways, created lighter, airier structures among the Maya. The round building and curved corners had not been seen with frequency even in the Preclassic and now reappeared in other forms. Causeways and roads had been initiated at El Mirador but did not become widespread until the seventh century when they often linked buildings and outlying areas to a central acropolis or another site.

SUMMARY

Early Classic:
A.D. 1–400

Teotihuacán emerged to dominate the Basin of Mexico and surrounding highlands, becoming a huge urban center with subsistence base guaranteed by intensive agriculture supported by irrigation. Exploitation of nearby obsidian sources led to an obsidian commercial enterprise outside the city at Tepeapulco, an expanding market system, and a long-distance trade network extending to Guatemala and Belize. To support these enterprises, Teotihuacanos were sent off to colonize and to exploit turquoise and exotic mineral resources in the north and west.

East of the Isthmus of Tehuantepec, the characteristic features of Maya civilization were already apparent with the spread of Chicanel and Protoclassic pottery styles, corbel-vaulted architecture, Long Count dating, and the stela cult throughout the southern lowlands. Although the northeast Petén was seen as the heartland, it was Tikal itself that emerged as the dominant center of the lowland Maya. A gradual growth of power and authority can be seen emerging from the most dominant family lineage of the older Preclassic centers. By the fourth century A.D., a royal dynasty was established at Tikal. Main settlements grew up along rivers and *bajos*. Fortifications were constructed at Tikal and Becán.

Middle Classic: (Early)
A.D. 400–550

Teotihuacán, now a city of 22.5 km² with 100,000–200,000 population, reached the peak of its influence and expansion. The Oaxaca Barrio was well established in the western part of the city. The relationship between Monte Albán and Teotihuacán is not clear but contact was peaceful. From commercial colonies in the Chalchihuites culture in Zacatecas, expeditionary groups penetrated New Mexico in search of turquoise. Other colonies established in Jalisco exploited turquoise and minerals and in northern Querétaro extracted cinnabar.

A port-of-trade developed in Guatemala Valley in which Teotihuacán-influenced Kaminaljuyú dealt with the Amatitlán chiefdom, which represented elite groups from every Maya region. Tikal became the most powerful urban center of the southern Maya lowlands where dynastic rulers recorded their histories on altars, stelae, and lintels. The corbelled arch was a standard architectural feature and massive masonry temples, pyramids, and palaces were grouped around courts and plazas. Two of Tikal's rulers may have come from Kaminaljuyú bringing Teotihuacán influence. Teotihuacán-style artifacts are found in elite burials and tombs, and its influence is seen in art. The lidded cylindrical tripod vessel of Teotihuacán was imported at this time. Characteristic of Maya ceramics was the Tzakol basal-flanged bowl decorated in geometric or naturalistic designs in polychrome. Commerce thrived as the elite class wanted products lacking in the Petén such as obsidian, hard stone for grinding tools, salt, jade, sea shells, and foreign-made goods. In turn the Maya exported its fine polychrome pottery, skins, feathers, and tropical-forest products.

Teotihuacán withdrew, or its trade networks were cut off by rival competitors. The impact of its former influence was still reflected in the art and iconography in the Peripheral Coastal Lowlands and Maya regions. The great urban city continued to prosper in the highlands and the Quetzalpapálotl Palace was built, but its power and prestige were diminished.

After a hiatus of 60 years and some disruption, Maya civilization underwent a realignment of political power, with new centers emerging in peripheral areas where trade was brisk and prosperous. Tikal was forced to share authority with Palenque, Calakmul, and Copán. Maya civilization reached its brilliant cultural climax in artistic and intellectual levels.

The two great centers in the Peripheral Coastal Lowlands, Tajín and Cotzumalhuapa, rose to prominence, and their influence was spread through the ball-game cult which became very important at a third center, Chichén Itzá. Trade flourished and new sea routes around Yucatán to Belize left central Yucatán and the Petén culturally isolated. After A.D. 600 secularization and warfare were more in evidence.

The Guatemalan chiefdoms in the highlands broke up.

Middle Classic: (Late)
A.D. 550–700

In the Basin of Mexico, Teotihuacán suffered a fire, its population was reduced to 50,000, and economic ruin was complete. The Basin was reduced to six small centers of which Teotihuacán was the largest. Coyotlatelco red-on-buff pottery was the new ceramic style of the highlands with one production center at Teotihuacán itself. Having lost control over the Tepeapulco obsidian industry including access to the Cerro de las Navajas source, Teotihuacán set up new workshops with Otumba gray obsidian. Tula may have begun to compete for land and resources.

In the Maya area, beautiful polychromed cylindrical jars (Late Tepeu phase) were painted with scenes showing human and animal figures, at times banded at the rim by rows of decorative hieroglyphs. However, the great civilization began to crumble, although even as the Maya reduced their territorial borders, some centers embarked on great rebuilding programs. Deterioration continued and by A.D. 900 activity ceased.

Multiple causes were responsible, among them the over-exploitation of the environmental potential, too large a population for the land available with no further expansion possible, a large dependent and demanding elite which was too expensive to maintain, and growing inequalities in the stratified society. Although internal sociopolitical stresses can be detected, the effect of foreign contact and external influences hastened the end. The Putún Itzá (Chontal-speaking Maya from Tabasco) invaded and occupied Chichén Itzá. Some went south through central Yucatán and took over Seibal in A.D. 830, prolonging

Late Classic:
A.D. 700–900

its history until the end of the century. Warfare and conflict were recorded at Becán and Usumacinta centers in the west. One by one the southern lowlands collapsed, all building ceased, many sites were abandoned or reduced to small villages.

There was no corresponding collapse in the north. The Puuc cities prospered and the new architectural style of veneer masonry use of concrete and mosaic decoration spread rapidly. By now every major center had at least one ball court. Mexican influence from Veracruz, Oaxaca, Teotihuacán, as well as Toltec, could be found in art and architecture. Maya influence was carried west to Guerrero, and north to central Mexico. Another route was via the Gulf Coast. It was strongly felt at Teotihuacán, at El Tajín, and in Cacaxtla. Monte Albán was abandoned soon after A.D. 700, but valley centers continued without interruption. In highland Guatemala nucleated settlements took up defensive positions on hilltops. The inhabitants of the sparsely settled lowlands lived in dispersed villages. In Yucatán, regionalism once more prevailed.

In the Peripheral Coastal Lowlands, Maya influence could be distinguished at Cotzumalhuapa, Matacapan, and Tajín. This region, which had initiated so many changes and innovations, at no time formed any kind of political union. The new power structure was at Tula. By the year A.D. 900, the shift in power had been completed.

Early Postclassic Developments: Tula and Chichén Itzá

As we approach the beginnings of legendary history, it is indeed curious that this brief period should be so confusing and so poorly known archaeologically. In these 300 years Mesoamerica had to readjust to many changes that resulted from the crises suffered by the major centers at the close of the Classic period. Tula rose to assume the role of leadership formerly held by Teotihuacán; this was a geographical shift of less than 160 km in central highland Mexico, but one that placed the new capital closer to the northern limits of agriculture. In the Maya region, the key area from this time on was Yucatán. However, despite many years of archaeological work and the advantage of the first legendary–historical records, there are great gaps, conflicting views, and many unsolved problems relating to the events of this unsettled period.

By A.D. 900 the highland Maya were moving out of the valleys to occupy defensive positions on the hilltops. The old Petén region was never totally abandoned. Ceramic remains there show occupation by people who manufactured a very inferior pottery, largely monochrome and unslipped. The former elegant polychrome painted wares had disappeared. Among students of Maya ceramics this period is known as the New Town Horizon. It is well represented at Barton Ramie in Belize but only meagerly at Tikal. This new material, bearing no resemblance to earlier traditions, could be due to a reoccupation of the area by strangers (Willey *et al.* 1967).

As already mentioned, the peninsula of Yucatán was prospering from events taking place elsewhere around A.D. 900. Dzibilchaltún provides a continuous record since it was never abandoned. Buildings were erected with stone mosaic facades and art became largely geometric. The interest displayed in public buildings emphasizes a secular rather than religious trend. Glyphs look more Mexican than Maya and cannot be translated. Teotihuacán influence as well as Toltec can be identified. The great sites of Uxmal and Chichén Itzá have a mixture of architectural styles and intrusive influence dating back to Middle and Late Classic periods. There is not much known about the final occupation of the Puuc sites, but the architectural style survived at least to A.D. 1000 at some centers.

By this time, various Mexican and Toltec influences were manifest at Chichén Itzá. Before trying to sort out what impact these had on Yucatán, let us first return to highland Mexico where Tula was emerging as the next great power.

THE TOLTECS
(SI–2)

The most important Toltec site is Tula, the legendary Tollan Xicocotitlán, which in 1941 was identified with the modern town of Tula in the state of Hidalgo (Jiménez Moreno 1941). Its geographical location is vitally important in that it was situated very close to the northern boundary of Mesoamerica, which from A.D. 900 to 1200 reached its northernmost limits and thereafter began to recede. The advantages of being on the Tula River, a tributary of the Pánuco, made for easy communication with people in northern Veracruz, the Huasteca. To the west contact was facilitated by the great Lerma River, which flowed out of the nearby Valley of Toluca. As we will see, these were the areas of greatest Toltec impact.

Legends of the Toltecs tell us that they were a most extraordinary people, taller than any people known today, and that they excelled in sports and in all arts and sciences. Their proud decendants attributed to them all major achievements. In studying the skeletal remains from Tula, we find that Toltecs were in fact just a little taller than most Mesoamericans, and had big noses and projecting faces. Less attractive features were bad teeth and poor hearing. If anything made them look distinguished it might have been a high intellectual forehead (Benfer 1974). It is said that they could grow cotton in colors and raise gigantic ears of corn. Above all, hunger and misery were unknown, everything was plentiful, and all were rich and happy. Is it any wonder that at the time of the Spanish Conquest groups all over Mesoamerica claimed descent from these people? By then the Toltecs, whose fame was enriched with the passing of time, had become mythical heroes. To identify oneself with them was to claim a superior birth-right (Armillas 1950). By then too, Quetzalcóatl had lost his earlier connotation as a warrior, migration leader, and founder (?) and was popularized as a priest-figure, pacific and penitent (Keber 1979).

The history of the Toltecs as reconstructed by the archaeological record is in sharp disagreement with the foregoing (Acosta 1956–1957), as it portrays them as constantly engaged in strife and conflict. Innovations under the Toltecs include alterations in religious architecture and new art styles in stone carving and ceramic production. Change, however, is not necessarily synonomous with improvement, and Toltec pottery and figurines, with their characteristic stiffness and monotony are a far cry from the imaginative elegance achieved by their Preclassic and Classic ancestors (see Plate 11, p. 370). Indeed, the remains at the site of Tula give the impression of having been put together in haste, skilled and unskilled alike having a hand in the carving and modeling. From a densely populated base that gradually grew up in Late Classic years, Tula fairly exploded into prominence after A.D. 900 only to suffer a major disaster. It has been estimated that this surge and demise could have happened in only 100 years (Sanders, Parsons, and Santley 1979). Nicholson (1978) suggests anywhere from 150 to 300 years.

It is often said that the historical record begins with Tula, but fact and fiction are so confused and distorted that interpretation is not easy. Toltec history is culled from the writings of Sahagún, Muñoz Camargo, Motolinía, and such anonymous sources as La Historia de los Mexicanos, Anales de Cuauhtitlán, and the Historia Tolteca–Chichimeca. Torquemada's and Ixtlilxóchitl's writings contain additions that must have been derived from still other sources, plus colorful embellishments of their own. These records relate oral traditions that had been handed down from mouth to mouth for approximately 400 years. The same event may be told differently in six different accounts, and the order of events is muddled, can skip, or even be reversed. These early records provide invaluable information but must be studied critically, realizing that myth, errors, contradictions, tailoring the facts to accommodate Christian beliefs and biases, and confusion arising from consulting various calendrical systems require that one must not accept the written word at face value as historical fact.

The word *Tollan* refers to a "place of reeds or rushes" which came to mean metropolis, or a great congregation of people "as thick as rushes." Eventually Tollan had the connotation of a place where craftsmen, that is, skilled or knowledgeable people, gathered (Davies 1977; Feldman 1974). Consequently Tollan could, and in all likelihood did, refer to a number of localities, but the first Tollan of concern to us here was probably Teotihuacán, home of the legendary Toltecs who brought to their world knowledge of science, arts, and crafts. Tula, Hidalgo is believed to be the Tollan Xicocotitlán of the chronicles which became the political capital of the Toltec "empire" after the fall of Teotihuacán. Finally we can also speak of later Toltecs who lived at Cholula (Tollan Cholollan) and produced some of the most beautiful pottery in all Mesoamerica's history (Davies 1977).

We have already seen that Teotihuacán was not suddenly abandoned but that squatters and neighboring peoples moved in or stayed on, living among the ruins of the great metropolis. Some of these were Olmeca–Xicalanca people who also inhabited the region of Puebla–Tlaxcala at this time. These were people believed to have come to the highlands from the Gulf Coast region, affiliated with the Nonoalca who were one of the ethnic lowland groups associated with Tula, Hidalgo. In the great displacement of peoples around A.D. 900 some of these people may have stayed on in the Puebla Valley to rebuild Cholula, for this great center had also undergone the same deterioration that affected Teotihuacán.

Some of the Toltecs of Tula, Hidalgo may well have formed part of Teotihuacán's rural population, maybe aided its downfall, usurped its lands, and even lived among its ruins as makers of Coyotlatelco pottery, the earliest ware at Tula. The northern part of the Basin of Mexico was densely settled, especially in the Zumpango region, and this concentration of population was somehow related to the growth of the new center at Tula.

Other Toltecs were Chichimec peoples (Tolteca–Chichimeca) who, according to tradition, came down to Tula from the northwest. We do know that Mesoamerican peoples had settled in the northwest by A.D. 200, and Teotihuacanos colonized some mining centers shortly thereafter. Mesoamerican traditions can be seen in the archaeology of the Chalchihuites culture which stretched from northern Durango to San Miguel de Allende on the present boundary between the states of Guanajuato and Querétaro (Kelley 1966). Early Mazapanoid figurines and Toltec pottery appear in Guanajuato and to the west somewhat earlier than at Tula itself, lending credence to a western or northwest priority for some Toltec traits (Braniff 1974; Kelly 1980).

Still another Toltec ingredient was the Nonoalca, people from the southern Veracruz–Tabasco region, who made their way north to the Huasteca and to Tula via Tulancingo. These people were presumably more refined and had more skills than the Tolteca–Chichimeca. Thus, in Toltec culture we can find a Teotihuacán background, combined with that of the northwestern Tolteca–Chichimecas, Nonoalca peoples from the Gulf Coast, along with Mixtecs and other neighboring groups.

History, Myth, and Quetzalcóatl The history of Tula is intimately related to the legendary adventures of Quetzalcóatl, and some version of this was familiar to all later Mesoamerican peoples. The most widely accepted account of this remarkable figure is that interpretation of Jiménez Moreno (1941, 1966). According to this popular version, Ce Técpatl Mixcóatl was the leader of a great northern horde of Tolteca–Chichimecas, who settled in the Valley of Mexico near the Cerro de la Estrella at Culhuacán. His son was Ce Acatl Topiltzin Quetzalcóatl, who became ruler after his father's death and moved the capital to Tula, Hidalgo in the year A.D. 968. There he became a religious reformer, assuming the title of high priest of the plumed serpent, Quetzalcóatl. Under his leadership the arts were stimulated and metallurgists, feather workers, sculptors, and craftsmen of every type were assembled from other regions and encouraged to produce their finest work. Quetzalcóatl's rival, Tezcatlipoca, God of the Night and the North, succeeded in humiliating Quetzalcóatl by intoxicating him and consequently causing him to neglect his religious obligations. In total disgrace, he sadly left Tula in A.D. 987 and with a band of faithful followers crossed the Valley of Mexico, passed between the two volcanoes, and proceeded to the Gulf of Mexico. There, according to one source, he set fire to himself and rose to the heavens to become the Morning Star. In a different version, he set sail eastward on a raft of serpents, prophesying that in another year Ce Acatl, the anniversary year of his birth, he would return to conquer his people. Meanwhile 97 years passed at Tula, until Huémac, the final sovereign, took over for a very long reign. Fresh barbaric attacks from the north resulted in the violent destruction of Tula, and Huémac abandoned the city, fleeing to Chapultepec in A.D. 1168 or 1178 (?) where he finally committed suicide.

A second interpretation of Toltec history is that based on the Memoria Breve de Chimalpahin and Sahagún. According to Kirchhoff (1955), Quetzalcóatl and Huémac were contemporaries and ruled simultaneously at Tula, Quetzalcóatl as religious leader or priest and Huémac as king or secular authority. Friction between the two resulted in the abandonment of Tula in A.D. 1168 (?), first by Quetzalcóatl, and later on in the same year by Huémac. According to this interpretation, our Toltec history would be greatly shortened because all events would occur during the joint reign of Quetzalcóatl and Huémac instead of extending over 200 years.

According to the first version, Quetzalcóatl's reign is placed at the beginning of Tula's history rather than at the end, leaving a period of 97 years between Quetzalcóatl and Huémac. If Quetzalcóatl was disgraced, it seems rather unlikely that all the officials would have followed him, leaving no intellectuals behind to mastermind the building of an empire.

In the second version, the two rulers who might have been heads of two dynasties, rule contemporaneously: Topiltzin Quetzalcóatl as leader of the Tolteca–Chichimecas and Huémac as leader of the Nonoalca. As Davies points out, these were two very different groups from opposite ends of Mesoamerica who might well have had trouble getting along with one another. Both had religious connotations: Topiltzin Quetzalcóatl as priest, associated with the morning star and the planet Venus, and Huémac associated with Tezcatlipoca. The personalities could also be interpreted as representing a struggle for control between secular and religious power. Most sources agree that Huémac, upon leaving Tula, went to Chapultepec and met a violent end by hanging. Topiltzin Quetzalcóatl is variously reported as leaving for the "east," or immolating himself to become the morning star, or the planet Venus, or as simply going to Tenayuca and from there to Culhuacán, that is, returning to his original home in the Basin of Mexico where he died.

Nicholson feels this is all highly speculative. The date of the establishment of Tula as a capital can vary greatly but A.D. 900 is generally accepted. The problems of interpretation are so complex that there is little agreement among the sources. To grasp the depth of the problem, one should read Nicholson's evaluation of the source material (1978) as well as Davies (1977). For the moment it seems wise to depend largely on the archaeological record and supplant it where possible with the ancient chronicles. We should always keep in mind that these are part myth and that what comes to us has passed through the hands of the Aztecs who, in addition to not having a clear picture themselves, certainly had their own ancestral interests at stake.

All ancient Mexicans believed that the gods had sacrificed themselves to create the Fifth Sun under which we live today. It was thanks to these gods that man was not forced to live in darkness. Known as the Leyenda de los Soles, this myth relates how the world formerly had been illuminated by four previous suns, but each time all living creatures had died when the suns were destroyed in turn by jaguars, fire, wind, and water (Caso 1958). Sahagún says the suns (the worlds) before the Toltecs were destroyed by water, the earth, wind, and fire. The era of the earth was the reign of the "giants" at Teotihuacán. This world was destroyed by wind and the Olmeca–Xicalanca who came in boats. (Most groups are originally supposed to have arrived in boats or "over water.") The Fourth World was destroyed by fire, after which the Toltecs rose to assume the reins of leadership. The Aztecs believed that we owe the Fifth Sun, which lights our present world, to Quetzalcóatl himself who gave his own life and blood by jumping into the fire to be consumed. This is supposed to have happened at Teotihuacán where guides may point out the exact spot. The Aztecs believed that our sun too will one day be destroyed by another evil force—earthquake.

It is not clear whether feathered serpents of all periods were related to this later concept of Quetzalcóatl, but their association with rain or water dates back to the Preclassic horizon, Joralemon's God VII, when perhaps Tlaloc and the plumed serpent were derived from the jaguar cult (Covarrubias 1946). At Teotihuacán the plumed serpent is represented, but the emphasis there is on Tlaloc. Plumed serpents are found in stone carvings in the Ciudadela and on pottery. The Quetzalcóatl image is found in the mural paintings of Zacuala as well as in the later *códices* of the Maya, Mixtecs, and central Mexicans. Representations of feathered serpents are found sculptured and painted in many Maya sites of the Classic and Postclassic periods. The Postclassic Quetzalcóatl is associated with the morning star or the east (Tlahuizcalpantecuhtli) and with the wind god, Ehécatl, and is intimately related to round temples and the Huasteca. Davies (1977) sees a radical transformation of Quetzalcóatl from Classic to Postclassic periods already apparent at Tula, where there are far more representations of Quetzalcóatl as the morning star than as the feathered serpent.

By the sixteenth century some sources identify Quetzalcóatl as a god, while others refer to him as a priest–king. Among the Aztecs, Quetzalcóatl was known as a dignitary or the holder of a titled position in the priesthood. He was still represented as Ehécatl and as the morning star, with his twin, Xólotl, the evening star or the planet Venus. Here again is the concept of duality.

The conflicting accounts interwoven with legends, history, and problems of chronology have been studied by Davies (1977), who has brought together a wealth of information on the Toltecs and the Quetzalcóatl saga. He points out, for example, that no single individual could be in all the places and do all the feats attributed to Quetzalcóatl; so at the outset, it is clear that this is part fable or that Quetzalcóatl represents a concept rather than fact. If a person did exist he probably lived in the late Classic period at Teotihuacán where an account of drunkenness and subsequent humiliation is exactly the same as that related by Sahagún about a Huastec leader. Quetzalcóatl is highly touted as being opposed to human sacrifice, but this could well be colored by Christianized versions. Archaeology reveals the custom as being well rooted in Mesoamerica; at Tula, one is constantly reminded of the bloody practice.

Tula, Hidalgo

Archaeology shows that Tula was settled around A.D. 650, its early center being what is known today as Tula Chico. This is an area of mound complexes and several small ball courts arranged much like that of the Main Ceremonial Precinct, located 2 km to the southwest. Slightly north of Tula Chico is another center, El Corral, probably contemporaneous. It has a round temple, and the area yields Tlamimilolpa- and Metepec-phase ceramic material. From these early settlements made by rural population from the Basin of Mexico, Tula grew and spread out to become a major center in the tenth century. It is even possible that the Tula region was controlled in its early days by Teotihuacán (Matos Moctezuma 1978).

The Main Ceremonial Precinct one sees today (Photo 57), which was burned around A.D. 1178 (?) and ravaged by every succeeding group, gives but a hint of the greatness once achieved by the people of Quetzalcóatl. This center has been known for many years and was excavated in the 1940s and 1950s. In addition, there are smaller civic–ceremonial plazas scattered through the vast residential areas only now being excavated. Tula lies 60 km north of Mexico City and is easily reached today by either automobile or train. The Main Ceremonial Precinct

PHOTO 57. Aerial view of central Tula, Hidalgo. The ball court is at upper left, Pyramid B center, and Building C lower right. (The photo was taken before the Atlantean figures were returned to their original location as in Photo 58.) (Courtesy of Compañia Mexicana Aerofoto, S. A.)

PHOTO 58. Pyramid B, dedicated to Quetzalcóatl, Tula, Hidalgo. (Photographed by the author.)

overlooks the modern town of Tula at the confluence of the Tula and Rosa rivers. Perched on a high promontory, it would have been easy to defend, for the stone-faced retaining walls are 10–15 m in height. There is a large central plaza faced on two sides by pyramids; to the east is Building C, a pyramid almost completely destroyed when the original stone facings were removed, probably by the Aztecs. The smaller but more impressive structure is Building B, the pyramid to the north of the plaza (Photo 58). It was built to support a temple to Quetzalcóatl in his aspect as Venus or the morning star, hence its official designation as the Pyramid of Tlahuizcalpantecuhtli. In the willful destruction of Tula, the temple was defaced and the great warrior Atlantean figures that supported the roof with their flat-topped heads were disjointed and hurled into a deep trench cut into the heart of the pyramid, along with dismembered feathered-serpent columns and carved pillars.

Now, after many seasons of excavation and reconstruction, these great stone Atlantean figures have been reassembled and returned to their original places on top of the pyramid (Photo 59). Each one is made

PHOTO 59. Colossal Atlantean figures that supported the temple roof, Pyramid B, Tula, Hidalgo. The figures represent warriors with an *atlatl* and a bag of incense. Height: 4.6 m. (Photographed by the author.)

in four sections, which are doweled together. A complete figure measures over 3.5 m high and represents a warrior richly attired, wearing rectangular ear pieces, a pectoral representing an upside-down bird, a belt that clasps in the rear with a great disk, necklace, bracelets, anklets, and sandals decorated with plumed serpents. The smooth elliptical mouth and eye sockets were probably inlaid with shell or obsidian. One hand holds an *atlatl*, the other a curved sword and a bag of incense. Even today one sees traces of the red and white pigment with which the warriors were painted. Similar warriors adorn pillars of the same height that supported the roof beams in the rear chamber of the temple, where small Atlantean figures with raised arms held up an altar or shrine (Figure 28-a). The lintel of the temple doorway rested

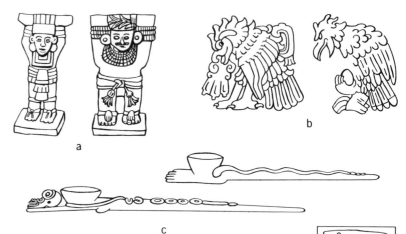

a

b

c

FIGURE 28. Comparative features: Tula and Chichén Itzá. (a) Atlantean figures (Bacabs?) (left, Tula; right, Chichén Itzá); (b) eagles with human heart from sculptured panels (left, Tula; right, Chichén Itzá); (c) pottery pipes (upper, Tula; lower, Chichén Itzá); (d) jaguars in relief (top, Tula; bottom, Chichén Itzá); (e) figures from sculptured columns (left, Tula; right, Chichén Itzá). (From the following sources: a(left, right), d(bottom), Tozzer 1957, courtesy of the Peabody Museum, Harvard University, copyright © 1957 by the President and Fellows of Harvard College; b(left), Marquina 1951; b(right), c(bottom), Morris, Charlot, and Morris 1931; c(top), Acosta 1945; d(top), e(left, right), Acosta 1941.)

d

e

on cylindrical serpent columns, which, although incomplete, may have been assembled like those at Chichén Itzá with their heads on the ground while their tails supported the lintel itself. Stone sculpture at Tula is largely concerned with architecture: columns, atlantids, or relief panels. In the 1979 excavations, carved stones were found which depict a corn goddess, as well as Quetzalcóatl and Coyolxauhqui; these may be of later date. In the old Ceremonial Precinct, deity representations and idols have not been found.

The five tiers of the pyramid originally were completely faced with sculptured panels of walking jaguars (Figure 28-d, top), coyotes, eagles devouring human hearts (Figure 28-b, left), and fantastic heads composed of human, bird, and serpent elements. Of these, only the panels on the east and north sides have survived. An enormous colonnaded court or gallery spanned the front and west side of the pyramid. Around the walls of both colonnaded halls are low benches carved with processions of richly attired figures wearing great plumed headdresses, jew-

Chichén Itzá

Tula

FIGURE 29. A comparison of benches carved in relief from Tula and Chichén Itzá. Each shows a procession of richly attired figures. Rattlesnakes adorn the cornice above. (Top, from Marquina 1951; bottom, from Acosta 1945.)

elry, and short skirts, and carry darts and shields. The red, blue, yellow, white, and black colors in which they were originally painted are still remarkably well preserved. Rattlesnakes adorn the cornice above the processional figures in the frieze (Figure 29).

The so-called Burnt Palace west of Building B has two large colonnaded halls with similarly decorated benches around the walls as well as altars, fire pits, and sunken central patios. One patio was the scene of *patolli* playing, a welcome hint of recreation for all its possible religious overtones. Patterns on the plaster floor can be recognized as the same game the Aztecs played at Conquest time (p. 450). This was a game of chance much like our modern Parcheesi, played on a cross-like board marked off into spaces through which a counter moved according to the throw of bone dice (Erasmus 1950).

As far as we know, the Teotihuacanos were the first to play the game, as a *patolli* board was scratched into the floor of their Zacuala Palace in the seventh or eighth century. Palenque, Seibal, Uxmal, Dzibilchaltún, and Belize (Benque Viejo, Stann Creek) also have *patolli* boards either painted or incised on floors. The Palenque, Seibal, and Belize examples are almost identical to those at Tula and most are estimated to date from the Terminal Classic period. Precise dating is uncertain since the pattern could have been placed on the floors at any time (Smith 1977).

Adjoining Building B on the east of the ruins at Tula, a number of structures believed to have been residences were erected against the pyramid. Much of this construction has been destroyed, but the walls were originally of adobe, faced with stone, stuccoed, and painted.

A new architectural feature makes its appearance at Tula and thereafter continues as an integral part of the Mesoamerican pattern. This is the serpent-wall, or *coatepantli*, which does not surround the Pyramid of Quetzalcóatl at Tula, as is the custom in many of the later Aztec complexes, but simply extends along its northern side. This too was toppled during Tula's destruction but has now been restored. Between two friezes of geometric design on the *coatepantli*, a gruesome scene repeated on every two slabs shows a serpent that has swallowed a dead person except for his head, which protrudes from its jaws. Dismembered arms and legs are enmeshed with the serpent's body.

To date, six ball courts have been identified. A large one, cleared and restored, looks like a copy of the one at Xochicalco, being of the same size and shape. Both are similar to Classic Maya courts. The large Tula court lies across the northern plazas from Building B and possesses a drainage system so remarkable that, freed of debris, it continues to function today. Panels and friezes once faced the ball court, but these were carried off by the later Aztecs. Originally, stone rings, through which the ball had to pass, protruded from the walls, but today only the empty holes for their insertion are visible. No one knows the purpose of the niches located diagonally at the ends of the courts, but similar ones are found in the court at Monte Albán and Atzompa in Oaxaca.

Also left to speculation is the meaning or purpose of the curious sculpted stone figures known as *chacmools* (see Plate 12-d, p. 380) of which two have been found. Elsewhere these rest at the top of stairs at the entrance to temples, perhaps for offerings or to serve as sacrificial stones (?). These life-sized figures, always found in a reclining posture with legs flexed, hold either a receptacle or flat slab on their abdomens as they gaze vacantly off to one side. Whatever their role in ceremonial life, it seems to have been fundamental to the Toltecs. We find *chacmools* among their contemporaries and descendants until Conquest times. These figures are prominent among the Postclassic Tarascans, Aztecs, and Maya. There is no precedent for this figure in central Mexico nor even in the Maya area where they are more common. An old specimen from Quiriguá is the only one reported from the southern Maya lowlands; unfortunately it is undated (Richardson 1940). They are found as far south as Costa Rica (Chapter 9). *Chacmools* of the Early Postclassic are not related to any specific deity, but the later Aztecs associated them with Tlaloc.

Few doubt that Tula was the capital of the legendary Quetzalcóatl. His name and attributes are amply recorded for us in a variety of forms including feathered-serpent columns and Tlahuizcalpantecuhtli carved in relief panels. In addition, the central motif of the *coatepantli* represents the planet Venus, Quetzalcóatl's twin, Xólotl, as the evening star. All the processional figures in the benches advance toward a central figure, Quetzalcóatl himself. The symbol of the planet Venus is carved in one remaining slab belonging to Building C. The famous rock-carving above Tula which bears the date 1 Reed 8 Flint (A.D. 980) is, however, considered by Nicholson to be work of the Aztecs (see discussion in Keber 1979). Another carved petroglyph of Quetzalcóatl discovered in 1980, and as yet not dated, depicts a feathered serpent richly attired and bedecked with ornaments. Accompanying this scene is one of the corn goddess who holds in each hand an ear of corn from which water flows. What of Quetzalcóatl's victorious rival, the scurrilous Tezcatlipoca? Of him, not a trace.

Artisans at Tula may have been plentiful, but the quality of the workmanship is not extraordinary, despite Toltec claims of superiority. Coyotlatelco ware, popular among valley peoples from the time of the destruction of Teotihuacán, continued to be used by the Toltecs. This ware features a red-on-buff decoration, predating Mazapan which is decorated with parallel wavy red lines on buff (Plate 11–e) and is the ware most characteristic of Tula. There was surprisingly little Coyotlatelco found in the residential areas; much more is found in the urban center itself. Although Coyotlatelco and the succeeding Mazapan are

PLATE 11. Toltec-period pottery.

a. Hollow jaguar figure with Zapotec style claws and mouth, Monte Albán II (?). Possibly Toltec from Oaxaca. Height: 38 cm. (Courtesy of the Museo Nacional de Antropología, Mexico.)

b. Clay spindle whorls (*malacates*), incised decoration, Central Mexico. Diameter largest: 6 cm. (Courtesy of the Museum of the American Indian. Heye Foundation, N.Y. [22/8559].)

c. Vessel with ringstand and handle representing Tlaloc, painted blue. Height: 13 cm. (Courtesy of the Museo Nacional de Antropología, Mexico.)

d. Negative-painted *olla*, Tlacotepec, State of Mexico: Early Postclassic period. Height: 14 cm. (Courtesy of the Museum of the American Indian, Heye Foundation, N.Y. [8/8773].)

e. Mazapan red-on-buff bowl. Height: 13 cm. (Courtesy of the Museo Nacional de Antropología, Mexico.)

f. Large orange-ware tripod with stamped decoration. Height: 28 cm. (Courtesy of the Museo Nacional de Antropología, Mexico.)

g. Plumbate effigy vessel, Department of Suchitepéquez. Guatemala. Height: 13 cm. (Courtesy of the Museum of the American Indian. Heye Foundation, N.Y. [16/3463].)

both red-on-buff potteries, and both made in the form of tripod bowls, the latter did not evolve out of Coyotlatelco, and the two are very different. Even though both are found at Teotihuacán, they are usually well separated stratigraphically (Cobean 1974). The pottery of Cholula is not found at Tula and very little Coyotlatelco and Mazapan occur at Cholula, which was probably undergoing hard times.

A painted pottery, known as *blanco levantado* or Tula Watercolored, is present although by no means common. The same can be said of cloisonné. These wares are found across Guanajuato and in parts of the Bajío and are related to a west Mexican tradition. *Blanco levantado* may be derived from Colima's early shadow-striping (p. 117).

Plumbate was found in great quantity which is a clear indication of trade with Guatemala. Four polychrome vessels from Nicaragua or Costa Rica are other notable imports. Aztec II, III, and IV pottery shows continued occupation of the area long after the Toltecs had ceased to live there (Cobean 1974). In general terms the local ceramic sequence is Coyotlatelco (A.D. 800–1000), Mazapan (A.D. 1000–1200), Aztec II (after A.D. 1200). Aztec II pottery was being made at the time of the destruction of Tula and has nothing to do with the Aztecs themselves. There seems to be no overlap with Mazapan. Aztec III, of which there is very little, and Aztec IV pottery which is well represented, belong to the Late Postclassic period and are associated with the Aztec occupation of the region.

Metallurgy finally made its entrance into Mesoamerica around A.D. 900, very possibly in a two-pronged intrusion from Guatemala and through western Mexico or coastal Guerrero, where excellent craftsman worked with tin, gold, copper, and silver ores, exhibiting great sophistication in their control of alloying and cold-working of metals (Pendergast 1962a, 1962b; Brush 1969). These regions were all well situated to receive stimulation from Central or South America via the Pacific Ocean. Few articles of metal have been found at Tula itself, but gold and copper ornaments began to appear at other early Postclassic sites.

Clay smoking pipes were an innovation at this time (Figure 28-c) (Thompson 1970). The typical Tula pipe is of orange ware with a small conical bowl, short flaring platform, and long stem decorated by an undulating serpent. Tobacco was used for medicinal purposes, taken as snuff, and smoked by both North and South American Indians at the time of the Conquest, but clay smoking pipes dating prior to the Postclassic period are rarely found in Mesoamerica. Several pipes in private collections are attributed to Tlatilco, and others to the Olmec culture. Peter Furst (personal communication) reports that stone pipes decorated with animal and human effigies from northern Jalisco are dated at about A.D. 100–200. In addition to this possible early evidence representations of smoking cigars or tubular pipes are known from the Classic Maya, but it was not until the Postclassic period that pipe smoking attained an appreciable popularity. Even then the habit was not universal in Mesoamerica, as the distribution of clay smoking pipes follows an arc from the Pacific, through the Basin of Mexico, to the Gulf Coast (Porter 1948). Since pipe smoking was a well-established practice among the Indians of the southeastern United States prior to A.D. 900, it may be that this practice diffused southward from this region to Mesoamerica (Porter 1948; Thompson 1970). Switzer (1969) has dated California stone pipes at around 4000 B.C., which, if correct, makes the west another possible source.

Also common now are the *malacate* or spindle whorl, a perforated round disk of clay used as a weight in spinning thread, and the *molcajete* (Figure 30-e, f), a tripod pottery bowl with a heavily scored interior floor for grinding fruit and chile. Preclassic "grater bowls" presumably made for this same purpose are sometimes called *molcajetes* also but are easily distinguishable (compare Figure 6-e, p. 76 with Figure 30-e and f).

The physical appearance of Tula must have been very different from that of Teotihuacán. Except for some apartment-like structures near the

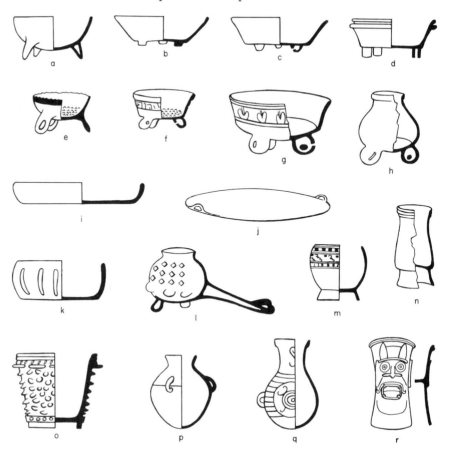

FIGURE 30. Ceramics of the Toltec period: (a), (b), (c) tripods, Tula; (d) coarse brown tripod, Tula; (e), (f) *molcajetes*, Tula; (g), (h) Z Fine Orange ware, Chichén Itzá; (i) brownware bowl, Tula; (j) *comal*, Tula; (k) gadrooned plain ware, Tula; (l) handled censer, Tula; (m) black-on-orange ring stand, Aztec I; (n) X Fine Orange, incised and painted in black, Chichén Itzá; (o) hobnail-decorated coarse ware, Tula; (p) red-on-brown jug, Tula; (q) black-on-orange jar, Aztec II; (r) Tlaloc incense burner, Tula. (From the following sources: a, k, q, Acosta 1945; b, c, d, e, f, i, j, l, o, p, r, Acosta 1956–1957; g, h, n, Brainerd 1941; m, Piña Chán 1960.)

Main Ceremonial Precinct and at Tula Chico, Tula was more spread out. Most people lived in small residential units that housed extended families, more like later Tenochtitlán than Teotihuacán. Houses faced inside and could only be reached via a narrow L-shaped entrance to the house group (Figure 31). There were marked status differences

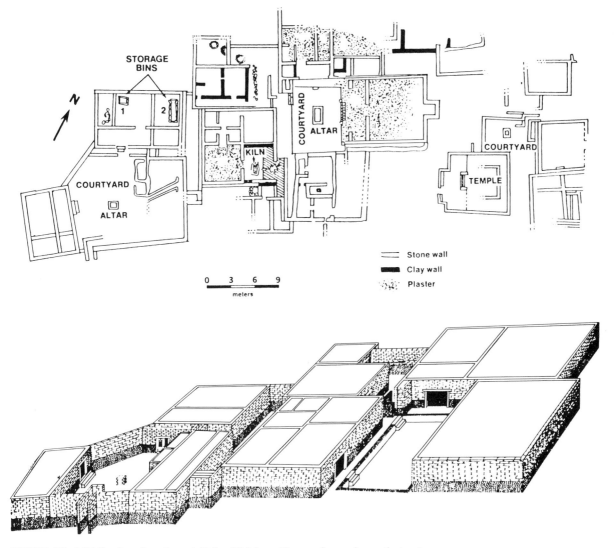

FIGURE 31. Middle-class housing at Tula, Hidalgo. Upper: floor plans of structures clustered around courtyards. Polychrome and Plumbate vessels from Central America were found in storage bin 2. Lower: hypothetical reconstruction showing most of houses in plan above. Lower walls were constructed of stone laid in mud mortar; the upper walls were made of adobe bricks. (From Diehl and Benfer 1975. Reprinted from *Archaeology Magazine*, vol. 28, no. 2, copyright © 1975 Archaeological Institute of America.)

within the same group as size and quality of construction varied (Healan 1977). Houses were made of stone and adobe walls and covered in some cases with lime plaster. Many were more substantial than anything we have previously seen. Floors were of packed earth, or plastered; roofs were covered over with beams. Patios usually had a shrine and one small Tlaloc temple served the ritual needs of the residential community. These people were not farmers but craftsmen and artisans. Not even gardens were cultivated within the city. Specializations are believed to have included obsidian, ceramic drain tubes, *ixtle* fiber thread, and perhaps mold-made figurines (Healan 1977). The farming community lived farther out.

The Toltecs are believed to have irrigated their fields, and ancient terraces are still visible. The most productive maize was grown close to the city. Good lime deposits were found to the south, and it is possible that the Zumpango region provided additional lime as it had done for Teotihuacán. Cotton, a very important crop, was grown in irrigated river bottomlands to the north in the area of Ixmiquilpan (Feldman 1974). Beyond lay the land of the Chichimecs, the very edge of Mesoamerica. A great quantity of spindle whorls is indicative of the importance of weaving. Cotton cloth and *ixtle* fibers would have been good export items.

Obsidian could have been obtained from various sources to the east. Like Teotihuacán, Tula probably owed part of its prosperity to the Pachuca obsidian mines. From Tula, these mines lay about 50 km to the east, and other obsidian deposits of Meztitlán, Tulancingo, and Teotihuacán Valley were within exploitation range. The Tepeapulco obsidian industry and redistributive network operated so efficiently by the Teotihuacanos is believed to have been continued under Toltec control (Charlton 1978). Two workshops have been located at Tula which are believed to have employed full-time specialists.

Population is estimated at 60,000 for the 12 km^2 of Tula's center, with another 60,000 rural dwellers (Sanders, Parsons, and Santley 1979). The combined population of 120,000 for greater Tula compares favorably with that of Teotihuacán, making it one of the truly great urban cities of ancient Mesoamerica. The size of the city came as a surprise to those who have seen the Main Ceremonial Precinct, for it seems very small and unimpressive to have been the capital of the great Toltec "empire." The metropolis was later greatly expanded (to 16 km^2) to reach the Hill of the Malinche. The current excavations being conducted by the Instituto Nacional de Antropología e Historia, under the direction of Rafael Abascal, are revealing residential areas with avenues, residences, *temescals,* complex drainage systems, and small civic–ceremonial plazas. It is not yet known how much of this belongs to the Toltec era itself. As we shall see, the Aztecs themselves claimed a Toltec heritage and rekindled interest in the ancient capital.

Toltec expansion may have had a military base coupled with intensive agriculture and the beginning of confiscation of food surpluses, later formalized as tribute payments. The capital of Tula swept many different peoples of diverse languages into the Toltec fold, and Mesoamerica's frontier was briefly pushed northward again as people were exposed to power, centralized authority, and "civilization." The Huastecs too took advantage of the good farming conditions for they either colonized or strongly influenced San Luis Potosí as seen at the site of Buenavista Huaxcama. To the west the farming belt extended along both the eastern and western flanks of the Sierra Madre Occidental to the southern border of Chihuahua.

Despite their fame as warriors, the actual extent of a Toltec "empire" or sphere of influence was not very large. Certainly it was not comparable to that of the Olmecs, Teotihuacán or the later Aztecs. But traded goods did find their way as far north as Casas Grandes, which was transformed from a small village to a major trading center around A.D. 1050 (see section to follow). It is not clear if the Toltecs themselves made contact with Casas Grandes people or if central Mexican ideas and artifacts were diffused via the west coast cultures. But these influences penetrated as far as Chaco Canyon in northern New Mexico, and the Southwest cultures have many motifs and ritual artifacts that are akin to Mesoamerica.

Trade to the south may have been somewhat hampered by other competitors. Tajín and Cempoala were potential rivals of Tula and could have blocked any attempt at eastern communication with the southern lowlands. At least this might explain the paucity of Toltec remains in these regions. We are not sure what was happening at Cholula, but there are no indications that the Toltecs were in the area to any great extent.

To the south, one might expect to find that the Toltecs occupied the Basin of Mexico and Morelos. Archaeology indicates that they controlled only the northern part of the Basin of Mexico. The southern portion was closely allied to the area of Puebla. In Morelos, Mazapan pottery is largely confined to the eastern part, the area of the Amatzinac Valley, always attractive for its cultivation of cotton. This may have been under Toltec domination in late times for it is Mazapan pottery, rather than Coyotlatelco that is found (Hirth 1977). In western Morelos, by A.D. 900 Xochicalco had ceased to be a center of any importance. There is little in this area to indicate contact with the Toltecs, although this void is not attributed to competition from a strong center.

The most likely communication to the far south could have taken place from Tula through the Toluca Valley to Ixtapan and Tonatico, State of Mexico, to northern Guerrero, and from there to the Middle Balsas and the Pacific Coast. This would also have been the most logical route for the entry into central Mexico of the Silho Fine Orange and

Toltec Expansion and "Empire"

Plumbate wares (Litvak-King 1978). Maya polychromes and other pottery attributed to Yucatán and Quintana Roo are among imports found in Tula. Four trade vessels of Papagayo or Nicoya Polychrome from Costa Rica or Nicaragua were found with Plumbate in a storage bin of a house at Tula where precious items had been put away (see Figure 31) (Diehl, Lomas, and Wynn 1974). No wealthy or elite tombs or graves have been found but data of this nature may be forthcoming from the major excavations in progress.

In the Toluca Valley, the great site of Teotenango is mentioned in Chimalpahin as another "Tollan." It was apparently settled by Teochichimecas and was also visited by some Nonoalco on their way to Tula, Hidalgo. The huge site of Teotenango, now restored by the State of Mexico under the direction of Román Piña Chan (1975), crowns the end of a steep hill overlooking the southern part of the Valley of Toluca (Photo 60). An enormous wall on the north makes that side impenetrable, while the other three sides fall off sharply to the valley below.

The area was first inhabited around A.D. 650 and saw a stream of visitors; it was occupied in turn by Teochichimecas, Otomís, and Matlatzincas. From A.D. 750–1162 it grew to an imposing civic–ceremonial center with spacious plazas and temple-platforms with *talud* and cornices somewhat like Teotihuacán. Altars, a Tula–Xochicalco-like ball court, streets, residences, markets, and Coyotlatelco pottery place it in the mainstream of central Mexican events in the Classic to Postclassic period. Architecturally it has features of Teotihuacán, Calpulalpan, and Tepeapulco (Piña Chan 1975).

Prior to A.D. 1162 the inhabitants of Teotenango were already conducting mass sacrifices. Ixtlilxóchitl (1952) says that after the fall of Tula legitimate heirs were sent out to live in the high mountains of Toluca to preserve the Toltec line. It is not clear if Teotenango was taken by the Toltecs or not, but the area was at least heavily influenced by them. Nopaltzin, the son of the famous Chichimec leader Xólotl (p. 419), is supposed to have married a Toluca girl, after which the residents of the valley are called Matlatzincas, another group professing legitimate Toltec ancestry. By A.D. 1255, the Matlatzincas are reported to have settled at Teotenango. They are famous for their adeptness with the sling used for war and hunting alike. Great rivalry existed between the Toluca towns, and no unification took place until the area fell to the Aztecs in A.D. 1476 (Piña Chan 1975) (see Map 12, p. 458).

What then, in summary, comprised the Toltec "empire?" The heartland of the Toltecs was the Tula to Tulancingo area, with strongest influence exerted in an east–west band from the Huasteca, across Guanajuato and Querétaro and the Bajío to Jalisco, and to a lesser extent north as far as the Chalchihuites culture. Mazapan pottery and figurines are scattered through Michoacán, Jalisco, and Nayarit; a curious crude *chacmool* occurs in the Lake Pátzcuaro area at a later date. But these do

PHOTO 60. General view of Teotenango, State of Mexico. (Courtesy of Román Piña Chan.)

not represent colonization or conquest. Data from the Basin of Mexico survey indicate Toltec control of the northern part of the valley only. Eastern Morelos would have been a valuable region to acquire with its cultivation and spinning of cotton fibers. This area may have been under Toltec domination in late times but few traces of Mazapan ware are found at Xochicalco, where considerable recent work has been done. Morelos probably cannot be included. The Toltec domain seems to have integrated no more than the northern Basin of Mexico, Hidalgo, perhaps the Tulancingo area, parts of the Bajío, and areas of the Lerma River drainage.

The Fall of Tula

The Tollan Studies report of 1974 (Diehl 1974) did not reveal much new information about the final days of Tula (A.D. 1168–1179?). It is usually felt that the final violent destruction of Tula was due to a dramatic climatic change that resulted in the desiccation of northern and central Mexico and the retraction of Mesoamerica's northern frontier. Unable to continue farming and faced by drought and starvation, Chichimec groups were forced to leave their lands. Their mass exodus in turn exerted pressure on more established settlements, of which the most vunerable was, of course, Tula. The accounts we read of ideological struggles, civil disorders, and political disaster are probably due in large part to very real ecological problems that faced the centers of power, resulting in inevitable conflicts, competitions, and reshuffling of population. Diehl wonders if, even more importantly, Tula might have lost control over its obsidian sources.

Acosta (1956) tells us that Tula itself was burned and sacked. The Burnt Palace provides evidence of adobe bricks fired hard and blackened by the conflagration. Fragments of burned wood, ash, and carbon abound. Much of the population left; the Nonoalcas going to Puebla and perhaps on as far as Veracruz. Others went to the Basin of Mexico, notably Culhuacán, and still others remained at Tula, joined we think by Otomís. The ceramic sequence shows continual occupation until Aztec times when the area was revered and resettled as a special place with ancestral ties.

The Toltecs have been well treated by later history. Tales of their glory and accomplishnents were preserved and embellished for generations. One great achievement attributed to them is empire building, yet little is known of the organization of their society or of the extent of their hegemony. We are left wondering if the same types of exchange networks still functioned or if the concept of exacting tribute was initiated during these years. The strong military flavor emphasizing a shift to a more secular outlook is seen elsewhere in Postclassic Mesoamerica, yet the most important public architecture at Tula is of the older temple–pyramid type resembling the ancient ceremonial center. In contrast there was a substantial interest in fine residential dwellings. There are many paradoxes and contradictions in our present knowledge of Tula and its famous inhabitants, many of which will surely be clarified by future excavations.

Tula and Chichén Itzá

Along with its association with Quetzalcóatl, Tula is probably best known for its relationship with Chichén Itzá in Yucatán. What can be said about Tula and the Maya area?

After A.D. 600, Yucatán was the scene of great movement of goods and people as the result of increased intercommunication and commerce led by the new peripheral centers operating under the efficiency of the Putún merchants. Yucatán found itself incorporated into a thriving exchange network. Not only were foreigners welcomed, but during the Middle and Late Classic periods many examples of Mexican influences had reached this Maya region. During the late phases there are many features suggestive of Teotihuacán, Monte Albán, Toltec, and Peripheral Coastal Lowlands' origins present in northern Yucatán. The ball-game cult was widely distributed.

One may logically ask: If the Main Ceremonial Precinct at Tula was not yet built, from where did the early Toltec influence in Yucatán derive? Perhaps it would be more correct to call it simply Mexican influence, although we now know Tula itself was settled at least as early as A.D. 650. Early contact with Yucatán is postulated through the Toltec–Nonoalca–Putún relationship (p. 346). Thus the Toltec influence seen in Yucatán must be very early Toltec accompanying other Mexican traits. Even Seibal exhibits Toltec-style stone carving around A.D. 830.

Between the fire of Teotihuacán and A.D. 900, the Maya or their Putún agents penetrated as far west as central highland Mexico. It was at this time that many of the Mexican features in Yucatán, having now acquired a Maya cast, could have been transmitted back to Mexico. These transformed features inspired the bas-reliefs and Maya-like ball court of Xochicalco and the Main Ceremonial Precinct of Tula, Hidalgo and its ball court. Kubler (1975) has long held the belief that Tula is a colonial outpost of Chichén Itzá rather than the reverse, a view also shared by Piña Chan. If, as now seems possible, much Toltec influence in Yucatán proves to be of Classic date, this idea would receive further support.

Maya influence at Tula is seen in the imported polychrome pottery, as well as in the bas-relief carvings on stelae. Stelae have no precedent in central Mexico, so the two at Tula are of particular interest. The frontal figures so closely parallel representations of rulers at Piedras Negras that these Tula figures may be rare examples of dynastic art. The warrior figure has a headdress bearing the face of Tlaloc and the year-sign emblem (Plate 12-b). Tlaloc with the year-sign is, as we have already noted, an emblem of Teotihuacán derivation found at many Maya sites in the seventh and eighth centuries. These stelae may date to Tula's early occupation and provide a dynastic link with Teotihuacán (Pasztory 1979).

Jaguars beneath round Mexican shields, which predate the prowling jaguars of Tula, are sculpted on the inner Temple of Kukulcán at Chichén Itzá. The Caracol at Chichén Itzá has both Puuc and Toltec features dating no later than the Late Classic period. In fact, there is nothing at Tula as yet that can account for the earliest Toltec art at Chichén Itzá, whereas there are abundant Maya precedents for such features as colonnaded doorways and Atlantean columns (Kubler 1975). It is also possible that the ball courts with Toltec-style reliefs underlying the Monjas and Red House construction at Chichén Itzá may

a

b

c

d

PLATE 12. Toltec stone carving.
a. A Toltec warrior. Height: 1.24 m. (Courtesy of the Museo Nacional de Antropología, Mexico.)
b. Early Toltec stela with frontal-view warrior wearing Tlaloc with year-sign headdress. Height: 122 cm. (Photographed by the author.)
c. Jaguar carved in stone relief. Height: approximately 122 cm. (Courtesy of the Museo Nacional de Antropología, Mexico.)
d. *Chacmool* figure, life size. Tula, Hidalgo, Height: 63.5 cm. (Courtesy of Museo Nacional de Antropología, Mexico.)

be of Classic rather than Postclassic date, which would further support a priority of Chichén Itzá (Cohodas 1978a, 1978b).

Diehl (1976) points out that in lacking an overall plan, the Main Ceremonial Precinct at Tula resembles more a Classic Maya ceremonial center than Teotihuacán, or even Tenochtitlán. However, unlike Maya centers, Tula's population settled in among the ceremonial structures with houses built right against each other.

There is much yet to learn from Tula and many questions are un-answered, but it is very tempting to speculate that what we see today in Tula's Main Ceremonial Precinct is a nostalgic attempt to recreate on foreign soil many features of the civic–religious center of Chichén Itzá. This is a highly complex problem, which is currently being reappraised.

THE NORTH AND THE WEST

By the Postclassic years northwest Mexico was drawn into the main current of events. This could have been triggered by the introduction of metallurgy from the west as well as transmitted knowledge of Teo-tihuacán's earlier mineral exploitation which might have stimulated the Toltecs to try their luck. What is the evidence?

The movement of Toltecs into the north probably followed the same routes of the older Teotihuacanos several hundred years earlier. All across Guanajuato, Querétaro, and the Bajío, people were producing pottery decorated with *blanco levantado*, cloisonné, and even Mazapan style. The Carabino phase at Morales, Guanajuato looks very Toltec with Plumbate, Fine Orange, and all of the Mazapan characteristics. *Blanco levantado* is the most common domestic ware in this region and is also widespread in the western states of Colima, Jalisco, and Sinaloa. In Guanajuato it has a continuous presence since the Late Preclassic period (Braniff 1972).

The huge site of La Quemada in the southern part of the state of Zacatecas has been very difficult to place chronologically as little is known of its culture history. It is usually dated around A.D. 900–1250 but could have earlier beginnings, for many features of its construction have Classic-period prototypes. Strategically located across a natural north–south route, it is an excellent example of a fortified citadel which may have been built to hold back the encroaching Chichimecs as well as to control the rich agricultural region of the Malpaso Valley (Weigand 1975). This is probably the most northern farming group in central Mexico. A fire marks the end of its occupation, but we do not know when this occurred or if it was done by later peoples. Perhaps a clue is provided by the Huichol Indians of Jalisco.

In ancient Huichol mythology, a site, whose description matches that of La Quemada, is frequently mentioned as lying on the route of the

Huicholes from their homeland to San Luis Potosí, where they went in search of peyote. This cactus, valued for its hallucinogenic powers, was marketed in a brisk trade network which also moved salt, feathers, and shells. When a large settlement (La Quemada ?) interfered, it was savagely destroyed and burned, not by the Chichimecs, who are usually blamed, but by Mesoamericans living to the west (Weigand 1975).

Situated at an altitude of 1950 m, the ruins of La Quemada cover most of a large hill. A great stone wall encircles the hilltop, while lower on the hillside are stone masonry pyramids, colonnaded courts, great stairways, and a subterranean passage, perhaps roofed by a corbelled arch. A large I-shaped ball court adjoins the Votive Pyramid (Photo 61). The large colonnades and much of the construction are built from small flat slabs of stone and adobe brick. Groups of structures are connected by raised causeways such as those found in Xochicalco and Yucatán.

PHOTO 61. Votive Pyramid at La Quemada, Zacatecas. (Courtesy of the Instituto Nacional de Antropología e Historia, Mexico.)

The Toltecs would have passed by La Quemada as they pushed into the northwest following along the eastern flanks of the Sierra Madre Occidental or crossing the mountains and going up the coast.

The Chalchihuites culture is about the last truly Mesoamerican culture encountered going north (see Maps 1, p. 11, and 5, p. 113). At Alta Vista where the Teotihuacanos had once mined exotic minerals, the Río Tunal phase (A.D. 950–1150) now reflects the impact of the Toltecs. This time the Mesoamerican imports seem to have come over the mountains from Guasave, Sinaloa in the form of polychrome pottery, spindle whorls, elbow pipes, needles, awls, rings, and bells of copper.

In Sinaloa two periods precede that of Guasave. Chametla (Kelly 1938) is believed to be the oldest manifestation or phase of the Aztatlán complex; Culiacán overlaps in part and follows chronologically with a greater range of traits; and Guasave represents the most recent and richest phase of all with iron-pyrite beads, onyx and alabaster vases, paint cloisonné, and turquoise mosaics, pendants, and beads (Kelley and Winters 1960).

Paint cloisonné is a technique of decoration applied to gourds and is associated with 34 graves at Guasave. This process of decoration consists of applying a layer of paint to the surface and cutting away the paint of the design area, then filling in the hollow with another color. The result is a perfectly smooth surface. The same technique is used by modern Tarascans of Uruapan and the Lake Pátzcuaro region of Michoacán to decorate wood and gourds. It is possible that this modern lacquer work represents the survival of an ancient pre-Columbian craft. The technique has a wide distribution in the New World, and examples are known from Snaketown, Arizona and all through western Mexico, including the Chalchihuites cultures and even the Valley of Mexico. It is interesting that far to the south, among the Inca culture of Peru, a similar paint-cloisonné decoration was applied to wooden cups (Ekholm 1942).

In a variation of this technique, two layers of paint are applied and part of the top of one is cut away to expose the color beneath. In this case the design feels raised to the touch. Pre-Columbian stone *metates* and *manos* and even conch shells decorated in this way have been found near Queréndaro, Michoacán. The technique, still applied today to wood and gourds, is a popular craft of Olinalá, Guerrero.

Paint cloisonné is an ingredient of the Aztatlán complex, which has features of the Mixteca–Puebla culture (p. 462). Whereas once thought to represent an actual migration out of central Mexico, Meighan (1974) now believes this was a widespread cultural Postclassic complex that was manifested all along the west coast, spreading through Jalisco, Nayarit, and Sinaloa around A.D. 1000–1350. It did not arrive suddenly but emerged out of the Classic tradition. The elaborate pottery was in all likelihood carried from the coast over the mountains to settlements farther north.

In Chihuahua, the remains become simpler, and as one proceeds north, an increasing influence of the Hohokam and Mogollon cultures of Arizona is found. For example, the Loma San Gabriel culture, with a pattern of hilltop ceremonial centers with small valley farms, lacks the stone masonry, paint cloisonné, copper objects, and *malacates* of its southern neighbors. It is probably transitional to the Río Conchas–Bravo Valley cultures, which culturally belong to the southwestern United States. There is no gap, no great hiatus, between the two culture areas throughout their continuous sedentary occupation.

Casas Grandes (Map 1, front endpapers) grew up as an extension of the southwestern culture. After A.D. 1000 as the result of the visit of some precocious merchants from the Pacific Coast, Casas Grandes rebuilt itself (Paquimé phase) with some Mesoamerican features (Di Peso 1974). It is easy to imagine that trading expeditions from Sinaloa and other areas further south introduced knowledge of hydraulic farming, copper objects, and architectural features which appear in the Medio period, of which the Paquimé phase represents the peak (A.D. 1205–1261).

From rather simple single-storied house clusters, now massive housing of multistoried, high-rise apartment complexes were built, covering as much as 36 ha. About this giant construction were plazas, special-function buildings, ball courts, markets, and effigy mounds. There were special quarters for copper and shell workers, jewelers, slaves, skin-workers, and dealers in peyote. From here, trading expeditions went north to New Mexico and Arizona.

By A.D. 1261 the economy had perhaps over-extended itself and a general stagnation was reported all across the north, affecting even the Chichimecs. A severe drought is believed to have triggered a cultural decline, and it is hard to imagine a more catastrophic event in an already arid region. During the Diablo phase at Casas Grandes (A.D. 1261–1340), not only did construction cease but also maintenance. The dead were miserably buried in the now dry water systems and drains of the city.

Thus, the far north was stimulated directly or indirectly by the Toltecs, who sent their merchants into the northwest presumably extending commercial operations and carrying a new religious cult. The northern regions reciprocated by providing salt, alum, peyote, incense, and raw copper. It was a contact of limited duration, and after this period the relationship was never resumed. The northwestern provinces did not prosper under the subsequent domination of the Aztecs to the south. As we shall see, Aztec interests lay largely in the richer areas of the east and south, and by A.D. 1400 the Chalchihuites culture and those of its neighbors had largely withered away.

The northeastern periphery of Mesoamerica, the region of northern Veracruz and eastern San Luis Potosí known as the Huasteca, reached its real peak of cultural attainment not in the Classic period as might be expected but in Postclassic times. The close bond between the Huasteca and southern Veracruz, Tabasco and the lowland Maya region that existed during the earlier Preclassic horizon had been abruptly severed, perhaps by the intrusion of Náhuat-speaking peoples into central Veracruz during the Classic period. It will be remembered that the Tajín and Remojadas cultures were strongly influenced by Teotihuacán. Although the Huasteca, lying immediately to the north of this area, also reflects these events (as seen in "portrait"-type figurines and negative or resist painting), the most significant Huastec development took place after A.D. 900. This could be the result, possibly indirect, of Toltec movements and shifting of peoples, new religious beliefs, and the ideas of weaponry and militarism that swept across all of northern Mesoamerica. This is Las Flores phase in the Huasteca sequence (Ekholm 1944).

We do not know the nature of Huastec exposure to Toltec culture, but it does not seem to have been through outright conquest. Pánuco pottery is similar to Fine Orange wares from the Isla de Sacrificios, Veracruz and other details are shared with El Tajín and Cerro Montoso in Veracruz, Cholula and early Aztec pottery. True Plumbate, however, has not been reported from the Huasteca. For the first time, objects of copper, clay smoking pipes, stamps, *malacates*, engraved shells, and wheeled figures are found. With the exception of the wheeled objects, most of the other artifacts have parallels at Tula as well as in the far western cultures of coastal Sinaloa. Lines of communication seem to have been well established across northern Mesoamerica at this time, very possibly a reflection of Toltec influence.

In addition to the relationships that link the Huasteca with major developments in highland Mexico in this early Postclassic period, local innovations gave unique distinction to this northeast periphery. The use of asphalt as paint or glue is found here as well as in the Classic Veracruz cultures such as Remojadas. Thin layers of asphalt were also used to cover floors and even to surface mounds from the Late Classic period onward. The application of asphalt, regardless of how desirable it might have been, depended entirely on natural seepages, so of necessity the technique was geographically limited. Stone carving is one medium that reflects a totally new artistic expression (Photo 62), the style of which is flat and slab-like. Figures often wear a conical-shaped headdress backed by a fan-like shield, and a cavity in the chest may have held an inlay of some kind.

Perhaps the Huasteca is most famous for its round structures, which are found here in greater numbers than in any other region of Mesoamerica and are the prevalent form of architecture. At the sites of Las Flores, Pavón, and Tancol, round structures predominate. Nu-

THE HUASTECA

PHOTO 62. Priest performing autosacrifice by running a stick of thorns through his tongue. Huastec Culture. Huilocintla, Veracruz. Height: 124 cm. (Courtesy of the Museo Nacional de Antropología, Mexico.)

merous others have been reported from the mountains as well as the coast and from as far west as Buenavista Huaxcama in San Luis Potosí. Round structures, wherever found in Mesoamerica, are generally associated with Quetzalcóatl in his aspect as the wind god, Ehécatl. Quetzalcóatl is also closely linked to the east as a cardinal point. The great concentration of round structures suggests that this east coast region was a likely center of origin (Ekholm 1944). One asphalt-surfaced conical structure at the Pavón site is estimated to date from the Late Classic period; others may prove to be of even earlier origin.

Round structures are known from various sites in central and southern Mesoamerica but are never common and generally date from the Toltec or Aztec periods. Notable exceptions are the structure shaped like a fluted cone at La Venta, the conical structure at Cuicuilco, and Structure 79 at Seibal. It may be that not all round structures were associated with Quetzalcóatl, and thus there need not necessarily be a connection between these pyramids and later Huasteca developments.

Huasteca pottery and figurines followed local styles of development. Basically the clay was fired very well, and has a characteristic cream or pinkish color. In late Postclassic times a very distinctive black-on-white decoration became extremely popular (see Figure 34-m, p. 434). Styles incorporating teapot forms, flat ribbon-like handles, and spouts were common. This new pottery has no counterpart elsewhere and does not have a long tradition in the Huasteca region itself. It appears fully developed. Sudden changes in the archaeology of this area are frequent, and the region is still very inadequately known. It remains a challenging peripheral area that retained a local flavor throughout its long history of occupation. By Conquest times, a few towns in the south had succumbed to the Aztec yoke, but on the whole the Huasteca was its own master.

The geographical position of the Huasteca makes it the best potential link between Mesoamerica and the southeastern cultures of the United States. But in sharp contrast to the northwestern frontier of Mesoamerica, which shows a blending into the southwestern United States, the northeastern seaboard seems to have had but sporadic contact with its northern neighbors. This point will be taken up again in Chapter 9, which examines Mesoamerica's relationships with cultures beyond her borders.

Cholula is a site we would all like to know more about, feeling that somehow the key to many questions lie in this region just east of the volcanoes in the Valley of Puebla. A modern map of Mexico shows highways radiating from the Valley of Puebla in four directions. The valley has always been strategically situated to attract travelers, merchants, and pilgrims from the earliest pre-Conquest days to the present. The control of the Puebla–Tlaxcala region may have been necessary to maintain major stability in the central highlands for any length of time. The foundations of Cholula had been laid hundreds of years earlier by Preclassic people. After reestablishing Cholula in the Early Postclassic,

CHOLULA AND THE BASIN OF MEXICO

following its abandonment to Cerro Zapotecas, the old pyramid was gradually enlarged four times until it eventually covered 16 ha and reached a height of 55 m, the largest single structure ever erected in the New World. Today it is easily mistaken for a hill, as the pyramid is covered with soil and grass, and is crowned by a Catholic Church, an effort by the Spaniards to substitute their religion for the old (Photo 63).

Excavations have revealed a veritable maze of superimposed platforms, walls, patios, open and covered stone drains. Chronology is based largely on ceramic correlations with other areas (Noguera 1954, 1965). The Early Postclassic phases known as Cholulteca I and II are characterized by *molcajetes,* negative painting, handled censers, griddles with high walls, and Coyotlatelco ware, introduced in the last days of Teotihuacán. Mazapan, with parallel wavy red lines on buff is found in small quantities. Plumbate and Culhuacán wares, the latter from the Basin of Mexico, are more common. Fine Orange vessels from the Isla de Sacrificios are proof of continuing ties with the eastern lowlands. All of these ceramics are the new wares and styles typical of the Early Postclassic.

Although Cholula lay outside the survey limits of the Basin of Mexico project of Sanders, Parsons, and Santley, it is only 40 km east of the Chalco region, and they found it to be closely allied to the history of the southern Basin. After the fall of Teotihuacán, some of its inhabitants may have drifted over to the Puebla Valley as we know the population in the Basin of Mexico was greatly reduced. It seems likely that Cholula controlled, or at least was in close contact with, the southern part of the Basin, while Tula dominated the north.

How strong was Cholula? Could Tula and Cholula have been political and economic rivals? If so, it would explain the lack of contact between the two centers. A more likely explanation is that Cholula was still impoverished and her circumstances would not have permitted much participation in interregional trade. Certainly the two sites have little in common.

Cholula seems to have retained her autonomy during the great period at Tula. It is sometimes reported that the Olmeca–Xicalanca ruled Cholula as tyrants in this period, but others believe they had been driven out around A.D. 850. (See discussions in Davies 1977; García Cook and Merino 1979; Nicholson 1978.) Davies thinks they left much more slowly. Indeed, some sources say there were Olmeca–Xicalanca in the region when the later Tlaxcalans moved in during the Late Postclassic period. Archaeologically Cholula looks relatively weak and was only beginning to revitalize the old ceremonial center. It is hard to see how the Toltecs would have been blocked in any expansion or commercial enterprise by an impoverished Cholula. Her major growth took place in the Late Postclassic. It was about the time Tula collapsed that Cholula entered her greatest period of prosperity and influence.

PHOTO 63. Excavations on the south side of the large pyramid at Cholula on which the church is built. (Photographed by the author.)

An elaborate art style known as Mixteca–Puebla (Nicholson 1961a) is believed to have grown up in the area of Cholula in early Postclassic years, reaching its greatest florescence thereafter. The style gradually dominated central Mexico and it can best be understood as a synthesis of the styles of Teotihuacán, Veracruz, and Xochicalco. Excellent examples are found in *códices* such as the Borgia, murals of Tizatlán, and in the polychromed ceramics. The influence of this distinctive pottery reached the far western cultures of Mexico; it forms part of the Aztatlán complex of Jalisco, Nayarit, and Sinaloa and was traded north to Casas Grandes, Chihuahua in its Medio period (p. 384).

In Late Postclassic years, Cholula became not only a major focus for merchants but also for pilgrims, as Tollan Cholollan attracted people from every direction to her tremendous temple–pyramid dedicated to Quetzalcóatl. The beautiful polychrome pottery and unexcelled craftsmanship of minor arts helped spread the fame attributed to the "Toltecs," perhaps referring not to Tula Toltecs, but to these latter-day Toltecs of Cholula.

OAXACA

The southern extension of Toltec influence is poorly known as there are few traces of their culture between central highland Mexico and northern Yucatán. But according to the *códices*, there was a close relationship between the Toltecs and Mixtecs. In the Codex Nuttall, the pictorial history of a Mixtec leader, Eight Deer, shows him a typical Toltec dress, while those surrounding him are clearly Mixtecs. Eight Deer is believed to have ruled over Tilantongo, a separate Mixtec domain, between A.D. 1030 and 1063 (Spores 1967; for an alternative view of the Toltec–Mixtec relationships see Chadwick 1971). To judge from one codex, Eight Deer actually made a trip to Tula for the investiture of office, where he was given his turquoise nose plug as a symbol of his rank. This suggests that Tula exercised some influence over this southern region. As already pointed out, the chronology of these *códices* is still uncertain (p. 159). To judge from the archaeological record, Tula made very little impact on the Oaxaca area.

Significantly absent from the Valley of Oaxaca are a whole range of objects we have come to associate with the Early Postclassic horizon. Oaxaca produced no *chacmools*, or Atlantean figures, and no stone sculpture of Toltec influence. Also lacking or extremely few in number are clay smoking pipes, *malacates*, circular pyramids, *molcajetes*, pottery flutes, whistles, and bone rasps. The pottery jaguar with claws and a bell around its neck is considered to be one of the few objects of Toltec influence (Paddock 1978) and its Monte Alban II label is probably incorrect (Plate 11-a, p. 370). Two Plumbate vessels have been found and quantities of Balancan Fine Orange ware were copied locally at Lambityeco (Sharp 1978), but Oaxaca has yielded no Mazapan or Aztec I ceramics. The impact of the Toltecs and later Aztecs on Oaxaca was weak (Paddock 1966a).

The well-known site of Mitla in the eastern part of the Oaxaca Valley is probably Zapotec with Mixtec influence, a mingling of traits also repeated at Yagul (Bernal 1965). Mitla consists of five groups of buildings, still not completely excavated. A typical group is made up of rectangular patios bordered by apartments of long, narrow rooms. The core of the construction was mud and stone, which was covered with plaster or well-cut trachyte. The facades and door frames are decorated with mosaics of small stones combined to form a wide variety of geometric patterns such as the stepped fret (Photo 64). Beams from wall to wall supported the roofs, which were covered with small slabs, then gravel, and finally plastered over. Roofs were made with a gentle slope to direct the rain water toward the patio.

At nearby Yagul, in a more attractive setting on the slopes of the hill northeast of Tlacolula, the buildings are constructed in exactly the same way, but the workmanship is not as fine. Tombs, often elaborate cruciform structures with antechambers, are similarly built. Enormous rectangular slabs on the roofs were heaved into final position by ropes passed through small holes. These tombs are probably the result of mingled Mixtec and Zapotec influences in the valley.

The Yagul ball court, partially decorated with stone mosaics, is larger than the ball court at Monte Albán and, unlike the latter, has no niches, central stone markers, or rings. Even in Mixtec *códices*, ball courts are illustrated without rings. The *códices* also show a variety of other structures such as temples, palaces, shrines, and even sweat baths. The structures at Yagul and Mitla are overwhelmingly civic rather than religious in nature, conforming to the general trend toward secularization seen elsewhere in Postclassic times.

A secular design, the *greca* motif (Photo 64) is especially prominent at Mitla. This was first painted on walls or used to decorate pottery, but by Late Classic and Early Postclassic periods, it was made in stone mosaics that decorated facades of buildings, residences, and tombs. It always seems to be associated with the elite, decorating their cloaks in the *códices*, and their tombs. A secular design, its presence indicates a close relationship between the areas of Oaxaca, Veracruz (Tajín), and Yucatán (Puuc sites) (Sharp 1978).

There is little evidence of the Toltecs until we reach Yucatán. The ninth century Toltec influence at Seibal would reflect earlier contact. However the similarities between Chichén Itzá and Tula have been compared to earlier relationships between Teotihuacán and Kaminaljuyú (Parsons and Price 1971). Despite the unsettled chronology in the case of Chichén Itzá and Tula, the relationship was probably initiated through trade and may have been a far more diffused or indirect contact than in the case of Teotihuacán and Kaminaljuyú.

PHOTO 64. Interior of palace structure at Mitla, Oaxaca. Construction technique is mosaic veneer masonry. Note variety of *greca* motifs. (Photographed by the author.)

CHICHÉN ITZÁ   About half the size of Teotihuacán (6.5 by 3.2 km²), Chichén Itzá is located in the center of the flat northern plains, undoubtedly attracting early settlers by the presence of two dozen *cenotes*. Most of these have now dried up, but the two most important still have water. The Sacred Cenote is reached by a long causeway that links it to the heart of the northern ruins. Most imposing of all *cenotes*, with very steep sides, it was used primarily for receiving ritual offerings. Water for practical purposes was more easily available from the Xtoloc Cenote in the center of Chichén Itzá where one could descend to the water level by two masonry staircases. In addition, *chultuns* which caught rain water are found throughout the area.

Between the two large *cenotes* is the North Terrace Group of structures located on an enormous artificial platform which supports the Great Ball Court, the Castillo or Temple of Kukulcán, the Temple of the Warriors, and Court of a Thousand Columns (Photo 65). Ruz Lhuillier

PHOTO 65. Aerial view of Chichén Itzá showing the Temple of the Warriors (in foreground) and Kukulcán. (Courtesy of Compañia Mexicana de Aerofoto, S. A.)

(1951) tells us that these structures were enclosed by a high wall forming an irregular polygon with entrances at the four cardinal directions, the sides of which were faced with dressed stone. The wall is now entirely destroyed, so it is not known if it had a parapet, nor can its dimensions be determined.

There was no feeling of limitation or crowding of buildings (Photo 66). On the contrary, buildings were widely dispersed along a consistent orientation 17° east of north, the common arrangement in central Mexico. Earlier Maya ceremonial structures had been built with thick walls, narrow doorways, and dark, mysterious interiors symbolizing the heart of the earth from which the priests would dramatically emerge. A new concept in religion replaced the earth gods with celestial worship of the sun, moon, and stars; consequently buildings and courts are open to the heavens for more effective mass communication between the gods and men. Human sacrifice, a deeply rooted Mesoamerican trait, was a matter of public record and therefore expedited under conditions of maximum spectator participation, pomp, and ceremony.

The I-shaped Great Ball Court has been the subject of study and controversy for many years, as it embraces Puuc, Petén, Usumacinta, and central Mexican architectural styles and motifs. Located on the northern edge of the platform, one of seven courts known to exist at Chichén Itzá, it has a playing alley 146 m long and 37 m wide—the

PHOTO 66. View of Toltec Chichén Itzá with the ball court and Temple of the Tigers in the foreground, the Temple of Kukulcán at right, and the Temple of the Warriors at rear. (Courtesy of the Instituto Nacional de Antropología e Historia, Mexico.)

PHOTO 67. View looking down the central playing alley of the Great Ball Court of Chichén Itzá. Note the position of stone rings high on the lateral walls. (Courtesy of the Instituto Nacional de Antropología e Historia, Mexico.)

giant of all Mesoamerican courts (Photo 67). The most dramatic features are the great vertical walls rising 8 m in height with stone rings still set in place. Six carved reliefs show the decapitation of a ball-player. A small temple is located at either end, but the most imposing structure is the Upper Temple of the Jaguars above the east wall. Feathered-serpent columns support the lintels of its doorways, above which on the exterior facade is a procession of jaguars carved in relief, paralleled by the prowling jaguars of Pyramid B at Tula. Frescoes decorating the inner walls portray the gory details of a battle scene that is often considered to represent a Toltec invasion of Yucatán. Thompson (1970) has presented another interpretation. He points out that the attackers' dress shows some elements of Toltec attire but that their round shields and feathers denote another group, which he identifies as Putún Itzá. The people they are attacking are not Yucatec Maya, and therefore this scene did not take place in Chichén Itzá. Rather several different ethnic groups are shown, making it likely that this commemorative mural records an attack by the Putún Itzá on groups in Tabasco.

Directly behind this temple at ground level, outside the court proper, is the Lower Temple of the Jaguars with low-carved and painted designs over the whole exterior surface. The entrance is decorated with Atlantean figures. This temple is partially covered over by the pyramidal base for the later Upper Temple of the Jaguars. Often missed by the casual visitor are the carved piers and the marvelous interior reliefs of the North Temple at the end of the ball court, depicting narrative scenes with naturalistic figures, plants, and animals along with some processions in progress.

Near the ball court is a macabre *tzompantli,* or skull rack, completely decorated with carved human skulls, a constant reminder of man's obligation to supply the deities with human hearts and blood.

The Temple of Kukulcán, also called the Castillo, is only a short walk south from the ball court and forms the center of Toltec Chichén. Nearly square, with steep staircases leading up on all four sides, the temple commands one of the best views of the entire site. Maya corbelled vaulting is found here along with reliefs of Toltec warriors, and the base is decorated in a series of alternating recessed and projecting panels recalling Monte Albán (Kubler 1975). This is the structure that encases an earlier Classic one with a temple–pyramid preserving prowling jaguars in bas-relief and the famous jaguar throne (p. 343). The Temple of Kukulcán is impressive for its severe but simple style. Greatly contributing to its grandeur is the fact that it rises in lonely splendor from an immense clearing. Thousands could have gathered on every side to share in the spectacle of the music, fires, and processions and to hear the voices of the gods. From the height of the Temple of Kukulcán one can look across at the Temple of the Warriors and observe that the plan is basically the same as the Temple of Quetzalcóatl (Building B) at Tula. Here, however, it is much larger and more skillfully executed. Maximum spaciousness, light, and air were admitted through great colonnaded courts, which perhaps served as meeting places or council halls as suggested by the dais or thrones. The Group of the Thousand Columns, a huge open plaza of several acres, is completely surrounded by colonnades. The great plaza may well have served as a marketplace, for certainly a central area was needed for exchange of goods.

One enters the Temple of the Warriors by passing through one of these great colonnaded courts of square columns, which are carved on all sides with typical Toltec warriors (see Figure 28-e, p. 366). The Temple of the Warriors is constructed with four stages resembling the architecture of Teotihuacán more than anything else. Climbing the wide staircase, one is greeted by a rather refined *chacmool* at the entrance to the temple, again supported by feathered-serpent columns at the doorway. At the back of the temple is a shrine or altar supported by small Atlantean figures such as are found at Tula (see Figure 28-a). The walls were frescoed with battle scenes between the Putún and groups of Maya; the frescoes are in such a deteriorated state that they are best viewed in the literature. The Temple of the Warriors contains an earlier structure known as the Temple of the Chacmool. Paintings on the benches of this structure clearly depict two protagonists: Toltecs seated on jaguar thrones, and Maya nobles holding scepters and seated on jaguar skins thrown over stools. The latter may not be Yucatec Maya, judging by the dress, ornamentation, and paraphernalia. Very confusing is the profile of the supporting pyramid of this inner structure, virtually identical to the outer one of the Castillo in which Kubler sees resemblances to both Monte Albán and the Petén.

Minor structures such as two dance platforms are completely Mexican in flavor. Their sloping *talud* and vertical *tablero* are not unlike the profile of Xochicalco and are covered with Toltec themes of eagles and jaguars eating human hearts. Although these low platforms are not to be compared with the great ceremonial structures, they were undoubtedly an important integrative factor in religious life. Here, Bishop Landa tells us, dances and public spectacles were held, affording vicarious participation by the populace.

To the south of these buildings is the section of Puuc-style structures linked by the cylindrical Caracol in between. These have been dealt with in Chapter 6. The striking resemblances and parallels between Chichén Itzá and Tula are seen mostly in relief sculpture, carved square piers, and colonnaded halls. Distribution of buildings and the structures themselves are very different. Many architectural features may be of Mexican style (Teotihuacán, Tajín, Monte Albán, Xochicalco) but not specifically Toltec. The narrative scenes, both painted and carved in stone, have no parallel at Tula, but processions of human figures and jaguars are shared by both.

Once again we look to two main sources for the historical interpretation of these remains: (1) the early chronicles and sixteenth-century information, and (2) the archaeological record. These in turn permit several possible explanations.

CHICHÉN ITZÁ, TULA, AND CHRONOLOGY

What is commonly and rather ambiguously referred to as the Mexican period in Yucatán are the years from A.D. 987 to A.D. 1250, when Chichén Itzá exhibited strong Toltec influence. It is not easy to trace movements of peoples and correlate conflicting historical sources with archaeology and the Maya calendar. By this time the calendar recorded only Short Count dates, and abbreviated date-recording system that replaced the earlier Long Count (see p. 172). Bishop Landa (Tozzer 1941), our most important Spanish source, for example, is unclear as to whether the Itzás arrived with Kukulcán and conquered Chichén Itzá, or came prior to, or even following this event. Itzá history is reconstructed from a few historical narratives mentioned by sixteenth-century Spaniards and from historical references in the katun prophecies. These are largely contained in the Books of Chilam Balam, written during Colonial times in the Maya language using Spanish script. The complicated blending of Toltec and Yucatec traditions has been interpreted by Thompson in 1970, aided by the scholarly writings of Ralph Roys (Roys 1966; Scholes and Roys 1948). This traditional version is pieced together as follows.

After Quetzalcóatl was humiliated and outwitted by Tezcatlipoca in Tula, he was forced to abandon the capital. With his followers, he left Tula, spent some time at Cholula (?), and then either immolated himself to become the morning star or the planet Venus, or sailed off to the "east." In precisely the same year, A.D. 987, Kukulcán (feathered-serpent in Maya) arrived in Yucatán leading a second group of Toltecs. Their exact route is not clear. Little evidence of their culture has been found in the Putún heartland, and it is likely that their passage through this area was relatively swift as they fled from their enemies. Thompson points out that their passage could have been greatly facilitated by the Putún, already well disposed toward Mexicans, who could have conducted them to Chichén Itzá, another area of their domain, along already well-established routes. Thus a second group of Putún Itzá is postulated to have accompanied Kukulcán and his Toltecs to Chichén Itzá in A.D. 987, katun 8 Ahau.

These Toltecs, after firmly establishing their seat of power at Chichén Itzá, soon managed to dominate Yucatán, a simple task in view of the backing and sponsorship of the Putún Itzá. Thus a kind of Toltec empire developed in Yucatán that spread the cult of Kukulcán and continued to promote commercial interests from Tabasco to Honduras.

It is further postulated that a new section of Toltec structures was added to Chichén Itzá: the Temple of Kukulcán, the Mercado, the Great Ball Court with its temples, the Temple of the Warriors, and minor structures. This final period would have lasted about 200 years during which Chichén Itzá was transformed into what we see today.

Although this hangs together very well in some respects, there are some worrisome inconsistencies. For the origin of Mexican elements, whether in murals, architecture, or sculpture, one usually points a finger at the Toltecs, whose influence is traditionally placed from the eleventh to the thirteenth centuries. For a number of years there have been some cracks in the scheme that are now growing wider, or more confusing. In her study of Maya sculpture, Proskouriakoff (1950) felt that the Itzá must have been in Chichén Itzá at least 100 years prior to A.D. 987. Lothrop (1952) reached the conclusion that the Toltec and Maya were contemporaries for a long period of time, based on his studies of the finds from the Sacred Cenote. Rands (1954), after studying floral motifs, said that the Toltec of Chichén Itzá and Late Classic Maya were contemporaries. Piña Chan (1964) expressed discontent with the dating of the Great Ball Court at Chichén Itzá since he felt their reliefs were contemporaneous with the Puuc murals of Mul-Chic. Andrews V sees an overlap of Yucatán Fluorescent and Toltec in architectural techniques. Years ago, Pollock felt that the Toltecs of Chichén were contemporaneous with the Late Classic of the Petén. A new voice has now been added, that of Cohodas (1978a, 1978b), who attempts to justify an even earlier Classic dating for the Great Ball Court as well as the other Toltec structures at Chichén Itzá. At the same time he challenges the reliability of using post-Conquest sources for reconstructing history 800–900 years prior to the Conquest.

By this time the Maya were using the Short Count, so a date could be placed within a 260-day period, but nothing indicates which 260-day period corresponds to the katun 4 Ahau supposed to mark the Itzá arrival. The year A.D. 987 has been widely accepted, but should be regarded as speculative (Cohodas 1978b; Nicholson 1978). The inaccuracies of the early chronicles have already been mentioned. The fact that the theme of the legend of Quetzalcóatl—sin and punishment—is widespread among traditions of the Maya and the Mixtecs leads Cohodas to consider this a myth rather than historical record. Relying on the archaeological record and ^{14}C dates available, he offers the following version as an alternative interpretation (Cohodas 1978a, 1978b).

Returning for a moment to the Classic period, he believes that several architectural styles in northern Yucatan were contemporaneous during the seventh century:

1. Puuc style with features of veneer masonry, pyramids, roof combs, flying facades, decoration in stucco and stone, masks, and temple and palace structures, which appeared by A.D. 600, but did not spread out of the core Puuc region until A.D. 700.

2. Regional styles with block masonry, no roof combs or flying facades, and decoration limited to stucco carving; associated with elaborate causeways. Examples: Oxkintok and Cobá.

3. Chichén Maya: multiroom palace-type structures, block masonry, and little architectural decoration, with distribution limited to Chichén Itzá.

4. Chichén Toltec: one- or two-room buildings and veneer masonry, typically having multiple columns and colonnades, feathered serpents on balustrades or entrance columns, with distribution limited to Chichén Itzá.

Accordingly, block masonry of the Early Classic was gradually replaced by veneer masonry in the latter part of the Middle Classic, with some overlap. In effect, Cohodas believes the Toltec buildings at Chichén Itzá can be dated prior to A.D. 900. Nearly all the carbon–14 dates fall between A.D. 869–889. The oldest Mexican influence on the inner temple of El Adivino at Uxmal is dated at A.D. 569 ± 50, and the ball-court rings at A.D. 649. This leads to Cohodas' central argument: He estimates the construction of the Great Ball Court of Chichén Itzá at A.D. 650!

We have seen that the ball game became a widespread cult during the Middle Classic Period. It is at this time that it could have been introduced by merchants into Yucatán, which became a major center of the cult along with Cotzumalhuapa and El Tajín. Much controversy has centered around the chronology of this Great Ball Court and a Middle to Late Classic dating would be welcomed by many who have studied the art and iconography. However, it could also be viewed as a later renaissance structure (Kubler 1975).

According to this Toltec chronology, there is no need for a second immigration of Toltecs. Toltec with various other Mexican influences came in during the Middle and Late Classic periods at a time of great interarea communication and commercial enterprise. The Toltec structures at Chichén Itzá would therefore exhibit this early blending of various Mexican and Maya styles. Chichén Itzá is seen to outlast the Puuc sites and flourish into the Early Postclassic period.

Archaeologically there is remarkably little information on a late Toltec intrusion, a fact pointed out by Thompson. No Mazapan pottery is found in Yucatán. Plumbate, although found at both Tula as well as Chichén Itzá, was a Guatemalan product, not specifically Toltec. Likewise, Silho Fine Orange, another marker of the period, is of lowland origin. A strong case can thus be made for a Classic dating of Toltec and other Mexican influences that persisted in Yucatán into the Postclassic period.

Returning to the legendary record, in order for the Toltecs of Tula, Hidalgo to have inspired the Toltec stone carvings and construction at Chichén Itzá, the Toltec elite would have had to leave Tula in the tenth century, at the very beginning of its rise to power. This is very unlikely. The later version in which Quetzalcóatl was contemporary with Huémac would place a migration in the twelfth century, too late to account for the long Yucatecan development. It seems possible that the legend of Quetzalcóatl was a popular one which eventually reached Yucatán and was incorporated into the local traditions concerning Chichén Itzá, where feathered serpents abound.

If a Classic-period dating of Toltec features at Chichén Itzá is accepted, the westward penetration of Maya influences could have reached Tula, Hidalgo and may be reflected in the main ball court, the two stelae, and the Main Ceremonial Precinct at this site (see discussion, p. 379). The relationships between Tula and Chichén Itzá and the dating of their buildings is of great importance for history and interpretation of archaeology during these several hundred years. It is a matter that cannot be settled here, but the issue has been raised and this latter version should be taken into account as a possible alternative interpretation of Toltec presence in Yucatán.

YUCATÁN UNTIL THE ABANDONMENT OF CHICHÉN ITZÁ

On a more positive note, we know that after A.D. 1000 northern Yucatán did in fact become a powerful commercial center under the leadership of Chichén Itzá. Just how this was accomplished we do not know, but it seems to have been at the expense of the Puuc sites. Yucatán had been opened up to trading networks in the Classic period. These were further stimulated in the Postclassic years, for great quantities of Silho Fine Orange pottery made in the southern Veracruz–Tabasco region are found in Yucatán. This mass production of Fine Orange pottery is an indication of the scale of trade involved, for it reflects the Putún merchants' efficiency in planning and organization as well as skills as accomplished sailors. They must have been hard-to-beat competitors and as they traveled back and forth around the peninsula, their language became kind of a lingua franca from Veracruz to Honduras, facilitating communication and commercial partnerships.

Silho Fine Orange and Tohil Plumbate are two distinctive ceramic types that were widely distributed at this time and are now helpful markers for the archaeologists. But salt was the commodity most responsible for the success of the Yucatán trade. Other products available from Yucatán were cotton cloth, honey, and slaves. Slaves could be provided since agricultural labor was not needed in Yucatán during a good part of each year. At the same time, slaves were always needed to work in the cacao groves of Tabasco and Honduras. Another Yucatecan export could have been the much admired blue coloring that was used in ritual, associated with sacrifice, and painted on Classic and Postclassic figurines and pottery. The source of blue comes from indigo or a clay mineral called *attapulgite* (Littman 1980). Near the village of

Sacalum, 55 km south of Mérida, a *cenote* was apparently mined to extract this substance (Arnold and Bohor 1975).

Ball (1977c) has offered a plausible reconstruction of these Early Post-classic years. As the Putún Maya invaded northwestern Yucatán in their eager search for salt, the Puuc centers in the west organized themselves to accommodate this new trade. Large centers like Uxmal, Kabah, and Labná expanded to facilitate the collection, storage, and movement of salt. Yet over in Chichén Itzá the Mexicanized Itzás continued to grow wealthy and more powerful, a fact resented and resisted by the Puuc centers. This tension may have led to the fortification of Chacchob, Cuca, and possibly other Puuc sites. Chacchob was the earliest, with rather plain Puuc architecture, but with a wall 1.5 to 3 m in height! Cuca would have offered a more effective defense with two concentric walls that look as if they had been added on to an older settlement (Webster 1978). However, despite their efforts, northern Campeche may have been simply by-passed after A.D. 1000, as port facilities built in the Tabasco region allowed the trade to be completely seaborne to northern Yucatán. This would account for the lack of Tohil Plumbate and Silho Fine Orange at the Puuc sites. In turn, Chichén Itzá asserted its power by constructing defensive outposts or control centers for the salt industry in the west at Xcopte and at Isla Cerritos in the east. Thus outmaneuvered, the Puuc sites were finally abandoned.

Around A.D. 1100 a small settlement destined to alter Yucatecan history was made to the west of Chichén Itzá. Mayapán, according to Landa, was founded by Quetzalcóatl and a group of Itzás from Chichén Itzá (Tozzer 1941), but archaeologists suggest the town was settled from the east coast island of Cozumel (Pollock, Roys, Proskouriakoff, and Smith 1962). Its leading family, the Cocoms, were instrumental in bringing about the end of the Itzá occupation of Yucatán. This is related in the oft-told tale of Hunac Ceel, a Tabascan mercenary imported by the Cocoms who rose to leadership at Mayapán. This colorful figure had become something of a hero by surviving the sacrificial ordeal of the Sacred Cenote at Chichén Itzá. After being thrown in the pool, he somehow survived all night and brought back to the world on the following morning the prophecy of the rain god concerning prospects for a good crop in the forthcoming year. Once he became chief of Mayapán he schemed to rid himself of his rivals at Chichén Itzá. Through the aid of sorcery, he persuaded the ruler of Chichén Itzá to abduct the bride of the chief of Izamal during the wedding feast. Then full of feigned indignation, Hunac Ceel and some Mexicans drove the Itzá from Chichén.

Fleeing from the conflicts of Yucatán, the Itzás eventually made their way south through the Petén jungle to settle in peace on five small islands in Lakes Petén and Ekixil. Their main settlement was at Tayasal, a peninsula opposite Noh Petén, today known as Flores. Here their descendants were visited many years later, in 1524, by Hernán Cortés, who was on his way to put down a revolt in Honduras. They were not actually conquered by the Spanish until 1697. These Itzás were ruled jointly by a head chief and a high priest. Under them were four minor officials, *batabs*, each of whom presided over a *barrio*, which was in turn subdivided. At the time of their conquest, they were well aware of their ancestral background in Yucatán, worshiped several of the same ancient deities, retained the katun count, and still practiced human sacrifice (Thompson 1951).

In Yucatán, the Itzás were heard from no more, and the Toltecs too had by then long since vanished from the record, probably completely absorbed into the Maya way of life. Although the Maya aristocracy seems to have maintained its identity during the Early Postclassic period, it was subsequently lost, and all battles, confrontations, and sacrifices happily forgotten. By the sixteenth century, all the upper classes claimed Mexican descent. It was the Toltecs who were immortalized, and their stay in Yucatán was recalled nostalgically as a golden age of peace, justice, and religious worship.

SIGNIFICANT FEATURES OF THE EARLY POSTCLASSIC PERIOD

There was a trend toward increasing secularization seen in pronounced emphasis on militarism. Weapons and warriors were prominently displayed in relief carvings.

Metallurgy from South America was introduced via west coast cultures of Nayarit and Guerrero. Central America was another possible entry point of metal. However, very little metal is found at Tula itself.

Traits Shared by Chichén Itzá and Tula, Hidalgo

• New architectural pattern of construction with long colonnaded courts.
• Processions of warriors with nearly identical clothing and weapons.
• Small Atlantean figures with upraised arms, supporting altars (?) or sanctuary repositories. The colossal Atlantids at Tula have no precedent or parallel in central Mexico.
• *Chacmool* stone figure. Two examples at Tula, 14 at Chichén Itzá. Origins unknown.
• Feathered-serpent columns (incomplete at Tula).
• Relief sculptures of jaguars, eagles, skulls and crossed bones, and human hearts.

Ceramic Markers

• Coyotlatelco: red-on-buff ware, transitional Classic–Postclassic in central highland Mexico.
• Mazapan: red-on-buff ware, Toltec culture, very wide distribution in north central Mexico.
• Aztec I and II: black-on-orange ware. Two styles probably contemporary with different geographical distributions in central highland Mexico. Aztec I: southern Basin of Mexico and Cholula. Aztec II: found at Tula and northern Basin of Mexico and late Toltec sites.

- Plumbate: distinctive Guatemalan trade ware found throughout Mesoamerica.
- Silho Fine Orange: fine-paste ware, widely traded at this time from Veracruz–Tabasco region. Mass production.
- *Blanco levantado* (Tula Watercolored): specialized ceramic decoration with limited distribution: Tula, Basin of Mexico, Guanajuato, Querétaro, Colima, Nayarit, Jalisco.
- Cloisonné: decorative technique shared by Toltec and northwestern cultures.
- Mixteca–Puebla: distinctive art style resembling that of Borgia *códices*. More characteristic of Late Postclassic. Probably originated in Puebla region, spread to west coast of Mexico, seen on polychrome pottery.

SUMMARY

Toltecs

Founded in the days of Teotihuacán, Tula became the leading center west of the Isthmus of Tehuantepec from A.D. 900 to 1150. The city consisted of 60,000 urban dwellers and an equal number of rural farmers. Tula is unusual for having a somewhat small Main Ceremonial Precinct accompanied by extensive excellent housing.

Economic prosperity was based on local subsistence farming and control of the obsidian industry at Tepeapulco. Specializations are believed to include obsidian working, textiles, fibers, and ceramic drain tubes.

The Toltec "empire" has probably been exaggerated. Its sphere of influence seems to have been limited to immediate regions in a transverse band north of Tula, Hidalgo. Trade extended from far northern Mexico to Lower Central America, with notable lack of contact with Puebla–Tlaxcala, the Gulf Coast, western Morelos, and Oaxaca. Communication south may have taken place via Toluca Valley, Guerrero, coastal Oaxaca to the Isthmus region (?).

Toltecs comprised a number of different peoples: Tolteca–Chichimeca from the north, Nonoalca from the Gulf Coast area, various Mexican groups including descendants of Teotihuacanos and possibly Mixtecs (?).

HISTORICAL ACCOUNTS: TULA

1. Tula was the legendary city of Topiltzin Quetzalcóatl who traditionally founded this capital around A.D. 968 and brought arts and learning to his people. He was eventually tricked, disgraced by his rival Tezcatlipoca, and forced to leave in A.D. 987. He fled to Yucatán where he appeared in the same year as Kukulcán in Maya chronicles. Nearly 100 years later, the last ruler of Tula, Huémac ascended the throne.

2. According to another version, Topiltzin Quetzalcóatl and Huémac were corulers (secular and religious (?)), the evil forces of Tezcatlipoca being represented by Huémac. This compresses Toltec history into a much shorter time frame. Quetzalcóatl and Huémac abandoned Tula together around A.D. 1168 or 1178 (?) and went to the Basin of Mexico. Huémac committed suicide at Chapultepec, and Quetzalcóatl probably returned home to Culhuacán, or went to Puebla (?).

In both accounts Tula was destroyed by fire and ravaged by northern barbarians around A.D. 1175–1179 (?). The Toltecs dispersed, with some going to the Basin of Mexico, others going east to Puebla. Some remained at Tula, which was continuously occupied until taken over by the later Aztecs.

HISTORICAL ACCOUNTS: YUCATÁN

1. In Yucatán, a second coming of Kukulcán (Quetzalcóatl) is traditionally placed at A.D. 987 at which time the Toltecs settled at Chichén Itzá and a new section of the city was added, with many sculptured and architectural features of Tula, Hidalgo.

2. Or, there was no second Toltec invasion. The earlier Classic Toltec influences spread west with Maya features in the ninth or tenth century (?) and inspired the constructions at Tula, which reflect architectural details of Chichén Itzá. At the latter site, a number of architectural styles, including Toltec, existed side by side until around A.D. 1000 when the Puuc cities were abandoned.

The Short Count dating system replaced the earlier Long Count of the Classic period.

The Puuc cities flourished until overtaken by the greater power of Chichén Itzá. Conflict and competition led to fortification of some towns. Decline and abandonment of Puuc cities was complete.

Chichén Itzá controlled trade in northern Yucatán. There was a thriving maritime commerce from Tabasco to Honduras in salt, slaves, honey, blue coloring, Fine Orange pottery, Plumbate, *ixtle* fibers, and perishables.

After A.D. 1000 Chichén Itzá flourished as a commercial center until overcome by a new rival, the city of Mayapán, around A.D. 1250.

Other Areas

Cholula. The center was reestablished after a period of weakness following the fall of Teotihuacán. Olmeca–Xicalanca hegemony (?) prevailed. Around A.D. 1100 a huge pyramid was enlarged to final gigantic proportions. The city (Tollan Cholollan) was dedicated to Quetzalcóatl. Fine polychrome ceramics decorated in the Mixteca–Puebla style reached the west coast of Mesoamerica. This distinctive art style attained its peak in the Late Postclassic period.

Oaxaca. There was a return to regionalism. Centers such as Yagul and Mitla were scattered in the Oaxaca Valley. Significant architectural developments include mosaic stone masonry and use of *greca* motif.

Huasteca. This was a period of great florescence, with contact with the Toltecs. Intense regional development resulted. Distinctive ceramics, an art style, and use of bitumen outcrops for glue and paint were characteristics.

Highland Guatemala. Hilltop defensible settlements became widespread.

Strife, Empires, and Europeans: The Late Postclassic Period

CHAPTER 8

The site of Chichén Itzá had probably originally been chosen because of its proximity to one of the great natural wells or *cenotes* on the northern plains of Yucatán. Eventually a cult that reached its peak in Postclassic times evolved around this Sacred Cenote. Even after the Spanish Conquest it was a center of pilgrimages. The *cenote* measures some 60 m in diameter and is 21 m deep. The symmetrical walls rise sharply from the water to the ground level, some 20 m above. Into this depth both human victims and valuable objects were thrown as offerings to the rain god and as a form of divination to predict abundance of future crops. A small temple at the edge of the *cenote* marks one end of a causeway connecting the pool with the Temple of Kukulcán. Presumably, sacrifices were made from this point (Tozzer 1957). The romantic idea that young Maya virgins were the sacrificial victims was hastily discarded once a sample of skeletons was studied by Dr. Ernest Hooton of Harvard University. The great majority proved to be children, a fair number were adult males, and the few women were beyond the normal age of marriage. Along with the skeletons, dredging brought up great amounts of jade, gold, and copper objects, jewelry of all types, weapons, copal, and rubber objects, wearing apparel, and fragments of textiles and baskets. Apparently, anything of value was offered to the gods in the hope of increasing precipitation.

Chichén Itzá was not the only center that attracted pilgrims. The Island of Cozumel was famous for the shrine of Ix Chel, goddess of medicine and patron deity of women. A paved road connected the nearest point on the mainland to Tabasco, Xicalanco, Champotón, and Campeche. A third shrine, honoring the sky god Itzamná, was located at Izamal, to which people swarmed to be cured of disease. Izamal was

MAP 10. The Postclassic Maya.

always a rich center owing to the excellent salt beds on the nearby coast. As a religious shrine, it prospered from Classic times until the eventual fall of Mayapán (Map 10).

Around the mid-thirteenth century, Mayapán, which had been founded about A.D. 1100, became the capital of Yucatán. Following a brief revival of the Kukulcán cult, a period of great debauchery set in. Legends are filled with tales of sorcery, adultery, homosexual practices, and much erotic conduct apparently associated with the *plumería* flower (frangipani). An Itzá lineage by the name of Cocom enlisted the aid of Mexican mercenaries from Tabasco and, with their help, seized the reins of government in Mayapán. The mercenaries are usually credited with introducing the bow and arrow into Yucatán, where it met with great success. Prior to its introduction, *atlatls* and darts brought in by the Toltecs, spears, blowguns, and traps were used. Under the leadership of the Cocoms, Mayapán gained control of all northern Yucatán. A prosperous period followed, led by rulers who were reputedly just and benevolent. The centralized government in Mayapán brought all the heads of other city states to live in the capital. By this means, coupled with their control of Chichén Itzá and Izamal, they eliminated their rivals.

The ruins of Mayapán cover an area of about 5 km² (Pollock, Roys, Proskouriakoff, and Smith 1962). Nine kilometers of defensive walls completely surrounded the city, which had only two entrances and interior steps leading up to the parapet. The Cocoms could thus have maintained a tight control over the inhabitants of the 3600 structures that have been mapped within the walls. Some houses were much more elaborate than others as they varied from two-room dwellings to elegant residences, but all had built-in benches as a standard feature. The finest homes had a family shrine and people often buried their dead closeby. Most of the house sites were arranged around small courtyards without any discernable master pattern. Religious structures, degenerate in scale and construction, were concentrated in a small ceremonial center at the heart of the city. A tiny temple dedicated to Kukulcán is a miserable replica of the one at Chichén Itzá, and some sort of round structure once existed where rubble stands today. Religion must have occupied a minor position in daily affairs and was largely reduced to individual household shrines. No one bothered to raise corbelled vaults, and columns were crudely assembled, with mistakes camouflaged by stucco. No ball courts, *tzompantlis*, or sweat baths have been found. Ceramics are largely monochrome; typically crude and ostentatious incense burners bear representations of both Mexican and Maya deities. Is the abundance of incense burners a sign of decadence,

MAYAPÁN AND THE LAST OF MAYA CIVILIZATION

anxiety, and distress? They have also been much in evidence during the final days of Kaminaljuyú and Teotihuacán (pp. 225, 261). When compared to the striking beauty of the Puuc cities and the craftsmanship and skill manifested by the architects of Chichén Itzá, Mayapán seems shoddy, tasteless, and presents a low in cultural achievements. The contrast may be due in part to a reorientation of priorities and interests, for Mayapán now became the capital or administrative center of the peninsular maritime trade.

The population has been estimated at around 11,000–12,000. With local rulers forced to reside at Mayapán, luxury goods flowed in as tribute and a brisk trade was carried on. It is believed that, aside from the nobility, the residents were craftsmen, merchants, and soldiers. Farmers would have had to live in the country and carry their products into the city.

The east coast of Yucatán now entered into its period of greatest glory, despite the frequent archaeological label as "Decadent period." We have seen that the Putún merchants, although commercially oriented, had been the vehicle for spreading the ball-game cult and all its paraphernalia in the Classic period. These people were seemingly inexhaustible. Although winds may suddenly arise and the treacherous coral reefs off Yucatán are the despair of modern ships, the experienced Putún in his large trading canoe could overcome these obstacles more easily. If it was necessary, he could take refuge in any number of protective inlets. At the southern end of Belize, he could put in at Nito, a large trading post at the mouth of the Río Dulce.

In the Late Postclassic, many of the so-called Toltec elements found at Chichén Itzá were transmitted via trade to the east coast: serpent columns and balustrades, columns decorated with figures in relief or stuccoed, *chacmools*, round structures, colonnaded halls, and Mixtec and Toltec elements in murals (Andrews and Andrews 1975). Let us take a brief look at some of the most outstanding east-coast sites.

There is a great proliferation of archaeological remains along the coast of Quintana Roo. Approximately 500 masonry structures are reported within a 60-km strip. Most of these date to the Late Postclassic period when this area was the scene of great commercial activity. The healthy climate is today being rediscovered and exploited by tourist resorts, but the combination of arable land, fresh water close to the coast, marine resources, and adequate rainfall was also appreciated in ancient times as seen in the dense population in the days of Mayapán. The most important sites from north to south are: Xcaret and the Island of Cozumel, Xelhá, Tancah, Tulum, and to the far south Ichpaatun and Santa Rita (northern Belize) (Map 10). Cobá, a well-known earlier inland site had been one of the first Classic Maya centers to collapse (A.D. 682). By this time, Cobá had lost its importance as activity was now concentrated on the coast where merchants could put in with their boats carrying merchandise. Although seemingly isolated from the leading center or capital of Mayapán, archaeological remains indicate that these scattered sites maintained a close relationship to it. For example, clay figurines at Santa Rita, Belize are almost indistinguishable from those of Mayapán.

Until A.D. 1250 the Putún Itzá based at Chichén Itzá exercised great control over the Yucatán waters. But after Chichén Itzá was virtually abandoned, Mayapán took over this lucrative trade and worked closely with Cozumel. Work on the island has led Sabloff and Friedel (1975) to interpret the role of Cozumel as a local administrative center of port facilities for Mayapán. Taken as a cultural unit, the west side offered the great shrine to Ix Chel. Although this may have been located more centrally earlier, it is believed that wherever shrines were found along the coast, they served both ritual needs as well as being watch towers. Boats could have docked at either end of Cozumel, while storage facilities were located safely inland at San Gervasio. Trade in obsidian and hard stone was carried on all year, but such seasonal items as salt, honey, and cacao required storage for which Cozumel was ideally suited (Sabloff 1977; Sabloff and Friedel 1975).

Xcaret, the Polé of Colonial days, on the central coast just opposite Cozumel, had a large population at this time. Although there is no early architecture, Late Preclassic ceramics indicate a long history of occupation. Like many other late coastal settlements, Xcaret was enclosed by walls.

Xelhá, north of Tulum, was a smaller fortified town. A causeway leading inland from the main plaza passes a structure that has both a vaulted roof and mural paintings. At one time it must have been covered with paintings, many of which are lost. But enough remain to show that these were probably copied from Tulum. They are not as finely executed, and the figures look rather uncomfortable wearing oversized headdresses. The usual theme that goes back to Classic times shows a triparte division of the Maya world: the sky, the earth, and the underworld (Farriss, Miller, and Chase 1975).

Tancah, just 4 km north of Tulum, was occupied continuously from Preclassic to Postclassic. This is one region where *Strombus gigas* shells are abundant, and could account for the continual use of the area. These shells were part of the ritual paraphernalia of the Classic period and may possibly be the ones represented in the Teotihuacán murals. Obsidian, granite, pyrite, jade, and Puuc slate vessels are part of the great variety of imported goods found at Tancah.

Tulum has the most dramatic setting of all, perched on a cliff overlooking the blue waters of the Caribbean (Lothrop 1924). Its other three sides are effectively protected by a massive, 800-m long wall that is 2 m high and has five gates and interior stairs at various points. In contrast to Mayapán, Tulum looks like a planned city. It is organized around a main-street axis, bordered by both civic and residential buildings, and includes a marketplace. Stone palaces suggest a greater interest in secular than religious structures, which were concentrated within a walled enclosure. One structure is outstanding for its Chichén-like serpent columns. Both Tulum and Mayapán are examples of Late Postclassic nucleated settlements in which residences are packed into the center of town.

Bishop Landa (Tozzer 1941) described such a pattern in sixteenth-century Yucatán: "The natives lived together in towns . . . in the middle of the town were their temples with beautiful plazas, and all around the temples stood the houses of the lords and the priests, and then those of the most important people . . . and at the outskirts of the town were the houses of the lowest class . . . [p.62]."

The mural paintings at Tulum have fortunately been restored for they are some of the most interesting and complex of all pre-Columbian examples. Themes are similar to those at Xelhá, and elaborately attired figures are commonly paired with one standing, one seated. Both the Temple of the Frescoes (Structure 16) and the Temple of the Diving God (Structure 5) date from A.D. 1450–1500, and are very strongly influenced by the Mixtec art style (Miller 1973b). So similar are the style and execution of Tancah and Tulum murals to Mixtec art that Miller (1977) believes it possible that the elite of Quintana Roo brought Mixtec mural painters in to decorate their halls.

Santa Rita too has murals that are more Mixtec than Mayan in technique, although the themes are clearly Mayan. Now gone, the glyphic text that once accompanied the murals of Santa Rita was the only one ever reported.

This whole area became a prominent regional cult center for this was the "east," that land where the gods of Ix Chel the moon and Kukulcán as the planet Venus were reborn. That this was a cult center is shown in the iconography of a cave in the Tancah Cenote. Here the murals depict a sequence of Maya relations with the sea. At first there is fear of the sea, gradually replaced by exploitation of its resources, which finally culminated in complete control and domination of the sea. This art may be no older than A.D. 1450, just 100 years before the arrival of the Spanish. The area was so densely populated that the Spaniards were forced to delay its conquest (Miller 1977).

This picture of Late Postclassic life is far from decadent. In contact with many parts of Mesoamerica, this part of Yucatán enjoyed a lively trade, well organized and administered from Mayapán, well protected by fortified towns, and with inland storage facilities on Cozumel. Religious pilgrimages also encouraged travel and intersite contact.

While the east coast prospered and grew wealthy, at Mayapán the Itzá empire under Cocom leadership was subtly undermined. A Mexican group known as the Xiu had, according to Landa, wandered about Yucatán for some 40 years and eventually settled near the old ruins of

Uxmal. They made friends with their neighbors and, by exercising a little diplomacy, managed to participate in the administration of Mayapán, becoming second in power to the Cocoms. This arrangement, however, was short-lived. The nobles of Mayapán soon rose up in revolt, with the full cooperation of the Xiu. All the Cocoms were overwhelmed and summarily put to death, except for one son who was off on a trading expedition to Honduras. This reportedly occurred in another katun 8 Ahau, probably not historically accurate.

The Xiu then improved their position by moving south of Mayapán to a well-populated area offering better resources than Uxmal. They established a small but powerful kingdom at Maní. When the Spanish arrived, they remained bystanders until they saw which way the tide was turning, whereupon they allied themselves with the foreigners.

The collapse and destruction of Mayapán in A.D. 1441 marks the end of the last centralized government in Yucatán. Thereafter political control was of three different types (Roys 1966). In one case a single lord reigned as a kind of monarch over his town and was recognized by a few others. In case of need, he could call all warriors to battle. Examples of this type of authority are found at Maní, Sotuta, Ah Kinchel, and Cochuah. The second type of political organization was a kind of lineage rule such as that of the Canul and Cupul, two lineages or name groups. This was a rather loose arrangement whereby the heads of groups of towns belonged to the same lineage and would unite to defend each other when necessary. Finally, in the third form, towns might simply ally themselves to form a kind of province. They sometimes aided one another, but this was not obligatory. The area of Chakan, which included Mérida, was such a region.

This political situation endured for almost 100 years, from the fall of Mayapán to the conquest of the northern end of the peninsula. These years are filled with accounts of petty quarrels, local competitions, and struggles. Chichén Itzá continued to be the object of pilgrimages but supported no concentrated population. Mayapán, in shambles, shuddered with relief to be rid of the Cocoms and no one else chose to live there. The Puuc cities had been abandoned for many years. Dzibilchaltún managed to maintain itself, though with no particular distinction. Surely these surviving Maya must have felt abandoned and cast out by their gods as disaster after disaster befell them. In 1464 they weathered a devastating hurricane, followed in 1480 by a plague. Worse still was the smallpox epidemic that swept through Yucatán in 1514, 3 years after some shipwrecked Spaniards had been cast ashore. It is any wonder that, with the exception of a few bloody uprisings, the Spanish Conquest of Yucatán met with little resistance?

By the time the Spanish had arrived and Landa wrote his account of the Yucatecan Indians, the greatest period of Maya development had passed. He found the Maya leading a simple village life, competing with neighboring towns for prestige, and constantly warring over any trivial dispute. Central Mexican influences had made considerable impact two or three centuries earlier and by now were thoroughly blended with native Maya culture. The ancient calendar had been condensed and reduced to recording only a katun ending date, the Short Count. Many drastic changes had taken place in Maya life since the peak of its civilization, but we have written documentation for only the last centuries of life in Yucatán (Roys 1965). Even the existing *códices* are thought to date from the Postclassic period and were probably painted in Yucatán. European influences are usually easily spotted, but those from central Mexico are less easily seen, for, after all, Mesoamerican cultures shared many basic features and attitudes. However, Maya culture had a special flavor and the Landa's sixteenth-century account may permit some inferences about the earlier Classic civilization.

Agriculture, for example, was basically the same everywhere in its reliance on the cultivation of maize, chili peppers, beans, squash, cotton, and fruit trees, although techniques varied according to local conditions. Some plants such as cacao, which needed well-drained land, heavy rainfall, and limited sunlight, could only be grown in particular locations and had to be traded to other regions. Landa speaks of individual houses as having gardens and fruit trees where papaya, custard apple, avocado, and the ramon tree were grown. Agricultural lands were located away from the centers of population. Dogs and turkeys were the only domesticated animals known, and were raised for food. Native stingless bees were important to the Maya because honey was a prominent export commodity and the wax was used in rituals. In addition to gathering wild honey in the woods, most families kept hives of bees. Hollowed tree trunks served as hives, the ends of which were closed with mud or a piece of wood or stone so that the honey could be easily extracted; the bees entered through a small hole in the side. Honey was also combined with water and soaked with the pounded bark of the *balché* tree to make a fermented ceremonial drink. Although bee keeping was probably limited to Yucatán, the practice of slash-and-burn agriculture, house garden plots, and the general range of cultivated plants are all features found in the Classic Petén.

Commerce was always vitally important to every region. Chief commodities in Yucatán were slaves, honey, salt, and cotton cloaks. Trade was carried out on land by foot travel using tump-lines (head or chest straps), but probably even more merchandise was moved by sea, for we know that the Maya had large dugout canoes with sails, capable of carrying 40 people, and that they traveled from the Bay of Honduras around Yucatán to the big port at Xicalanco. The Putún distinguished themselves as merchant seamen as early as the seventh or eighth century. This long-distance trade will be more fully described when we deal with the *pochteca*, the Aztec merchants. It is assumed that the

Maya had equivalent traders, although an association such as that of the *pochteca* is not described. Maya merchants operated under the auspices of Ek Chuah, God of the North, who was their patron. He can easily be identified in the *códices* by his black face (see Figure 32).

There is no reason to believe that the Maya house in Classic times was any different from that seen today in villages of Yucatán. Rectangular, often with rounded corners, houses were set on stone-faced platforms with walls made of stone rubble and plaster sometimes combined with poles. The roofs were of thatched palm and floors were covered with gravel or plaster. This is the same house as that depicted in the mosaic stone facade of the Nunnery at Uxmal, and it has been constructed by the Maya for centuries.

Landa's description of towns has been mentioned earlier. It is not certain how long the Maya had been living in tightly nucleated centers. Classic settlements present a great variety of patterns due in some cases, but not all, to the local topography. Because houses of mud, reed, and plaster are not preserved, we have little information on the arrangements and distribution of private homes prior to Postclassic Yucatecan settlements. There is some indication that Tikal may have resembled the late urban city of Mayapán in having an ungridded residence pattern and structures scattered about at random. The contrasting terrain of these cities could account for some differences, and the defensive wall of Mayapán reflects the troubled times of Postclassic years. Haviland sees in Mayapán a logical outgrowth of earlier Petén settlements in contrast to central Mexican city planning, which was very different (Haviland 1969).

Technology likewise remained stable for hundreds of years. It was based on the digging stick, *metate* and *mano*, bark beaters, and the use of obsidian, flint, granite, limestone, and quartzite for knives, pounders, polishers, and scrapers. The *atlatl* may have been in use during the latter part of the Classic period, but its manufacture was given new impetus as a result of the Toltec invasion. The bow and arrow were introduced even more recently, probably from the area of Tabasco. Metals were also a Postclassic addition, as the Classic Maya had relied exclusively on stone tools.

All this information is documented archaeologically. The patterns of ritual, religion, and social and political organization, however, are much more inferential, and for this information we rely heavily on written accounts of sixteenth-century Yucatán to look for either supporting evidence or lack of it from the archaeological record. There is no question that Maya society was strongly stratified. Landa reports ruling families and tells of the great respect with which chiefs and lords were treated. Society was highly structured. At the top were the nobles, an aristocracy that contained the civic, religious, and military leaders. Merchants and artisans were next in rank, followed by the peasants or commoners and slaves. Only the priests and lords knew the art of writing, and they were in charge of educating sons of the first families in writing, astronomy, calendrics, and astrology. With the exception of military leaders, for whom there is little evidence at present, the structuring of society applies equally well to what we know of life in late Classic times, as evidenced in the riches of tombs and paintings of elaborately attired individuals who must have belonged to the hierarchical elite (Adams 1970).

The Maya concept of the world is not well known and has been interpreted from the written documents, legends, sculptures, and painted representations of deities and ceremonies. It is possible that the Maya, like the Aztecs, believed that the world rested on the back of a huge crocodile in the center of a pond (Barrera Vásquez and Morley 1949; Thompson 1970).

The Maya pantheon was crowded with deities but this may have been a rather late phenomenon. Preclassic and Classic Maya art show supernatural beings that were often combined with animal forms such as jaguars, iguanas, snakes, crocodiles, quetzals, and parrots. These might be considered more as vital forces such as wind or "spirits" than as deities (Marcus 1978). The concept of deities and idols is more characteristic of later periods and Marcus suggests this was a change brought about by contact with the central Mexicans. In the Postclassic period the Maya conceived of groups of deities, who were both individual and multiple at the same time. Maya gods are not as well known as Aztec ones, and the data at hand refer largely to Yucatán (Morley 1956; Thompson 1954, 1970). Representations of deities are found in stone, stucco, pottery, and in the three surviving *códices* (Figure 32).

Itzamná, a sky god, was the supreme deity who, with his wife Chebel Yax, the creation goddess, begat all the other gods and goddesses. Itzamná, who is the father of science and the arts, is shown with the face of an old man; he has a prominent aquiline nose and a single tooth.

Kukulcán, the feathered-serpent deity of Yucatán, was known as Gucumatz among the highland Quichés. He did not assume prominence until early Postclassic times and is closely associated with the Toltecs. Feathered serpents are present earlier, however, in sculptures of many Classic sites, including Tikal.

Yum Cimil or Hun Cimil was the god of death, and can be identified in the *códices* by his fleshless backbone, skull head, and body with black spots denoting decay. An owl or the Moan bird often accompanies him. Other deities dealt with epidemics, mass deaths, suicides, death by hanging, and being caught in a trap. The war god seems to have also presided over human sacrifice and violence.

The nature deities were very important, for they were vitally concerned with man's subsistence activities such as agriculture and fertility.

Cosmic and celestial bodies, wind, water, and vegetation all had patron deities. Chac, the rain god, was unrivaled in importance. Associated with the five cardinal points—east, west, north, south, and the center of the universe—he was at the same time benefactor, creator, and father of agriculture. It is his long hooked nose that adorns the Puuc buildings. His helpers, the Bacabs, stood at the four sides of the world and held up the sky.

The sun god, Kinich Ahau, is usually shown with filed teeth and large square eyes. He was the patron deity of Izamal, where at noontime he took the form of a macaw and swooped down to devour any offerings made to him.

Of almost equal importance and prominence in the Maya pantheon is Ah Mun, the corn god, represented as a handsome young man who often has a maize plant sprouting from his head.

Although there were a great number of deities, power was concentrated in a few; the others were remembered on special occasions when

Itzamná   Chac   Ah Mun

Yum Cimil   Ek Chuah   Xaman Ek

FIGURE 32. Maya deities. *Itzamná*, the head of the Maya pantheon, patron of day Ahau, the last and most important of the 20 days. *Chac*, the rain god. *Ah Mun*, the god of corn and agriculture, usually shown as a young man, often with an ear of corn or corn plant as a headdress. *Yum Cimil*, the god of death, patron of the day Cimi, shown with a skull for a head and fleshless body with bare ribs and exposed vertebrae. *Ek Chuah*, the black war captain with a large drooping underlip; also the god of merchants. *Xaman Ek*, the god of the North Star, shown with a snub-nosed face, who somewhat resembles a monkey. (From the following sources: Itzamná, Ah Mun, Yum Cimil, Xaman Ek, Codex Dresden, Villacorta and Villacorta 1930; Chac, Ek Chuah, Codex Tro-Cortesiano, Villacorta and Villacorta 1930.)

their help was needed. The gods were not particularly charitable, as their favors were dispensed in exchange for offerings of incense, food, and blood. No important move was made without consulting their wishes, and they indicated the most propitious time for planting and harvesting. They regulated marriages, baptisms, and the selection of names and advised when to embark on a trip or trading expedition, when to fish, and when and where to hunt. Supplications were made in public and in private, but the activities of continence, fasting, prayer, and making offerings went on incessantly. The Maya were very superstitious and exhibited a real concern with lucky and unlucky days, charms, amulets, and magic. Eclipses of the sun or moon caused great fear, which was partly alleviated by banging on doors or seats and making as much noise as possible.

Some beliefs recorded by the Spanish are not typical of aboriginal American thinking and may well represent the teachings of the Spanish friars. We suspect that one example of this is the concept of reward and punishment meted out in a heaven or hell depending on how one behaved on earth. However, the practices of baptism, incense burning, and a kind of confession were already part of native Indian religion, which facilitated the substitution of Catholicism in the sixteenth century.

The Maya were as vain as we are today, and went to great lengths to improve their natural appearance. Elongated heads with receding foreheads forming a straight line with the nose were so admired that infants' skulls were artificially deformed to produce the coveted profile. This was accomplished by lashing two boards together, one flat against the back of the head, the other on the forehead. Four or five days of this treatment were sufficient to alter permanently the shape of the skull. Head deformation has a very long history in the Maya region, including the Classic period years. Greatly admired too were squinting and slightly crossed eyes, which could be induced by suspending a little stone or ball of resin between the eyes. Other beauty aids included filing the teeth to create interesting patterns and encrusting them with jade or iron pyrites. Finally, the body might be decorated by tattooing, scarification, or painting. Much of this may have had symbolic or ritual significance as well, for we know that colors had special meanings. These traits, along with hair styles and modes of dress, are documented by clay figurines and murals. Figurines from Jaina and the murals of Bonampak show styles of skirts, turbans, mantles, flowing robes, animal skins, and masks as well as the expressions, stances, and gestures of the various social ranks (see Plate 9-h, i; Photos 43, p. 312, and 44, p. 313).

The Maya loved their children and believed in discipline. Children were punished by pinching their arms and ears or rubbing chili pepper on them. Marriages were arranged by a professional matchmaker and the spouse was chosen from a prescribed group, usually when a young man was about 20. After a wedding feast the husband lived with his father-in-law for 5 or 6 years, an indication of matrilineal ties. However, property was passed on patrilineally and family ties were important for joint enterprises such as exchange of labor. The ability to trace both parents' descent groups was a necessary key to prestige in the community. Usually a man had only one wife, but desertion and divorce were common. On the whole, women were chaste and hard working but extremely jealous and prone to erupt into violent rages. Men and women ate and danced separately. We are told that the Maya loved dancing and banquets. A dinner invitation incurred an obligation to return the favor, and presents were exchanged. Music was produced by wooden drums, flutes, whistles, conch-shell trumpets, and rattles.

Upon the death of a person, relatives showed signs of great distress. During the day they wept in silence, but at night they howled and cried aloud. People were usually buried in the house or just behind it, and the dwelling was then deserted unless the family was so large that desertion was impractical. This long-standing practice of deserting a house upon death of a member of the family has caused some anxiety among archaeologists when using house-mound counts to estimate ancient populations (see the discussion on pp. 273–274, Thompson 1971). The more privileged members of society were cremated and their ashes placed in an urn. The Cocoms of Mayapán preserved the head by cooking it, removing the flesh, and sawing it in half from top to bottom. The front half was covered with wax and modeled to resemble the deceased. This then was kept in the family shrine and revered, where it was provided with offerings from time to time.

Warfare was common during the last years before the Conquest. In the Classic period weapons consisted of clubs and a kind of battle axe. Later the bow and arrow and *atlatl* were introduced from Mexico with great success. The cotton quilted armor described for Yucatán may have been inspired by that of the central Mexicans. Wars were fought in the day time, and war paint, along with much shouting and hissing, was designed to frighten the enemy.

Thompson (1954) characterized the spirit of the Maya as devout, exercising moderation, and possessing great discipline. Many scholars now share M.D. Coe's belief (1980) that this picture is not realistic. Coe sees them instead as quarrelsome, doting on warfare, and fiercely competitive in their struggle for political gain. Archaeological facts appear to lean toward a more theocratic organization in the early years of Maya history with the constant building and rebuilding of religious structures and the ceremonial center, whereas toward the end of the Classic period, elite residences, palaces, and civic buildings show an increasing interest in mundane affairs. This is further supported by the personal glorification and dynastic records of personal histories that are recorded on the stone monuments. Human sacrifice, although practiced earlier, became more common and on a larger scale. Defensive walls were raised around Yucatecan cities, weapons were more plentiful and diversified, and actual scenes of battles were portrayed in murals. This secular trend became more and more prevalent and has parallels in other Postclassic cultures, a current coexisting with, but not replacing the religious.

The discussion now returns to central highland Mexico.

THE CHICHIMEC PERIOD
(SI–3)

From the fall of Tula, roughly A.D. 1200, until A.D. 1370, marked by the accession of Tezozomoc as ruler of the Tepanecs at Azcapotcalco, the Basin of Mexico was occupied by various central Mexican peoples and groups of Chichimecs who had come in at various times. It was a troubled period of conflict between these seminomads of the north and the sedentary farmers who had been in residence over a longer period of time.

The Basin of Mexico survey (Sanders, Parsons, and Santley 1979) concedes that this is one of the most difficult periods to assess archaeologically. The difficulty is partly because of an identity problem with the later material, and partly because modern Mexico City chose to inhabit the same terrain. In general the northern end of the valley was inexplicably almost devoid of people. The central part (Map 11) was dominated by Azcapotzalco and Tenayuca to the west of Lake Texcoco; and Huexotla and Coatlichan on the east, each with a population estimated at 10,000 to 15,000 people. The southern part was the most densely populated of all with regional centers of Culhuacán, Xochimilco, Cuitláhuac, Mixquic, Chalco, Xico, and Amecameca. Chalco was probably the largest. This area is the best watered and most desirable area for living and had been the first choice of settlers back in Preclassic days. At this time, people were beginning to settle down near the lake shore and to experiment with *chinampa* cultivation.

The historical record that follows deals mainly with the Aztecs, but there is a wealth of source material for the entire region (Nicholson 1978).

The early history of the Aztecs is sketchy, and until the reign of Nezahuacóyotl in Texcoco in the fifteenth century, we trace events in the Valley of Mexico through oral traditions. Later history is pieced together from the Spanish chronicles and the pre-Hispanic and Colonial *códices*. Excellent ethnographic data and genealogic and chronologic information abound in the writings of Conquest witnesses such as Cortés (1908). Sahagún (1946), and Diaz del Castillo (1944), and later authors such as Torquemada (1943) and Durán (1967). Best of the native sources are the *Tira de la Peregrinación, Historia de los Mexicanos por sus*

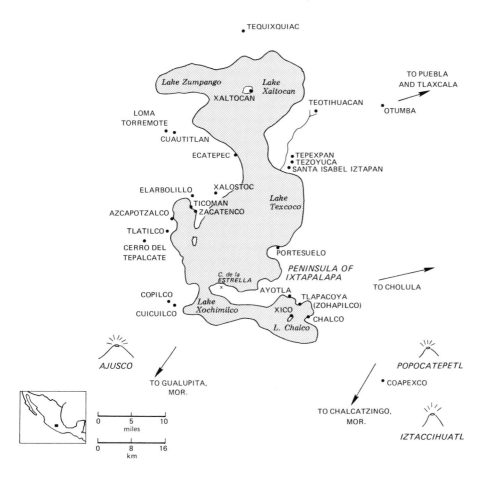

MAP 11. The Basin of Mexico, A.D. 1519.

Pinturas, Codex Xólotl, the Tlotzin and Quinatzin maps, and the interpretations of Ixtlilxóchitl (1952), for despite exaggerations and confu-
sions resulting at times from the bias of the latter author, an essentially
coherent picture emerges. In the Aztec period, we are dealing with
historical archaeology; history and archaeology merge, confirming and
amplifying one another. For other works dealing with this period see
Acosta Saignes (1945, 1946), Barlow (1949), Bray (1972a, 1977c), Brundage (1972), Carrasco (1971), Caso (1958, 1967), M. D. Coe (1962), Cook
(1947), Davies (1973), Jiménez Moreno (1962), Kelly and Palerm (1952),
Kirchhoff (1954–1955), León-Portilla (1963), Monzón (1949), Peterson
(1959), Soustelle (1964), Wolf (1959), and Wolf and Palerm (1955).

Accordingly, we know that after the destruction of Tula, a great
Chichimec leader, Xólotl, settled first at Tenayuca and later moved his

capital to Texcoco, which was to play a vital role in the history of the Basin of Mexico. But of the several Toltec groups, the lineage at Culhuacán was the most prestigious and the most sought out for marriage. Before long, the best land for cultivation in the Basin of Mexico was in use, the lake shore was settled by Náhuat- and Otomí-speaking peoples and by descendants of refugees from the old centers of Teotihuacán and Tula.

With the choice areas already taken, no one welcomed an additional band of immigrant Chichimecs with the unpleasant habits of stealing women and practicing human sacrifice. These were *tamime,* or semicivilized Chichimecs, not as barbaric as the Teochichimecs such as Xólotl and his followers. The *tamimes* had a knowledge of the 52-year cycle and the ball game; they cultivated a few crops with irrigation, constructed in stone, and dressed in maguey fiber clothing. They also had a *calpulli*-type organization (see p. 445). We call this Náhuat-speaking group *Aztec,* a word derived from Aztlán, "place of the seven legendary caves." There these "warriors of the sun" were spawned. They, however, did not call themselves Aztecs. They were known at various times as Tenochca, Mexica, or more specifically, the Culhua–Mexica. As Tenochca they followed their early tribal leader, Ténoch, under whom they straggled into the Valley of Mexcico as unwanted squatters and for whom they later named their city Tenochtitlán. Stressing their association with the Toltec lineage at Culhuacán, they eventually became known as the Culhua–Mexica. But they are frequently called simply the Mexica, a name that came to be known and dreaded from coast to coast. Today the term Aztec is more common.

The story of the Aztecs' or Mexica's rise to power is a dramatic rags-to-riches tale. This miserable band, despised by all, was driven from one location to another around the western lake shore. There they lived as they could on fly eggs, snakes, and other vermin. Between A.D. 1250 and 1298 they served as vassals to the Tepanecs at Azcapotzalco but they later pushed on further south. Before long the king of Culhuacán engaged their aid in a war against the neighboring Xochimilco, but he was affronted by their barbarous customs, such as severing ears from each prisoner as proof of Aztec prowess in war. On another occasion the Aztecs requested the hand in marriage of the daughter of the king of Culhuacán in order to initiate a lineage of their own. When the king granted this wish, Aztec gratitude was so profound that they sacrificed the unfortunate girl by flaying her. When the king arrived for the supposed marriage festivities of his daughter, he was confronted instead by a priest dancing about in his daughter's skin. To escape the fury of the Culhuacanos, the Aztecs took refuge in the tall reeds of the lake shore, and finally in desperation moved to some swampy islands in the lake.

According to legends, their tribal war god, Huitzilopochtli, led them to this place. Here an eagle, sitting on a cactus with a serpent in its beak, told them to build their temples and nourish the sun with the sacrifice of human victims. To sustain the sun and other deities with sacrificial blood became the purpose and mission of the Aztecs in this world, and here the prophecy was to be fulfilled. The legend is depicted on the Mexican flag today.

Accounts vary as to the date of the founding of Tenochtitlán, but it probably occurred close to A.D. 1345, the date given by Jiménez Moreno and Davies. Kirchhoff prefers A.D. 1369–1370 (see Nicholson 1978). An eagle may or may not have been waiting, but the fact remains that the Aztecs had exhausted the tolerance of their littoral neighbors and were badly in need of refuge. Another group of Aztecs went over to a nearby island in 1358 and founded another settlement, Tlatelolco. These two cities were to thrive side by side for many years, the former becoming a great mercantile center, the latter growing steadily in military strength. Rivalry between the twin cities was unavoidable, and Tlatelolco was finally taken over by Tenochtitlán under Axayácatl in A.D. 1473, after 128 years of jealous, competitive coexistence.

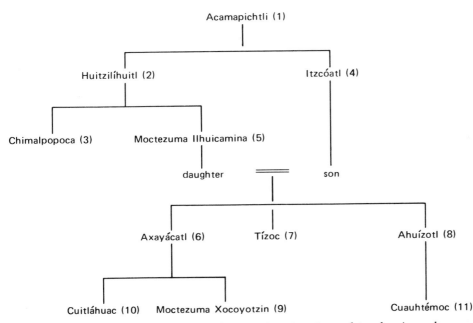

FIGURE 33. Genealogy of Aztec rulers. This genealogy is not complete, showing only the probable relationship between rulers. There often are conflicting accounts in the chronicles. For example, some sources list Chimalpopoca rather than Huitzilíhuitl as the father of Moctezuma Ilhuicamina, and Itzcóatl as the son of Huitzilíhuitl rather than his brother. Numbers refer to order of succession. (Based on Carrasco 1971.)

The rise of Aztec power and events in the Basin of Mexico can be followed by tracing the succession of kings and outstanding personalities of the times. Although preceded by tribal leaders, Acamapichtli was the first king and the founder of a lineage because of his kinship ties with Culhuacán.

In the Chichimec period the Aztecs were led by Acamapichtli, his son Huitzilíhuitl, and his grandson Chimalpopoca (Figure 33). During this time the Aztecs served as mercenaries to the Tepanecs, the people of Azcapotzalco, who were led by a ruthless but extraordinarily gifted ruler, Tezozomoc. Undoubtedly the Aztecs benefited greatly under this master warrior and administrator, but at the same time they seethed under the yoke of tribute and subjugation. Tensions were eased temporarily by intermarriage with the Tepanecs, only to worsen in the reign of Chimalpopoca, when the Aztecs were accused of becoming arrogant and demanding. Accounts vary as to whether Chimalpopoca was poisoned, strangled, starved in a cage, or committed suicide, but in all likelihood the Tepanecs were responsible (Ixtlilxóchitl 1891, vol. 2).

THE AZTECS OR MEXICA (LH)

Emergence as a Political Power

The subsequent election of Itzcóatl in Tenochtitlán took place after the tyrant Tezozomoc had died in Azcapotzalco, and with the rule of Itzcóatl a new phase was initiated. Aided by Texcoco and Huexotzingo, Azcapotzalco was finally conquered, ruthlessly sacked, and its people brutally massacred. All the pent-up vengeance of years gone by was unleashed on the defeated Tepanecs. The surviving Tepanec town of Tlacopan, today's Tacuba, had been sufficiently neutral to be selected as the weakest member of a Triple Alliance formed with Tenochtitlán and Texcoco. Henceforth, all three cities were to receive part of the tribute exacted from subservient towns; Tenochtitlán and Texcoco were entitled to two-fifths each, and Tlacopan received the remaining fifth.

The defeat of Azcapotzalco in 1428 established the Aztecs as the dominant power in the Basin of Mexico, a position they were to maintain until struck down by the Spaniards. The victory over Azcapotzalco not only gave them independence and political power, but a foothold on the mainland as they confiscated the rich *chinampas*, increasing their wealth and prestige and strengthening their class structure. The year 1428 launched the Aztecs on their way to statehood and empire.

Itzcóatl, Obsidian Snake, was a strong ruler himself and his rein is intimately associated with two of the most important figures in the history of the Valley of Mexico: Tlacaélel and Nezahuacóyotl. Tlacaélel, a half-brother of Moctezuma Ilhuicamina, occupied a position of power, an office known as the *cihuacóatl*, or Snake Woman. In early times this office included some priestly duties along with acting as advisor to the king, but eventually the religious aspect seems to have been discarded. Tlacaélel was a famous *cihuacóatl* who served under three successive kings. He emerges in history as a very able administrator who exercised great influence. To him we may owe the book burning that took place during Itzcóatl's reign. At that time the Aztecs gained their freedom from the Tepanecs, and it was decided to wipe out their inglorious and degrading past and to rewrite history to their liking. Thus, every available record of the Aztecs as conquered peoples was destroyed and a new indoctrination begun extolling the glories of the Warriors of the Sun.

Nezahuacóyotl of Texcoco is linked with both Itzcóatl and his successor in Tenochtitlán, Moctezuma Ilhuicamina. When only a child, Nezahuacóyotl, from his hiding place in a tree, witnessed the murder of the king, his father, at the hands of the Tepanecs. He grew up in exile knowing that he was responsible for carrying on the ancient Chichimecan lineage. Helpless against the powerful Tepanecs, he sought refuge with eastern friends and relatives in Tlaxcala and Huexotzingo, secretly visiting Texcoco and Tenochtitlán to plot his rightful restoration of power. Allying himself with Itzcóatl, he took part in the destruction of Azcapotzalco, which effectively ended Tepanec power in the Valley. One by one other cities fell around the lake shore: Culhuacán, Xochimilco, Huexotla, Coatlichan, and Coatepec. After subduing all the Tepanec strongholds in the Texcocan region, Nezahuacóyotl returned to his home covered with glory and was restored to power as king of Texcoco in a great ceremony at Tenochtitlán.

His reign was unparalleled in cultural achievements and learning. He codified Texcocan law, which was more severe than that of the Aztecs, and constructed a great dike across Lake Texcoco to hold back the brackish water of this lake from the fertile *chinampas* (a system of agriculture, see p. 426) of the sweet water of Lake Chalco. He initiated an intricate system of canals and dams to increase agricultural production; he helped Moctezuma Ilhuicamina build the aqueduct that carried sweet water to Tenochtitlán from Chapultepec; and he stimulated arts and crafts, offering prizes for the finest achievements in gold and feather working, music, and poetry. His summer residence at Texcotzingo, in ruins today, still retains elements of the former beauty of its stairways, temples, fountains, aqueducts, and baths, which were either cut out of bedrock or constructed of mortar. It is said that commoners and nobles were equally represented on Nezahuacóyotl's governing councils, and merchants were consulted on economic affairs. The early chroniclers stress his monotheistic tendencies and opposition to human sacrifice. Nezahuacóyotl preferred an invisible god who had both masculine and feminine qualities and who could not be represented materially. This god, Tloque Nahuaque, lived in the highest point in the heavens and all things depended on him. It did not intervene directly in man's affairs; therefore, Tloque Nahuaque was never very popular. We know, however, that although Nezahuacóyotl did erect a large temple to this one almighty god, in which there was no sacrificial stone, he also honored other deities. Nezahuacóyotl emerges as a very fair administrator and an exceptional thinker and poet, yet he too participated in many battles and, as a product of his times, ordered sacrifices and executions. Under Texcocan law, his favorite son was put to death as a traitor, because even the king's son could not be an exception. While Texcoco, under his administration, became famous as a center of learning, Tenochtitlán grew in military strength and eventually prevailed as a political power.

Tenochtitlán undoubtedly owes more to Texcoco than is usually admitted. Texcoco had its own history of conquests and tribute rolls prior to Aztec supremacy (Palerm and Wolf 1954–1955). After the fall of Azcapotzalco, it was through Texcoco's leadership that the eastern regions were brought under control of the Triple Alliance. Texcoco and Huexotzingo were long-standing friends, and it was the towns in the Puebla Valley that gave refuge and support to Nezahuacóyotl and enabled him to regain the throne. Thus, some conquests claimed by Tenochtitlán had already been achieved by Texcoco. Unwittingly or not, Texcoco was gradually dispossessed of its role as leader and upstaged by its aggressive island neighbor.

The Triple Alliance provided Tenochtitlán with a base for its scramble to power. Under Itzcóatl's nephew, Moctezuma Ilhuicamina, Archer of the Sky, the Aztecs began their great expansion. Their domain was extended to the Gulf Coast, an area of special commercial interest. Influenced and aided by his friend and ally Nezahuacóyotl, Moctezuma built botanical and zoological gardens. Every known plant, bird, and animal was collected at Huastepec, Morelos. It was also during his reign, about A.D. 1450, that Tenochtitlán suffered privation under a great 4-year drought. Hunger was so great that the Aztecs became frantic; wild animals emerged from the forests and attacked people for lack of food. So desperate was the situation that many Aztecs sold themselves as slaves to the lowland Totonacs of Veracruz, where corn was plentiful. Later they were to serve as spies reporting vital information about the alien country. In a final spasm of desperation, the Aztecs appealed to their powerful gods through mass human sacrifice. From this time on, human sacrifice on a large scale formed part of the Aztec pattern of life. The two great leaders, Moctezuma Ilhuicamina (Moctezuma I) and Nezahuacóyotl, died within a few years of each other, and the stage was set for the final thrust of Aztec militarism. The great urban center was by now made up of very diverse groups including foreigners. These were all absorbed into the urban labor force and civil disorders were severely suppressed. The growing population of Tenochtitlán–Tlatelolco was composed of full-time occupational specialists, not peasant farmers.

Axayácatl, the first of Moctezuma Ilhuicamina's grandsons to succeed him, spent much time reconquering territory and suppressing rebellions. He attempted western expansion, only to be met with firm resistance from the Tarascans (see Map 12, p. 458). But he finally took Tlatelolco, which from A.D. 1473 on was governed from Tenochtitlán. Upon his death his brother Tízoc reigned, but only for a short time. Tízoc has been branded in history as a coward because his love of battle did not match that of his brothers. However, the third brother, Ahuízotl, thrived on war. Under him Aztec influence was extended from coast to coast to include the Balsas basin and coastal Guerrero, and he pressed his claims to the Guatemalan border. He was especially gifted as a military leader. At home he managed to complete the Great Temple of Tenochtitlán, dedicated jointly to Huitzilopochtli and Tlaloc, each of whom was honored by a temple atop a pyramid with a double stairway, the hallmark of Aztec architecture although earlier examples are known at Tenayuca and at Teotihuacán. So important were the dedication ceremonies, which lasted 4 days, that 20,000 victims were stretched over the sacrificial blocks to have their hearts removed while multitudes watched and rejoiced.

The Aztecs in A.D. 1519

Moctezuma Xocoyotzin, son of Axayácatl, is remembered largely for his tragic fate and forced surrender of Tenochtitlán to the Spanish. Usually unnoticed is the fact that he was a very powerful, well educated, and able ruler who continued military expeditions in the area of Oaxaca and adjacent regions and dealt with his share of uprisings. In his day, Tenochtitlán was transformed into a beautiful city with a great concentration of population, estimated at between 200,000 and 300,000, which embraced hereditary nobles, priests, specialized artisans in a variety of crafts, merchants, and an enormous peasantry.

The first city the Spaniards saw was Cempoala on the Veracuz coastal plain where they were amiably received by the Totonac ruler. This was a large urban center with five temple–pyramids and a round temple dedicated to Quetzalcóatl–Ehécatl. The city was neatly walled in and raised above the ground level, which served both for defense and for protection from floods. The Spanish must have felt some surprise at finding fresh water provided to dwellings and marveled at the gorgeous multicolored pottery in Mixteca–Puebla or Isla de Sacrificios style. But this could in no way prepare them for what lay ahead.

As they made their ascent to the *altiplano* they could hardly have anticipated the sight of the great metropolis that awaited them as they passed between the snow-covered volcanoes of Popocatépetl and Iztaccíhuatl. There, spread beneath them, stretched the vast sweep of the Basin of Mexico, some 7700 km², enclosed by forested mountains and embracing in the center a chain of five lakes. Coming closer, they saw an island city with towering temple–pyramids connected to the mainland by three great causeways, a city of canals rather than streets.

Banding the island were *chinampas*, some of the most fertile gardens in the New World (Photo 68). Here the Aztecs grew corn, squash, beans, chili, *chia*, amaranth, innumerable vegetables, and flowers. The ingenious system of *chinampa* cultivation was initially begun by digging ditches in swampy lake-shore areas or on natural islands (Armillas 1971). The ditches drained off water to reveal plots of soil where plant-

PHOTO 68. *Chinampa* at Mixquic, Valley of Mexico. (Courtesy of Victoria Bach.)

ing could be done. Aerial photographs show a very carefully laid out grid network of canals. From canoes they renewed the soil by scooping up and spreading mud from the lake bottom, extremely rich in organic matter. Eventually the *chinampas* became more elevated, which reduced the danger of flooding, always a threat with the arrival of summer rains. This system was ideally suited for the island dwellers of Tenochtitlán for it provided tillable land and easy transport of produce by canoe. Owing to the constant renewing of the soil, *chinampas* never wore out.

The *chinampas* were cultivated from Tenochtitlán and Tlatelolco south to the shore of Lake Xochimilco and then east into Lake Chalco. Smaller systems were located in Lake Texcoco and Xaltocan where enough sweet water was provided by local springs to counteract the salinity of the lakes. We know that the Aztecs worked hard to protect these valuable lands. The greatest threat to their existence was the possibility of infiltration of nitrous salts from the eastern part of Lake Texcoco. Eventually they constructed a network of dikes built of stones, earth, poles, and branches, with sluice gates to protect the western part of Lake Texcoco from the salty waters of the east.

Although it is possible that the system had an earlier start, the massive planned colonization and development of *chinampas* dates from the fifteenth century. Sanders, Parsons, and Santley (1979) believe it was carefully planned by a central government.

At the center of Tenochtitlán was a great court enclosed by a *coatepantli*, or serpent wall, within which were the main religious structures, 72 according to Sahagún's count (Photo 69). The main temples of Huitzilopochtli and Tlaloc and those dedicated to Tezcatlipoca, Xipe Totec, and Quetzalcóatl, together with the ball courts, grisly *tzompantlis*, altars,

PHOTO 69. Reconstruction of the ceremonial center of Tenochtitlán. Note the Great Temple at center rear. (Courtesy of the Instituto Nacional de Antropología e Historia, Mexico.)

houses of retreat, and minor structures, were all located within the walls. Outside this main center were the sumptuous palaces of the nobility, lay buildings, humble dwellings, plazas, and marketplaces, all interlaced by canals. The latter separated the different private holdings in the city. Sweet water was carried to the Great Temple by an aqueduct from Chapultepec. What a magnificent spectacle it must have been, this island-city with its painted temples and whitewashed houses gleaming in the bright valley sun. What a pity that it was so completely ruined!

In the 90-day siege against the Spaniards, many buildings were destroyed to fill in the canals. The Aztecs hurled stones and debris from temples, houses, and bridges in a desperate attempt to save their city. The battle was heroic but futile. Cortés had much more on his side than the obvious superiority of weapons. Moctezuma Xocoyotzin, who had been a student at the *calmécac,* had trained for the priesthood, and was thoroughly indoctrinated in his Toltec ancestral history, knew well the prophecy of Quetzalcóatl to return in a year Ce Acatl. Thus, when the fair and bearded Cortés arrived in Veracruz precisely in that year, who could be certain that Quetzalcóatl had not returned? In addition to the monarch's own superstitions, uncertainty, and apprehension, which were heightened by numerous bad omens, the centralized government of Tenochititlán did not extend throughout the Aztec "empire." The decisive impetus was given by the Tlaxcalans, who joined the Spaniards and contributed both their manpower and knowledge of native warfare.

It is not clear exactly how Moctezuma Xocoyotzin met his death in the year 1520, but surely he must have felt that his gods had failed him. Having welcomed the Spanish into the city, he soon found himself their prisoner. In the heat of a bloody battle in which the Spaniards were forced to flee the city and retreat to Veracruz, Moctezuma Xocoyotzin perished. He was succeeded by his brother Cuitláhuac, who ruled only 4 months and died of illness the same year. Their nephew Cuauhtémoc, the last of the Aztec kings, fought savagely in the defense of Tenochtitlán and is regarded today as a national hero. In the final death throes of Tenochtitlán, every Aztec fought valiently, persistently, but in vain. The city was shattered in the struggle and, after the battle ended, the Spaniards completed the destruction of its temples and idols to facilitate the substitution of a new order. Still not feeling completely secure, however, Cortés took Cuauhtémoc on an expedition to Honduras rather than risk leaving him behind. In the jungle country of Chiapas the last Aztec king was cruelly hanged in A.D 1524.

Archaeology   What can archaeology add to the wealth of data provided by the chroniclers? We know, for example, that the religious center of Tenochtitlán underlies the civic center of modern Mexico City. The location of the Great Temple had been known since Manuel Gamio excavated the southwest corner of the pyramidal base in 1936. In fact the whole ceremonial precinct of the Aztecs had been very carefully mapped, and Ignacio Marquina made a reconstruction of the Great Temple in 1960. For years one could look down behind the main cathedral of Mexico City and see a big carved serpent head by the edge of the base of the Great Temple. A slight rise in the street accommodated the rest of the pyramidal structure.

In February 1978 the Instituto Nacional de Antropología e Historia was notified that some unusual stones were being uncovered by workmen. This led to the discovery of a new great stone monolith and the decision to expose completely the entire twin-pyramid complex that was the Great Temple. The decision was not made lightly in view of the necessity to tear down buildings, divert traffic, and cause considerable inconvenience in the busy heart of Mexico City a block north of the Zócalo. However, thanks to the personal interest of President López Portillo, the work progressed rapidly. The scientific excavations were guided by Eduardo Matos Moctezuma and his well-trained staff of specialists.

These excavations provide a good example of the Mesoamerican custom of periodically rebuilding or renovating structures. This was done to commemorate a special calendrical or historical event, or to honor a new king. In the case of the Great Temple, there were at least four complete pyramidal structures with several additional facades. The Spaniards saw the latest structure and did their best to destroy it, along with any sculptures, paintings, and reliefs. But beneath lay earlier structures, all believed to have been basically similar. The Great Temple was a twin-pyramid complex with two staircases leading to two temples on top: To the south was the Temple of Huitzilopochtli, the war god; adjacent to it on the north was the Temple of Tlaloc, god of rain. Both temples faced west across the great ceremonial precinct (Photo 69). At the base of the stairway leading to the Temple of Huitzilopochtli was a huge stone representing Coyolxauhqui (see p. 438). It is the most spectacular single find to date, but there are other discoveries of great archaeological importance. On the east side a magnificent brazier representing Tlaloc was found beside a beautifully carved serpent head. A large stone was placed in the open serpent mouth, believed to have helped protect and preserve it when this was covered over to erect the next structure. A great many offerings have been found beneath floors of staircases or in other prominent locations in stone-lined cists. These were made as gestures of reverence by people from all parts of the Aztec empire.

Cist 1, for example, was placed beneath a stucco floor of an earlier construction. It was lined completely with black and red *tezontle* stone and measured approximately 1 m². Its contents numbered more than 800 pieces and required several months to excavate by carefully removing layer by layer of objects. Contents included copper bells; stone, shell, and turquoise beads; seated stone figures; two magnificent stone Tlaloc vases with lids, 17 flint sacrificial knives decorated with shell; 6 human skulls, some probably decapitated; a beautifully polished obsidian mace; turquoise mosaics; human skulls with lateral openings for the insertion of *tzompantli* poles; many shells; vegetal fibers; and plant remains. Earplugs of shell were decorated with turquoise. All of this rested on a bed of fine sand with great amounts of fish scales, bone, and bird remains. Faunal remains included crocodiles, a complete fish, eagle, and jaguar, corals, and marine objects from the Gulf of Mexico, the Caribbean, and the Pacific Coast. A large green stone figure (another Coyolxauhqui ?) and 8 other figures were found leaning against the pyramid. Great quantities of pottery await study, along with the identification of plant, fauna, and marine specimens of all kinds.

South of the Great Temple is a small shrine containing a round altar (?). The walls are beautifully painted in a red and white geometric design, topped by large stone rings also painted red.

Of particular interest are the remains of the earliest temple, for superstructures are rarely found in this area. Inside, the base that supported the wooden cult statue of Huitzilopochtli can still be seen, while before him at the top of the stairs, the sacrificial stone was found *in situ*. In this case it is a simple slab of *tezontle,* about 45 cm in height, over which the victim was arched to have his heart torn out. In the adjacent Temple of Tlaloc, in place of the sacrificial stone, reclines a well preserved *chacmool.* The entrance to the sanctuary is flanked by two stone pillars still gaily painted in stripes and human figures. The most sacred area contains a long bench on which the cult statue of Tlaloc stood.

Well over half the small stone figures and carvings from these excavations come from the State of Guerrero, and are those commonly associated with the Mezcala style. Other exotic finds include a gorgeous green jade jaguar; many representations of Xiuhtecuhtli, the fire god, seated with his arms folded, and innumerable Tlalocs with inlaid eyes of shell and obsidian. There is surprisingly little metal of any sort; copper is scant and gold is extremely rare. Once again the Great Temple of Tenochtitlán has become the center of pilgrimages of sorts, attracting Mexicans and foreigners alike to see the ancient pyramids and the great Coyolxauhqui.

Across the city, the ruins of Tlatelolco, including part of its great temple, can be seen. Literally tons of stone sculpture, pottery, and artifacts of all kinds have poured out of each freshly dug foundation and street construction as well as from the excavations for the Metro, which passes through the heart of the ancient capital. Tenochtitlán lies hopelessly beyond the possibility of restoration, but, from reading the Spanish accounts and visiting the ruins today, it is easier to visualize the great metropolis.

In addition, there are numerous remains of the Aztecs' ancient contemporaries from surrounding sites such as Tenayuca, Tezcotzingo, Calixtlahuaca, Teotenango, Malinalco, Teopanzolco, Tepozteco, and Cholula. These give an excellent idea of the final Mesoamerican construction and are easily accessible today from Mexico City.

Tenayuca, that old settlement of Xólotl near the modern town of Tlalnepantla, was enlarged many times (Photo 70). The temple's final construction with a double staircase was probably very similar to that of the main temple of Tenochtitlán. Three sides of this pyramid are encircled by a *coatepantli* consisting of once brightly colored coiled serpents made of mortar with great carved heads. Two large fire serpents with crested heads are coiled on either side of the stairways. Only 3 km away is the small pyramid of Santa Cecilia, completely restored even to the stone temple on top. It is one of the finest visible examples of Late Postclassic architecture (Photo 71).

Calixtlahuaca in the Valley of Toluca, home of the Matlatzinca, was a center closely allied first to the Tepanecs and then to the Aztecs. Particularly outstanding is a round structure believed to have been dedicated to Quetzalcóatl as the wind god, Ehécatl. Axayácatl, ruler of the Aztecs, swept through the area in A.D. 1474 and 2 years later had added Calixtlahuaca, Teotenango, and Malinalco to the Aztec tribute rolls. Teotenango could not have been an easy prey located as it is high above the valley (see Photo 60, p. 377). The tremendous amount of construction that is visible today represents only one-fourth of the

PHOTO 70. Pyramid of Tenayuca, Tlalnepantla. (Courtesy of the Instituto Nacional de Antropología e Historia, Mexico.)

PHOTO 71. Restored pyramid and temple of Santa Cecilia at Tenayuca. (Courtesy of the Instituto Nacional de Antropología e Historia, Mexico.)

archaeological remains. There are few structures built by the Aztecs. Elite graves have yielded rich offerings of obsidian, rock crystal, turquoise, gold, and copper. After the city fell to the Aztecs in 1476, energy was devoted to keeping their tribute installments up to date.

Southeast of Toluca near the modern town of Tenancingo is Malinalco, which was also incorporated into the Aztec domain. Its unique main temple was actually hewn out of the bedrock of the mountainside. Jaguar sculptures flank the main staircase, which leads to a circular chamber through a doorway shaped like the jaws of a serpent. The interior shrine resembles the *kiva* (ceremonial chamber) of the southwestern United States in several features. A low bench was built into the circular wall. On it was the sculptured stone skin of a jaguar flanked by stone eagle skins. In the center of the floor is another sculpted eagle

PLATE 13. Aztec-period vessels.

a. Cholula polychrome vessel with ring stand. Height: 24 cm. (Courtesy of the Museum of the American Indian, Heye Foundation, N.Y. [16/3394].)

b. Polychrome goblet with humming bird, Tomb 2, Zaachila, Oaxaca. Height: 9 cm. (Courtesy of the Museo Nacional de Antropología, Mexico.)

c. Onyx monkey-effigy vessel with inlaid obsidian eyes, Isla de Sacrificios, Veracruz. Height: 13 cm. (Courtesy of the Museo Nacional de Antropología, Mexico.)

d. Onyx tripod vessel, Isla de Sacrificios, Veracruz. Height: 22 cm. (Courtesy of the Museo Nacional de Antropología, Mexico.)

e. Tlaloc brazier, central Veracruz: Late Postclassic. Height: 152 cm. (Courtesy of the Museo Nacional de Antropología, Mexico.)

f. Red-ware "teapot" vessel with stirrup-spout handle, Michoacán: Tarascan culture. Height: 20 cm. (Courtesy of the Museum of the American Indian, Heye Foundation, N.Y. [24/3025].)

g. Black-on-white spouted vessel, Veracruz: Huasteca culture. Height: 19 cm. (Courtesy of the Museum of the American Indian, Heye Foundation, N.Y. [66/46].)

433

with outspread wings that looks out the door. Sculptures of eagles, jaguars, and serpents abound. Malinalco was a very holy place, and to judge from its unique features, it must have been a very special Aztec shrine.

In the state of Morelos, another twin-pyramid can be seen at Teopanzolco, across the tracks from the railroad station at Cuernavaca. But far more spectacular, because of its setting, is the simple pyramid of Tepozteco, which clings to the cliffs overlooking the village of Tepoztlán.

In addition to the Aztec ruins themselves, small objects used in daily living as well as a vast array of ceremonial paraphernalia have been unearthed (Plate 13). Díaz del Castillo (1944) mentions that multicolored pottery vessels were especially favored by the rulers. We know that this reference is to the famous Cholula polychrome or Mixteca–Puebla ware (Figure 34-a,b,c,d,f; Plate 13-a,b). The plates, goblets, bowls, cups,

FIGURE 34. Ceramics of Late Postclassic period. (a), (b), (c), (d), (f) Cholula polychrome; (e) red-on-white bowl, skull-and-crossbones motif; (g) polished black-on-red pitcher; (h) black-on-red goblet; (i) black-on-orange *molcajete;* (j) black-on-orange tripod; (k) monochrome unslipped censer, with a circular central vent in the base, Burial 5, Tikal; (l) Ixpop polychrome tripod vessel, rattle supports, surface debris, Temple II, Tikal; (m) black-on-white vessel, Huasteca culture. (From the following sources: a, Piña Chán 1960; b, d, Noguera 1965; c, Noguera 1950; e, Covarrubias 1957, redrawn from *Indian Art of Mexico and Central America,* by Miguel Covarrubias, copyright © 1957 by Alfred A. Knopf, Inc., reprinted by permission of the publisher; f, g, Toscano 1952; h, j, m, Marquina 1951; i, Museum of the American Indian, Heye Foundation, N.Y. [8/8694]; k, l, Adams and Trik 1961, The Tikal Project, The University Museum, University of Pennsylvania.)

and pitchers are truly worthy of royalty. Although these prized wares were manufactured either by Mixteca–Puebla residents of Tenochtitlán or imported from their eastern homeland, the Aztecs also made great quantities of a well-fired pottery decorated in black on orange. The tripod forms, plates, and pitchers made by earlier groups were continued, but supports now were either thin solid slabs or sharp spikes. *Molcajetes* with deeply scored interiors are common (Figure 34-i). A fine, highly polished red ware sometimes decorated in black is very characteristic. Stamps (Plate 14-j), smoking pipes (Plate 14-g), *malacates* (Plate 11-b, p. 370), and mold-made figurines representing deities (Plate 14-h) were all very standardized and produced in great quantities. The finest wares are the imports of which many, such as elaborate long-handled censers (Figure 30-l, p. 372) were designed strictly for ceremonial use.

Art and Iconography

The greatest artistic expression of the Aztecs was achieved in stone carving. It is here that symbolism is seen as an important dimension in Mesoamerican art. The free-standing figures of Aztec deities are true idols (Photo 72). Many insignia of the deities are just beginning to be understood, and they can usually be identified by the face, headdress or clothing, and posture. Facial painting seems to be diagnostic: Blue with horizonal and yellow stripes identifies Huitzilopochtli; black with horizontal lines indicates Tezcatlipoca; vertical lines through the eyes may be Xipe Totec or Ehécatl–Quetzalcóatl; a white butterfly motif around the mouth is characteristic of Xochipilli (Nicholson 1973). Ear and nose ornaments, pectorals, and objects held such as shields all help identification. Female figures are shown kneeling (Photo 73) whereas male figures often with ankles crossed, sit on stools. Stone sculpture falls into two very distinct groups: (1) colossal sculptures made for temples, such as the Calendar Stone, the Stone of Tízoc, the Stone of Coyolxauhqui; and (2) smaller deity images that personified nature, spirits, and objects of all kinds. These were very popular, less well crafted, and possibly mass produced (Nicholson 1973; Pasztory 1979).

Earlier cultures depicted their gods in ceramics and in mural paintings. There are large clay sculptures from Oaxaca, Veracruz, and central Mexico. But the Aztecs were seemingly obsessed with representing deities and documenting important events to last an eternity, so they initiated great free-standing sculptures in stone. This is partly explained by their ignoble background. They heard tales of the brilliant and clever Toltecs who could excel in any field. They made pilgrimages to make offerings at the revered ancient site of Teotihuacán, which, though in ruins, must still have been very impressive. They clung to Toltec myths, loudly proclaiming a Toltec heritage but nonetheless vividly remembering their humble beginnings in the Basin of Mexico, and were anxious to leave a fine permanent record of their achievements in stone.

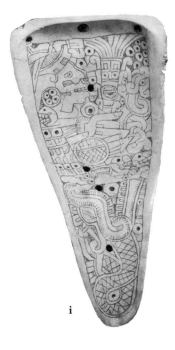

i

j

PLATE 14. Miscellaneous small artifacts of the Postclassic period.

a. Obsidian lip plugs or labrets, showing front, lateral, and interior surfaces, Aztec culture. Length: 3 cm. (Courtesy of the Metropolitan Museum of Art, The Michael C. Rockefeller Memorial Collection of Primitive Art, Bequest of Nelson A. Rockefeller, 1979.)

b. Ground obsidian ear spool associated with grave, Tzintizuntzan, Michocán. Maximum diameter: 5.7 cm. (Courtesy of the Museo Nacional de Antropología, Mexico.)

c. Pair of obsidian ear plugs: Aztec culture. Height each: 3 cm. (Courtesy of the Metropolitan Museum of Art, The Michael C. Rockefeller Memorial Collection of Primitive Art, Bequest of Nelson A. Rockefeller, 1979.)

d. Necklace of pink shell beads, Oaxaca. Bead diameter: 3 mm. (Courtesy of the Museo Nacional de Antropología, Mexico.)

e. Necklace of rock crystal beads: Mixtec culture. Maximum bead diameter: 1.8 cm. (Courtesy of the Museo Nacional de Antropología, Mexico.)

f. Carved jaguar bone: Mixtec culture. Length: 13 cm. (Courtesy of the Museo Nacional de Antropología, Mexico.)

g. Aztec polished red clay pipe, Federal District of Mexico. Height: 7 cm. (Courtesy of the Metropolitan Museum of Art, The Michael C. Rockefeller Memorial Collection of Primitive Art, Bequest of Nelson A. Rockefeller, 1979).

h. Mold-made clay figurine. Valley of Mexico: Aztec culture. Height: 15 cm. (Courtesy of the Museum of the American Indian, Heye Foundation, N.Y. [22/1025].)

i. Conch-shell pendant, carved in design of warrior. Veracruz: Huastec culture. Length: 16 cm. (Courtesy of the Museum of the American Indian, Heye Foundation, N.Y. [23/9573].)

j. Clay stamps or seals. Dimensions of specimen on right: 5 × 6 cm. (Courtesy of the Museum of the American Indian, Heye Foundation, N.Y. [left: 23/5490, right: 23/5489].)

437

PHOTO 72. (*Left*) Stone statue of Xipe Totec, Tlalpan, Valley of Mexico. Height: 76 cm. (Courtesy of the Museum of the American Indian, Heye Foundation, N.Y. [16/3621].)

PHOTO 73. (*Right*) Aztec water goddess, Chalchihuitlicue. Height: 66 cm. (Courtesy of the Trustees of the British Museum.)

Moctezuma I may have been the first king of Tenochtitlán to conceive the idea of having his portrait carved on the stone cliffs at Chapultepec. Durán (1967) tells how he commissioned two figures to be carved, himself and that of Tlacaélel. Upon completion he declared his greatness would be as lasting as that of Topiltzin Quetzalcóatl. Moctezuma II also added his image to the Chapultepec cliffs (Nicholson 1961b). Unfortunately these are now barely visible. It is amusing that the Aztecs themselves carved the image of Topiltzin Quetzalcóatl at Tula in an effort to provide a parallel dynastic image with which to associate their tradition (Keber 1979).

Eventually huge stone sculptures were commissioned to commemorate great victories such as the defeat of Azcapotzalco, or the inauguration of a new ruler. Examples of these are the famous Coatlícue, the Stone of Tizoc, the Jaguar Sacrificial stone, and Coyolxauhqui. The latter, mentioned before, found *in situ* before the Temple of Huitzilopochtli in the Great Temple, is an 8 ton sculptured stone representing the Aztec moon goddess, sister of Huitzilopochtli (Garcia Cook and Araña 1978) (Photo 74). It was found in a horizontal position on the landing of the temple. The almost circular sculpture is approximately

PHOTO 74. Aztec sculptured monolith representing a dismembered Coyolxauhqui, moon goddess. Found *in situ* at base of stairs leading to the Temple of Huitzilopochtli, Tenochtitlán. Diameter: 3.26 m. (Courtesy of the Museo Nacional de Antropología, Mexico.)

3.26 m in greatest diameter with a depth varying between 5 and 8 cm. Only the top surface is sculptured, and this is done in deep relief. It was once painted red. The andesite stone could have come from the northern part of the Basin of Mexico. In a marvelous state of preservation, defaced only by a single crack, probably due to settling in place, the relief represents a female creature (Coyolxauhqui) who has been dismembered and decapitated. Another famous representation of Coyolxauhqui, in the National Museum of Anthropology in Mexico City, consists of just the decapitated head, beautifully executed in polished green diorite. The Aztecs liked to see their deities and have them about in their temples and sacred places, so scores of gods and goddesses were realistically sculptured in their various aspects (Photos 72 and 73).

The famous so-called Calendar Stone, a relief carving nearly 4 m wide, is actually a representation of the sun god who emerges from the underworld out of the central symbol for 4 Earthquake (movement), the date on which, according to legend (Codex Chimalpopoca 1945), this world will end with an earthquake. According to Klein (1976) the central figure is actually the night/dead sun; according to Navarrete and Heyden (1974) and Townsend (1979) it is the face of the earth. 4 Jaguar, 4 Wind, 4 Rain, and 4 Water, each responsible for a disaster wiping out former worlds, are also represented, and all of this is enclosed by a band of the 20 day signs, solar symbols, and two fire-serpents. Unnoticed by most observers in the midst of the complex relief are dates of 13 Reed and 1 Flint, along with a noncalendrical glyph identified as the name of Moctezuma II. Townsend (1979) and Umberger (1979) demonstrate the complexities of Aztec iconography in tracing the various meanings of 13 Reed and 1 Flint. The style and hieroglyphs lead Umberger to believe the stone was commissioned in the days of Moctezuma II to celebrate some great event like the defeat of the Tepanecs in the year 1 Flint, A.D. 1428. The combination of hieroglyphs denote at the same time several other meanings for the date 1 Flint such as the beginning of the Aztec migration, the name of Huitzilopochtli, and a day of great ceremony. The Calendar Stone is believed to have been a sacrificial stone, placed horizontally somewhere in the main ceremonial center of Tenochtitlán. It is an excellent example of the interlacing of semimythical tribal history with actual events.

Another monumental stone is that of Tízoc, carved to validate his rule (Townsend 1979). (See also Wicke 1976.) Around the edge of the great wheel-like stone is Tízoc himself, identified by his name glyph, as he leans toward another figure that he grabs by the hair, signifying the figure's capture. There are 15 nearly identical scenes of paired figures that in effect publicize Aztec conquests up to his time (Wicke 1976). This stone was found in 1791 when repaving the Zócalo of Mexico City. The central hollow on the top and a groove leading to the edge are post-Aztec mutilations of some sort.

Atlantean figures and *chacmools*, a survival of Toltec art forms, continued to be carved. The latter often represent Tlaloc and are characteristically more elaborate than the known Toltec examples. Pre-Aztec *chacmools* had no deity association. With the lapse of time involved, the Aztecs probably knew no more about the meaning of the figure than we do. They ascribed to it their own view of Toltec beliefs. So for them, Tlaloc was a Toltec deity who represented the glorious past they wanted to perpetuate (Pasztory 1979). After a rather subdued role under the Toltecs, Tlaloc became elevated to the highest rank of Aztec deities and shared honors with Huitzilopochtli in the Great Temple. During the 1978 excavations of this structure, the most gorgeous *chacmool* of Mesoamerica was found—gorgeous because not only is he carefully carved, but he is brilliantly painted in red, blue, white, and black. Perfectly preserved, the only discordant note is his lumpy nose of black bitumen (*chapopote*). Reclining *in situ* at the top of the stairs of Tlaloc's temple, he gazes today out over the excavations that have replaced his earlier view of the great ceremonial precinct of Tenochtitlán. Located precisely in the place of the sacrificial stone, he might have supported Tlaloc's victims while the priests performed their gory duty.

Although most sculptures are life size or even larger, there are a series of smaller outstanding carvings of coyotes, serpents, grasshoppers, and plant forms. All have a religious connotation and were probably cult objects placed in sacred areas, for Aztec art was highly symbolic and the gods often assumed animal forms. There are also stone blocks, perhaps used as pedestals, and stone boxes. Even wooden drums (*huéhuetl*) and the *xiuhmolpilli* or year bundle (representing the completion of a 52-year cycle) were copied in stone. We know that these were also carved in wood and buried. As Nicholson (1973) has pointed out, friezes and panels, popular among earlier peoples, were rare. Symbolism and freestanding sculpture characterizes Aztec art.

For craftsmanship in textiles, wood, and feathers, one must rely on descriptions rather than actual specimens. We know that feathers were worked into cloaks and shields and were highly valued. A few weathered examples have survived in European museums, but the selection cannot possibly be representative of what once existed. Some beautiful wooden drums, undoubtedly made for ceremonial use, have been preserved. Wooden drums were of two kinds. One was the *huéhuetl*, a vertical drum over the top of which a skin was stretched (see Photo 43, p. 312). It was played with the palms and fingers like an Afro-Cuban bongo drum. The other, the *teponaztli*, was a horizontal cylinder in the top of which one or two tongues of wood were carved (Plate 15-f). These tongues were struck with sticks, the points of which were covered with rubber. The different length of the tongues produced different sonorous and penetrating sounds. Some of these were beautifully carved with religious motifs and were probably sacred instruments. Small drums made of pottery are also known. Music also was made by striking a turtle shell with splinters of deer bone. Rattles, copper bells, bone rasps, conch-shell trumpets, pan pipes, whistles, and *ocarinas*, along with various kinds of simple and composite flutes, were all utilized in honoring the gods. Music was probably not used for aesthetic enjoyment; rather, it constituted one of the emotional props in religious fanaticism. No funeral procession, ritual, or warfare took place without its appropriate musical setting (Plate 15) (Martí 1968).

The very finest gold work is usually attributed to the gifted Mixtecs of northwestern Oaxaca, who perfected the "lost wax," or *cire perdue*, method of gold working to produce the greatest masterpieces of this

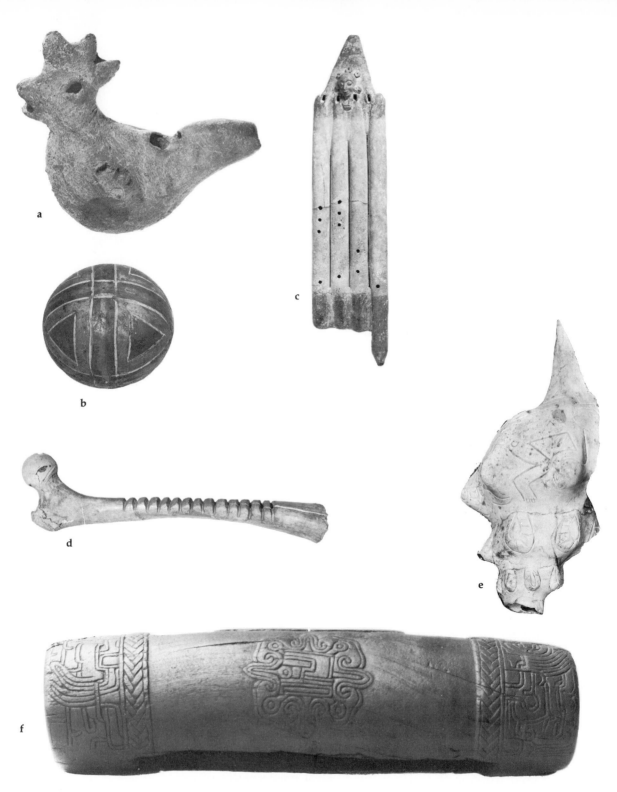

type in the New World. The labrets and ear spools, beads, nose and breast ornaments, pendants, and rings made by these skilled metal-lurgists are nothing short of exquisite. Pearls, jade, turquoise, amber, rock crystal, and amethyst were combined with gold or obsidian. Even ceremonial vessels might be fashioned of jade or rock crystal. The famed Tomb 7 of Monte Albán yielded some of the finest grave goods of this type ever recovered in the New World (Caso 1965a). The use of copper and silver was less spectacular but these metals were also worked into jewelry. (See Plate 16, pp. 464–465.)

With the possible exception of those made by the Tarascans, who excelled in copper and bronze work, tools had changed but slightly since Preclassic days. The digging stick, *manos* and *metates*, bark beaters, pounders, and obsidian blades, knives, and scrapers remained standard equipment.

Social Structure

When one king died, the next was elected from the royal lineage by a council composed of nobles, titled warriors, and important priests. Although the council gathered to "elect" a new king, the foregoing genealogical chart (p. 421) illustrates how tightly the reins of succession were held, usually passing from brother to brother before descending to the following generation. The hereditary nobility, from which the king was chosen, reckoned its descent from the Toltecs and enjoyed certain privileges not shared by others. The king claimed that he was selected by the god Tezcatlipoca and was the god's representative on earth. Furthermore, he claimed descent from deified ancestors, not real ones. As might be expected, the king had special insignia and the finest clothing. He, as well as his own court, was permitted to have many wives and to send his male children to the *calmécac*, a strict, elite school for sons of the nobility, where formal education was given in the arts

---

PLATE 15. Mesoamerican music.
a. Clay whistle in the form of a bird, Tlatilco. Length: 10 cm. (Photographed by Spence Gustav. Author's collection.)
b. Rattle in the shape of a game ball, Tlacotepec, Toluca Valley. Diameter: 9 cm. (Courtesy of the Museum of the American Indian, Heye Foundation, N. Y. [8/8752].)
c. Pottery pan pipes, Tabasco, Mexico. Length: 57 cm. (Courtesy of the Museum of the American Indian, Heye Foundation, N.Y. [23/902].)
d. *Omichicahuaztli* (bone rasp) made of human femur, Valley of Mexico. Length: 26 cm. (Courtesy of the Museum of the American Indian, Heye Foundation, N.Y. [2/6719].)
e. Incised conch-shell trumpet, Oaxaca: Mixtec culture. Length: 24 cm. (Courtesy of the Museum of the American Indian, Heye Foundation, N.Y. [22/6377].)
f. Carved wooden *teponaztli* drum, Axzotla, Puebla. The base is hollowed out and the top is slitted to form two tongues. Length: 44 cm. (Courtesy of the Museum of the American Indian, Heye Foundation, N.Y. [16/3373].)

and sciences, but with emphasis being placed on basic religious instruction. There were six such institutions in Tenochtitlán; at these schools much time was devoted to sacrifice, prayers, ritual purification, bloodletting, and autosacrifice, wherein the students pierced their ears and tongues with the sharp spines of the maguey. These young boys became the *pillis* and *tecuhtlis,* a privileged group including the king (*tlatoani*), from which people were chosen to occupy posts as governors, ministers of justice, and coordinators. This group owned land but did not work it themselves. Although they formed a hereditary nobility, another group of nobility was eventually created. A warrior who distinguished himself in battle might be singled out for honors and thus be elevated to a special nobility, freed from his *calpulli* and the requirement to work its lands. There is some indication that this neo-nobility was somewhat in conflict with the hereditary one (Monzón 1949). The crucial step that provided the *pillis* with economic as well as political power was the resounding defeat of the Tepanecs. Only then did the Aztecs gain mainland acreage and begin their rise to political power.

Commoners and laborers who made up the bulk of the population were, of course, very poor. They were free commoners with direct access to land of the state which they could use but not own, for they could not pass it on to their heirs. If they distinguished themselves in commercial enterprises or on the battlefield, they might be rewarded with certain privileges and thus improve their social position. The ruler might bestow on one the right to dedicate a captive for sacrifice, the right to wear a special insignia on his cloak, or jewelry. They had only one wife each, and their meager belongings consisted of stones for grinding corn, a *petate* to sleep on, and the clothes they wore. Their male children might attend the *telpochcalli* schools, of which there was one in each district of Tenochtitlán. These schools did not produce leaders. They turned out Aztec citizens who learned what their place was in society and how to be good citizens and warriors (Bray 1977c). This was a popular school, less severe than the *calmecac.* Boys were instructed in the arts of warfare and were given some religious training. There were other schools that taught dance, song, and the playing of musical instruments, but all were basically religious in orientation. Girls were educated in separate schools receiving instruction in domestic arts as well as in religion.

Another social group was the *mayeques,* or bondsmen, often called slaves. They worked the land of others but could neither own or inherit land. Of these there were different categories and for some the status was only temporary. A person might voluntarily go into slavery or temporarily place his children in bondage to pay off a debt. Women and children captured in war were treated as slaves, as were criminals, who were sometimes forced to work for the family they had offended.

The *mayeques* were used as beasts of burden, but their children were free. This was a special fluctuating social category. As a servile group, they worked the lands of the *pillis*.

Much has been written about the *calpulli*, which originally was a kind of tribal organization, but came to mean a barrio or district. The 20 *calpullis* in Tenochtitlán seem to have been based on kin groups or clans with endogamous tendencies; thus, they were permanent, land-holding groups with hereditary headmen. Not all *calpullis* had equal status; some owned more land than others and embraced all kinds of people (Monzón 1949). It functioned as a corporate body, owning land and paying taxes. The exact role of the *calpulli* is not clearly understood and it apparently underwent changes. There seems to have been a tendency for certain craft specializations to be associated with particular *calpullis*.

Law and Justice

At the time of the Conquest, the highest authority was, of course, the king himself, who was considered to be semidivine and so supreme that only those of the very highest rank were permitted to look at him directly. When approaching the king, one had first to touch the ground and then his mouth with his hand, a sign of humility and reverence. The king ate alone and received visitors and foreign dignitaries only after they had removed their sandals and covered their fine clothes with a humble maguey fiber cape. The king was carried about in a litter and did not touch his foot to the earth. How many changes had taken place since the first unwanted Aztecs had straggled into the Valley of Mexico under the command of their tribal leader!

A complex juridical system grew out of early customs and was probably influenced by Nezahuacóyotl, king of nearby Texcoco, whose far-reaching code of law has been preserved (Ixtlilxóchitl 1952). Aztec law dealt with all aspects of human relations—civil, criminal, and legal matters as well as foreign affairs of the state. The entire structure of the legal system was taught at the *calmécac*.

The advisory position of *cihuacóatl* (Snake Woman) was originally one of considerable power with administrative and juridical authority. Probably the most famous *cihuacóatl* was Tlacaélel who served as advisor to Moctezuma Ilhuicamina, and participated in all major decisions. However, thereafter the monarch's power increased and the position of *cihuacóatl* gradually declined in importance. One of the chief duties of the *cihuacóatl* was to preside over a supreme court, which was composed of four judges. A very difficult case could be referred to the king who was the ultimate authority. He was aided by 13 wise men who formed a special high court that met about every 12 days. Their verdict was passed on to the king who then pronounced judgment. There were also lower courts of justice, provincial courts, and a kind of local judge in each town. Sahagún (1946) stresses that these offices were filled from the ranks of well-qualified nobles, who had been educated in the *calmécac*.

Because of the nature of Aztec law, there was little need for jails or prisons. Most crimes were punished by some kind of death: flogging, sacrifice, decapitation, or by being placed in slavery either temporarily or for life, depending on the nature of the offense. Small wooden cages housed those who committed minor crimes. If Aztec law seems brutal today, it was clearly understood by the society that the law-abiding citizen was protected and could feel secure under the justice of the land. The law was harsh, yet it contained certain rather charming exceptions. For example, stealing corn was punishable by death, but a person in need was permitted to help himself to four ears from those rows planted along the road for his immediate use without castigation. An interesting concept of Aztec law was that the severity of punishment was measured in accordance with the offender's station in life. A high priest would be put to death for a crime that might be tolerated if committed by a bondsman. That is, a man of high office assumed greater moral responsibilities and his conduct was expected to be beyond reproach. Laws were designed to preserve the family, the society, and the state. Nobles had the right to defend themselves and be heard in private, but they were duly punished if found guilty. Under no circumstance was the individual permitted to take action or settle a dispute on his own. The state only was authorized to make decisions and mete out punishment.

A good law-abiding Aztec was careful about his conduct and was anxious to do what was right and appropriate as well as gain approval of others. He wanted to be highly regarded, but his conduct on earth was in no way connected with a belief in reward or punishment after death (León-Portilla 1963).

Religion

To understand the Aztec attitude toward many of their activities and the functioning of their society, it is necessary to know something of their religious beliefs. Indeed, commerce, warfare, and religion were the most time-consuming occupations of the Aztecs. Because all aspects of a functioning society are interrelated and integrated, it is impossible to discuss one feature as an isolated entity. It is necessary, for example, to realize that warfare was both a privilege and duty of every able-bodied man and was carefully reinforced by religious beliefs. After important battles honors and titles were handed out for bravery or for capturing four or five prisoners; in this way nobility could be achieved. Every young man was considered to be a potential warrior dedicated to providing prisoners of war for sacrifice. The sacrifice of human hearts was the "food" necessary to sustain the sun in its daily flight across the sky, and was not the sun necessary to life itself?

Aztec religion with over 200 deities, each with multiple forms, seems to us an exaggerated polytheism (Caso 1958). Full of fear, dread, and apprehension, the Aztec mirrored in their gods their own preoccupation with magic and divination and forces of good and evil. With the exception of Nezahuacóyotl's Tloque Nahuaque, the multitude of gods were represented in human form and were felt to have human problems and weaknesses. The war god, Huitzilopochtli, was the Aztecs' own tribal god and one of the most important deities. Like Quetzalcóatl, Tezcatlipoca, and Mixcóatl, who are so familiar to us from the chronicles, the deities are seldom represented materially. Pasztory points out (1976b) that these gods were venerated largely by the elite and had no popular cults. If these main deities were only represented as cult statues in temples, they were rapidly destroyed by the Spanish. In the case of Huitzilopochtli, this was not difficult as his main idol was of wood. Every spring when the festival in his honor came around, a huge idol of his likeness was made of dough. Great quantities of amaranth (*huauhtli*) were combined with toasted maize, kneaded with honey, and made into a life-sized statue. This was carried on a litter all about Tenochtitlán, even to the suburbs before being returned to the temple, broken up and eaten as flesh and bones of Huitzilopochtli, the only food consumed that day. Everyone participating, which was the whole populace including secular and religious officials, had to give a tithe of amaranth. This event is described in the Codex Ramirez and by Sahagún and discussed at length by Sauer (1950).

In general, Aztec religion had great flexibility and a unique capacity to embrace deities of both ancestral peoples and contemporaries. Thus the ancient gods of fire (Huehuéteotl), rain and water (Tlaloc), springtime (Xipe Totec), and the feathered serpent (Quetzalcóatl) still occupied important roles, although their meaning and symbolism may well have undergone reinterpretations (Figure 35). For example, we have seen how the Aztecs associated the *chacmool* with Tlaloc, and Quetzalcóatl is featured as priestlike, pacific, and religious in contrast to his earlier record at Tula (Keber 1979).

Tezcatlipoca (Smoking Mirror) is familiar from Toltec days as the adversary of Quetzalcóatl. His talisman was the smoking mirror which often takes the place of a foot in representations of him (Figure 35). By gazing into this mirror he could predict events. He was eventually assimilated into the religious beliefs of Tloque Nahuaque, chief deity of Texcoco, where he emerged as a very civilized god opposed to human sacrifice! No idols have been found of him (Townsend 1979). Under the Aztecs, Tezcatlipoca had perhaps the greatest variety of attributes and prerogatives. He was intimately associated with the night and therefore the stars and moon, but he also had affinities with death, evil, and destruction. Eternally young, he was the patron deity of magicians and robbers. The overlapping of roles of this and other deities

FIGURE 35. Aztec deities. *Tlaloc*, the god of rain and lightning, probably one of the oldest gods; known as Chac among the Maya, Tzahui among the Mixtecs, and Cocijo among the Zapotecs. *Xipe Totec*, the Flayed One, god of planting, springtime, and jewelers; in his honor, victims were flayed and their skins worn by a priest. He is also the red Tezcatlipoca. *Quetzalcóatl*, the feathered-serpent deity, god of learning and the priesthood. He is also god of life, the morning, the planet Venus, and twins and monsters. In various aspects, he may be called Ehécatl, Tlahuizcalpantecuhtli, Ce Acatl, or Xólotl. *Tezcatlipoca*, the Smoking Mirror, appears in many forms. He is associated with the nocturnal sky, the moon, and the forces of evil, death, and destruction. (From the following sources: Tlaloc, Codex Telleriano-Remensis 1889; Xipe Totec, Codex Borbónico 1899; Quetzalcóatl, Codex Fejéváry-Mayer, 1830–1848; Tezcatlipoca, Stone of Tizoc, drawn after Tozzer 1957, courtesy of the Peabody Museum, Harvard University, copyright © 1957 by the President and Fellows of Harvard College.)

sometimes seems a hopeless jumble. For example, Tezcatlipoca of the east was red and associated with Xipe, while Huitzilopochtli, both war and sun god, was at the same time the blue Tezcatlipoca of the south. The white Tezcatlipoca of the west was one form of Quetzalcóatl. The night deity, of course, was none other than a northern black Tezcatlipoca.

Much confusion arises because one god could appear in different forms. Quetzalcóatl, for example, might be the wind god, god of life, god of the morning, the planet Venus, or god of twins and monsters, and he could only be recognized by particular attributes that distinguish his various names: Ehécatl, Tlahuizcalpantecuhtli, Xólotl, or Ce Acatl. Toltec history is bound up with legends of Quetzalcóatl, and we suspect that the Aztecs revitalized Tula; there they expanded the ancient confines of the city and revered it as the city of Quetzalcóatl. We know too that after A.D. 1200 he was honored as the patron deity of Cholula.

It is difficult for us to understand the complexities of Aztec religion if we try to visualize the deities as distinct entities, which they were not. The concept of duality, the forces of good and evil being represented by different aspects of the same deity, was a common feature of this religion. Common people busied themselves with satisfying their immediate household deities and looked to the priests for guidance, interpretation, words of caution, and advice in such religious matters.

All Aztecs were aware that they were living under the constant threat of doomsday, which they tried to ward off as long as possible by human sacrifices. Although many cultures have some kind of blood sacrifice, there is probably no historical parallel that can be made to the attitude of the Aztecs, expressed in such acts as the slaughter of 20,000 victims at the dedication of the Great Temple of Tenochtitlán under Axayácatl. How was it possible to create this state of mind?

The beliefs surrounding Quetzalcóatl and Huitzilopochtli are good examples of the fanatic Aztec preoccupation with war, blood, and death, into which every child was indoctrinated from birth. Quetzalcóatl, god of air and life, went down to the underworld and, gathering up all the bones of past generations, sprinkled them with his own blood, and thus recreated humanity. Since man's very existence depended on the gods, he had to ensure their well-being by providing them with human sacrifices, which supplied that magic substance of life found only in blood and human hearts.

In his aspect as the sun, Huitzilopochtli is a young warrior and is born every morning in the womb of the earth and who dies every night to illuminate the underworld of the dead. Each morning the young warrior, armed with his fire serpent, has to fight off his sister, the moon, and his brothers, the stars. By winning this daily struggle, he ensures a new day of life for man. Victorious, he is borne to the center of the heavens by the souls of those glorious warriors who have had the good fortune to perish either in battle or on the sacrificial block. In the afternoon, the souls of women who died in childbirth, that is, in giving their lives for a warrior, carry the sun to the west, where he is now visualized as an eagle who falls and dies, only to be gathered up by the earth. This daily struggle of Huitzilopochtli was the Aztecs' struggle, for they were the people of the sun, chosen to be warriors. From birth, children learned that their reason for existence was to prepare for the sacred war necessary to nourish Huitzilopochtli. Thus, man's collaboration with the gods was indispensable.

Several types of sacrifices were performed. Most common was that of stretching a victim over a convex sacrificial stone at the entrance to the temple, where four priests held the limbs while the fifth made a sharp slice through the chest and, reaching in, wrenched out the still palpitating heart. Placed in a special stone eagle vase, or *cuauhxicalli*, it was burned for the gods' consumption. Flaying the victim was a sacrifice performed in honor of Xipe Totec. Another form was a "gladiatorial combat" in which the prisoner, tied to a gigantic stone, was forced to defend himself with a wooden club against Aztec warriors armed with obsidian-edged swords. Occasionally his defense was so excellent that the victim was spared. A special sacrifice involved tying the prisoner to a wooden frame and shooting him with arrows. Both the gladiatorial combat and arrow sacrifice were Chichimec customs that were brought into vogue with the Aztecs (Historia Tolteca–Chichimeca 1947). Whatever form was chosen, however, the sacrifice was always carried out to nourish the gods and for the eternal glorification of the Aztecs.

Religion touched almost every aspect of Aztec society. Art, of course, was almost exclusively of a religious and symbolic nature, and religious instruction was an integral part of education for both sexes. Even games were played under divine guidance. Sahagún tells us that the two ball courts in Tenochtitlán were dedicated to the sun and the moon. The game *tlachtli* had been known in some form for probably 2000 years, and a match always met with enthusiastic anticipation. Which side would the gods favor? All knew that the decision was made in the heavens.

The game of *patolli* also had religious overtones and was played under the auspices of the god of games. *Patolli* is surprisingly like the game of pachisi (or the modern Parcheesi), which spread to the Western world from India. Both are played on a similar cross-shaped board with safety zones and progression of counters. We have already noted (p. 368) that this game was known to the Teotihuacanos, Toltecs, and Maya. The Aztecs used marked beans instead of dice. Many years ago the striking similarities caught the attention of one of the early anthropologists, Edward B. Tylor; this set off a lively discussion of the principles of diffusion as a cultural process. Students are still fascinated by the pachisi–*patolli* game, without ever having settled its history or histories of development (Erasmus 1950).

The area devoted to the *volador* occupied a prominent place near the center of Tenochtitlán. Not a dance, and certainly not a game, it was more of a spectacular ritual ceremony involving a giant pole capped by a kind of revolving platform. The *códices* illustrate men dressed as birds or gods who threw themselves off the revolving frame and descended to earth with the aid of a rope fastened to the waist, which unwound as they "flew." Today the *volador* is still performed by the Totonac Indians of the Papantla region of Veracruz and in parts of the state of Puebla. One man remains on top of the pole and stomps out a dance while playing a flute and beating a drum. The music gives the signal for the "flyers" to begin their perilous flight to earth.

The Aztecs lived in such constant fear of the gods that they were perhaps reluctant to enjoy worldly pleasures. Thus, mothers withheld outward manifestations of pride in their sons and the long-distance traders known as *pochteca* dressed humbly so as not to incite wrath or jealousy on the part of the gods (or perhaps the nobility). Strict religious discipline may help to explain the high moral code of the Aztecs. As man respected the gods, so he also respected his superiors and his parents. Discretion and sobriety were expected and demanded, as were women expected to be chaste and faithful to their husbands. A good *macehual* obeyed the harsh laws, met his tribute deadlines promptly, had only one wife, and carefully observed the rules of sexual continence and drinking restrictions. Drunkenness was a crime against the state, and only after the age of 70 was drinking to excess permitted.

The Economic System

The large nucleated settlements of Tenochtitlán–Tlatelolco were composed of full-time occupational specialists rather than farmers. By 1519 the population is estimated at 150,000–200,000 people in an area of 12 km^2 (Calnek 1976). With no arable land in the immediate vicinity, the island habitat presented a very difficult problem of provisioning; great attention was therefore devoted to acquiring *chinampas* and increasing local agricultural production as well as procuring new markets, controlling sources of raw materials, and developing trade and commerce. In effect, the Aztec economy relied on tribute, the market system, and "rents" from landed estates that supported the administrative personnel.

In addition to Tenochtitlán, Texcoco occupied 4 km^2 with a population of 20,000–30,000 people and smaller urban developments included Azcapotzalco, Tlacopan, and Coyoacán. Five different rural settlement types have been defined by the Basin of Mexico survey (Sanders, Parsons, and Santley 1979): (1) nucleated radial villages, (2) dispersed line villages, (3) dispersed radial villages, (4) zonal hamlets, and (5) isolated households. The most common of these were the dispersed radial villages characteristic of the Texcoco region and Teotihuacán Valley, and the zonal hamlet pattern which usually lacked a civic–ceremonial precinct. Hilltop shrines such as the Hill of Tlaloc attracted pilgrims and crowds on occasion but were not residential areas.

Sanders believes that the subsistence base of Tenochtitlán could have been met by the Basin of Mexico itself. In the Chalco–Xochimilco area alone there were 9500 ha of *chinampas,* although these may not all have been in production at the same time. Parsons (1976) calculates that this region might have contributed one-half to two-thirds of the subsistence base needed. A tremendous labor force was required to construct the drainage ditches, put in the flood-control devices, and work in the fields. Even given the very high productivity of the *chinampas,* there was still a short-fall. This was alleviated by bringing more land under cultivation, that of the upper piedmont area which had thinner soils and was formerly sparsely settled. Sophisticated farmers were put to work terracing and arranging for flood-water irrigation. This was probably a state-directed resettlement project.

It seems likely that most of the smaller centers in the Basin of Mexico were totally dedicated to farming, with the exception of specialized obsidian crafts at Otumba and salt production near Ecatepec. The Basin of Mexico survey reveals that the concentration of full-time non-food producers at Tenochtitlán was much higher than previously thought and a clear dichotomy appears to have existed between the great metropolis of non-food producers and the rest of the Basin of Mexico.

The economic support of greater Tenochtitlán, facilitated by lake transport, must have dominated the entire activity of the Basin of Mexico. The functioning of the whole economic system is best understood not in terms of Tenochtitlán alone, but by considering the entire basin (urban and rural) as a unit. This is a comparable situation to that seen earlier on a smaller scale in the case of Teotihuacán.

With land at a premium, it is no wonder that land ownership was tightly controlled. Some lands were owned communally by the *calpullis* and were given to individuals or families to work during their lifetimes; other land was worked to maintain temples, schools, palaces, civil service, and warfare, but hereditary ownership was limited to the nobility. It was not until the defeat of the Tepanecs that the real transition was made from a rural to an urban economy (Calnek 1976). This marked the beginning of the rapid increase in private wealth among the elite, which in turn emphasized class differentiation, desire for more foreign and exotic goods, and the emergence of a complex statehood.

With this development in mind, we turn to other economic factors: trade and tribute.

The greatest unifying factor among the diverse areas of Mesoamerica continued to be commercial activity. The strong desire for products of other regions goes back at least to Preclassic times. Trade stimulated contact among different groups and forced lines of communication to remain open, regardless of competition or warfare. The establishment of commercial relations provided a natural vehicle for the exchange of, or at least exposure to, all forms of cultural activity. The structure of Aztec trade relations is well documented in the literature. This complex system had been gradually elaborated through the years by predecessors of the Aztecs.

Basically, two kinds of trading systems operated simultaneously but independently (Chapman 1957). The local market system, which functioned like a neighborhood general store, was carefully preserved by the Spanish and has survived to our day in native Latin America. Daily local markets were held in such cities as Tenochtitlán, Texcoco, and Cholula, with larger gatherings every fifth day. The urban centers had huge markets with as many as 60,000 in attendance, but smaller settlements too had local markets for their daily needs. The market at Tlatelolco particularly dazzled the Spanish, for it was held in the wide paved area that stretched before the great Temple of Huitzilopochtli, where boats could draw up in the canal at one side to unload their merchandise. Every imaginable product was available and occupied its designated place; vendors of vegetables, fish, and fruit products squatted in orderly rows with their merchandise in neat piles before them on *petates* (Sahagún 1946, Vol. 2). Merchandise included not only finished products such as mantles, baskets, pottery, tools, jewelry, and feather work, but also slaves and raw materials such as unrefined gold ore, stone, untanned hides and skins, lime, and wood. From the list of commodities offered, it would seem that not everyone built his or her own house, produced his or her own food and tools, and wove his or her own cloth, but that specialists and middlemen existed. The goods were taxed as they were brought in and sales were carefully regulated by special courts and judges, and for this reason transactions were forbidden outside the markets. Misdemeanors were severely punished; anyone caught pilfering was immediately stoned to death. Accordingly, business was orderly and the marketplace respected. It also functioned as a social and religious gathering place for gossip and worship (Acosta Saignes 1945; Chapman 1957; Sahagún 1946, Vol. 2; Torquemada 1943).

A favorite drink of the nobility, cacao, or chocolate, was also used as a medium of exchange. Other types of money were cotton cloaks, quills filled with gold dust, and small copper axes. Because of the widespread use of cacao both as money and as a beverage, the areas of production were of considerable importance. The most productive regions were Tabasco and northern Oaxaca, central and southern Veracruz, southern Chiapas, southwestern Guatemala, and Honduras. We believe that cacao had been produced for at least 1000 years prior to the Conquest, and it was a product often listed on the tribute rolls (R. Millon 1955).

Another type of trade was carried on over long distances by professionally trained merchants known as *pochteca* (Acosta Saignes 1945; Chapman 1957). They also acted as spies and confidence men. They dealt exclusively with foreigners and imports outside the Aztec domain. Once an area was conquered, however, trade became tribute, which was no concern of the *pochteca*. Occupying a special status in Aztec society roughly equal to that of skilled craftsmen, they were granted private ownership of a piece of land, like the *pilli,* but they were not nobles. The *pochteca* of 18 towns in the Valley of Mexico banded together in a kind of association and resided in Tlatelolco. Theirs was a hereditary occupation. They had their special god, Yiacatecuhtli, and their own rites, feasts, courts, hierarchy, and insignia.

If the day was auspicious for a trade caravan to leave Tenochtitlán, the band of merchants would travel together to Tuxtepec in Oaxaca, laden with such goods as gold ornaments and precious stones, rich garments, slaves, obsidian knives, and copper bells, needles, and combs. Tuxtepec was the end of the first lap of the journey. Here the caravan split, part heading east, the others south to meet their counterparts at a specified location where fleets of canoes and other caravans converged from foreign regions. (See Map 12, p. 458.)

The return to Tenochtitlán was carefully planned so that the *pochteca* arrived at night on a day of good luck. A merchant would deposit his acquired goods, typically raw materials such as feathers, precious stones, cacao, animal skins, and gold, in the home of a relative and would then report to the officials. One wonders at this furtive nocturnal entry. In addition to being a protective measure, it may have served to conceal success, for the *pochteca* were careful not to appear too prosperous. We know that those who were conspicuous about accumulating wealth were put to death. A model *pochteca* was humble, self-effacing, and stayed well within the limits of propriety.

Long-distance trade was a separate institution from that of the daily market. The former was organized for dealing with luxury items and took place at special geographical locations called ports of trade. Near lagoons or rivers for convenient access by canoe, these meeting places were located in areas traditionally removed from political conflict. The most important were Xicalanco in Tabasco, Soconusco on the Pacific coast of Guatemala, the region of Acalán on the lower Usumacinta River, and more distant areas on the Bay of Chetumal and Gulf of Honduras (see Map 12, p. 458). In all these areas, with the exception of Soconusco, Putún traders had been active around A.D. 800 (Thompson 1970), so that the regions had a very long history of commercial transactions. The *pochteca* probably dealt with professional counterparts in Xicalanco, who handled the trade to the south, traveling around Yucatán by sea to the Bay of Chetumal. These sea-going traders along the coasts of Yucatán and Honduras reportedly used large canoes 2 m wide by 15 m long in which the heaviest cargo could be carried. It must be remembered that on land all goods were transported on human backs. The maximum load permitted was 50 pounds per person. One would like to feel that such a limitation shows some concern by the state for the welfare of its people, but the limitation may simply have proved to be most efficient in the long run. It is interesting that the Spanish allowed this long-distance trade to dry up, since they had no use for it, whereas they themselves depended on the market system, which has consequently survived to the present day. Both kinds of trade were carried out under the auspices of particular gods, but trade was primarily a business operation of a secular nature.

Sanders, Parsons, and Santley (1979) tend to minimize the importance of trade as a major factor in the formation of the state and sustaining the city. Not all scholars are in agreement (Tolstoy in press). Although everyone understands that it might have been easiest to provision the city from within the Basin itself, where heavy loads could be moved by canoe across the lakes, the Aztecs do not seem to have concerned themselves with the difficulties of transport as long as they had the manpower at their disposal. In fact, it is known that slaves, once relieved of their burdens, were themselves sold in the marketplaces (Scholes and Roys 1948); this made transport of goods highly profitable. The accounts of the volume of tribute are almost beyond belief. For example, Soconusco, 800 km and many mountain ranges away from Tenochtitlán, paid 200 loads (5 tons!) of cacao alone every 6 months in addition to other items (R. Millon 1955). *Huauhtli* (amaranth) was a great basic food crop which along with maize and beans was sent as tribute from Toluca. A granary held 10,000 bushels and towns were forced to fill one or two granaries with amaranth a year (Sauer 1950).

The empire was, as we shall see, largely a design for exercising the threat of force over defeated towns for economic exploitation.

The Aztec Empire

The Aztec "empire" was a curious thing indeed. "Sphere of influence" is in one sense a more descriptive term, but it does not convey the oppression, cruelty, and harsh demands inflicted by the Aztecs on their conquered peoples. Military expeditions were two-fold in purpose. The first and foremost goal was to exact heavy tribute to meet the increasing demands in Tenochtitlán for all the food, cloth, feathers, raw materials, and slaves necessary to maintain the highly structured urban society of the island city. The Aztecs were materialistic. Seemingly insatiable, the nobility demanded cotton, cacao, feathers, and raw materials such as jade, gold, and precious stones in order to manufacture all the luxury items produced in Tenochtitlán for their delight and support, as well as for the enrichment of the temples and religious hierarchy. Another goal was to maintain an ever-ready supply of sacrificial victims to satisfy the gods. A coordinated, centralized political empire never emerged, but the strong state power of Tenochtitlán maintained itself through force and threat of force.

The *pochteca* doubled as government spies, and often the Aztec war council would act on their information. When the order went out for war, every able-bodied man received his weapons and paraphernalia from the local storehouse as no standing army was maintained. The weapons were obsidian-edged wooden swords, *atlatls*, spears, bows and arrows, slings, and blow-guns. Shields were made of reeds and feathers and were sometimes jeweled. The Aztec warrior decked himself out in fantastic headdresses, nose and ear ornaments, and cotton-quilted armor, and the outfits of the nobility were even more dazzling. Thus geared for war, *pillis* and *macehuales* alike plunged into battle to the music of trumpets and drums. Warfare, justified partly on religious grounds, is more readily understood in the light of economics, for expansion and conquest were calculated to increase the flow of goods into Tenochtitlán.

The lack of any true, cohesive political empire is seen in the fact that many towns were constantly reconquered. Once a town was taken, the Aztecs sent tribute collectors, but otherwise the region usually continued under the same local administration. When the *pochteca* reported signs of unrest, or were themselves captured or put to death, immediate retribution would follow in the form of a sweeping attack by the dreaded Triple Alliance of the Aztecs, to which resistance was useless. The defensive sites and fortifications were built in strategic areas such as hilltops, and walls and moats were also constructed with an eye to defense. But there is nothing in the record to indicate permanent occupation by troops or a professional army. Tenochtitlán itself was not a fortified city. Its best means of defense was its natural position in the lake and it possessed no special military structures. In the battle for its life, fighting raged from housetops, temples, aqueducts, and bridges (Díaz del Castillo 1944; Sahagún 1946).

A good example of a Postclassic fortress is Tepexi el Viejo (Gorenstein 1973). Located 50 km southeast of Puebla, it is not far north of the Mixteca Baja and was closely related to both the central highland cultures and the Mixteca. Early in its history it was allied to Tlatelolco through marriage. Typical of its day, it seems to have fought constantly with its neighbors. Tepexi el Viejo was the center of a small community whose lord exercised jurisdiction over nearby hamlets. Beyond these was its tributary territory, which rendered tribute but otherwise retained independence over its own internal affairs.

Located at 1700 m elevation, the fortress perched on a hill with deep canyons on three sides. In addition, a series of massive walls enclosed the main precinct. The walls served both for defense and the prevention of erosion. The defense was formidable. Tunneling would have been useless since the ground level within was far above that of the surface below. Gates, probably two, were located so the attacker had to expose his right (unshielded) side to the defenders. Walls were 3–5 m high, straight, smooth, and plastered, which discouraged any potential climber. This enormous outlay of manpower and labor provided the defense, for there was no standing army, no specialized military structure or equipment.

When the enemy appeared, everyone brought out his darts, slings, *atlatls*, and bow and arrows. Swords, axes, and lances were also used. For bodily protection they either put on a short vest of padded cotton, or threw on an animal skin worn like a poncho. Although Tepexi el Viejo was located on a hilltop, the position was not strategic in relation to its territory. When taken by the forces of Moctezuma II in 1503, it was not destroyed or ruined. The people lived much as they had before, but were now forced to send tribute periodically to the Basin of Mexico. In 1520 it fell to Cortés with the help of the Tlaxcalans.

Gorenstein feels that greater military specialization is a necessary prerequisite for successful political centralization. The decentralized political structure of the small city-state like Tepexi el Viejo combined with its lack of military specialization provided no future power base beyond the tribute system.

Tlaxcala was a rather special traditional enemy, which always maintained its independence. It is well known that the Tlaxcalans were well prepared for war. They possessed fortifications as well as a good mercenary army of Otomís and refugees from the Basin of Mexico eager for revenge (Davies 1968, 1973). Possibly more important than the uncertainty of success in an all-out military effort against the city was the fact that Tlaxcala represented no great economic prize. From the time that Moctezuma Ilhuicamina extended the Aztec empire to the Gulf Coast, thus cutting off the Tlaxcalans' communications and supplies with this eastern region, they became notoriously poorly clothed and suffered from lack of salt. Indeed, the area offered so little in the way of economic resources that its conquest may not have been worth the effort involved. Indications are, however, that enmity was real and feeling strong on both sides. It is not true, as some have thought, that the two cities maintained a friendly arrangement for battle engagements (Davies 1968, 1973).

The Aztec sphere of influence lay east and south of its capital Tenochtitlán. As we have seen, these had always been the areas of greatest economic interest. The vast north and northwest, exploited by the Toltec, were largely ignored by the Aztecs, to whom they seemed of little economic value. The land of the Tarascans, immediately to the west, was a different matter. Here conquest was desired and attempted, but never accomplished. The Aztecs were ever aware of a large independent kingdom located directly at their backs.

The maximum extent of the Aztec empire is shown on Map 12. It includes central Mexico as far west as the western edge of the Toluca Valley where a line of forts extended south through Guerrero to mark the line of demarcation with the Tarascans. To the north, the boundary was set by Mesoamerica itself, which did not extend far north of Tula, and northeast to Tamuín in the Huasteca. To the east and south, all regions fell to the Triple Alliance as far as the Valley of Oaxaca and the Gulf Coast. At times the Aztecs reached the modern boundaries of Guatemala. There were a few pockets of independence such as Tlaxcala, the Mixteca kingdoms, the Tarascans, and the ports-of-trade. Although few had kind words for these Warriors of the Sun, they were nonetheless highly respected for their power.

Aztec warfare may seem like a senseless exercise in which military campaigns were fought only to be fought again. Such was not the case. Warfare, in addition to providing tribute in staples and luxury goods,

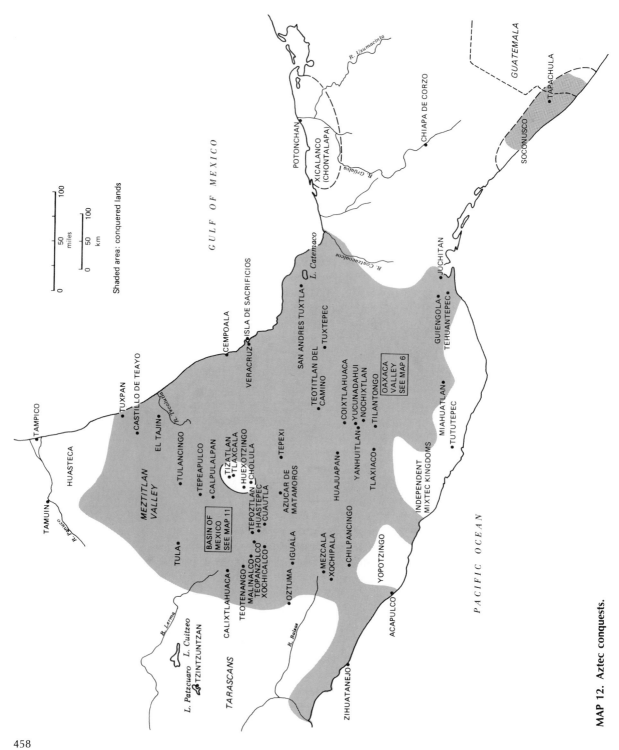

MAP 12. Aztec conquests.

458

was a social mechanism that helped reinforce the stringent class stratification, contributed to the redistribution of wealth, and was a valuable factor in the integration of religion. We can now see how the whole system functioned.

Aztec Civilization

The Aztecs were newcomers to the Basin of Mexico, reputedly a backward tribal people from the frontier regions who in 200 years became the urban leaders of the most extensive empire in Mesoamerican history. Their well-documented evolution from seminomads to a stratified statehood affords a unique opportunity to observe one example of adaptive cultural processes in pre-Columbian America.

In the course of this transformation, the acquisition of land was a key factor. Settling on the islands because the rest of the valley was occupied and because they had antagonized other groups in residence, the Aztecs were faced with a severe land shortage. There was little alternative but to become vassals of the Tepanecs on the western shore at Azcapotzalco. Humiliated but obedient, they observed the astute Tezozomoc in power, and in the process they were learning and conniving. Wars against other valley groups such as Chalco, Xaltocan, and Texcoco sharpened the Aztecs' wits and gave them valuable political experience. Finally, in 1428, as members of the Triple Alliance, they succeeded in the defeat of the Tepanecs and the expropriation of their valuable *chinampas*. This was a major turning point allowing Tenochtitlán to become an urban city of at least 150,000.

Acquiring land was essential to the maintenance of the huge urban city of non-food producers. *Chinampas* were carefully planned and laid out in grids for maximum efficiency of maintenance and production. No effort was spared in developing intensive agriculture; the protection of the sweet waters of Chalco and Xochimilco by a huge dike with sluice gates to keep back the saline waters of Lake Texcoco was particularly important.

Meanwhile the city itself was transformed from a rural to an urban society. Poorly made huts were replaced by substantial homes of adobe and stone. The upper class of nobles had become landowners with the confiscation of lakeshore property. Thus they now commanded services of others to work their lands, while they devoted themselves to asserting their status by ostentatious display of wealth accumulated through their continuing commercial ventures.

Rank was displayed in dress and ornaments. An Aztec was not permitted to purchase or wear objects beyond his station in life. The *pochteca*, professional traders, carried on a long-distance trade with rich areas to the east and south. From there they brought back fine luxury goods and reports of wealth and weaknesses of foreign areas. Tenochtitlán, Tlacopan, and Texcoco, the Triple Alliance, had unprecedented power, which allowed them to sweep through new regions to the glory of Huitzilopochtli, Quetzalcóatl, and Tezcatlipoca. Tribute in staples of maize, beans, amaranth, cacao, and cotton was moved on human backs to the storehouses of the Aztec *tlatoani*. Raw materials, rare exotic goods, and fine finished crafts flowed into Tenochtitlán where markets such as Tlatelolco offered a dazzling selection of goods from great distances.

The well-functioning economic base worked in conjunction with the religious to reinforce the tight stratification of society. Rulers of tributary regions were required to spend a certain amount of time in Tenochtitlán annually. There they witnessed for themselves the tremendous scale of craft production, the handling of produce, and the redistribution of raw materials and manufactured goods. The great religious ceremonies celebrating an anniversary, a victory, the advent of a new king, or the inauguration of a temple brought out the entire populace including *pillis* and *tecuhtlis,* both religious and secular, in their finest garments and paraphernalia to honor the gods in massive displays of human sacrifice. Visiting heads of state, dignitaries, and their retinues all had to be housed and fed, thus making Tenochtitlán a truly cosmopolitan city. At the same time, visitors, however well treated, were more than a little shaken by the impressive display of power and coercion, and all returned home eager to comply with their tribute quotas, for none wanted to fall victim to the penalties or retributions meted out by the Triple Alliance.

The role of warfare can hardly be over-emphasized. Warfare increased stratification since it provided a way to gain rank through honors and gifts of insignia or even land, bestowed by the ruler. Warfare also extended the empire by incorporating other regions into the Aztec fold for the prime purpose of exacting tribute. In addition, warfare provided prisoners for sacrifice, an essential ingredient of Aztec religion. Thus, warfare was vital to the economic, social, and religious functioning of Aztec civilization.

The strategy was excellent. As population swelled, more land was reclaimed and more settlers were sent higher into the piedmont area where they applied their talents to building terraces for the increase of food production. The arrival of luxury goods only created demand for more, so that the ruling class was able to increase its power and wealth. Social classes were strictly defined and carefully promoted through ownership of land and other wealth, education, occupational specialization, and control of rights and privileges. Laws and regulations were very clear; infringements were harshly punished. The whole system was further reinforced by the religious belief that the Aztecs were the people chosen to render homage to and placate their deities by providing the requisite number of sacrificial victims. The Aztecs were realists in the sense of capitalizing on the dramatic and making good use of propaganda. Obsessed with their desire to legitimize their birthright, they burned and destroyed all existing records. They rewrote history to their own advantage by documenting current events by the commission of monumental stone sculptures. The rulers themselves left their portraits carved in the Chapultepec cliffs, a kind of genealogical record designed to last an eternity.

Just how the Spaniards achieved their conquest should now be clear. They arrived both with firearms, for which darts and arrows were no match, and with the bewildering horse. They found a loosely structured empire with members eager to rebel against the hated authority in highland Mexico. Rather than conquering the Aztecs with a small band of soldiers, the Spanish arrived to lead a revolt, gathering thousands of allies with supplies along the way. The Spaniards were fighting a war of conquest, while the Aztecs, struggling to catch a live Spaniard for sacrifice, were shot in the process. With Moctezuma himself uneasy with malevolent prophecies, omens, and the possibility that Cortés might after all be Quetzalcóatl, the outcome, however delayed, was never really in doubt.

THE MIXTECS

To the Mixtecs the Mesoamericans owed many of the finer things of life. For the most beautiful examples of pottery, exquisite work in metallurgy, and fine lapidary art of all kinds, we turn to the Mixtecs who were the teachers of the Texcocans and Aztecs. Their crafts were in great demand by the Aztec nobility, and the finest jewels sent to Charles V of Spain were undoubtedly turned out by their expert hands.

The Mixtec region, often called simply the Mixteca, consists of three subareas. The Mixteca Baja is centered in western and northwestern Oaxaca. To the east and south lies the Mixteca Alta, an area of high, cold, fertile valleys surrounded by mountains. This region borders on and is most intimately related to the Zapotec remains. Finally there is the Mixteca de la Costa or the coastal lowlands of Oaxaca (Spores 1967).

Confusion often arises because the term Mixteca–Puebla culture is used to refer to the development around Cholula and Tlaxcala in Toltec and Aztec times (Nicholson 1961a). The elaborate polychrome pottery of Cholula is indistinguishable from the sumptuous wares manufactured in the Mixteca Alta (Plate 13-a, b, p. 433). The red-on-cream pottery may be Coyotlatelco-derived, and Mixtec figurines certainly resemble those of Mazapan and later Aztec ones. Many features of native writing are also shared with groups in the Puebla region.

Cholula may be the home of the lacquered polychrome ware of the Postclassic but a strong case can also be made for a Mixtec origin and northward spread (Bernal 1965). The small sample found in the Nochixtlán Valley suggests that this area should be eliminated as a possible origin. The predominant ware there is a red-on-cream. Paddock (1966a) thinks it could have developed out of the Ñuiñe local style, whereas Nicholson (1978) suggests that the origins lie somewhere in southern Puebla or adjoining regions of Veracruz or Oaxaca, an idea with which most researchers agree. Related varieties of this remarkable pottery are Isla de Sacrificios V, Cholulteca III, and the Chalco polychrome of the Basin of Mexico, all outstanding examples of Mesoamerica's ceramic art.

The Mixteca–Puebla art style mentioned in Chapter 7 is closely related to that of the Borgia group of *códices* with very precise, clear figures in bright, vivid colors. This same style is also seen in mural paintings of the same period from Tizatlán, Tlaxcala, Mitla, Oaxaca, and from the Yucatán Peninsula. The Tizatlán murals are painted on altars, and they depict Tezcatlipoca with his smoking-mirror foot and Tlahuizcalpantecuhtli, as well as a lake scene with animal and human figures, all in Codex Borgia style. The Mitla murals adorn palace structures and also seem to be copied from the *códices*. A great geographical hurdle to the southeast reveals similar mural paintings in eastern Yucatán at Tulum, Xelhá, and Tancah, as well as at Santa Rita, Belize (see Map 10, p. 406).

Aside from murals the Mixteca–Puebla art style can also be seen in stone carvings and in pottery decoration widely distributed throughout central Mexico and extending as far south as Nicaragua and Costa Rica (Stone 1972). In west Mexico we have noted strong manifestations of the Mixteca–Puebla style in the pottery of Nayarit and Sinaloa. After this ware ceased to be made in Cholula, it continued in use in the Mixteca. Despite close interaction with the Puebla–Tlaxcala region, the Mixtecs had a distinctive culture of their own, and although it is hard to say exactly when and where this culture first emerged, it is a Postclassic development.

Major Mixteca centers were Tilantongo, Coixtlahuaca, Tlaxiaco, Yanhuitlán, and Tututepec (Map 12). Each of these headed a tributary territory but no one great center ever emerged, and there was never a unified Mixtec empire. Probably the largest and most stable was that of Tututepec on the Oaxaca Coast. The ties between a center and its tributary territory were weak and the latter did little more than comply with its required tribute.

The Mixtecs were a proud people with royal lineages and a class structure based on an intricate ranking system. At the top were a privileged kin group, the ruler, who was an absolute monarch, and his immediate family. This small class of nobility was succeeded in rank by the great mass of commoners, with servants and slaves occupying the lowest positions in the social scale. Through historical sources we know that marriages were contracted to strengthen alliances and to preserve and limit prerogatives. The careful structuring of society was duplicated in each valley that formed a distinct political entity (Spores 1967). At the time of the Conquest, one of the most important centers was Tilantongo. The lords of Tilantongo exercised such power that they could appoint members of their royal family to fill vacancies in certain towns where the ruling cacique or lord had no legitimate offspring. This royalty was supported by farmers who produced maize, squash, beans, and chili in the bottomlands and on artificial terraces. This diet was supplemented by the gathering of wild plants, fruits, roots, and herbs, and to a minor extent by hunting deer and birds.

Archaeologically the Mixteca culture is best known from the east–central zone known as the Mixteca Alta (see Map 7, p. 188). This includes sites of Coixtlahuaca, Tilantongo, Chachoapan, and the Nochixtlán Valley.

The Nochixtlán Valley (Spores 1972) has a long cultural history reaching back to 1300 B.C. Its urban Classic center of Yucuñadahui was located high on a mountain and dominated the whole valley of perhaps 30,000 population. For some reason, the population became more dispersed and moved off the hilltop sites and settled around Yanhuitlán at the northern end of the valley. For a few hundred years prior to the Conquest, this area of the Mixteca enjoyed a stable, relatively peaceful existence under their own petty-state rulers. In the late fifteenth century, the Triple Alliance under Ahuízotl had no trouble adding this region to the Aztec empire (Map 12).

Coixtlahuaca and Tilantongo are two other well-known sites in the Mixteca Alta. Little is known of their architecture, but some Zapotec influence is represented in walls covered with mosaics like those of Mitla and Yagul. A very common pottery vessel is an open bowl decorated with red or brown geometric designs on the natural base color. Curiously enough, though many aspects of Mixteca culture spread to the Valley of Oaxaca, this vessel form did not. The elegant polychrome wares shared with the Valley of Puebla are particularly outstanding but are not associated with tomb material of the Mixtec.

One exceptional tomb at Coixtlahuaca consisted of three chambers with a common entrance, a unique example. The usual Mixtec tomb was not constructed but simply dug into the *tepetate,* much like the shaft-and-chamber tombs of western Mexico, only much smaller (Bernal 1965).

No ball courts are known from either Coixtlahuaca or Tilantongo, but the Mixtecs must have known the game because courts are amply represented in their *códices.* This apparent absence could be due to either inadequate excavation or lack of recognizable traces on the surface.

The Mixteca Alta never produced a major ceremonial center of the magnitude of Monte Albán, but they eventually mingled with Zapotec culture, spread throughout parts of the Valley of Oaxaca, and occupied sites such as Mitla and Yagul on the eastern edge of the valley (Map

6, p. 121). These towns, built by Zapotecs in Monte Albán IV, incorporated some Mixtec ideas.

In the Valley of Oaxaca we know that Monte Albán was almost deserted by Postclassic times. Period V remains found there are limited to tombs, burials, and offerings from the Mixtec occupation.

Mixtec craftsmanship was highly prized and greatly sought out by others (Plate 14-d, e, f, p. 436; Plate 16-b, d, e), and this area was a great center for the production of small, fine luxury items such as gold objects, jade and turquoise mosaics, small carvings in hard stone, and beautiful polychrome ceramics. Turquoise was as favored by Mixtec jewelers as jade, which had always been the preferred precious stone of earlier cultures.

PLATE 16. Mesoamerican metallurgy.

a. Copper bells from Ulua River Valley, Honduras. Length of largest: 9 cm. (Courtesy of the Museum of the American Indian, Heye Foundation, N.Y. [left to right: 4/312, 18/4724, 20/3469, 4/3920, 4/3921].)

b. Gold-filigree ring representing an eagle. Monte Albán V. Oaxaca: Mixtec culture. Height: 2 cm. (Courtesy of the Museum of the American Indian, Heye Foundation, N.Y. [16/3447].)

c. Copper figurines, Michoacán: Tarascan culture. Height largest figurine: 5.5 cm. (Courtesy of the Museo Nacional de Antropología, Mexico.)

d. Gold necklace. Oaxaca: Mixtec culture. Length: 51 cm. (Courtesy of the Museum of the American Indian, Heye Foundation, N.Y. [16/345].)

e. Gold labret respresenting jaguar head with flexible tongue, Ejutla, Oaxaca: Mixtec culture. Length: 6 cm. (Courtesy of the Museum of the American Indian. Heye Foundation, N.Y. [18/756].)

f. Pendant, needles, and pins of copper from graves at Tzintzuntzan. Michoacán. Maximum length needle: 7 cm, maximum width pendant: 5.5 cm. (Courtesy of the Museo Nacional de Antropología, Mexico.)

g. Copper axe hafted to wooden handle from grave at Tzintzuntzan, Michoacán. Length: 11 cm. (Courtesy of the Museo Nacional de Antropología, Mexico.)

h. Copper tweezers. Michoacán: Tarascan culture. Height largest: 7 cm. (Courtesy of the Museo Nacional de Antropología, Mexico.)

465

The most fabulous treasure ever recovered in the New World is that of Tomb 7 at Monte Albán (Caso 1965a). The tomb itself was Zapotec, constructed in Period IIIb and reused by the Mixtecs to inter a high official. Thereafter it remained undisturbed until Alfonso Caso discovered it in 1932. Twenty-four silver objects, 121 gold objects, and 8 vessels of *tecali* were found as well as necklaces formed of beads of jet, jade, pearl, amber, coral, and shell. Other finds, including rock crystal jewels and vases, disks, rings, ear and nose ornaments, obsidian ear plugs less than 1 mm thick, and beautifully carved jaguar bones, demonstrate the beauty, precision, and superb craftsmanship of the Mixtec artists. The cylindrical drill had long been known, but perfection in stone working was achieved by cutting with flint, using special sands as abrasives, and polishing with wood, bone, and bamboo. No finer gold work was ever achieved in the Americas. Techniques of hammering, fusing, soldering, filigree, repoussé, overlaying of metals, and gilding were all known. The most exquisite gold work was made by the "lost wax" or *cire perdue* method.

Contrary to popular belief, metal working was not exclusively limited to jewelry. The extensive list of practical tools includes such items as hoes, axes, spades, chisels, helmets, awls, punches, shields, tweezers, needles, pins, and lances. Tin and lead were known in addition to gold, silver, and copper. We do not know to what extent bronze was used. It may have been restricted to the coastal regions of Guerrero, Nayarit, and the Tarascan region (Brush 1969). Studies in this field are still in progress. There is no doubt, however, that the Mixtecs were very sophisticated craftsmen in the arts of metallurgy and working fine precious stones (Plate 16-b, d, e).

At the same time they made thousands of crude little human figures of stone, known as *penates*. Carved from a greenish or white stone, their features summarily indicated by straight incised lines or drilled circles, they are the antithesis of the beauty and perfection of the jewels just described. They may have been mass-produced to satisfy a large popular demand. Caso (1965a) has suggested that they might represent dead ancestors. They are very characteristic of the Mixtec period (Monte Albán V).

Talent of another kind is reflected in writing and calendrical inscriptions. The Códices Vindobonensis, Nuttall, Bodley, Colombino, Seldens, and Beckers are all beautiful examples of picture writing from this area. These deal primarily with genealogies and historical data but divinatory manuals are also included that have a wealth of symbols and representations of deities. The writing is fundamentally symbolic and iconographic, but Caso felt that there was some phonetic value associated with toponyms (place names). Many personal and place names, dates, representations of astral bodies, geographical localities, and animals can be interpreted. Of particular interest are the prized ethnographic data provided by illustrations of houses, temples, palaces, weapons, dress, ornaments, and evidence of rank. Although these *códices* are closely related to those from Puebla–Tlaxcala, they retain a distinctive flavor. The Mixtec calendar was of the typical Mesoamerican system already described (Chapter 5). The earlier use of a bar to represent 5 was replaced by both the Zapotecs and the Mixtecs with dots up to 13 (Caso 1967). These *códices* are the subject of studies in progress (Troike 1978).

Although the Mixtec and Zapotec cultures mingled and overlapped in certain areas of Oaxaca, each had a very individual development. The Mixtecs seem to have been as secular as the Zapotecs were religious. No great center of urban life comparable to Tenochtitlán ever emerged, nor do we find any truly extensive ceremonial centers. The settlement pattern was one of rather limited valley enclaves. As there was no incentive to conquer territory, warfare was never more than a matter of raids and local intervillage wars. Numerous sites, such as Diquiyu, were mountain settlements that doubled as defensive posts. The fortified Zapotec sites of Mitla and Yagul were probably more like Tepexi el Viejo than Guiengola (see p. 468) and would have offered only temporary resistance. About the time the Spaniards arrived, Tilantongo was trying to recapture Miahuatlán for the second time.

Miahuatlán was a valuable prize as it was a busy commercial town between the Valley of Oaxaca and the Pacific Coast (Map 12). No architecture has yet been excavated there, but the ceramics have revealed contact with other areas such as Monte Albán and Lambityeco in the Classic period, and Mitla and Yagul in the Postclassic. It produced a Mixteca polychrome ware that is almost identical with that of the coast. This is but one of three local ceramics that have separate traditions: Mixtec polychrome, a bichrome ware, and a gray pottery. Following an earlier idea of Covarrubias, Brockington has postulated that Mixtec can best be understood as representing a group of elite-oriented traits, copied or imitated locally, which could account for the Miahuatlán polychrome. The use of elite goods could have been restricted which we know occurred at Tenochtitlán where dress, ornaments, and valuables were specifically confined to particular social groups. Spores (1967) has shown that a rigid class structure existed among the Mixtecs. Where permitted, styles of the elite might have been copied by subordinates and the copies in turn diffused. When a prestigious item is involved, such as the Mixtec-style polychrome, the spread might be very fast. This could also account for the west Mexican distribution of the elegant Mixteca–Puebla polychrome style (Brockington 1973).

In Postclassic times, Oaxaca found itself crossed by trade routes in several directions (Map 12). The belligerent Huexotzincans and Tlaxcalans to the east of the Basin of Mexico sometimes made it difficult for the Aztecs to use the old time-honored routes to the eastern lowlands. A bypass could be made, leaving the Basin via Chalco, Amecameca, and Cuautla to Izúcar de Matamoros, from which point merchants could reach their markets in Tuxtepec, Tlaxiaco, Coixtlahuaca, and Cuilapan in Oaxaca. Another route took off east from Izúcar de Matamoros to Teotitlán del Camino. This was an independent kingdom that lay on the route east which, by special relationship with the Triple Alliance, did not pay tribute and was a major center for the *pochteca* in their constant travels (Barlow 1949). Once traders reached Tuxtepec from Teotitlán del Camino, they had no trouble reaching Xicalanco or crossing the Isthmus to the Pacific Coast and Soconusco.

In addition, there is another route of considerable importance although less well known. This is a west Mexico–Oaxaca coastal network which circulated copper money axes, other metal objects, and luxury goods of the hot country (Ball and Brockington 1978). Participants included the Tarascans, the people of Yopotzingo, the Tututepec mini-empire, and the Tehuantepec and Chiapanec kingdoms. The big market town of Miahuatlán mentioned before participated somewhat but had other interests. So active was the coastal trade that some of it could have been conducted by sea between Tututepec and Central America. At the same time, the coastal route may have formed a valuable link with the other two highland-to-coast systems.

The Mixtec communities were so well known for their wealth of jewels, precious stones, plumes, and fine mantles that they made prime targets for the economically ambitious Aztecs (Barlow 1949). Around 1497 the Mixtecs banded together with the Zapotecs to deal the Aztecs a resounding defeat from Guiengola, a hilltop fortress 15 km west of Tehuantepec. This is one of the most famous fortresses in Mesoamerica and, in contrast to Tepexi el Viejo, this was a specialized military site of the Zapotecs (Peterson and MacDougall 1974). It never had a large resident population; little domestic refuse and none of the elegant polychrome pottery have been found. Guiengola has a dramatic setting on the east flanks and ridges of a high mountain. There is only one easy access path and a stairway entrance. The site is enclosed by possibly 40 km of massive double walls, 1.5 m thick by 3 m in height. Two pyramids, and I-shaped ball court, patios, rooms, and a "tower" make up one building complex. There is an elite residential area with a kind of look-out room with a view of the river as far as Tehuantepec. Two other ruins on high points also afford great visibility. Unlike Tepexi el Viejo, Guiengola has two large natural wells and many holes to catch run-off water. There are other sites on cliffs along the river. This was a natural corridor for travel between Soconusco and Xicalanco that would have been used by merchants taking the Tuxtepec route to the central highlands.

Eventually, in the fifteenth century, the greater part of the rich Mixteca Alta fell to the forces of Tenochtitlán. Taking Coixtlahuaca was one of Moctezuma II's greatest victories. This town and Tlaxiaco were the richest of the tribute provinces in the region. Thereafter, the native rulers of the Mixteca were allowed to retain their power (Spores 1967), but in humiliation they watched their subjects, heads bent against the weight of the tump-line, make their long journey through the mountains to deliver the tribute eagerly awaited in Tenochtitlán.

THE TARASCANS AND LATE DEVELOPMENTS IN THE WEST

The western Mexican development we know most about in Late Postclassic years is the culture and empire of the Tarascans, centered at Lake Pátzcuaro and thriving at the time of the Spanish Conquest. Source material for this region is not as extensive as that for the Aztec because the conquerors of Michoacán left no personal history. Fortunately, the Spanish monarchs requested geographical and historical information about New Spain, and these records, called the "Relaciones," provide invaluable data for us. Other early sources are the traditions recorded by members of the religious orders, sixteenth-century *códices* and land titles, and references to the Tarascans in the Mexican *códices*. We know of no pre-Columbian Tarascan *códices*. The sixteenth century *codex* called the Lienzo de Jucutácato, found near Uruapan, shows a definite Hispanic influence. Both a Nahua and Tarascan document, it traces a migration of peoples from Veracruz to the Valley of Mexico and hence to Zacapu and Uruapan. Eventually they split up into four groups: three went off to look for mines and one headed for the Pátzcuaro region. The basic work on the Tarascans is the *Relación de Michoacán*, believed to have been written by a Franciscan friar around 1538 (Brand 1943; León 1904). Reference has already been made to the Tarascans as the group that repeatedly repelled the Aztec warriors who probed their eastern frontier, undoubtedly with an eye on their fine copper and bronze tools as well as other excellent Tarascan products (Sauer 1948).

The Tarascans were people who mingled with the Chichimecs and occupied the northern shores of Lake Pátzcuaro in the twelfth century, after the fall of Tula. The affinities of the Tarascan language are unknown, but some similarities have been noted with the far-flung Quéchua of South America. Today the language is still spoken by the descendants of the Tarascans, who occupy the land of their forefathers, the richly endowed modern state of Michoacán. Proud of their Chichimec dynasty, the Tarascans made their capital at Tzintzuntzan on the shores of Lake Pátzcuaro. Here they constructed a huge platform on the slopes of the mountainside to support a tight row of five temple–pyramids called *yácatas*. Each *yácata* was roughly T-shaped, combining a rectangular with a circular structure, the first tier being common to all five structures (Photo 75). From this religious and ad-

PHOTO 75. Panoramic view of the giant ceremonial platform supporting five *yácatas* at Tzintzuntzan, Michoacán. (Courtesy of Román Piña Chán.)

ministrative center, the Tarascan kings waged wars of exploitation against their neighbors from A.D. 1370 to 1522, and reputedly conquered the northwestern part of Michoacán and adjacent Jalisco, part of the *tierra caliente*, the hot lowlands of Michoacán and northwestern Guerrero. Both the Tarascans and the Aztecs maintained a line of forts separating their domains. These were usually situated on hills or promontories commanding views of the rivers, and also served as signal stations. The Tarascan military expeditions were probably similar to those of the Aztecs. A favorite eastern raid had as its goal the fine salt deposits of Ixtapan. Tarascans were also interested in deposits of copper, gold, and silver; cinnabar; and products of the Balsas and Tepalcatepec rivers such as honey, cotton, cacao, feathers, hides, skins, and oleoresins like copal. It is uncertain how far south of the Balsas River the Tarascans reached. To the north, their frontier fluctuated from time to time as they endeavored to push back the Chichimecs and Otomís. Raids reached as far west as Guadalajara, Jalisco but the "empire" itself probably included only the lands in modern Michoacán (Brand 1943).

Among the Tarascans, the most ancient and revered deity was the fire god Curicaueri and his feminine counterpart. These gods throve on human sacrifice, and in their honor the Tarascans drew blood from their ears and threw it into the fire. Because the sun is a great ball of fire, Curicaueri was logically the sun god too. As among the Aztecs, a vast pantheon of deities is found, each with many attributes and prerogatives associated with colors, animals, directions, and certain calendrical days. We do not know the names of the Tarascan days, but we do know that at least in the area of Lake Pátzcuaro the Tonalpohualli employed symbols similar to those of the Aztecs (Caso 1967).

Today the five *yácatas* of Tzintzuntzan command a view of the lake over the mestizo pottery-making village below. Because no mortar was used in building, the interiors, formed of small slabs, easily collapse once the outer cut-stone facings are gone, making restoration work hazardous. Nonetheless, several *yácatas* have been reconstructed. Excavations at the site have yielded much resist-painted pottery and many stirrup handles and teapot spouts (Plate 13-f, p. 433), miniature tripods, and clay smoking pipes. Notched bones are also common, as are axes, copper bells, and ornaments. Although none have been found at Tzintzuntzan itself, *chacmools* form part of the Tarascan complex. The nearby site of Ihuatzio across the lake has rectangular *yácatas* and has produced some rather charming simple sculptures of coyotes rearing up on their hind legs.

Excavations by the Instituto Nacional de Antropologiá e Historia in the patios of Yácata V (that is, in the angles where the round structure joins the rectangular one) revealed rich multiple burials (Rubín de la Borbolla 1944). The five burials in the southwest patio contained female skeletons and were probably secondary graves. Offerings consisted of many miniature objects of ritual use. Some vessels had been "killed" by chipping a small hole through the bottom. Many copper objects were found, including brooches decorated with animal heads and two dangling bells, simple bells, needles (Plate 16-f), and a lip plug of rock crystal. The east patio was more complex. A primary multiple grave with nine skeletons had been interred beneath a layer of stones. The arm of each skeleton was interlocked with that of his neighbor. They had been placed upon *petates*, with pottery vessels at their heads. Copper bells were found near their ankles, and copper bracelets on their wrists. Also found were long-stemmed clay smoking pipes, obsidian lip and ear plugs of incredible perfection, and a pair of silver tweezers (Plate 16-h). We know from early descriptions that tweezers were customarily worn around the neck of a priest. Another body was buried with a copper axe hafted to a wooden handle, which was partially preserved by the oxidation of the copper (Plate 16-g). Two gold earrings, simply made and bearing one flat square pendant, were found with this skeleton. In other excavations multiple graves with objects of obsidian, gold, rock crystal, and turquoise were recovered in the patio of Yácata IV.

How can we account for these simultaneous burials, in which several bodies were interred with distinctive goods? The descriptions of the colorful funeral services of a Tarascan king in the *Relación de Michoacán* (León 1904) and the writings of Torquemada (1943) provide a reasonable answer. When the king died, we read, he was washed and clothed elegantly. His ankles were adorned with gold bells, his wrists with bracelets of turquoise, and his head with an elaborate jeweled and plumed headdress. He also wore elegant necklaces and ear plugs of gold. Two gold bracelets were tied on his arms and a green lip plug put in place. The body then was placed on a platform and attention turned to selecting those who were to accompany him in the next world. According to law, when the king died, those servants that were to attend him in the hereafter must also die. They were selected by the new king from both sexes. Seven women were chosen to occupy the following positions: chamber maid or jewel keeper, caretaker of the lip plugs, server of drinks, caretaker of water for washing hands, the cook, and her servants. The men to be killed were more numerous: caretaker of clothes, hairdresser, garland weaver, chair carrier, woodcutter, adventurer, shoemaker, incense carrier, boat oarman, boatman, doorman for the king and doorman for the women, feather worker, silversmith, custodian of the bows and arrows, two or three mountain climbers, several doctors, storyteller, musicians, and dancers. It is said that all these people offered to die willingly and volunteered spontaneously. It may well be that they felt treatment at the hands of their chief in the next world would be preferable to that offered by his successor in this one.

Precisely at midnight the bier was brought out of the palace, preceded by all those who were to perish. They wore garlands of flowers on their heads and played crocodile bones on turtle shells. Amid many lights, the trumpets and shells sounded, the tones mingling with voices raised in song. Those who did not take part in the ceremonies were busy sweeping and cleaning off the paths leading to the patios of the temple, where the bier was placed on a huge pyre of dry wood. While the king burned, all his future servants were killed. First they were intoxicated to remove the fear of death, and then were killed with clubs and knives of wood edged with obsidian. They were buried behind the temple with all their adornments, jewels, and instruments. By sunrise the great bier had been reduced to ashes, and all the jewels and precious stones that had escaped the fire were bound up together with the bones and, adorned with a mask and gold shield, were placed inside a large funeral urn. This was set on a wooden couch in a tomb decorated with very fine *petates* and surrounded by many *ollas* and jars filled with food and drink. Fine cloaks and robes were thrown on top, and the rest of the tomb was filled in with bundles of feathers and ornaments worn by the king during festivities. Finally the tomb was carefully covered over with beams and planks.

The account does not say where the tombs were located, and they still await discovery somewhere at Tzintzuntzan. The retainers who were "buried in the patios behind the temples" are in all likelihood the multiple burials. Instead of graves, excavations of other patios have yielded remains of walls and earlier structures. A cemetery with primary graves with much more modest offerings was located on a lower hillside. Secondary burial (that is, bones interred after decomposition of the flesh) and cremation were also practiced at Tzintzuntzan.

When the Spaniards were making their way up to Tenochtitlán, the Aztecs sent some emissaries to the Tarascans to ask for aid. The latter, not knowing what to do, solved this dilemma by sacrificing the visitors. Later, when Tenochtitlán lay in ruins, they belatedly questioned their hasty actions. When their own turn came to face the Spaniards in A.D. 1522, the last Tarascan king, Tangaxoan II, offered little resistance.

The Tarascans are probably representative of many groups of Mesoamericans at the time of the Conquest. They left no evidence of truly urban centers, yet they undoubtedly had a structured society with nobility, commoners, and slaves; craft specialization; and commercial interests. We do not know of any ports of trade in this area, but exploitation of the hot country was important to them. Of their material goods, we would like to know where they found the inspiration for their stirrup-spouted handles on pottery vessels and their advanced techniques of metallurgy. Some of the answers may be provided by the coastal regions, where many influences converged.

The vast amount of gold reported by the chroniclers from western Mexico has never been substantiated archaeologically. From numerous field seasons at Tzintzuntzan some gold jewelry and tweezers were found, but gold is even more rare at other western Mexican sites. Rather, copper ornaments and tools are found in quantity. Gilding of copper has been reported from Tzintzuntzan (Rubín de la Borbolla 1944) and from Amapa, Nayarit (Pendergast 1962a). The addition of tin to copper makes it yellowish in appearance, which, together with gilding, may account for the widespread reports of gold in the sixteenth century.

Quantities of metal have been found near Zihuatanejo on the coast of Guerrero. The finds consist of hundreds of open rings, often hooked together in jumbles, along with bells, thin sheets of gold, a grey metal resembling silver, and two pieces of slag. Ellen and Charles Brush excavated nearby at the Barnard site and recovered metal associated with polychrome pottery and large quantities of *malacates*. They believe the site to have been occupied briefly just after A.D. 900 (Brush 1969).

Analysis of the metal shows that much of it is bronze, probably deliberately compounded of copper and tin alloy. Tumbaga, an alloy of silver, copper, and gold, is characteristic of pre-Columbian Mexican metallurgy (Bray 1978). The silver is present as a natural impurity and may constitute 25% of the total weight, whereas the copper is intentionally added. Tumbaga is easier to cast and very fine decorative details can be achieved.

Bronze at the Barnard site was recovered from household refuse, an indication that it was not a luxury product. We do not yet know how extensively bronze was used in Mexico, but upon analysis some "copper" objects from Michoacán have proved to be bronze. Should this account for the renowned superiority of the Tarascans in warfare, it might imply that the knowledge of bronze was restricted. Chunks of slag found at the Barnard site indicate that smelting was performed on the spot. There are traces of silver, copper, tin, and gold, and alloyed ores do exist in the region.

Amapa, Nayarit was another metal-working center active by A.D. 900. A great variety of artifacts have been recovered including fish-hooks, ear spools, axes, awls, knives, pins, needles, numerous kinds of bells, and plaques. Located about 50 km from the Pacific Coast on the north bank of the Santiago River, Amapa would have been as accessible to commerce by sea as coastal Guerrero.

Metal artifacts in Mesoamerica have been studied by Bray (1972b, 1977b, 1978) and Pendergast (1962a, 1962b). The latter has suggested some patterning in their distribution. Two areas seem to have functioned as primary metal-working centers. One was the southern Maya region, which influenced other Maya groups as well as southern, eastern, and central Mexico. A second center, in western Mexico, included coastal Nayarit and Guerrero, from where the art is believed to have spread rapidly to central Mexico, in particular to areas in the far north reaching into the southwestern United States. The inhabitants of the Oaxaca region, able craftsmen though they were, apparently had less influence on surrounding areas than might be expected.

The concept of metal working was understood in these areas by A.D. 900 and became widespread in Mesoamerica shortly thereafter. This is considerably later than in South America, where the knowledge was well advanced by A.D. 300. Although specific resemblances have been pointed out between Amapa artifacts and some from Ecuador, others can be found with Central America. The almost simultaneous appearance of metal-working centers in the southern Maya area and on the Pacific coast of Mexico lends support to maritime travel as the means of introduction.

Another area of western Mexico, known largely from the excavation of one site, is the Tepalcatepec Basin, lying northwest of Guerrero in the *tierra caliente* of Michoacán. This area, somewhat isolated from others discussed, lies in a depression bordered by the escarpment of the highland plateau on the north and the mountains of the Sierra Madre del Sur on the south. Here, at Apatzingán, I. Kelly (1947) identified a sequence of cultural remains chronologically extending from Classic to Conquest times. Ring stands, *molcajetes*, resist painting, pyrite mirrors, and copper smelting are widespread Postclassic Mesoamerican features, but in addition Apatzingán has a distinctive local flavor that isolates it in many ways from Tarascan sites and the Jalisco–Colima complex. Now, many years after the publication of the Apatzingán report, there is little archaeological knowledge that can be added, a fact that emphasizes the need for intensive field work in western Mexico.

Although the Aztec, Mixtec, and Tarascan states were largest and most powerful at the time of the Conquest, smaller, less well-defined kingdoms, located east and south of the Valley of Mexico (see Map 12, p. 458) existed. It is by no means clear how much autonomy or political unity these areas enjoyed, but they do not appear to have paid tribute to Tenochtitlán.

OTHER KINGDOMS

The history of the Puebla region is intimately tied to events in the Basin of Mexico as well as to the Spanish Conquest itself. Tlaxcala was as traditionally the good friend of Texcoco as it was the enemy of Tenochtitlán. Therefore, the rise of Tenochtitlán in the Triple Alliance naturally increased the hostility of the latter toward Tlaxcala.

Although Tlaxcala was the dominant center in the Valley of Puebla at the time of the Conquest, the towns of Huexotzingo and Cholula were earlier leaders. The independent kingdom of Tlaxcala therefore should be remembered as possessing three centers, with a very old history that reached back to the time of Teotihuacán supremacy. Cholula, once dominated by the Olmeca–Xicalanca, was at one time the leading political and mercantile power in the area. Huexotzingo eventually conquered Cholula in A.D. 1359 and retained its position of strength until the reign of Moctezuma Ilhuicamina. After the long and bitter war over Chalco in the Valley of Mexico, many people from Chalco took refuge in Huexotzingo, contributing to its importance. In the wars of Aztec expansion that resulted in the isolation of the Tlaxcala–Huexotzinco area, these refugees did not take a firm stand or active role, but encouraged other towns to resist the Aztecs.

Gradually Tlaxcala emerged as the most important center in Puebla and actively engaged Tenochtitlán in battle. How was it possible for such a small group to maintain its independence? Partial explanation has already been given (see p. 457), from the viewpoint of the Aztecs. As for Tlaxcala itself, the economic problems created by its isolation did not greatly alter its effectiveness in warfare because few imports were needed. It is also possible that the Aztec encirclement was not as effective on the eastern side as on the west. There is some evidence that around the time of the Conquest Aztec patience was finally wearing thin and that they were actually attempting to strangle Tlaxcalan independence and complete their domination of the Puebla–Tlaxcala *altiplano*. In the final showdown, the Tlaxcalans threw in their lot with the Spanish and participated in the seige of Tenochtitlán, which could have been a deciding factor.

Two other kingdoms lay north and south of Tlaxcala (Davies 1968). To the north lay Meztitlán, a region embracing parts of the modern states of Puebla, Tlaxcala, Hidalgo, and Veracruz. It was a region rich in agricultural land but poor in salt. It was constantly threatened by the Aztecs during their early days as mercenaries of Azcapotzalco.

To the south lay Yopotzinco (Map 12, p. 458), which was more like a confederation of tribes with no true urban settlements, located in the harsh mountainous environment of Oaxaca and Guerrero. This is believed to be the homeland of that famous deity Xipe Totec (Caso and Bernal 1952) (Figure 35, p. 448; Photo 72, p. 438; Plate 7–e, p. 210). Perhaps the region had some special religious and traditional significance for the Aztecs, which could have been a factor in maintaining its autonomy.

In contrast, Tututepec del Sur, with well-defined borders and single capital, had greater cohesion as an independent kingdom. Both Toltec and Mixtec influences met and mingled in this coastal region of Oaxaca, the childhood home of the famous Mixtec king, Eight Deer. The Codex Nuttall depicts scenes from his youth in a temple and ball court of Tututepec, which can be identified by the accompanying name glyph. Apparently the region reached its greatest extension in the years between the Toltec and Aztec supremacies. After the Mixtecs formed a confederation following the rule of Eight Deer, Tututepec established itself as a separate kingdom. A cotton and cacao-producing area, self-sufficient in salt, it was a rich, prosperous region. Tribute was rendered in gold dust, jewels, and copper. Eventually its boundaries were reduced as a result of Aztec expansion, but it retained its independence.

The political status of Teotitlán del Camino, an area lying between Oaxaca and Tlaxcala, is not clear. It may have been subject to the Aztec yoke at the time of the Conquest. Support for this belief comes from the Aztecs themselves, who traditionally invited their enemies to Tenochtitlán on special occasions to witness great sacrifices. As Teotitlán del Camino was not included in the invitations, it already may have been subservient to the Aztecs (Davies 1968).

It will be remembered that the Toltecs who settled at Tula were only the best known of many groups that claimed the name. One of these groups that eventually settled in El Salvador and Nicaragua was also Toltec. Their descendants in historic time are known as the Pipils. Migrations may have resulted from displacement of peoples at both the break up of Teotihuacán and Tula, and would account for the presence of many Mexican features and place names that persisted until Spanish times in regions further south.

The highland Maya peoples were among many that claimed Toltec ancestry (Recinos and Goetz 1953). We do not know for certain whether these claims were real or fictitious. Certainly some Toltec penetration of the Maya highlands made a strong impact and these communities retained a Toltec flavor until the Conquest. The Postclassic period in the northern Guatemalan highlands was also characterized by a series of independent states which devoted themselves to warring among their aggressive kingdoms.

The Quiché were a warrior group who entered the Guatemalan highlands from the eastern lowlands around A.D. 1250 after the abandonment of Chichén Itzá in Yucatán (Fox 1978). The earliest settlements were in rather remote but defensible positions. Gradually they acquired more productive land, and in the early 1400s they conquered much of the Guatemalan highlands, establishing their capital at Utatlán. Each of the four sections of the city had its own temple mounds, ball court, and house platforms.

After the long gradual development over 1200 years, the changes of the fourteenth century were very abrupt. Ceramic styles became very standardized. Twin temples were built on a single pyramidal base, ball courts were enclosed, metallurgy became well developed, and the annals record new lineages.

Before long, revolts fractured the system. The most successful group was that of the Cakchiquels who established their own state and founded a capital at Iximché around 1486(?) (Guillemin 1977). A typical fortress of the period, Iximché was in fact a huge city well protected by deep ravines on three sides. The central ruins resemble an old ceremonial center with 10 temples and 2 ball courts. Residential areas extend far beyond the protective ravines, and in case of serious conflict, the populace could take refuge within the city. Two of the four main groups of structures in the center are especially imposing and may represent residential, administrative, ceremonial, and religious facilities for the two ruling families who shared the supreme power.

Archaeology reveals many similarities to central Mexico in these years immediately preceding the Conquest. The two main cult deities correspond to those of Huitzilopochtli and Tezcatlipoca. Human sacrifice was well established and *tzompantlis* and sacrificial stones are prominently displayed. All centers, unless very insignificant, played the sacred ball game as a symbolic reenactment of a cosmic event.

Utatlán and then Iximché were capitals of the largest city-states of the Quiché and Cakchiquels, but there were others of lesser importance such as the Pokomam with their capital of Mixco Viejo, the Mam at Zaculeu, and the Zutzughil nations. When the old center of Zacualpa was conquered by the early Quiché king, Quicab, it was not destroyed but simply reoccupied (Wauchope 1975). Warfare was a way to capture slaves and to increase wealth and prestige. Tribute was imposed much as we have seen among the Aztecs. But unlike the latter, the Quichés put to death any conquered leaders and incorporated the wives of these dead leaders into the local ruling lineages.

The Aztecs traded with all these groups and may have had a friendship treaty with the Cakchiquels. There is some disagreement over the language spoken, but probably the bulk of the population spoke a Maya tongue. The calendar in operation at the time of the Conquest was synchronized with that of Tenochtitlán. All these groups claimed Toltec ancestry. There are indications that power was becoming increasingly centralized and distances between elite centers were diminished (Fox 1978). The great Iximché capital was finally burned by Alvarado after the Conquest in 1526. According to the sources, this was the punishment meted out to the Cakchiquels for not wanting to join the Spanish on their march to Honduras.

SUMMARY

The Aztecs

The Aztecs left their legendary Seven Caves of Aztlán and entered the Basin of Mexico as seminomadic Chichimecs from the north. The valley was already occupied by farming groups, the southern area being most densely populated. The Aztecs served others as vassals and mercenaries, and finally settled on islands in Lake Texcoco (A.D. 1345).

Acamapichtli was the first dynastic ruler of Tenochtitlán. Aztecs served as subject of Tepanecs in wars against Chalco, Xaltocan, and Texcoco during succeeding reigns of Huitzilíhuitl and Chimalpopoca. Under Itzcóatl, the Triple Alliance defeated the Tepanecs of Azcapotzalco (A.D. 1428), and the Aztecs gained their independence; they thereafter rose rapidly to become the most powerful group in all Mesoamerica.

Tenochtitlán became an urban city of nonfarmers, with a tightly nucleated gridded metropolis, occupied by specialists of all kinds. The height of power and prestige and the maximum extent of the Aztec empire were attained. Tlatelolco was taken over by Tenochtitlán in 1473. Power and authority were concentrated in the hands of the ruler and nobility at Tenochtitlán. Land was strictly controlled; the social organization was tightly stratified with limited mobility. Aztec law was harsh but effective.

The expansion of the empire was initiated by Itzcóatl and continued under Moctezuma I. There was a successful Toluca campaign under Axayácatl. Tízoc was a relatively weak ruler followed by Ahuízotl who again subjugated Toluca Valley and took over the Huasteca, coastal Guerrero, part of Oaxaca, and the Isthmus of Tehuantepec. In 1502 Moctezuma II ascended the throne. War with Tlaxcala and Mixteca Baja began. Conquests brought tribute, prestige, and power, and reinforced the social and religious systems. The role of *pochteca* as professional traders was important politically and economically (A.D. 1428–1519).

Cortés arrived at Veracruz in February, 1519; he entered Tenochtitlán in November. In A.D. 1520, Moctezuma II died. The phenomenal success of the Spaniards was due in part to finding subjugated peoples eager to revolt. The Spaniards provided the firearms and leadership and were joined by local inhabitants who knew the terrain, customs, and intrigue, and could provision the foreigners. Tlaxcala was a key ally for the Spanish. From April to August, 1521, Tenochtitlán was besieged by Spaniards. August 13, 1521 saw the fall of Tenochtitlán and capture of Cuauhtémoc.

Other Areas

Yucatán enjoyed great commercial prosperity under the leadership of Mayapán. The east-coast cities flourished with the trade passing between Yucatán and Honduras. Cozumel became an eastern depot for storing merchandise and an administrative port for Mayapán. Important towns were Tulum, Xelhá, Tancah, San Gervasio (Cozumel), Santa Rita, and Ichpaatun, Belize. Eventually the Cocoms of Mayapán were overthrown by the Xius of Uxmal, and the political authority in Yucatán was soon distributed among small city-states. The Spanish Conquest of Yucatán met considerable resistance by the east-coast cities, but by A.D. 1550 they too succumbed.

Highland Guatemala saw the rise of several prominent city-states, the most important being those of the Quiché at Utatlán and the Cakchiquels at Iximché. Others were located at Pokomam, Mixco Viejo, and Zaculeu. All claimed Toltec ancestry, and religion, calendar, and architecture were heavily influenced by Postclassic central highland Mexico.

The Mixtecs of Oaxaca were famous as outstanding artisans and craftsmen recruited by the Aztecs to produce jewelry, feather work, and ceramics. Although eventually conquered by the Aztecs, they had strong regional traditions of lineages and class-structured society, and they engaged in alliances and local conflicts.

The Tarascans of Michoacán were a strong independent nation never conquered by the Aztecs. Their own calendar, deities, and pattern of culture were typically Mesoamerican. This was a region where metal, especially copper, was worked into bells, celts, knives, axes, and jewelry. After the conquest of Tenochtitlán, the Tarascan capital at Tzintzuntzan fell to the Spanish with little resistance.

TRENDS AND INNOVATIONS OF THE LATE POSTCLASSIC PERIOD

The most outstanding feature is the lack of innovation and the continuity and adaptation of older features of the Mesoamerican pattern, many of which date back to the Preclassic horizon. Many of these are restructured and given new emphasis that make Aztec culture seem unique.

Fortifications of Guiengola and Tepexi el Viejo are notable, although, in the area of Tlaxcala, defensive structures have a very long history. Warfare never involved standing armies, but was organized on a larger scale than previously seen.

Aztec stone sculpture is distinctive. The three-dimensional stone carvings of idols and the commemorative monumental stone sculptures are particularly notable.

Urbanism at Tenochtitlán, an island city, is remarkable. Earlier precedents for the grid pattern of dense settlement can be found at Teotihuacán.

The political organization with very effective concentration of authority represents the culmination of dynastic rule by a semidivine king.

A tribute-based empire grew out of the earlier exchange and trading networks. The Aztecs were excellent politicians, utilizing the *pochteca* to good advantage.

The sophisticated hydraulic system utilized to bring fresh water to Tenochtitlán, the construction of aqueducts, dikes with sluice gates, and flood-water irrigation of terraces indicate the depth of learning, of knowledge acquired and applied in the years between approximately A.D. 1350–1450. The engineers and technical skill stemmed from Texcoco. The cultivation of *chinampas,* although perhaps begun earlier, was now state-planned and directed on a huge scale, yielding a large percentage of the necessary food for the capital.

In the field of architecture, constructions seem familiar, based as they are on those of earlier peoples. The Aztecs took the old idea of placing twin temples on a single pyramidal base for their distinctive style in religious building. Among the familiar pantheon, Huitzilopochtli was the Aztecs' own tribal deity.

The increasing trend toward secularization was somehow reinforced by the role of religion.

Religion, commerce, and warfare were interrelated and inseparable. Upon this state-controlled triad rested the Aztec civilization.

Mesoamerica
and Its Neighbors

In viewing Mesoamerica as a major culture area in the New World and the northern center of Nuclear America, one should note that its boundaries did not function as cultural barriers and that contacts were maintained with neighboring areas. The reverse is often the unfortunate impression given by culture area maps in which by necessity boundaries are clearly and decisively drawn. Such maps have the advantage of facilitating the grouping of tribes and concentrating or clustering traits for study, but they do not reflect the blending of cultures that takes place in peripheral regions.

In this chapter, the relationship of Mesoamerica to neighboring cultures is briefly summarized, followed by comparative comments on more distant regions. In so few pages, the complex question of diffusion, and the processes and implications involved, cannot be adequately treated. Scarcely more than a few similarities and possible inferences can be presented. The aim is to give some perspective to Mesoamerica within the total context of New World cultures rather than to abandon its cultural history at the sixteenth-century frontiers. Mesoamerican studies should not be bounded by these limitations, and it is becoming increasingly clear that the civilization of Mesoamerica needs to be viewed in the broader context of New and Old World cultures in order to understand its evolutionary development.

MESOAMERICA AND THE SOUTHWESTERN UNITED STATES

It has already been pointed out that no great gap existed between the cultures of northwestern Mesoamerica and southwestern United States. Between 7000 and 5000 B.C. these two areas shared features of the Desert preceramic cultural tradition and were probably indistinguishable. It was after 5000 B.C. that people of Mesoamerica began to cultivate plants such as the bottle gourd, squash, corn, cotton, and beans, their appearance antedating that in the Southwest. *Chapalote* maize reached the Southwest as early as 3000 B.C. and was introduced to the ancestral people of the Mogollon culture. The impact was hardly noticeable, however, for sedentary villages did not grow up among the desert people of the Hohokam in the arid basin-and-range lowlands of Arizona until a hybrid form of maize was produced that could grow at lower elevations and in more arid regions. This event took place around 100 B.C. or slightly earlier. At the same time the sedentary Mogollon people of the semiarid mountains of southeastern Arizona and southwestern New Mexico were making pottery and figurines, also inspired by their high-culture southern neighbors. The Hohokam culture could have derived its knowledge of pottery making and village farming either from the Mogollon or from a separate Mexican stimulus. However the introduction of diffused ideas took place, it was the Hohokam rather than Mogollon peoples who ultimately manifested the strongest and most enduring ties with Mesoamerica. Excellent discussions of the relationships between these cultures and areas are to be found in the publications by Jennings (1968), J. C. Kelley (1956, 1960, 1966), Sears (1964), Sociedad Mexicana de Antropología (1944), and Willey (1966).

There were two main routes by which we believe that people, ideas, and artifacts might have made contact. One path lies along the Pacific coastal plain of Nayarit and Sinaloa to Sonora, where the river drainage pattern could be followed northward to southwestern United States. The other lies along the eastern slopes of the Sierra Madre Occidental range, which was occupied by farming communities of the Chalchihuites and Canutillo cultures, leading up to Casas Grandes and from there to the Southwest (Di Peso 1974). Although some of these western regions are not considered to have formed part of Mesoamerica until A.D. 600, they were important as transmitters of culture traits.

Opinions vary regarding the process by which diffusion took place. Large, direct group migration; small, sporadic group contacts; trade excursions; and individual journeys have all been suggested as mechanisms. Probably various patterns, involving both direct and indirect diffusion, were employed, because these two routes seem to have been used for a very long period of time.

The coastal route may have been the first used. There are some vague similarities between the San Blas complex of Nayarit and the Pioneer period of the Hohokam in pottery decoration (or lack of it), clay human figurines, and stone ornaments (Mountjoy 1970). There may well be other such estuary settlements to the north that will reveal a greater extension of Preclassic population in this region.

Inland along the eastern edge of the Sierra Madre Occidental, farming villages of the Chalchihuites and Canutillo cultures stretched in an unbroken line northward from Zacatecas, Durango, and Chihuahua, providing a kind of cultural corridor for the movement of trade items and ideas. Because the whole region shared the same basic environment, the diffusion of cultigens would have been very easy. The southwestern cultures of the United States were located at the northern end of this route (see Map 1, p. 11).

Following A.D. 600 Mesoamerican flavor is seen in Hohokam design motifs such as positive- and negative-painted small animals, simple and interlocking plain and fringed scroll designs, quadrant bowl interior patterns, vessel supports, and basket handles, but perhaps above all in the red-on-buff pottery itself. Other such items include stone bowls, mortars, three-quarter grooved and polished stone axes, troughed *metates*, shell work, conch-shell trumpets, and turquoise mosaics. The ball game and ball courts, mosaic pyrite mirrors, *chacmool*-like figures carved in stone, and cotton weaving are further evidence of Mesoamerican influence, along with platform mounds of earth and adobe. The copper bells are Mesoamerican in shape and were manufactured by the "lost wax" method of casting. In view of the early tradition of metal working at Amapa, Nayarit (Meighan 1976b; Mountjoy 1969; Pendergast 1962a), the coastal route would have been the most logical for the diffusion of these copper bells, which arrived in the Southwest by A.D. 1000. Hohokam canal irrigation may be a local development and is not necessarily derived from Mesoamerica.

It will be remembered that around A.D. 1000 coastal Sinaloa was the center of the extraordinary Aztatlán development, which reflects a close relationship with the central Mexican Mixteca–Puebla cult (Ekholm 1942). During the Aztatlán horizon the Anasazi southwestern expansion took place, bringing the two groups closer together and thus facilitating interaction (Kelley and Winters 1960).

Many Mesoamerican motifs—life forms and mythological beings such as ceremonial mural art with birds, masked dancers, eagle men, stylized plumed serpents, sun symbols, crosses, and feathers—are very significant features in the Southwest. It has been suggested that the *katchina* ceremonialism (*katchinas* were supernatural beings of the pueblos of southwestern United States) may have been introduced from Mesoamerica as a variant of the Tlaloc cult (J. C. Kelley 1966). It is difficult to trace specific sources in this case, since the Aztatlán complex shared many features of the Chalchihuites cultures to the east, and both of these in turn were related to cultures further south. Somewhere in western Mexico the stirrup-spout bottle is believed to have lingered on after its early occurrences in Colima, at Tlatilco and, later, Chupícuaro. Its appearance in the Anasazi cultures of the Southwest is believed to be the result of diffusion out of Mesoamerica. Eventually the form traveled eastward, via the Arkansas River trade route, where it became popular among late cultures in the Mississippi Valley after A.D. 1200 (Ford 1969).

The Puebloan Southwest developed a rich style of its own, which grew out of an infiltration of Mesoamerican ceremonialism with concepts of fire, sun, and a twin war god associated with an early Quetzalcóatl and a basic rain fertility cult.

Around A.D. 1350 the Guasave phase on coastal Sinaloa collapsed and disappeared, and the inland Chalchihuites cultures rapidly followed suit. In the Southwest, the Pueblo cultures retreated, and in the intermediate area of southern New Mexico, Arizona, and Sonora, a cultural and geographic hiatus developed that had not existed previously. This resulted in the virtual isolation of the Pueblo cultures. As we have seen, it was at this time also that Mesoamerica turned its attention to the east and south under Aztec leadership.

It is therefore particularly interesting that the Casas Grandes culture in the northwestern part of Chihuahua close to the border of New Mexico reached such extraordinary complexity after A.D. 1000. As the fertile Casas Grandes Valley parallels the main range of the Sierra Madre Occidental, the mountains provided useful natural resources for valley farmers who settled along the rivers. Here one could find stands of pine to be used for building and fuel, quartz and sandstone to be quarried, natural outcroppings of raw copper, and white kaolin deposits to make fine pottery. Deer and turkeys were hunted, the latter sometimes kept in pens in the valleys (Di Peso 1966).

Of the three main periods of development at Casas Grandes, Mesoamerica exerted a strong influence only in the last one. Prior to A.D. 1000 the Viejo period inhabitants were in contact with southwestern peoples as seen in their pit-house dwellings, pottery, and the *kiva* or underground ceremonial chamber. In the succeeding Medio period, grave goods were more plentiful, the people commonly being buried beneath the house floors, and polychrome pottery was added to earlier styles. The population greatly increased during this time, for the water systems were more elaborate, now including irrigation canals and subterranean drains. A building boom resulted in the erection of walls and stairs, with the ceremonial *kiva* retaining its importance.

The peak of Casas Grandes was reached in the Paquimé phase of the Medio period. A number of Mesoamerican features suddenly appeared—I-shaped ball courts, platform mounds, truncated pyramids, town courts, round stone houses, and human sacrifices—presenting a startling new orientation with a Mesoamerican flavor. The plumed-serpent motif, copper bells, and needles also may have been Mexican-derived. But Casas Grandes also exhibits some non-Mesoamerican characteristics during this period. An extraordinary polychrome pottery produced in abundance was probably locally inspired, while the multiroomed and multistoried dwellings have their closest parallel among the southwestern Anasazi people. Di Peso (1966) suggests that the Mesoamerican influence could have resulted from a take-over by a powerful religious group from central Mexico. It is also possible, however, that inhabitants of the Mimbres region to the north migrated south to Casas Grandes, and subsequently were heavily influenced by Mesoamerica (Willey 1966). At the height of prosperity, Casas Grandes, with its master building plan, religious architecture, specialized labor, and intricate water system and communication network, ranks as the most powerful center of the northern mountain area. Its natural resources and strategic location in northwestern Chihuahua could have established Casas Grandes as a major trading center. Influences were carried from here by *pochteca*-like merchants in the Early Postclassic period as far north as Chaco Canyon, New Mexico (Di Peso 1974).

In the final phase of its pre-Columbian history, a rapid architectural decline took place at Casas Grandes, manifested by makeshift and flimsy construction, which was followed by razing and burning. Diehl (1976) notes that despite the Mexican features at Casas Grandes, the culture still seems more Southwestern than Mesoamerican.

Thus far, we have dealt largely with the diffusion of Mesoamerican influence to the north and west. What, if anything, did the southwestern United States area contribute to Mesoamerica? One possibility is the domesticated turkey, which appears earlier in this region than in Mesoamerica, where our first record of it is found in the Palo Blanco phase of the Tehuacán Valley (MacNeish 1967). Another interesting possibility is the smoking pipe. Conical stone pipes were smoked on the California coast as long ago as 4000 B.C., the earliest documented evidence of pipe smoking in the Americas (Switzer 1969). From here the use of pipes diffused into the Great Basin and into the Southwest where they attained great popularity. Tubular basalt pipes have been found in pit houses in western New Mexico in the Pine Lawn Valley as early as 500–400 B.C. Although clay smoking pipes are largely a Postclassic feature in Mesoamerica, the antiquity of Mexican smoking pipes is difficult to trace owing to the possible existence of perishable early instruments. At the present time, the southwestern United States is at least as likely a source of clay smoking pipes as any other.

Whatever the origin of the smoking pipe, it is entirely possible that many of the religious beliefs and concepts surrounding the ceremonialism of pipe smoking entered the southwest from Mexico. The Tlalocs and their assistants, the Tlaloques, closely parallel the Pueblo rain chiefs, who also were concerned with rainmaking and identified with mountain tops. Switzer (1969) believes that some of the Mexican religious concepts could have spread to areas of southwestern United States at a very early time, along with corn and squash. This supposition in no way conflicts with the history of the smoking pipe since there is no necessary correlation of the spread of agriculture and the use of tobacco for chewing and smoking.

MESOAMERICA AND THE EASTERN CULTURES OF THE UNITED STATES

Peoples of eastern United States also felt the impact of the strong neighboring civilizations during both the Woodland and Mississippi traditions, and possibly even as early as the Late Archaic period (Ford 1969; Griffin 1966; Jennings 1968; Willey 1966).

Prior to 8000 B.C. these eastern peoples shared the hunting tradition of other North American groups, but thereafter a shift can be seen in which local groups exploited their immediate environments in a pattern much like that of Mesoamerica's Tehuacán and Tamaulipas cave dwellers. The earliest pottery from southeastern United States is a crude, fiber-tempered ware, dated at about 2400 B.C. It was found at a site on the Georgia coast called the Stallings Island complex. The shapes and decorations of these vessels have some parallels in the very early Valdivia pottery of coastal Ecuador. Ford (1969) has speculated that the resemblances are the result of contact with maritime voyagers who made their way along the eastern coast of Panama and, aided by the Gulf Stream, were able to navigate through the straits of Yucatán and Florida to the Georgia coast. According to Ford, another settlement, the Orange complex, located some 150 miles south of Stallings Island on the Florida coast, likewise is related to Ecuador. The first possible Mesoamerican influence is reflected in pottery made after 1300 B.C., when wide, flat rims on flat-based vessels are found in the early Atlantic coastal sites. These early features are also shared with northern South America (Map 13).

About this time the Olmecs rose to prominence in Mesoamerica, and some of their influence could have reached the lower Mississippi Valley soon after 1200 B.C. The curious site of Poverty Point appears to have been occupied from 1300 to 200 B.C. Mesoamerican-type *manos* and *metates* have been found, and these, together with material from the inland living sites, provide indirect evidence of maize cultivation. Earth mounds forming concentric ridges are located 8° left of the true cardinal directions, an orientation paralleled by construction at the Olmec sites of La Venta and Laguna de los Cerros. The long prismatic flakes struck from prepared cores found at these sites have parallels in Mesoamerica, and the work in jasper is much like the Olmec lapidary art in jade. Both cultures share unzoned rocker-stamping and the *tecomate* vessel form. Despite careful excavations, Poverty Point is still hard to fit into the more general scheme of southeastern archaeology (Ford 1969; Jennings 1968).

As this early period, sometimes called Archaic, blends into the early Woodland culture, exemplified by the Baumer and Red Ocher sites in Illinois and Tchefuncte in Louisiana, pottery making and construction of burial mounds became very widespread. Wicke (1965) interprets the latter as being Mesoamerican inspired. The cord-marked, rocker-stamped, zone-decorated Woodland pottery is often seen as the result of stimulation from northeastern Siberia, although it also resembles pottery

MAP 13. Mesoamerica and its neighbors.

found in some Middle Preclassic Mesoamerican sites. Scandinavia has been proposed as an alternate source of this Woodland pottery, as the pottery was found at an appropriate chronological depth (Kehoe, 1962). The perplexing possibility of outside stimulation on these eastern cultures therefore remains very much open at the present time.

By 1000 B.C. attention shifts to the Woodland cultures of the Ohio River valley and Great Lakes area. Both mound building and maize agriculture seem to have preceded pottery making in this area. A car-

bonized ear of maize from an Adena burial in Ohio has been dated
with radiocarbon at 280 B.C. Also found in the Adena remains was
skeletal material showing the intrusion of a brachycephalic population
that practiced occipital and frontooccipital head deformation. Here a
direct migration of peoples from the south, possibly even from Central
America, is implied, for earlier eastern populations were dolichoce-
phalic. Other traits that may have diffused northward from Mesoamerica are the celt axe form, perhaps conical mounds over cremations
on floors (which has some parallel at La Venta), sandstone saws, bird
motifs, and ear spools. Flat tablets (stamps?) and finger rings probably
should also be included.

The Hopewell culture replaced that of Adena and flourished until
A.D. 300. It spread over a large area but most significantly southward,
to Louisiana and Mississippi. Though somewhat retarded, Olmec influence can be found even here, in such traits as the bent-knee stance
of figures, burial of green stone celts, and tombs made of logs that are
similar to the basalt column tombs of La Venta and the log tombs of
Kaminaljuyú. Pan pipes and blades struck from prepared cores represent further southern influence. As noted before, the rocker-stamped
pottery of this culture need not be derived from Mesoamerica. Indeed,
it more closely resembles the ceramics with zoned stamping of the
Chavín horizon in Peru, or may even stem from entirely different Si-
berian or Scandinavian traditions (Jennings 1968).

From a southern Hopewellian manifestation called Marksville emerged
the Mississippian culture, in which the peoples of the eastern United
States after A.D. 600 attained their greatest complexity of development.
Although its geographic center lay along the Mississippi Valley from
Natchez, Mississippi to St. Louis, Missouri, related cultures extended
from Oklahoma to Florida and Georgia and north to Michigan. Temple–pyramids, enlarged many times, were found grouped around plazas in a layout familiar to every student of Mesoamerica. This period
is well described and summarized by Jennings (1968).

Of particular interest to us is the wave of Mesoamerican influence
that can be recognized in this culture around A.D. 900 or 1000. Contact
is believed to have been made via the overland route rather than
through coastal settlements, although Wicke (1965) thinks that maritime
contacts are a good possibility. That contact was made is generally
conceded, but the circumstances under which it took place are largely
speculative. The areas lying between northeastern Mexico and Texas
were poorly suited for early agriculture, and there was no uniform
environmental corridor of farming peoples uniting the areas, as we
have just noted in the case of northwestern Mexico and southwestern
United States. Nevertheless, the most likely overland route passed from
northern Mexico across Texas and eastward to the Mississippi Valley.
The Gulf Coast would not have offered a useful route as the shore line

consists of mud flats and sand dunes, and could not have supported year-round occupation.

A number of Mexican artifacts have been recovered in the area between Mesoamerica and southeastern United States, but these are usually isolated discoveries without any associations and are difficult to place chronologically. One of the most significant features shared by both regions was an engraved pottery design into which red paint was rubbed. This technique was centered in the so-called Caddoan area that extended from eastern Oklahoma to the Mississippi Valley and is believed to be the result of contact with Mesoamerican peoples around A.D. 700–900, in the early part of the Mississippi period, which lasted until the seventeenth century.

The Mississippi period after A.D. 900 is probably the best-known eastern culture. An intensive agricultural village life with temples and mounds arranged around a central plaza reflects the typical Mesoamerican pattern. This configuration is almost certainly related to new agricultural developments. A number of traits attributed to Mesoamerica are found in this Mississippi tradition. The most outstanding features relevant to this discussion have been outlined by Griffin (1966) and are briefly reviewed here.

Negative painting as a decorative technique was known earlier but only became common in the period from A.D. 1000 to 1500. In Mexico its long history currently dates back to 1200 B.C. (Tolstoy and Paradis 1970). The eastern examples most closely resemble those of Mesoamerica's Late Classic and Early Postclassic periods, which would be chronologically compatible with the influx of other Mesoamerican features. For example, tooth mutilation was common in Classic and Postclassic Mesoamerica, and it occurs after A.D. 1000 in Illinois. Some very close parallels in art styles are seen in the combination of skull–hand–heart and long-bone motifs relating to the religious and ceremonial ideology of Postclassic Mesoamerica. The Southeast Ceremonial complex, dated at A.D. 1000-1400, contains many features of this nature. Perhaps ties were strongest of all during the Early Postclassic period, when the Toltec peoples were more concerned with the northern frontier and peripheral regions than the succeeding Aztecs. The Toltecs also smoked tobacco in pottery pipes, and during their day pipe smoking was taken up by certain groups in Mesoamerica. The smoking of pipes has a long history among eastern peoples of the United States, and the chronological distribution of pipes suggests this region as a source for their diffusion to Mesoamerica (Griffin 1966). Another possibility, as we have seen, could have been southwestern United States. Cord-marked pottery may represent a very late diffusion from the area of the United States to Mexico. Although some examples have been reported from Soconusco and Veracruz at a very early time (M. D. Coe 1961), it was never important in Mesoamerica until the Aztec period.

In Late Mississippi cultures, the shoe-shaped vessel and stirrup-spout bottle occur, the latter having been ultimately derived from Mesoamerica via the Southwest (Ford 1969). There are undoubtedly many more specific resemblances that could be mentioned, but the most significant contribution of Mesoamerica to this area was the knowledge of agriculture and the religious and cultural ideas associated with it, which were reflected in the material culture. The result, however, was not the spread of Mesoamerican civilization, but the emergence of a distinctive pattern of southeastern cultures that chose a very different lifestyle.

THE CARIBBEAN

Despite the fact that Yucatán is located less than 200 km from Cuba, there is scant evidence to suggest that much contact occurred between these two regions prior to the arrival of the Spanish. It is believed that the Lesser and Greater Antilles were largely populated from various parts of northern South America, and archaeological evidence indicates that the closest ties were with mainland Venezuela. In the reconstruction of Caribbean history it is a significant fact that the remnants of the earliest and simplest inhabitants, the Ciboney, are found on the westernmost tip of Cuba, which geographically lies closest to Mesoamerica. More complex cultures, those of the Arawak and later Carib, are found in the central region, and on the islands of Hispaniola and Puerto Rico.

Should Ford (1969) prove to be correct, sea-going travel has a very long history among aboriginal Americans. We know that the Caribs had fine canoes, and that Arawak canoes were outfitted with sails and oars and carried 40 to 50 people. Mesoamericans also had the technical knowledge to make long voyages, for we know that merchant ships skirted the eastern coastline and transported merchandise to and from Xicalanco from ports in Yucatán and Honduras. Despite this knowledge of navigation, neither archaeological studies nor early written sources lead us to believe that contacts were either regular or frequent between the Caribbean islands and the Mesoamerican mainland.

The Chilam Balam of Chumayel (Roys 1933) mentions that some unclothed strangers arrived in Yucatán about 1359 "looking for people to eat." Occasionally a ship strayed off its course, and sporadic shipwrecks were inevitable. Such accidents would account for the presence of a Jamaican Indian girl found on the island of Cozumel by the Spaniards in A.D. 1518. She told of strong currents that had swept a fishing group off course 2 years earlier, carrying their canoe west to Cozumel, where all the men ended up on the sacrificial block.

Pertinent archaeological evidence pointing to possible contact revolves around a discussion of maize agriculture, *metates* and *manos*, and the ball game, hammock, and certain religious beliefs (Rouse 1966).

Although maize was grown by the Arawak, it was not the staple crop of the islands and was always second in importance to manioc. The Arawak preferred roasting ears of corn in the fire to the Mesoamerican method of preparation, which was based on soaking it in lime water overnight to be subsequently ground on the *metate* and made into tortillas. The *metates* and *manos* found in Cuba, Jamaica, and Puerto Rico resemble those of southern Central America more than Mesoamerican ones. If Mexico was the source of Caribbean maize, it probably reached them via Central America and northern South America.

The best evidence of direct contact is provided by the ball game. Arawak courts were not bordered by elaborate stone construction as in Mesoamerica, but they did outline courts with earth or slab walls, which was not done in South America. Ekholm (1961) has argued convincingly that Arawak stone "collars" and "elbow stones" were in all probability used as protective ball-game belts, in much the same way as the Mexican "yokes." The presence of these belts and the delineation of courts support direct diffusion as the means of introduction. The game itself was played more like that of the modern Arawak of the Orinoco Valley, thus providing some basis for the postulated introduction of the game into the Antilles via South America.

The hammock may well be a Caribbean import to Mesoamerica, either directly or indirectly through Central American peoples. It is hard to ascertain when the hammock was introduced into Yucatán, but its pre-Columbian presence is documented by a painting on a Late Classic Maya vase that shows a chief in a jaguar-skin hammock.

Rouse (1966) believes that the best ties between the two areas in the fields of religion and social organization are yet to be found. However, it does not seem likely that the Caribbean and Mesoamerican peoples ever maintained contact to any significant degree. This may not be true in the case of South America.

LOWER CENTRAL AMERICA

The scenic land bridge of lower Central America to South America is not a uniform archaeological area and is still very imperfectly known. The best information comes from the base of the Nicoya Peninsula (the northern part of Guanacaste Province in Costa Rica and the Isthmus of Rivas in Nicaragua), which Haberland (1978) calls Greater Nicoya, and the Chiriquí and Coclé regions of Panama.

The earliest known cultural phase from Greater Nicoya, which is also found on Ometepe Island (Lake Nicaragua), is called the Dinarte phase, dated at 1000 B.C.–500 B.C. (Haberland 1978). Its pottery bears some resemblance both to the Cuadros phase of Guatemala and Machalilla in Ecuador, providing a much sought-out link in the Preclassic horizons of those regions. Later in this period Olmec influences reached the

Ulua River valley, Lake Yojoa region, and the Cuyamel Caves of Honduras (p. 149). Olmec influence is also seen in small portable objects such as carved jades in the Nicoya Peninsula and other parts of lower Central America, but these are difficult to date as they were treasured as heirlooms and continued to circulate many years after their manufacture.

The Zoned Bichrome horizon (500 B.C.–A.D. 500), with combinations of incised and painted decoration, is marked by the appearance of maize agriculture, considered to have spread from Mesoamerica south to these manioc farmers. Some of the forms and decoration of the pottery from the northern part of lower Central America resembles the Early and Middle Preclassic pottery of Mesoamerica at this time. A chronological lag is apparent here when compared to dates further north. This is seen both in the carbon dates and the presence of some Usulután decorated pottery in the Nicoya area.

Thereafter, polychrome pottery makes its appearance, possibly as early as A.D. 200 in the south, but later in Nicoya since this feature may have spread northward out of South America. It is not until at least A.D. 800 that Mesoamerican influence is seen in the polychrome designs of Nicoya along with whistling vessels, jadeite celts with Maya motifs, and marble Ulua-type vessels. The use of stone calls attention to other Mesoamerican influence in some of the Nicaraguan and Costa Rican stone sculpture. This seems to have penetrated the eastern regions where in the Gulf of Chiriquí there are stone pillars capped by a small human or animal figure that somewhat resembles shaft figures from Tres Zapotes and Tonalá, the Guatemalan highlands, western El Salvador, and Honduras. Something similar is found around A.D. 800 at Río Cano, Coclé (Stone 1972). Although Haberland has worked out a chronology for the Greater Nicoya area, this cannot be applied to the rest of lower Central America, so after A.D. 500 one must deal largely with regional styles (Willey 1978).

After A.D. 900 the religious concepts of lower Central America had a more Mexican cast, probably due to actual movement of peoples. The unsettled conditions further north are reflected in the Nicoya Peninsula and as far south as western Panama.

It is often speculated that a group of Nonoalca, Náhuat-speaking people, after an early migration to Central America, returned to the central highlands of Mexico and settled at Tula. If so, they could have taken along such things as the knowledge of metallurgy, working green stones and alabaster, as well as certain religious beliefs. In Postclassic times groups of Náhuat–Pipil pushed south through Chiapas, Guatemala, El Salvador, and Honduras to become the Nicarao. Tohil Plumbate, the distinctive trade ware made in the Guatemalan highlands, found its way south to Panama. The Mixteca–Puebla style can be found on tripod censers in Honduras and northern Costa Rica. A few pieces occur as trade ware even farther south. The *chacmool* figure (Plate 12-d, p. 380) associated with the Toltec period also appears in Costa Rica.

In the other direction, we can find lower Central American traits in Mesoamerica. From either Nicaragua or the Nicoya Peninsula, four beautiful examples of Papagayo Polychrome ware were taken north to Tula where they were carefully put away (p. 376). This type of polychrome is often decorated with representations of Quetzalcóatl–Ehécatl. Examples of Panamanian gold work have been found in the Sacred Cenote at Chichén Itzá. Polychrome pottery from the Yestla–Naranjo area of central Guerrero is strongly reminiscent of Nicaraguan and Costa Rican wares. This same ware, at times with loop supports, is known from the coastal Barnard site. Characteristic of both Postclassic Guerrero and Central America is a design consisting of a row of dots bordered by vertical lines.

This is the kind of archaeological evidence we have to go on at the present time. The ceremonial center and urban development of Mesoamerica had no counterpart here. These people were more closely associated with the Amazonian tradition based on a personalized religious following of a particular chief.

In the Late Postclassic period other Mexican groups are believed to have migrated to lower Central America. Aztec motifs are displayed on Nicoya pottery, and *molcajetes* are present as well as Cholula–Tlaxcala pottery styles. At the time of the Conquest, the Spanish reported Náhuat-speakers living in the border area between Nicaragua and Honduras as well as in eastern Costa Rica; it is no surprise, therefore, to find the spread of Mexican religious beliefs and the use of cacao as a medium of exchange.

More significant relationships, which may have been more important to the development of Mesoamerica, are found much further south and are much earlier in time.

Many years ago, Spinden (1917) postulated the existence of an early "archaic" culture that spread from Mexico to the Andean area and involved such shared traits as maize agriculture, pottery, and clay figurines. At that time, it was felt that the area of initial maize domestication would also prove to be the heartland of the other features, which together formed a complex that spread throughout this vast geographical area. Now we know that maize was not the first cultivated plant, but probably had multiple origins, and that in the case of Mesoamerica, cultivated plants preceded pottery making by several thousand years. Still, in one way Spinden's vision of a common "archaic" (now called Preclassic or Formative) period may have been prophetic, for indeed it is during this horizon, prior to A.D. 1, that the greatest

THE INTERMEDIATE AND ANDEAN CULTURE AREAS

evidence of contact and most pronounced similarities among centers of Nuclear America are to be found. The following discussion is based on writings of Badner (1972), Ford (1969), Grove (1971), Lanning (1967), Lathrap (1966, 1970, 1973, 1975), Meggers, Evans, and Estrada (1965), Paulsen (1977), Reichel-Dolmatoff (1965), and Willey (1962b, 1971, 1978), all of whom have dealt with this problem.

The most important Preclassic sites with ceramics that are pertinent to the discussion here are the following, listed from north to south (see Map 13, p. 487):

Panama: Monagrillo, a shell midden on the Pacific Coast of Panama on the Parita Peninsula (2140 B.C.) (Willey and McGimsey 1954).

Colombia: Puerto Hormiga, north coast between the Magdalena and Sinú Rivers (3000 B.C.), nearby Momíl (1500 B.C.) (Reichel-Dolmatoff 1965).

Ecuador: Loma Alta, inland riverine site (3100 B.C.–2700 B.C.); Valdivia, coastal site both on the Guayas Peninsula (either 3000 B.C.–1500 B.C. or 2700 B.C.–1500 B.C.). Machalilla phases at nearby coastal sites (either 2000 B.C.–1000 B.C. or 1500 B.C.–1100 B.C.). Chorrera-phase sites located along rivers, inland on the Guayas Peninsula (either 1500 B.C.–500 B.C. or 1100 B.C.–300 B.C.) (Meggers, Evans, and Estrada 1965; Willey 1978).

Peru: coastal sites: Guañape, Las Haldas, and Asia (1500 B.C.). Cupisnique, Ancón (900 B.C.) (Lanning 1967).

highland sites: Waira-jirca Kotosh (1800 B.C.–600 B.C.) (Izumi and Sono 1963); Chavín de Huantar (900 B.C.) (Bennett 1944).

eastern lowland sites: Tutishcainyo (1800 B.C.) (Lathrap 1958, 1970, 1975).

Pottery making and certain pottery forms and decorations make their earliest appearance in northwestern South America. With the discovery of early agriculture, early animal domestication, and a semisedentary existence in the highlands of Peru in dry caves near Ayacucho (MacNeish 1969), we recognize a familiar pattern roughly paralleling that of the Tehuacán Valley. Just as each ecosystem in Mesoamerica was developing its own program of exploitation of resources and cultivation of local plants, so throughout Nuclear America there must have been any number of local cultures responding in a variety of ways to their environmental potentials. Because of the great distances between the small village communities of this period, it is all the more remarkable to find that Preclassic peoples of Nuclear America were in contact with one another, probably by sea as well as land (Edwards 1978; Paulsen 1977; West 1961).

The earliest ceramic site may be Puerto Hormiga on the north coast of Colombia where around 3000 B.C. builders of shell mounds made pottery, some of which resembles ceramics from Valdivia. Rocker-stamping is found on the oldest ware both here and in Valdivia; unzoned rocker-stamping is found in Ecuador, whereas both zoned and dentate types have been found in Colombia. By 2140 B.C. the same technique is found on pottery at Monagrillo, Panama, along with excising and the *tecomate* form (Willey and McGimsey 1954).

The archaeological sequence for Ecuador is of considerable interest to this discussion for not only is it here that some of the earliest pottery in the New World has been found, but also that relationships are seen here with Mesoamerica. There is, however, some disagreement regarding chronology, sequence, and origins.

Meggers, Evans, and Estrada (1965) believe that the art of pottery making, along with certain decorative techniques was ultimately derived from the Old World, specifically Japan, where they see early parallels between the Jomon pottery of Japan and that of Valdivia on the Ecuadorian coast. This early settlement would have subsisted on a sea-based economy. (See also McEvan and Dickson 1978.)

An opposing view is that of Lathrap (1973, 1975), who believes the Valdivia-style pottery originated in the tropical forest area of South America and from there was spread to Ecuador by farmers who cultivated maize (*Zea mays*, Zevallos *et al.* 1977) and manioc as evidenced by stone bladelets for mounting in grater boards. If one does not take into account the single ^{14}C date of 3200 B.C. which is out of context stratigraphically, the earliest ceramic Valdivia phase on the coast would date to 2700 B.C.

An important site of Valdivia culture, Loma Alta, is located 15 km up the Valdivia River on a hill above the fertile valley floor, where farming was possible without irrigation due to the high water level. Valdivia culture is also known from several sites to the south on the Sta. Elena Peninsula. One of these, Real Alto, on the Río Verde, has yielded 72 burials dating to Valdivia III (2920 B.C.–2770 B.C.). The site was occupied as early as 3400 B.C. by a sedentary group who gradually took up the cultivation of maize (Klepinger 1979). Thus Lathrap believes that the Valdivia culture originated in a farming riverine environment, and the coastal manifestation represents a westward spread. The two chronologies line up as follows (Willey 1978):

Meggers	Lathrap
Chorrera phase: 1500 B.C.– 500 B.C.	Engoroy (Chorrera): 1100 B.C.– 300 B.C.
Machalilla phase: 2000 B.C.–1000 B.C.	Machalilla phase: 1500 B.C.–1100 B.C.
Valdivia phase: 3000 B.C.–1500 B.C.	Valdivia subphases 1–8: 2700 B.C.–1500 B.C.
	Real Alto (Valdivia culture): 3400 B.C.–1500 B.C.

Notice that in the Meggers sequence there is an overlap between Valdivia and Machalilla that Lathrap does not find.

It is interesting that there is yet another ceramic tradition represented

in the lowest levels at other Valdivia sites that is not found in the
coastal Valdivia phase; this hints of still earlier pottery (Lathrap 1975).
There is surely more to come, for Valdivia pottery is a product of potters
who have fully mastered their craft. No one has yet found what is
believed to be an early experimental stage of pottery making.

The Machalilla phase of coastal Ecuador is represented at sites north
of Valdivia extending into the Manabí province. Although chronologically overlapping with Valdivia sites and dating from 2000 B.C.–1500
B.C., this phase shows distinctive traits that stem from an unknown
source. This is of interest to us here because of the early appearance
of the stirrup-spout and bottle forms (Evans and Meggers 1966; Lathrap
1975). These also occur together at Kotosh, Peru about 1100 B.C. and
are a well-known ingredient of the Chavín-horizon pottery.

Of particular interest to this discussion is the matter of relationships
with Mesoamerica. Although the chronology at both ends (i.e., Mesoamerica and northwestern South America) still needs refining, cultural resemblances are particularly strong at an early time.

The earliest hint of contact with South American cultures may be the
appearance of pottery itself (Chapter 4) about 2300 B.C. (Belize, Guerrero
and the Basin of Mexico), as it spread northward from South America.
There is some evidence that this was accompanied by manioc cultivation, which would tend to support the linkage of traits that Lathrap
sees earliest in the Ecuadorian sequence (Lathrap 1975).

The discovery of the Capacha phase ceramics of Colima in west
Mexico (Kelly 1980) has helped define these early relationships. Capacha
pottery shares with Valdivia pottery of Ecuador generalized features
of form and decoration and specific resemblances in broad-line incision
combined with various forms of punctuated designs. In addition, it is
believed that the shaft tombs such as El Opeño form part of the Capacha
complex extending back as far as 1500 B.C. Some of the shaft and
chamber tombs of western Mexico resemble those from the Cauca Valley
and central Andes of Colombia. In Mesoamerica, these tombs are almost
entirely limited to the states of Jalisco, Colima, and Nayarit. Although
it was once felt that they represented a diffusion northward from South
America, this is now questioned on the basis of dating.

With Ecuador's Machalilla phase, the Capacha complex shares a particular type of cranial deformation known as *tabula erecta*, as well as
some pottery forms, specifically the stirrup-spout vessel. The origin of
this curious shape is as yet undetermined but felt to have been a unique
event. The form appears early in west Mexico, central Mexico, and in
Honduras. A related form is Capacha's trifid vessel (Plate 4-c, p. 93)
known also from coastal Sinaloa and Arkansas in the United States.
South of the Machalilla culture of Ecuador, the stirrup-spout became
a popular vessel form of the Chavín and subsequent Mochica cultures
of Peru while one trifid is known from the highlands (Kelly 1980).

Although the distribution of this shape is discontinuous, a recognizable early tradition of which it is a part can be found in the complexes of Panama (Monagrillo), Colombia (Puerto Hormiga, Barrancoid, Barlovento), and Ecuador. Contact between these areas and Mesoamerica could have been made by following the Pacific Coast or directly across the sea. Honduras may represent an intermediate point along the Caribbean side, and influences from both directions might have converged on central Mexico (see discussion in Kelly 1980).

Another area of Mesoamerica to profit from this maritime travel was that called Soconusco (coastal Guatemala and Chiapas). No stirrup-spouts or trifids have been found in this region but at Altamira, Chiapas, Green and Lowe (1967) found ceramic ties between the early Barra and Chorrera material. A striking similarity was noticed by M. D. Coe (1960a, 1961) and Meggars, Evans, and Estrada (1965) between Ocós pottery and that from the Chorrera phase of Ecuador, sites approximately equivalent in date. It should be remembered that Ocós represents an early, very wide-spread stylistic tradition that predates the Olmec civilization. The Chorrera (or Engoroy) phase succeeds the Valdivia and Machalilla phases of Ecuador already mentioned. Both Ocós and Chorrera yield pottery decorated by a kind of iridescent painting in bands or circles. To the same Ecuadorian phase belong napkin-ring ear spools, annular bases, and obsidian flakes and blades seen by Meggers as Mesoamerican influence. Again, rocker-stamping occurs.

The Preclassic ceramic resemblances between Mesoamerica and northwestern South America can be summed up as follows: The Barra phase pottery of Altamira (red slip, incising, grooving, fluting, zoned decoration, cordmarking) ties in with Machalilla, Ecuador and with Puerto Hormiga and Barlovento, Colombia. The widespread Ocós complex (flaring wall bowls, dentate and plain rocker-stamping, cordmarking, zone burnishing, iridescent painting) is related to the Chorrera phase of Ecuador. Zoomorphic effigy representations of Ocós parallel those of Puerto Hormiga and Momíl. The long solid vessel supports (spider-leg tripods) of Tlatilco are found in Momíl II and Early Tutiscainyo. From west Mexico at the Morett site, Meighan (1969, 1972) ties his red-and-white zoned ware to that of the Chorrera and Tejar phases of Ecuador.

If Chorrera proves to be earlier than currently dated, which Lathrap anticipates, the hollow figurine complex that has a long tradition on the Guayas Peninsula could be ancestral to the whole hollow figurine complex of Mesoamerica. He also believes the hollow pottery dogs of Colima, whistling jars, and multitiered vessels of west Mexico can all be ultimately attributed to Ecuador, which has a long experimental history in these features, extending back to 3000 B.C. (Lathrap 1975).

Knowledge of metal working, which became widespread after A.D. 900, is, along with pottery making, the most significant feature believed to be imported from the south. The art in Ecuador goes back to 2000 B.C. (Lathrap 1975). The Tarascans were famed metal workers, as were the Mixtecs. Two possible centers of introduction have already been mentioned—the southern Maya area and western Mexico (Pendergast 1962b), which would mean that the old Preclassic lines of communication were kept open. Mountjoy (1969) has drawn attention to specific similarities between metal artifacts from Amapa, Nayarit, and those from Ecuador. Not only are metal objects, mostly copper, abundant, but the fact that they were used for common domestic implements such as tweezers, fish hooks, and needles shows that metal was not a luxury but had become accessible to everyone. This idea is further supported by the discovery of discarded metal objects in ordinary refuse, as well as the fact that the crescent-shaped "money" knives used in other parts of Mesoamerica are not found in western Mexico. Metal had become an everyday article. An important point advanced by Meighan (1976b) is that Andean metal workers may have spent some time on the west coast in order to demonstrate technological knowledge rather than merely engaging in traded objects. In addition, there is some archaeological evidence of metallurgy workshops at the Barnard site on the Pacific coast of Guerrero, west of Acapulco (Brush 1969).

Evidence of this inter-American contact evidence has been brought together by Paulsen (1977), who feels there is now enough chronological evidence to postulate a network of maritime trade between Ecuador and Mesoamerica between 1500 and 600 B.C. as well as a lively trade between Guangala, Ecuador, and Costa Rica from 100 B.C. to A.D. 600.

In Colombia, near the old Puerto Hormiga site, early Momíl inhabitants at 1500 B.C. were sedentary villagers who planted manioc and baked it on large, circular, rimmed griddles. They already were decorating some vessels with negative or resist painting, which has a long tradition in Nuclear America. However, in Momíl II a few hundred years later maize agriculture was practiced, as evidenced by stone *metates* and *manos*. Other Mesoamerican-like traits appearing at this time are bowls with basal flanges, mammiform-shaped supports, tall solid tripods, tubular spouts, red-zoned incisions, red pigment rubbed in incised lines, flat and cylindrical stamps, and zoomorphic whistles.

Later influence and contact seem more sporadic and less generalized. It is possible that Mesoamerican settlers colonized the Pacific coast of Colombia from time to time. The Tumaco culture near the border of Ecuador had a well-defined complex of ceramic traits resembling some on the Gulf coast of Mesoamerica. Other similarities have been found in such diverse areas as Oaxaca, the highlands of Mexico, and Guatemala, and in some Central American cultures. We find thin, red-slipped, and incised pottery, double-bridged spouts, basal flanges, white-on-red painting, thin pointed vessel supports, anthropomorphic figurines, and large *metates* and *manos* without any antecedents in the older local tradition. Reichel-Dolmatoff (1965) believes that this complex moved eastward away from the coast and gradually spread up the river valleys to the intermountain valleys near the headwaters of the Magdalena River, introducing such traits as deep-level pit graves, elaborate figurines, head deformation, vessel suports, and perhaps double-spouted jars, stamps, *malacates*, and whistles. Here the inhabitants of San Agustín and Tierradentro carved great shaft-and-chamber tombs into the earth, a local specialization closely paralleled in western Mexico. Their chronological range is still undetermined. (See discussion in Kelly 1980.) It is in this region that a sub-Andean culture pattern eventually developed. By Conquest times, some political cohesion had been achieved, and many late customs are similar to those seen in Mesoamerica: warfare for the purpose of capturing sacrificial victims; sacrifice by removal of the heart, flaying, and arrows; exhibition of trophy skulls; frontooccipital head deformation; tooth mutilation; and bee keeping. Chibcha traditions speak of a bearded man who brought the knowledge of arts and crafts to his people before eventually ascending to the sky, recalling the legend of Quetzalcóatl.

Turning now to Peru, a number of shared traits around the years 1500 B.C.–500 B.C. have been compiled: ear spools; finger rings; mirrors; effigy vessels; stirrup spouts; flat-based, straight-sided bowls; *tecomates*; and the decorative techniques of zoning, paneling, burnishing, and roughening of fields using rocker-stamping, excising, and punctating. It may be significant that in both areas the first great art styles, those of Chavín and the Olmecs, were spreading. The presence of the jaguar or feline motif as a common ingredient is often pointed out in these two styles. Although the jaguar motif is a recurrent theme in both, there are highly significant differences. The Olmec jaguar is usually a were-jaguar, more human than animal, whereas in Chavín the animal overshadows the human attributes. The style and execution are very different in both areas and Willey (1962b) has argued against a close relationship other than a possible sharing of ancient mythological concepts, which if they existed at all, have left no trace in the intermediate areas. For example, neither Puerto Hormiga nor the later site of Momíl on the northern Colombian lowlands has produced any artifacts reflecting the jaguar art theme although Mesoamerican influence is much in evidence.

The question of Olmec–Chavín relationships has been widely discussed for many years. These were once postulated in part on the mistaken assumption that the unusual features at Tlatilco were Olmec (see Grove 1974). We now know that bottles and stirrup-spouts are not Olmec traits, and may represent different traditions that met in highland central Mexico. The similarities often pointed out between Olmec and Chavín ceramics and iconography may be due more to derivation from an earlier widespread tradition than from any direct contact between the two cultures.

Still later resemblances can be found between art styles of Izapa

(Mexico) and Chavín (Peru) and between west Mexican ceramics with the Moche culture (Badner 1972). On this later horizon, there are two striking specific similarities with Peru in the *chimera* decoration—an imaginary monster in Mochica art which was used as a pottery design on a bowl from Amapa, Nayarit (Meighan 1969) and the Nazca-style gold disks of western Mexico (Furst 1965). Guerrero has also produced several isolated features that hint of southern origins. For example, at Arcelia, a small mound explored by looters exposed an interior three-storied adobe structure the trapezoidal doorway of which is very Incan in form.

Both South and Central American influence is evident in the Mixteca–Puebla culture, some features of which have been noted in the Aztatlán complex. One Mixteca–Puebla polychrome vessel in the National Museum of Anthropology of Mexico is decorated with an interlocking serpent motif much in the style of textile designs from coastal Peru. Finally, the linguists, with understandable caution, tell us that the Tarascan language, with no known relative in Mesoamerica, may be affiliated with Penutian languages, which also embrace the Quéchua-Aymará in Bolivia (Swadesh 1956; see discussion in Wolf 1959).

In summary, the evidence for contact between centers of Nuclear America is found from early to late horizons. Around 1500 B.C. the contact seems to have been stronger and suggests some kind of organization, while later influences were more sporadic. In reviewing the recent archaeological material, Colombia and Ecuador appear to have been the hearth of many cultural innovations that spread to both centers of Nuclear America. If overland travel by foot or voyages by sea at this early time seem incredible, the task of defending any alternative explanation is a burden of equal proportion. In a study of possible maritime contacts, Edwards (1978) points out that sea travel would not have been as difficult as is often depicted. The trip could have been made directly by sea, in large ocean-going rafts or canoes, and if the course was in doubt, one could easily have tacked toward land now and then to check on progress. The trip was also possible in a smaller craft such as a dugout by following a course close to shore and running up on a beach to search for food or to wait out an impending squall. (See discussion in Paulsen 1977.)

Reflecting on the emergence of civilization in Mesoamerica, one wonders what influence any of these outside contacts might have had. If we are correct in believing that maize was transmitted south from Mesoamerica and that the art of pottery making traveled north from South America, these would be both the earliest and most significant features ever exchanged. Of the other elements mentioned, many are trivial and nonessential in nature and would hardly have affected the on-going equilibrium. Metallurgy, the most significant later import, arrived in Mesoamerica long after the patterns of civilization had crystallized, and served only to enrich an elaborate society already set in its ways. Although it is not yet possible to understand the trading mechanism or the nature of contact, it is significant that interaction and exchange of ideas were taking place.

Similar problems concerning the effect of possible diffusion arise in relation to the current trans-Pacific studies, which attempt to trace Old World influences on New World cultures. Here interest centers around an old question in archaeology: Did New World civilizations arise independently, or were their origins and development significantly influenced by the Old World?

OLD WORLD CONTACTS

When similarities are found in different cultures, they may be explained on the basis of convergence. That is, if environments pose similar problems to different peoples, they might be expected to solve them in similar ways, leading to independent inventions of the same custom or technique. On the other hand, a cultural trait may have been shared or widely copied, resulting in its geographical spread by the process called diffusion. For example, most people have no difficulty in accepting the diffusion of agriculture from Mesoamerica to southwestern United States where chronological, ecological, and geographical factors reinforce the archaeological data. The assumption of diffusion between such widely spaced areas as the New and Old Worlds, however, has set up a lively controversy. To admit the intrusion of an Old World trait into the western hemisphere is felt by many to somehow deprive our cultures of their native genius or to undermine the status of New World civilizations. Part of the controversy involves such intangibles as the very nature and "psychic unity" of man. For example, some feel that pottery making is so unique a concept that it could only have been invented once in the history of the world. Others see it as a simple technique easily explained by a number of possible origins, including inspiration by natural forms such as gourds, imitation of stone receptacles, or accidental invention resulting from the observation of clay drying in the sun or hardening through proximity to fire.

Those who have difficulty in accepting the idea of trans-Pacific contacts want to know how man managed to transport himself across the Pacific Ocean and ask for explanations of time, place, and means of contact. They feel that such traits as metallurgy and pottery making are not so complex that they could not have had multiple origins, and they cite numerous historical cases of reinvention. Stylistic convergences can—and have been known to—occur. The fact that the only antecedents we have for the Olmec culture are the stone carvings of Abaj Takalik need not mean that more antecedents will not be found, thus it is not necessary to invoke voyages across the Pacific to provide their roots. The history of the domestication of maize in the Mexican highlands has proved that it could have taken place locally and that New World domestication of plants is no longer challenged. The botanical evidence for Old World–New World origin of plants has been widely discussed over the years, and the most recent opinions have been summarized in Chapter 3 (Baker 1971; Flannery 1973; Tolstoy 1974). Even if sporadic contacts did somehow take place, the foreign influence may not have been sufficiently early or significant to be decisive in influencing the emergence of New World civilizations (Phillips 1966).

Those favoring trans-Pacific contacts are not dismayed by these challenges. They believe that early voyages did take place, perhaps accidentally in some instances, as a result of voyagers being swept off course and carried away by currents. They admit that evidence will be difficult if not impossible to produce, but they do not see transportation as an overriding problem in view of the convincing nature of the evidence itself. Meggers believes that an excellent case for diffusion can be supported by such factors as the uniqueness of a trait, the lack of local antecedents, the absence of functional causality, and the clustering of traits. In this view, Old World influence in Mesoamerica is reflected primarily in styles and motifs and in some technical processes. The brief summary presented here is based largely on the writings of Ekholm (1964), Heine-Geldern (1959, 1966), D. H. Kelley (1960, 1969), and Tolstoy (1963, 1974).

The oldest trans-Pacific influence in Mesoamerica is postulated for the Early Preclassic period coming in from Valdivia, coastal Ecuador, and corresponding to the Early Bronze age in China during the Shang dynasty (1700–1027 B.C.) (Meggers, Evans, and Estrada 1965). At this time the art of jade working and the jaguar or feline motif could have been introduced to Mexican lowland cultures. This has been seriously challenged by Lathrap and others. Tolstoy (1963) has made a strong case for the introduction of stone beaters for making bark cloth from Asia into upper Central America and the Isthmus of Tehuantepec around 1000 B.C. This study is backed by statistical analyses of detailed attributes and takes into account the alternatives, nonessential aspects, and degrees of similarity. Kelley (1969) has attempted to derive the Mesoamerican calendar from the Chinese lunar zodiac.

The cylindrical tripod vessel of Early Classic Teotihuacán has parallels in the bronze and pottery vessels of the Han period in China. Details of form, the conical lid, and the frequent use of a bird at the apex, as well as the use of a mold for producing appliqued ornaments, are shared by both regions. During the Classic period clay figurines were produced in molds, replacing the earlier hand-modeled technique. Might not this change represent a new application of the mold originally used to make the bronze vessels? About the same time the distinctive Tajín art style spread its interlaced design through most major centers of Mesoamerica. This scroll pattern is paralleled in late Chou art in China. The fresco technique for decorating walls and pottery and wheeled clay figures as miniature reproductions of bronze carts are both traced to Han China by Ekholm (1964).

Ekholm sees a second wave of influence during the Late Classic and Postclassic periods in Mesoamerica that seems to stem not from China but from the Hindu–Buddhist civilizations of India and Southeast Asia. This influence is seen in phallic sculptures and themes in bas-relief panel carvings such as the lotus motif, tiger thrones, and the "tree of life." The relief carvings of Palenque contain much of this flavor, and some is present in later periods at Chichén Itzá and in central Mexico. As interest in this old field of research has been renewed, many scholars have recently engaged in comparative analyses of conch shells, panpipes, metal casting, calendrical concepts, mythology, architecture, sacrifice, languages, and botanical studies. There is interest in the transfer of knowledge as an event and also in diffusion as an explanation of culture change.

This whole subject of Old and New World contacts has been reviewed and articulately presented by Davies (1979). In summing up the evidence both trans-Atlantic and trans-Pacific, he presents four periods in New and Old World relationships prior to 1492. These are as follows:

(1) 40,000 B.C.–10,000 B.C. in which bands of hunters entered the New World from northeast Asia.

(2) 10,000 B.C.–A.D. 1. During this period agriculture is believed to have developed independently in the New World. The proposed diffusion of pottery-making from Japan to South America seems less plausible now than it did a few years ago. To my knowledge nothing has come to light to reinforce this theory, while pottery in Ecuador seems to be earlier inland than on the coast, thus weakening the argument for diffusion from Japan. It is during this period that contact is evident between North and South America.

Maize agriculture is believed to have diffused south out of Mesoamerica while pottery-making and manioc cultivation made their way north from South America. Around 1500 B.C. an early widespread ceramic tradition is found in northwestern South America, certain locations in Panama, Honduras, and on the Pacific Coast of Mesoamerica as far north as Sinaloa.

The great Olmec and Chavín civilizations flourished thereafter. They may have been aware of each other or may reflect their common earlier background resulting in iconographic similarities. Although the Olmec and Chavín cultures were contemporary with the Egyptian New Kingdom and the Shang Dynasty in China, there is nothing that hints of transoceanic voyages to place these latter cultures in contact with those of the Americas.

(3) A.D. 1–A.D. 800 are years marked by the great New World civilizations of Teotihuacán and the Maya in Mexico, Nazca and Mochica

in Peru. Davies (1979) notes that although the Chinese may have been capable of a chance oceanic crossing at this time, accounting for some Teotihuacán ceramic designs, as yet there is no evidence that this occurred.

(4) A.D. 800–A.D. 1492 could have witnessed the arrival of Polynesian boats on the shores of Peru (or even Peruvian sailing rafts reaching the Polynesian islands), but to date no pre-Columbian material has been found that includes anything of Polynesian manufacture.

The Vikings did visit America in pre-Columbian times, but their landing made little impact on the world at large. Likewise the ancient Mexicans had small wheeled clay animals but since the principle of the wheel was never applied in a utilitarian way, we say the wheel was lacking in the New World. As Kroeber (1948) pointed out: An invention (or discovery) is no invention until accepted socially. Thus, in this sense, America was not fully "discovered" by the Europeans until 1503 when Amerigo Vespucci identified it as a New World (Davies 1979).

The two Ra expeditions of Thor Heyerdahl demonstrated that Egyptian reed boats might have successfully reached America. Heyerdahl is careful however not to speculate as to when this may have happened, nor does he suggest that the Nile civilization was in any way responsible for those of America. Davies cites pertinent examples of how people washed ashore on foreign soil have adapted their way of life to the local culture rather than initiate changes they may remember from their homeland. One is therefore led to question how great an impact any chance survivor might have had on New World civilizations.

This rather negative note may be misleading as I have touched only certain aspects of the problems. For more detailed discussion, the reader is urged to consult Benson (1977), Davies (1979), Riley *et al.* (1971), and Tolstoy (1974).

If we now restate the problem of diffusion in the light of the latest studies, we are left with a very basic question: Assuming that contact did occur, how far does it go toward explaining such basic factors as the function and configuration of the socioeconomic pattern of Mesoamerica, the "core" features of its culture, and its rise to civilization? To affect substantially basic cultural development, the influence would presumably have been absorbed early in the Preclassic horizon, before the pattern of civilization crystallized. Second, the influence would have had to be of a nature that would affect the existing equilibrium in the religious, political, social, or economic systems. To present evidence in support of this thesis is a difficult task, but the present atmosphere of challenge, discussion, and weighing of evidence is producing stimulating results. Trans-Pacific contacts have yet to be proven convincingly, but analytical studies in progress mark the first step in a truly scientific approach that is replacing the older, emotional one.

Mesoamerica in Retrospect

By now the reader has become familiar with Tikal, Tlatilco, Dzibil-chaltún, and Kaminaljuyú, and an endless assortment of names difficult to retain and harder to spell. Does it matter which people painted their pots and which added legs? Are pipes and Plumbate worth remembering? The answer must indeed be yes, for just as every piece is necessary to complete a puzzle, so in archaeology each bit of evidence is precious and has its rightful place in the record. Interrelated and arranged chronologically, these fragments of knowledge, pieces of culture, form the factual record from which inferences and interpretations of the history of Mesoamerican civilization are drawn. Thus, this record will serve as a testing ground for the ultimate disproof or verification of the ever-increasing number of hypotheses and models, regardless of source. Furthermore, and even more important, this systematic knowledge is a necessary prerequisite toward an understanding of the processes at work in the evolution of a civilization, wherever it may be found.

CIVILIZATION DEFINED: THE MESOAMERICAN EXAMPLE

It is time to see what is meant by the term *civilization* and in what way it applies to Mesoamerica. It is commonly felt that a "civilized" person is one who is a member of a permanent, large, complex society with an orderly government, as contrasted with a member of a small independent group, perhaps leading a nomadic or primitive life. The inference here is that the concept of civilization is closely related to that of the state, which is true. This political aspect is only part of its character, however. In attempting to define what is meant by civilization, the views of anthropologists often reflect their particular regional interests. For example, Childe (1952a, 1952b), whose primary concern has been with Old World cultures, in particular those of the Near East, feels that writing and urbanism are achievements correlated with civilization. Often mention is made of specific techniques such as metallurgy, use of the wheel, and domestication of beasts of burden. However, if we try to apply these kinds of criteria to cultures throughout the world we run into difficulty for some New World civilizations clearly do not conform to this pattern. Furthermore, the simple possession of one or more such features does not indicate the existence of a highly complex society as some of these traits may be found among very primitive people. To embrace all civilizations of both the Old and New Worlds such a definition must be cased in more general terms to express a quality or style of life. The forms that these may take are the specific characteristics of each individual civilization unique to it. Among those general qualities implicit in the word *civilization* we find many relating to a well-developed social structure, such as stratification of rank; complex division of labor resulting in occupational specialization; intensive agriculture; efficient methods for the distribution of food, raw materials, and luxury items; some large concentration of population; monumental architecture; and political and religious hierarchies in whose hands rests the administration of the state. Characteristics of civilized societies include some form of writing or recording device which seems functionally very important for administrative purposes, and a high art in which sophistication, symbolism, and language of form are present. If a culture embraces not only one or two but all of these features, we say it has attained that degree of complexity called civilization.

There is further agreement among scholars that a civilization must have as its base sufficient efficiency in food production to produce a surplus so that some members of the community can dedicate their full time to crafts, trade, religious, administrative, or other pursuits, by which means advances are made in technological, political, and social control. The fact that agriculture is practiced by many simple cultures does not necessarily imply that a surplus of food is produced. Some motivation must be present to produce more food than is needed for mere subsistence. When the reasons for such a motivation are exposed, more will be known about the processes that lead to the rise of civilization, an issue that we will take up shortly.

Let us look at Mesoamerica as a civilization. It possesses all the general complexities just mentioned, excelling particularly in monumental public works and scientific and intellectual achievements. I shall try to outline what I consider to be the fundamental aspects of Mesoamerican civilization—those ingredients that give it its particular style. First, it possessed an elaborate religious hierarchy closely integrated with a formalized political system, wherein lay the administrative powers. The belief in a fatalistic cosmology was accompanied by man's perpetual struggles to influence the deities on his behalf. Special features became of primary importance in carrying out man's mission in life such as human sacrifice, the ritualistic ball game, a special complex calendrical system and method of counting, periodic markets, and institutionalized trade. In this civilization the principle of the wheel was never put to any practical use nor was any beast of burden domesticated. The first case is not easily explained because the wheel could have been used to great advantage both by ceramicists and for transporting goods. Its absence is all the more remarkable since an excellent working model existed in miniature wheeled objects. In the second case, the lack of a suitable native animal to domesticate is one obvious explanation. This situation indicates that domesticated animals as a source of energy are not a determining factor in the growth of civilization. Metallurgy, usually considered to be a vital technology, was introduced to Mesoamerica from cultures further south. However, this occurred long after the attainment of its cultural climax, and therefore is not seen as either a prerequisite or an inducement to the rise of civilization in this part of the world. Another special characteristic of Mesoamerican civilization as a whole is the multiplicity of centers of development. Never in its long cultural history was there one capital, one political center, or seat of power. In earliest times, small cultural centers were the general rule, and these were eventually succeeded by larger settlements, some of which reached urban proportions. At no time, however, was there a centralization of administration that can approach that of the Inca state in Peru, for example. As a result specific civilizations within Mesoamerica can be identified. One can properly speak of an Olmec civilization in Preclassic times; the Classic Teotihuacán, Zapotec, and Maya civilizations; and numerous Postclassic examples. Nonetheless these regional cultures differ from each other only by degree. Their basic pattern was very similar. For example, they shared religious concepts although deities had local names; they ate the same staple foods with local environmental supplements; whether they put feet or annular bases on their pots or painted or incised them or both was a matter of taste and local tradition. But to use Kroeber's term, the ethos of Mesoamerican culture persisted in space and time. One of its most striking aspects is its continuity from 1200 B.C. to A.D. 1521.

Having looked at regional developments, we can now review the whole with more perspective. To study the Olmecs in terms of their own local development would make little sense for they were involved with peoples from Guerrero to El Salvador. Teotihuacán's prosperity depended on its foreign markets. With these cut off, it withered away. The lowland Maya civilization is not yet fully understood but it is usually conceded that contact with Teotihuacán made such an impact that when direct relationships ended, the Maya underwent many socioeconomic changes, which may have eventually affected its collapse. The Yucatecan Maya and the Toltecs were surely related, sharing and copying styles and concepts. The Maya had settled into small city-states and highland kingdoms by the time the Aztecs expanded their empire, but the areas were in contact. The Aztecs in 1519 had not gone beyond a tributary empire or developed a politically united state, but their history was interrupted by the Spaniards' arrival.

At the risk of oversimplification, the following pages emphasize these widespread relationships between regional centers. If seemingly repetitious at times, it is the continuity of basic concepts that run like threads binding into a single entity the diverse areas, and these are the fundamentals that give cultural unity to Mesoamerica.

EARLY BEGINNINGS

In the beginning, which in this area is around 22,000 B.C., our base is a diverse geographical area dominated by two north–south mountain ranges and a transverse volcanic axis that fractured the face of the land into very different environmental habitats. Their geographical range includes altitudes from 2400 m to sea level, rivers, lakes, estuaries, swampy settings, deserts to tropical forests, each with a variety of fauna and flora.

Until approximately 8000 B.C., this part of the New World we call Mesoamerica was culturally indistinguishable from its neighbors. Population was not heavy, and man lived by hunting large and small game animals and supplementing his diet by natural foods that could be gathered or foraged at will with no effort on his part to replenish nature's stores. The transition from the terminal Pleistocene to the modern age was not dramatically marked by climatic changes in Mesoamerica. Likewise, man's way of life did not undergo abrupt changes, for the hunting of large game animals in this region had never been as important as smaller game and wild plant food.

TRANSITION TO FARMING

Around 8000–7000 B.C. are the first signs that some alterations were being made. Our information comes mainly from highland Mexico and Belize where there is ample evidence that this area was occupied early. Tamaulipas, Tehuacán, Oaxaca, and the Basin of Mexico also provide evidence of this transition from nomadic hunting and gathering to a sedentary life with agriculture. The first three areas are arid or semiarid highlands, whereas the Basin of Mexico was a forested, lacustrine environment with adequate rainfall. The domestication of plants seems to have been a very gradual process for the advantages were not immediately apparent and it required many years to develop a high-yield race of plants that would make it worth man's while to give up his mobile existence. In the arid environments, man moved seasonally to exploit plant life according to their production schedules. In the Basin of Mexico, an early sedentary life was possible because of the abundant lacustrine, piedmont, and forest food resources. Although early agriculture is not easily recognized, it is believed (Bray 1977a) that man was under no pressure or stress, but that he simply drifted into domestication of plants by accident, possibly beginning with garden plots beside the kitchen door. Domesticated maize, which had evolved around 5000 B.C., is currently believed to have evolved from *teosinte*, a native grass. Beans, squash, and the bottle gourd were among other early domesticates. If indeed maize developed from *teosinte*, known only from the Mexican area, its distribution would constitute evidence of early diffusion, for by 3000 B.C. maize had reached the southwest and southeast of the United States and as far south as highland Peru.

In return, South America contributed its tropical forest cultigen, manioc, which we believe to have been present in Mesoamerica by 2000 B.C., brought in along with the art of pottery making. Thus there is evidence of widespread communication soon after the beginnings of settled life. The urge for some to move around was ever present.

Focusing on Mesoamerican events, domestication may have taken place in various regions of the highlands. The earliest corn samples from Tehuacán and Tlapacoya are already *Zea mays*, a corn well down the evolutionary road. Its early forms or origins are yet to be discovered. Maize cultivation spread from the highlands to the lowlands where it was enthusiastically received by Pacific coastal peoples who immediately substituted it for manioc.

With the appearance of pottery by 2000 B.C. near the coasts of Guerrero, Chiapas, and Belize, we say the Preclassic period begins. Because these earliest known ceramics are too high quality to be rudimentary efforts, I have dated Preclassic beginnings at 2500 B.C. as a conservative estimate. Over the 5500 years from 8000 to 2500 B.C., the shift from the Desert tradition as a way of life to one based on agriculture, Mesoamerica had unwittingly set her course, one that was to culminate in a brilliant civilization.

The Preclassic years, 2500 B.C. – A.D. 1, are those which transform the simple agricultural villages into a variety of settlements; some became much larger and wealthier than others with increasingly complex sociopolitical organization and expanding interregional exchange networks. Although the development of agriculture and sedentarism seems to have taken place in a highland environment, it was in the lowland regions that the most spectacular cultural advances were made. By 1200 B.C. Mesoamerica had spawned its first civilization, that of the Olmecs.

THE OLMECS   Olmec civilization probably developed largely where we find it, around the Los Tuxtlas areas of Veracruz where basalt stone was available within 50 km and the rich flood lands produced bountiful food crops. Although the stone carvings and relief sculptures have no local antecedents, the ceramics follow a logical sequential development out of the earlier widespread Ocós horizon. Some forerunners of the Olmec sculptural style are found at Abaj Takalik, Guatemala. The dramatic rise to civilization was related to a desire for resources lacking in the homeland area such as obsidian, salt, and good hard stone. The effort to acquire these products led to the development of exchange networks, and could be one reason for the emergence of a wealthy elite and stratification of society. A complex religious system emerged, which in turn demanded considerable scheming to sanctify rituals, resulting in even more complex sociopolitical organization. The cultivation of maize on such rich lands produced a surplus, resulting in competition for the remaining land available. Thus a land-owning group furthered the stratification of society. Eventually the wealthy elite saw in a new ideology an opportunity to legitimize semidivine lineages and emphasize royal descent which would reinforce their power. The kings, who had their portraits carved into colossal stone heads, believed themselves semidivine descendants of a jaguar–human primordial pair. The werejaguar, fire-serpent, and their symbols are predominant artistic themes. The crocodile too may have played a larger role than once thought. Left unanswered is what sparked the initial demand for foreign goods. How important a role did religion play? It is easy to see how once an elite was formed, it worked to maintain itself.

Whether acquisition of power was quite this calculated we do not know, but the reasoning fits the archaeological facts. All explanations of the rise of the Olmec civilization ultimately involve long-distance exchange networks. These people needed not only daily or utilitarian commodities, but the elite had an insatiable desire for luxury goods such as jade and ilmenite, displayed as badges of authority, power, and prestige. The control of this trade contributed to the wealth of the elite and the unequal distribution of goods. Religion, land ownership, and trade are all related factors that were conducive to stratification and creation of a rich upper class.

Products were procured via exchange with high-status individuals in other developing societies in Oaxaca, Morelos, the Basin of Mexico, Soconusco, and the Maya area. The commercial trail is marked by small portable art objects, sculptured rock carvings and cave paintings. The few militaristic themes outside the Olmec heartland are not sufficient to suggest any attempt at conquest.

The pursuits of the Olmec may have provided the stimulus for other great developments seen in Oaxaca and the Basin of Mexico. In these areas too, farming communities were developing along similar lines with emergent elitist societies. The Olmecs provided them with a model for becoming rich and powerful. Being astute pupils, the Oaxaqueños thus realized their own potential, and their subsequent development permitted them to outstrip the Olmecs and develop their own civilization.

At San Lorenzo and La Venta some of the architectural concepts that became basic features of later Mesoamerica are seen in mounds grouped around courts, astronomical orientation of buildings, tombs, and caches with elaborate offerings emphasizing social stratification and ritual. Never an urban city, but a well-maintained ceremonial center supported by a large hinterland population, San Lorenzo prospered until 900 B.C. at which time it was violently destroyed, perhaps as a reaction against a ritualistic system that could no longer be maintained. A somewhat similar and disastrous cycle repeated itself at La Venta.

By 400 B.C. the Olmec civilization was spent. It produced Mesoamerica's first great art style, built up elaborate exchange networks, and left a legacy of ritual, religious beliefs, and architectural planning for the great civilizations to follow. Its complex iconography may have prepared the groundwork for a writing system. The Olmec civilization produced no cities, nor would it be called a state, for there is no evidence of administrative functions of large bureaucratic organization. It was strongly oriented toward the interrelated concepts of a religious philosophy and development of trade. In this the legacy of the Olmecs was enormous, for they established much of the cultural pattern on which future Mesoamerican civilizations were to build.

And now we are confronted with our first vanishing civilization in Mesoamerica. What happened to the Olmecs? As to the people themselves, some may have dispersed and moved on to other regions of Mesoamerica. One of these may have been the eastern region of Tabasco, from where they could have followed the great rivers to live among the Maya, who spoke the same or a related language. As to their civilization, it is suggested that internal weaknesses brought it down, through the inability to maintain such elaborate and demanding ritual and elite class structure. It is entirely possible too that they had stimulated other regions to the point where they themselves were eclipsed, by Oaxaca for example, who had much greater environmental potential for growth of civilization than did the Gulf lowlands. But the Olmecs will be remembered for setting Mesoamerica on its course of future growth.

The Classic period developed or emerged gradually from a Preclassic foundation and is not represented uniformly throughout Mesoamerica nor do its manifestations occur simultaneously. Probably as a result of the contact with the precocious Olmecs, the next major developments took place in the highland area of Oaxaca, the Basin of Mexico, and among the lowland Maya. The Mexican regions have histories older than the lowlands but their Preclassic development was less complex.

As the Olmec civilization developed, however, it was the highlands that controlled the desired resources, that could concentrate great populations in urban developments as a result of high-yield agriculture based on irrigation. These were primary factors in the shift of leadership to the highlands of central Mexico.

Monte Albán is unique in representing a conscious communal effort to found a political capital on neutral land. This is one of the best examples of a fledgling state with a ranked authoritarian administrative system. It was these masters of organization that gave us the beginnings of the Mesoamerican calendar. Although Monte Albán dealt commercially with its neighbors, colonized a district of Teotihuacán, and shared its scientific knowledge, it retained a staunchly regional flavor as center of the Zapotec culture. Fiercely loyal, warlike, and ambitious, the Zapotecs' sphere of influence was limited to the confines of the Oaxaca region.

The two most important civilizations following the Olmec were, therefore, those of Teotihuacán and the Maya. Teotihuacán led the way with its trading networks based in highland Mexico.

TEOTIHUACÁN

It will be recalled that among the Preclassic settlements in the Basin of Mexico, Teotihuacán had made an unimpressive beginning as a village settlement in the north, selecting a rather arid region shunned by earlier settlers who preferred the better agricultural land to the south. Settlement was made possible by the availability of water from natural springs, but the choice was probably dictated by the desire to control several obsidian sources closeby. Almost immediately obsidian tools began to be produced in the area of the Old City, while builders, masons, and planners laid out the four quarters of the huge ceremonial center. An important force that motivated the people behind its leaders was undoubtedly religion. Its role should not be underestimated, as it is linked to both politics and economics. Teotihuacán's major rival, Cuicuilco, was soon eclipsed culturally by the larger city, and then physically overcome by great volcanic eruptions. Now without competition, the population of Teotihuacán grew rapidly as people were drawn from the Basin of Mexico and the valleys of Puebla and Tlaxcala as well. By A.D. 400 Teotihuacán dominated all the central region including eastern Morelos, and accommodated two-thirds of its population in the city itself. The result was a true urban city, centered around a gigantic civic–ceremonial axis and marketplace surrounded by elite residences for administrative officials and priests and apartment-like compounds for the masses composed of craftsmen, workmen of all professions, and farmers. In contrast to other Mesoamerican cities, at Teotihuacán farmers lived within the city and commuted daily to their fields. The huge city is estimated to have had a population between 100,000 and 200,000. Although the development of hydraulic agriculture permitted the dense nucleation, and the massive ceremonial complex must have attracted both settlers and pilgrims to the great religious center, the wealth and prosperity of the city depended on its commercial, nonagricultural enterprises.

A great obsidian industry was developed northeast of the city at Tepeapulco, which processed the raw material quarried and brought in from nearby sources. This industry was promoted and strictly controlled from Teotihuacán which handled the redistribution. Other raw materials such as turquoise, jadeite, and chert were procured from the Chalchihuites culture in Zacatecas, cinnabar from Querétaro, minerals and other exotic stones from Jalisco and Guerrero. These were brought into the city to be fashioned by specialized craftsmen into the fine products that eventually reached all corners of Mesoamerica. By A.D. 400 green obsidian had found its way into caches at Altun Há, Belize, and Becán in the Petén.

To set the stage for its commercial expansion, the Basin of Mexico was first incorporated into the city. This area provided all building materials and many perishable foodstuffs. The Amatzinac Valley of Morelos was also taken over to provide cotton for the city's spinning industry. The eastern lowlands were particularly valuable for their cacao and rubber, and soon the eager Teotihuacános sought out control of the greatest prize of all, the cacao lands of Soconusco. Thus, the port-of-trade was established in the Valley of Guatemala, which was ideally situated to keep an eye on the cacao production while a brisk trade could be conducted with both the highland and lowland Maya. Commerce was beneficial to all but the effect on the lowland Maya elite was profound. The exposure to a new ideology and the opportunity to associate themselves with foreigners of status and wealth who ostentatiously displayed the advantages of power and authority were not wasted on the emerging Maya civilization. Teotihuacán never established a lowland colony, but the ruling dynasty of Tikal may have included a Mexican–Kaminaljuyú personage.

Teotihuacán too was influenced by it foreign contacts. Maya features can be identified in murals and in ceramics, but Maya writing and sophisticated calendrics, two of their most distinctive traits, were not adopted. A group from Oaxaca founded its own colony at Teotihuacán but relationships were closest with Tajín and peoples of the east coast.

THE SOUTHERN MAYA

Southeast of the Isthmus of Tehuantepec, the Petén Maya had settled near rivers and *bajos* where water was available. There they began to farm and build civic–ceremonial centers. Uaxactún and Tikal emerged as prominent early centers, where the corbelled vault was no longer restricted to tomb construction, but was used for roofing temples and palaces as well. Long Count dating appeared on stelae, and polychrome pottery became widespread. The Floral Park complex may represent intrusions of people from El Salvador who had seen their homes disappear under the ash and lava blown out of Mt. Ilopango. As they moved down the rivers they looked for new lands on which to cultivate their cacao and cotton and found Belize, riverine gateway to the Petén, climatically well suited for their production. This was a period of considerable homogeneity characterized by the spread of similar ceramic and architectural styles and scientific knowledge.

The entire Maya area was now populated, including northern Yucatán, but until the ninth century the most important developments took place in the southern lowland region. By A.D. 300 the pattern of Maya civilization was well established.

The old Preclassic communities were composed of pole-and-thatch houses, but some were grouped around patios and are believed to have housed extended families. These patio-group arrangements might in turn be clustered into larger settlements as were found at Copán where they were composed of 5 to 12 such family units or lineages. At Altar de Sacrificios it is possible to trace the development of an early patio-group through its enlargement to finally become a Maya center complete with temple–pyramids and elite residences. Thus there is archaeological evidence for the gradual accumulation of power and prestige by a family lineage to emerge as a local ruling dynasty.

Tikal, located in the northeastern Petén, became the largest and the most dominant center of the southern Maya lowlands in the Early Classic period. The contrast with Teotihuacán is notable. Whereas the latter was located in semiarid terrain, the Petén setting was that of a tropical forest. In the dispersed villages and clustered groupings around the large civic–ceremonial centers, nothing exists that is comparable to Teotihuacán's apartment-house compounds. The ruler, who handed out advice on when to plant, whom to worship, when and whom to ask for rain, may have been both political and religious. At the same time we believe the constant warfare between centers was an elite activity and trade in exotic products was also carefully controlled as was the distribution of goods. At least by the fourth century A.D. power was in the hands of an established lineage at Tikal.

The rise of Maya civilization in such a seemingly unlikely environment has been attributed to a number of factors including: the role of religion, trade resulting from certain local resource deficiencies, the increased occupational specialization and accentuation of class differences growing out of the demands of the civic–ceremonial center, and warfare in cases where population pressure created a need for intensification of agricultural production that had reached its limitations.

Here too, conflict over water control and land ownership is often emphasized as leading to stratification of society. There was no single cause and Maya civilization arose, as did all the others, in response to many interrelated factors. Of primary importance is believed to be the interrelationship between diverse regions, or interregional diffusion. Among the many groups in contact with each other, the Teotihuacanos in particular would have had a profound influence on the young Maya civilization. Timing was just right to impress the Maya elite with the advantages and possibilities of power. Although Teotihuacán influence would only have been one input, it is hardly coincidental that, after contact with the central Mexicans, the Maya sought to increase their power and authority through greater centralization of government. That this was done by establishing ancestral ties and divine descent as criteria for rulership was merely one of the methods the Maya used to achieve their ends.

We find interregional contact or diffusion a factor in every area of Mesoamerica, whether between Oaxaca and the Olmecs, or Tajín and Teotihuacán. It will be remembered that the Petén region was initially settled from different regions, each group bringing knowledge from its home base. In addition there was deliberate exchange of lowland–highland products to the benefit of each. An example may be the early development of the Maya calendar, which is believed to have been passed along from the Peripheral Coastal Lowlands possibly via the Guatemalan highlands. There are innumerable examples of sites that owe their prosperity not only to their own environmental potential, but also to being located favorably for contacts with ongoing trade networks. Such settlements are called gateway communities and examples are Laguna Zope, Chalcatzingo, Sakajut, Cerros, and perhaps Altar de Sacrificios.

In the lowlands, a curious hiatus or break occurred from A.D. 534 to 593 when few stelae were erected and construction almost ceased. This is somehow related to the breakdown of relations with Teotihuacán. The fire and collapse of the great highland center did not occur for several decades, so the decline evident at its foreign posts was not yet apparent at Teotihuacán itself. The highland port-of-trade closed down in the Guatemala Valley, and it seems likely that other trade routes shifted away from the Petén and merchants began circumventing Yucatán by sea.

As Teotihuacán neared collapse, other regional centers competed with each other to take its place: El Tajín, Xochicalco, Ñuiñe, and possibly Tula. This is the moment when many shifts of power and realignments took place. At Tikal where something is known of the sequence of events, some kind of a power struggle ensued during the hiatus. Tikal recovered by A.D. 593, and embarked on a great building spree under a new dynasty. Ruler A may in fact be the descendant of

Stormy Sky, suggesting that the traditional, more conservative political faction won out. During this surge of activity, many new centers emerged, centers located in the peripheral areas, conveniently located to participate in the prosperous coastal and riverine trade. When Tikal relinquished its earlier leadership, it was forced to share authority with three other centers. These so-called capitals in turn had dependencies, which resulted in four layers of authority, with main cities displaying their own emblem glyphs. Every effort was made to enhance the cities, attract merchants, and reinstate long-distance trade. Throughout the lowlands, Teotihuacán influence was still manifested in art and iconography, but many elements are vague or diffused. Some influence commonly attributed to Teotihuacán may, in fact, have stemmed from the Gulf Coast which enjoyed great prestige at this time.

From this area the ball-game cult spread rapidly, transmitted by the merchants and their cacao trade. The distribution of ball-game paraphernalia provides good indications of a trading network that encircled Yucatán by sea from the Gulf of Mexico to Belize and up the rivers to the west. Every major site had at least 1 ball court, but Tajín had 11, Chichén Itzá 7. A third great center was Cotzumalhuapa.

Much Mexican influence is present at Puuc sites in Yucatán, which until recently has been considered Postclassic in date. A reevaluation suggests that much of this may belong to the seventh century. The Toltecs were establishing themselves at Tula and traits often attributed to them can be found in northern Yucatán at this time. It seems likely that there was more travel between Yucatán and central Mexico than heretofore suspected. A trail of Maya elements leads westward along the coast of Oaxaca, to Guerrero, and then north to Xochicalco in Morelos, and finally to Tula. Maya influence is also an ingredient of the eclectic art of the murals of Cacaxtla, probably as a result of other Maya influences that spread out of Tabasco north to Matacapan and Tajín. Still more Maya traits are present in Cotzumalhuapa art. The intense trade and communication of the Late Classic or Protoclassic years are unequalled in Mesoamerican history. It is as if each region tried to fill the void left by the collapse of Teotihuacán. What effect did this have on the Maya civilization?

The peak of Maya civilization was reached after the hiatus in the years A.D. 593–830 when in addition to great accomplishments in the fields of writing, astronomy, and mathematics, artistic achievements reached a brilliant climax. Architectural complexes of temple–pyramids, staircases, courts, sweat baths, ball courts, palaces, or long buildings of multiple rooms are impressive creations produced without the benefit of metal. When these are complemented and accompanied by the rich contents of elite tombs and caches, fine stone carving, stucco sculpture, painted murals, exquisite carving on jade, bone and obsidian, pottery decorated in as many as six colors depicting scenes of ceremonial life or ritual, it is possible to reconstruct the life of the ancient Maya. What emerges is a highly stratified class society, headed by a dynastic nobility eager for wealth, prestige, and power, and concerned with legitimizing their rights of rulership. Warfare, conflict, and human sacrifice were widespread, yet made no less palatable because of the artistic skill of their portrayal. Petén centers were now urban cities of at least 45,000 (?) population. Sophisticated farming on terraces and raised fields had been developed to help cope with population pressure in a region of limited arable land. Yet despite intellectual achievements, more advanced techniques of food production, and providing defense for its population, the Maya civilization seemed to corrode from within. Pressure from without was the final blow. Why could it not have adapted and survived the new political and economic developments taking place in other areas?

When the direct relationship with Teotihuacán ended around A.D. 550 it must have had a profound effect on the Maya economic system. We have noted that some kind of major political shake-up took place during the hiatus. The rise of peripheral centers and many new centers indicates that some effort was made to adjust to the new trading networks. By following a sea route, the new networks left the older Petén areas isolated. The frenzy of building and creating more craft workshops at Tikal might be interpreted as a desperate attempt to revitalize the old system. The older ceremonial-type center with dispersed population had gradually been replaced by more city-dwellers, and more specialists, placing a heavier burden on the farmers who had moved closer. The result was the development of large nucleated urban centers. Given the level of technology of the Late Classic Maya, it is believed that great stress was put on their agricultural and social organization during these years. It is entirely possible that soil depletion and crop failures may have contributed to internal problems. A great surplus was necessary to support all the non-food producing craftsmen, workmen, administrative officials and nobility. Any slight alteration in the delicate balance among the subsistence base, the procurement of raw materials, craft production, and import–export exchange could have had disastrous effects. In this case the Maya may have overexploited their environment and not have known how to cope. One reaction may have been to turn to their deities for help, putting everyone to work enlarging temples, and thus setting in motion greater demands on food resources and services that could not be met.

Compounding their problems, the aggressive Putún Maya chose this moment to invade from northern Yucatán as well as from Tabasco, penetrating the western river systems. The Maya civilization was not equipped to deal with this challenge from without, which constituted the final nudge over the brink to collapse. By the end of the ninth century A.D., the main centers were abandoned and cities fell prey to the encroaching jungle.

THE
NORTHERN MAYA

Yucatán did not share the depressing fate of its southern neighbors for it was enjoying prosperity brought about by trade with the Chontal Maya. Central Yucatán, however, was caught in the middle. First in a strategic position between north and south, Becán and the other Río Bec sites flourished as they drew strength from both neighboring regions. But the situation was not an enviable one as each extreme sought to dominate, while Becán tried in vain to maintain its individuality behind its formidable defenses. In addition to north–south rivalry, there was also east–west communication from Belize to Laguna de los Términos. The success of the Putún maritime operations eventually left central Yucatán to the same fate as the southern centers, and by the Postclassic period the area was rapidly deteriorating.

In the rich stone mosaic facades and temples of the northern Puuc cities, Mexican influences from various sources are notable. The ball game was embraced with enthusiasm. The Putún Itzá made Chichén Itzá their capital and soon outdistanced all other centers. Puuc and Mexican features from a variety of regions, including Toltec influences, are incorporated into the art and architecture of Chichén Itzá. There is no consensus as to when all the construction was done, but everyone agrees on the very eclectic nature of the site. Feathered-serpent columns, *chacmools*, prowling jaguars, *tzompantlis*, Atlantean figures, and Toltec warrior-reliefs have their counterparts at Tula, Hidalgo. The narrative murals are Mayan rather than Mexican, but depict foreigners in some scenes.

The wealth of Chichén Itzá was founded on and supported by the long-distance trade from Tabasco to Honduras. Yucatecan commodities were salt, slaves, honey, and possibly textiles and blue coloring. Through this network circulated fine-paste pottery from the Tabasco area and Plumbate ware from Guatemala. Did a Quetzalcoátl–Kukulcán figure invade Yucatán in the late tenth century with another infusion of Toltec culture? There is little evidence of such a movement in the intervening regions, and the remains at Chichén Itzá are subject to various interpretations. The problem is more likely to be resolved by the archaeologists and art historians than by a strict reliance on the ancient chronicles for which allowance must be made for calendrical adjustments, legendary content, and later personal biases. In any event, Chichén Itzá retained the political leadership of northern Yucatán until about A.D. 1250 when its power and prestige were replaced by that of Mayapán.

The Mayapán hegemony is the last centralized government in Yucatán prior to the Conquest. The city itself had none of the inspired grandeur of its Puuc or Chichén Itzá predecessors although there was a feeble attempt to copy some of the latter's public buildings. Farmers lived in rural communities outside the city walls. Once again commerce is seen as sustaining late Postclassic prosperity. Cozumel became Mayapán's administrative center for port facilities and controlled the organized trade to Nito and Honduras. Walled port cities, religious shrines, and polychromed mural paintings of Mexican style distinguish settlements along eastern Yucatán.

All the main themes of Postclassic Mesoamerica are brought together here: interregional communication, religious pilgrimages, human sacrifices, militarism, and commercial enterprises. The separation of the capital of Mayapán from its offshore administrative center was a unique regional development. When Mayapán was eventually overthrown by an internal revolt, Yucatán was no longer a powerful force in the larger framework of Mesoamerica.

In central highland Mexico, the largest single center to emerge from the unsettled conditions following Teotihuacán's demise was Tula, Hidalgo. It had been settled as early as A.D. 650 at the confluence of two rivers about 10 km northwest of Teotihuacán, closer to the great Chichimec hordes to the north. Taking over the Tepeapulco obsidian industry, Tula became wealthy and eventually supported a dense urban center of 60,000 with a rural population of equal size. In addition to food crops, cotton may have been raised in the fertile bottomlands, and textiles would have been a valued commercial commodity.

THE TOLTECS

Archaeologically Tula is a Mesoamerican maverick. Despite the large population, its ceremonial complex is surprisingly small and suggests a hurried construction. Colonnaded halls, *chacmool* and Atlantean figures, stone reliefs of jaguars and warriors look like imitations of the northern section of Chichén Itzá, which combined Maya with earlier Toltec influence. Stelae, of which Tula has two, are a Maya feature with no central Mexican precedent. Like one at Xochicalco, a Tula ball court was built in Maya style.

We say legendary history begins with Tula, which means that fact is mixed with legend. Written sources date from the sixteenth century, 400 years after the Toltecs, but by then history had been rewritten by the Aztecs to provide themselves with the ancestral dignity they so desired. Were the Toltecs as handsome, clever, capable, and benevolent as the ancient sources would have us believe? Did they really have a priest–king called Topiltzin Quetzalcóatl who quarreled with his rival Huémac–Tezcatlipoca and had to leave in disgrace, promising to return at a later date?

Although the 300 years of Toltec history between A.D. 900 and 1200 are some of the most confusing and least well understood in Mesoamerica, the following information seems substantiated.

The people we know as Toltecs were made up of some seminomadic Chichimecs from the north, together with Nonoalca people of the Gulf

Coast and undoubtedly some descendants of Teotihuacán and other Basin of Mexico inhabitants. They continued the great commercial tradition of Teotihuacán and the ancient Olmecs and intensified the militaristic orientation of society. Tula is replete with warriors, weapons, skull racks, themes of sacrifice, and eagles devouring human hearts. However, their "empire" seems to have consisted of little more than the northern part of the Basin of Mexico and the regions immediately northeast and west of Tula. It would be interesting to know if the concept of tribute was instigated by the militant Toltecs, but information is still inadequate on this point. Trading expeditions took them to the far north to Casas Grandes, spreading Mesoamerican religious concepts and art forms in their quest for exotic minerals and peyote. Toltec merchants may have been instrumental in spreading the newly acquired knowledge of metallurgy which we believe to have been introduced into west Mexico from South America. Polychrome vessels from Yucatán and lower Central America were carried to Tula as well as quantities of the great trade ware called Plumbate, produced in southwestern Guatemala.

On one hand the Toltecs seem to have had but slight impact on Tlaxcala–Puebla, Morelos, Oaxaca, and the Gulf Coast regions, while on the other, their influence is very much in evidence in both Yucatán and highland Guatemala. As we have seen, some of this may date from an early association with their Putún allies, and it is also possible that upon the destruction of Tula in the twelfth century some people went south. These migrations would have been too late to inspire the Toltec structures at Chichén Itzá, but could account for the Toltec traits and legends in the northern highlands of Guatemala. As for Topiltzin–Quetzalcóatl, we cannot be sure, but he may have moved home to Culhuacán in the Basin of Mexico where he was born. In retrospect we still have many gaps in our knowledge of Tula's political affairs and nature and extent of its "empire." The Toltecs were of considerable importance in perpetuating the older traditions of the Teotihuacanos, to which they added their own militaristic and commercial stamp, before passing them on as a legacy to the Aztecs.

THE AZTECS   After the fall of the Toltecs, a short period ensued in which various groups vied for power in the Basin of Mexico. We refer to these tumultuous years until the rise of the Tepanecs as the Chichimec period.

The Aztecs, or Mexica, were another group of "barbaric" Chichimecs who served the Tepanecs as vassals until, through cunning and their political skills, they put together the Triple Alliance. This powerful force, composed of Texcoco, Tlacopan, and Tenochtitlán, eventually succeeded in destroying the Tepanec power at Azcapotzalco in A.D.

1428. This event set the shrewd Aztecs on their dramatic rise to power, culminating in the most powerful empire ever achieved in Mesoamerica. From their island capital, they consciously absorbed from their neighbors the skills and knowledge of their predecessors while promoting in every way possible a claim to a Toltec heritage.

To further this end, a book-burning spree was followed by rewriting history as they wanted it recorded. Monumental stone carvings were commissioned to commemorate important current events such as the inauguration of a temple, an outstanding conquest, the accession of a king. The Aztecs did not plan to be forgotten.

The physical limitations of an island city mean that nothing could be left to chance. The city was carefully laid out in a gridded pattern that dictated the efficient use of space. The heart was the civic–ceremonial precinct which, aside from its public buildings, provided open space for ostentatious state religious festivities, a great unifying force. The nonfarming population of 200,000 (?) was rigidly stratified. Feeding such a metropolis was a primary consideration necessitating control over both land and people of the Basin of Mexico. Once this was accomplished, the Aztecs exploited every possible means of agricultural potential. Next they devoted their attention to expanding their domain beyond the central regions to which end they brought into play their considerable political and military skills.

Theirs was a tributary empire; conquests were made to subjugate kingdoms for the purpose of economic exploitation. Warfare in turn reinforced religion by supplying victims for sacrifice. The first step in expansion would begin by initiating a trade relationship with a foreign power. This responsibility fell to professional merchants, the *pochteca*, who in addition to commercial activities engaged in spying to prepare the way for conquest. Once the warriors of the Triple Alliance swept through the region, this area was then required to pay annual tribute to Tenochtitlán, and no longer dealt with the *pochteca*, who moved on in search of new targets for exploitation. By these means the Aztecs managed to bring a large portion of Mesoamerica under their control, while trading operations extended as far south as lower Central America. The empire was only loosely integrated by tax collectors, but the heads of conquered regions were kept in line by "invitations" to Tenochtitlán to witness mass sacrificial ceremonies and displays of power and wealth. Fear, threats of coercion, and retribution effectively kept the tribute flowing and discouraged revolt. When the Spaniards arrived in 1519, the Aztecs were on the verge of consolidating their empire.

The economic system was sustained by heavy tribute payments and the local market system and revenue from property worked for the benefit of the state. Social organization was rigidly stratified. Power and authority were tightly held by the king and his nobility who filled the administrative posts. Religion and warfare served to reinforce and bind the whole system into a smoothly operating mechanism.

In retrospect, the Aztecs had no reason to be concerned with securing a place in history. Scheming and ruthless they undoubtedly were, but in less than 200 years they had transformed their simple nomadic society into the most powerful empire in Mesoamerica. This was effected by a deliberate adoption of the Mesoamerican way of life.

EVOLUTIONARY TRENDS

This brief sketch of Mesoamerican culture history is not meant as a summary but is aimed at emphasizing certain fundamental trends and traditions that characterize this unusual New World civilization. In the Aztec civilization we can see the amalgamation of all that had transpired in the long 2700 years of cultural development since the Olmecs started moving earth at San Lorenzo. In the Aztec capital at Tenochtitlán one can find religious, political, architectural, social, and economic concepts that have some antecedents in the first civilization of the Olmecs.

Many specific features were common to all Mesoamerican peoples such as the use of obsidian, the value placed on jade, certain deities like the rain god and feathered serpent, *metates* and *manos*, the counting system, observance of the 52-year cycle, and the ritual ball game. The list (as compiled by Kirchhoff 1943) could include many more features with ancient roots. What matters most is not the actual trait, but the continuity or persistence that these have in the archaeological record.

For many, more important than the description and the nature of Mesoamerican civilization is the discovery of how it came about. A vital prerequisite or precondition lay in the nature of the land. How often have references been made here to highland versus lowland situations and to the location of raw materials and resources. How important obsidian was to those who lacked it, and for an Olmec king an iron-ore mirror was not a luxury but a necessity. Thus the varied face of the land, altitude, water resources, and access to raw materials were of vital importance, in addition to the more obvious factors such as the diversity of plant and animal foods and agricultural potentials. Ecological differentiation became a primary factor in stimulating interregional contact and establishing exchange networks.

A related factor was the flow of ideas between these diverse regions. A much respected and wealthy member of the Olmec elite would undoubtedly have fired the ambitions of the headman of San José or Chalcatzingo to follow his example. Perhaps the most important result of the Teotihuacán–Kaminaljuyú relationship was the model of centralized authority and power that diffused to the lowland Maya. A visible result is seen for several hundred years in the art and iconography of the Maya, but we suspect that there were more subtle changes in the political and economic fields. Thus the potential of interregional diffusion of ideas should not be underestimated. Commerce provided the vehicle.

Contact with neighbors beyond the limits of Mesoamerica has been briefly summarized. Not only does archaeology confirm its existence, but of particular interest is the fact that some of the strongest evidence is among the oldest. About 1500 B.C. cultural similarities between Mexico and Ecuador were so remarkable as to suggest regular communication. Thereafter, contact seems to have been more sporadic. Earlier still, maize agriculture spread in every direction out of Mesoamerica, and manioc cultivation came north from tropical areas in South America, possibly bringing with it the idea of pottery making.

How much influence did these other cultures have on the developing civilization in Mesoamerica? Probably very little. Mesoamerica was by and large a self-contained cultural unit. It domesticated its basic food plants and lived within its own rich environmental potential. A ceramic decoration or a new art style was not likely to alter the course of events. If these were accompanied by political or socioeconomic ideas, the situation would be different, but there is no evidence that this was the case. Even a knowledge of metallurgy, which was such an advantage to Old World cultures and which became a sophisticated craft early in South America, did not reach Mesoamerica until A.D. 900, too late to shape Teotihuacán or Mayan civilizations. Even thereafter, metal was largely used for jewelry rather than put to much practical use.

The most significant import may have been pottery making, which seems to be a universal ingredient of high culture. Its origins are not yet known and may be multicentered, but at present the craft has a longer history in South America than anywhere else in the western hemisphere.

In a thoughtful summary of the rise of civilization in Mesoamerica, Lamberg-Karlovsky and Sabloff (1979) have singled out six trends in the process of cultural evolution in this area:

1. The early ceremonial centers developed into large urban centers which in two cases exceeded 100,000 population.
2. Power and authority became centralized in these urban centers.
3. Trade expanded to maintain the urban centers. Thus control and distribution of raw materials and finished products became essential, in turn increasing the wealth and power of a growing elite.
4. The volume of trade led to the rise of a separate merchant class.
5. Social organization evolved from a simple peasant–elite relationship to a highly stratified class system.
6. The role of militarism and warfare increased. This was of real concern to an expanding state as well as a necessity for protecting the vitally important trade routes.

Another trend, that of increasing secularization, might be added. I would agree with Lamberg-Karlovsky and Sabloff that religious beliefs among the Aztecs were linked as closely to other aspects of their culture as were those of the Olmecs. But in a material way, there was increasing interest in personal glorification, marriage alliances, dynastic histories, finer residences, display of wealth, control of land and labor. One suspects that, over time, religion might have become the pretext for manipulating the lower classes for the benefit of the nobility.

Some of these factors, such as interrelationships between highland and lowland peoples, between areas with and areas without resources, and between geographically similar and diversified potentials, are also paralleled in the development of civilization in the Old World. The lack of beasts of burden, metal tools, and the wheel in Mesoamerica have often been cited as deficiencies hard to overcome on the long road to complex societies. Yet when one looks out over the temples of Palenque or climbs the monuments of Teotihuacán, one wonders how great a difference these really made. What constitutes a necessity? The Aztecs from their seminomadic foundation have shown how flexible and adaptable a culture can be. The Maya provide a graphic illustration of the disastrous effects of over-exploiting an environmental potential combined with the extraordinary increase of non-food-producing urbanites. Given the advantages of hindsight they would surely have devoted some effort to long-range projections. When we stop to think of the diverse problems resolved by the urban planners of Teotihuacán and Tenochtitlán, there is still much we can learn from the study of these ancient peoples.

Selected List of Mesoamerican Deities[1]

Ah Mun Maya god of maize, symbolized by day glyph Kan and associated with the number eight. Represented in the *códices* as a handsome young man, often with a maize plant sprouting from his head. Classic and Postclassic representations (Figure 32).

Bacabs Four Maya deities, brothers, who held up the sky. Atlantean figures may represent Bacabs and date back to Classic period. Bacabs associated with the fate of the incoming year, bees, and the apiary.

Bolonti-Ku Nine Maya Lords of the Underworld, who ruled in unending sequence over a cycle of 9 nights. Glyphs included in Long Count inscriptions (Figure 16).

Centéotl, see also Chicomecóatl Aztec god of the maize plant, as distinguished from Xilonen (goddess of the young tender ear of corn) and Ilamatecuhtli (goddess of the old dried ear of corn). The three were intimately associated with Chicomecóatl, general goddess of sustenance. All may be distinguished by some attribute of the maize plant. Possibly derived from Olmec God II.

Chac, see also Tlaloc Yucatec name of rain god or group of rain deities. Rain-god cult is very old lowland tradition recorded in inscriptions and *códices*. Many concepts parallel the Mexican Tlaloc such as the ancient association of rain deities with the snake. Chac represented with long pendulous nose, a scroll beneath the eye, often toothless. Four Chacs were associated with the cardinal points: east, west, north, and south with colors red, black, white, and yellow, respectively. Many lesser Chacs (Figure 32).

[1] Based primarily on Caso 1958, Joralemon 1971, Sahagún 1946, and Thompson 1970.

Chebel Yax Wife of the great Maya creator, Itzamná. Depicted in *códices* as the old red goddess with hank of cotton or cloth, who presided over weaving activities.

Chicomecóatl Most important of Aztec vegetation deities, whose name signifies "seven serpent," also called "seven ears of corn." Sculptured in stone, she often holds two ears of corn in each hand.

Coatlícue Aztec earth goddess and mother of Huitzilopochtli, typically shown wearing a skirt made of entwined serpents. She presided over the rainy season which was directly related to her concern with the soil and agriculture.

Cocijo, see Tlaloc (Plate 7-g).

Coyolxauhqui Aztec moon goddess and ill-fated sister of Huitzilopochtli. Decapitated by her brother (Photo 74).

Curicaueri Tarascan fire and sun god. Postclassic, western Mexico.

Ehécatl, see also Quetzalcóatl Quetzalcóatl in his aspect as the wind god, shown with a projecting mouth mask. Aztec (Figure 11-b).

Ek Chuah, see also Xamen Ek Yucatec god of merchants and cacao, normally painted black and often shown traveling with a staff and back pack. Possibly of Putún origin. Classic and Postclassic periods (Figure 32).

Gucumatz, see Quetzalcóatl

Huehuéteotl The old fire god, also known as Xiuhtecuhtli. One of the most ancient of Mesoamerican deities, often shown as an old man with wrinkled face and toothless, who bears a brazier on his head. Traced back to Preclassic cultures in the Basin of Mexico and God I of the Olmecs.

Huitzilopochtli Special war and sun god of the Aztecs, chief deity of Tenochtitlán. Identified by his special weapon, the fire-serpent. He is also the blue Tezcatlipoca, associated with the south.

Itzamná Most important and supreme deity of the Maya, abundantly represented in Classic and Postclassic art. Creator deity with multiple aspects affecting every phase of man's life. Both celestial and terrestrial associations (Figure 32).

Itztlacoliuhqui God of curved obsidian knife, variant of Tezcatlipoca as deity of the ice and cold, of sin and misery. Represented in Teotihuacán and Aztec art.

Ix Chel Leading Putún deity with great shrine at Cozumel. Goddess of the moon, childbirth, procreation, and medicine, associated with lakes, wells, and underground water. Wife of Yucatec sun god, Kinich Ahau.

Kinich Ahau   Yucatec name of sun god. Sun deity is abundantly represented in Classic and Postclassic Maya art with a square eye and prominent aquiline nose, closely associated with Itzamná as the old sun god in the sky. His head glyph personifies the number four. The sun may also appear as a young man with an almond shaped eye, personifying the day Ahau.

Kukulcán, see also Quetzalcóatl   The feathered-serpent deity in Yucatán. The Codex Dresden relates the feathered serpent to the planet Venus, or Quetzalcóatl as the morning star. Many associations link the cult to the Putún Maya who brought it to Yucatán.

Mictlantecuhtli   God of death who resided in the underworld in darkness. He is usually represented wearing a mask in the form of a skull. Possibly derived from Olmec God VIII.

Quetzalcóatl, see also Kukulcán   The feathered-serpent deity, bearded god of learning and the priesthood, father and creator, brother of Xipe Totec, Tezcatlipoca, and Huitzilopochtli. He brought to man all knowledge of the arts, agriculture, and science. His many different aspects include: the wind god (Ehécatl), the morning star (Tlahuizcalpantecuhtli), and the evening star (Xólotl, his twin). Counterparts: Kukulcán and Gucumatz among the Maya. A feathered-serpent deity is prominent throughout Mesoamerican art, Classic and Postclassic periods. Preclassic representations include Olmec God VII (Figure 35).

Tezcatlipoca   A god of creation possessing many diverse forms, often identified by a smoking mirror that replaces his foot, which was wrenched off by the earth monster. God of night closely associated with deities of death, evil, and destruction. Patron deity of sorcerers and robbers. Very important because of his direct intervention in the affairs of man. Attained prominence among Toltecs as the adversary of his brother, Quetzalcóatl. Revered later not only in Tenochtitlán but as the tutelary god of Texcoco and known in many parts of Mexico. Depicted on columns at Chichén Itzá (Figure 35).

Tlahuizcalpantecuhtli, see also Quetzalcóatl   Quetzalcóatl, the planet Venus as the morning star. He appears with two faces: that of a living man and the other a skull. Postclassic Central Mexico.

Tlaloc, see also Chac   Rain god, "he who makes things grow." Aztec. Associated with serpent, mountains, flooding, drought, hail, ice, and lightning. Probably one of the most ancient Mesoamerican deities, traced to Olmec God IV. Rings around the eyes, fangs, and a volute over the mouth are frequent distinguishing characteristics (Plate 1-e; Plate 8-j; Plate 13-e; Figure 30-r). Rings around the eyes, fangs, and a volute over the mouth are frequent distinguishing characteristics. Three different Tlalocs are associated with art of the fifth to seventh centuries: (1) *the* rain deity with crocodilian features, (2) god of water and the underworld with jaguar features and net symbols, (3) patron deity of Teotihuacán (?) associated with warrior cult (Plate 10-d). In seventh- and eighth-century art Tlaloc often wears a headdress with the year sign (Plate 12-b). Counterpart among other Mesoamerican cultures: Chac (Lowland Maya), Tajín (Totonacs), Tzahui (Mixtecs), Cocijo (Zapotecs).

Tloque Nahuaque   Abstract invisible god revered in Texcoco under Nezahuacóyotl. Supreme deity who could not be represented materially. Worshipped in temples without idols.

Tonatiuh   The sun god of the Aztecs, closely associated with the young warrior, Huitzilopochtli, the sun himself. Best-known representation is that of the so-called "calendar stone" in which the central figure is Tonatiuh who clutches in his taloned eagle claws hearts of human beings, his sustenance. (See discussion, p. 440.)

Xamen Ek, see also Ek Chuah   Maya god of the north star and the guide of merchants, logically associated with Ek Chuah. His name glyph is the hieroglyph for cardinal point north. Frequently represented in *códices* (Figure 32).

Xipe Totec   Aztec god of springtime, seeding, and planting; the red Tezcatlipoca associated with the west. In his honor a priest dressed in the skin of a flayed victim, a ritual signifying the renewal of vegetation in the spring. Also called Yopi. Believed to have been brought to central Mexico from Oaxaca–Guerrero borders. Ultimate origins may be found in Olmec God VI. Revered in central Mexico, especially Tlaxcala. Represented also in Maya area in Campeche, Oxkintok, Chichén Itzá, and Mayapán (Figure 35; Plate 7-e; Photo 72).

Xólotl, see also Quetzalcóatl   Aztec god of the planet Venus as the evening star, twin brother of Quetzalcóatl. Represented as having the head of a dog. Postclassic central Mexico. Also name of Chichimec leader who established his capital at Tezcoco in Early Postclassic.

Yiacatecuhtli   Aztec god of the long-distance merchants. Shares some attributes with Quetzalcóatl. Symbol is a bamboo staff. Postclassic central Mexico, especially Cholula, Tenochtitlán–Tlatelolco.

Yum Cimil   Maya god of death and evil who presides over luckless days. In the *códices* his head often replaced by a skull; the ribs and backbone are exposed to view. Associated with the south, the color yellow, the number ten and day sign Cimi. Other names: Cizin and Hun Ahau (Figure 32).

Glossary of Terms Frequently Used in Mesoamerican Archaeology[1]

aguadas   Seasonal water holes in lowland Maya region.

amate   Paper used for making *códices;* derived from the inner bark of the wild fig tree.

Atlantean figures   Figures of men used as supporting or decorative columns (Chichén Itzá and Tula) (Figure 28-a; Photo 59).

atlatl   Spear thrower; a short, grooved stick with finger loops at one end used to propel a dart or lance (Figure 4-h; Plate 10-d).

Aztecs   Also known as Mexica. Late inhabitants of the Basin of Mexico who created the largest empire in Mesoamerica. Conquered by the Spaniards in 1521.

Bajío   Lerma River drainage basin from Guanajuato to Jalisco.

bajos   Broad, swampy depressions in Petén area that fill with water during summer months. Many were cultivated like *chinampas* by the Classic Maya.

baktun,   see Long Count

blanco levantado   An unburnished painted decoration of white transparent streaky lines, usually rectilinear. Also known as Tula Watercolored. Widespread in Bajío region and central highlands during Classic and Early Postclassic periods. May be derived from early shadow-striped decoration of Colima.

calendar round   Cycle of 52 years produced by the permutation of the 260-day cycle and the 365-day true year.

calmecac   Strict Aztec school for the male children of the king and nobility.

[1] For a more comprehensive treatment, see Muser 1978.

calpulli   Kin units, "conical clans," division of the Aztec tribe of which there were 20 in Tenochtitlán, occupying designated sectors of the city.

candelero   Small clay incense burner characteristic of Teotihuacán (Figure 22-d).

celt   Ungrooved axe, popular wood-working tool.

cenote   Natural underground well in Yucatán, a major source of water for drinking and bathing (Photo 3).

chacmool   Life-size stone figure in reclining position, legs flexed, head turned to one side. Usually found at entrance to temples as sacrificial stones or to receive offerings. Postclassic (Plate 12-d).

champ-levé   Decorative ceramic technique in which part of the design area is heavily carved, characteristic of Classic Teotihuacán.

chapalote   Ancient indigenous race of Mexican maize found in Tehuacán area.

Chichimecs   A generic term loosely applied to a multitude of peoples considered to be uncivilized barbarians, living beyond the northern limits of Mesoamerica. They were non-farming, nomadic people. Also called *Teochichimecas*.

chinampa   Very productive system of agriculture created by ditches made in swamps, and built up by repeated resurfacing with muck from the lake bottom. Popularly called "floating gardens" in the Basin of Mexico (Photo 68).

chultun   Bottle-shaped underground cistern in northern Yucatán, used for water storage; in the southern lowland Maya area, smaller lateral chambered *chultuns* were dug for food storage, particularly of the ramon nuts of the breadfruit tree.

cloisonné   Method of decorating pottery, wood, or gourds in which a layer of paint is applied to the surface. A design is marked off and the paint cut out within the design area. The hollow spaces are then filled in with another color and the surface remains smooth. Several layers of paint can be worked in this way (cultures of northern and western Mexico).

coa   Digging stick, principal farming instrument.

coatepantli   Serpent wall, forming part of sacred precincts in Postclassic highland Mexico.

codex (plural: **códices**)   Painted book made from amate paper or deer skin that folds like a screen (Photos 19, 20).

comal   Clay griddle for cooking tortillas (Figure 30-j).

cord marking   Decorative technique in which a fine cord was wrapped around a paddle and pressed against an unfired clay vessel, leaving a characteristic imprint.

Coyotlatelco ware Distinctive red-on-buff pottery tradition of Early Postclassic horizon, central Mexico.

cuauhxicalli So-called "eagle cup," stone receptacle for burning and storing of human hearts (Aztec).

"Danzantes" Life-size carvings of prisoners or sacrificed victims in bas-relief on stone slabs at Monte Albán. Preclassic (Plate 1-d).

double-line-break Incised decoration on pottery in which one or two lines run parallel to the lip or rim and then turn sharply and disappear over the edge. Middle Preclassic tradition (Figure 6-e).

excising Decorative technique applied to pottery in which deep grooves, channels, or fields were carved from the surface; recessed areas often left rough and coated with red cinnabar. Preclassic (Figure 6-k; Plate 4-g).

Fine Orange ware Fine-grained, untempered pottery with several distinct varieties. Manufactured in Gulf Coast plains and lower Usumacinta region (Figure 30-g, h, n).

florero Pottery jar with tall restricted neck and flaring rim. Classic Teotihuacán (Figure 22-f).

Haab Maya calendar year of 365 days, corresponding to Aztec Xíhuitl.

hacha ('thin stone head') Beautifully carved stone, associated with the ball-game cult, often with a notch or projecting tenon at back for attachment (Classic Veracruz cultures) (Plate 8-g).

huéhuetl Vertical drum with skin head, played with palms and fingers (Photo 43).

incensario A pottery vessel made for ceremonial purposes to hold coal and incense (Plate 7-j).

Initial Series, see Long Count

katun, see Long Count

kin, see Long Count

Long Count Total number of days elapsed from a mythical starting point in the past, 3113 B.C. (GMT correlation); recorded by the Maya in number of *baktun* (144,000 days or 20 *katuns*), *katun* (7200 days or 20 *tuns*); *tun* (360 days or 20 *uinals*); *uinal* (20 days or 20 *kins*); and *kin* (1 day). Classic lowland Maya (Figure 16; Plate 6-b).

"lost wax" (*cire perdue*) Method of casting metals; the desired form was carved in wax, coated with charcoal and clay, and the whole encased in an outer pottery form leaving ducts. The wax melted and ran out one duct as molten metal was poured in via another duct replacing the wax model. After cooling, the clay casing was broken, and the finished product extracted, each one an original (Plate 16-e).

macehual Commoner or laborer (Aztec).

malacate   Spindle whorl, usually of pottery; a perforated round disk used as a weight in spinning thread (Plate 11-b).

mano, see metate.

mayeque   Bondsman or "slave" in Aztec society.

Mazapan ware   Pottery decorated by wavy parallel red lines on buff-colored vessel. Toltec (Plate 11-e).

metate   Stone basin (quern) for grinding maize, often trough-like, accompanied by a hand stone (**mano**) (Figure 4-s).

Mexica , see Aztecs.

molcajete   Bowl, usually tripod, with interior scoring or roughening for grinding fruits and vegetables (Figure 30-e, f; 34-i).

Nahua   Language of Uto-Aztecan group; also applied to people.

Náhuat   An old linguistic form of Nahua, in contrast to the more recent close relative, Náhuatl, the language of the Aztecs.

Náhuatl   Language derived from Nahua which became the *lingua franca* of the Aztecs.

negative painting,   see resist painting

Nemontemi   Five unlucky days at year end of Aztec calendar, corresponds to the Maya Uayeb (glyph, Figure 13-c).

Nonoalca   Inhabitants of Tula who came from the southeast (Tabasco) neighbors of the Chontal, Putún. These were people of high skills and culture who co-existed with the Tolteca–Chichimeca at Tula, Hidalgo.

olla   Pottery jar with flaring neck (Figure 4-p).

omichicahuaztli   Musical instrument made of a notched bone, often human or deer, played by rasping a stick along the serrations (Plate 15-d).

palma ('palmate stone')   Carved fan-shaped stone with smooth dorsal surface, associated with ball-game cult. Classic Veracruz culture (Plate 8-h).

patolli   Game played by Aztecs, Toltecs, Teotihuacanos, and Maya, on cross-shaped board much like modern Parcheesi.

penate   Small stone figure produced in large quantity by the Mixtecs, serving as an amulet (?).

petate   Woven straw mat.

pilli   Privileged class in Tenochtitlán.

Pipil   Term applied rather loosely to the speech and culture of migratory Nahuat-speaking groups in Central America.

pisote   Coati (*Nasua*); a small, raccoon-like arboreal animal.

Plumbate   Fine exture ware with a high percentage of iron compounds; upon firing, the surface acquires a hard, lustrous vitrified finish, often with a metallic iridescence. Two varieties: San Juan (Classic Maya),

Tohil (Post-Classic Maya). Manufactured in region of Tajumulco, Guatemala, and widely traded. Similar wares produced in Veracruz and El Salvador.

pochteca Professional traders and spies of Aztecs. Term is often applied generically to all long-distance traders in Mesoamerica.

"pot" irrigation Irrigation of cultivated plots of land where the water table is high by sinking wells at intervals in fields; water is drawn out by buckets or scoops and distributed around plants.

Pox pottery A ware pitted by lack of control in the firing process.

Putún Chontal Maya inhabiting southern Campeche and delta regions of the Usumacinta and Grijalva rivers of Tabasco (Xicalanco); outstanding seamen and merchants who extended their commercial interests throughout the Yucatán Peninsula.

quexquemitl A sleeveless blouse formed of two rectangular pieces united in such a way that it hangs in a point in front and in back.

resist painting (negative painting) Technique of decoration of pottery in which the design may be covered before firing with some substance, probably wax, and paint applied; the wax is subsequently removed, revealing the design in base color. An alternative method is by firing the vessel and then applying clay slip over design area; vegetable substance is then rubbed on and a low heat applied. The clay slip can subsequently be rubbed off, creating the same effect. Isabel Kelly (personal communication) suggests that the somewhat shadowy effect might also be created through smoke absorption rather than by direct application of pigment.

rocker-stamping Decorative technique in which a curved sharp edge, probably shell, is "walked" back and forth on pottery vessel creating a curved zig-zag incised line. Preclassic (Figure 6-o; Plate 4-m).

roof comb (or crest) A tall stone superstructure built on roof of lowland Maya temples, adding height and grandeur to the temple–pyramid complex. Openings were sometimes made to relieve the massive weight. Roof combs were often elaborately stuccoed, carved, and painted (Figure 26, Tikal, Palenque; Photos 39, 49).

sacbé Maya causeway, constructed of huge blocks of stone, leveled with gravel and paved with plaster (Photo 54).

Short Count Abbreviated date recording system utilized by the Maya in Late Postclassic Yucatán, consisting of 13 *katuns* (13 × 7200 days or 256 1/4 years), each *katun* bearing the name of the day on which it ended, always Ahau. Thus a Short Count date (as referred to in the Books of Chilam Balam) might read *katun* 9 Ahau, or *katun* 7 Ahau.

slash-and-burn agriculture Swidden agriculture, in which fields are cleared, burned, and planted until yield decreases, then allowed to lie fallow for several years to regain fertility.

slip   A wash of clay applied to vessel before firing.

Soconusco (Xoconusco)   Geographical province of Pacific coastal plains of Chiapas and Guatemala, important port of trade in the Late Postclassic period (Maps 3, 9).

stela (plural: **stelae**)   Stone column monument (Plate 6).

stirrup-spouted jar   Distinctive ceramic form with two hollow tubes that rise from the body of the vessel to form a single spout (Preclassic) (Figure 6-ff; Plates 4-b, 13-f).

talpetate,   see tepetate

talud–tablero   Architectural feature consisting of a sloping apron (**talud**) surmounted by a horizontal, rectangular panel (**tablero**); Teotihuacán (Figures 21, 27).

tamimes   semicivilized Chichimecs of Late Postclassic period, of which the Aztecs are an example. They spoke Náhuat, had a knowledge of the 52-year cycle, the ball game, dressed in maguey-fiber clothes, and practiced some agriculture.

tecali   Mexican onyx, either a banded calcite, travertine, or alabaster (Plate 10-k).

tecomate   Spherical pottery vessel with restricted opening and no collar (Figure 6-m,o,s; Plate 4-g). A very early form.

tecuhtli   Privileged class in Tenochtitlán; also used as an honorary title.

telpochcalli   Aztec schools for *macehuals*, standard training, instruction in warfare.

temescal   Sweat bath, often used for ritual purification.

teosinte   Early wild grass, forerunner and closest relative of maize (*Zea mays*).

tepetate (**talpetate**)   A fine-grained compact yellowish substance of volcanic origin.

teponaztli   Horizontal cylindrical wooden drum with slotted tongues, struck with sticks with points covered with rubber (Figure 17-b; Plate 15-f).

tezontle   A porous volcanic stone, red, gray, or black, common in the Basin of Mexico.

Thin Orange ware   Fine-paste, thin-walled pottery, widely traded in the Classic period. Redistributed by Teotihuacán, actual place of origin unknown (Plate 7-c).

tlachtli   Ancient ritual ball game.

tlacolol agriculture   A variant of the slash-and-burn system in which cultivable land is divided into sectors, some of which are planted for 2 to 3 years, then left to fallow for 3 to 4 years; usually practiced on slopes.

tlatoani   The king (Aztec).

Tolteca-Chichimecas   People who came to Tula from the "northwest" and spoke Náhuat. They probably included some Otomís. They occupied an intermediate cultural level between the Chichimecs and the more civilized groups like the Nonoalca.

Tonalpohualli   Cycle of 260 days, Aztec, composed of 20 days combined with 13 numbers, corresponding to the Maya Tzolkin.

Tripsacum   Wild grass that ranged from Texas to South America.

tump-line   Carrying strap passed over either the chest or forehead, facilitating transportation of a burden packed on the back (see figure heading, Chapter 2).

tun,   see Long Count (glyphs, Figure 15).

Tzolkin   Cycle of 260 days, Maya, composed of 20 days combined with 13 numbers, corresponding to Aztec Tonalpohualli.

tzompantli   Skull rack, usually located near temple, to which heads of sacrificial victims were skewered. Postclassic.

Uayeb   Remaining 5 unlucky days at year end of Maya calendar; known as Nemontemi among the Aztecs (glyph, Figure 12).

uinal,   see Long Count (glyphs, Figure 15).

Usulután ware   Pottery decorated with a resist technique producing groups of wavelike yellowish lines on a dark orange or brown background; the center of manufacture is thought to have been western El Salvador. Preclassic (Plate 4-a).

volador   Ceremony in which men, dressed as gods or birds, descended to earth from a rotating platform erected at the top of a high pole; the men were tied at the waist by ropes that unwound as they circled to earth. Still performed today in the states of Veracruz and Puebla, Mexico.

white-rimmed black ware   Pottery with a contrast in surface color produced by differential firing (Plate 4-l).

Xicalanco   Gulf-coast region of Tabasco (home of Putún), important port of trade in the Late Postclassic period (Map 12).

Xíhuitl   Aztec calendar year of 365 days, corresponding to Maya Haab.

Xoconusco,   see Soconusco

yácata   Tarascan mound or pyramid (Photo 75).

yoke   U-shaped stone, often elaborately carved, believed to be imitation of the protective belt worn by ball-players. Classic Veracruz cultures (Plate 8-k).

References

Abascal, R., P. Dávila, P. J. Schmidt, and D. Z. de Dávila
  1976   La arqueología del sur-oeste de Tlaxcala (primera parte). *Comunicaciones Proyecto Puebla-Tlaxcala* No. 11.
Acosta, J. R.
  1941   Los últimos descubrimientos arqueológicos en Tula, Hgo. 1941. *Revista Mexicana de Estudios Antropológicos* 5:239–248.
  1945   La cuarta y quinta temporada de excavaciones en Tula, Hidalgo, 1943–1944. *Revista Mexicana de Estudios Antropológicos* 7:23–64.
  1956   Resumen de las exploraciones arqueológicas en Tula, Hidalgo, durante los VI, VII y VIII Temporadas 1946–1950. *Instituto Nacional de Antropología e Historia, Anales* 8:37–116.
  1956–   Interpretación de algunos de los datos obtenidos en Tula relativos a la época
  1957   Tolteca. *Revista Mexicana de Estudios Antropológicos* 14:75–110.
  1964   El Palacio del Quetzalpapálotl. *Instituto Nacional de Antropología e Historia, Memorias 10.*
  1965   Preclassic and Classic architecture of Oaxaca. *Handbook of Middle American Indians* (Vol. 3), edited by R. Wauchope. Austin, Texas: University of Texas Press. Pp. 814–836.
Acosta Saignes, M.
  1945   Los Pochteca. *Acta Antropológica* 1 (1).
  1946   Los Teopixque. *Revista Mexicana de Estudios Antropológicos* 8:147–205.
Adams, R. E. W.
  1970   Suggested Classic period occupational specialization in the southern Maya lowlands. *Peabody Museum, Harvard University, Archaeological and Ethnological Papers* 61:487–498.
  1971   The ceramics of Altar de Sacrificios. *Papers of the Peabody Museum* 63(1). Cambridge, Massachusetts: Harvard University.
  1977a   *Prehistoric Mesoamerica.* Boston: Little, Brown and Co.
  1977b   Comments on the glyphic texts of the "Altar Vase." In *Social process in Maya prehistory: Studies in memory of Sir Eric Thompson,* edited by N. Hammond. London: Academic Press. Pp. 409–420.

1977c (Ed.) *The origins of Maya civilization.* Albuquerque, New Mexico: University of New Mexico Press.

1978 Routes of communication in Mesoamerica: The northern Guatemalan highlands and the Petén. In *Mesoamerican communication routes and cultural contacts,* edited by T. A. Lee, Jr. and C. Navarrete. *Papers of the New World Archaeological Foundation* No. 40: 27–35.

Adams, R. E. W., and A. S. Trik
1961 Temple 1 (Str. 5D-1): Post-constructional activities, *Tikal Reports,* No. 7, *Museum Monographs,* The University Museum, Philadelphia, Pennsylvania.

Adams, R. M.
1961 Changing patterns of territorial organization in the central highlands of Chiapas, Mexico. *American Antiquity* 26(3):341–360.

Agrinier, P.
1975 Mounds 9 and 10 at Mirador, Chiapas, Mexico. *Papers of the New World Archaeological Foundation* No. 39.

Anderson, W. F.
1971 Arithmetic in Maya numerals. *American Antiquity* 36:54–63.

Andrews, E. W., IV
1960 Excavations at Dzibilchaltún, northwestern Yucatán, Mexico. *American Philosophical Society, Transactions* 104(3):254–265.

1965 Archaeology and prehistory in the northern Maya lowlands. *Handbook of Middle American Indians* (Vol. 2), edited by R. Wauchope. Austin, Texas: University of Texas Press. Pp. 288–330.

Andrews, E. W., IV, and A. P. Andrews
1975 A preliminary study of the ruins of Xcaret, Quintana Roo, Mexico. With notes on other archaeological remains on the central east coast of the Yucatán Peninsula. *Middle American Research Institute Publication* No. 40.

Andrews, E. W., V
1974 Some architectural similarities between Dzibilchaltún and Palenque. *Primera Mesa Redonda de Palenque, Part I,* edited by M. G. Robertson. Pebble Beach, California: The Robert Louis Stevenson School. Pp. 137–147.

1976 The archaeology of Quelepa, El Salvador. *Middle American Research Institute Publication* No. 42.

1977 The southeastern periphery of Mesoamerica: A view from eastern El Salvador. In *Social process in Maya prehistory: Studies in memory of Sir Eric Thompson,* edited by N. Hammond. London: Academic Press. Pp. 115–134.

Armillas, P.
1950 Teotihuacán, Tula, y los Toltecas. *Runa* 3:37–70.

1969 The arid frontier of Mexican civilization. *Transactions of the New York Academy of Sciences (Series II)* 31:697–704.

1971 Gardens in swamps. *Science* 174:653–661.

Arnold, D. E., and B. F. Bohor
1975 Attapulgite and Maya blue: An ancient mine comes to light. *Archaeology* 28(1):23–29.

Ashmore, W. (Ed.)
1980 *Maya lowland settlement patterns.* Albuquerque, New Mexico: University of New Mexico Press.

Aufdermauer, J.
1973 Aspectos de la cronología del preclásico en la cuenca de Puebla-Tlaxcala. *Comunicaciones Proyecto Puebla-Tlaxcala* No. 9.

Aveleyra, L.
1950 *Prehistoria de Mexico.* Mexico, D.F.: Ediciones Mexicanas.

1956 The second mammoth and associated artifacts at Santa Isabel Iztapan, Mexico.

American Antiquity 22:12–28.

1963   *La estela teotihuacana de La Ventilla, México.* Mexico, D.F.: Museo Nacional de Antropología.

1964   The primitive hunters. In *Handbook of Middle American Indians* (Vol. 1), edited by R. Wauchope. Austin, Texas: University of Texas Press. Pp. 384–412.

Aveleyra, L., and M. Maldonado-Koerdell

1953   Association of artifacts with mammoths in the Valley of Mexico. *American Antiquity* 18:332–340.

Aveni, A. F., and R. M. Linsley

1972   Mound J. Monte Albán: Possible astronomical orientation. *American Antiquity* 37:528–531.

Badner, M.

1972   A possible focus of Andean artistic influence in Mesoamerica. *Studies in Pre-Columbian Art and Archaeology* No. 9. Washington D.C.: Dumbarton Oaks.

Baker, H. G.

1971   Section III Commentary. In *Man across the sea: Problems of Pre-Columbian contacts,* edited by C. L. Riley, J. C. Kelley, C. W. Pennington, and R. Rands. Austin, Texas: University of Texas Press. Pp. 428–444.

Ball, H. G., and D. L. Brockington

1978   Trade and travel in prehispanic Oaxaca. In *Mesoamerican communication routes and cultural contacts,* edited by T. A. Lee, Jr. and C. Navarrete. *Papers of the New World Archaeological Foundation* No. 40:107–114.

Ball, J. W.

1974a   A Teotihuacán-style cache from the Maya lowlands. *Archaeology* 27(1):2–9.

1974b   A coordinate approach to northern Maya prehistory: A.D. 700–1200. *American Antiquity* 39:85–93.

1977a   The archaeological ceramics of Becán, Campeche, Mexico. *Middle American Research Institute Publication* No. 43.

1977b   The rise of the northern Maya chiefdoms: A socioprocessual analysis. In *The origins of Maya civilization,* edited by R. E. W. Adams. Albuquerque, New Mexico: University of New Mexico Press. Pp. 101–132.

1977c   A hypothetical outline of coastal Maya prehistory: 300 B.C.–A.D. 1200. In *Social process in Maya prehistory: Studies in memory of Sir Eric Thompson,* edited by N. Hammond. London: Academic Press. Pp. 167–196.

Barlow, R. H.

1949   The extent of the empire of the Colhua-Mexica. *Ibero-Americana,* No. 28.

Barrera Vásquez, A., and S. G. Morley

1949   The Maya chronicles. *Carnegie Institution of Washington, Contribution,* No. 48.

Baudez, C. F.

1970   *Central America.* London: Barrie and Jenkins.

Baudez, C. F., and P. Becquelin

1973   Archéologie de Los Naranjos, Honduras. *Études Mesoamericaines* (Vol. II). Mission archéologique et etnologique Française au Mexique, México.

Becker, M. J.

1979   Priests, peasants and ceremonial centers: The intellectual history of a model. In *Maya archaeology and ethnohistory,* edited by N. Hammond and G. R. Willey. Austin, Texas: University of Texas Press. Pp. 3–20.

Bell, B.

1972   Archaeological excavations in Jalisco, Mexico. *Science* 175:1238–1239.

1974   (Ed.) *The archaeology of west Mexico.* Ajijíc, Jalisco, Mexico: West Mexican Society for Advanced Study.

Benfer, R. A.

1974   The human skeletal remains from Tula. In *Studies of ancient Tollan: A report of the University of Missouri Tula archaeological project,* edited by R. A. Diehl. *University of Missouri Monographs in Anthropology* No. 1. Columbia, Missouri: Department of Anthropology, University of Missouri. Pp. 105–116.

Bennett, W. C.
1944   The north highlands of Peru: Excavations in the Callejón de Huaylas and at Chavín de Huantar. *American Museum of Natural History, Anthropological Papers 39,* Part 1.

Bennyhoff, J. A.
1967   Chronology and periodization: Continuity and chance in the Teotihuacán ceramic tradition. *Teotihuacán, Onceava Mesa Redonda.* Mexico, D.F.: Sociedad Mexicana de Antropologia. Pp. 19–30.

Benson, E. P. (Ed.)
1977   *The sea in the Pre-Columbian world.* Washington, D.C.: Dumbarton Oaks Research Library and Collections.

Berlin, H.
1958   El glifo "emblema" en las inscripciones mayas. *Journal de la Société des Americanistes* 47:111–119.

Bernal, I.
1965   Archaeological synthesis of Oaxaca. In *Handbook of Middle American Indians* (Vol. 3), edited by R. Wauchope. Austin, Texas: University of Texas Press. Pp. 788–813.
1973   Stone reliefs in the Dainzú area. In *The iconography of Middle American sculpture.* New York: Metropolitan Museum of Art. Pp. 13–23.

Blanton, R. E.
1978   *Monte Albán: Settlement patterns at the ancient Zapotec capital.* New York: Academic Press.

Blom, F., and O. La Farge
1926–   Tribes and temples. *Middle American Research Institute, Tulane University, Pub-*
1927   *lication No. 1.* 2 vols.

Borhegyi, S. F.
1965   Archaeological synthesis of the Guatemalan highlands. In *Handbook of Middle American Indians* (Vol. 2), edited by R. Wauchope. Austin, Texas: University of Texas Press. Pp. 3–58.

Bove, F. J.
1978   Laguna de los Cerros: An Olmec central place. *Journal of New World Archaeology* 2(3).

Brainerd, G. W.
1941   Fine Orange pottery in Yucatán. *Revista Mexicana de Estudios Antropológicos* 5:163–183.
1951   Early ceramic horizons in Yucatán. In *The civilizations of ancient America,* edited by S. Tax. New York: Cooper Square. Pp. 72–78.
1958   The archaeological ceramics of Yucatán. *University of California Anthropological Records 19.*

Brand, D. D.
1943   An historical sketch of geography and anthropology in the Tarascan region, Part 1. *New Mexico Anthropologist* 6:37–108.

Braniff, B.
1972   Secuencias arqueológicas en Guanajuato y la cuenca de México: Intento de correlación. In *Teotihuacán XI Mesa Redonda, Mexico.* Sociedad Mexicana de Antropología. Pp. 273–323.
1974   Oscilación de la frontera septentrional mesoamericana. In *The archaeology of west Mexico,* edited by B. Bell. Ajijíc, Jalisco, Mexico: West Mexican Society for Advanced Study. Pp. 40–50.

Bray, W.
1972a   The city state in central Mexico at the time of the Spanish conquest. *Journal*

of Latin American Studies 4(2):161–185.

1972b   Ancient American metal-smiths. *Proceedings of the Royal Anthropological Institute 1971.* Pp. 25–43.

1977a   From foraging to farming in early Mexico. In *Hunters, gatherers and first farmers beyond Europe,* edited by J. V. S. Megaw. Leicester, England: Leicester University Press. Pp. 225–250.

1977b   Maya metalwork and its external connections. In *Social process in Maya prehistory: Studies in memory of Sir Eric Thompson,* edited by N. Hammond. London: Academic Press. Pp. 365–403.

1977c   Civilizing the Aztecs. In *The evolution of social systems,* edited by J. Friedman and M. J. Rowlands. London: Duckworth. Pp. 373–398.

1978   Gold-working in ancient America. *Gold Bulletin* 11(4):136–143.

Brockington, D. L.
1973   Archaeological investigations at Miahuatlán, Oaxaca. *Vanderbilt University Publication in Anthropology* No. 7.

Bronson, B.
1966   Roots and the subsistence of the ancient Maya. *Southwestern Journal of Anthropology* 22(3):251–279.

Brown, C. N.
1972   Pattern of erection of stelae at Piedras Negras. *Katunob* 8(1):50–53.

Brown, K. L.
1977a   The Valley of Guatemala: A highland port-of-trade. In *Teotihuacán and Kaminaljuyú: A study in prehistoric culture contact,* edited by W. T. Sanders and J. W. Michels. University Park: The Pennsylvania State University Press. Pp. 205–395.

1977b   Toward a systematic explanation of culture change within the Middle Classic Period of the Valley of Guatemala. In *Teotihuacán and Kaminaljuyú: A study in prehistoric culture contact,* edited by W. T. Sanders and J. W. Michels. University Park: The Pennsylvania State University Press. Pp. 411–440.

Bruhns, K. O.
1980   Plumbate origins revisited. *American Antiquity* 45:845–848.

Brundage, B. C.
1972   *A rain of darts: The Mexica Aztecs.* Austin and London: University of Texas Press.

Brush, C. F.
1969   A contribution to the archaeology of coastal Guerrero, Mexico. Ph.D. dissertation, Department of Anthropology, Columbia University, New York.

Brush, E. S.
1968   The archaeological significance of ceramic figurines from Guerrero, Mexico. Ph.D. dissertation, Department of Anthropology, Columbia University, New York.

Calnek, E. E.
1976   The internal structure of Tenochtitlán. In *The Valley of Mexico,* edited by E. R. Wolf. Albuquerque, New Mexico: University of New Mexico Press. Pp. 287–302.

Canby, J. S.
1951   Possible chronological implications of the long ceramic sequence recovered at Yarumela, Spanish Honduras. In *The civilizations of ancient America, selected papers of the 29th International Congress of Americanists,* edited by S. Tax. Pp. 79–85.

Carlson, J. B.
1976   Astronomical investigations and site orientation influences at Palenque. In *Segunda Mesa Redonda de Palenque,* edited by M. G. Robertson. Pebble Beach, California: The Robert Louis Stevenson School. Pp. 107–122.

Carneiro, R. L.
1960   Slash and burn agriculture: A closer look at its implications for settlement

patterns. In *Men and cultures,* edited by F. C. Wallace. Philadelphia: University of Pennsylvania. Pp. 229–234.

1970   A theory of the origin of the state. *Science 169:*733–738.

Carr, R. F., and J. E. Hazard

1961   Map of the ruins of Tikal, El Petén, Guatemala. *Tikal Reports,* No. 11, *Museum Monographs,* The University Museum, Philadelphia, Pennsylvania.

Carrasco, P.

1971   Social organization of ancient Mexico. In *Handbook of Middle American Indians* (Vol. 10), edited by G. F. Ekholm and I. Bernal. Austin, Texas: University of Texas Press. Pp. 349–375.

Caso, A.

1958   *The Aztecs, people of the sun.* Norman, Oklahoma: University of Oklahoma Press.

1960   *Interpretation of the Codex Bodley 2858* (translated by Ruth Morales and revised by John Paddock). Mexico: Sociedad Mexicana de Antropología.

1965a   Lapidary work, goldwork and copperwork from Oaxaca. In *Handbook of Middle American Indians* (Vol. 3), edited by R. Wauchope. Austin, Texas: University of Texas Press. Pp. 896–930.

1965b   Zapotec writing and calendar. In *Handbook of Middle American Indians* (Vol. 3), edited by R. Wauchope. Austin, Texas: University of Texas Press. Pp. 931–947.

1965c   Mixtec writing and calendar. In *Handbook of Middle American Indians* (Vol. 3), edited by R. Wauchope. Austin, Texas: University of Texas Press. Pp. 948–961.

1967   *Los Calendarios Prehispánicos.* Mexico, D.F.: Universidad Nacional Autónoma de México, Instituto de Investigaciones Históricas.

Caso, A., and I. Bernal

1952   Urnas de Oaxaca. *Instituto Nacional de Antropología e Historia, Memorias 2.*

1965   Ceramics of Oaxaca. In *Handbook of Middle American Indians* (Vol. 3), edited by R. Wauchope. Austin, Texas: University of Texas Press. Pp. 871–895.

Chadwick, R.

1971   Native pre-Aztec history of central Mexico. In *Handbook of Middle American Indians* (Vol. 11), edited by G. F. Ekholm and I. Bernal. Austin, Texas: University of Texas Press. Pp. 474–505.

Chapman, A. M.

1957   Port of trade enclaves in Aztec and Maya civilizations. In *Trade and market in early empires,* edited by K. Polanyi and C. M. Pearson. Glencoe, Illinois: Free Press of Glencoe. Pp. 114–153.

Charlton, T. H.

1978   Teotihuacán, Tepeapulco and obsidian exploitation. *Science 200:*1227–1236.

n.d.   Teotihuacán: Trade routes of a multi-tiered economy. Unpublished manuscript.

Cheek, C. D.

1977a   Excavations at the Palangana and the Acropolis, Kaminaljuyú. In *Teotihuacán and Kaminaljuyú: A study in prehistoric culture contact,* edited by W. T. Sanders and J. W. Michels. University Park: The Pennsylvania State University Press. Pp. 1–204.

1977b   Teotihuacán influence at Kaminaljuyú. In *Teotihuacán and Kaminaljuyú: A study in prehistoric culture contact,* edited by W. T. Sanders and J. W. Michels. University Park: The Pennsylvania State University Press. Pp. 441–452.

Childe, V. G.

1952a   The birth of civilization. *Past and Present,* No. 2:1–10.

1952b   *New light on the most ancient East.* London: Routledge & Kegan Paul.

Cleland, C. (Ed.)

1976   *Cultural change and continuity: Essays in honor of James Bennett Griffin.* New York: Academic Press.

Clune, F. J.
1976   The ball court at Amapa. In *The archaeology of Amapa, Nayarit. Monumenta Archaeologica* (Vol. 2), edited by C. W. Meighan. Los Angeles, California: The Institute of Archaeology, University of California. Pp. 276–298.

Cobean, R.
1974   The ceramics of Tula. In *Studies of ancient Tollan: A report of the University of Missouri Tula archaeological project*, edited by R. A. Diehl. *University of Missouri Monographs in Anthropology* No. 1. Columbia, Missouri: Department of Anthropology, University of Missouri. Pp. 32–41.

Codex Borbónico
1899   In *Manuscrit Mexicain de la Bibliotéque de Palais Bourbon*, edited by M.E.T. Hamy: Paris.

Codex Chimalpopoca
1945   *Anales de Cuauhtitlán y Leyenda de los Soles*, translated from Náhuatl by Primo F. Velazquez. Mexico, D.F.: Universidad Nacional Autónoma de México, Instituto de Historia.

Codex Dresden
1930   In *Códices Maya*, edited by J. A. Villacorta and C. A. Villacorta. Guatemala City: Tipografía Nacional.

Codex Fejéváry
1830–   In *Antiquities of Mexico*, edited by Lord E. K. Kingsborough (Vol. III). London:
1848   Robert Havel & Calnaglie, Son & Co.

Codex Florentino
1905   In *Historia General de las Cosas de Nueva España, Facsimile Edition of Vol. 5*, edited by Fray B. de Sahagún, Francisco del Paso y Troncoso. Madrid: Hauser y Menet.

Codex Laud
1966   (Ms. Laud misc. 678) Bodleian Library Oxford. Gras, Austria. Akademische Druck Verlagsanstalt.

Codex Magliabecchiano
1904   *Manuscrit Mexicain Post-Colombien de la Bibliothèque National de Florence*. Rome: Duke of Loubat.

Codex Matritense de la Real Academia de la Historia
1907   In *Historia General de las Cosas de Nueva España, Facsimile Edition of Vol 8*, edited by Fray B. de Sahagún, Francisco del Paso y Troncoso. Madrid: Hauser y Menet.

Codex Mendoza
1830–   In *Antiquities of Mexico*, edited by Lord E. K. Kingsborough (Vol. I). London:
1848   Robert Havel & Calnaglie, Son & Co.

Codex Nuttall
1902   In *Facsimile Edition*, introduction by Zelia Nuttall. Cambridge, Massachusetts; Peabody Museum of American Archaeology and Ethnology.

Codex Telleriano-Remensis
1889   In *Facsimile Edition*, Commentary by E. T. Hamy. Paris: Duke of Loubat.

Codex Tro-Cortesiano
1930   In *Códices Maya*, edited by J. A. Villacorta and C. A. Villacorta. Guatemala City: Tipografía Nacional.

Coe, M.D.
1957   Cycle 7 monuments in Middle America: A reconsideration. *American Anthropologist 59*:597–611.

1960a   Archaeological linkages with North and South America at La Victoria, Guatemala. *American Anthropologist 62*:363–393.

1960b   A fluted point from highland Guatemala. *American Antiquity 25*:412–413.

1961   La Victoria, an early site on the Pacific Coast of Guatemala. *Peabody Museum, Harvard University, Archaeological and Ethnological Papers 53.*

1962   *Mexico.* New York: Praeger.

1965a   Archaeological synthesis of southern Veracruz, and Tabasco. In *Handbook of Middle American Indians* (Vol. 3), edited by R. Wauchope. Austin, Texas: University of Texas Press. Pp. 679–715.

1965b   The Olmec style and its distribution. In *Handbook of Middle American Indians* (Vol. 3), edited by R. Wauchope. Austin, Texas: University of Texas Press. Pp. 739–775.

1965c   *The jaguar's children: Preclassic Central Mexico.* New York: Museum of Primitive Art.

1968a   San Lorenzo and the Olmec civilization, *Dumbarton Oaks Conference on the Olmec*, Trustees for Harvard University, Washington, D.C., 1968. Pp. 41–71.

1968b   *America's first civilization: Discovering the Olmec.* New York: American Heritage.

1970   The archaeological sequence at San Lorenzo, Tenochtitlán, Veracruz, Mexico. *Contributions of the University of California, Archaeological Research Facility*, No. 8: 21–34.

1972   Olmec jaguars and Olmec kings. In *The cult of the feline*, edited by E. Benson. Washington, D.C.: Dumbarton Oaks Research Library and Collections. Pp. 1–18.

1973   *The Maya scribe and his world.* New York: Grolier Club.

1976   Early steps in the evolution of Maya writing. In *The origins of religious art and iconography in Preclassic Mesoamerica*, edited by H. B. Nicholson. Los Angeles, California: Latin American Center. Pp. 109–122.

1977   Olmec and Maya: A study in relationships. In *The origins of Maya civilization*, edited by R.E.W. Adams. Albuquerque, New Mexico: University of New Mexico Press. Pp. 183–195.

1980   *The Maya.* London: Thames and Hudson, Ltd.

Coe, M. D., and R. Cobean

1970   Obsidian trade at San Lorenzo, Tenochtitlán, Mexico. Paper presented at the 35th Annual Meeting, Society for American Archaeology, Mexico, D.F.

Coe, M. D., and K. V. Flannery

1964   Microenvironments and Mesoamerican prehistory. *Science 143*:650–654.

1967   Early cultures and human ecology in south coastal Guatemala. *Smithsonian Contributions to Anthropology 3.*

Coe, W. R.

1957   Environmental limitation on Maya culture: A re-examination. *American Anthropologist 59*(2): 328–335.

1959   Piedras Negras archaeology: Artifacts, caches, and burials. *Museum Monographs*, The University Museum, Philadelphia, Pennsylvania.

1962   A summary of excavation and research at Tikal, Guatemala, 1956–1961. *American Antiquity 27*:479–507.

1965   Tikal: Ten years of study of a Maya ruin in the lowlands of Guatemala. *Expedition, Bulletin of the University of Pennsylvania 8*(1):5–56.

1967   *Tikal: A handbook of the ancient Maya ruins.* Philadelphia: University of Pennsylvania.

Coe, W. R., and J. J. McGinn

1963   The north acropolis of Tikal and an early tomb. *Expedition, Bulletin of the University of Pennsylvania 5*(2):24–32.

Coggins, C.

1979   A new order and the role of the calendar: Some characteristics of the Middle Classic Period at Tikal. In *Maya archaeology and ethnohistory*, edited by N. Hammond and G. R. Willey. Austin, Texas: University of Texas Press. Pp. 38–50.

1980   The shape of time: Some political implications of a four-part figure. *American Antiquity 45*:727–739.

Cohodas, M.
  1978a   Diverse architectural styles and the ball game cult: The Late Middle Classic Period in Yucatán. In *Middle Classic Mesoamerica A.D. 400–700*, edited by E. Pasztory. New York: Columbia University Press. Pp. 86–107.
  1978b   The great ball court at Chichén Itzá, Yucatán, Mexico. New York: Garland Publishing Co., Inc.
Cook, S. F.
  1947   The interrelation of population, food supply and building in pre-Conquest central Mexico. *American Antiquity 13:*45–52.
Cortés, H.
  1908   *The letters of Cortés to Charles V* (F. A. MacNutt, translator). New York and London: Oxford University Press. 2 vols.
Covarrubias, M.
  1946   El arte "Olmeca" o de la Venta. *Cuadernos Americanos 28*(4):153–179.
  1957   *Indian Art of Mexico and Central America.* New York: Knopf.
Cowgill, G. L.
  1964   The end of Classic Maya culture: A review of recent evidence. *Southwestern Journal of Anthropology 20:*145–159.
  1979   Teotihuacán, internal militaristic competition, and the fall of the Classic Maya. In *Maya archaeology and ethnohistory*, edited by N. Hammond and G. R. Willey. Austin, Texas: University of Texas Press. Pp. 51–62.
Cowgill, U. M.
  1962   An agricultural study of the southern Maya lowlands. *American Anthropologist 64*(2):273–286.
Culbert, T. P.
  1970   Sociocultural integration and the Classic Maya. Paper presented at the 35th Annual Meeting, Society for American Archaeology, Mexico, D. F.
  1973   (Ed.) *The Classic Maya collapse.* Albuquerque, New Mexico: The University of New Mexico Press.
  1977   Early Maya development at Tikal, Guatemala. In *The origins of Maya civilization*, edited by R. E. W. Adams. Albuquerque, New Mexico: University of New Mexico Press. Pp. 27–43.
Cyphers Guillén, A.
  in press Una secuencia preliminar para el valle de Xochicalco. *Anales de Antropología, Instituto de Investigaciones Antropológicos.* Universidad Nacional Autónoma de México.
Dahlin, B. H.
  1979   Cropping cash in the Proto-Classic: A cultural impact statement. In *Maya archaeology and ethnohistory*, edited by N. Hammond and G. R. Willey. Austin, Texas: University of Texas Press. Pp. 21–37.
Davies, C. N.
  1968   Los señorios independientes del imperio azteca. *Serie Historia 19.* Instituto Nacional de Antropología e Historia.
  1973   *The Aztecs: A history.* New York: MacMillan.
  1977   The Toltecs until the fall of Tula. Norman, Oklahoma: University of Oklahoma Press.
  1979   *Voyagers to the New World: Fact and fantasy.* London: MacMillan.
De Terra, H., J. Romero, and T. D. Stewart
  1949   Tepexpan Man. *Viking Fund Publications in Anthropology*, No. 11.
Diaz del Castillo, B.
  1944   *Historia Verdadera de la Conquista de la Nueva España.* Mexico, D.F.: Editorial Pedro Robredo. 3 vols.
Dibble, C. E.
  1940   El antiguo sistema de escritura en Mexico. *Revista Mexicana de Estudios Antropológicos, 4:*105–128.

Dickson, D. B.
1980   Ancient agriculture and population at Tikal, Guatemala: An application of linear programming to the simulation of an archaeological problem. *American Antiquity* 45:697–712.

Diehl, R. A.
1974   (Ed.) Studies of ancient Tollan: A report of the University of Missouri Tula archaeological project. *University of Missouri Monographs in Anthropology* No. 1, Columbia, Missouri: Department of Anthropology, University of Missouri.
1976   Prehispanic relationships between the Basin of Mexico and north and west Mexico. In *The Valley of Mexico*, edited by E. R. Wolf. Albuquerque, New Mexico: University of New Mexico Press. Pp. 249–286.

Diehl, R. A., and R. A. Benfer
1975   Tollan, the Toltec capital. *Archaeology* 28(2):112–124.

Diehl, R. A., R. Lomas, and J. T. Wynn
1974   Toltec trade with Central America: New light and evidence. *Archaeology* 27(3):182–187.

Dillon, B. D.
1975   Notes on trade in ancient Mesoamerica. *University of California Archaeological Research Facility Contribution* No. 24:80–135.

Di Peso, C. C.
1966   Archaeology and ethnohistory of the northern sierra. In *Handbook of Middle American Indians* (Vol. 4), edited by R. Wauchope. Austin, Texas: University of Texas Press. Pp. 3–25.
1974   Casas Grandes: A fallen trading center for the Gran Chichimeca. *Amerind Foundation Publication* 2(9). Flagstaff, Arizona: Northland Press.

Drennan, R. D.
1976   Religion and social evolution in Formative Mesoamerica. In *The early Mesoamerican village*, edited by K. V. Flannery. New York: Academic Press. Pp. 345–368.

Drucker, P.
1943a   Ceramic sequences at Tres Zapotes, Veracruz, Mexico. *Bureau of American Ethnology, Bulletin* 140.
1943b   Ceramic stratigraphy at Cerro de las Mesas, Veracruz, Mexico. *Bureau of American Ethnology, Bulletin* 141.
1952   La Venta, Tabasco: A study of Olmec ceramics and art. *Bureau of American Ethnology, Bulletin* 153.

Drucker, P., and R. F. Heizer
1960   A study of the *milpa* system of La Venta Islands and its archaeological implications. *Southwestern Journal of Anthropology* 16:36–45.

Drucker, P., R. F. Heizer, and R. J. Squier
1959   Excavations at La Venta, Tabasco, 1955. *Bureau of American Ethnology, Bulletin* 170.

Drucker, R. D.
1974   Renovating a reconstruction: The Ciudadela at Teotihuacán, Mexico. Construction sequence, layout and possible uses of the structure. Ph.D. dissertation, Department of Anthropology, University of Rochester, Rochester, New York.

Dumond, D. E.
1961   Swidden argiculture and the rise of Maya civilization. *Southwestern Journal of Anthropology* No. 4: 301–316.

Dumond, D., and F. Muller
1972   Classic to Post Classic in highland central Mexico. *Science* 175:1208–1215.

Durán, Fray D.
  1967   *Historia de las Indias de Nueva España e Islas de la Tierra Firme* (2 vols.), edited
          by A. M. Garibay K. Mexico: Porrua.

Earle, T. M., and J. E. Ericson (Eds.)
  1977   *Exchange systems in prehistory.* New York: Academic Press.

Eaton, J. D.
  1974   Chicanna: An elite center in the Río Bec region. In *Archaeological investigations
          on the Yucatecan Peninsula. Middle American Research Institute Publication* 31:133-
          138. New Orleans, Louisiana.
  1975   Ancient agricultural Maya farmsteads in the Río Bec area. *University of California
          Archaeological Research Facility Contributions* No. 27:56–82.

Edwards, C. R.
  1978   Pre-Columbian maritime trade in Mesoamerica. In *Mesoamerican communication
          routes and cultural contacts,* edited by T. A. Lee, Jr. and C. Navarrete. *Papers
          of the New World Archaeological Foundation* No. 40:199–209.

Ekholm, G. F.
  1942   Excavations at Guasave, Sinaloa, Mexico. *American Museum of Natural History,
          Anthropological Papers* 38:23–139.
  1944   Excavations at Tampico and Pánuco in the Huasteca, Mexico. *American Museum
          of Natural History, Anthropological Papers* 38:321–509.
  1948   Ceramic stratigraphy at Acapulco, Guerrero. In *El Occidente de México, Mesa
          Redonda.* Mexico, D.F.: Sociedad Mexicana de Antropologia. Pp. 95–104.
  1961   Puerto Rican stone "collars" as ballgame belts. In *Essays in pre-Columbian art
          and archaeology,* edited by S. F. Lothrop *et al.* Cambridge, Massachusetts:
          Harvard University Press. Pp. 356–371.
  1964   Transpacific contacts. In *Prehistoric man in the New World,* edited by J. D.
          Jennings and E. Norbeck. Chicago, Illinois: University of Chicago Press, 1964.
          Pp. 489–510.

Ekholm, S. M.
  1969   Mound 30A and the Early Preclassic ceramic sequence of Izapa, Chiapas,
          Mexico. *New World Archaeological Foundation, Papers.* No. 25.
  1979   The Lagartero figurines. In *Maya archaeology and ethnohistory,* edited by N.
          Hammond and G. R. Willey. Austin, Texas: University of Texas Press. Pp.
          172–186.

Erasmus, C. J.
  1950   Patolli, pachisi and the limitation of possibilities, *Southwestern Journal of An-
          thropology* 6:369–387.

Evans, C., and B. J. Meggers
  1966   Mesoamerica and Ecuador. In *Handbook of Middle American Indians* (Vol. 4),
          edited by R. Wauchope. Austin, Texas: University of Texas Press. Pp. 243–264.

Farriss, N. M., A. G. Miller, and A. F. Chase
  1975   Late Maya mural paintings from Quintana Roo, Mexico. *Journal of Field Ar-
          chaeology* 2:5–10.

Feldman, L. H.
  1974   Tollan in Hidalgo: Native accounts of the central Mexican Tolteca. In *Studies
          of ancient Tollan: A report of the University of Missouri Tula archaeological project,*
          edited by R. A. Diehl. *University of Missouri Monographs in Anthropology* No.
          1. Columbia, Missouri: Department of Anthropology, University of Missouri.
          Pp. 130–149.

Fladmark, K. R.
  1979   Routes: Alternative migration corridors for early man in North America.
          American Antiquity 44:55–69.

Flannery, K. V.

1968a   The Olmecs and the valley of Oaxaca: A model for inter-regional interaction in formative times. *Dumbarton Oaks Conference on the Olmec*, Trustees for Harvard University, Washington, D.C., 1968. Pp. 79–110.

1968b   Archaeological systems theory and early Mesoamerica. In *Anthropological archaeology in the Americas*, edited by B. J. Meggers. Washington, D.C.: The Anthropological Society of Washington. Pp. 67–87.

1973   The origins of agriculture. *Annual Reviews of Anthropology* (Vol. 2). Palo Alto, California: Annual Reviews, Inc. Pp. 271–310.

1976a   The early Formative household cluster on the Guatemalan Pacific Coast. In *The early Mesoamerican village*, edited by K. V. Flannery. New York: Academic Press. Pp. 31–34.

1976b   (Ed.) The early Mesoamerican village. New York: Academic Press.

Flannery, K. V., A. V. Kirkby, M. J. Kirkby, and A. W. Williams

1967   Farming systems and political growth in ancient Oaxaca, Mexico. *Science* 158:445–454.

Folk, R. L., and S. Valastro, Jr.

1976   Successful technique for dating of lime mortar by carbon 14. *Journal of Field Archaeology* 3:203–208.

Foncerrada de Molina, M.

1965   La escultura arquitectónica de Uxmal. *Instituto de Investigaciones Estéticas*. Estudios y fuentes del arte en México (Vol. 20). Universidad Nacional Autónoma de México.

1978   The Cacaxtla murals: An example of cultural contact? *Ibero-Amerikanisches Archiv*. Neue Folge Colloquiem Verlag Berlin. Pp. 141–160.

Ford, J. A.

1969   A comparison of formative cultures in the Americas. *Smithsonian Contributions to Anthropology 11*.

Fox, J. W.

1978   *Quiché conquest: Centralism and regionalism in highland Guatemalan state development*. Albuquerque, New Mexico: University of New Mexico Press.

Friedel, D. A.

1978   Marine adaptation and the rise of Maya civilization: The view from Cerros, Belize. In *Prehistoric coastal adaptations*, edited by B. L. Stark and B. Voorhies. New York: Academic Press. Pp. 239–265.

1979   Culture areas and interaction spheres: Contrasting approaches to the emergence of civilization in the Maya lowlands. *American Antiquity* 44:36–54.

Furst, P. T.

1965   West Mexico, the Caribbean and northern South America: Some problems in New World interrelationships. *Antropológica*, No. 14.

Galinat, W. C.

1975   The evolutionary emergence of maize. *Bulletin of the Torrey Botanical Club* 102(6):313–324.

García Cook, A.

1973   Una punta acanalada en el Estado de Tlaxcala, México. *Comunicaciones Proyecto Puebla-Tlaxcala* No. 9:39–42.

1974   Transición del "clásico" al "post-clásico" en Tlaxcala: Fase Tenanyecac. *Revista Cultura y Sociedad, Mexico* 1(2):83–98.

1978   Tlaxcala: Poblamiento prehispánico. *Comunicaciones Proyecto Puebla-Tlaxcala* No. 15:173–187.

García Cook, A., and R. M. Araña A.

1978   *Rescate arqueológico del monolito Coyolxauhqui*. Instituto Nacional de Antropología e Historia. Mexico, D.F.

García Cook, A., and B. L. Merino C.
1977   Nota sobre caminos y rutas de intercambio al este de la cuenca de México. *Comunicaciones Proyecto Puebla-Tlaxcala* No. 14:71–92.
1979   Grupos huastecos en el norte de Tlaxcala. *Comunicaciones Proyecto Puebla-Tlaxcala* No. 17:57–63.

García Cook, A., and F. Rodríquez
1975   Excavaciones arqueológicas en "Gualupita las Dalias," Puebla. *Comunicaciones Proyecto Puebla-Tlaxcala* No. 12.

García Cook, A., and E. C. Trejo
1977   Lo Teotihuacano en Tlaxcala. *Comunicaciones Proyecto Puebla-Tlaxcala* No. 14:57–78.

García Payón, J.
1957   *El Tajín, Guia Oficial.* Mexico, D.F.: Instituto Nacional de Antropología e Historia.

Gay, C. T.
1967   Oldest paintings in the New World. *Natural History* 76(4):28–35.
1972   *Xochipala: The beginnings of Olmec art.* Princeton, New Jersey: University Press.

Gorenstein, S.
1973   Tepexi el Viejo: A Post-Classic fortified site in the Mixteca-Puebla region of Mexico. *American Philosophical Society Transactions* 63(1).

Graham, J. A.
1973   Aspects of non-Classic presences in the inscriptions and sculptural art of Seibal. In *The Classic Maya collapse,* edited by T. P. Culbert. Albuquerque, New Mexico: University of New Mexico Press. Pp. 207–219.
1976   Maya, Olmecs and Izapans at Abaj Takalik. *Actes du XLII Congrès International des Américanistes* 8:179–188.
1977   Discoveries at Abaj Takalik, Guatemala. *Archaeology* 30(3):196–197.

Graham, J. A., R. F. Heizer, and E. M. Shook
1978   Abaj Takalik 1976: Exploratory investigations. *University of California Archaeological Research Facility* No. 36:85–114.

Graham, J. A., T. R. Hester, and R. N. Jack
1972   Sources for the obsidian at the ruins of Seibal, Petén, Guatemala. *University of California Archaeological Research Facility Contribution* No. 16:111–116.

Green, D. F., and G. W. Lowe
1967   Altamira and Padre Piedra, early Preclassic sites in Chiapas, Mexico. *New World Archaeological Foundation, Papers.* No. 20

Greengo, R. E., and C. W. Meighan
1976   Additional perspectives on the Capacha complex of western Mexico. *Journal of New World Archaeology* 1(5):15–23.

Grennes-Ravitz, R. A.
1974   The Olmec presence at Iglesia Vieja, Morelos. In *Mesoamerican archaeology: New approaches,* edited by N. Hammond. Austin, Texas: University of Texas Press. Pp. 99–108.

Griffin, G. G.
1972   Xochipala, the earliest great art style in Mexico. *American Philosophical Society Proceedings* 116:301–309.
1976   Portraiture in Palenque. In *Segunda Mesa Redonda de Palenque,* edited by M. G. Robertson. Pebble Beach, California: The Robert Louis Stevenson School. Pp. 137–147.

Griffin, J. B.
1966   Mesoamerica and the eastern United States in prehistoric times. In *Handbook of Middle American Indians* (Vol. 4), edited by R. Wauchope. Austin, Texas: University of Texas Press. Pp. 111–131.

Grove, D. C.
  1968a Chalcatzingo, Morelos, Mexico: A reappraisal of the Olmec rock carvings. *American Antiquity* 33:486–491.
  1968b The Preclassic Olmec in central Mexico: Site distribution and inferences. *Dumbarton Oaks Conference on the Olmec,* Trustees for Harvard University, Washington, D.C., 1968. Pp. 179–185.
  1971 The Mesoamerican Formative and South American influences. Primer Simposio de Correlaciones Antropológicas Andino–Mesoamericano, Salinas, Ecuador. Mimeographed copy.
  1973 Olmec altars and myths. *Archaeology* 26(2):128–135.
  1974 The highland Olmec manifestation: A consideration of what it is and isn't. In *Mesoamerican archaeology: New approaches,* edited by N. Hammond. Austin, Texas: University of Texas Press. Pp. 109–128.
Grove, D. C., K. G. Hirth, D. E. Bugé, and A. M. Cyphers
  1976 Settlement and cultural development at Chalcatzingo. *Science* 192:1203–1210.
Grove, D. C., and L. I. Paradis
  1971 An Olmec stela from San Miguel Amuco, Guerrero. *American Antiquity* 36:95–102.
Guillemin, G. F.
  1968 Development and function of the Tikal ceremonial center. *Ethnos* 33:1–35.
  1977 Urbanism and hierarchy at Iximché. In *Social process in Maya prehistory: Studies in memory of Sir Eric Thompson,* edited by N. Hammond. London: Academic Press. Pp. 227–264.
Haberland, W.
  1978 Lower Central America. In *Chronologies in New World archaeology,* edited by R. E. Taylor and C. W. Meighan. New York: Academic Press. Pp. 395–430.
Hammond, N.
  1972 Obsidian trade routes in the Mayan area. *Science* 178:1092–1093.
  1974 (Ed.) *Mesoamerican archaeology: New approaches.* Austin, Texas: University of Texas Press.
  1975a Preclassic to Postclassic in northern Belize. *Actas del XLI Congreso Internacional de Americanistas* 1:442–448.
  1975b Lubaantún: A Classic Maya realm. *Peabody Museum Monographs 2.* Cambridge: Peabody Museum of Archaeology and Ethnology, Harvard University.
  1977a Ex Oriente Lux: A view from Belize. In *The origins of Maya civilization,* edited by R. E. W. Adams. Albuquerque, New Mexico: University of New Mexico Press. Pp. 45–76.
  1977b The early Formative in the Maya lowlands. In *Social process in Maya prehistory: Studies in memory of Sir Eric Thompson,* edited by N. Hammond. London: Academic Press. Pp. 77–101.
  1977c (Ed.) *Social process in Maya prehistory: Studies in memory of Sir Eric Thompson.* London: Academic Press.
Hammond, N., A. Aspinall, S. Feather, J. Hazelden, T. Gazard, and S. Agrell
  1977 Maya jade: Source location and analysis. In *Exchange systems in prehistory,* edited by T. K. Earle and J. E. Ericson. New York: Academic Press. Pp. 35–67.
Hammond, N., D. Pring, R. Wilk, S. Donaghey, F. P. Saul, E. S. Wing, A. G. Miller, and L. H. Feldman
  1979 The earliest lowland Maya? Definition of the Swasey Phase. *American Antiquity* 44:92–110.
Hammond, N., and G. R. Willey (Eds.)
  1979 *Maya archaeology and ethnohistory.* Austin, Texas: University of Texas Press.
Harrison, P. D.
  1977 The rise of the *bajos* and the fall of the Maya. In *Social process in Maya prehistory: Studies in memory of Sir Eric Thompson,* edited by N. Hammond. London: Academic Press. Pp. 469–508.

Harrison, P. D., and B. L. Turner II (Eds.)
1978   *Prehistoric Maya agriculture.* Albuquerque, New Mexico: University of New Mexico Press.

Haviland, W. A.
1969   A new population estimate for Tikal, Guatemala. *American Antiquity* 34:429–433.
1970   Tikal, Guatemala, and Mesoamerican urbanism. *World Archaeology* 2(2):186–198.
1975   The ancient Maya and the evolution of urban society. *Museum of Anthropology, University of Northern Colorado, Miscellaneous Series* No. 37.
1977   Dynastic genealogies from Tikal, Guatemala: Implications for descent and political organizations. *American Antiquity* 42:61–67.

Hayden, J. D.
1976   Pre-altithermal archaeology in the Sierra Pinacate, Sonora, Mexico. *American Antiquity* 41:274–289.

Healan, D. M.
1977   Architectural implications of daily life in ancient Tollan, Hidalgo, Mexico. *World Archaeology* 9(2):140–156.

Healy, P. F.
1974   The Cuyamel Caves: Preclassic sites in northeast Honduras. *American Antiquity* 39:435–447.
1978   Excavations at Río Claro, northeast Honduras. *Journal of Field Archaeology* 5(1):15–28.

Heine-Geldern, R.
1959   Chinese influence in Mexico and Central America: The Tajín style of Mexico and the marble vases from Honduras. *Actas del 33 Congreso Internacional de Americanistas, San José, Costa Rica* 1:195–206.
1966   The problem of transpacific influences in Mesoamerica. In *Handbook of Middle American Indians* (Vol. 4), edited by R. Wauchope. Austin, Texas: University of Texas Press. Pp. 277–295.

Heizer, R. F.
1960   Agriculture and the theocratic state in lowland southeastern Mexico. *American Antiquity* 26:215–222.
1968   New observations on La Venta. *Dumbarton Oaks Conference on the Olmec*, Trustees for Harvard University, Washington, D.C., 1968. Pp. 9–36.

Heizer, R. F., and J. A. Bennyhoff
1958a   Archaeological investigation of Cuicuilco, Valley of Mexico. *Science* 127:232–233.
1958b   Excavations at Cuicuilco in 1957. Unpublished manuscript.

Heizer, R. F., and S. F. Cook
1959   New evidence of antiquity of Tepexpan and other human remains from the Valley of Mexico. *Southwestern Journal of Anthropology* 15:32–42.

Hellmuth, N. M.
1975   Pre-Columbian ball game: Archaeology and architecture. *Foundation for Latin American Anthropological Research.* 1(1).
1978   Teotihuacán art in the Escuintla, Guatemala region. In *Middle Classic Mesoamerica A.D. 400–700*, edited by E. Pasztory. New York: Columbia University Press. Pp. 71–85.

Hernández Ayala, M. I.
1976   Una estela olmeca en el area del Usumacinta. *Instituto Nacional de Antropología e Historia, Epoca II, Boletín* 16:22–28.

Heyden, D.
1970   Nueva interpretacíon de las figuras sonrientes, señalada por las fuentes históricas. *Tlalocan* 6(2):159–162.
1975   An interpretation of the cave underneath the Pyramid of the Sun in Teotihuacán, Mexico. *American Antiquity* 40:131–147.

Hirth, K. G.
  1977   Toltec–Mazapan influence in eastern Morelos, Mexico. *Journal of New World Archaeology II*(1):40–46.
  1978a   Teotihuacán regional population administration in eastern Morelos. *World Archaeology* 9(3):320–333.
  1978b   Interregional trade and the formation of prehistoric gateway communities. *American Antiquity* 43:35–45.

Historia Tolteca-Chichimeca
  1947   *Anales de Quauhtinchan* (prologue by P. Kirchhoff). Mexico, D.F.: Antigua Librería Robredo, de José Porrua e Hijos.

Ixtlilxóchitl, F. de A.
  1952   *Obras históricas*, 2 vols. Editoria Nacional, México. D.F.

Izumi, S., and T. Sono
  1963   *Andes 2: Excavations at Kotosh, Peru, 1960*. University of Tokyo, Scientific Expedition to the Andes. Tokyo: Kadokawa Publ.

Jack, R. N., T. E. Hester, and R. F. Heizer
  1972   Geologic sources of archaeological obsidian from sites in northern and central Veracruz. *University of California Archaeological Research Facility Contribution* No. 16:117–122.

Jennings, J. D.
  1968   *Prehistory of North America*. New York: McGraw-Hill.

Jiménez Moreno, W.
  1941   Tula y los Toltecas según las fuentes históricas. *Revista Mexicana de Estudios Antropológicos* 5:79–83.
  1962   La historiografía Tetzcocana y sus problemas. *Revista Mexicana de Estudios Antropológicos* 18:81–85.
  1966   Mesoamerica before the Toltecs. In *Ancient Oaxaca, discoveries in Mexican archaeology and history*, edited by J. Paddock. Stanford, California: Stanford University Press. Pp. 1–82.

Joesink-Mandeville, L. R. V.
  1977   Olmec–Maya relationships: A correlation of linguistical evidence with archaeological ceramics. *Journal of New World Archaeology* 2(1):30–39.

Johnson, F., and R. S. MacNeish
  1972   Chronometric dating. In *The prehistory of the Tehuacán Valley* (Vol. 4), edited by R. S. MacNeish. Austin, Texas: University of Texas Press. Pp. 3–55.

Jones, C.
  1977   Inauguration dates of three Late Classic rulers of Tikal, Guatemala. *American Antiquity* 42:28–60.

Joralemon, P. D.
  1971   A study of Olmec iconography. *Dumbarton Oaks, Studies in Pre-Columbian Art and Archaeology*, Trustees for Harvard University, Washington, D.C. No. 7.

Kaufman, T.
  1976   Archaeological and linguistic correlations in Mayaland and associated areas of Meso-America. *World Archaeology* 8(1):101–118.

Keber, E. Q.
  1979   The Aztec image of Topiltzin Quetzalcóatl. Paper presented at the XLIII International Congress of Americanists. Vancouver, B.C. August 1979.

Kehoe, A. B.
  1962   A hypothesis on the origin of northeastern American pottery. *Southwestern Journal of Anthropology* 18(1):20–29.

Kelley, D. H.
  1960   Calendar, animals and deities. *Southwestern Journal of Anthropology* 16:317–337.
  1962a   Glyphic evidence for a dynastic sequence at Quiriguá, Guatemala. *American Antiquity* 27:323–335.

1962b Fonetismo en la escritura Maya. *Estudios de Cultura Maya* 2:277–318.

1962c A history of the decipherment of Maya script. *Anthropological Linguistics* 4(8).

1969   Culture diffusion in Asia and America. In *The alphabet and the ancient calendar signs*, edited by H. A. Moran and D. H. Kelley. Palo Alto, California: Daily Press. Pp. 125–139.

1972   The nine lords of the night. *University of California Archaeological Research Facility Contribution* No. 16:53–68.

Kelley, J. C.

1956   Settlement patterns in north-central Mexico. In *Prehistoric settlement patterns in the New World*, edited by G. R. Willey. Viking Fund Publications in Anthropology, No. 23. Pp. 128–139.

1960   North Mexico and the correlation of Mesoamerican and southwestern cultural sequences. In *Selected Papers, 5th International Congress of Anthropological Sciences, Philadelphia, Pennsylvania*, edited by A. P. C. Wallace. Pp. 566–573.

1966   Mesoamerica and the southwestern United States. In *Handbook of Middle American Indians* (Vol. 4), edited by R. Wauchope. Austin, Texas: University of Texas Press. Pp. 94–110.

1971   Archaeology of the northern frontier: Zacatecas and Durango. In *Handbook of Middle American Indians* (Vol. 11), edited by G. F. Ekholm and I. Bernal. Austin, Texas: University of Texas Press. Pp. 768–801.

Kelley, J. C., and H. D. Winters.

1960   A revision of the archaeological sequence in Sinaloa, Mexico. *American Antiquity* 25:547–561.

Kelly, I.

1938   Excavations at Chametla, Sinaloa. *Ibero-Americana*, No. 14.

1947   Excavations at Apatzingán, Michoacán. *Viking Fund Publications in Anthropology*. No. 7.

1970   Vasijas de Colima con boca de estribo. *Instituto Nacional de Antropologia e Historia, Boletín* 42:26–31.

1974   Stirrup pots from Colima: Some implications. In *The archaeology of west Mexico*, edited by B. Bell. Ajijíc, Jalisco, Mexico: West Mexican Society for Advanced Study. Pp. 206–211.

1978   Seven Colima tombs: An interpretation of ceramic content. *University of California Archaeological Research Facility Contribution* No. 36:1–26.

1980   *Ceramic sequence in Colima: Capacha, an early phase. Anthropological Papers of the University of Arizona No. 37.* Tucson, Arizona: University of Arizona Press.

Kelly, I., and A. Palerm

1952   The Mexican conquests in *The Tajín Totonac*, Part 1, Publication 13. Washington, D.C.: Smithsonian Institution, Institute of Social Anthropology. Pp. 264–317.

Kelly, I., and B. Braniff de Torres

1966   Una relación cerámica entre Occidente y la Mesa Central. *Instituto Nacional de Antropología e Historia, Boletín* 23:26–27.

Kidder, A. V.

1947   The artifacts of Uaxactún, Guatemala. *Carnegie Institution of Washington, Publication 576.*

Kidder, A. V., J. D. Jennings, and E. M. Shook

1946   Excavations at Kaminaljuyú, Guatemala. *Carnegie Institution of Washington, Publication 561.*

Kirchhoff, P.

1943   Mesoamerica. *Acta Americana* 1:92–107.

1954– Land tenure in ancient Mexico. *Revista Mexicana de Estudios Antropológicos*
1955   14(Part 1):351–362.

1955   Quetzalcóatl, Huémac y el fin de Tula. *Cuadernos Americanos* 84(6):163–196.

Klein, C. F.
1976   The identity of the central deity on the Aztec calendar stone. *The Art Bulletin* *58*(1):1–12.

Klepinger, L. L.
1979   Paleodemography of the Valdivia III phase at Real Alto, Ecuador. *American Antiquity 44*:305–309.

Knorozov, Y. V.
1958   The problem of the study of the Maya hieroglyphic writing. *American Antiquity 23*:284–291.
1967   *The writing of the Maya Indians (Russian Translation Series)* (Vol. 4). Cambridge, Massachusetts: Harvard University Press.

Kroeber, A. L.
1948   *Anthropology*. New York: Harcourt.

Krotser, P. H., and G. R. Krotser
1973   The life style of Tajín. *American Antiquity 38*:199–205.

Kubler, G.
1967   The iconography of the art of Teotihuacán. *Dumbarton Oaks, Studies in Pre-Columbian Art and Archaeology,* Trustees for Harvard University, Washington, D.C. No. 4.
1970   Paper presented at Before Cortés Symposium, Metropolitan Museum of Art, New York, October 5–9.
1972   La iconografía del arte de Teotihuacán. In *Teotihuacán XI Mesa Redonda,* Mexico. Sociedad Mexicana de Antropología. Pp. 69–86.
1975   *The art and architecture of ancient America*. Harmondsworth, England: Penguin Books, Ltd.

Lamberg-Karlovsky, C. C., and J. A. Sabloff
1979   *Ancient civilizations: The Near East and Mesoamerica*. Menlo Park, California: The Benjamin/Cummings Publishing Co., Inc.

Langenscheidt, A.
1970   Las minas y la minería prehispánica. In *Minería prehispánica en la Sierra de Querétaro, México*. Secretaría del Patrimonio Nacional. Pp. 45–48.

Lanning, E. P.
1967   *Peru before the Incas*. Englewood Cliffs, New Jersey: Prentice-Hall.

Lathrap, D. W.
1958   The cultural sequence at Yarinacocha, eastern Peru. *American Antiquity 23*:379–388.
1966   Relationships between Mesoamerica and the Andean areas. In *Handbook of Middle American Indians* (Vol. 4), edited by R. Wauchope. Austin, Texas: University of Texas Press. Pp. 265–276.
1970   *The upper Amazon*. New York: Praeger.
1973   The antiquity and importance of long-distance trade relationships in the moist tropics of pre-Columbian South America. *World Archaeology 5*:170–186.
1975   *Ancient Ecuador: Culture, clay and creativity*. Chicago: Field Museum of Natural History.

Lee, T. A., Jr.
1969   The artifacts of Chiapa de Corzo, Chiapas, Mexico. *Papers of the New World Archaeological Foundation* No. 26.

Lee, T. A., Jr., and C. Navarrete (Eds.)
1978   Mesoamerican communication routes and cultural contacts. *Papers of the New World Archaeological Foundation* No. 40.

León, N.
1904   *Los Tarascos*. Mexico, D.F.: Museo Nacional.

León-Portilla, M.
1963   *Aztec thought and culture, a study of the ancient Náhuatl mind*. Norman, Oklahoma: University of Oklahoma Press.

Linné, S.
1942   Mexican highland cultures: Archaeological researches at Teotihuacán, Cal-
        pulalpan, and Chalchicomula in 1934–1935, Publication No. 7. Stockholm:
        Ethnographical Museum of Sweden.

Littmann, E. R.
1980   Maya Blue—a new perspective. *American Antiquity* 45:87–100.

Litvak-King, J.
1978   Central Mexico as part of the general Mesoamerican communications system.
        In *Mesoamerican communication routes and cultural contacts*, edited by T. A. Lee,
        Jr., and C. Navarrete. *Papers of the New World Archaeological Foundation* No.
        40:115–122.

Long, J. R.
1974   The Late Classic and Early Post-Classic ceramics from the eastern portion of
        the coast. In *The Oaxaca Coast Project Reports Part II, Vanderbilt University Pub-
        lications in Anthropology*, Publication 9:40–98.

Long, S. V.
1966   Archaeology of the Municipio of Etzatlán, Jalisco. University Microfilms, Inc.
        1970. Ann Arbor, Michigan.

Longyear, J. M., III.
1952   Copán ceramics: A study of southeastern Maya pottery. *Carnegie Institution
        of Washington, Publication 597.*

Lorenzo, J. L.
1970   Cronología y la posición de Tlapacoya en la prehistoria americana. Paper
        presented at the 35th Annual Meeting, Society for American Archaeology,
        Mexico, D.F.

Lothrop, S. K.
1924   Tulum: An archaeological study of the east coast of Yucatán. *Carnegie Institution
        of Washington, Publication 335.*
1952   Metals from the Cenote of Sacrifice, Chichén Itzá. *Memoirs of the Peabody
        Museum of Archaeology and Ethnology* (Vol. 10, No. 2). Cambridge: Harvard
        University Press.

Lowe, G. W.
1959   Archaeological exploration of the upper Grijalva River, Chiapas, Mexico. *New
        World Archaeological Foundation, Papers.* No. 2.
1975   The Early Preclassic Barra Phase of Altamira, Chiapas. *Papers of the New World
        Archaeological Foundation* No. 38.
1978   Eastern Mesoamerica. In *Chronologies in New World archaeology*, edited by R.
        E. Taylor and C. W. Meighan. New York: Academic Press. Pp. 331–393.

Lowe, G. W., and J. A. Mason
1965   Archaeological survey of the Chiapas coast, highlands and upper Grijalva
        Basin. In *Handbook of Middle American Indians* (Vol. 2), edited by R. Wauchope.
        Austin, Texas: University of Texas Press. Pp. 195–236.

MacNeish, R. S.
1954   An early archaeological site near Pánuco, Veracruz. *American Philosophical So-
        ciety, Transactions* 44(Part 5):543–646.
1958   Preliminary archaeological investigations in the Sierra de Tamaulipas, Mexico.
        American Philosophical Society, Transactions 48(Part 6).
1961   First annual report of the Tehuacán archaeological botanical project, Project
        Reports No. 1. Andover, Massachusetts: R. S. Peabody Foundation.
1962   Second annual report of the Tehuacán archaeological botanical project, Project
        Reports No. 2. Andover, Massachusetts: R. S. Peabody Foundation for
        Archaeology.
1967   A summary of the subsistence. In *Prehistory of the Tehuacán Valley* (Vol. 1),
        edited by D. S. Byers. Austin, Texas: University of Texas Press. Pp. 290–309.

REFERENCES

1969   First annual report of the Ayacucho archaeological botanical project. Andover, Massachusetts: R. S. Peabody Foundation for Archaeology.

1970   Megafauna and man from Ayacucho, Highland Peru. *Science 168*:975–977.

MacNeish, R. S., and A. Nelken-Terner

1967   Introduction. In *Prehistory of the Tehuacán Valley* (Vol. 2), edited by D. S. Byers. Austin, Texas: University of Texas Press. Pp. 3–13.

MacNeish, R. S., A. Nelken-Terner, and A. D. García Cook

1970   *Second annual report of the Ayacucho Archaeological–Botanical Project.* Andover, Massachusetts: R. S. Peabody Foundation.

MacNeish, R. S., and F. A. Peterson

1962   The Santa Marta rock shelter, Ocozocoautla, Chiapas, Mexico. *New World Archaeological Foundation, Papers.* No. 14, Publication 10.

Maldonado-Koerdell, M.

1964   Geohistory and paleogeography of Middle America. In *Handbook of Middle American Indians* (Vol. 1), edited by R. Wauchope. Austin, Texas: University of Texas Press. Pp. 3–32.

Mangelsdorf, P. C.

1974   *Corn: Its origin, evolution and improvement.* Cambridge, Massachusetts: Harvard University Press.

Mangelsdorf, P. C., R. S. MacNeish, and W. C. Galinat

1967   Prehistoric wild and cultivated maize. In *Prehistory of the Tehuacán Valley* (Vol. 1), edited by D. S. Byers. Austin, Texas: University of Texas Press. Pp. 178–200.

Marcus, J.

1976a   *Emblem and state in the Classic Maya lowlands.* Washington, D.C.: Dumbarton Oaks Research Library and Collections.

1976b   The origins of Mesoamerican writing. *Annual Reviews of Anthropology* (Vol. 5). Palo Alto, California: Annual Reviews, Inc. Pp. 35–67.

1978   Archaeology and religion: A comparison of the Zapotec and Maya. *World Archaeology 10* (2):172–191.

1980   Zapotec writing. *Scientific American 242*(2):46–60.

Marquina, I.

1951   Arquitectura prehispánica. *Instituto Nacional de Antropología e Historia, Memorias 1.*

Martí, S.

1968   Instrumentos musicales precortesianos. Instituto Nacional de Antropología e Historia, Mexico, D.F.

Mathews, P., and L. Schele

1974   Lords of Palenque: The glyphic evidence. *Primera Mesa Redonda de Palenque,* Part I, edited by M. G. Robertson. Pebble Beach, California: The Robert Louis Stevenson School. Pp. 63–76.

Matos Moctezuma, E.

1978   The Tula chronology: A revision. In *Middle Classic Mesoamerica A.D. 400–700,* edited by E. Pasztory. New York: Columbia University Press. Pp. 172–177.

Maudslay, A. P.

1889–   *Archaeology, Biologia Centrali-Americana.* London: E. Du Cane Godman & Osbert
1902   Salvin. Text in 4 vols.

McDonald, A. J.

1977   Two Middle Preclassic engraved monuments at Tzutzuculi on the Chiapas Coast of Mexico. *American Antiquity 42*:560–566.

McEvan, G. F., and D. B. Dickson

1978   Valdivia, Jomon fishermen and the nature of the north Pacific: Some nautical problems with Meggers, Evans and Estrada's (1965) transoceanic contact thesis. *American Antiquity 43*:362–371.

Medellin Zeñil, A.
1960   *Cerámicas del Totonacapán: Exploraciones en el centro de Veracruz.* Jalapa, Veracruz: Universidad Veracruzana, Instituto de Antropología.

Meggers, B. J., C. Evans, and E. Estrada
1965   Early Formative period of coastal Ecuador: The Valdivia and Machalilla phases, *Smithsonian Contributions to Anthropology 1.*

Meighan, C. W.
1969   Cultural similarities between western Mexico and Andean regions. *Mesoamerican Studies* No. 4:11–25. Research Records of the University Museum, Southern Illinois University, Carbondale, Illinois.
1972   Morett site. *University of California Publications in Anthropology* (Vol. 7).
1974   Prehistory of west Mexico. *Science* 184:1254–1261.
1976a   (Ed.) *The archaeology of Amapa, Nayarit. Monumenta Archaeologica* (Vol. 2). Los Angeles, California: The Institute of Archaeology, University of California.
1976b   The archaeology of Amapa, Nayarit. In *The archaeology of Amapa, Nayarit. Monumenta Archaeologica* (Vol. 2), edited by C. W. Meighan. Los Angeles, California: The Institute of Archaeology, University of California. Pp. 1–162.
1978   California. In *Chronologies in New World Archaeology,* edited by R. E. Taylor and C. W. Meighan. New York: Academic Press. Pp. 223–240.

Michels, J. W.
1977   Political organization at Kaminaljuyú: Its implications for interpreting Teotihuacán influence. In *Teotihuacán and Kaminaljuyú: A study in prehistoric culture contact,* edited by W. T. Sanders and J. W. Michels. University Park: The Pennsylvania State University Press. Pp. 453–467.
1979   *The Kaminaljuyú chiefdom.* University Park: The Pennsylvania State University Press.

Miller, A. G.
1973a   *The mural painting of Teotihuacán.* Washington, D.C.: Dumbarton Oaks.
1973b   Archaeological investigations of the Quintana Roo mural project: A preliminary report of the 1973 season. *University of California Archaeological Research Facility Contribution* No. 18:137–147.
1977   The Maya and the sea: Trade and cult at Tancah and Tulum, Quintana Roo, Mexico. In *The sea in the Pre-Columbian world,* edited by E. P. Benson. Washington, D.C.: Dumbarton Oaks Research Library and Collection. Pp. 97–135.

Millon, C.
1966   The history of mural art at Teotihuacán. Paper presented at 11th Mesa Redonda, Mexico, D.F., August 10.
1973   Painting, writing and polity at Teotihuacán, Mexico. *American Antiquity* 38:294–314.

Millon, R.
1955   When money grew on trees. Ph.D. dissertation, Department of Anthropology, Columbia University, New York.
1973   The Teotihuacán map. In *Urbanization at Teotihuacán, Mexico* (Vol. 1, part 1), edited by R. Millon. Austin, Texas and London, England: University of Texas Press.
1976   Social relations in ancient Teotihuacán. In *The Valley of Mexico: Studies in prehispanic ecology and society,* edited by E. Wolf. Albuquerque, New Mexico: University of New Mexico Press. Pp. 205–248.

Millon, R., R. B. Drewitt, and G. L. Cowgill
1973   The Teotihuacán map. In *Urbanization at Teotihuacán, Mexico* (Vol. 1, part 2), edited by R. Millon. Austin, Texas: University of Texas Press.

Moedano K., H.
1948   Breve noticia sobre la zona de Oztotitlán, Guerrero. In *El occidente de México.*

Cuarta reunión de Mesa Redonda sobre problemas antropológicos de México y Centro-América, México. Sociedad Mexicana de Antropología. Pp. 104–105.

Moholy-Nagy, H.
1975   Obsidian at Tikal, Guatemala. *Actas del XLI Congreso Internacional de Americanistas, México 1:*511–518.
1978   The utilization of Pomacea snails at Tikal, Guatemala. *American Antiquity 43:*66–73.

Molloy, J. P., and W. Rathje
1974   Sexploitation among the Late Classic Maya. In *Mesoamerican archaeology: New approaches,* edited by N. Hammond. Austin, Texas: University of Texas Press. Pp. 431–444.

Monzón, A.
1949   *El Calpulli en la Organización Social de los Tenochca.* Mexico, D.F.: Universidad Nacional Autónoma de México, Instituto de Historia.

Morley, S. G.
1915   An introduction to the study of the Maya hieroglyphs. *Bureau of American Ethnology, Bulletin 57.*
1920   The inscriptions of Copán. *Carnegie Institution of Washington, Publication 219.*
1956   *The Ancient Maya* (3rd ed., revised by G. W. Brainerd). Stanford, California: Stanford University Press.

Morris, E. H., J. Charlot, and A. A. Morris
1931   The Temple of the Warriors at Chichén Itzá, Yucatán. *Carnegie Institution of Washington, Publication 406.* 2 vols.

Moser, C. L.
1973   Human decapitation in ancient Mesoamerica. *Studies in Pre-Columbian art and archaeology* No. 11. Washington, D.C.: Dumbarton Oaks.

Mountjoy, J. B.
1969   On the origin of west Mexican metallurgy. *Mesoamerican Studies,* No. 4:26–42. Research Records of the University Museum, Southern Illinois University, Carbondale, Illinois.
1970   Prehispanic culture history and cultural contact on the southern coast of Nayarit, Mexico. Ph.D. dissertation. Department of Anthropology, Southern Illinois University. University Microfilms. Ann Arbor, Michigan.
1978   Prehispanic cultural contact on the south-central coast of Nayarit. In *Mesoamerican communication routes and cultural contacts,* edited by T. A. Lee and C. Navarrete. *Papers of the New World Archaeological Foundation* No. 40. Pp. 127–139.

Mountjoy, J. B., and D. Peterson
1973   Man and land at prehispanic Cholula. *Vanderbilt University Publication in Anthropology* No. 4.

Muser, C.
1978   *Facts and artifacts of ancient Middle America: A glossary of terms and words used in the archaeology and art history of pre-Columbian Mexico and Central America.* New York: E. P. Dutton.

Nations, J. D.
1979   Snail shells and maize preparation: A Lacandon Maya analogy. *American Antiquity 44:*568–571.

Navarrete, C.
1974   The Olmec rock carvings at Pijijiapan, Chiapas, Mexico and other Olmec pieces from Chiapas and Guatemala. *Papers of the New World Archaeological Foundation* No. 33.

Navarrete, C., and D. Heyden
1974   La cara central de la Piedra del Sol. Una hipótesis. *Estudios de Cultura Náhuatl XI:*355–376.

Nelson, F. W., Jr.
 1973   Archaeological investigations at Dzibilnocác, Campeche, Mexico. *Papers of the New World Archaeological Foundation* No. 33.
Nelson, F. W., Jr., K. K. Nielson, N. F. Mangelson, M. W. Hill, and R. T. Matheny
 1977   Preliminary studies of the trace element composition of obsidian artifacts from northern Campeche, Mexico. *American Antiquity* 42:209–225.
Nicholson, H. B.
 1961a The use of the term "Mixtec" in Mesoamerican archaeology. *American Antiquity* 26:431–433.
 1961b The Chapultepec cliff sculpture of Motecuhzoma Xocoyotzin. In *El Mexico Antiguo*. Tomo especial de homenaje consagrado a honrar la memoria del ilustre antropologo Dr. Hermann Beyer. Mexico, D.F. *Sociedad Alemana Mexicanista* IX:379–423.
 1973   The late prehispanic central Mexican (Aztec) iconographic system. In *The iconography of Middle American sculpture*. New York: The Metropolitan Museum of Art. Pp. 72–97.
 1976a Preclassic Mesoamerican iconography from the perspective of the Postclassic: Problems in interpretational analysis. In *The origins of religious art and iconography in Preclassic Mesoamerica*, edited by H. B. Nicholson. Los Angeles: Latin American Center. Pp. 159–175.
 1976b (Ed.) *The origins of religious art and iconography in Preclassic Mesoamerica*. Los Angeles: Latin American Center.
 1978   Western Mesoamerica A.D. 900–1520. In *Chronologies in New World Archaeology*, edited by R. E. Taylor and C. W. Meighan. New York: Academic Press. Pp. 285–329.
Niederberger, C.
 1976   Zohapilco, cinco milenios de ocupación humana en un sitio lacustre de la Cuenca de Mexico. *Departamento de Prehistória. Colección Científica* No. 30. Mexico: Instituto Nacional de Antropología e Historia.
 1979   Early sedentary economy in the Basin of Mexico. *Science* 203:131–142.
Noguera, E.
 1942   Exploraciones en El Opeño, Michoacán. *Proceedings 27th International Congress of Americanists*. Pp. 574–586.
 1950   El horizonte Tolteca-Chichimeca. *Enciclopedia Mexicana de Arte* No. 4. Mexico, D.F.: Ediciones Mexicanas.
 1954   *La cerámica arqueológica de Cholula*. Mexico, D.F.: Editorial Guaranía.
 1965   *La cerámica arqueológica de Mesoamerica*. No. 86. Mexico, D.F.: Universidad Nacional Autónoma de México, Instituto de Investigaciones Historicas.
Oliveros, J. A.
 1974   Nuevas exploraciones en El Opeño, Michoacán. In *The archaeology of west Mexico*, edited by B. Bell. Ajijíc, Jalisco, Mexico: West Mexican Society for Advanced Study. Pp. 182–201.
Paddock, J.
 1966a Oaxaca in ancient Mesoamerica. In *Ancient Oaxaca, discoveries in Mexican archaeology and history*, edited by J. Paddock. Stanford, California: Stanford University Press. Pp. 83–242.
 1966b (Ed.) *Ancient Oaxaca, discoveries in Mexican archaeology and history*. Stanford, California: Stanford University Press.
 1978   The Middle Classic Period in Oaxaca. In *Middle Classic Mesoamerica A.D. 400–700*, edited by E. Pasztory. New York: Columbia University Press. Pp. 45–62.
Paillés, H. M.
 1978   The process of transformation at Pajón: A Preclassic society located in an estuary in Chiapas, Mexico. In *Prehistoric coastal adaptations: The economy and*

ecology of maritime Middle America, edited by B. L. Stark and B. Voorhies. New York: Academic Press. Pp. 81–95.

Palerm, A., and E. R. Wolf
1954–   El desarrollo del area clave del imperio Texcocano. *Revista Mexicana de Estudios*
1955   *Antropológicos 14:*337–349.
1957   Ecological potential and cultural development in Mesoamerica. *Social Science Monographs* (Vol. 3). Washington, D.C.: Pan American Union. Pp. 1–38.

Parsons, J. R.
1976   The role of *chinampa* agriculture in the food supply of Aztec Tenochtitlán. In *Cultural change and continuity: Essays in honor of James Bennett Griffin,* edited by C. Cleland. New York: Academic Press. Pp. 233–262.

Parsons, L. A.
1969   Bilbao, Guatemala: An archaeological study of the Pacific Coast Cotzumalhuapa region. *Publications in Anthropology* No. 12. Milwaukee, Wisconsin: Milwaukee Public Museum.
1978   The Peripheral Coastal Lowlands and the Middle Classic Period. In *Middle Classic Mesoamerica* A.D. *400–700,* edited by E. Pasztory. New York: Columbia University Press. Pp. 25–34.

Parsons, L. A., and P. S. Jenson
1965   Boulder sculpture on the Pacific Coast of Guatemala. *Archaeology 18*(2):132–144.

Parsons, L. A., and B. J. Price
1971   Mesoamerican trade and its role in the emergence of civilization. In *Observations on the emergence of civilization in Mesoamerica,* edited by R. F. Heizer and J. A. Graham. *University of California Archaeological Research Facility Contribution* No. 11:169–195.

Pasztory, E.
1972   The historical and religious significance of the Middle Classic ball game. In *XII Mesa Redonda, Mexico.* Sociedad Mexicana de Antropología. Pp. 441–455.
1974   The iconography of the Teotihuacán Tlaloc. *Studies in Precolumbian Art and Archaeology* No. 15. Washington, D.C.: Dumbarton Oaks.
1976a   *The murals of Tepantitla, Teotihuacán.* New York and London: Garland Publishing, Inc.
1976b   *Aztec stone sculpture.* New York: Center for Inter-American Relations.
1976c   The Xochicalco stelae and a Middle Classic deity triad in Mesoamerica. *XXIII International Congress of the History of Art* (Granada 1973) 1:185–215.
1978a   Artistic traditions of the Middle Classic Period. In *Middle Classic Mesoamerica* A.D. *400–700,* edited by E. Pasztory. New York: Columbia University Press. Pp. 108–142.
1978b   (Ed.) *Middle Classic Mesoamerica* A.D. *400–700.* New York: Columbia University Press.
1979   The Aztec Tlaloc: God of water and antiquity. Paper presented at the XLIII International Congress of Americanists. Symposium on Postclassic iconography. August, 1979, Vancouver, B.C.

Paulsen, A.
1977   Patterns of maritime trade between south coastal Ecuador and western Mesoamerica. 1500 B.C.–A.D. 600. In *The sea in the Pre-Columbian world,* edited by E. P. Benson. Washington, D.C.: Dumbarton Oaks Research Library and Collection. Pp. 141–160.

Pendergast, D. M.
1962a   Metal artifacts from Amapa, Nayarit, Mexico. *American Antiquity. 27:*370–379.
1962b   Metal artifacts in prehispanic Mesoamerica, *American Antiquity. 27:*520–545.
1969   Altun Há, British Honduras (Belize): The sun god's tomb. *Royal Ontario Museum of Art and Archaeology, Occasional Paper* No. 19.

Peterson, D. A., and T. B. MacDougall
  1974   Guiengola: A fortified site in the Isthmus of Tehuantepec. *Vanderbilt University Publication in Anthropology* No. 10.

Peterson, F. A.
  1959   *Ancient Mexico: An introduction to the pre-Hispanic cultures.* New York: Capricorn Books.

Phillips, P.
  1966   The role of transpacific contacts in the development of New World pre-Columbian civilizations. *Handbook of Middle American Indians* (Vol. 4), edited by R. Wauchope. Austin, Texas: University of Texas Press. Pp. 296–315.

Piña Chan, R.
  1955   *Las culturas preclásicas de la Cuenca de México.* Mexico, D.F.: Fondo de Cultura Económica.
  1958   *Tlatilco.* Serie Investigaciones, No. 1, 2. Mexico, D.F.: Instituto Nacional de Antropología e Historia.
  1960   Mesoamerica. *Instituto Nacional de Antropología e Historia, Memorias* No. 6.
  1964   Algunas consideraciones sobre las pinturas de Mul-Chic Yucatán. *Estudios de Cultura Maya* (Vol. 4). Mexico, D.F.: Universidad Nacional Autónoma de México. Pp. 63–78.
  1968   *Jaina.* Mexico, D.F.: Instituto Nacional de Antropología e Historia.
  1975   Teotenango: El antiguo lugar de la muralla. 2 vols. Dirección de Turismo, Gobierno del Estado de México.

Pires-Ferreira, J. W.
  1975   Formative Mesoamerican exchange networks with special reference to the Valley of Oaxaca. *Memoirs of the Museum of Anthropology* No. 7. Ann Arbor, Michigan: University of Michigan Press.
  1976   Shell and iron-ore mirror exchange in Formative Mesoamerica, with comments on other commodities. In *The early Mesoamerican village,* edited by K. V. Flannery. New York: Academic Press. Pp. 311–328.

Pires-Ferreira, J. W., and K. V. Flannery
  1976   Ethnographic models for Formative exchange. In *The early Mesoamerican village,* edited by K. V. Flannery. New York: Academic Press. Pp. 286–292.

Pohorilenko, A.
  1977   On the question of Olmec deities. *Journal of New World Archaeology* 2 (1):1–16.

Pollock, H. E. D.
  1965   Architecture of the Maya Lowlands. In *Handbook of Middle American Indians* (Vol. 2), edited by R. Wauchope. Austin, Texas: University of Texas Press. Pp. 378–440.

Pollock, H. E. D., R. L. Roys, T. Proskouriakoff, and A. L. Smith
  1962   Mayapán, Yucatán, Mexico. *Carnegie Institution of Washington, Publication 619.*

Porter, M. N.
  1948   Pipas precortesianas. *Acta Antropológica* 3(2).
  1953   Tlatilco and the Pre-Classic Cultures of the New World. *Viking Fund Publications in Anthropology* No. 19.
  1956   Excavations at Chupícuaro, Guanajuato, Mexico. *American Philosophical Society, Transactions 46,* Part 5.

Porter Weaver, M.
  1967   Tlapacoya pottery in the museum collection. *Indian Notes and Monographs, Miscellaneous Series* No. 56. New York: Museum of the American Indian, Heye Foundation.
  1969   A reappraisal of Chupícuaro. In *The Natalie Wood collection of pre-Columbian ceramics from Chupícuaro, Guanajuato, Mexico,* edited by J. R. Frierman. Los Angeles, California: University of California. Pp. 3–15; appendix, pp. 81–92.

Potter, D. F.
  1976   Prehispanic architecture and sculpture in central Yucatan. *American Antiquity* 41:430–448.

Pring, D. C.
  1977   Influence or intrusion? The Proto-Classic in the Maya lowlands. In *Social process in Maya prehistory: Studies in memory of Sir Eric Thompson*, edited by N. Hammond. London: Academic Press. Pp. 135–165.

Proskouriakoff, T.
  1946   An album of Maya architecture. *Carnegie Institution of Washington, Publication 558*.

  1950   A study of Classic Maya sculpture. *Carnegie Institution of Washington, Publication 593*.

  1954   Varieties of Classic Central Veracruz sculpture. *Carnegie Institution of Washington, Contribution* No. 58:63–100.

  1960   Historical implications of a pattern of dates at Piedras Negras, Guatemala. *American Antiquity 25:454–475*.

  1961   The lords of the Maya realm. *Expedition, Bulletin of the University of Pennsylvania* 4(1):14-21.

Puleston, D. E.
  1971   An experimental approach to the function of Maya *chultuns. American Antiquity* 36:322–335.

  1975   Richmond Hill: A probable early man site in the Maya lowlands. *Actas del XLI Congreso Internacional de Americanistas I:522–533*.

  1977   The art and archaeology of hydraulic agriculture in the Maya lowlands. In *Social process in Maya prehistory: Studies in memory of Sir Eric Thompson*, edited by N. Hammond. London: Academic Press. Pp. 449–467.

  1979   An epistemological pathology and the collapse, or why the Maya kept the Short Count. In *Maya archaeology and ethnohistory*, edited by N. Hammond and G. R. Willey. Austin, Texas: University of Texas Press. Pp. 63–71.

Puleston, D. E., and D. W. Callender, Jr.
  1967   Defensive earthworks at Tikal. *Expedition, Bulletin of the University of Pennsylvania 9(3):40–48*.

Pyne, N. M.
  1976   The fire-serpent and were-jaguar in Formative Oaxaca: A contingency table analysis. In *The early Mesoamerican village*, edited by K. V. Flannery. New York: Academic Press. Pp. 272–282.

Quirarte, J.
  1973   Izapan style art: A study of its form and meaning. *Studies in Pre-Columbian Art and Archaeology* No. 10. Washington, D.C.: Dumbarton Oaks.

  1976   The relationship of Izapan style art to Olmec and Maya art: A review. In *The origins of religious art and iconography in Preclassic Mesoamerica*, edited by H. B. Nicholson. Los Angeles: Latin American Center. Pp. 73–86.

  1977   Early art styles of Mesoamerica and early Classic Maya art. In *The origins of Maya civilization*, edited by R. E. W. Adams. Albuquerque, New Mexico: University of New Mexico Press. Pp. 249–283.

Rands, R.
  1954   Artistic connections between the Chichén Itzá Toltec and the Classic Maya. *American Antiquity 19:281–282*.

  1974   A chronological framework for Palenque. *Primera Mesa Redonda de Palenque*, part I, edited by M. G. Robertson. Pebble Beach, California: The Robert Louis Stevenson School. Pp. 35–39.

  1977   The rise of Classic Maya civilization in the northwestern zone: Isolation and integration. In *The origins of Maya civilization*, edited by R. E. W. Adams. Albuquerque, New Mexico: University of New Mexico Press. Pp. 159–180.

Rands, R. L., and Smith, R. E.
  1965   Pottery of the Guatemalan highlands. In *Handbook of Middle American Indians* (Vol. 2), edited by R. Wauchope. Austin, Texas: University of Texas Press. Pp. 95–145.

Rathje, W. L.
  1970   Socio-political implications of lowland Maya burials: Methodology and tentative hypotheses. *World Archaeology* I(3):359–374.
  1971   The origin and development of lowland Classic Maya civilization. *American Antiquity* 36:275–285.
  1973   Classic Maya development and denouement, a research design. In *The Classic Maya collapse*, edited by T. P. Culbert. Albuquerque, New Mexico: University of New Mexico Press. Pp. 405–454.
  1977   The Tikal connection. In *The origins of Maya civilization*, edited by R. E. W. Adams. Albuquerque, New Mexico: University of New Mexico Press. Pp. 373–382.

Rattray, E. C.
  n.d.   Craft production at Teotihuacán in the Coyotlatelco phase. Manuscript. Instituto de Investigaciones Antropológicos. Universidad Nacional Autónoma de México.
  1978   Los contactos entre Teotihuacán y Veracruz. *XV Mesa Redonda* (Vol 2). Mexico. Sociedad Mexicana de Antropología. Pp. 301–311.
  1980   Anaranjado delgado: Cerámica de comercio de Teotihuacán. In *Interacción cultural en Mexico central*, edited by E. C. Rattray, J. Litvak-King, and C. D. Oyarzabal. Instituto de Investigaciones Antropológicos. Universidad Nacional Autónoma de México. Pp. 74–107.

Recinos, A.
  1950   *Popol Vuh: The sacred book of the ancient Quiché Maya*. Norman, Oklahoma: University of Oklahoma Press.

Recinos, A., and D. Goetz
  1953   *The Annals of the Cakchiquels*. Norman, Oklahoma: University of Oklahoma Press.

Reichel-Dolmatoff, G.
  1965   *Colombia*. New York: Praeger.

Reyna Robles, R. M., and L. Gonzalez Quintero
  1978   Resultado del analysis botánico de formaciones troncocónicas en Loma Terremote, Cuautitlán. Estado de México. In *Arqueobotánica: métodos y aplicaciones. Departamento de Prehistoria, Colección Científica* No. 63. Mexico, D.F.: Instituto Nacional de Antropología e Historia. Pp. 33–41.

Richardson, F. B.
  1940   Non-Maya monumental sculpture of Central America. In *The Maya and their neighbors*, edited by C. Hay. New York: Appleton. Pp. 395–416.

Riley, C. L., J. C. Kelley, C. W. Pennington, and R. Rands (Eds.)
  1971   Man across the sea: Problems of Pre-Columbian contacts. Austin, Texas: University of Texas Press.

Robertson, M. G.
  1974   (Ed.) *Primera Mesa Redonda de Palenque. A conference on the art, iconography and dynastic history of Palenque*, parts I and II. Pebble Beach, California: The Robert Louis Stevenson School.
  1975   Stucco techniques employed by ancient sculptors of the Palenque piers. *Actas del XLI Congreso Internacional de Americanistas, Mexico* 1:449–472.
  1976   (Ed.) *Segunda Mesa Redonda de Palenque. The art, iconography and dynastic history of Palenque*, part III. Pebble Beach, California: The Robert Louis Stevenson School.
  1977   Painting practices of the Palenque stucco sculptors. In *Social process in Maya*

prehistory: Studies in memory of Sir Eric Thompson, edited by N. Hammond. London: Academic Press. Pp. 297–326.

Robertson, M. G., M. S. R. Scandizzo, M.D., and J. R. Scandizzo, M.D.
1976   Physical deformities in the ruling lineage of Palenque and the dynastic implications. In *Segunda Mesa Redonda de Palenque,* edited by M. G. Robertson. Pebble Beach, California: The Robert Louis Stevenson School. Pp. 59–86.

Rouse, I.
1966   Mesoamerica and the eastern Caribbean area. In *Handbook of Middle American Indians* (Vol. 4), edited by R. Wauchope. Austin, Texas: University of Texas Press. Pp. 234–242.

Roys, R. L.
1933   The Book of Chilam Balam of Chuyamel. *Carnegie Institution of Washington, Publication 438.*

1965   Lowland Maya native society at Spanish contact. In *Handbook of Middle American Indians* (Vol. 3), edited by R. Wauchope. Austin, Texas: University of Texas Press. Pp. 659–678.

1966   Native empires in Yucatán. *Revista Mexicana de Estudios Antropológicos* 20:153–175.

Rubín de la Borbolla, D. F.
1944   Orfebrería Tarasca. *Cuadernos Americanos* 3:127–138.

Ruppert, K., J. E. S. Thompson, and T. Proskouriakoff
1955   Bonampak, Chiapas, Mexico. *Carnegie Institution of Washington, Publication 602.*

Ruz Lhuillier, A.
1951   Chichén Itzá y Palenque, ciudades fortificadas, *Homenaje al doctor Alfonso Caso.* Mexico, D.F.: Imprenta Nuevo Mundo, S.A. Pp. 331–342.

1960   *Palenque, official guide.* Mexico, D.F.: Instituto Nacional de Antropología e Historia.

1963   *Uxmal, official guide.* Mexico, D.F.: Instituto Nacional de Antropología e Historia.

Sabloff, J. A.
1975   Excavations at Seibal, Department of Petén, Guatemala: Ceramics. *Memoirs of the Peabody Museum of Archaeology and Ethnology* 13(2).

1977   Old myths, new myths: The role of sea traders in the development of ancient Maya civilization. In *The sea in the Pre-Columbian world,* edited by E. P. Benson. Washington, D.C.: Dumbarton Oaks Research Library and Collection. Pp. 67–88.

Sabloff, J. A., and D. A. Friedel
1975   A model of a Pre-Columbian trading center. In *Ancient civilizations and trade,* edited by J. A. Sabloff and C. C. Lamberg-Karlovsky. Albuquerque, New Mexico: University of New Mexico Press. Pp. 369–405.

Sabloff, J. A., and C. C. Lamberg-Karlovsky (Eds.)
1975   Ancient civilizations and trade. Albuquerque, New Mexico: University of New Mexico Press.

Sáenz, C. A.
1961   Tres estelas en Xochicalco. *Revista Mexicana de Estudios Antropológicos* 17:39–65.
1962   Xochicalco, Temporada 1960. Instituto Nacional de Antropología e Historia, Mexico, D.F. *Colección Informes,* No. 11.

Sahagún, Fray B. De
1946   *Historia General de las Cosas de Nueva España.* Mexico, D.F.: Editorial Nueva España. 3 vols.

Salazar, P.
1966   Maqueta prehispánica teotihuacana. *Instituto Nacional de Antropología e Historia, Boletin* 23:4–11.

Sanders, W. T.
1956   The central Mexican symbiotic region. In *Prehistoric settlement patterns in the New World*, edited by G. R. Willey. Viking Fund Publications in Anthropology, No. 23. Pp. 115–127.

1973   The cultural ecology of the lowland Maya: A reevaluation. In *The Classic Maya collapse*, edited by T. P. Culbert. Albuquerque, New Mexico: University of New Mexico Press. Pp. 325–365.

1977a   Ethnographic analogy and the Teotihuacán horizon style. In *Teotihuacán and Kaminaljuyú: A study in prehistoric culture contact*, edited by W. T. Sanders and J. W. Michels. University Park: The Pennsylvania State University Press. Pp. 397–410.

1977b   Environmental heterogeneity and the evolution of lowland Maya civilization. In *The origins of Maya civilization*, edited by R. E. W. Adams. Albuquerque, New Mexico: University of New Mexico Press. Pp. 287–297.

Sanders, W. T., and J. W. Michels
1969   The Pennsylvania State University Kaminaljuyú Project—1968 Season. Part 1, The Excavations. *Pennsylvania State University, Occasional Papers in Anthropology*, No. 2.

Sanders, W. T., J. R. Parsons, and R. S. Santley
1979   *The Basin of Mexico: Ecological processes in the evolution of a civilization.* New York: Academic Press.

Sanders, W. T., and B. J. Price
1968   *Mesoamerica: The evolution of a civilization.* New York: Random House.

Satterthwaite, L.
1965   Calendrics of the Maya Lowlands. In *Handbook of Middle American Indians* (Vol. 3), edited by R. Wauchope. Austin, Texas: University of Texas Press. Pp. 603–631.

Sauer, C. O.
1948   Colima of New Spain in the sixteenth century. *Ibero-Americana* No. 29.

Sauer, J. D.
1950   The grain amaranths: A survey of their history and classification. *Annals of the Missouri Botanical Garden* 37(4)561–632.

Schele, L.
1976   Accession iconography of Chan-Bahlum in the Group of the Cross at Palenque. *Segunda Mesa Redonda de Palenque*, edited by M. G. Robertson. Pebble Beach, California: The Robert Louis Stevenson School. Pp. 9–34.

Schmidt, P.
1977   Rasgos característicos del area maya en Guerrero: Una posible interpretación. *Anales de Antropología*, vol. XIV. Mexico: Universidad Nacional Autónoma de México. Pp. 63–73.

Schoenwetter, J.
1974   Pollen records of Guilá Naquitz cave. *American Antiquity* 39:292–303.

Scholes, F. V., and R. L. Roys
1948   The Maya Chontal Indians of Acalán-Tixchel. *Carnegie Institution of Washington, Publication 560.*

Schöndube B., O., and J. J. Galván V.
1978   Salvage archaeology at El Grillo-Tabachines, Zapopan, Jalisco, Mexico. In *Across the Chichimec sea. Papers in honor of J. Charles Kelley*, edited by C. L. Riley and B. C. Hedrick. Carbondale, Illinois: Southern Illinois University Press. Pp. 144–164.

Sears, W. H.
1964   The southeastern United States. In *Prehistoric man in the New World*, edited by J. D. Jennings and E. Norbeck. Chicago, Illinois: University of Chicago Press. Pp. 259–287.

Sedat, D. W., and R. J. Sharer
 1972   Archaeological investigations in the northern Maya highlands: New data on
         the Maya Preclassic. *University of California Archaeological Research Facility Con-
         tribution* No. 16:23–35.
Séjourné, L.
 1966   *Arqueología de Teotihuacán, la cerámica.* Mexico, D.F.: Fondo de Cultura Económica.
Sharer, R. J.
 1978a Archaeology and history at Quiriguá, Guatemala. *Journal of Field Archaeology*
         5(1):51–70.
 1978b *The prehistory of Chalchuapa, El Salvador.* 3 vols. Philadelphia, Pennsylvania:
         University of Pennsylvania Press.
Sharer, R. J., and D. W. Sedat
 1973   Monument 1, El Portón, Guatemala and the development of Maya calendrical
         and writing systems. *University of California Archaeological Research Facility Con-
         tribution* 18:177–193.
Sharp, R.
 1978   Architecture as interelite communication in preconquest Oaxaca, Veracruz and
         Yucatán. In *Middle Classic Mesoamerica A.D. 400–700,* edited by E. Pasztory.
         New York: Columbia University Press. Pp. 158–171.
Sheets, P. D.
 1979   Maya recovery from volcanic disasters. Ilopango and Cerén. *Archaeology*
         32(3):32–42.
Shepard, A. O.
 1948   Plumbate, a Mesoamerican trade ware. *Carnegie Institution of Washington, Pub-
         lication 573.*
Shook, E. M.
 1951   The present status of research on the Preclassic horizons in Guatemala. In
         *The Civilization of Ancient America, Selected Papers of the 29th International Congress
         of Americanists,* edited by S. Tax. Pp. 93–100.
 1958   The Temple of the Red Stela. *Expedition, Bulletin of the University of Pennsylvania*
         1(1):26–33.
 1960   Tikal, Stela 29. *Expedition, Bulletin of the University of Pennsylvania* 2(2):28–35.
Shook, E. M., and M. P. Hatch
 1978   The ruins of El Bálsamo, Department of Escuintla, Guatemala. *Journal of New
         World Archaeology* 3(1).
Shook, E. M., and A. V. Kidder
 1952   Mound E-III-3, Kaminaljuyú, Guatemala. *Carnegie Institution of Washington,
         Contribution 53.*
Siemens, A. D., and D. E. Puleston
 1972   Ridged fields and associated features in southern Campeche: New perspectives
         on the lowland Maya. *American Antiquity* 37:228–240.
Simmons, M. P., and G. F. Brem
 1979   The analysis and distribution of volcanic ash-tempered pottery in the lowland
         Maya area. *American Antiquity* 44:79–91.
Smith, A. L.
 1977   Patolli at the ruins of Seibal, Petén, Guatemala. In *Social process in Maya
         prehistory: Studies in memory of Sir Eric Thompson,* edited by N. Hammond.
         London: Academic Press. Pp. 349–363.
Smith, A. L. and A. V. Kidder
 1951   Excavations at Nebaj, Guatemala. *Carnegie Institution of Washington, Publication
         594.*
Smith, R. E., and J. C. Gifford
 1965   Pottery of the Maya Lowlands. In *Handbook of Middle American Indians* (Vol.

2), edited by R. Wauchope. Austin, Texas: University of Texas Press. Pp. 498–534.

Sociedad Mexicana de Antropología
1944   El norte de México y el sur de Estados Unidos. *Tercera Reunión de Mesa Redonda, Mexico, D.F.*

Soustelle, J.
1964   *The daily life of the Aztecs.* London: Pelican Books.

Spinden, H. J.
1917   The origin and distribution of agriculture in America. *Proceedings 19 International Congress of Americanists.* Washington, D.C. Pp. 269–276.

Spores, R.
1967   *The Mixtec kings and their people.* Norman, Oklahoma: University of Oklahoma Press.
1972   An archaeological settlement survey of the Nochixtlán Valley, Oaxaca. *Vanderbilt University Publication in Anthropology* No. 1.

Stark, B. L., and B. Voorhies (Eds.)
1978   *Prehistoric coastal adaptations: The economy and ecology of maritime Middle America.* New York: Academic Press.

Stirling, M. W.
1943   Stone monuments of southern Mexico. *Bureau of American Ethnology, Bulletin 138.*

Stocker, T., S. Meltzoff, and S. Armsey
1980   Crocodilians and Olmecs: Further interpretations in Formative Period iconography. *American Antiquity 45:*740–758.

Stone, D.
1972   *Pre-Columbian man finds Central America. The archaeological land bridge.* Cambridge, Massachusetts: Peabody Museum Press.

Stromsvik, G.
1947   Guide book to the ruins of Copán. *Carnegie Institution of Washington, Publication 577.*

Strong, W. D., A. V. Kidder, and A. J. D. Paul
1938   Preliminary report on the Smithsonian Institution–Harvard University Archaeological Expedition to Northwest Honduras, 1936. *Smithsonian Miscellaneous Collections 97*(1).

Swadesh, M.
1956   Problems of long-range comparisons in Penutian. *Language 32:*17–41.

Switzer, R. R.
1969   Tobacco, pipes, and cigarettes of the prehistoric Southwest. Special Report No. 8, El Paso Archaeological Society.

Taylor, R. E.
1978   Dating methods in New World archaeology. In *Chronologies in New World archaeology,* edited by R. E. Taylor and C. W. Meighan. New York: Academic Press. Pp. 1–27.

Taylor, R. E., and C. W. Meighan (Eds.)
1978   *Chronologies in New World archaeology.* New York: Academic Press.

Thompson, J. E. S.
1939   Excavations at San José, British Honduras, *Carnegie Institution of Washington, Publication 506.*
1942   *The civilization of the Mayas,* Leaflet 25. Chicago, Illinois: Field Museum of Natural History, Anthropology.
1943   A trial survey of the southern Maya area. *American Antiquity 9:*106–134.
1951   The Itzá of Tayasal, Petén, *Homenaje al doctor Alfonso Caso.* Mexico, D.F.: Imprenta Nuevo Mundo, S.A. Pp. 389–400.

1954 *The rise and fall of Maya civilization.* Norman, Oklahoma: University of Oklahoma Press.

1959 Systems of hieroglyphic writing in Middle America and methods of deciphering them. *American Antiquity 24:*349–364.

1962 A catalogue of Maya hieroglyphics. Norman, Oklahoma: University of Oklahoma Press.

1965a Archaeological synthesis of the southern Maya lowlands. In *Handbook of Middle American Indians* (Vol. 2), edited by R. Wauchope. Austin, Texas: University of Texas Press. Pp. 331–359.

1965b Maya hieroglyphic writing. In *Handbook of Middle American Indians* (Vol. 3), edited by R. Wauchope. Austin, Texas: University of Texas Press. Pp. 632–658.

1970 *Maya history and religion.* Norman, Oklahoma: University of Oklahoma Press.

1971 Estimates of Maya population: Deranging factors. *American Antiquity 36:*214–216.

1974 Canals of the Río Candelaria Basin, Campeche, Mexico. In *Mesoamerican archaeology: New approaches,* edited by N. Hammond. Austin, Texas. University of Texas Press. Pp. 297–302.

1975 *Maya hieroglyphic writing.* Third edition. Norman, Oklahoma: University of Oklahoma Press.

Tolstoy, P.

1963 Cultural parallels between Southeast Asia and Mesoamerica in the manufacture of bark cloth. *Transactions of the New York Academy of Sciences (Series II)* 25(6):646–662.

1974 Transoceanic diffusion and Nuclear America. In *Prehispanic America,* edited by S. Gorenstein. New York: St. Martin's Press. Pp. 124–144.

1975 Settlement and population trends in the Basin of Mexico. Ixtapaluca and Zacatenco phases. *Journal of Field Archaeology 2:*331–349.

1978 Western Mesoamerica before A.D. 900. In *Chronologies in New World archaeology,* edited by R. E. Taylor and C. W. Meighan. New York: Academic Press. Pp. 241–284.

in press Review of *The Basin of Mexico: Ecological processes in the evolution of a civilization,* W. T. Sanders, J. R. Parsons, R. S. Santley (New York: Academic Press, 1979). *American Scientist.*

Tolstoy, P., and S. K. Fish

1975 Surface and subsurface evidence for community size at Coapexco, Mexico. *Journal of Field Archaeology 2:*97–104.

Tolstoy, P., S. K. Fish, M. W. Boksenbaum, K. B. Vaughn, and C. E. Smith

1977 Early sedentary communities of the Basin of Mexico. *Journal of Field Archaeology* 4:91–106.

Tolstoy, P., and L. I. Paradis

1970 Early and Middle Preclassic culture in the Basin of Mexico. *Science 167:*344–351.

1971 Early and Middle Preclassic culture in the Basin of Mexico. In *Observations on the emergence of civilization in Mesoamerica, Contributions of the University of California Archaeological Research Facility,* edited by R. F. Heizer and J. A. Graham, No. 11. Pp. 7–28.

Torquemada, J. de

1943 *Monarquía Indiana* (facsimile edition). Mexico, D.F.: Editorial Chávez Hayhoe. 3 vols.

Toscano, S.

1952 *Arte Precolombino de Mexico.* Mexico, D.F.: Universidad Nacional Autónoma de Mexico.

Townsend, R. F.

1979 State and cosmos in the art of Tenochtitlán. *Studies in Pre-Columbian Art and Archaeology* No. 20. Washington, D.C.: Dumbarton Oaks.

Tozzer, A. M.
1941   Landa's Relación de las cosas de Yucatán, a translation. *Peabody Museum, Harvard University, Archaeological and Ethnological Papers 18.*
1957   Chichén Itzá and its *cenote* of sacrifice. *Peabody Museum Memoirs 12.*

Troike, N. P.
1978   Fundamental changes in the interpretation of the Mixtec códices. *American Antiquity 43*:553–568.

Turner, B. L., II
1974   Prehistoric intensive agriculture in the Mayan lowlands. *Science 185*:118–124.
1979   Prehispanic terracing in the central Maya lowlands: Problems of agricultural intensification. In *Maya archaeology and ethnohistory,* edited by N. Hammond and G. R. Willey. Austin, Texas: University of Texas Press. Pp. 103–115.

Turner, B. L., II, and W. C. Johnson
1979   A Maya dam in the Copán Valley, Honduras. *American Antiquity 44*:229–305.

Umberger, E.
1979   Myth, history and the calendar stone. Paper presented at the XLIII International Congress of Americanists, August 1979, Vancouver, B.C. (Revised and expanded.)

Vaillant, G. C.
1930   Excavations at Zacatenco. *American Museum of Natural History, Anthropological Papers 32*:1–197.
1931   Excavations at Ticomán. *American Museum of Natural History, Anthropological Papers 32*:199–439.
1935   Excavations at El Arbolillo. *American Museum of Natural History, Anthropological Papers 35*:137–279.

Vaillant, G. C., and S. B. Vaillant
1934   Excavations at Gualupita. *American Museum of Natural History, Anthropological Papers 35*:1–135.

Villacorta, J. A., and C. A. Villacorta
1930   *Códices Maya.* Guatemala City: Tipografía Nacional.

Villagra Caleti, A.
1949   Bonampak, la ciudad de los muros pintados. *Instituto Nacional de Antropología e Historia, Anales Suppl. 3.*

Voorhies, B.
1976   The Chantuto people: An archaic period society of the Chiapas littoral, Mexico. *Papers of the New World Archaeological Foundation* No. 41.

Wauchope, R.
1975   Zacualpa, El Quiché, Guatemala. An ancient provincial center of the highland Maya. *Middle American Research Institute Publication* No. 39.

Webb, M. C.
1973   The Maya Petén decline viewed in the perspective of state formation. In *The Classic Maya collapse,* edited by T. P. Culbert. Albuquerque, New Mexico: University of New Mexico Press. Pp. 367–404.
1974   Exchange networks: Prehistory. *Annual Review of Anthropology* (Vol. 3). Palo Alto, California: Annual Reviews, Inc. Pp. 357–383.

Webster, D.
1975   Warfare and the evolution of the state: A reconsideration. *American Antiquity 40*:464–470.
1976   Lowland Maya fortifications. *Proceedings of the American Philosophical Society 120*:361–371.
1977   Warfare and the evolution of Maya civilization. In *The origin of Maya civilization,* edited by R. E. W. Adams. Albuquerque, New Mexico: University of New Mexico Press. Pp. 335–371.

1978   Three walled sites of the northern Maya lowlands. *Journal of Field Archaeology* 5:375–390.

Weiant, C. W.

1943   An introduction to the ceramics of Tres Zapotes. *Bureau of American Ethnology, Bulletin 139.*

Weigand, P. C.

1974   The Ahualulco site and the shaft-tomb complex of the Etzatlán area. In *The archaeology of west Mexico,* edited by B. Bell. Ajijíc, Jalisco, Mexico: West Mexican Society for Advanced Study. Pp. 120–131.

1975   Possible references to La Quemada in Huichol mythology. *Ethnohistory 22* (1):15–20.

Weigand, P. C., G. Harbottle, and E. V. Sayre

1977   Turquoise sources and source analysis: Mesoamerica and the southwestern U.S.A. In *Exchange systems in prehistory,* edited by T. K. Earle and J. E. Ericson. New York: Academic Press. Pp. 15–34.

West, R. C.

1961   Aboriginal sea navigation between Middle and South America. *American Anthropologist 63*:133–135.

1964   The natural regions of Middle America. In *Handbook of Middle American Indians* (Vol. 1), edited by R. Wauchope. Austin, Texas: University of Texas Press. Pp. 363–383.

Wicke, C.

1965   Pyramids and temple mounds: Mesoamerican ceremonial architecture in eastern North America. *American Antiquity 30*:409–420.

1976   Once more around the Tízoc stone: A reconsideration. *Actas del XLI Congreso Internacional de Americanistas,* Mexico. II:210–221.

Wilkerson, S. J. K.

1973   An archaeological sequence from Santa Luisa, Veracruz, Mexico. *University of California Archaeological Research Facility Contribution* No. 18:37–50.

1975   Pre-agricultural village life: The late preceramic period in Veracruz. *University of California Archaeological Research Facility Contribution* No. 27:111–122.

1979   The cultural ecology project in Mexico: A summary of the 1977–1978 season. *Mexicon 1*(3):28–29.

1980   Man's eighty centuries in Vera Cruz. *National Geographic Magazine 158*(2):203–231.

Wilkinson, R. G., and M. C. Winter

1975   Cirugía craneal en Monte Albán. *Instituto Nacional de Antropología e Historia, Boletín epoca II*(12):21–26.

Willey, G. R.

1962a   Mesoamerica. In *Courses toward urban life,* edited by R. Braidwood and G. R. Willey. *Viking Fund Publications in Antropology,* No. 32. Pp. 84–105.

1962b   The early great styles and the rise of the pre-Columbian civilizations. *American Anthropologist 64*:1–14.

1966   *An introduction to American archaeology.* Vol. 1, *North and Middle America.* Englewood Cliffs, New Jersey: Prentice-Hall.

1970   Type descriptions of the ceramics of the Real Xe complex, Seibal, Petén, Guatemala. *Peabody Museum, Harvard University, Archaeological and Ethnological Papers 61*:315–355.

1971   *An introduction to American archaeology.* Vol. 2, *South America.* Englewood Cliffs, New Jersey: Prentice-Hall.

1973   The Altar de Sacrificios excavations: General summary and conclusions. *Peabody Museum Papers 64*(3).

1974   The Classic Maya hiatus: A rehearsal for the collapse? In *Mesoamerican archaeology: New approaches,* edited by N. Hammond. Austin, Texas: University of Texas Press. Pp. 313–334.

1977a The rise of Classic Maya civilization: A Pasion Valley perspective. In *The origins of Maya civilization*, edited by R. E. W. Adams. Albuquerque, New Mexico: University of New Mexico Press. Pp. 133–157.

1977b The rise of Maya civilization: A summary view. In *The origins of Maya civilization*, edited by R. E. W. Adams. Albuquerque, New Mexico: University of New Mexico Press. Pp. 383–423.

1978 A summary scan. In *Chronologies in New World archaeology*, edited by R. E. Taylor and C. W. Meighan. New York: Academic Press. Pp. 513–563.

1980 Towards an holistic view of ancient Maya civilization. *Man* 15(2):249–266.

Willey, G. R., and W. R. Bullard, Jr.
1965 Prehistoric settlement patterns in the Maya lowlands. In *Handbook of Middle American Indians* (Vol. 2), edited by R. Wauchope. Austin, Texas: University of Texas Press. Pp. 360–377.

Willey, G. R., W. R. Bullard, Jr., J. B. Glass, and J. C. Gifford
1965 Prehistoric Maya settlements in the Belize Valley. *Peabody Museum, Harvard University, Archaeological and Ethnological Papers 54.*

Willey, G. R., T. P. Culbert, and R. E. W. Adams
1967 Maya lowland ceramics: A report from the 1965 Guatemala City Conference. *American Antiquity* 32:289–315.

Willey, G. R., and N. Hammond
1979 Introduction. In *Maya archaeology and ethnohistory*, edited by N. Hammond and G. R. Willey. Austin, Texas: University of Texas Press. Pp. xi–xvii.

Willey, G. R., and R. M. Leventhal
1979 Prehistoric settlement at Copán. In *Maya archaeology and ethnohistory*, edited by N. Hammond and G. R. Willey. Austin, Texas: University of Texas Press. Pp. 75–102.

Willey, G. R., R. M. Leventhal, and W. L. Fash, Jr.
1978 Maya settlement in the Copán Valley. *Archaeology* 31(4):32–43.

Willey, G. R., and C. R. McGimsey
1954 The Monagrillo culture of Panama. *Peabody Museum, Harvard University, Archaeological and Ethnological Papers 49(2).*

Willey, G. R., and D. B. Shimkin
1973 The Maya collapse: A summary view. In *The Classic Maya collapse*, edited by T. P. Culbert. Albuquerque, New Mexico. University of New Mexico Press. Pp. 457–503.

Willey, G. R., and A. L. Smith
1969 The ruins of Altar de Sacrificios, Department of Petén, Guatemala, an introduction. *Peabody Museum, Harvard University, Archaeological and Ethnological Papers 62(1).*

Willey, G. R., A. L. Smith, G. Tourtellot III, and I. Graham
1975 Excavations at Seibal, Department of Petén, Guatemala. Introduction. The site and its setting. *Memoirs of the Peabody Museum of Archaeology and Ethnology 13(1).*

Winter, M., and W. O. Payne
1976 Hornos para cerámica hallados en Monte Albán. *Instituto Nacional de Antropología e Historia, Boletín epoca II(16):37–40.*

Wolf, E. R.
1959 *Sons of the shaking earth.* Chicago, Illinois: University of Chicago Press.

1976 (Ed.) *The Valley of Mexico. Studies in prehispanic ecology and society.* Albuquerque, New Mexico: University of New Mexico Press.

Wolf, E. R., and A. Palerm
1955 Irrigation in the old Acolhua domain. *Southwestern Journal of Anthropology* 11:265–281.

Zeitlin, R. N.
  1978   Long-distance exchange and the growth of a regional center: An example from the southern Isthmus of Tehuantepec, Mexico. In *Prehistoric coastal adaptations: The economy and ecology of maritime Middle America,* edited by B. L. Stark and B. Voorhies. New York: Academic Press. Pp. 183–210.
Zevallos, M. C., W. C. Galinat, D. W. Lathrap, E. R. Leng, M. Klump, and K. Klump
  1977   The San Pablo corn kernel and its friends. *Science 196*:385–389.

Author Index

Numbers in italics refer to the page on which the complete reference can be found.

Subject Index

CHRONOLOGICAL CHART

			Years	NAYARIT COAST				COLIMA JALISCO BORDER / INT.	COLIMA ARMERIA AXIS	COLIMA ARMERIA NW-S	MICHOACAN	NORTH WEST FRONTIER	BASIN OF MEXICO	TLAXCALA	PUEBLA (TEHUACAN)	MORELOS	GU...
LH	POSTCLASSIC	MID-DLE / LATE	1500		SANTIAGO				PERI-QUILLO	EL CHANAL	TARASCAN	CASAS GRANDES	AZTEC	TLAXCALA	MIXTECA PUEBLA STYLE	AZTEC	
			1400														
SI 3		MID-DLE	1300		IZCUINTLA								CHICHIMEC				
			1200	SANTA CRUZ								RIO TUNAL	TOLTEC (MAZAPAN)			LOCAL REGIONAL CENTERS	
SI 2		EARLY	1100			IXTLAN DEL RIO			?	ARMERÍA	TINGAMBATO	QUERENDARO		LATE TEXCALAC EARLY			XOCHIPALA
			1000		CERRITOS							LAS JOYAS	COYOTLALTECO OXTOTIC PAC			XOCHICALCO	
			900														
SI 1	CLASSIC	LATE	800							COLIMA		RETOÑO	METEPEC		LATE PALO BLANCO		
MH 5			700	LOS COCOS				LATE MORETT				CALICHAL				TEOTIHUACAN DOMINATION OF AMATZINAC VALLEY	
MH 4		MIDDLE	600		?								XOLALPAN	TENANYECAC			
MH 3			500								AMECA	ALTA VISTA	TLAMIMILOLPA				
MH 2/1			400	EARLY IXTLAN	AMAPA			COMALA			SAN SEBASTIAN	CANUTILLO	MICCAOTLI				
FI 11		EARLY	300														
FI 10			200										TZACUALLI		EARLY PALO BLANCO		
			100 A.D. / B.C.		GAVILÁN	SHAFT AND CHAMBER TOMBS		EARLY MORETT			CHUPÍCUARO GRAVES (GUANAJUATO)		PATLACHIQUE	TEZOQUIPAN			
FI 9		EPI-OLMEC	100	?													
FI 8			200					ORTICES				TICOMÁN		LATE SANTA MARIA		
FI 7	PRECLASSIC		300													
FI 5		OLMEC	500	SAN BLAS										TEXOLOC		
FI 4			600									ZACATENCO	EARLY SANTA MARIA	CANTERA	
FI 3			700												
FI 2			800	?										BARRANCA	
FI 1			900								MANANTIAL	TLATEMPA			
EH 4			1000											
EH 3			1100				AYOTLA / COA-PEXCO				LATE AJALPAN		
EH 2			1200											AMATE
EH 1			1300								? NEVADA	EARLY AJALPAN	
		PRE-OLMEC	1400	MATANCHEN				CAPACHA COMPLEX		EL OPEÑO		TZOMPANTEPEC		
			1500										?	
			1600								TLALPAN ?		
IP			1800										PURRON	
			2000								ZOHAPILCO		
			2300									?	
			2400									PRECERAMIC PHASES	
			2500											

LH-LATE HORIZON SI-SECOND INTERMEDIATE (PHASES 1-3) MH-MIDDLE HORIZON (PHASES 1-5)
FI-FIRST INTERMEDIATE (PHASES 1-11) EH-EARLY HORIZON (PHASES 1-4) IP-INITIAL PERIOD